Forbidden Acts

Forbidden Acts

Pioneering Gay & Lesbian Plays of the Twentieth Century

Edited and with an Introduction by

Ben Hodges

APPLAUSE
THEATRE & CINEMA BOOKS

Forbidden Acts: Pioneering Gay & Lesbian Plays of
the Twentieth Century
Edited and with an Introduction by Ben Hodges

Cover and interior photos reprinted with permis-
sion from the Billy Rose Theatre Collection, The
New York Public Library for the Performing Arts,
Astor, Lenox, and Tilden Foundations and the John
Willis Theatre World/Screen World Archive.

Book design by Michelle Thompson

Library of Congress Cataloging-in-Publication Data:
Forbidden acts: pioneering gay & lesbian plays of
   the twentieth century/
   edited and with an introduction by Ben Hodges.
   p. cm.
   Includes bibliographical references.
   ISBN 1-55783-587-X
   1.   Gay   men—Drama.
   2.   Lesbians—Drama.
   3.   Drama—20th   century.
   4.   Gays'   writings.
   I. Hodges, Ben (Benjamin A.)
   PN6120.G43F67 2003
   808.82'0086'640904–dc21   2003014043

British Library Cataloging-in-Publication Data
   A catalog record of this book is available from the
   British Library

APPLAUSE THEATRE & CINEMA BOOKS
151 West 46th Street, 8th Floor
New York, NY 10036
PHONE: (212) 575-9265
FAX: (646) 562-5852
EMAIL: info@applausepub.com
INTERNET: www.applausepub.com

Sales & Distribution
NORTH AMERICA:
   Hal Leonard Corp.
   7777 West Bluemound Road
   P. O. Box 13819
   Milwaukee, WI 53213
   PHONE: (414) 774-3630
   FAX: (414) 774-3259
   EMAIL: halinfo@halleonard.com
   INTERNET: www.halleonard.com
UK:
   Roundhouse Publishing Ltd.
   Millstone, Limers Lane
   Northam, North Devon Ex 39 2RG
   PHONE: (0) 1237-474-474
   FAX: (0) 1237-474-774
   EMAIL: roundhouse.group@ukgateway.net

For my family

Contents

Acknowledgments 9
Editor's Note 11
Introduction 13

God of Vengeance 25
Sholom Asch

The Captive 83
Edouard Bourdet

The Children's Hour 173
Lillian Hellman

Oscar Wilde 239
Leslie and Sewell Stokes

The Immoralist 303
Ruth and Augustus Goetz

The Killing of Sister George 361
Frank Marcus

Boys in the Band 443
Mart Crowley

Bent 519
Martin Sherman

As Is 593
William Hoffman

Love! Valour! Compassion! 653
Terrence McNally

Acknowledgments

I am deeply indebted to Mark Glubke at Applause Books for acquiring this anthology as well as for providing crucial input at its inception. I also wish to thank authors Alysia Abbott, John Clum, Mart Crowley, Stephen Fife, Joe E. Jeffreys, Ken Furtado, Esther Harriot, Sheridan Morley, Caraid O'Brien, and Don Shewey for helping point me in the right direction.

Ken Furtado's *We Can Always Call Them Bulgarians* and Alan Sinfield's *Out on Stage* have both been invaluable resources in my research, especially considering the dearth of literature on gay and lesbian drama during the early twentieth century.

My own personal editor, Brad Hampton, and friends Epitacio Arganza, Nicole Boyd, Liz and Ron Briggs, Jason Cicci, Tim Deak, Juliet Furness, Laura and Tommy Hanson, Bob and Renee Isely Tobin, Aaron and Gretchen Kerr, Gail Miller, Carolyn and David Rapp, Hannah Richman Slosberg, Wilson Valentin, Rachel Werbel, and Robin Whitehouse, have all dispensed wise advice and provided unfaltering support as well as intermittent opportunities for rest and relaxation.

Kenyon Harbison at the William Morris Agency, Buddy Thomas at ICM, Caryn Burtt at Random House, and Rick Miramontez at the Richard Kornberg Office have all gone above and beyond the call of duty in processing permissions requests.

Theatre World editor John Willis, my mentor and friend, continues to teach me the value of the work we do as archivists and historians through our *Theatre World* annuals, as well as the proper way to do it, and also generously granted me unlimited access to his vast archive.

The indefatigable staff of the New York Public Library for the Performing

Arts at Lincoln Center—especially Jeremy Megraw—has been indispensable in providing assistance with tracking down elusive photographs and production information.

At Applause Theatre and Cinema Books, managing editors Kallie Shimek and Jenna Bagnini have both been incredibly valuable in helping determine which titles would ultimately be included in this anthology, and have continued to provide encouragement toward its successful completion. Michelle Thompson's thoroughly captivating cover design and editorial advice were crucial to the actualization of this publication, as was publicist Kay Radtke's public relations expertise. John Cerullo and Michael Messina have guided this project from its infancy, assuring that it received the attention it required, as they do on an ongoing basis with our *Theatre World* series.

To all of the above, I am forever grateful.

Editor's Note

When I first set out to create this anthology, I had anticipated assembling a collection that would focus on the playwrights that had emerged from downtown New York's Caffe Cino and La Mama scenes of the late 1950s and early 1960s—the cradle of modern gay and lesbian theatre and the Off-Off-Broadway theatre movement. But gradually, as I began to examine the history of gay and lesbian theatre, I understood that in order to properly illustrate the emergence of a gay and lesbian presence on the twentieth century stage, I needed to also acknowledge some of the genre's more obscured progenitors. Many of these early works are still disputed for their (by contemporary standards) mostly quiet queer content. But a collective voice was doubtlessly gaining strength in those early works, and no anthology on this subject would be complete without their inclusion.

Forbidden Acts is structured as a timeline of the emergence of gay and lesbian theatre in the broadest sense. The chronological approach is a pragmatic device that I've decided to use to locate each work's gains in a rapidly changing society over the course of a century, not a suggestion that one work necessarily seamlessly influenced the next and so on. More than anything, my primary intent is to *make available* to readers the texts of plays that locate major ordinal points in the history of the genre, to bring together a string of plays that illustrate the growth of an influential movement in the theatre, one which grew exponentially in strength and resonance with each passing decade.

The publishing of *Forbidden Acts* marks the first time that a collection of works of this scope on this subject has been assembled. For many, it will simply be a convenience—a greatest hits of "remastered" classics and favorites. For others, it will provide an accessible overview of the emergence of a queer presence on the mainstream American stage over the course of a century. For those involved in critical examinations of gay and lesbian theatre history, *Forbidden Acts* will be a companion compilation, a reference text to many of the plays that are often cited (and debated) in critical histories as well as classrooms.

I chose to use a set of criteria for inclusion in this anthology that I hope will serve it well. All of the plays included here are notable for having explored gay or lesbian themes in what might be loosely termed a "pioneering" way. In early cases (*God of Vengeance, The Children's Hour, The Captive, Oscar Wilde, The Immoralist*), when homosexuality had not been openly explored on stage, these themes were mostly buried or implied, although clearly recognizable to gay and lesbian audience members (and often still wrapped in the derogatory stereotypes of mainstream society). Other, later plays are notable for their unapologetic, happenstance presentation of gay characters (*The Killing of Sister George*) or the never-before-seen view into gay life that they provided (*The Boys in the Band*). Still others are to be recognized for the exploration of various aspects of gay culture and history (societal and governmental oppression, AIDS, community, queer identity) that they brought to the stage (*Bent, As Is, Love! Valour! Compassion!*).

These ten plays also bridge a range of theatrical genres: drama, tragedy, romance, comedy, farce. They remain vibrant and relevant not only as studies of gay and lesbian history, but also as testaments to art's irrepressible ability to persevere in the face of oppression, to collect and make audible the voices of unheard and misunderstood communities and to deepen understanding of them once they have developed a presence. *Forbidden Acts* traces the obscure infancy of a genre and sees it through to a breakthrough mainstream presence of profound proportions. Its landmark voices are due to be heard again, to be allowed to continue to influence and inspire, and to assure the continued vibrancy and vitality of a gay and lesbian identity in contemporary theatre.

Introduction

"'GOD OF VENGEANCE' AN OBSCENE PLAY; 13 FOUND GUILTY" [1]

I t was May 24, 1923 when this provocative headline in the *New York Morning Telegraph* announced the outcome of the obscenity trial surrounding the truncated production of Sholom Asch's *God of Vengeance*. It was, according to a report in the *New York Tribune*, the first time in the history of American law that the owner and cast members of a dramatic production had been convicted by a jury of presenting an allegedly "indecent" play. [2]

As the press reported it, the trial was mainly concerned with the fact that several scenes in *God of Vengeance* are set in a brothel. However, read between the lines and it becomes clear that it was most certainly one brothel scene in particular involving a lesbian seduction between two prostitutes that actually ignited the controversy:

> In theory we have always maintained that there is nothing which cannot be said or done upon the stage if the intent is sincere and the artist great... "The God of Vengeance" has been translated into many languages and played all over the world. That does not help us any. The scene between the young girl and a harlot in her father's establishment made us a little sick. From the point of view of expediency our position is stronger than it is in theory. After all, the American stage has not yet achieved absolute frankness in dealing with the more traditional and conventional vices. We can afford to wait until that fight has been won before ventures into decadence. (Heywood Broun, *New York World*) [3]

> Yekel's daughter, in spite of all of her father's care, takes the path of her mother's early life and her father's profession. The terrible details need not be recorded here. They are almost too terrible to look upon in the theatre. (*New York Evening Telegram*) [4]

> Ugly, sordid, and repellent beyond any play that has yet been presented on the contemporary English speaking stage, "The God of Vengeance," by Sholom Asch, . . . is absorbing, though often offensive. . . . (Rivkele's) perverted curiosity makes her the easy victim of her sex, and she escapes with Manke, a lesbian companion, to her predestined fate. (Maida Castellun, *The Call*) [5]

The play, which had enjoyed popular performances for more than a decade throughout Germany and Russia, as well as in New York in its original Yiddish, had finally made its English language debut, no sooner than to be effectively outed as trafficking in "unspeakable" themes. The producer, Harry Weinberger, and star Rudolph Schildkraut were each fined $200, while the sentences of the eleven actors were suspended. In imposing the sentences, the presiding judge declared that his verdict had "forever answered the question of censorship of the stage." [6] Not quite, but the stage was now set for a decades-long battle for playwrights who wished to represent homosexual life, situations or characters in their work on the American stage.

Three years later, in 1926, Arthur Hornblow, Jr.'s *The Captive*, an adaptation of Edouard Bourdet's *La Prisonnière*, debuted on Broadway. *La Prisonnière* had opened in Paris earlier in the year, giving the New York drama critics time to prepare themselves—and their public—for its subject matter. The play's stateside reception was also bolstered by the reputation of the actress Helen Menken who portrayed Irene De Montcel—the play's eponymous captive. Menken, who was already a well-known stage actress and wife of actor Humphrey Bogart, undoubtedly helped lend credibility to the play, which was generally well-reviewed on its merits, possibly inoculating it initially against public outcry over its unsubtle lesbian themes. It also couldn't have hurt that the seductress is never seen. This obscuring device also conveniently allowed the critics and many audience members to comfortably bypass true acknowledgement of the subject matter and indeed, prompted some critics to wonder what all the fuss was about:

> The town's busybodies had it that M. Bourdet had written stuff unfit for the American ears and suggested calling the police . . . For "The Captive"

is too tragical to be tawdry; too honest to be smut. It ventures on accustomed ground, ground treacherous with misunderstanding and crowded with the mountain of prejudice and caverns of ignorance. It is plagued by all the fogs that all smugness has wrapped around sex and its solemn errors until some charts were made, pitifully inept, but anyway charts trying feebly to straighten out a tangled mess of morals, instincts, and conduct. (John Anderson, *New York Evening Post*) [7]

Appauling rumors had been brought from Paris by shy tourists that "La Prisonnaire" dealt with dreadful sex-specters, the nature of which is customarily discussed in nervous whispers. This it did, but no blanched faces were to be seen, and so far as could be noticed, there were none who crawled under their chairs to hide embarrassment. (Percy Hammond, *New York Herald Tribune*) [8]

But *The Captive* could not hide its not-so-secret bombshell forever. Amidst increasing pressure from religious leaders, New York Governor Al Smith, and New York City Mayor Jimmy Walker, *The Captive* was finally raided by the police during its February 9, 1927, performance, leading to its untimely closing. This was in part facilitated by the concurrent appearance of Mae West's sensational *The Drag*, which, quite conversely, had happily flaunted its homo bent. This collective onslaught of nouveau naughtiness proved to be too much for city and state leaders to swallow and the general crackdown began, sweeping *The Captive* and *The Drag* up in the same indiscriminating net.

In November 1934, when Lillian Hellman's *The Children's Hour* opened on Broadway, the sapphically charged witch-hunt plot once again rang the city's taboo alarms, and flashbacks to *The Captive* were inevitable:

Eight years have passed since M. Bourdet's "La Prisonnière" was produced as "The Captive" at the Empire...At Maxine Elliott's Theater "The Children's Hour" dwells even more determinedly on the affection that passes normal understanding and the wreckage it is able to create in otherwise well-ordered lives. (Robert Garland, *New York World-Telegram*) [9]

There was once a play, "The Captive," which, when it was produced here, I called a most decent and honorable play...and, though editors growled and policemen snorted, I would not eat those adjectives. "The Children's Hour" makes minor use of the same theme. So, what with the changes which Father Time and Mother Nature, adversity, perversity, and Uncle Havelock Ellis have wrought in us, I take even greater pains to point to "The Children's Hour" as a thoroughly decent and wholly honorable play . . . But, when all is said and sobbed, you wonder if people are as blindly intolerant as that nowadays. (Gilbert Gabriel, *New York American*) [10]

Miss Lillian Hellman has written a sound tragedy in "The Children's Hour" and one that will make your two eyes start from their sockets as its agitating tale is unfolded with honest audacity and honest craftsmanship. Its subject has been forbidden in the Theater as unfit for public illustration and a previous attempt to discuss it in "The Captive" was discouraged by the forces of law and order . . . Miss Hellman, with a gallant indifference to what has been termed the proprieties, speaks out, although with artistic direction, and she leaves not even the most innocent drama lover in the dark. No tot, attending a matinee with its mother, will need to inquire: "Mama, what is it all about?" (Percy Hammond, *New York Herald Tribune*) [11]

But the early signs of a slow paradigm shift were beginning to show. The New York critics, and audiences in general, were beginning to test new waters and, with the law staying out of the theatre this time around, the play was actually able to capitalize on its controversial subject matter:

There will be those to whom the subject matter will seem distasteful; On the other hand the undercurrent whispering about the fact that the play deals with homosexuality will bring it a certain amount of box office strength. (*Variety*) [12]

Many things have happened to increase the nationally breadth of mind since Bourdet's delicate "The Captive," having enjoyed several fat months of success, was suddenly discovered to be improper and hurried from the stage, and "The Children's Hour," a more sincere and less mysterious treatment of the same topic, should now be safe. No doubt it will cause rabid discussion, but its honest bluntness and the depressing tragedy of it save it the curse of sensationalism—and no doubt will rob it, too, of a deserved popularity. (Arthur Pollock, *Brooklyn Daily Eagle*) [13]

Although *The Children's Hour* managed to emerge from its New York debut relatively unscathed, it would later be banned in Boston and London until 1936 and author Lillian Hellman was overlooked in consideration for the

Pulitzer Prize when the committee members deemed the play's subject matter objectionable.

By the late 1930's, having now racked up nearly two decades' worth of controversial lesbians, the American stage was ready to take the next step and present a gay man — and not just any gay man — but one of history's most notorious: Oscar Wilde. Leslie and Sewell Stokes' *Oscar Wilde* debuted in New York in the fall of 1938 becoming the first English-language play to dramatize the life of the bon vivant. For his characterization of the title character, Robert Morley received that era's equivalent of the Tony Award® for Best Actor. For their play, the Stokes also received their share of acclaim for the general quality of the play and its production, which tended to overshadow some of the usual morally fretful buzz:

> There were reports that it was a "dirty" piece before it arrived. I question the wisdom of doing the play at all, but I admit freely that it has been well done. (Burns Mantle, *New York Daily News*) [14]

> A story of homosexuality that is never cheap or disgusting…Theatrical exhibits on such a theme are generally embarrassing to watch, but "Oscar Wilde" handles its materials with such tactfulness and yet dramatic directness that it is, in its inescapably painful fashion, a dignified, intelligent drama of genuine power. (Richard Watts, Jr., *New York Herald Tribune*) [15]

> Plays dealing with deviations from normal relationships between humans generally leave me either in a state of anger or nausea. This one doesn't, first, because it is excellently written, second because it shows a shrewd appreciation of the psychology involved in the case, third, because it is neither sly nor vicious. (Sidney B. Whipple, *New York World-Telegram*) [16]

The Stokes may have been somewhat shielded from the kind of backlash that was widely expected because of the prominent profile of their protagonist. The public knew whom they were dealing with and most were aware of Wilde's biography. This allowed the play to unambiguously present its homosexual character in the spotlight, with all his conflicts and humanity on the surface, judged as he inevitably was — in life before and now on stage. Still, *Oscar Wilde* was as unapologetic a portrayal of a homosexual character as had ever been seen on the American stage, marking the latest step toward the closet door for gay and lesbian theatre.

In 1954, sixteen years after *Oscar Wilde*, Ruth and Augustus Goetz's *The Immoralist* (based on Andre Gide's autobiographical novel of the same name) again brought homosexual characters to the New York stage. Opening less than a year after Robert Anderson's *Tea and Sympathy*, which circled ambiguously around the issue of homosexuality, *The Immoralist* was less tentative, despite an open ending that stopped well short of an endorsement of its protagonist's proclivities. Like *Oscar Wilde*, *The Immoralist* was also rooted in biography (or here autobiography) and this also tipped the moral outrage scales more toward a distanced, condescending judgment of its protagonist (and his "misfortune" read "homosexuality") than inspiring any kind of public uproar:

> Let's not imply that "The Immoralist" is a "pleasant play"... The subject is depressing... But given the theme and the source, it is difficult to see how Mr. and Mrs. Goetz could have gotten closer to the sort of tragedy that goes beyond will into the awful areas of fate... Like Gide, who spent a career wrestling with his soul over his misfortune, the play has to be accepted and respected. (Brooks Atkinson, *New York Times*) [17]

The cast of *The Immoralist* was particularly memorable for its high-profile diversity. Geraldine Page continued her ascent as a promising new stage actress playing the alcoholic wife to screen star Louis Jourdan (in his Broadway debut) who portrayed the conflicted homosexual Arab confidante, a characterization that hinted at a changing homosexual sensibility, prompting the character to later be called "the first homophilic character in American drama." [18] Also notable was a heavily made-up James Dean who raised eyebrows as the sexually opportunistic Arabian houseboy.

1966's controversial *The Killing of Sister George* brought a new kind of lesbian portrayal to the stage in full force (and, some would maintain, farce). The play's markedly unflattering portrayal of its gay protagonists has transformed it into the one of the pariahs of the gay/lesbian play canon, disputed for its derogatory and stereotyped characterizations (bull-dyke, femme predator, opportunist tart) but inarguably notable for its unapologetically happenstance presentation of its characters' sexual orientation.

In a 1966 interview ("Author Sees George as Study in Oppression") that appeared shortly after the play's Broadway debut, author Frank Marcus urged that the main theme of his play is oppression. We are not, according to Marcus, to interpret the characters' manipulation of one another as a comment on the nature of their sexual orientation:"For me this is a love relationship, and like most precarious love relationships one oppresses the other. The fact they are homosexuals is only incidental." [19] In fact, it has been maintained that Marcus, in an attempt to avoid a libel suit, had actually changed his main character's gender from male to female in order to disguise his dramatization of what was purportedly a true incident involving a male English television personality (what became the Sister George role). [20] Regardless of its motivations, the play made an indelible impression in its presentation of a compelling human drama whose characters just happen to be gay.

It could be said that the curtain was finally fully and irreversibly raised on the presentation of gay life in the theatre when Mart Crowley's *The Boys in the Band* exploded onto the Off-Broadway stage in 1968. Critics were united in their assessment of the play's instant groundbreaking status:

> The play, which opened last night at Theater Four, is by far the frankest treatment of homosexuality I have ever seen on the stage. We are a long way from "Tea and Sympathy" here. The point is that this is not a play about a homosexual, but a play that takes the homosexual milieu, and the homosexual way of life, totally for granted and uses this as a valid basis for the human experience. Thus it is a homosexual play, not a play about homosexuality. (Clive Barnes, *New York Times*) [21]

> All the once forbidden words are there, and the action is highly explicit, but the play by Mart Crowley, now off-Broadway at Theater Four, doesn't strike me as a mere exercise in sensationalism... When I saw it last Thursday night at one of the previews, most of the spectators appeared to regard it as the merest of larks, and I think they were being unfair to it... Yet it is basically a sad and rather wistful play, it certainly has no truck with the theory with that the third sex—"queens," "queers" and "fags" it prefers to call them—lead happy and wistful lives. (Richard Watts, Jr., *New York Post*) [22]

Like *Sister George*, the play juggled gay stereotypes but presented its all-gay cast of characters in vivid, explosive emotional full-frontals (the real thing would have to wait), with all their human foibles exposed. But the stark contrast between the euphemistic and ambiguous homosexuality in *Tea and Sympathy* fourteen years before and the in-your-face portrayal of every aspect of gay life in *The Boys in the Band* could hardly have been more pronounced. *Boys* was, in essence, a harbinger of the tectonic shift about to occur in the gay community; it was a coming out party for gay and lesbian theatre that ushered in the Stonewall era, the iconic mark against which all future plays with gay themes would be compared.

While some critics dismissed it as overly melodramatic, Martin Sherman's *Bent* was broadly regarded as an incredibly powerful and moving love story when it debuted on Broadway in 1979. *Bent* was one of the first widely seen plays to graphically address society's—in this case Nazi Germany's—oppression of gays. Set in a Nazi concentration camp, *Bent* presented characters that manage to love in the face of a violent oppression. It was a potent analogue for many gay viewers to modern society's continued prejudice against gays and lesbians and, in retrospect, at the dawn of the AIDS era, a hauntingly prescient fable of love's power in the face of death and destruction. It was precisely this unwavering focus on the universality of love—not the sexual orientation of the characters in love—that set *Bent* apart:

> "Bent" may be regarded as pro-gay in that it displays no social or moral qualms about anyone's being gay. (T.A. Kalem, *Time*) [23]

> There will be many people who will doubtless claim the homosexual element in the play is incidental, and the reality of the theme is simply that it is about survival and a man discovering in himself the ability to love and make sacrifices. Possibly—but the homosexual orientation of the play is very evidently stressed. (Clive Barnes, *New York Post*) [24]

William Hoffman's *As Is*, (1985) (although beating Larry Kramer's *The Normal Heart* to the stage by less than a month), wasn't the first play about AIDS to open in New York. It had been preceded eight months earlier by Robert Chelsey's *Nightsweat* at the Meridian Gay Theater, and Stephen Holt's *Fever of Unknown Origin* at the Theater for the New City. While *The Normal Heart* focused on the political ramifications of AIDS, *As Is* dealt with the disease's social and personal fallout:

> A wonderful and frightening play has turned up at the Circle Repertory, and I commend it to both you and your conscience...I do believe it is valuable simply in drawing graphic attention to a socio-medical problem that needs more attention than it is receiving. (Clive Barnes, *New York Post*) [25]

As Is brought the alienation, fear and loss of AIDS into the open and attached it to people, lives and emotions. Its personalization of the nascent epidemic allowed theatregoers to glimpse the tragedy of AIDS from the perspective of the community most devastated by it. That the characters were gay was no longer a device or agenda, it was a plea for understanding.

By 1994, when Terrence McNally's *Love! Valour! Compassion!* debuted at the Manhattan Theatre Club, a decade and a half had passed and the lighthearted bathhouse landscape of *The Ritz* had been completely transformed by the specter of AIDS. Concurrent with Tony Kushner's epic *Angels in America, Love! Valour! Compassion!* tightened its focus even more closely on the personal experience of gay life in the shadow of AIDS, revealing powerfully intimate portraits of contemporary gay men, their lives and their relationships:

> First there was "Boys in the Band" in 1968. Then "Torch Song Trilogy" in 1982...Now gay theatre reaches another watershed with Terrence McNally's "Love! Valour! Compassion!"..."Love!" gives us something rare in the depiction of homosexuals on stage: three ordinary summer weekends with a group of friends laughing, loving, hating, and crying. (David Sheward, *Back Stage*) [26]

> McNally seduces an audience, straight and gay, into testing the borders of its own fears. (Jan Stuart, *New York Newsday*) [27]

> McNally has written the deepest, wittiest, most satisfying play of his impressive career—indeed—one of the major plays of our time. But he has also written his most ambitiously unambiguous gay work, infused with open and playful eroticism, naked emotions and naked men, presented simply, without underestimating audiences with stage gadgets and spectacles and emotional compromises. (Linda Winer, *New York Newsday*) [28]

With *Love! Valour! Compassion!*, McNally kept the trend in gay and lesbian theatre to focus on the individual and the "ordinary," underscoring the theme of survival and perseverance, universal themes that resonate not only in the gay and lesbian community in the age of AIDS, but themes that reflect on the flourishing of a long oppressed genre.

> To a certain extent, the history of New York theater in the last decade has been the history of gay theater. Terrence McNally's "Love! Valour! Compassion!"...is a key moment in that history.... It documents the

moment when the word "gay," which used to mean merry and mirthful,
as well as "homosexual," has come to mean bittersweet, if not sorrowful.
(Howard Kissel, *New York Daily News*) [29]

These plays that follow represent but a sampling of the gains that have been
made over the last century. Gay and lesbian theatre (as well as all walks of
queer theatre and performance) is still in its infancy; it is a genre that will
continue to develop in tandem with the diverse communities that it
addresses and who produce it. Let there be no mistake: there are still hurdles
to be overcome and breakthroughs to be made. And with every new gay and
lesbian play that hits the stage, progress is being made and with it, a lot of
great theatre.

—Ben Hodges
New York
August, 2003

The greatest compliment most of these people think they can give the show
is to say, "It's not a gay play, but a play about people." I'd much rather have
them say . . . "It's a gay play, but it's good. It's about queers, but they're kinda
funny."

—Harvey Fierstein [30]

Notes

1. "'God of Vengeance': An Obscene Play; 13 Found Guilty," *New York Morning Telegraph*, May 24, 1923.
2. "God of Vengeance," *New York Tribune*, May 24, 1923.
3. Heywood Broun, "The New Play," *New York World*, December 20, 1922.
4. "The Elder Schildkraut in Devastating Play," *New York Evening Telegram*, December 20, 1922.
5. Maida Castellun, "The Stage," *The Call*, December 21, 1922.
6. "Producer Likewise Punished, but Sentence on Members of Cast Is Suspended," May 28, 1923.
7. John Anderson, "The Play," *New York Evening Post*, September 30, 1926.
8. Percy Hammond, "The Theaters," *New York Herald Tribune*, September 30, 1926.
9. Robert Garland, "Children's Hour a Moving Tragedy," *New York World-Telegram*, November 21, 1934.
10. Gilbert Gabriel, "The Children's Hour," *New York American*, November 21, 1934.
11. Percy Hammond, "The Theaters," *New York Herald Tribune*, November 21, 1934.
12. "The Children's Hour," *Variety*, November 27, 1934.
13. Arthur Pollock, "The Theater," *Brooklyn Daily Eagle*, November 21, 1934.
14. Burns Mantle, "'Oscar Wilde': A Sympathetic Retelling of an Old Scandal," *New York Daily News*, October 11, 1938.
15. Richard Watts, Jr., "The Theaters," *New York Herald Tribune*, October 11, 1938.
16. Sidney B. Whipple, "Play on Oscar Wilde Sparkles with Wit," *New York World-Telegram*, October 11, 1938.
17. Brooks Atkinson, "First Night at the Theatre," *New York Times*, February 9, 1954.
18. Kaier Curtin, *We Can Always Call Them Bulgarians* (Boston: Alyson Publications Inc., 1988), 292.
19. Interview with Frank Marcus, Francis Herridge, "Author Sees 'George' as Study in Oppression," *New York Post*, 1966.
20. Interview with actress Paddy Croft, November 22, 2002.
21. Clive Barnes, "Theater: 'Boys in the Band' Opens Off Broadway," *New York Times*, April 15, 1968.
22. Richard Watts, Jr., "A Birthday Celebration Among the Homosexuals," *New York Post*, April 15, 1968.
23. T.E. Kalem, "Walpurgisnacht," *Time*, December 17, 1979, p. 84.
24. Clive Barnes, "On the Town," *New York Post*, December 3, 1979.
25. Clive Barnes, "Healthy Production of 'As Is,'" *New York Post*, March 12, 1985.
26. David Sheward, "Love! Valour! Compassion!," *Back Stage*, 1985.
27. Jan Stuart, "Terrence McNally Gets Naked," *New York Newsday*, November 6, 1994.
28. Linda Winer, "It's 'Love' on Broadway," *New York Newsday*, February 15, 1995.
29. Howard Kissel, "What's Not to 'Love'?," *New York Daily News*, February 15, 1995.
30. Interview with Harvey Fierstein, Jonathan Mandell, "Say Goodnight, Arnold," *The Sunday News Magazine*, May 1, 1983.

The God
of Vengeance

Sholom Asch

*Authorized translation from
the Yiddish "Gott fun Nekoma"
by Isaac Goldberg*

Preface

The birth of Yiddish literature in Russia and the beginning of the great Jewish exodus from that country to America are two effects of one and the same cause. The same anti-semitic crusade that forced the Children of Israel to go beyond the seas in search of a safe home, aroused them to a new sense of their racial self-respect and to an unwonted interest in their native tongue.

Prior to the anti-Jewish riots of 1881 educated Jews were wont to look upon their mother tongue as a jargon beneath the dignity of cultured attention. Yiddish, more especially in its written form, was the language of the untutored. People with modern training spoke and wrote Russian. As for the intellectual class of the Talmudic type, it would carry on its correspondence and, indeed, write its essays, verse and fiction, in the language of Isaiah. One wrote Yiddish to one's mother, for the mothers of those days were not apt to understand anything else. For the rest, the tongue of the Jewish masses was never taken seriously and the very notion of a literature in "a gibberish that has not even a grammar" would have seemed ludicrous.

Popular stories and songs were written in Yiddish long before the end of the nineteenth century, but, barring certain exceptions, these were intended exclusively for the most ignorant elements of the populace, and were contemptuously described as "servant-maid literature." (As for Yiddish poetry, it was almost wholly confined to the purposes of the wedding bard.) The exceptions here mentioned belong to the sixties and the seventies, when some brilliant attempts were made in the direction of literature in the better sense of the term by S. J. Abramovitch. But Abramovitch's stories were not even regarded as vanguard swallows heralding the approach of Spring. They aroused an amused sort of admiration. Indeed, it required a peculiar independence of mind to read them at all, and while they were greeted with patronizing applause, it was a long time before they found imitators.

All this changed when the whip of legal discrimination and massacres produced the "national awakening" of the educated Jew. Thousands of enlightened men and women then suddenly made the discovery, as it were, that the speech of their childhood was not a jargon, but a real language, — that instead of being a wretched conglomeration of uncouth words and phrases, it was rich in neglected beauty and possessed a homely vigor full of artistic possibilities. A stimulus was given to writing Yiddish "as the Gentiles do their mother tongues." Abramovitch was hailed as "the father of Yiddish literature" and his example was followed by a number of new writers, several of whom proved to be men of extraordinary gifts.

The movement bears curious resemblance to that of the present literary renaissance of Ireland.

Some truly marvelous results were soon achieved, the list of writers produced by the new literature including the names of men like Rabinovitch (Sholom Aleikhem) and Peretz, whose tales were crowned with immense popularity.

Sholom Asch belongs to a younger group of Yiddish story-tellers and now that Abramovitch, Rabinovitch and Peretz are in their graves (they have all died during the last two years) he is the most popular living producer of Yiddish fiction.

His narratives and plays are alive with a spirit of poetic realism, with a stronger leaning toward the poetic than toward reality, perhaps, but always throbbing with dramatic force and beauty. Sholom Asch's passion for color and melody manifests itself as much in his rich, ravishing style as in the picturesque images it evokes. The "jargon of servant maids" becomes music in his hands.

His "God of Vengeance," which is his strongest play, is one of the best things he has written in any form. Absorbingly interesting and instinct with human sympathy, it mounts to a natural climax of cataclysmal force and great spiritual beauty.

The theme, while thoroughly original and unique, reflects the artistic traditions of the country in which the author was born and bred. It was a matter of course that the young literature of which he is a conspicuous representative should shape itself under the influence of the much older and richer literary treasures of Slavic Russia and Poland. If it was natural for the novel of countries like France, Germany, Norway or Italy to fall under the sway of Turgenev, Tolstoi, Dostoyevski, Chekhov and Gorki, how much more so was it for a non-Russian fiction produced on Russian soil to seek guidance, directly or indirectly, in the same source.

Human sympathy is the watchword. Pity for and interest in the underdog—the soul of Russian art—became, from the very outset, the underlying principle of the new-born Yiddish art. No human being is so utterly brutalized as to possess not a single spark worthy of the artist's sympathetic, though ruthlessly impartial, attention,—this is the basic rule of Yiddish letters.

Himself a creature of the gutter, Yekel Tchaftchovitch, the central figure of "The God of Vengeance," is stirred by the noblest ambition known to a father in the world of orthodox Judaism. Imbedded in the slime that fills Yekel's soul is a jewel of sparkling beauty. But the very income by which he seeks to secure his daughter's spiritual splendor contains the germs of her loathsome fall and of his own crushing defeat.

The clash between Yekel's revolting career and his paternal idealism, and the catastrophe to which it inevitably leads form one of the strongest and most fascinating situations known to the modern drama.

I cannot conclude without a word of well-earned praise for the English version of "The God of Vengeance." Dr. Isaac Goldberg's translation is not only a thoroughly correct and felicitous equivalent of the original, but a piece of art in itself.

Abraham Cahan, editor
of the "Jewish Daily Forward" and
author of "Yekl," "The White
Terror and the Red," "The Rise of
David Levinsky," etc.
New York City
April, 1918

Introduction

Sholom Asch is one of the chief authors in contemporary Yiddish letters,—a literature at present enjoying a renaissance that attests the remarkable vitality of a people long oppressed in intellectual no less than in economic domains,—a literature that has much to teach America in the way of fearlessness before the facts of life, frankness in their interpretation and persistent idealism in face of the most degrading and debasing environment. Indeed, the conjunction of squalid surroundings, sordid occupation and idealistic yearning to be met so frequently in Jewish writers arises most naturally from the peculiar conditions of much of the life in ghettos the world over.

It is interesting to consider Asch's "The God of Vengeance" in connection with a play like "Mrs. Warren's Profession." To be sure, there is no technical resemblance between the two dramas; nor, despite an external similarity in backgrounds, is there any real identity of purpose. Shaw's play is essentially sociological, and is a drama of disillusionment. Asch's piece glows with poetic realism and recounts an individual tragedy not without symbolic power. Yet the essentially (though not conventionally) moral earnestness of both Shaw and Asch brings the circles of their themes in a sense tangent to each other.

Mrs. Warren cherishes no delusions about her dubious profession,—neither the delusion of that sentimentalization of the prostitute which Dumas helped so much to effect and which Augier strove to combat, nor the delusion of the conservative, conventional horror before an institution for the perpetuation of which conservatism and conventionalism are much to blame. If Yekel and his wife (in Asch's play) are not so enlightened as Mrs. Warren in their views upon the traffic off which they live, they are in their own crude way equally sincere in beholding in it a business quite as legitimate as any other. With the same inconsistency with which Hindel implores Heaven for aid in achieving her nefarious aims, after which she promises to be a model wife and mother (See Act Two), Mrs. Warren at the end of Shaw's play swears by Heaven that henceforth she will lead a life of evil.

In the case of Yekel and his wife, as in Mrs. Warren's, another touch of inconsistency is added by the agreement that theirs is not the best of professions. Crofts, too, in the English play, discusses the business with all the matter-of-factness of Asch's Shloyme, yet considers himself a gentleman none the less.

Rifkele, of course, is no Vivie. Asch's simple-minded Jewish girl is a victim, not a rebel. Yet in either case the daughter is lost to the parents, and the power of money is of no avail to win the child back. And just as Yekel, in his impotence, blasphemously thrusts the Holy Scroll from his household, so does Mrs. Warren, defeated in her attempt to win hack her daughter, cry "From this time forth, so help me Heaven in my last hour, I'll do wrong and nothing but wrong. And I'll prosper on it." Perhaps, too, the retribution which in each case is visited upon the parent arises from the fact that both Mrs. Warren and Yekel have, in Vivie's accusatory words, "lived one life and believed in another."

"The God of Vengeance," despite conclusions too easily drawn, is not a sex play. When Asch wishes to deal with sex as sex he is not afraid to handle the subject with all the poetry and power at his command. Such a play as his "Jephthah's Daughter" treats the elemental urge of sex with daring, beauty and Dionysiac abandon. Here, too, a golden symbolism wafts through the piece. Again, in his powerful novel "Mottke the Vagabond," Asch has given us scenes from the underworld of Warsaw that are unparalleled for unflinching truth to detail. "The God of Vengeance," however, despite the sordid environment in which the play takes place, possesses a certain moral beauty,—a beauty much dimmed, perhaps, by the repellant human beings who are its carriers, but a beauty none the less. Its symbolism and its poetry lift it far above the brothel in which it takes place. And what a strong conception is the Holy Scroll, itself one of the chief characters, and how frightfully eloquent in the mysterious, religious power that the dramatist has woven around it! ★

First produced by the famous director Max Reinhardt, at the Deutsches Theater, Berlin, in 1910, Asch's powerful play quickly made its way to the chief stages of Europe. It has been played all over Germany, Austria, Russia,

---

★The Holy Scroll, the religious significance of which is fully explained in the course of the play, is a parchment manuscript containing the first five books of the Bible, together known as the Torah, or Law. (Pentateuch).

Poland, Holland, Norway, Sweden and Italy. In Italy it created a marked impression during the entire season of 1916. "The God of Vengeance" has been translated into Hebrew, German, Russian, Polish, Dutch, Swedish, Norwegian, Italian and French.

Asch himself is yet a young man, having been born near Warsaw, some thirty-seven years ago. He is at present settled in New York, where pages flow in rapid succession from his prolific pen. Among his better known works are the following:

The Town: A collection of sketches depicting Yiddish life in the "staedtil" of the Old World. It was this work that brought him into prominence at the age of twenty-four.

Meri and *The Road to Self*: A pair of novels forming a continuous whole, in which the author, with a wealth of color and episode, depicts the wanderings of Jewish souls in search of self-realization. The background, mainly that of the Russian revolution of 1905, shifts to various parts of the globe. The books are rich in poetry and movement, and have been referred to as the epic of the Yiddish part in the revolution of 1905. Besides this the love story of Meri Rosenzweig and Misha, and the figures of Rachel and Kovalski the artist, lend to the novels all the charm that love can add to adventure and beautiful language to both.

Mottke the Vagabond: (Translated into English.) A powerful tale of life in the underworld of Warsaw, and the career of a Yiddish "cellar-child." American critics have found Asch, in this book, comparable in various respects to such authors as Hugo, Dickens and Gorki.

The Sinner: (Translated into English.) A one-act symbolic play of intense power, which has been likened for its atmosphere to certain of Maeterlinck's dramas. The story, which deals with the refusal of a Jewish grave to receive the corpse of a man who has sinned by marrying out of the faith, is developed with penetrating skill and impartial outlook.

Our Faith: A full-length drama upon a theme similar to that just touched upon. The author's refusal to cater to orthodox views shows his artistic independence.

Short Stories: The best of the numerous short stories that Asch has published in his various collections attain a high degree of artistic excellence. That same nervous prose as distinguishes his longer pieces, that same linguistic iridescence, — one might term it, — as he achieves in such remarkable places as Chapter XIII (Part One) of "Meri" and Chapter XLI (Part Two) of "The Road to Self," are encountered often in his many shorter tales.

In his more notable work Asch glows with a spontaneous artistry. It is this part of Asch's work that holds much pleasure in store for an increasing number of American readers who are awakening to the beauties of Yiddish literature.

Isaac Goldberg
Roxbury, Mass.
April, 1918

Actress Dorothee Nolan (Manke), who, along with other members of the cast, was arrested for her appearance in *The God of Vengeance*. (Photograph reprinted with permission from the Billy Rose Theatre Collection, The New York Public Library for the Performing Arts, Astor, Lenox, and Tilden Foundations.)

Sholom Asch's *The God of Vengeance* was first produced by the famous director Max Reinhardt, at the Deutsches Theater, Berlin, in 1910, under the personal direction of Rudolph Schildkraut, who also created the role of Yekel. Asch's powerful play quickly made its way to the chief stages of Europe. It has been played all over Germany, Austria, Russia, Poland, Holland, Norway, Sweden, and Italy. In Italy, it created a marked impression during the entire season of 1916, as it recently did on the Jewish stage in this country when it was produced at the Jewish Art Theatre. Mr. Schildkraut chose Yekel as his first role on the English speaking stage, and it is the third language in which he plays the part. *The God of Vengeance* has been translated into Hebrew, German, Russian, Polish, Dutch, Swedish, Norwegian, Italian, French, and English.

The English translation of *The God of Vengeance* was first presented in New York on December 20, 1922 at the Provincetown Theatre by The Players Company, Inc. It was staged under the personal direction of Mr. Schildkraut, and the settings were designed and executed by Cleon Throckmorton.

Cast

(in order of appearance)

Rifkele, daughter of Shepshovitch.	Virginia Mac Fadyen
Sarah, her mother	Esther Stockton
Yekel Shepshovitch	Rudolph Schildkraut
A Poor Woman	Marjorie Stewart
Shloyme	Lou Sorin
Hindel	Mae Berland
Reb Ali, a matchmaker	Sam Jaffe
Reb Aaron, a pious scribe	Morris Carnovsky
Manke	Dorothee Nolan
Basha	Aldea Wise
Reizel	Lillian Taiz
Reb Yankev	James Meighan
Poor Men and Women of the Neighborhood. .	Samuel Selden, Roland Twombly, Ruth Mahrer, Bess Goodman, Eleanor Rowe

For the Players Company

Ewing Rafferty . . . . Executive Manager
Benjamin Kauser . . . . Stage Director
Lucy HuVaker . . . . Press Representative
James Meighan . . . . Stage Manager
Oscar Liebetrau . . . . Stage Carpenter
Samuel Selden . . . . Electrician

The Players Company gratefully acknowledges the valuable assistance of
Seldon Bennett in this production.

The God of Vengeance transferred to the Apollo Theatre in New York on
February 19, 1923, and was produced by Harry Weinberger.

Cast

(in order of appearance)
Rifkele, daughter of Shepshovitch . . . . Virginia Mac Fadyen
Sarah, her mother . . . . Esther Stockton
Yekel Shepshovitch . . . . Rudolph Schildkraut
A Poor Woman . . . . Marjorie Stewart
Shloyme . . . . Irwin J. Adler
Hindel . . . . Mae Berland
Reb Ali, a matchmaker . . . . Sam Jaffe
Reb Aaron, a pious scribe . . . . Morris Carnovsky
Manke . . . . Dorothee Nolan
Basha . . . . Aldea Wise
Reizel . . . . Lillian Taiz
Reb Yankev . . . . James Meighan
Poor Men and Women of the Neighborhood . . Samuel Selden, Roland
Twombly, Ruth Mahrer,
Serette Marshel, Eleanor
Rowe, Mitzi Salzman,
Bess Goodman, Eleanor
Rowe

A note on the text: There have been many subsequent English translations of *The God of Vengeance* since it was originally translated by Dr. Isaac Goldberg from the Yiddish *Gott fun Nekoma* in 1918. The version which follows is Dr. Goldberg's translation.

Act One
The private dwelling of Yekel Tchaftchovitch
An afternoon in early Spring

Act Two
In the cellar of Yekel's dwelling
A night in Spring

Act Three
Same as Act One
At dawn the next day

Persons of the Drama

YEKEL TCHAFTCHOVITCH: *Familiarly known as the*
    "Uncle"; the owner of a brothel.
SARAH: *His wife; formerly a prostitute.*
RIFKELE: *Their daughter; a young girl of about seventeen.*
HINDEL: *First girl of the brothel; a girl of some thirty odd*
    years, but much older in appearance.
MANKE: *Second girl; rather young.*
REIZEL: *Third girl.*
BASHA: *A country lass, recently arrived.*
SHLOYME: *A procurer; Hindel's betrothed, a handsome chap*
    of twenty-six.
REB ALI: *A matchmaker; neighbor of the "Uncle."*
REB YANKEV: *A pious Scribe.*
A STRANGER: *Father of Rifkele's proposed husband.*
A POOR WOMAN: *Blind in one eye.*
Poor Men and Women of the neighborhood.

Time: *The present.*
Place: *One of the larger towns of a Russian province.*

Act One

Scene: *The "Uncle's" private dwelling on the ground floor of an old wooden house. Below, in the cellar, is the brothel. A flight of rickety wooden stairs, whose creaking announces the coming of all visitors, leads from the outside into the home, which consists of a large room with a low ceiling. The furniture is new, in the cheap Warsaw style, and does not at all harmonize with the old-fashioned structure. On the wall hang pictures embroidered upon canvas, depicting scenes from the Bible, such as "Adam and Eve at the Tree of Knowledge," etc. These are evidently a young girl's handiwork. At the rear, the door leading to the outside. To the right, a door leading to RIFKELE's room. At each side of this door, placed against the wall, a bed piled high with bedding. To the left, two low windows, hung with curtains and provided with shutters that close from the inside. Before the windows, pots of flowers; between, a cupboard; at the side of one of the windows, a bureau.*

The finishing touches are being put to the cleaning of the room...Evidently guests are expected...Extra tables and benches have been placed about, laden with baskets of bread, cake, fruit, etc.

An afternoon in early spring.

SARAH and RIFKELE are discovered as the curtain rises. SARAH is a tall, slender, prepossessing woman. Her features have become coarsened, yet they retain traces of her former beauty, which has even now a tone of insolence. On her head lies a wig, through which, from time to time, shows a lock of her alluring hair. She is dressed quite soberly, as befits a mother, yet a vulgar display of jewels spoils this effect. Her movements, too, reveal that she is not quite liberated from the influences of the world out of which she has risen.

RIFKELE is a fascinating girl, dressed very neatly and modestly; still in short dresses, with two long braids hanging across her shoulders. She is busy decorating the room.

RIFKELE: [*As she pins some paper flowers to the curtain.*] There! That's the way, mamma dear. And now to decorate the mirror. See, mamma dear. Won't this be pretty?

SARAH: [*Busy arranging the table.*] Hurry, daughter dear, hurry. Your father has already gone to ask the guests to bring the Holy Scroll home.

RIFKELE: Won't that be lovely! We'll have a house full of people . . . There'll be playing and singing . . . Yes, mamma dear?

SARAH: Yes, my darling. It's a sacred event,—a great merit in the eyes of God . . . Not everyone can have a Holy Scroll written. Only a man of dignity, a person of standing.

RIFKELE: And will there be girls, too? And dancing? Really, mamma dear? [*Suddenly.*] I'll have to buy myself a waist, ma. And a pair of white slippers. [*Sticking out her shoes.*] You can't dance in shoes, can you?

SARAH: When you'll be engaged, in God's good time. Next Passover I'll make you a long dress and buy you slippers. Girls will come, fine young ladies, respectable ones. And you'll chum with them.

RIFKELE: [*Stubbornly.*] You're always putting things off until Passover. I'm a grown-up girl already. [*Looking into the mirror.*] See, ma. I'm a big girl. [*Showing her hair.*] And just see how long my braids are. Why, Manke tells me . . . [*Interrupting herself.*] And Manke will be there, too, won't she, mamma dear?

SARAH: No, my darling. Only nice, respectable girls. For you are a respectable child, a decent Jewish daughter . . .

RIFKELE: Why not, mamma dear? Manke sketched a David's shield for me on the cover of the Holy Scroll . . . I'm going to embroider it now in silk thread,—a wreath of leaves and a garland of flowers. You'll see how beautiful it'll be, ma. [*Points to the pictures on the wall.*] A hundred times prettier than these . . .

SARAH: [*With deep concern.*] Woe is me! Don't tell that to your father! He'll scold and fly into a rage when he hears of it.

RIFKELE: Why, mamma dear? It's for the Holy Scroll, isn't it?

SARAH: Your father will rave! [*Footsteps are heard.*] Hush, Rifkele, father is coming.

YEKEL: [*Still without.*] What? Do they think I'll get down on my knees and beg them? Not on their lives! [*Enters. He is a tall, strong man of about forty, stout; swarthy countenance, covered with dark hair; his black beard cut round. He speaks in loud, gruff tones, at the same time making coarse gestures and grasping the lapel of the man whom he happens to be addressing. Despite this, his face and person beam with a certain frank geniality.*] So they won't come! They don't have to! . . . So I got together some poor folks . . .

Don't you worry...We'll have plenty of customers for our honey-cakes and our geese. [*Noticing* RIFKELE, *he sits down.*] Come here, my little Rifkele, come to papa.

SARAH: [*Angered, but trying to conceal her feelings, continues to set the table.*] Do they think they'll soil their pedigree by coming to you? And when they need to borrow a hundred-rouble note...or take a charity contribution...they're not at all ashamed of your company then... The Gentile is impure, but his money's untainted.★

YEKEL: She's afraid already. Something new to worry about, eh? Never fear, it'll spoil nothing of yours...[*Calls* RIFKELE.] Well, well, come to daddy, won't you?

RIFKELE: [*Approaches her father very unwillingly, in fear.*] What does papa dear want?

YEKEL: Don't be afraid, Rifkele, I won't hurt you. [*Takes her hand.*] You like your father, don't you?

RIFKELE: [*Nods "yes."*]

YEKEL: Then why are you afraid of him?

RIFKELE: I don't know.

YEKEL: Don't be afraid of papa. He loves you. Very, very much. Today I'm having a Holy Scroll written. It costs a good deal of money. All for you, my child, all for you. [RIFKELE *is silent. Pause.*] And with God's help, when you are betrothed, I'll buy your sweetheart a gold watch and chain—the chain will weigh half a pound...Papa loves you very dearly. [RIFKELE *is silent. She lowers her head bashfully. Pause.*] Don't be ashamed. There's nothing wrong about being engaged. God has ordained it. [*Pause.*] That's nothing. Everybody gets engaged and married. [RIFKELE *is silent. Pause.*] Well, now. Do you love daddy?

RIFKELE: [*Nodding, and speaking softly.*] Yes.

YEKEL: Well, then. What do you want me to buy you? Tell me, Rifkele. [*She makes no reply.*] Tell me, now. Don't be afraid. Your daddy loves you. Tell me, like a good little girlie. What shall I buy you? [RIFKELE *is silent.*]

SARAH: [*Busy at the table, to* RIFKELE.] Well, why don't you answer when your father speaks to you?

RIFKELE: I don't know...

SARAH: [*To* YEKEL.] She wants a silk waist and a pair of white slippers.

YEKEL: Is that it? A silk waist and a pair of white slippers? Eh?

RIFKELE: [*Nods "yes."*]

★The force of this in the original is increased by the use of the terms 'trayf' and 'kosher,' i.e., that which, according to the Mosaic dietary laws, is unfit or fit to be eaten.

YEKEL: You certainly deserve them. [*From his pockets, which jingle with coins, he takes out a gold-piece and offers it to* RIFKELE.] Here, give this to mamma. And let her buy them for you. [RIFKELE *takes the money and hands it to her mother. On the stairs outside is heard the noise of the poor folk whom* YEKEL *has invited.* YEKEL *turns to* SARAH.] See? You said [*He opens the door.*] that you would have no guests. [*Calls.*] Now then. Come in. Come in. [*Enter a crowd of poor people, men and women, at first singly, as if they were stealing in; then more boldly, in groups. All greet* YEKEL, *some of them ironically.*]

PEOPLE IN THE CROWD: Good day to you, host! [*To* SARAH.] Good day to you, hostess.

SARAH: [*Puts on an apron, places in it loaves of white bread, rolls, honey-cakes and so forth, and distributes them among the guests.*]

ONE OF THE POOR MEN: Long life to you, hostess, and may you live to celebrate joyous events beyond number.

A WOMAN: May the Holy Scroll bring good fortune and be a blessing to your home.

YEKEL: [*Throwing slices of white bread to the poor people. To* SARAH.] Give them a whole pound of cake apiece. And a bottle of brandy to take home with them. Let them know that I'm celebrating today... Never mind. I can well afford it.

A WOMAN, BLIND IN ONE EYE: [*Praising* YEKEL *and* SARAH *before her poor neighbors.*] This is a house for you, such luck may I have. Nobody ever leaves this place empty-handed. There's always a plate of soup for the sick, a shirt for a poor fellow. What then? Do you think you can get anything over there where the proud purses live? ★ [SARAH, *as if not hearing the woman's words, throws into the apron of the latter a few more portions of food. The old woman holds up her apron and continues to talk.*] Whenever there's a celebration here... whoever you are... however humble your trade...

OTHER POOR FOLKS: [*Among themselves.*] That's so. May we know such luck... May such good fortune be ours!..

YEKEL: [*Takes out a handful of small change and casts it into* RIFKELE'S *apron.*] Here, divide this among the poor folks. [RIFKELE *distributes the money.*]

THE BLIND WOMAN: [*Now enthusiastic, pointing to* RIFKELE.] And show me, in the whole town, another girl as respectable as she!... [*To the other women.*] Why, Rabbis haven't such virtuous children! [*More softly, yet loud enough for* YEKEL *and* SARAH *to hear.*] God alone knows how such

---

★ Literally, 'under the high windows.'

a pure child came to them...Imagine, brought up in such a place,—may Heaven not punish us for mentioning it. [*Louder.*] And they guard her like the apple of their eye...They weigh and measure every step she takes. It's a delight to look at her. [*Goes over to* YEKEL.] Never mind. Everybody knows it. [*Pointing to* RIFKELE.] If I had a Rabbi for a son, I'd choose her for his bride.

THE OTHER WOMEN: [*Among themselves.*] Everybody knows it. It's the talk of the town.

YEKEL: Just wait till I lead her under the wedding canopy, in God's good time. You'll all get a whole goose apiece, and a pickerel just out of the water, and roubles galore. And if I lie, then my name isn't Yekel Tchaftchovitch!

THE BLIND WOMAN: And I tell you, it's just as if she had been brought up in a synagogue,—Heaven pardon the word in this place. So pure and modest...finer than any child of the most respectable family.

THE OTHER WOMEN: Folks will learn all about it. It's the talk of the town.

YEKEL: [*Distributing glasses of brandy. Blurts out, before he realizes what he is saying.*] Even though her father *is* Yekel Tchaftchovitch...

SARAH: [*Giving out glasses.*] Look at the people before whom he must boast!

YEKEL: [*Pouring brandy into glasses. With passionate unrestraint.*] It makes no difference to me,—poor or rich. Let everybody know,—let the whole town know. What *I* am, I am. [*Points to his wife.*] What *she* is, she is...It's all true,—everything. But let them not breathe a word against my daughter...And if anyone dares to do so, I'll break his head with this bottle here. Even if it's the Rabbi himself, it'll make no difference to me!...She's purer than his own daughter. [*Pointing to his neck.*] You may slash my throat if that isn't so!

SARAH: [*Stops passing around the brandy.*] We've heard all that before...That's enough. [*Rubs her hands and goes to a corner for the broom.*] We must clean the room now for our guests. [*Turning to the poor folk.*] You're not offended, I hope?

THE POOR PEOPLE: Not at all, hostess. May happiness and joy be yours forever... [*They leave the room singly, uttering profuse blessings.* YEKEL, *behind his wife's back, throws them more food. The last woman speaks to* RIFKELE, *loud enough for the others to hear.*] Go, Rifkele, and prepare the robe for the Holy Scroll. Reb Ali will soon come, and the Scribe, too. [RIFKELE *goes into her room.*]

SARAH: [*Sweeping the floor.*] To think that he had to boast before such people! I tell you!...And otherwise, do you imagine, they wouldn't have come to you? Make a celebration every day, and every day you'll have them here. In respectable houses people know how to act so that they'll be looked up to. What do you think, — they're all like you, with your "Hello, good brother!" right away? What kind of host are you, anyway?

YEKEL: Do you expect respectable folks to come to your home? Have you forgotten who you are, perhaps?

SARAH: "Who you are!" What! Have you stolen anything? You have a business. Everybody has his own business. You don't compel anybody, do you? You may deal in what you please, can't you, if you yourself do no wrong? . . . Just try to give them some money, and see whether they'll take it from you or not!

YEKEL: They'll take it from you, all right, but they'll look upon you as a dog, just the same . . . And at the synagogue you'll have the back seat, and they'll never call you up to the altar, to read from the Holy Book.

SARAH: Do you really believe that they're any better than you? You don't need their favors! . . . That's the way of the world these days: if you've got the money, even so pious a Jew as Reb Ali comes to your home, — a Pietist,★ mind you, — and accepts handsome alms from you. He asks no questions, — whether you got it by theft or by murder. So long as you have the cash. That's the chief point!

YEKEL: Don't climb too high, Sarah. Do you hear? Not too high . . . For if you do, some fine day you'll fall and break your neck. [*Shakes a warning finger at her.*] And don't try to break into the upper crust. Don't, I tell you. You've a home of your own, — stay there. You've got bread, — eat. But don't intrude where you're not wanted . . . Every dog must know his own kennel. [*Leaving the table, with a gesture of apprehension.*] The whole business is beginning to make me uneasy . . . I'm afraid that this will bring the downfall of our hopes . . .

SARAH: [*Stops her work, placing her arms akimbo.*] And you're a man! Shame yourself! I'm only a woman, but I can say to myself, "The past is gone forever." Whiz! Flown away! . . . There's nobody to be ashamed of. The whole world isn't any better. Why, if it were, people would have to go about with their heads bowed to the earth. [*Coming nearer to him.*] In a little while you'll have money. You close up shop and not a rooster crows . . . Who needs to know what we were?

YEKEL: [*Meditatively.*] That would be best . . . [*Pause.*] To buy a pack of horses and smuggle them across the border, just like Eisikl Furman did . . . And become a respectable person . . . not have people eye you like a thief.

★ 'Khossid.' The 'Khassidim' are noted for the religious frenzy of their worship.

SARAH: [*Considering the matter.*] Just the same it's too bad to go out of our business... You'll never make such good money from your horses. Here, at least, it's all cash.

YEKEL: That's certainly so.

SARAH: [*Goes into the next room, returns with a tray of plates and begins to arrange them upon the table.*] And just see what a daughter we have. Thank God, more decent than all the daughters of the best families in town. She'll marry some highly esteemed fellow, raise a respectable family... Isn't that so? Then what's wrong?

YEKEL: [*Arising.*] Yes, with an example like you as her guide. Go, let Manke steal up to her from downstairs... Have her here, in this room, all the time!

SARAH: Just see how he's carrying on! I once asked Manke to teach Rifkele how to embroider on canvas. Rifkele's a young lady, you must remember. Has she any companions at all? You don't let her step out into the street... [*Pause.*] If you don't want her to have anything to do with Manke, then she won't.

YEKEL: No, I don't want her to! Do you hear? I don't! I don't want my home to mix with downstairs. [*Points to the cellar.*] My home must be kept apart from that place! Understand? Just like pure and impure!★ Below [*Indicating the cellar.*] is a brothel, and here lives a pure girl, worthy of marrying the best of men. Do you hear? [*Bangs his fist upon the table.*] A pure, virtuous maiden lives here! Keep the two places apart!... [*Footsteps are heard outside.*]

SARAH: All right. Just as you say. Only don't make such a racket. [*Listening.*] Hush. People are coming. It's Reb Ali [*She thrusts her hair back underneath her wig and pulls off her apron.* YEKEL *strokes his beard and straightens his coat. Both stand by the door, expectantly... The door opens wide. Enter* SHLOYME *and* HINDEL. *The first is a tall, sturdy chap; wears long boots and a short coat. He is a knavish fellow, whose. eyes blink with stealthy cunning as he speaks. The second is a rather old girl, with a wan face and wearing clothes much too young for her years.* SHLOYME *and* HINDEL *are evidently at ease and feel at home.*]

YEKEL: [*To* SARAH.] Take a look at these guests of mine, will you? [*To* SHLOYME.] I do no business here. Down below. Everything down below. [*Pointing to the cellar.*] I'll be down right away.

SHLOYME: What's the hurry to get rid of us? Are you already ashamed of our company?

★ Cf. previous note on 'trayf' and 'kosher.'

YEKEL: Well, what have you got to say for yourself?

SHLOYME: You're having a celebration today, aren't you? So we came in to wish you good luck. Old friends... eh, what?

SARAH: Look at our "old friends," will you?

YEKEL: That was all once upon a time. From today on, — all over! You want to talk business with me? All right. But everything downstairs. [*Indicating the basement.*] Here I don't know you, nor do you know me, — from now on. You're welcome to a glass of brandy. [*Pours out brandy.*] But be quick. Somebody might come.

SHLOYME: [*Taking his glass, speaks to* HINDEL, *roguishly.*] You see? It's a great thing to get married. You become a somebody, on a par with everybody else. And you have Scrolls of the Law written. Not like us chaps, us scamps. [*To* YEKEL.] Yes, and I've really taken an example from you and have today become engaged to this thing here. [*Points to* HINDEL.] She'll make a dandy housewife, eh? You'll see. She'll put on a wig and she'll be the living image of a Rabbi's wife. As true as we're alive...

YEKEL: May I always hear such good news! So! You're engaged, are you? And when will the wedding take place, — may it be with luck!

SARAH: Just see with whom he's stopped to talk! It really becomes him! With outcasts, God forgive my words. Reb Ali and the Scribe will be here at any moment!

SHLOYME: When'll the wedding take place, you ask? When does one of our kind ever have a wedding? When we'll get a couple of girls we'll get married and open a house of our own. What else can one of us become? Certainly not a Rabbi. But the girls must be something fine, — first class. Fiery and hot-blooded. [*Winking to* YEKEL.] Otherwise it doesn't pay.

YEKEL: And what do you want of me, I'd like to know?

SHLOYME: What do I want of you? A mere trifle. [*Points to* HINDEL.] She's your woman, isn't she? And she's my sweetheart. She has a claim upon you. [*Takes from* HINDEL *her wagebook.*] From this day on you'll have to deal with me. Today I ask a mere bagatelle. Ten roubles, on this book. [*Slaps the book.*] It's good money, safe money. [*Looking at* HINDEL.] She wants to buy herself a hat.

YEKEL: All that downstairs. Down below. I'll be down soon and we'll transact all business down there. Here I don't even know you. Here I do no business with you at all.

SHLOYME: It's all the same to me. Above or below. Downstairs live no strangers, nor upstairs either. Same thing. The same devil.

YEKEL: Get a move on! Off with you! Do you hear? We're expecting people!

SARAH: May an evil night descend upon their heads, their hands and their feet. They came here to spoil our celebration... [*Looks at* HINDEL *with scorn.*] It pays to have so much vexation over such a slut!

HINDEL: If I'm not good enough to be one of your women, go down into the cellar yourself.

SHLOYME: [*To* HINDEL.] Tell her to send her daughter down there. [*To* SARAH.] Upon my word, you'd do a rushing business.

YEKEL: Curse me, — do you hear? [*Points to* SARAH.] Curse her, too. We're your kind. But don't dare to breathe my daughter's name. Understand? [*Coming closer to* SHLOYME.] Don't dare to mention her name, or I'll rip your bowels open. Do you hear? She doesn't know you, and you don't know her!

SHLOYME: Then I *will* know her. She's the daughter of a fellow-tradesman, so we're quite closely related.

YEKEL: [*Seizing* SHLOYME *by the throat.*] I'll rip your bowels open... You may slap my face; kick me about, if you will, but don't mention my daughter's name! [YEKEL *and* SHLOYME *engage in a struggle.*]

SARAH: [*Running over to them.*] A curse has been visited upon me! There he goes, starting a fight with such low-lives! Somebody's liable to come in at any moment, woe is me. Yekel! — Reb Ali and the Scribe... Yekel, for God's sake! [*Dragging him away from* SHLOYME.] What's come over you? [*Heavy footsteps are heard outside.*] Yekel, Yekel! Reb Ali is coming, — the Scribe is here! This is a shame and a disgrace before people!

YEKEL: Let me go. Right on this spot I'll... [*Tightening his grasp upon* SHLOYME.]

REB ALI'S VOICE: Right here, Scribe. This is the home of the Scroll's donor. [REB ALI *appears in the doorway, first thrusting in his large head, with a pipe between his teeth.*] What's all the noise about? In the home of one who has a Scroll of the Law written, all must be joy and happiness. Not quarrelling. [*To the* SCRIBE *outside.*] This way, please, Scribe. [YEKEL, *at the sound of* REB ALI'S *voice, releases* SHLOYME. SARAH *runs over to* SHLOYME *and thrusts into his hand a piece of paper money which she has taken from her stocking. She shoves* HINDEL *and* SHLOYME *toward the door; the latter two encounter the* SCRIBE *and* REB ALI *on the threshold. The pious men stand back from the woman, making way for her and* SHLOYME.]

SHLOYME: [*To* HINDEL, *as they leave.*] Take a peek at the folks he's hob-nobbing with these days. He'll become head of the town before long. [*They go off, conversing in indistinct tones.*]

REB ALI: [*A short, corpulent fellow, who speaks rapidly, making ingratiating gestures as he does so. He appears to be much at home, and evidently entertains a high opinion of himself.*] I beg your pardon, Scribe; I beg your pardon. [*Quietly, to* YEKEL *and* SARAH.] You ought to act more decently. It's high time. People are coming and…

THE SCRIBE: [*Enters. A tall old man, whose long, thin body is enveloped in a broad overcoat. His beard is long, white and sparse. He wears spectacles and has an air of cold aloofness and mystery.*]

REB ALI: [*Pointing to* YEKEL.] This is the donor of the Scroll.

THE SCRIBE: [*Proffering his hand to* YEKEL, *at the same time surveying him.*] Greetings. Peace be to you, fellow Jew.

YEKEL: [*Thrusts out his hand, uncertainly.* SARAH *reverently steps to one side.*]

REB ALI: [*Takes a seat at the table and pushes a chair over toward the* SCRIBE.] Be seated, Scribe. [*To* YEKEL.] Take a seat. [*The* SCRIBE *sits down.* YEKEL, *still uncertain, sits down opposite him, next to* REB ALI. *The latter addresses the* SCRIBE.] This is the gentleman on whose behalf I ordered the Holy Scroll. [*He helps himself to brandy, first pouring out a glass for the* SCRIBE.] He has no son, so he desires to do honor to the Lord with a Scroll of the Law. Such is the custom among the people of Israel,—and a very beautiful one, too. So we must aid him… Your health, Scribe. [*Gives his hand to the* SCRIBE, *then to* YEKEL.] Your health, host. Today you are the Master of Festivities. [YEKEL *stretches out his hand, at a loss.* REB ALI *drinks.* SARAH *approaches the table and pushes toward* REB ALI *some jelly preserves.* YEKEL *pulls her by the sleeve and signals her to withdraw from the table.* REB ALI, *after drinking, turns to the* SCRIBE.] Drink, Scribe. [*To* YEKEL.] Drink, host. Today you must rejoice. God has favored you with the means of having a Holy Scroll written. It is a divine merit indeed. A very great one.

THE SCRIBE: [*Holding his glass in his hand, to* REB ALI, *referring to* YEKEL.] Who is this man?

REB ALI: What is the difference? A Jew… And if he isn't a learned scholar, must all men be scholars? A Jew wants to earn a divine blessing. Then we must befriend him. [*To* YEKEL.] Drink a health. Here's joy to you.

THE SCRIBE: Will he know how to take care of the Holy Scroll?

REB ALI: And why not? He is a Jew, isn't he? And what Jew doesn't know the holy significance of a Scroll? [*Drinks.*] Your health, your health. And may the Lord send His blessings to His people.

THE SCRIBE: [*Gives his hand to* YEKEL.] Your health, host. [*Admonishing him.*] And know, that a Holy Scroll is a wondrous possession. The whole world rests upon a Scroll of the Law, and every Scroll is the exact counterpart of the tablets that were received by Moses upon Mount Sinai. Every line of a Holy Scroll is penned in purity and piety…

Where dwells a Scroll, in such a house dwells God himself...So it must be guarded against every impurity...Man, you must know that a Holy Scroll...

YEKEL: [*Awed; he stammers.*] Rebbi, rebbi ★...I want to tell the Rebbi the whole truth,—the honest truth...I am a poor sinner...Rebbi, I'm afraid...

REB ALI: [*Interrupting* YEKEL. *To the* SCRIBE.] The man is a sincere penitent and it is our duty to befriend him. The Talmud counsels us to. Of course he understands the significance of a Holy Scroll. He's a Jew, after all. [*To* YEKEL.] You must have reverence for a Scroll of the Law. Great reverence,—precisely as if a noted Rabbi were under your roof. In the house where it resides no profanity must be uttered. It must dwell amidst purity. [*Speaks to* SARAH, *looking toward her but not directly at her.*] Wherever a Holy Scroll is sheltered, there no woman must remove the wig from her head...[SARAH *thrusts her hair more securely under her wig.*] Nor must she touch the Scroll with her bare hands. As a reward, no evil overtakes the home that shelters a Scroll. Such a home will always be prosperous and guarded against all misfortune. [*To the* SCRIBE.] What do you imagine?—That he doesn't know all this? They're Jews, after all...[SARAH *nods affirmatively.*]

THE SCRIBE: You hear, sir, that the whole world rests upon the Scroll. The fate of our race lies rolled up in that parchment. With one word,— with a single word, God forbid, you can desecrate the Law and bring down upon all the Jews a grievous misfortune,—God forbid.

YEKEL: [*Arising from the table.*] Rebbi, I'll confess everything...Rebbi [*Comes nearer to* REB ALI.] I know that you are a holy man. I am not worthy, Rebbi, of your presence in this house...under my roof... Rebbi, I am a sinner. She [*Pointing to his wife.*] is a sinner. We have no right to a Holy Scroll...Inside that room. [*Pointing to the door at the right.*] For her sake, Rebbi...[*Goes into* RIFKELE's *room and returns, leading her by the hand. She holds a velvet cover of a Scroll, upon which she is embroidering a David's shield in gold thread.*] Rebbi, she [*Pointing to* RIFKELE.] may go about a Holy Scroll. She is as pure as the Lord's Law itself. It is for her that I ordered it. [*Indicating her embroidery.*] See, Rebbi, she's embroidering a cover for the Scroll. She may, Rebbi, for her hands are pure. I, Rebbi, [*Striking himself over the heart.*] I promise

---

★ 'Rebbi' is a term usually applied to teachers of Hebrew. It is often interchanged with the more dignified 'Rabbi,' which means, properly, a doctor of Hebrew law. The term 'Reb' is a form of address used by Jews before first names only. Cf. the Spanish 'Don.'

not to touch your Holy Law. She [*Pointing to his wife.*] will not touch your Holy Scroll. She [*Resting his hand upon* RIFKELE'*s head.*] will carry it. It will be placed in her room. [*To* RIFKELE.] And when you are married and leave my roof, take the Scroll of the Law with you to your husband's home…

REB ALI: [*To* YEKEL.] In other words, when you marry off your daughter, you'll give her the Holy Scroll as her dowry. Isn't that it?

YEKEL: Reb Ali, when my daughter is married, I'll give her as a dowry a pile of money, and I'll say to her: "Go out of your father's house and forget…forget your father…forget your mother…and have pure children, Jewish children, just like every Jewish daughter." That's what I'll say to her.

REB ALI: That is, you will present the Holy Scroll as a wedding-gift to your son-in-law. That's the idea, isn't it? [*To the* SCRIBE.] Do you see, Reb Aaron, there are still pious Jews in the world; here's a man with a daughter, and has a Scroll of the Law written for her future husband…How beautiful that is, — how virtuous…I tell you, Reb Aaron, that the spirit of Israel, the Jewish spark…the…ahem…ah!…ah!… [*Smacking his lips.*]

YEKEL: [*Leads* RIFKELE *back into her room. He closes the door after her.*] Rebbi, I can speak plainly to you. We're alone. My wife may hear it, too. We are sinners. I know, God will punish us. Let Him punish. That doesn't bother me. Let Him cripple me, disfigure me; let Him make me a pauper, so that I'll have to go begging from door to door…Anything but *that*… [*More softly.*] Rebbi, when a man has a son who goes to the bad — the devil take him. But a daughter, Rebbi. If a daughter falls, it is as if the mother had sinned in her grave. So I went to the holy synagogue and approached this man [*Pointing to* REB ALI.] and I said to him: "Give me something that'll guard my home from evil"…So he said to me: "Have a Holy Scroll written and place it in your home." Rebbi, as for us, our souls belong to the devil anyway…For her, and in her room I'll place the Scroll; for her to have as a companion. As for us, we dare not, we must not… [REB ALI *bends over to the* SCRIBE, *whispers something to him, making various gestures and pointing to* YEKEL. *The latter and* SARAH *stand at the table in tense expectancy. Pause.*]

THE SCRIBE: [*After brief consideration.*] And where are the guests in honor of the Holy Scroll?

REB ALI: We'll go to the synagogue and gather a quorum ★ of Jews. It will

---

★ 'Minyan'. The quorum of ten males above the age of thirteen required for all religious services.

be easy enough to find men who are willing to honor the Law. [*Arises from the table, pours brandy into the glasses, slapping* YEKEL *on the shoulder.*] There, there! God will help you! Rejoice, host! The Lord befriends the sincere penitent...Don't worry. You'll marry your girl to some proficient scholar; you'll take some poor Yeshiva ★ student for a son-in-law, and support him while he sits and studies the Holy Law. And the blessings of the Law will win you the Lord's forgiveness. [*Pause.*] I've really been thinking about it, and have a certain fellow in view,— a jewel of a chap,—smart head on his shoulders...his father is a highly respected man. [*Abruptly.*] Are you going to give your daughter a large dowry?

YEKEL: Rebbi, take away all I own. I'll let you strip me bare...Take everything, everything...And I'll say to my girl, "Forget your mother... forget your father." And I'll send her and her husband all they need, in a roundabout way. "Here's your food and drink, keep on studying in your holy books...I don't know you...you don't know me..."

REB ALI: Everything will be all right, in the virtue of the Scroll...Come, Scribe. Come, host, let's be off to the synagogue. We'll hunt out a quorum and celebrate the Holy Scroll...[*To the* SCRIBE.] Do you see, Reb Aaron? A Jew, even if he sins, still remains a Jew. A Jewish soul— seeks a pious scholar for a son-in-law...[*To* YEKEL.] Never you mind. Don't worry. God will help you...The Lord loves a repentant sinner. But you must give generous donations to the students of the Law. If you cannot study the Law yourself, at least support those who can, for the whole world rests upon the Holy Law...[*To the* SCRIBE.] Is that not so, Reb Aaron? And why not? [*Pointing to* YEKEL.] I knew his father...He was a fine man...a teamster...handsome chap...Believe me, the Lord will come to his aid, and he will become a Jew as worthy as any other. [*To* YEKEL.] The important thing is to repent deep in your heart,—that is, you must abandon the path of iniquity that you've followed hitherto...and you must contribute liberally to the support of the students of the Holy Word.

YEKEL: [*Summoning courage, he approaches* REB ALI.] Just let me make a little more money, Reb Ali, so that I can give my daughter a handsome dowry, and my name isn't Yekel Tchaftchovitch if I don't go out of the business altogether...I'll deal in horses, just as my father did, may his soul rest in peace. I'll get together a stable of horses and go to the Lovitch fair. And my son-in-law will be sitting inside there studying

---

★ 'Yeshiva'. An academy of Hebrew studies.

the sacred Law. I'll come home for the Sabbath and sit down right here and listen to him reading from the Commentaries. And if I lie, my name isn't Yekel.

REB ALI: Don't worry. It's all right. The Lord will come to your aid. Yes, God will help you. Isn't that so, Reb Aaron?

THE SCRIBE: Who can tell? Our Lord is a God of mercy and forgiveness, but He is also a God of retribution and vengeance. [*Leaving.*] Well, it's getting late. Let's be off to the synagogue. [*Leaves.*]

YEKEL: What did the Rebbi say?

REB ALI: It's all right. Don't worry. God will help you... He *must* help you... Come, come and take your Holy Scroll home in rejoicing. [*About to depart.* YEKEL *hesitates, undecided.* REB ALI *notices this.*] What? You want to speak a few words with your wife, — to tell her to prepare for our return with the Scroll?

SARAH: [*To* REB ALI.] Everything's ready, Reb Ali. Everything.

REB ALI: Well, what are you waiting for? The Scribe has already gone.

YEKEL: [*At the door, uncertain, pointing to himself.*] I, walk together with the Rebbi, through the streets?

REB ALI: Come, come. If the Lord pardons you, surely we may do so, too.

YEKEL: [*Enthusiastically.*] Reb Ali, you're a good Rebbi. [*About to embrace* REB ALI; *suddenly recalls himself and draws back.*] A good Rebbi, may I live so! [REB ALI *and* YEKEL *leave together. The evening shadows gather.*]

SARAH: [*Betakes herself assiduously to cleaning the room and setting the table. Calls into* RIFKELE's *room*] Rifkele, Rifkele, come in and help me out a bit. They'll soon be coming with the Holy Scroll.

RIFKELE: [*Appears on the threshold of her door, uncertain.*] Has father left already?

SARAH: Yes. He went to the synagogue with Reb Ali and the Scribe. The Rabbi will soon be coming, and other guests, too.

RIFKELE: [*Showing the cover for the Holy Scroll.*] See how nicely I've embroidered it.

SARAH: Yes, yes. I see. But comb your hair. Dress yourself. The guests will soon be here. Rabbi and...

RIFKELE: I'll call up Manke and have her comb me... I love to have her comb me. She does it so beautifully. Makes my hair so smooth... And her hands are so cool. [*Takes something and taps the floor with it, calling.*] Manke! Manke!

SARAH: [*Frightened.*] Rifkele! What are you doing? Don't! Your father will be furious! It isn't becoming for you to chum with Manke. You're already a marriageable young lady, a virtuous child. And we've just been talking about some good matches for you,—excellent matches with learned scholars...

RIFKELE: But I do love Manke so much!

SARAH: It's a shame for you to chum with Manke, I tell you! You are a decent girl; you'll have clean, respectable girls to go around with... We're arranging a match for you, an excellent match. Your father's just gone to see the bridegroom, Reb Ali said,... [*Goes into the next room.*] We must wash, dress, and put on our best clothes... The guests will be here at any moment.

RIFKELE: A bridegroom? What kind of bridegroom, mamma dear?

SARAH: [*From the other room.*] A sweetheart,—a golden one. A wonderful student, of a fine family.

MANKE: [*Appears in the doorway at the rear. First she thrusts in her head, shaking her finger playfully at* RIFKELE; RIFKELE *goes over to her, walking cautiously backwards, beckoning to her as she does so. The room is fast growing dark.*]

RIFKELE: [*Falls into* MANKE's *arms. To her mother.*] A handsome sweetheart, mamma dear? [MANKE *kisses her passionately.*]

SARAH: [*From within.*] Yes, daughter dear. A handsome sweetheart, with two jet-black temple-locks and a satin coat, and a velvet skull-cap, dressed just like a Rabbi. He's a Rabbi's son, Reb Ali said.

RIFKELE: [*In* MANKE's *embrace, caressing* MANKE's *cheeks.*] And where will he stay, mamma dear?

SARAH: [*From within.*] There in your room, where the Sacred Scroll will be kept. He'll live there with you and study the Holy Law.

RIFKELE: [*In* MANKE's *arms.*] And will he love me, mamma dear?

SARAH: [*As before.*] Ever so much, daughter dear, ever so much. And you'll have pure, respectable children, virtuous children...

[*Slow* CURTAIN...

Falling as they speak.]

Act Two

Scene: *In the cellar-brothel. A spacious basement in an old building; low-arched ceiling; high up on the wall, close to the ceiling, two deep, narrow windows, hung with curtains. On the sill, flower-pots. The rain is coming in through the windows. A flight of stairs leads to the door above, which is constructed like that of the entrance to a cabin on board ship. Half of the door is ajar, revealing the gloom of the night. Rain drips down. In the background of the cellar, several small compartments, separated from one another by thin partitions, and screened by thick black curtains. One of the curtains has been drawn aside; in the compartment are seen a bed, a wash-stand, a mirror and various toilet articles. A colored night-lamp sheds a dim light over the tiny room. The furniture of the cellar itself consists of several lounges, a table, benches and card-tables; on the walls, looking-glasses bedecked with gaudy ornaments; chromos representing women in suggestive poses . . .*

On one of the lounges sleeps SHLOYME; *his long boots reach to a nearby bench. It is a night in spring.*

The room is lighted by a large hanging-lamp.

HINDEL: [*Enters. Halts for a moment upon the top stair and looks down at* SHLOYME. *She is wrapped in a thin shawl, coquettishly dressed in a skirt much too short for her age. Descends into the cellar, stepping noisily so as to wake* SHLOYME.]
SHLOYME: [*Awakes. Looks around.*] It's you, is it? Why aren't you outside?
HINDEL: It's begun to rain.
SHLOYME: [*Sitting up.*] So you deign to answer me, milady? Have you, then, forgiven me?
HINDEL: I wasn't angry in the first place.
SHLOYME: So . . . Well if you wish, you can get angry again, for all I care.
    [*Lies down.*]
HINDEL: [*Looks around. Runs over to one of the screened compartments and listens,*

then runs back to SHLOYME.] Shloyme, I don't want to leave this place.
See, now we're all alone and nobody can hear us. Tell me, as truly as
there is a God in heaven,—tell me, do you really mean to marry me?

SHLOYME: Go, my grand dame. Make knots in your shirt and hide your
money there, and then run to "Uncle" Yekel and complain that I take
all your earnings,—that you haven't even enough to buy yourself a
hat...

HINDEL: Yes, I did tell him that. It made me furious and cut me to the
quick,—to have you tear the very clothes off my back and then go
and make eyes at that yellow bitch...I'll dash vitriol into her face.
Why, her breath smells terribly. How can anybody get near such a
thing? A fine young lady he's hunted out!

SHLOYME: Away from me! I'll give you such a crack between the eyes that
you'll see your great-great-granny's ghost!

HINDEL: Crack away! Tear strips of skin off my body...[*Pushing up one
of her sleeves and showing him her arm.*] You've covered me with black
and blue marks. [*Baring her other arm.*] Here, pinch, slash, whatever
you will. But tell me, here on this very spot, by the memory of your
father and as truly as you pray for the repose of his soul,—will you
really marry me?

SHLOYME: [*Still stretched out.*] Once I wanted to. Now I don't.

HINDEL: Then it's no. That's the way I like to do things. Only no deceit. Do
you want money?—Say the word. A coat?—Here's the price. Only
no fooling me. [*Walks off.*]

SHLOYME: That's all right. There are plenty of sweethearts. You'll catch your
fish all right.

HINDEL: [*Drawing aside the curtain of her compartment.*] Don't give yourself
any worry on my account.

SHLOYME: You object, do you? Have it your way. [*Pause.*] But you're not
too angry to pour a fellow a glass of tea, are you?

HINDEL: [*Fetches him a glass of tea from her compartment and places it upon the
cellar table. She then returns to her place and sits down before her trunk of
clothes, as if looking for something. After a brief silence she addresses* SHLOYME,
from her compartment.] So you like her, eh?...Well, well...You'll soon
be busy, all right,—buying towels to pad out her flat bosom, paying
dentists for putting a set of teeth into her jaws, and getting her a pair
of stilts to make her look human size. Then you can hire a barrel-
organ and take her around people's backyards. A fine hurdy-gurdyman
you'd make, upon my word. I'll throw you a two-kopeck-piece from
the window, I promise.

SHLOYME: Hold your tongue, I tell you!

HINDEL: And what'll you do if I don't?

SHLOYME: I'll beat you black and blue.

HINDEL: Ho, ho! There's no beating folks these days. Nowadays a beating is answered with a knife.

SHLOYME: [*Springing to his feet.*] And who'll do that? [*Striding into* HINDEL's *compartment.*] Who'll do the knifing, eh? [*He struggles with her, tearing from her grasp a red waist. He returns to the cellar.*] Now we'll see. [*He rips the waist open eagerly. A photograph falls to the floor.*] Aha! Moyshe the locksmith! So that's your champion, is it? And since when have you become so thick with him? [*Goes back to her room.*]

HINDEL: What business is that of yours?

SHLOYME: This is what business it is of mine! [*He gives her a hard slap; she falls upon her bed and begins to weep.*] So you're going around with Moyshe the locksmith, are you? Exchanging photographs, eh? A regular pair of sweethearts! And all behind my back? [*Silence. He returns to his table.*] And I knew nothing about it... [*Drinks more tea, arises, and mounts the stairs.*] And I knew nothing about it... [*He stops at the door.*] Hindel! [*She does not answer.*] Hindel! Come here this instant! [*No reply.*] Hindel! [*He stamps his foot, then runs down the flight of stairs in a rage.*] Come here, I tell you! Do you hear what I say!

HINDEL: [*Arises from her bed and walks over to him, hiding her face in her handkerchief.*]

SHLOYME: Have you spoken to Manke?

HINDEL: [*Whimpering.*] Yes.

SHLOYME: Well, what does she say?

HINDEL: [*Still crying.*] If we'll have our own "house," she'll come to us.

SHLOYME: Sure?

HINDEL: [*Drying her eyes.*] Yes. But she doesn't want to come alone. She wants to bring a chum.

SHLOYME: Certainly. Do you imagine you can make any money on one girl, — even enough to pay the rent?

HINDEL: We ought to have a fresh young girl...

SHLOYME: Upon my soul! Then we'd do business! But where can we get her?

HINDEL: I've got my eye on one, — as beautiful as the day.★ and still untouched.

★ Literally 'as beautiful as a tree.'

SHLOYME: [*Curious.*] Can we get her for the business?

HINDEL: I should say!...

SHLOYME: A girl...from a "house"?

HINDEL: No. A pure maiden.

SHLOYME: How do you come to know her?

HINDEL: She comes to Manke every night...Steals out of her home... Nobody sees her. Something seems to draw her here...she is so inquisitive...

RIFKELE: [*Thrusting her bare head through the window, beckoning to* HINDEL.] Ps-s-s! Is my father down there?

HINDEL: [*Signalling back.*] No.

RIFKELE: [*Disappears from the window.*]

SHLOYME: [*Eyeing* HINDEL *closely.*] She! "Uncle" Yekel's daughter! A genuine gold-mine!

HINDEL: Hush! She's coming!

RIFKELE: [*Slender and beautiful; dressed modestly, and wrapped in a black shawl; steals through the door, runs down the stairs with trembling caution. She speaks more with signs than with words.*] Where is Manke? There? [*Pointing to a screened compartment.*] There, with...?

HINDEL: [*Nods "yes."*]

RIFKELE: [*Approaches the curtain of* MANKE's *room and listens with passionate intentness, looking around every other moment with palpitant apprehension.*]

SHLOYME: [*Very softly, to* HINDEL.] Tomorrow we must go and take a look at that house on Pivna Street.

HINDEL: And when shall we be married?

SHLOYME: First we've got to have a home.

HINDEL: I wonder how much the Rabbi will ask for performing the ceremony.

SHLOYME: As long as there's enough left to buy some furniture with. The place must make a decent showing. [*The door is suddenly banged open and* YEKEL *bursts in.*]

YEKEL: [*His face still betrays signs of his cunning and of his youthful dissipation. He is dressed in dignified, orthodox fashion. Removes his hat and shakes the rain from it.*] A fine business! It has to rain! [*Suddenly noticing* RIFKELE, *he explodes with rage.*] What! You here! [*Seizes her by the collar and shakes her, clinching his teeth.*] What are you doing here?

RIFKELE: [*Terrified, stammering.*] Mam...Mamma told me...to...c-call... [*Bursting into tears.*] Papa, don't hit me!

YEKEL: Your mother...your mother sent you...here! [*With a loud outcry.*]

Your mother! [*Dragging her upstairs.*] She'll lead you to ruin yet! Something draws her to it!...She wants her daughter to be what the mother was...

RIFKELE: [*Crying.*] Papa, don't hit me!

YEKEL: I'll teach you to mind your father! [*Leads her out.* RIFKELE'*s crying is heard from without.*]

SHLOYME: There's a virtuous Yekel for you! It doesn't become his dignity for his daughter to be a brothel-woman. [*Through the ceiling is heard a noise of angry stamping, and the weeping of a woman.*] He must be giving it to his wife now, all right! Biff! Bang!

HINDEL: He's right. A mother should guard her daughter well...Whatever you were, you were, but once you marry and have a child, watch over it...Just wait. If God should bless us with children, I'll know how to bring them up. My daughter will be as pure as a saint, with cheeks as red as beets...I won't let an eye gaze upon her. And she'll marry a respectable fellow, with an orthodox wedding...

SHLOYME: [*Slapping her across the shoulders.*] We'll see about that, all in due season. But talk to Rifkele in the meantime. Work upon her, I say. Otherwise everything's lost.

HINDEL: Don't you worry about my part. I'll know how to go about it.

SHLOYME: We'll see, then. [*Silence.*] If you land her, bring her right to me. You know...

YEKEL: [*Enters, in anger.*] It's time to close up. It's raining. In any case no dog's going to stick his snout into this place tonight. [*With a sharp look at* SHLOYME.] Enough, enough of this billing and cooing. Time to close up. [*Mounts the steps, opens the door and calls.*] Reizel! To bed! Basha! Time to go to sleep! [*From without are heard girls' voices: "Soon. Right away!"*]

HINDEL: [*Points to* YEKEL *and signals* SHLOYME *to leave.*]

SHLOYME: [*Goes up the steps. As he is about to go out he comes face to face with* YEKEL. *They eye each other.*]

YEKEL: Get a move on. Time to close up. You've whispered secrets long enough.

SHLOYME: [*Thrusting his hands into his trousers pocket. Looks sharply at* YEKEL.] Since when have you become such a respectable personage?

YEKEL: Off with you, now. Get a move on. I'll tell you later.

SHLOYME: To the devil with you!

HINDEL: [*Runs up the stairs to* SHLOYME.] Shloyme, go home, I tell you. Do you hear? Go home!

SHLOYME: [*Leaving, with a defiant glance at* YEKEL.] There's a fine lout for you!

YEKEL: As if I need him here!...[*Pointing to* HINDEL.] Here! You may take your old carcass along with you and start a place of your own.

HINDEL: People don't open places with old carcasses. You merely lie down to rest with them. But little dolls...

YEKEL: [*Calling into the entry.*] Reizel! Basha! [*Enter two girls, running. Rain is dripping from their wet, filmy dresses and from their unbraided hair. They are in a merry mood and speak with laughter.* YEKEL *leaves, slamming the door behind him.*]

BASHA: [*A stout girl, with red cheeks. Naïve in manner; she speaks with a harsh accent.*] What a sweet odor the rain has!...[*Shaking raindrops off her clothes.*] Just like the apples at home drying, in the lofts. This is the first May rain.

HINDEL: Such a crazy idea: to stand in the rain. As if they'll attract the whole world...Nobody'd ever show up in a downpour like this... [*Goes into her compartment and sits down near her trunk, packing various articles.*]

REIZEL: [*Shaking off raindrops.*] To the deuce with the whole lot of them. I paid my account the day before yesterday...We were standing under the eaves, the rain is so fragrant...It washes the whole winter off your head. [*Goes over to* HINDEL.] Just look...[*Showing her wet hair.*] How fresh it is...how sweet it smells...

BASHA: At home, in my village, the first sorrel must be sprouting. Yes, at the first May rain they cook sorrel soup...And the goats must be grazing in the meadows...And the rafts must be floating on the stream...And Franek is getting the Gentile girls together, and dancing with them at the inn...And the women must surely be baking cheese-cakes for the Feast of Weeks. ★ [*Silence.*] Do you know what? I'm going to buy myself a new summer tippet and go home for the holidays...[*Runs into her room, brings out a large summer hat and a long veil; she places the hat upon her wet hair and surveys herself in the looking-glass.*] Just see! If I'd ever come home for the holidays rigged up in this style, and promenade down to the station...Goodness! They'd just burst with envy. Wouldn't they? If only I weren't afraid of my father!

REIZEL: Why? Would he hurt you?

BASHA: He'd kill me on the spot. He's on the hunt for me with a crowbar.

★ Pentecost.

Once he caught me dancing with Franek at the village tavern and he gave me such a rap over the arm with a rod [*Showing her arm.*] that I carry the mark to this very day. I come from a fine family. My father is a butcher. Talk about the fellows that were after me!...[*In a low voice.*] They tried to make a match between me and Nottke the meat-chopper. I've got his gold ring still. [*Indicating a ring upon her finger.*] He gave it to me at the Feast of Tabernacles★ Maybe he wasn't wild to marry me,—but I didn't care to.

REIZEL: Why didn't you care to?

BASHA: Because I didn't...He always smelled ox meat...Ugh! His name is Pshorik. Think of marrying Pshorik and having a little Pshorik every year! Ugh!

REIZEL: And how is it any better for you here?

BASHA: Here, at least, I'm a free person. I've got my chest of finery, and dress swell. Better clothes, upon my word, than the rich daughters of my village...[*Fetching from her compartment a brown dress.*] When I go walking on Marshalkovski street in this dress they all stare at me...Fire and flame! Mm! If I could only put in an appearance in my home town dressed in this fashion, here's how I'd promenade to the station. [*Struts across the room like a lady of fashion, raising her skirt at the back and assuming a cosmopolitan air.*] They'd die of jealousy, I tell you...They'd be stricken with apoplexy on the spot. [*Promenades about the room playing the grand dame.*]

REIZEL: [*Straightens the folds of* BASHA*'s dress in the back and adjusts her hat to a better angle.*] That's the way! Now raise your head a bit higher...Who needs to know that you were ever in a place of this sort? You'll tell them that you were with a big business house. A Count has fallen in love with you...

HINDEL: [*From her room, where she is still busy with her chest of clothes.*] And what's the matter with a place of this sort, I'd like to know? Aren't we every bit as good as the girls in the business houses, eh? The whole world is like that nowadays; that's what the world demands. In these days even the daughters of the best families aren't any better. This is our way of earning a living. And believe me, when one of us gets married, she's more faithful to her husband than any of the others. We *know* what a man is.

BASHA: [*Still strutting about the room.*] Ah! Do you imagine they wouldn't recognize me right away? Their hearts would tell them...You know,

★Succoth.

my mother died from the shock . . . She couldn't live through it . . . To
this day I haven't visited her grave . . . [*Suddenly comes to a halt.*]
Sometimes she comes before me . . . At night I see her in my dreams.
She appears to me in her shroud, covered with thorns and briers,
because of my sins. And she pulls me by the hair.

REIZEL: Oh, mother! And did you really see her? How does she look, your
dead mother? Is she pale?

HINDEL: Shut up, will you? Late at night they have to start telling stories
about the dead. No dead people can come here. Our boss has a Holy
Scroll upstairs . . . [*A sudden hush.*] What's wrong about our trade, I'd
like to know? [*She leaves her little room and goes into the cellar.*] Wasn't
our mistress in a house like this for fifteen years? Yet she married. And
isn't she a respectable God-fearing woman? . . . Doesn't she observe all
the laws that a Jewish daughter must keep? . . . And isn't her Rifkele a
pure child? And isn't our boss a respectable man? Isn't he generous?
Doesn't he give the biggest donations to charity? . . . And he's had a
Holy Scroll written . . .

REIZEL: But they say that you mustn't read from such a Holy Scroll, and
that the daughter of such mothers become what the mothers themselves were . . . that something draws them on like a magnet, and that
the Evil Spirit drags them down into the mire . . .

HINDEL: [*Frightened.*] Who said so?

REIZEL: An old fortune-teller, — a sorceress told it to me . . . it's just as if
such a daughter were in the power of an enchantment . . .

HINDEL: That's a rotten lie! . . . Where's the old gypsy who told you that? . . .
I'd scratch her eyes out for her! There is a God in heaven, I say! We
have a God in Heaven!

MANKE: [*Steals from her compartment into the cellar. She is half-dressed, with a
shawl thrown over her. Her colored stockings are visible, and her hair is in
disorder. Her eyes sparkle with wanton cunning. Her face is long, and insolently
pretty; she is quite young. A lock of hair falls over her forehead. Her eyes blink
as she speaks, and her whole body quivers. She looks about in surprise.*] What?
Nobody here?

REIZEL: [*To* MANKE.] Is it you, Manke? A good thing you came. [*Pointing to*
HINDEL.] She's almost made a Rabbi's wife of me. Where have you left
your guest?

MANKE: He fell asleep. So I stole out.

REIZEL: Some generous land-owner, perhaps? Maybe he'll stand for the
drinks?

MANKE: Bah! He's a fool. Third time he's come. And he keeps asking me, who's my father, who's my mother,—as if he intended to marry me... Whenever he kisses me he hides his face in my bosom, closes his eyes and smiles as if he were a babe in his mother's arms. [*Looks around. In a low voice, to* HINDEL.] Hasn't Rifkele been here yet?

HINDEL: [*With a soft laugh.*] She was here... and her father caught her... and maybe he didn't raise a rumpus...

MANKE: Good heavens! How long since?

HINDEL: Quite a while ago... He must be asleep by now. [*Softly.*] She'll surely be down again soon.

REIZEL: [*To* MANKE, *in a merry mood.*] Come, Manke, let's go out into the street. It's raining. The drops are like pearls... The first May shower. Who's coming out with me for a rain bath?

MANKE: [*Approaching the window.*] It's raining. And what a thin drizzle. And how sweet it smells... Let's go out.

BASIL: At home when we have a shower like this the gutters run over and flood the narrow lanes. And we take off our shoes and stockings and dance in the rain barefoot... Who's going to take her shoes off? [*Removes her shoes and stockings.*] Take off your shoes, Manke, and let's dance in the rain!

MANKE: [*Removes her stockings and lets down her hair.*] There! Now let the rain soak us from head to foot... Standing in a May shower makes you grow. Isn't that so?

BASHA: [*Runs over.*] Come. Let's splash each other... Let's sprinkle handfuls of raindrops over each other. [*She lets down her hair.*] Let's drench our hair just like the trees... Come!

HINDEL: Wait. Wait. "Uncle" isn't asleep yet. He might hear us. [*All listen, their ears directed to the ceiling.*]

REIZEL: Come along! Can't you hear him snoring?

MANKE: Wait... We'll tap softly for Rifkele. [BASHA *and* REIZEL *go out.* MANKE *takes a stick and taps in a corner of the ceiling, very softly. From outside comes the noise of the girls skipping about in the water. They take handfuls of raindrops and throw them in through the open door, calling "Come out! Come out!"*]

RIFKELE: [*Thrusts her head through the window. She is in her night clothes, covered by a light shawl.*] She whispers cautiously. Manke, Manke. Did you call me?

MANKE: [*Takes a chair and places it under the window; stands upon it and reaches to* RIFKELE's *hand.*] Yes, Rifkele. I called you... Come, we'll stand in the May rain, splash water over each other and grow taller...

RIFKELE: [*From above.*] Hush! Speak more softly. I stole out of bed. So that
pa wouldn't hear. I'm afraid, — that he'll beat me.

MANKE: Don't be afraid of your father. He won't wake up so soon. Come,
let's rather stand in the rain. I'll let your hair down. [*She undoes
RIFKELE's braids, reaching through the window to do so.*] There. And now I'll
wash them for you in the rain. Just like this.

RIFKELE: I have only a nightgown on. All night I lay in bed waiting for my
father to fall asleep, so that I might steal out to you. I heard your
tapping and sneaked away. So softly, barefoot, — so that my father
shouldn't hear me.

MANKE: [*Embraces her passionately.*] Come, Rifkele, I'll wash your eyes in the
rainwater. The night is so beautiful, the rain is so warm and the air is
so full of delightful fragrance. Come.

RIFKELE: Hush . . . hush . . . I'm afraid of my father . . . He beat me . . . He
locked the door . . . And hid the key near the Holy Scroll. I lay awake
all night . . . I heard you call me . . . You called me so softly . . . And
something drew me so irresistibly to you . . . and I stole the key from
the Scroll . . . My heart pounded so wildly . . . so wildly . . .

MANKE: Wait, Rifkele, I'm coming right out to you. [*Jumps down from the
chair and runs up the stairs.*] I'm coming out to you. Just a moment and
I'm with you. [*She leaves.* RIFKELE *disappears from the window.*]

HINDEL: [*From the curtain of her compartment she has been listening very intently
to the conversation between* MANKE *and* RIFKELE. *She now begins to pace up
and down the cellar excitedly, wrapt in thought and muttering to herself very
slowly.*] With God's help, if I can only get both of them, Rifkele and
Manke, this very night . . . I'll take them directly to Shloyme's . . . And
I'll say to him, "Here you are . . . Here's your bread and butter. Now
rent a place, marry me, and become a respectable man as well as any
other." [*Stops abruptly. Raises her hands toward the ceiling.*] Father in
Heaven, you are a Father to all orphans . . . Mother in your grave, pray
for me . . . Let my troubles come to an end. Let me at last be settled in
my own home! . . . [*Pause.*] If God is only good to me, I'll have a Holy
Parchment written in His honor . . . And every Sabbath I'll give three
pounds of candles to the House of Study. [*A long pause. She is lost in the
contemplation of her future prospects.*] Yes, he is a good God . . . a good
God . . . Father in Heaven . . . Mother, pray in my behalf . . . don't be
silent . . . pray for me . . . do your very best for me . . . [*She returns to her
compartment and begins hastily to pack her things.*] I can be ready, anyway.
[*A long pause. The stage is empty. Soon* MANKE *leads in* RIFKELE. *They are*

both wrapped in the same wet shawl... Their hair is dripping wet. Large drops of water fall from their clothes to the floor. They are barefoot... HINDEL, *behind her curtain, listens as before.*]

MANKE: [*Speaks with restrained passion and love,—softly, but with deep resonance.*] Are you cold, Rifkele darling? Nestle close to me...Ever so close...Warm yourself next to me. So. Come, let's sit down here on the lounge. [*Leads* RIFKELE *to lounge; they sit down.*] Just like this... Now rest your face snugly in my bosom. So. Just like that. And let your body touch mine...It's so cool...as if water were running between us. [*Pause.*] I uncovered your breasts and washed them with the rainwater that trickled down my arms. Your breasts are so white and soft. And the blood in them cools under the touch, just like white snow,—like frozen water...and their fragrance is like the grass on the meadows. And I let down your hair so...[*Runs her fingers through* RIFKELE's *hair.*] And I held them like this in the rain and washed them. How sweet they smell...Like the rain itself...[*She buries her face in* RIFKELE's *hair.*] Yes, I can smell the scent of the May rain in them...So light, so fine...And fresh...as the grass on the meadows...as the apple on the bough...So. Cool me, refresh me with your tresses. [*She washes her face in* RIFKELE's *hair.*] Cool me,—so. But wait...I'll comb you as if you were a bride...a nice part and two long, black braids. [*Does so.*] Do you want me to, Rifkele? Do you?

RIFKELE: [*Nodding.*] Yes.

MANKE: You'll be the bride...a beautiful bride...It's Sabbath eve and you are sitting with your papa and mamma at the table...I—I am your sweetheart...your bridegroom, and I've come as your guest. Eh, Rifkele? Do you like that game?

RIFKELE: [*Nodding.*] Yes, I do.

MANKE: Wait, now; wait. Your father and mother have gone to sleep. The sweethearts meet here at the table...We are bashful...Eh?

RIFKELE: [*Nodding.*] Yes, Manke.

MANKE: Then we come closer to one another, for we are bride and bride-groom, you and I. We embrace. [*Places her arm around* RIFKELE.] Ever so tightly. And kiss, very softly. Like this. [*Kisses* RIFKELE.] And we turn so red,—we're so bashful. It's nice, Rifkele, isn't it?

RIFKELE: Yes, Manke...Yes.

MANKE: [*Lowering her voice, and whispering into* RIFKELE's *ear.*] And then we go to sleep together. Nobody sees, nobody hears. Only you and I. Like this. [*Clasps* RIFKELE *tightly to herself.*] Do you want to sleep with me tonight like this? Eh?

RIFKELE: [*Looking about nervously.*] I do...I do...

MANKE: [*Drawing* RIFKELE *closer.*] Come...Come...

RIFKELE: [*Softly.*] I'm afraid of my father. He'll wake up and...

MANKE: Wait, Rifkele, wait a second. [*Reflects for a moment.*] Do you want to go away from here with me? We'll be together days and nights at a time. Your father won't be there, nor your mother... Nobody'll scold you...or beat you... We'll be all by ourselves... For days at a time... We'll be so happy. What do you say, Rifkele?

RIFKELE: [*Closing her eyes.*] And my father won't know?

MANKE: No. We'll run away this very night,—with Hindel, to her house...She has a house with Shloyme, she told me. You'll see how nice everything will be... Young folks will be there aplenty,—army officers...and we'll be together, all by ourselves, all day long. We'll dress just like the officers and go horseback-riding. Come, Rifkele,—do you want to?

RIFKELE: [*Trembling with excitement.*] And papa won't hear?

MANKE: No, no, He won't hear. He's sleeping so soundly...There, can't you hear him snoring?...[*Runs over to* HINDEL'*s compartment and seizes* HINDEL *by the arm.*] Have you got a place? Come! Take us away at once!

HINDEL: [*Waking with a start.*] Yes, yes. To Shloyme's, right away! [*She throws a dress over* RIFKELE.] He'll find us a place quickly enough.

MANKE: [*Hastily dressing* RIFKELE.] You'll see how nice everything'll be... What a jolly time we'll have. [*All dress, seizing whatever they happen to lay hands upon. Slowly they ascend the steps. At the door they encounter* REIZEL *and* BASHA *who, drenched to the skin, are just returning to the cellar.* REIZEL *and* BASHA *look at the others in surprise.*]

REIZEL and BASHA: [*Together.*] What's this? Where are you going?

MANKE: Hush! Don't make any noise. We're going for some beer,—and lemonade...[HINDEL, MANKE *and* RIFKELE *leave, followed by the amazed glances of* REIZEL *and* BASHA.]

REIZEL: There's something suspicious about this that I don't like.

BASHA: Same here.

REIZEL: Something's up...Good heavens!

BASHA: [*Stares at* REIZEL *in fright.*] What? You mean *that*?

REIZEL: It's none of our business. Let's put out the lamp and go to sleep. We know nothing about it. [*Turns down the wick of the lamp. The stage is bathed in gloom. The girls go to their respective compartments.*] That fortune-teller was certainly right, I tell you. She certainly was right!... [*She disappears. For a moment the stage is empty and in darkness.*]

BASHA: [*Comes running wildly from her room, with a hysterical outcry. She is in night clothes.*]

REIZEL: [*Thrusting aside the curtain of her compartment.*] What's the matter, Basha?

BASHA: I'm afraid to go to sleep. I feel that the ghost of my mother, with her thorns and her briers, is hovering about my room.

REIZEL: The Holy Scroll in the room above has been defiled. We have no one to shield us now!

BASHA: I'm afraid this is going to be a terrible night. My heart's thumping. [*Suddenly, from above, a din is heard. There is a scraping of chairs and tables. The girls, eyes distended with fear, listen intently. Soon there is the sound of something heavy falling down the outside stairs.*]

YEKEL: [*Outside.*] Rifkele, Rifkele! Where are you?

REIZEL: [*To* BASHA.] Let's lie down in our beds and pretend we're fast asleep... We know nothing at all, remember! [*Both go to their beds and feign deep sleep.*]

YEKEL: [*Rushes into the cellar, a burning candle in his hand. His hair is in disorder. Over his nightshirt he has thrown a coat. He shouts wildly.*] Rifkele! Rifkele! Is Rifkele here? [*No reply. He tears the curtains of the compartments violently aside.*] Rifkele! Where is she? [*Waking* REIZEL *and* BASHA.] Where is Rifkele! Rifkele! Where is she?

REIZEL and **BASHA**: [*Rubbing their eyes with their sleeves, as if awakened from sound sleep.*] What?... We don't know.

YEKEL: You don't know?... You don't know?... [*Rushes up the stairs, almost at a single bound. Goes out. Pause. There is a sound outside of something falling down the stairs. The door is suddenly banged open and* YEKEL *stumbles in, dragging* SARAH *by the hair. Both are in night attire.* YEKEL *pulls* SARAH *downstairs by the hair. Points to the cellar.*] Where is your daughter? Your daughter,—where is she? [BASHA *and* REIZEL *huddle close to the wall, trembling with terror.*]

Quick CURTAIN

Act Three

Scene: *Same as Act I. The cupboard and the bureau have been knocked out of place. Clothes and linen are strewn about the floor. The door to RIFKELE's room is open, and from within the light of a candle comes across the stage. SARAH, her hair dishevelled and her clothes in disarray, is going about the room picking up the things that lie scattered about. She packs them into a bundle, as if preparing to leave, yet eventually puts most of the articles back into their proper places.*

It is early morning. Through the closed shutters penetrates the gray light of coming day.

SARAH: Yekel! What's the matter with you, Yekel? [*Goes over to the door of* RIFKELE's *room and looks inside.*] Why are you sitting there like that? [*Turns back and continues to collect the scattered things.*] What a misfortune! He wants to bring the whole house to ruin. [*Returns to* RIFKELE's *door.*] Yekel! Why are you so silent? What's come over you? [*Turns back, tearfully.*] Did you ever see? A person sits down before the Holy Scroll and thinks and thinks. What is there to think about? A misfortune has befallen us. Go to the police, see the captain . . . Seek out the man by hook or crook . . . There is yet time. [*Returns to the door.*] Why don't you say something? [*She sits down upon a bundle of clothes near the door, buries her face in her hands and begins to weep.*] He sits there like a madman, staring at the Holy Scroll and mumbling. He neither sees nor hears. What on earth can have possessed him? [*Arises. To* YEKEL.] It makes no difference to me, — one place or another. If you want me to leave, all right. I'll go. The devil won't take me . . . I'll earn my bread, all right, wherever I may be. [*Resumes her packing, silently. Pause.*]

YEKEL: [*Enters from* RIFKELE's *room. He is without hat or coat; his hair is in disorder. His eyes have a wild glare, and he speaks slowly, with a subdued, hoarse voice.*] I'll go . . . You'll go . . . Rifkele will go . . . Everything and everybody will go . . . [*Pointing to the brothel.*] Down into the cellar . . . God won't have it otherwise . . .

SARAH: Yekel, what's possessed you? Have you gone crazy? [*Approaching him.*] Consider what you're doing. A misfortune has befallen us. Agreed. To whom don't misfortunes happen? Come. Let us hunt out Shloyme. We'll give him two or three hundred roubles and let him give us back our child. He'll do it, all right... Well, what are you sitting there moping about? What's the matter with you?

YEKEL: [*In the same hoarse voice, as he paces about the room.*] It's all the same to me now. My soul is given over to the devil. Nothing will help. It's no use. God won't have it... [*He stops before the window and peers through an interstice of the shutter.*]

SARAH: God won't have it, you say? You've merely talked yourself into that! It's *you* that won't have it. Do you love your daughter? Yekel! Yekel! [*Dragging him away from the window.*] What's come over you? Act while there is yet time! He might take her off somewhere while we're wasting time here. Let's be off to him at once. Hindel must surely have taken her to him. What are you standing there for? [*Abruptly.*] I've sent for Reb Ali. We'll hear what he has to say. [*Pause.* YEKEL *still peers through the shutter spaces.*] What are you staring at there? [*Pause.*] Why don't you say something? Good heavens, it's enough to drive a woman insane! [*Turns away and bursts into tears.*]

YEKEL: [*Pacing about the room as before.*] No more home... No more wife... no more daughter... Down into the cellar... Back to the brothel... We don't need any daughter now... don't need her... She's become what her mother was... God won't have it... Back to the cellar... Down into the brothel!

SARAH: So you want to go back to the cellar? — Into the cellar, then! Much I care! [*Resumes her packing.*] He wants to ruin us completely. What has come over the man? [*For a moment she is absorbed in reflection.*] If you're going to stand there like a lunatic, I'll get busy myself! [*Takes off her diamond ear-rings.*] I'll go over to Shloyme's and give him my diamond ear-rings. [*From her bundle she draws out a golden chain.*] And if he holds back, I'll add a hundred rouble note. [*She searches* YEKEL's *trousers pocket for his pocketbook. He offers no resistance.*] Within fifteen minutes [*Throwing a shawl over her shoulders.*] Rifkele will be here. [*As she leaves.*] Shloyme will do that for me. [*Slams the door behind her.*]

YEKEL: [*Walks about the room, his head bowed.*] It's all the same to me now... The devil got her, too. No more daughter... No more Holy Scroll... Into the brothel with everything... Back to the brothel... God won't have it... [*Long pause.* REIZEL *appears at the door, thrusting in her head.*]

Steals into the room and stops near the entrance. YEKEL *notices her, and stares at her vacantly.*]

REIZEL: [*Stammering.*] I went for Reb Ali. Your wife sent me. He'll be here soon.

YEKEL: [*With the same empty stare.*] The devil has won her, anyway. No use now. Too late. God won't have it.

REIZEL: She was such a nice girl. What a shame!

YEKEL: [*Eyes her with amazement.*]

REIZEL: [*Apologizing.*] Your wife told me to wait here until she came back.

YEKEL: Don't be afraid. I haven't gone insane yet. Not yet. God has punished me.

REIZEL Who could ever have expected such a thing? She was such a pure child. Oh! what a heartbreaking pity! As true as I live...

REB ALI: [*Enters, carrying a lantern.*] What's happened, that you had to call me before daybreak? [*Going to the window and peering through the shutter spaces.*] It's almost time for the morning prayers.

YEKEL: [*Not looking at* REB ALI.] The Holy Scroll has been violated, Reb Ali. Desecrated most foully.

REB ALI: [*Frightened.*] What are you saying? God forbid, the whole town will have to atone for the sin! What has happened? Speak, man! Good Lord in Heaven!

YEKEL: Down into the brothel... [*Pointing below. Then to* REIZEL.] Down below, with the rest of them. Down into the brothel. No more Holy Scroll.

REB ALI: Man! What words are these! What's happened here? Speak!

REIZEL: [*At the door. Reassuring* REB ALI.] No, Rebbi. Not the Holy Scroll. His daughter... Rifkele. The Holy Scroll is undefiled. [*Points to* RIFKELE'*s room.*] Still in there.

REB ALI: [*With a sigh of relief.*] Blessed be His name. But are you sure that the Scroll is undefiled?

REIZEL: Yes, Rebbi.

REB ALI: [*More calmly, spitting out.*] Blessed be His Name. I feel easier on that score. [*To* YEKEL.] What made you talk such nonsense? [*To* REIZEL, *without looking at her.*] Did she go away? Isn't she back yet? [*To* YEKEL.] Has anybody gone to look for her?

YEKEL: My daughter is holier to me than a Holy Scroll.

REB ALI: Don't talk nonsense. Just keep quiet and don't make any scenes. Has anybody gone yet to look for her? To bring her back? Well? What are you standing there for, instead of going after her?

REIZEL: My mistress went to get her.

REB ALI: Do they know where the girl went?

REIZEL: Yes. The mistress will soon fetch her home.

REB ALI: Fine! Then what's all this commotion about? The whole town will know all about it before long. Such things should be kept dark. They're not nice. If a prospective father-in-law ever got wind of the story, her dowry would have to be raised a couple of hundred roubles . . .

YEKEL: It's all the same to me now. Let everybody know. No more daughter . . . No more Holy Scroll . . . Into the cellar. Into the brothel with everything.

REB ALI: Fie! You're out of your head altogether. True, a misfortune has befallen you. May Heaven watch over all of us. Well? What? Misfortunes happen to plenty of folks. The Lord sends aid and things turn out all right. The important point is to keep it a secret. Hear nothing. See nothing. Just wash your hands clean of it and forget it. [*To* REIZEL.] Be careful what you say. Don't let it travel any further, God forbid. Do you hear? [*Turns to* YEKEL, *who is staring vacantly into space.*] I had a talk with . . . [*Looks around to see whether* REIZEL *is still present. Seeing her, he stops. After a pause he begins anew, more softly, looking at* REIZEL *as a hint for her to leave.*] With er, er . . . [*Casts a significant glance at* REIZEL, *who at last understands, and leaves.*] I had a talk with the groom's father. I spoke to him between the afternoon and evening prayers, at the synagogue. He's almost ready to talk business. Of course I gave him to understand that the bride doesn't boast a very high pedigree, but I guess another hundred roubles will fix that up, all right. Nowadays, pedigrees don't count as much as they used to. With God's help I'll surely be here this Sabbath, with the groom's father. We'll go down to the Dayon. ⋆ and have him examine the young man in his religious studies . . . But nobody must get wind of this tale. It might spoil everything. The father comes of a fine family and the son carries a smart head on his shoulders. There, there. Calm yourself. Trust in the Lord and everything will turn out for the best. With God's help I am going home to prepare for the morning prayer. And as soon as the girl returns, notify me. Remember, now. [*About to go.*]

YEKEL: [*Arises and grasps* REB ALI's *arm.*] Listen to me, Rebbi. Take your Holy Scroll along with you. I don't need it any more.

⋆ Assistant to the Rabbi, and usually well versed in religious law.

REB ALI: [*Thunderstruck.*] What are you talking about? What has possessed you? Have you gone stark mad?

YEKEL: My daughter has gone to a brothel. The Scroll has been desecrated. God has punished me.

REB ALI: [*Trying to interrupt him.*] What are you raving about?

YEKEL: I am a woeful sinner. I know it well. He should have broken my feet beneath me, — or taken away my life in its prime. But what did He want of my daughter? My poor, blameless daughter?

REB ALI: Hear me. You mustn't talk like that against the Lord.

YEKEL: [*Excited.*] And why not? I may speak everything. It's the truth. Yes, I am Yekel Tchaftchovitch, all right. The "Uncle" of a brothel. But the truth I may speak even to God. I'm afraid no longer. I went into the House of Study to you. I told you everything. So you advised me to have a Holy Scroll written. In there I placed it, — in her room. I stood before it night after night, and used to say to it, "You are really a God. You know everything I do. You will punish me. Very well. Punish me. Punish my wife. We have both sinned. But my poor, innocent daughter. Guard her. Have pity upon her!"

REB ALI: But no evil has befallen her. She will return. She will yet make a fine pious Jewish wife.

YEKEL: No use . . . The devil has won her. She'll be drawn to it. Once she has made a beginning . . . she'll not stop . . . If not today, tomorrow. The devil has won her soul. I know. Yes, I know only too well.

REB ALI: Don't speak folly, I tell you. Calm yourself. Pray fervently for the Lord's pardon. Give up this business of yours. With God's help your daughter will yet marry just like all Jewish women, and bring you plenty of happiness.

YEKEL: Too late, Rebbi. Too late. If only she had died in her childhood, I should have nothing to complain about . . . Then I'd know she was dead, — that I had buried an innocent creature . . . I would visit her grave and say to myself, "Here lies your child. Even if you yourself are a sinner, here lies a pure daughter of yours, a virtuous child." But as it is, what is left me on earth? I myself am a sinner. I leave behind me sinful offspring. And so passes sin from generation to generation.

REB ALI: Don't speak like that. A Jew must not utter such things. Trust in the Lord, and say "The past is dead and gone."

YEKEL: [*Interrupting.*] Don't try to console me, Rebbi. I know that it's too late. Sin encircles me and mine like a rope around a person's neck. God wouldn't have it. But I ask you, Rebbi, *why* wouldn't He have it? What harm would it have done Him if I, Yekel Tchaftchovitch, should have been raised from the mire into which I have fallen? [*He goes into* RIFKELE's *room, carries out the Sacred Parchment, raises it aloft and speaks.*] You, Holy Scroll, I know,—you are a great God! For you are our Lord! I, Yekel Tchaftchovitch, have sinned. [*Beats his breast with his closed fist.*] My sins... my sins... Work a miracle,—send down a pillar of fire to consume me. On this very spot, where I now stand! Open up the earth at my feet and let it swallow me! But shield my daughter. Send her back to me as pure and innocent as when she left. I know... to You everything is possible. Work a miracle! For You are an almighty God. And if You don't, then You're no God at all, I tell you. I, Yekel Tchaftchovitch, tell You that You are as vengeful as any human being...

REB ALI: [*Jumps up and snatches the Parchment from* YEKEL's *grasp.*] Do you realize whom you are talking to? [*Looks at him sternly, then takes the Scroll back to* RIFKELE's *room.*] Implore pardon of the Holy Scroll!

YEKEL: The truth may be spoken even before God's very face! [*Follows* REB ALI *into* RIFKELE's *room.*] If He's a true God, then let Him reveal His miracle here on this very spot!

SARAH: [*Runs in excitedly. Hastens over to the mirror and begins to arrange her hair with her hands. Calls.*] Come in, Shloyme. Why do you remain outside?

SHLOYME: [*From without.*] Where is Yekel? Let him know [*Comes in.*] that I'll do anything for one of our brotherhood. Even if he did insult me.

SARAH: [*Runs over to* RIFKELE's *door. Locks it, leaving* YEKEL *and* REB ALI *inside.*] Let him stay there. [*Smiling.*] These last few days he's turned into a saint... Seeks the company of pious Jews. [*Runs over to the entrance door and locks it.*] And what a bride you have picked out! Such a pest your Hindel is, I must say! You can't shake yourself rid of her! She trails after you as if you already belonged to her. I'll wager she's tracked you to this place, too! [*With a wily smile.*] Ah, Shloyme, Shloyme, such goods you've selected! [*She goes over to the window and opens the shutters. The room grows lighter.*] Why have they closed up the place, anyway? As if in mourning!

SHLOYME: Don't worry, I tell you. Once I've said "yes," I mean it. Whoever else I'd refuse, I'll do it for you. Even if you *have* treated me shabbily of late... Well, never mind. Hindel may go to perdition for all it'll help her.

SARAH: [*Glides over to him, seizes his hand and looks straight into his eyes.*] A fellow as young as you,—how can you take such a scarecrow as Hindel? Who is she? She's roamed around from one brothel to another. Why, a young chap like you! And you can make a tidy bit now. Then what do you need her for? With your couple of hundred roubles why can't you catch some fine, respectable girl? Why not?

Aren't you as young and handsome as any other, I'd like to know? [*Slaps him across the shoulders.*] You just listen to me, Shloyme. You know I was never unkind to you, even if I haven't been all I might have, lately. But I've always been Sarah to you. Isn't that so? [*Looking him straight in the eyes.*]

SHLOYME: [*Twirling his moustache.*] The devil! Deuce knows! I let my head be turned by the girl...Just for the time being...to get a few roubles...Do you really think I meant to marry her? My mother would have cursed every bone in my body. I have a respectable mother. And my sister?

SARAH: Haven't you any better business prospects than to tie yourself to such a fright and open a place with her? Much there is in the business these days, anyway. It doesn't pay to have to do with outcasts of her type. [*Comes close to him and thrusts her ear-rings into his hand.*] Here, take these and here's another hundred roubles. Now tell me where Rifkele is.

SHLOYME: What's true is true. You were once a good woman. [*Winks at her.*] Lately you've been spoiled. But that's another matter. Just remember that Shloyme is one of your own crowd. [*Pockets her ear-rings.*]

SARAH: And now tell me, Shloyme, where she is. You may tell me every-thing, even if I am her mother. You know, such things don't affect me. Tell me,—have you led her off somewhere to a...?

SHLOYME: She is very near...If I say I'll bring her here, you may depend upon me. And listen,—may I have such luck, what a prize she would make! Such eyes, such motions. And as clever as they make 'em!

SARAH: Ha! Ha! There's life to Sarah yet...But tell me, Shloyme, where have you put her? You may speak freely to me. [*Places an arm about him and slaps him over the shoulder with the other, looking into his eyes coquettishly.*] Come, tell me, good brother.

SHLOYME: Not far from here. Not far...[*A thumping of fists is heard on the door leading to the outside.*]

HINDEL: [*From without.*] You know nothing about her! Nothing at all!

SARAH: Let her hammer her head against the wall. Goodness me! How she holds him in her clutches! Ha, ha! He dare not leave her for a moment! [*Making eyes at him.*] Shame yourself, to have affairs with trash like that! [SHLOYME *meditates for a moment.* SARAH *seizes him by the arm and draws him aside.*] See here. What do you need her for? I'll get a girl for you. A dream. You'll see. [*Winks at him.*]

HINDEL: [*Forcing the door open, rushes in.*] What are they pestering him about? Bad dreams to them! Their daughter runs away...[*Seizing*

SHLOYME *by the hand.*] He doesn't know where she is. What do they want of you, anyway?

SARAH: [*Sits down, glances teasingly at* SHLOYME *and points to* HINDEL.] So that's your style, eh? That thing there? Ha, ha!

HINDEL: [*Looking around.*] She laughs like an evil spirit! [*To* SHLOYME.] You know nothing whatever about Rifkele. [*Takes him aside. Softly.*] Let's be off to Lodz at once. We'll marry there...Rent a house...With two girls like these we can...Consider what you're doing! [*Aloud.*] What are they pestering you for? You know nothing at all about her. [*Pulling him out.*] Come, Shloyme. [*He is undecided.*]

SARAH: [*Aloud, with a wily smile.*] Well, why don't you go along with her, Shloyme? She's come for you...to take you to Lodz...to get married...and set up house. Tee-hee! [*Comes close to* SHLOYME *and draws him away from* HINDEL.] A young chap like you, with a respectable mother, — and your father was a pious Jew...What does *she* want of you? What is *she* pestering you for?

SHLOYME: [*Resolutely.*] Come, Sarah. We'll get Rifkele.

HINDEL: [*Clapping her hand across his mouth.*] You'll not tell. You know nothing about her. [*She runs over to the door, shuts it and stands with her back against it.*] I won't let you go out. [*Runs over to* SHLOYME *and seizes his hand.*] Remember, Shloyme. It's all right for *them.* Then why not for *us?* Come, Shloyme. We'll leave this place...And we'll do such a business—such a flourishing business!

SHLOYME: We've heard all that...we've heard it before. [*Thrusts her away.*] We'll talk that over later. I haven't any time now. [*Goes out with* SARAH, *followed by* HINDEL.]

SARAH: [*Running back. Opens* RIFKELE'S *door and calls to the men inside.*] Rifkele is here!

HINDEL: [*From the entry.*] I'll not let you. You won't tell!

SHLOYME: [*In the doorway.*] Come, Sarah.

SARAH: [*Runs after him.*] I'm coming, Shloyme. [SARAH, SHLOYME *and* HINDEL *leave.*]

REB ALI: [*Enters, with* YEKEL.] Praised be the Lord! Praised be the Heavenly Father! [*Following* YEKEL, *who paces about the room.*] See how the Almighty, blessed be His Name, has come to your aid? He punishes, — yes. But he sends the remedy before the disease. Despite your having sinned, despite your having uttered blasphemy. [*Admonishing him.*] From now on see to it that you never speak such words, — that you have reverence, great reverence...Know what a Holy Scroll is, and what a learned Jew is...You must go to the synagogue, and you must make a generous donation to the students of the Law. You must fast in atonement, and the Lord will forgive you. [*Pause.* REB ALI *looks sternly at* YEKEL, *who has continued to walk about the room, absorbed in his thoughts.*] What? Aren't you listening to me? With the aid of the Almighty everything will turn out for the best. I'm going at once to the groom's father and we'll discuss the whole matter in detail. But be sure not to haggle. A hundred roubles more or less, — remember who you are and who he is. And what's more, see to it that you settle the dowry right away and indulge in no idle talk about the wedding. Heaven forbid, — another misfortune might occur! Such matters should not be delayed. [*Glares angrily at* YEKEL.] What! You pay no attention? I'm talking to you!

YEKEL: [*As if to himself.*] One thing I want to ask her. One thing only. But she must tell me the truth, — the whole truth. Yes, or no.

REB ALI: Don't sin, man. Thank the good Lord that He has helped you.

YEKEL: [*As before.*] I'll not lay a finger upon her. Just let her answer the truth. Yes, or no.

REB ALI: The truth. The truth. Heaven will help you . . . Everything will turn out for the best. I'm going to the young man's father directly. He's over at the synagogue and must surely be waiting for me. [*Looks around.*] Tell your wife to put the house in order in the meantime. And you, prepare the contract, and at once, so that he'll have no time to discover anything amiss and withdraw. Arrange the wedding date and have the bride go at once to her parents-in-law. No idle chatter, remember. Keep silent, so that nobody will learn anything about it. [*Ready to go.*] And cast all this nonsense out of your head. Trust in the Lord and rejoice in His comfort. [*At the door.*] Tell your wife to tidy up the place. [*Leaves.*]

YEKEL: [*Strides nervously to and fro.*] Let her only tell me the truth. The plain truth. [*A long silence.*]

SARAH: [*On the threshold.*] Come in. Come in. Your father won't beat you. [*Pause.*] Go in, I tell you. [*Pushes* RIFKELE *into the room.* RIFKELE *has a shawl over her head. She stands silent and motionless at the door, a shameless look in her eyes, biting her lips.*] Well, what are you standing there for, my darling? Much pleasure you've brought us . . . in return for our trouble in bringing you up. We'll square that with you later. [*Interrupting herself.*] Get into your room. Comb your hair. Put on a dress. We're expecting guests. [*To* YEKEL.] I just met Reb Ali. He's going for the groom's father. [*Looks about the room.*] Goodness me! How the place looks! [*She begins hastily to place things in order.*]

YEKEL: [*Seeing* RIFKELE, *fastens his gaze upon her, approaches her, takes her gently by the hand and leads her to the table.*] Don't be afraid. I'll not hurt you. [*He sits down.*] Sit down here beside me. [*Pushes a chair toward her.*] Sit down.

RIFKELE: [*Provoked, hides her face in her shawl.*] I can stand just as well.

YEKEL: Sit down. [*He seats her.*] Don't be afraid.

RIFKELE: [*From behind the shawl.*] Why should I be afraid?

YEKEL: [*Speaks in a faltering voice.*] Rifkele, tell me, Rifkele. You are my daughter. I am your father. [*Points to* SARAH.] She is your mother. Tell me, my daughter. Tell me the whole truth. Don't be afraid of me. Don't feel ashamed before me. I know,—not for *your* sins . . . not for *your* sins . . . For my sins, *mine* . . . For your mother's sins . . . *our* sins . . . Tell me, daughter.

SARAH: Just look at the way he's sat down to cross examine her! What does he want of her? The moment she arrives! Let her go in and dress. We'll soon be having company. [*About to take* RIFKELE *away.*]

YEKEL: Let her go, I say! [*Thrusts* SARAH *away from* RIFKELE.]

SARAH: He's gone crazy today. What's possessed the man? [*Resumes her cleaning.*]

YEKEL: [*Seating* RIFKELE *beside him.*] I'll not beat you. [*Clutching her slender throat with his fingers.*] If I had only twisted your neck for you, like this, before you ever grew up, it would have been better for you, and for me . . . But don't be afraid. I won't harm you. It's not for your sins that God has punished us. No. It's for ours. I guarded you like the apple of my eye. I had a Holy Scroll written for you. I placed it in your room and prayed to it for days and nights at a time. "Shield my child from evil! Visit your punishment upon me! On her mother! But spare my daughter!" You'd grow up, I planned, and I'd make a fine match for you. I'd get you a respectable young man for a husband. I'd keep you both here with me, at my expense. You would both live . . .

RIFKELE: [*Still hidden behind her shawl.*] There's plenty of time for me to marry. I'm not so old.

SARAH: And she has the impudence to argue with him!

RIFKELE: They want to turn me into a Rabbi's wife.★— Why didn't mamma marry early?

SARAH: Hold your tongue, or I'll slap you black and blue! Just listen to what she's picked up in a single night!

★ Colloquial expression signifying extreme piety.

RIFKELE: [*Misunderstanding.*] Yes, I know everything now.

YEKEL: Let her alone! [*With nervous haste.*] I want to ask her only one thing. One thing only. Tell me the truth . . . I'll not beat you. I'll not lay a finger upon you. You're not to blame. [*Almost unable to speak.*] Tell me frankly, the — the — whole truth tell me . . . The truth . . .

SARAH: What truth shall she tell you? What do you want of the girl?

YEKEL: I'm not asking you . . . [*Arises, seizing* RIFKELE *by the hand.*] Don't feel ashamed before me. I'm your father. You may tell me everything . . . Speak openly . . . Are you — are you still as pure as when you left this house? Are you still a virtuous Jewish daughter? [*Shouting.*] Yes, — a virtuous Jewish daughter?

SARAH: [*Tearing* RIFKELE *out of* YEKEL's *grasp.*] What do you want of the girl? The child is innocent of all evil. Let her go.

YEKEL: [*Holding* RIFKELE *firmly, and trying to look straight into her eyes.*] Just tell me the truth. I'll believe you. Look me straight in the face. Are you still an innocent Jewish child? Look me in the face! Straight in the eye! [RIFKELE, *despite* YEKEL's *efforts, hides her face in the shawl.*]

SARAH: Why don't you take that shawl off your head? You don't need it indoors. [*Removes* RIFKELE's *shawl.* RIFKELE *resists, but losing her grasp upon the shawl she hides her face in her gown.*]

YEKEL: [*Loudly.*] Tell me now. Don't be ashamed. I'll do you no harm. [*Holding her firmly by the hand and looking her directly in the eye.*] Are you still a chaste Jewish daughter? — Tell me, at once!

RIFKELE: [*Trying to hide her face.*] I don't know . . .

YEKEL: [*At the top of his voice.*] You don't know! You don't know! Then who *does* know? What do you mean, — you "don't know?" The truth, now! Are you still —

RIFKELE: [*Tearing herself from* YEKEL.] It was all right for mamma, wasn't it? And it was all right for you, wasn't it? I know all about it! . . . [*Hiding her face in her hands.*] Beat me! Beat me! Go on!

SARAH: [*Rushes over to* RIFKELE *with arms upraised, ready to strike her.* YEKEL *casts* SARAH *aside with a single blow, and falls into a chair, pale and breathing hard.* RIFKELE *sinks to the floor, weeping hysterically. A long pause.* SARAH, *plainly upset, paces aimlessly about the room. After a while she takes a broom and begins to sweep the room; her silence betrays a feeling of guilt . . . She then approaches* RIFKELE, *lifts her by the hand and leads her off stage into the room.* YEKEL *is rooted to his place.* SARAH *returns, runs over to* YEKEL, *grasps his hand and entreats him.*] Yekel, consider what you are doing, for God's sake! Who need know anything? [*Pause.*] Calm yourself. [*Pause.*]

79

Rifkele will get married and we'll live to have plenty of happiness from her. [YEKEL *is silent.*] Put on your coat,—they'll soon be here. [*Abruptly.*] Who need know anything at all about it?

YEKEL: [*Silent. Stares vacantly into space.*]

SARAH: [*Brings in* YEKEL'*s coat and hat and places them upon him. He offers no resistance.*] What a misfortune! What a misfortune! Who could have foreseen such a thing? [*She straightens* YEKEL'*s coat, then puts the room in order. Runs into* RIFKELE'*s room. She is heard hiding something there, and soon returns.*] I'll have a reckoning with you later. [*Putting the finishing touches to the room.*] Terrible days, these. Bring up children with so much care and anxiety, and...Ah! [*Footsteps are heard outside.* SARAH *runs over to* YEKEL *and pulls his sleeve.*] They're here! For the love of God, Yekel, remember! Everything can be fixed yet. [*Enter* REB ALI *and a stranger.* SARAH *hastily thrusts her hair under her wig and goes to the door to welcome the visitors.*]

REB ALI: Good morning.

SARAH: Good morning. Good year. Welcome. [*Somewhat confused, she places chairs before the guests and motions them to be seated.*]

REB ALI: [*In a cheerful mood.*] Well, and where is the bride's father? [*Looking about for* YEKEL.]

SARAH: [*Smiling, to her husband*] Why don't you show yourself, Yekel? [*She thrusts a chair toward him. The visitors express their greetings and take their seats.*]

REB ALI: [*Gesticulating.*] Let's get right down to business. [*To the stranger, pointing to* YEKEL.] This gentleman wishes to unite families with you. He has an excellent daughter and wants as her husband a scholar well versed in Rabbinical lore. He'll support the couple for life.

THE STRANGER: That sounds inviting.

YEKEL: [*Arising.*] Yes, my friend. A virtuous Jewish daughter...a model child...

REB ALI: [*To the stranger.*] He's ready to settle upon her a dowry of five hundred roubles cash at the time of the engagement...And he'll support the couple for life. He will treat your son as his own child.

THE STRANGER: Well,—there's little need of my boosting *my* goods. With two years more of study, he'll have the whole learning at his finger tips.

REB ALI: Naturally, naturally. This gentleman will guard him like the apple of his eye. He'll have the best of everything here. He'll be able to sit and study the Holy Law day and night, to his heart's content.

YEKEL: [*Indicating* RIFKELE'*s room.*] Yes, he'll sit inside there and study the sacred books...I have a virtuous Jewish daughter. [*Goes into the room and drags* RIFKELE *out by force. She is only half dressed, her hair in disorder. He points to her.*] Your son will marry a virtuous Jewish daughter, I say. She will bear him pure, Jewish children...even as all pious daughters. [*To* SARAH.] Isn't that so? [*Laughing wildly, to the stranger.*] Yes, indeed, my friend, —she'll make a pure, pious little mate. My wife will lead her under the wedding canopy...Down into the brothel! Down below! [*Pointing to the cellar.*] Down into the brothel! [*Dragging* RIFKELE *by her hair to the door.*] Down into the brothel with you! Down!

SARAH: [*Rushing madly over to* YEKEL.] Good God! He's gone stark mad! [*She tries to tear* RIFKELE *away from* YEKEL; *he thrusts* SARAH *aside and drags his daughter out by the hair.*]

YEKEL: Down into the brothel with you! [*He leaves together with* RIFKELE, *whose cries are heard from outside.*]

THE STRANGER: [*With amazement and fright.*] What is this? [REB ALI *beckons to him, pulls him by the sleeve and points to the door. The stranger stands motionless in his astonishment.* REB ALI *draws him to the door. They leave. Pause.*]

YEKEL: [*Enters, dragging back with him* REB ALI, *whom he has met on the stairs.*] Take the Holy Scroll along with you! I don't need it any more!

CURTAIN

The Captive

Edouard Bourdet

Introduction

During the summer and early autumn of 1926, rumors that an American producer was bringing to America an adaptation of Bourdet's "La Prisonnière" were received with a good deal of uncertainty by the more responsible citizens of New York. For the theatrical news from Paris, where this trenchant drama began its career, had stressed the audacity of the theme, with a general tintinnabulation about censorship and the decadence of the stage. And those who were already nauseated by the fetid smells of several plays then current were quite naturally distressed at the prospect of sensationalism in the form of abnormality. Surely, they complained, themes of this character are not fit subjects for open portrayal on the stage. Indeed, the audience assembled for the opening performance at the Empire Theatre was obviously prepared for a violent shock. But whatever the expectations may have been, the objective treatment of the theme and the austere quality of the performance cleared the humid air like a northwestern breeze. With Mr. Hornblow's adaptation and Mr. Miller's masterly direction "The Captive" became, as it was written, a restrained though uncompromising tragedy, rather than a malodorous truckling to low curiosity. Thus for the thousandth time it was evident that the motives of a dramatic production are of far greater importance than the details of the subject matter.

Not that M. Bourdet has cloaked his drama under the sanctimony of the crusader's armor. If one may judge by the haunting impression left by the grim performance, M. Bourdet is interested, not in the details of his theme, but in their illumination of human character; and he is by that sign preeminently a dramatist. None of the soul-flagellations of a Rousseau or a Strindberg alleviates the horror by distributing the blame among gods and men, or by sighing over the sensual temptations or the squalor. Choosing a Greek theme M. Bourdet treats of it, if not in the classical manner, then in the modern counterpart to that tragic inevitability. In fine, the play approaches its subject objectively. And since M. Bourdet understands his characters through and through, his conclusion is foreordained. In reading it we have no feeling that he is shaping it to prove an arbitrary thesis, or to lead his characters through theatrical adventures for lurid effects. So "The Captive" moves swiftly through three long acts; even before the nature of the malady is defined in the second act, doom swims over the play like a thick, black cloud.

Although, as the reader will soon discover, the occasion for "The Captive" is the fact of an abnormal relationship between two women, the interest is solely in its revelation of character. M. Bourdet has described his people as ordinary well-bred human beings, whatever their failings may be. Irene's tenderness towards her little sister, and her own humility and anguish, reveal her as a young lady of fine instincts; she is in no sense the neurotic debauchee of tawdry melodrama. Jacques Virieu, likewise, is a young man of high impulses; and of sufficient strength of character to fly recklessly in the face of danger to support an ideal. Unlike the contemporary school of pettifogging novelists and dramatists, with their garish sophistication, M. Bourdet does not excuse his characters on the score of congenital weakness or worldly disillusionment or pseudo-scientific buncombe. No, indeed, he is not interested in excuses; his is a tragedy of consequences. He shows Irene estranged from her father, playing false to her ingenuous sister, and fast losing all the friends with whom she once associated freely. He tortures her before Jacques. Once she was his ideal, a woman to whom he looked up; now she comes as a petitioner for mercy and pity rather than respect. In the second act, M. Bourdet shows the husband of the unseen Madame d'Aiguines—a simulacrum of a man, gray before his time, wretched and tormented, unable to escape from a poisoned home. All these characters, involved in various ways, have been withered a little by their proximity to the festered one. And if any proof were needed of the sincerity of M. Bourdet's purpose, his treatment of Madame d'Aiguines would be sufficient. They talk of her occasionally, but by keeping her in the background and by describing the blighted fruits of her influence, M. Bourdet retains the fine objectivity and austerity of his drama.

M. Bourdet casts his tragedy in the familiar three-act mold of crisp, economical playwrighting. Without bothering his head too much about details of craftsmanship, without wasting time over the motivation of exits and entrances, he pursues his course vigorously to the end. As the composer contrasts his main theme with fragile, minor developments, so M. Bourdet heightens his tragedy by rippling interludes with Gisele and Françoise Meillant, fresh, charming and frank. This is M. Bourdet's first notable play; he is still in his thirties. His first play was "Le Rubicon," put on at the Théâtre Michel in 1910. During the war M. Bourdet abandoned his career as a playwright to fight in the infantry; he was wounded twice, cited three times for bravery, and given the cross of the Legion of Honor. In the trenches he met as a fellow officer a young man who was deliberately seeking death in battle as an escape from the wretchedness of his home life. This man corresponds to the d'Aiguines of "The Captive," and was the germ of the present play. The planning and writing of the tragedy occupied M. Bourdet off and on for two years. Within a year after its first appearance in Paris, "The Captive" was played in Berlin, Vienna, Budapest and New York. Mr. Hornblow's notable adaptation communicates the precise flavor of the original.

—J. Brooks Atkinson
October, 1926.

Ann Andrews (Francoise) and Basil Rathbone (Jacques) in *The Captive*, at the Empire Theatre 1926. (Photograph reprinted with permission from the Billy Rose Theatre Collection, The New York Public Library for the Performing Arts, Astor, Lenox, and Tilden Foundations.)

La Prisonnière by Edouard Bourdet was presented for the first time on any stage at the Théâtre Femina in Paris on March 6th, 1926. Adapted by Arthur Hornblow, Jr., it was presented for the first time in English under the title of *The Captive* at the Empire Theatre in New York, on September 29th, 1926. The play was presented by the Charles Frohman Company and produced by Gilbert Miller.

Cast

De Montcel	Norman Trevor
Irene De Montcel	Helen Menken
Gisele De Montcel	Ann Trevor
Jacques Virieu	Basil Rathbone
d'Aiguines	Arthur Wontner
Françoise Meillant	Ann Andrews
Mlle. Marchand	Winifred Fraser
Josephine	Minna Phillips
Georges	Arthur Lewis

To Gilbert Miller
Whose splendid production of this play has
earned the admiration and gratitude of
the author and his translator.

The Characters

DE MONTCEL
IRENE DE MONTCEL
GISELE DE MONTCEL
JACQUES VIRIEU
D'AIGUINES
FRANÇOISE MEILLANT
MLLE. MARCHAND
JOSEPHINE
GEORGES

Act One
Irene de Montcel's room in her father's apartment; Paris.

Act Two
Jacques Virieu's study. One month later.

Act Three
The same. A year later.

Act One

Scene: IRENE's *room in her father's apartment, Paris. A door at the left leads to a dressing room; another in back gives onto the hall, a third at the right connects with* GISELE's *room.*

The room is furnished simply but with period pieces of uncommon taste; the bed lies in a recess, there is a small divan, some comfortable chairs and a table. On the latter stands a telephone.

On the walls hang several photographic copies of paintings of the Italian school. In the far corner stands an artist's easel, faced toward the wall.

When the curtain rises the room is empty; then the door at the right half opens and GISELE, *an attractive girl of seventeen, looks in.*

GISELE: [*Calls*] Irene? [*She enters and proceeds to the door at left.*] Irene? [*Looking off.*] She's not there. [MLLE. MARCHAND, GISELE's *governess enters at right.*]

MLLE. MARCHAND: I told you she hadn't come in yet. It's only six o'clock...that's much too early for her.

GISELE: But she told me she'd be back early to-night because of the dinner. She's supposed to help me fix the flowers for the table.

MLLE. MARCHAND: I wouldn't count on her too much if I were you. Would you like me to help you?

GISELE: Oh, I'd rather she did. If I do them without her they won't look like anything.

MLLE. MARCHAND: Very well.

GISELE: Isn't she tiresome always being late like this! What *am* I to do about my dress?

MLLE. MARCHAND: What about it?

GISELE: I've got to know what dress to put on!

MLLE. MARCHAND: Surely you don't need your sister to decide that?

GISELE: Well, you see we're the only two women at dinner to-night, and we must arrange that our dresses don't clash.

MLLE. MARCHAND: Ah, yes, that's so. [JOSEPHINE, *a maid, enters at the back, carrying a gown to be put away in the dressing room.*]

GISELE: Josephine, has Irene told you what dress she's wearing to-night?

JOSEPHINE: No, mademoiselle, she hasn't.

GISELE: Oh, Lord! Now I've no idea what to wear myself! [JOSEPHINE *goes out.*]

MLLE. MARCHAND: Wear your yellow dress. It's charming—and it's very becoming.

GISELE: My yellow dress! Don't be silly!

MLLE. MARCHAND: Gisele! A little more respect for your governess, if you please!

GISELE: I'm sorry, mademoiselle. I respect you, dear,—but when it comes to clothes I must say you don't know what you're talking about!

MLLE. MARCHAND: But what have you got against the yellow dress?

GISELE: Much too formal! It's just a little political dinner...papa said the men won't dress. We'll be only eight in all...a few antiques from the Foreign Office...and a couple of senators. It'll be a regular wilderness of whiskers!

MLLE. MARCHAND: Gisele! If you please!

GISELE: What's the matter?

MLLE. MARCHAND: If you're not a bit more careful in your language, you'll never get along in Rome, my dear. Please remember that you're to be very nearly an official personage there. The daughter of an ambassador is somebody. Every word of yours will be noticed and criticized, you may be sure.

GISELE: [*Smiling.*] Nonsense! [M. DE MONTCEL *appears at the back. He is a tall, distinguished looking man of fifty.*]

MONTCEL: Is Irene here?

GISELE: No, papa, she's not in yet.

MONTCEL: [*Half to himself.*] Naturally! [*Aloud.*] Good evening, mademoiselle. Don't get up. [*To* GISELE.] Please see that I'm told the moment she gets in.

GISELE: Very well, papa. [MONTCEL *starts to go.*]

GISELE: Papa?

MONTCEL: Yes?

GISELE: If it's about the dinner that you want to see Irene, you might tell me...

MONTCEL: No, it's not about the dinner.

GISELE: Oh.

MONTCEL: Have her inform me as soon as she comes in, won't you... Even if I have some one with me in the study.

GISELE: Yes, papa. [MONTCEL *goes out.*]

So! The storm's ready to break! Well, I felt it coming!

MLLE. MARCHAND: Is there something the matter between Irene and your father?

GISELE: Why, they haven't said a word to each other for over a week. "Good morning" "Good evening." That's all. Oh, it'll be jolly in Rome if things go on like this! At least here, papa is away three days out of four. But in Rome...

MLLE. MARCHAND: What's the quarrel about?

GISELE: Ah! That's a mystery! [*Pause.*] Do you remember a few days ago after luncheon... when Irene asked papa if she might speak to him alone... in his study?

MLLE. MARCHAND: Yes, I remember.

GISELE: It all began then. I've no idea what they said to each other. I tried to get it out of Irene but couldn't. She told me not to worry about it and that it would all come out all right. Then she changed the subject... I saw it was no use insisting.

MLLE. MARCHAND: Do you think it's because your father was vexed with Irene for having refused that young man?

GISELE: What young man?

MLLE. MARCHAND: The young man your aunt introduced here. You know perfectly well.

GISELE: Oh, good heavens, no! That's ancient history... why, it was over a month ago. No, no—that's been forgotten. Anyhow, that makes the third suitor that Irene's refused this year so I suppose papa's beginning to get used to it. No, it's something else.

MLLE. MARCHAND: Perhaps your father's beginning to notice that Irene leads a rather—rather odd life for a young unmarried girl.

GISELE: Oh, hullo! Back to the old subject! It's a long time since you've complained about Irene's behavior.

MLLE. MARCHAND: I'm not—complaining, my dear. In the first place it's not my concern... no longer my concern, at any rate, thank heaven. If

I were still responsible for her bringing up I might complain—and for good reason. But fortunately I'm not.

GISELE: Oh, come on,—surely you don't expect that at twenty-five Irene should lead the same existence I do at seventeen?

MLLE. MARCHAND: Why not? The elder Robien girl is twenty-four and her sister eighteen. Yet they lead precisely the same lives; they go about only with their mother or their companion.

GISELE: I hope you're not trying to compare that pill Valentine Robien with Irene!

MLLE. MARCHAND: They're girls of the same age and same class as you.

GISELE: You know perfectly well that Irene isn't anything like them!

MLLE. MARCHAND: And why not, pray?

GISELE: Do you know many girls as brilliant—as cultured—as attractive as Irene?

MLLE. MARCHAND: What of it?

GISELE: Well, certainly you can't expect a girl like that to spend her life in a nursery—with a kid sister and a wet nurse! She'd be bored to death!

MLLE. MARCHAND: I don't know whether she'd be bored to death as you so tactfully put it...but I *do* know it would be far better for her reputation than spending every minute away from home and alone... without ever telling anyone where she goes.

GISELE: What do you mean, "where she goes"? She goes to the studio, to her teacher. She works at her painting.

MLLE. MARCHAND: Very well.

GISELE: You don't believe that?

MLLE. MARCHAND: Yes, I believe it, my dear. I'm sure of it, but nevertheless it's no life for a girl of good family. You can't change my mind as to that. It's not the way to find a good husband.

GISELE: When it comes to that you needn't worry about Irene. The day she wants to—

MLLE. MARCHAND: The day she wants to may be too late. However, it's not my affair. It's your father's.

GISELE: Oh, as for papa's bothering!... [*Pause.*] Naturally, he'd prefer to see us both married so as to be rid of us,—and then he could take *all* his meals at Madame de Vallon's. He'd love that!

MLLE. MARCHAND: Gisele! You will kindly not speak in that way of your father!

GISELE: What have I said? It's entirely within papa's rights to prefer Madame de Vallon's cook to ours. It seems that she has a superb cook! I really can't conceive how papa will do without that cook in Rome!...

Perhaps he'll take her there—as he did to Brussels. Do you think he will?

MLLE. MARCHAND: Gisele!

GISELE: The *cook*, I mean!

MLLE. MARCHAND: Gisele, will you be still! The subject is not a proper one!

GISELE: All right! Don't be cross. I'll be still. [*She kisses* MLLE. MARCHAND, *laughingly.*] Poor mademoiselle! [*The door at the back opens and* IRENE *enters. She is smartly dressed and wears a bunch of violets.* GISELE *goes toward her gayly.*] Ah, there you are!

IRENE: [*Somewhat seriously; with the air of one who has something on her mind.*] What are you doing in here, you two?

GISELE: Waiting for you. Know what time it is?

IRENE: Yes, I'm late. I couldn't find a taxi.

GISELE: Tell me,—what dress are you going to wear to-night?

IRENE: What dress?

MLLE. MARCHAND: Gisele, don't forget your father's message to Irene.

GISELE: Oh, yes; papa said that you were to notify him the minute you got in.

IRENE: Oh.

GISELE: He said to let him know even if there were people in with him.

IRENE: [*As though to herself.*] Very well.

GISELE: Shall I tell him?

IRENE: Yes—if you don't mind.

MLLE. MARCHAND: [*To* GISELE.] Well, I'll say good night, my dear. It's after six. I must go home.

GISELE: Do wait a moment. I'll be right back. [*She runs out at back.*]

[IRENE *in a thoughtful mood removes her hat and cloak and puts them on a chair.*]

MLLE. MARCHAND: Well, Irene, how are you getting on with your painting? Are you satisfied?

IRENE: [*Inattentive.*] What? . . . Oh, yes, thank you, mademoiselle.

MLLE. MARCHAND: Are you making headway?

IRENE: Slowly, yes.

MLLE. MARCHAND: It still interests you very much, does it?

IRENE: Oh, yes, it still does. [*She puts her violets on the table. There is an awkward moment of silence.* GISELE *returns.*]

GISELE: Papa says he'll come in here.

IRENE: Very well.

MLLE. MARCHAND: Good night, Irene.

IRENE: Good night, mademoiselle. [*They shake hands.*]

MLLE. MARCHAND: [*To* GISELE, *kissing her.*] Till to-morrow, dear.

GISELE: [*Seeing her to the door.*] I've an Italian lesson at two. So will you come at about three?

MLLE. MARCHAND: At about three…

GISELE: We can take a walk through the park if it's fine…

[*They go out.* GISELE *returns almost at once. To* IRENE.] You haven't told me what dress you're going to wear?

IRENE: I don't know, dear. Whichever you prefer; it doesn't matter to me.

GISELE: Then wear your white, do you mind? I'll wear my blue, — you know, the new one, to try it out.

IRENE: All right. Tell me, dear, do you know why father wants to see me?

GISELE: No. I asked him if it were something about the dinner, but he said no. That's all I can tell you.

IRENE: What mood is he in?

GISELE: A little stern. But that means nothing… he's so often that way. [MONTCEL *appears at the back.*]

MONTCEL: Gisele, would you mind leaving us, child. I wish to speak with Irene.

GISELE: Yes, papa. [*She goes into her room and closes the door.*]

MONTCEL: [*After a pause.*] I might begin, my dear, by saying that what we have to discuss is extremely serious. My attitude toward you from now on must depend upon it. Before making any decision I wanted to give you ample time to think things over. Have you done so?

IRENE: Yes, father.

MONTCEL: Well? Then tell me what conclusion you've reached.

IRENE: I have not changed my mind, father.

MONTCEL: Which means?

IRENE: That I still ask you to let me stay here when you leave for Rome.

MONTCEL: So! This past week has gone for nothing. You persist in asking me something which you know perfectly well is impossible.

IRENE: I persist in asking it. But I cannot see that it's impossible.

MONTCEL: Very well. You also persist in withholding the reason for your extraordinary request.

IRENE: I've already given it to you, father.

MONTCEL: You've told me you wished to remain in Paris because of your work, your painting. That's it, isn't it?

IRENE: Exactly.

MONTCEL: Irene,—consider well, my child, what I'm asking you. Will you or will you not give me the true reason?

IRENE: There is no other.

MONTCEL: [*Irritated.*] Come, come, this is childish! If it were a question of your going to live on a desert island your excuse might take on the semblance of truth. But it's a question of your living in Rome, in the heart of Italy, the very cradle of art. Why, only last year you didn't stop begging me to let you go there,—and once you'd gone I had the devil's own time getting you to come back! [*Pause.*] Of course, it's true that it was there that you made the acquaintance of those people— those d'Aiguines—who since then seem to have become the very center of your existence.

IRENE: What have Monsieur and Madame d'Aiguines to do with this?

MONTCEL: Perhaps it's I who might ask you that. But I'll limit myself to saying that I deplore your constant association with them.

IRENE: Why?

MONTCEL: It is not a fit one for you.

IRENE: But what have you against them?

MONTCEL: Many things. To begin with, it's not to his credit that he had to leave the diplomatic service at the time of his marriage.

IRENE: Because he married a foreigner.

MONTCEL: An Austrian, I know.

IRENE: Well, then…

MONTCEL: If you don't mind, let's put aside the subject of the d'Aiguines. Let's get back to Rome, where as I was saying, you'll be in an excellent position to keep on with your painting.

IRENE: When one starts with a certain teacher it's not wise to change. Mine is not in Rome, he is here.

MONTCEL: Do you work a great deal with your teacher?

IRENE: Of course.

MONTCEL: Every day, I suppose?

IRENE: Practically, yes.

MONTCEL: That's not true.

IRENE: What?

MONTCEL: I've been to see your teacher.

IRENE: You've been to see him?

MONTCEL: To-day. I wanted to satisfy myself. I went to ask him if he were pleased with his pupil. I left his studio fully aware of the real place that painting occupies in your life.

IRENE: What did he tell you?

MONTCEL: That he had not seen you at his studio for a month!

IRENE: [*Faltering.*] I've been making a copy at the Louvre.

MONTCEL: Really! Well, in that case, my child, you have cause to be very pleased, for in Rome you'll find galleries where you'll be able to copy some of the most beautiful pictures in the world.

IRENE: Why are you so insistent that I come with you?

MONTCEL: Because the place of a young unmarried woman is with her family and because until you *are* married your family is your father... even if at times you appear to forget it.

IRENE: If I forget it, father, perhaps it's because you don't always remember it yourself.

MONTCEL: What do you mean by that?

IRENE: Oh, nothing...

MONTCEL: Excuse me... I insist that you explain your remark.

IRENE: If a daughter's place is with her father why did you never think of having us join you while you were in Brussels?

MONTCEL: I've already told you it was because of my quarters there.

IRENE: Only because of that, I suppose?

MONTCEL: [*With growing temper.*] Which of us two owes explanations to the other? You or I? Let that be enough. You are free to think of me what you wish; it makes no difference. But I am your father and I intend to exact obedience from you. [*Forcibly.*] I had thought until now that you were a serious-minded girl, well able to conduct herself properly... I have treated you accordingly. I was mistaken. I shall treat you in the future as you deserve. I shall leave for Rome as soon as my successor arrives here, which will be early next month. You and your sister will leave with me.

IRENE: [*Softly.*] No, father.

MONTCEL: What do you say?

IRENE: I shall not leave. I have already told you so.

MONTCEL: [*Thoroughly angered.*] You shall leave! You'll go or be *forced* to go!

IRENE: [*Willfully.*] As to that!...

MONTCEL: Take care, Irene. You should know me well enough to realize that when I've made up my mind to something it's dangerous to oppose me. I've broken stronger wills than yours in my career.

IRENE: And you should know me, father. I'm your daughter, and in that respect we are alike.

MONTCEL: Enough! I'll not tolerate your threats!

IRENE: [*Controls herself.*] They are not threats. But I'm twenty-five. I'm no longer a child and you must realize that I wouldn't have come to you the other day as I did if I had not also made up my mind.

MONTCEL: Made up your mind to what — remain in Paris?

IRENE: Yes.

MONTCEL: Where do you intend to live?

IRENE: Why — here.

MONTCEL: Oh, no, not here. I'm very sorry, but I've decided to sublet the apartment. It costs a great deal, and I'll have no reason for holding on to it after leaving Paris.

IRENE: Oh.

MONTCEL: That being the case, may I ask where you expect to go?

IRENE: Well . . . to an hotel, I suppose.

MONTCEL: And how will you support yourself? With what money? Not with mine. You'll not have a penny from me.

IRENE: But, father . . .

MONTCEL: Not a penny, let that be clear! As long as I live! . . . and I might inform you — at the risk of disappointing you — that the present state of my health gives no cause for alarm. [*Pause.*] That offers a new side to the question, eh?

IRENE: If you think you can force your will on me in any such way as that —

MONTCEL: If that way fails, there are others.

IRENE: What others?

MONTCEL: I'll tell you. Not only you'll never have a penny of mine but so far as I'm concerned you'll no longer exist. I shall never see you again. I realize that's probably the least of your worries. Your affection for me will readily bear that separation. But what may cause you more concern is to learn that I shall never again let you see your sister.

IRENE: [*Dismayed.*] Oh!

MONTCEL: Never!

IRENE: You'd do that?

MONTCEL: Most assuredly.

IRENE: It's wicked of you!

MONTCEL: Wicked or not, my plain duty is to guard her against you. I shall do so, believe me.

IRENE: Guard her against me! Do you know what you're saying, father? What would become of the poor child without me. Who'd take care of her? I'm all she has in the world.

MONTCEL: Really! I don't count, I suppose!

IRENE: You — oh, but father . . .

MONTCEL: I what? Come, come, finish your thought. She doesn't love me, is that it? She doesn't love me any more than you do!

IRENE: [*Quietly.*] And you, father ... do you love us? Have you ever given us a moment's concern, a moment's bother? I may as well say it, since we're on the subject. What has our childhood been? Not a happy one, father. Always alone with servants. If Gisele hadn't had me and I her, there'd have been little enough affection in our lives since mother's death.

MONTCEL: You're beginning that over again, eh?

IRENE: No, father ... It's finished ... You've done what you wanted to. It isn't for us to attempt to judge you. But, if after having accustomed us to be everything to each other for fifteen years, you think to separate us, you're mistaken, that's all.

MONTCEL: If that's the case, tell me, — since you believe yourself so necessary to your sister — how can you consider remaining here while she's in Rome? Eh, — tell me *that*?

IRENE: Why shouldn't she also stay here?

MONTCEL: With you? In your care? Are you quite mad? You don't really believe that I could trust that child to you. To *you*! That's superb!

IRENE: What do you mean?

MONTCEL: I mean that your sister is a sweet, innocent girl. I propose that she shall remain so! Now you have it!

IRENE: Oh! Father! ...

MONTCEL: I'm sorry, but I must say what I think, — what your behavior compels me to think. If I'm wrong you have only to justify yourself.

IRENE: There is no need for me to justify myself.

MONTCEL: God in heaven! If the reason you had for wishing to remain here were the kind that a daughter might tell her father, you'd have let me hear it long ago.

IRENE: I have told you it was my painting.

MONTCEL: [*Gazing steadily at her.*] I had thought you more intelligent than this. As things stand now I'd tell the truth if I were you. It would be better. [IRENE *is silent.*]

You don't want to? Don't you see that your silence is the most damning evidence against you? Do you think that with what I already take for granted and what I may guess it will still be difficult for me to find out the rest?

IRENE: What do you take for granted?

MONTCEL: You'd like to know?

IRENE: Yes.

MONTCEL: I take for granted that since you don't wish to come to Rome there is some one who holds you here. That's what I think! Am I not right?... Answer me! [*She is silent.*]

Listen, Irene... I'm determined to throw full light on this matter, do you understand? By keeping up this silence you will simply force me to take unpleasant steps which you can still prevent.

IRENE: What steps?

MONTCEL: Never mind! But I promise you I'll get at the truth. I'll insist upon it in a place where I know I can find it and where there'll be no evading it.

IRENE: Where?

MONTCEL: From those whom I must suppose are acquainted with the intimate facts of your life. Your devoted friends the d'Aiguines.

IRENE: [*Thunderstruck.*] That's mad, father!

MONTCEL: I think not.

IRENE: But—whatever gave you the idea—of asking the d'Aiguines about such a thing?

MONTCEL: The idea occurred to me after certain things I've observed.

IRENE: What have you observed?

MONTCEL: I must be allowed to keep that to myself for the present.

IRENE: But at least I have the right to know?—

MONTCEL: No, you have not! [*Pause.*] You seem curiously disturbed that I should take this step.

IRENE: I,—not at all! It's a matter of complete indifference to me.

MONTCEL: Really? Why, then, were you so agitated by my mention of the name d'Aiguines?

IRENE: [*Disturbed.*] I wasn't agitated.

MONTCEL: You were! Besides, it's very simple. [*Looks at his watch.*] We'll settle this right away.

IRENE: What are you going to do?

MONTCEL: Ask Monsieur d'Aiguines to come here and have a talk with me immediately.

IRENE: You won't do that, father!

MONTCEL: You'll see.

IRENE: Even if I tell you that it would be quite useless, that you will learn nothing?

MONTCEL: Ah! So you're already beginning to admit things! Listen,—listen to me—if within two minutes you have not spoken the name I wish to hear, I shall ask d'Aiguines for it whether you wish me to or not!

IRENE: Father, I beg you not to do this!

MONTCEL: Then tell me. On whose account do you wish to remain in Paris? Will you tell me,—yes or no?

IRENE: [*In despair.*] But, father—

MONTCEL: [*After a moment.*] All right, I'm through! [*He reaches the door, back.*]

IRENE: [*Imploringly.*] Father! No, father!

MONTCEL: [*At door.*] Well?

IRENE: It's on account—of—Jacques.

MONTCEL: [*Surprised*] Jacques? Jacques who? Jacques Virieu?

IRENE: Yes.

MONTCEL: [*Still surprised.*] It's on account of Jacques that you want to remain in Paris?

IRENE: [*Nervously.*] Well,—yes.

MONTCEL: Upon my soul! What's going on between you two?

IRENE: Nothing.

MONTCEL: What do you mean, nothing?

IRENE: Nothing serious, I assure you.

MONTCEL: Would you mind not juggling words with me. I warn you that all you say will be verified.

IRENE: Of course, father…

MONTCEL: So I advise you not to try to hide anything from me. Now, answer my question. What is going on between you?

IRENE: [*With difficulty.*] We've been fond of each other for some time and we had thought,—at least, *I* had thought that I might marry him,— that's all.

MONTCEL: You're telling me everything?

IRENE: Yes.

MONTCEL: So you and Jacques want to get married?

IRENE: I said that *I* wanted to,—that is, I'd like to.

MONTCEL: And he?

IRENE: I don't know.

MONTCEL: Do you mean to say he hasn't spoken of his intentions?

IRENE: No.

MONTCEL: Then how do things stand?

IRENE: He hasn't spoken yet.

MONTCEL: And you imagine that he's getting ready to? Eh? Speak! Explain yourself… don't make me force every word out of you!

IRENE: I'm not certain of anything.

MONTCEL: Then, as I understand it, you love him…if he were to propose you'd be inclined to say yes. Is that it?

IRENE: [*After a pause.*] Yes.

MONTCEL: And it's with this hope in mind that you'd prefer remaining in Paris?

IRENE: Yes.

MONTCEL: Well, for heaven's sake, my dear, why haven't you simply said so instead of keeping up this air of mystery?

IRENE: It wasn't my secret alone.

MONTCEL: Why, it isn't betraying a secret of that kind to tell it to one's father. Besides you must have known perfectly well that there's nothing about your idea that displeases me. Jacques's a distant relative of ours on his mother's side…You've known each other since you were children…he goes with the same sort of people we do. He's a fine boy, and I'm very fond of him. To make things complete his electrical concession in Morocco assures him a good income. There's no possible reason for my opposing your wish.

IRENE: I didn't want to tell you about something which may exist only in my imagination.

MONTCEL: Why not? Where's the harm?

IRENE: Well, it's not exactly pleasant having to confess oneself mistaken about a thing like that. You must understand.

MONTCEL: We must learn to pocket our pride at times. Instead of being afraid of me you should have looked upon me as your natural guide and adviser. I realize that *you* can't ask the young man to reveal the state of his feelings; that wouldn't be quite the thing. But *I* can do it easily, without your pride being hurt in any way.

IRENE: But father, that's impossible!…

MONTCEL: It's so far from being impossible, my dear, that I'll prove it by taking the matter up with Jacques to-morrow.

IRENE: You don't really mean to!

MONTCEL: Don't worry…I'll leave you out of it. I'll not even refer to our conversation, —

IRENE: But, father…

MONTCEL: [*Going on.*]…I'll merely tell him that for some time past a number of things have led me to believe that you were developing a deep affection for some one. That I have watched you closely and come to understand, without your saying a word, that your feelings concerned him. I'll then say that, as I'm about to leave Paris to be gone for some time I'd like to know if he has anything to say to me. Just that.

IRENE: Father, I beg you to do nothing of the sort...!

MONTCEL: I'm sorry to oppose your wishes, my dear, but under the circumstances I'm a better judge of what should be done than you. Some day you'll thank me for it.

IRENE: I don't want you to do it!

MONTCEL: Do you prefer going to Rome without knowing what he—?

IRENE: I prefer to wait, without rushing matters.

MONTCEL: Wait for what? For him to make up his mind? Don't forget that I'm leaving in three weeks' time.

IRENE: Well, naturally, we can't expect things to develop much in three weeks.

MONTCEL: Well, then?

IRENE: That's exactly why I want to stay behind.

MONTCEL: Under no conditions! Unless, of course, he has proposed formally, and even then...we'll see.

IRENE: But you've just said you had faith in him.

MONTCEL: No. Don't insist. It's quite useless. I shall speak to him, just as I've outlined and—

IRENE: Father, please!

MONTCEL: Don't be afraid. I'll talk with him as man to man in the friend-liest possible way. Whatever his sentiments may be he won't be able to take any exception to what is said.

IRENE: For the last time, father, I beg you not to do this!

MONTCEL: That's enough, my child. My mind is made up and I shan't change it. Let's leave it at that for this evening if you don't mind. It's already half past six and I must run around to the Foreign Office before dinner. [*He goes toward the door, back.*] By the bye, will you put Dardennes at your right and Couvreur at your left. Dinner's at eight-fifteen. [*He goes out.*]

[IRENE *seems tremendously disturbed as soon as she is alone. She drops into a chair, musing; then suddenly rising, goes to her table and lifts the telephone receiver.*]

IRENE: [*Into the telephone.*] Elysèes 24-51... Please. Hullo?... Elysèes 24-51?... May I speak to Monsieur Jacques Virieu? Oh, it's you, Jacques? I didn't recognize your voice... You knew mine?... I'm glad. Listen, Jacques, is there any way of my seeing you?... Yes—if you wish... But wouldn't it be possible right away?... Could you come here?... Thanks so much. I'll expect you... What?... Oh, I'll tell you, I can't over the telephone... Good-by! [*She replaces the receiver, and for a moment remains pensively where she is.* GISELE *enters at right.*]

GISELE: May I come in?

IRENE: Certainly, dear. Dressed so soon?

GISELE: But it's fairly late. And we haven't fixed the flowers yet.

IRENE: Oh! please do it without me. I simply won't have the time. [IRENE *goes to dressing room.*]

GISELE: All right. They'll be too awful, but what's the difference?

IRENE: [*From dressing room.*] Of course they won't. Don't be silly!... Ring for Josephine, dear, do you mind? I must dress.

GISELE: [*Rings bell.*] Irene?

IRENE: What, darling?

JOSEPHINE: [*Entering at the back, to* GISELE.] Did you ring, mademoiselle?

GISELE: No, — Irene.

IRENE: [*Still off.*] My crêpe de chine gown, Josephine... I'm going to dress right away.

GISELE: But you said you'd wear the white dress!

IRENE: So I did. My white dress, Josephine.

JOSEPHINE: Very good, mademoiselle. [JOSEPHINE *goes to dressing room.*]

GISELE: Irene!

IRENE: You wanted to ask me something?

GISELE: [*Going to door of dressing room and speaking off to* IRENE.] Oh, yes. I overheard something that papa said while I was in my room. Just a few words, but I'm dying to know what they meant.

IRENE: You heard something father said?

GISELE: Yes — not deliberately — I really wasn't listening at the keyhole. But for a moment papa spoke so loudly that I couldn't help hearing.

IRENE: What did you hear?

GISELE: He said, "You'll go or be forced to go!" Surely it wasn't Rome he was speaking about?

IRENE: Yes.

GISELE: What?... You're not coming to Rome!... Oh, Irene, you can't mean that!

IRENE: I'm not sure yet, dear. Don't bother your head about it.

GISELE: [*Leaving the door, almost in tears.*] You're not going to let me go there alone with papa?

IRENE: [*Enters in negligée.*] I may have to... [*Takes* GISELE'*s hand.*]

GISELE: [*Heartbroken.*] Oh!

IRENE: But you'll have a marvelous time in Rome... You've no idea how beautiful it is. You'll meet some delightful people... they'll give you any number of parties. Just think, dear, you'll be the only woman in the embassy... You'll have the time of your life!

GISELE: Without you?

IRENE: [*Tenderly.*] Yes, dearest, even without me.

GISELE: How can I—if you're not there?

IRENE: [*Holding her close.*] My dear!

GISELE: Oh, well, if you're going to desert me, then what will—

IRENE: Would you rather stay here with me?

GISELE: Oh, yes—much!

IRENE: But wouldn't you be sorry not to go to Rome?

GISELE: I'd like to have gone if you had gone. But without you—no—I'd much prefer to remain here.

IRENE: Are you sure?

GISELE: Sure.

IRENE: Well, would you like me to persuade father to leave you here too? It won't be easy, but if it's worked well he might consent.

GISELE: Yes, please do.

IRENE: All right, let me try! But you won't say a word to any one, not even to Mademoiselle Marchand, will you?

GISELE: Not a word!

JOSEPHINE: [*Entering left.*] Mademoiselle?

IRENE: Yes, yes. — I'm coming. [*She goes again into the dressing room.* JOSEPHINE *follows her off.*]

GISELE: Oh, Irene! You didn't say a thing about my new frock!

IRENE: [*Off.*] Oh! I'm so sorry! [GISELE *approaches the half-open door.*] I think it's a dream, dear.

GISELE: Don't you think the skirt rather long?

IRENE: [*Still off.*] No... I think it's all right that way.

GISELE: [*Raising her skirt a bit.*] Now—isn't that much better? Look?

IRENE: M-m-m—perhaps. But it was really all right before.

GISELE: Oh! You make me sick! Can't you give a poor woman a little friendly advice?

IRENE: Well... no, it *is* a little too short for you. It doesn't look quite modest.

GISELE: Really? But I raised it barely two inches...

IRENE: You've got plenty of time ahead in which to show your legs—

GISELE: Oh, you think so? And what if they begin wearing long skirts again next season, then where am I?

IRENE: There's something in that!

GISELE: Well, suppose I raise it one inch... Are you still horrified?

IRENE: No, go ahead... Shorten it one inch!

GISELE: [*To* JOSEPHINE *who crosses from the dressing room toward the right.*] You heard, Josephine. One inch.

JOSEPHINE: Yes, mademoiselle.

GISELE: I'll pin it up for you in the morning. It can stay like this for to-night. [JOSEPHINE *takes* IRENE's *coat and hat from chair.*] Who cares about to-night, anyhow?—Whiskers!

IRENE: [*Coming in now fully gowned.*] Josephine!

JOSEPHINE: Yes, mademoiselle?

IRENE: Monsieur Jacques Virieu will be calling to see me. As soon as he arrives, show him in here... do you understand?

JOSEPHINE: Yes, mademoiselle. [*Exits at back with coat and hat.* GISELE *has taken from the table the bunch of violets which* IRENE *brought in with her and is absent-mindedly inhaling their odor.*]

GISELE: [*Pleased; turns to* IRENE.] Jacques coming? [IRENE *sees the violets in* GISELE's *hand, a faint movement reveals some indefinable emotion as she takes them from her. She exits into the dressing room returning with the flowers in a vase which she places on the table.* GISELE *watches her, a bit surprised.*] I say, Irene—?

IRENE: What?

GISELE: Is Jacques coming?

IRENE: Yes... I'm expecting him.

GISELE: What fun!... Dear old thing! I *will* be glad to see him! But he isn't coming for dinner, is he?

IRENE: No. I asked him to come to see me for a minute because... I've something to tell him... Incidentally, Gisele, be an angel and leave me alone with him after you've said hullo.

GISELE: Righto!

IRENE: Thank you, darling... You're really a dear! You never ask questions... and you never ask me to explain a thing!

GISELE: Oh, I just try not to meddle in what isn't my business, that's all.

IRENE: Yes, but they're scarce, people who can do that! [JOSEPHINE *opens the door at back and admits* JACQUES. *He is about thirty-four and good looking.*] Hullo, Jacques! [*Gives him her hand.*]

JACQUES: How are you, Irene? [*To* GISELE.] Well, baby sister!

GISELE: Hullo, Jacques!

JACQUES: Lord, what a beauty! I'm bowled over... and to think that I once bounced *this* on my knee! I wouldn't dare try it now!

GISELE: Well, I should hope not! [*The girls laugh.*]

JACQUES: [*Noticing their costumes, to* IRENE.] But, see here, you didn't tell me this was a state occasion!

IRENE: State occasion?

JACQUES: Your gowns...!

IRENE: Don't be startled! Father's having some guests to dinner this evening.

JACQUES: Oh, I see. [*Pause.*] Well, what's going on?

GISELE: Before you start in, say good-by to me.

JACQUES: Are you leaving us?

GISELE: I must.

JACQUES: Farewell, beauteous one!

GISELE: When are you having that tea party for Irene and me?

JACQUES: You've only to name your day!

GISELE: The last time I saw you you promised us a sumpt'ous tea with caviar sandwiches. But that's as far as it ever got.

JACQUES: We'll arrange it, I promise!

GISELE: I'm counting on you, don't forget! I just love caviar! [*She goes out at back.*]

JACQUES: Well?

IRENE: Thanks for having come, Jacques.

JACQUES: Please... [*He sits.*] I'm very curious. What's happened?

IRENE: First I want you to swear that you'll never repeat a word of what we're going to say to a living soul...

JACQUES: Is it as serious as that?

IRENE: Yes... You'll swear it, won't you, Jacques?

JACQUES: Why, certainly.

IRENE: You've heard that father has just been appointed to the post in Rome?

JACQUES: Yes.

IRENE: He's decided that Gisele and I are to go with him.

JACQUES: Naturally.

IRENE: It's not so natural. Until now whenever he occupied a foreign post he's left us here. Why does he want to take us to Rome this time?... I can't help thinking he's been advised to do it.

JACQUES: By whom?

IRENE: The Foreign Office probably. It seems they're rather strict in Rome. Perhaps they felt at the Foreign Office that it would look well for him to have his daughters with him... and that it would prevent his taking

Madame de Vallon as he always has before. I don't think that was liked
any too well in Brussels.

JACQUES: Really?

IRENE: I can't be certain that's the reason, but it seems likely. Besides, it
doesn't matter. The main point now is that he's decided we're to go
with him. [*Pause.*] Only I have decided to remain in Paris.

JACQUES: Why?

IRENE: [*After a moment.*] . . . I told him it was because of my painting, — so
that I might continue to work here with my teacher . . .

JACQUES: Wasn't that true?

IRENE: No. Besides, to-day, father saw my teacher, who told him I hadn't
been at the studio for a month.

JACQUES: I see.

IRENE: He realized I had another reason for staying. We had a very trying
scene just now; he wound up by saying that he was sure my desire not
to go was due to some one who held me in Paris. He insisted on
knowing who it was.

JACQUES: And then?

IRENE: He tormented me with questions which I couldn't answer,
threatened to take steps which I couldn't let him take. I was nearly
crazy, and then a name came to my lips almost despite myself . . .
the name of the only friend I knew I could count on, the only being
I could confide in . . . yours.

JACQUES: Mine?

IRENE: Yes.

JACQUES: You gave him my name?

IRENE: Yes.

JACQUES: Then . . . your father believes it's on *my* account that you wish to
remain in Paris?

IRENE: Yes.

JACQUES: [*After a moment.*] Do you realize, Irene, what you've done?

IRENE: Yes.

JACQUES: What can your father thing?

IRENE: [*Not looking at him.*] Nothing. I told him that by leaving me in
Paris — that is, by not taking me away from where you were — a plan
which so far I was alone in forming might become a reality . . .

JACQUES: What plan?

IRENE: That of . . . our getting married.

JACQUES: You led him to believe that?

IRENE: Yes.

JACQUES: No!

IRENE: Yes, I know . . . I know everything you're thinking.

JACQUES: Wouldn't it have been better to tell him—the truth?

IRENE: [*Sharply, looking at him.*] What truth?

JACQUES: I don't know. But whatever it may be it's certainly better than this—this lie.

IRENE: [*Hopeless. Staring ahead.*] If I had told truth, no one would have understood it.

JACQUES: Why? [*She is silent.*] Tell me!

IRENE: It doesn't matter . . .

JACQUES: Can't you at least tell *me*?

IRENE: No.

JACQUES: Ah? [*Pause.*] Well, I confess it's pretty hard for me to understand how you could have disposed of me like this in such a serious situation—without even consulting me!

IRENE: Did I have time to consult you? I was frantic. Every argument I used was turned against me . . . I saw only one thing—that father had to be reassured about me at any cost . . . so that he'd look no further. That was my one anxiety.

JACQUES: Were you so certain that my name would be enough to reassure him?

IRENE: Yes.

JACQUES: You might have realized, Irene, that you should have used some other name . . . *any* other name. [*He rises impatiently.*]

IRENE: What choice had I? Do you think I have a single friend besides yourself of whom I could ask such a thing?

JACQUES: Didn't it occur to you that perhaps I was last one of whom you could ask such a thing?

IRENE: I thought you were fond of me.

JACQUES: You didn't remember that I had also loved you?

IRENE: Oh, Jacques . . . that's all in the past.

JACQUES: Are you so sure? [*Pause.*] Certainly it's not so far in the past that you've already forgotten it? Is it?

IRENE: I didn't think about it.

JACQUES: You should have understood that a girl doesn't ask a man to take part in a pretended engagement when he had hoped for the real thing . . . a man, who hardly a year ago had every reason to believe that his hope would be realized!

IRENE: Please, Jacques! Don't remind me of that! I've regretted it so much, believe me! I don't know what could have let you suppose that I'd ever had the idea of—

JACQUES: Of becoming my wife? Then why didn't you stop me right away the first time I told you that I loved you and that I wanted to marry you?...

IRENE: But... I didn't think you were really serious about it...

JACQUES: [*With ill-humor.*] Come now! Who jokes about such a thing? Besides if you had thought I was joking you would have replied in the same vein. Instead of that you asked for time to think things over... with real sincerity in your voice. [*His manner softens.*] You had to leave for Florence a month later. We saw each other every day before you went. I took you to the station the night you left, and on the platform during the last few minutes before the train pulled out, you said with a smile that I can still see that you were going to send me your answer. [*More coldly.*] Well, I'll never believe that the answer you were planning to send was the one that I finally received three weeks later.

IRENE: You're wrong.

JACQUES: I don't believe it.

IRENE: What—according to you—could have happened to make me change my mind?

JACQUES: I don't know. Something occurred in your life there that I know nothing about, that I haven't tried to find out, but that has changed you in many ways. Of course, it's none of my business... but surely I have the right to find it—shall we say unexpected—that you come to me after that, asking me to pose as your fiancé! You must admit it's a bit humorous!

IRENE: I thought you'd have a little more sympathy.

JACQUES: Oh, don't think I'm reproaching you. I just find it humorous, that's all. [*Pause.*] So you told your father that I wanted to marry you and that—

IRENE: I didn't tell him you wanted to marry me. I said merely that *I* wanted to marry... but that I was unaware of your intentions.

JACQUES: And your father believed that this desire came to you—like that —with nothing on my part to encourage it? Come, Irene, your father's fully aware of your pride... he can't help but think I'm on the verge of telling him I want to marry you.

IRENE: I swear that I've said nothing which might let suppose so... Anyhow, you'll see that for yourself,—he wants to speak to you.

JACQUES: [*Surprised.*] He wants to speak to me?

IRENE: I did my best to prevent it, but he wouldn't listen. He said he'd see you to-morrow.

JACQUES: Really?

IRENE: You'll see by what he says that I haven't "disposed" of you, as you say...In a moment of distress I turned to you as the one human being who could possibly help me. If you don't want to, there's nothing to compel it. When father questions you, you've only to act as though all this were news to you and surprises you. Say that there's some mistake—that it's a misunderstanding for which you're terribly sorry but which you did nothing to cause and that will be all. You may rest assured that's the last you'll hear of it.

JACQUES: And then,—what will you do?

IRENE: That, Jacques—[*She turns away.*]

JACQUES: Yes. That's none of my business, is that it?

IRENE: What can it matter to you?

JACQUES: [*After a moment.*] But tell me,—before calling me to help you, didn't it occur to you that I might not be free, that there might be some one else in my life.

IRENE: I know that there is some one else in your life.

JACQUES: You know it?

IRENE: Yes, of course.

JACQUES: Well, then, since you know it, how could you ask me to do this for you?

IRENE: Am I asking you to change your mode of existence in any way?

JACQUES: Well, what are you asking me? To pose as your fiancé, isn't that it?

IRENE: Not at all! It's simply—

JACQUES: Yes, yes, only so far as your father is concerned.

IRENE: But not even so far as he is concerned. All I ask is that you suggest to him that by taking me away from Paris he might lessen the—the possibility of a marriage between us some day...that's all.

JACQUES: In other words, you want to take advantage of the confidence your father has in me to hide something behind it.—I don't know exactly what, but *something*—that you can't confess to anyone. It amounts to that, doesn't it?

IRENE: I simply need a few days until father leaves. Afterwards—[*A gesture.*]

JACQUES: What afterwards?

IRENE: Afterwards, I'll manage somehow. [*Determinedly.*] I'll find some way of remaining here. I'll give you back your liberty, I promise you.

JACQUES: But why must you remain here at any cost? Mayn't I know?

IRENE: I don't wish to leave Paris; that's all I can say.

JACQUES: Irene! Let's have the truth. You don't want to leave some one who's in Paris. It's that, isn't it? Eh? [IRENE *is silent. A pause.*] So that's what you've come to. You! . . . You that I admired so much! You whom I've always thought incapable of anything low or cheap. And here you are mixed up in the cheapest of all things—a *lie*!

IRENE: If I lie, it's because I'm driven to it.

JACQUES: By whom?

IRENE: By everyone. There's no other course open to me.

JACQUES: That course isn't worth much, believe me . . . It won't lead you far. And, above all, it's unworthy of you, Irene. You're too fine for that!

IRENE: No, I'm not too fine for that! You've always cherished illusions about me, Jacques. How often I've asked you not to place me on a pedestal—don't you remember? Why have you always persisted in thinking me different?

JACQUES: Probably because I loved you.

IRENE: Ah! That's not my fault.

JACQUES: And then, *no*, it's not true! . . . You were different! Only you've changed . . . or rather they've changed you—

IRENE: [*Aggressively.*] They? Who?

JACQUES: No doubt the people you've been with such a lot this past year. In deserting your old friends for them it doesn't seem to me that you have profited by the change.

IRENE: These "people" as you call them . . . do you know them?

JACQUES: Not at all.

IRENE: Well, then—[*Pause.*] Think what you wish of them but don't tell me about it, do you mind?

JACQUES: [*Angrily.*] Very well! But since they mean so much to you why didn't you turn to one of them for the help you need? It seems to me that would be far more natural. Especially, as I'm not exactly the man for this sort of game.

IRENE: [*Beseeching.*] Jacques!

JACQUES: You must have some real friends among them—one surely—well, ask him.

IRENE: I have only one real friend—you . . . At least I thought you were my friend.

JACQUES: It's just because I am your friend that I haven't the right to do what you ask.

IRENE: Why?

JACQUES: Because it's unpleasant, dangerous—and, above all, useless. No good can come of a lie like that. It's doomed in advance.

IRENE: If you were really my friend, you'd let yourself be guided by your heart...instead of by the rules of middle class morality.

JACQUES: Middle class morality has its good points.

IRENE: [*Ironically.*] Yes...especially to those who profit by it!

JACQUES: What does that mean?

IRENE: Were you being prompted by the rules of that morality last year when you asked me to be your mistress? You remember that...?

JACQUES: Yes, I do.

IRENE: Highly moral, that?

JACQUES: Yes.

IRENE: Ah!

JACQUES: Yes, because if you had belonged to me, you'd have ended by loving me and marrying me. I'd have overcome your unwillingness to give up your liberty...It would have been a step toward the only solution of any girl's life—marriage.

IRENE: Then it was to convert me to marriage that you wanted me to give myself to you?

JACQUES: Yes.

IRENE: Really? [*Pause.*] I had thought it was merely because you wanted me.

JACQUES: Naturally I wanted you. I wanted you with all my heart. The thought of your body against mine stirred my blood—as it does at this minute, if you must know!

IRENE: Jacques!

JACQUES: I'm beginning to think I'll never get over my love for you. However, that's neither here nor there, and doesn't interest you... What I want to tell you is that it's always you of whom I think... even, before myself, do you hear? Even now. So that you won't doubt it, I'll say this:—swear to me that, this affair of yours—about which I don't ask to know anything—will eventually lead to a marriage worthy of you...just swear that and I'll do anything you want me to do. Can you swear it?

IRENE: [*Turning away.*] ...I won't swear to anything.

JACQUES: Very well. Then, I refuse. Think what you like...that I'm heartless, that I don't love you—I don't care. I refuse. And if my refusal makes you give up this affair a bit sooner than you expected; it will be better all around, you may be sure.

IRENE: [*With intense feeling.*] You ought to know me well enough, Jacques, to realize that I'll do what I've decided to do…even if doing so shatters everything.

JACQUES: Have you gone crazy?

IRENE: [*Wildly.*] No! But I will if I'm forced to leave…

JACQUES: Irene! [IRENE *lowers her head, repressing her emotion.* GISELE *enters, at back.*]

GISELE: Jacques, papa says not to go,—he wants to speak to you.

IRENE: [*Alarmed.*] How did he know Jacques was here?

GISELE: Why, I told him. He just got back. He took one look at the table and said it looked like nothing at all! So he told me to fetch you and I said you were with Jacques. [*Pause. Penitently to* IRENE.] Shouldn't I have said that?

IRENE: [*Embarrassed.*] That's all right, dear.

GISELE: So he sent me to ask Jacques to wait because he wanted to see him, that's all…[*To* JACQUES.] Did I put my foot in it…?

JACQUES: No, Gisele, it doesn't matter.

GISELE: Well, I couldn't know! You should have warned me. [*She goes out.* JACQUES *closes door.*]

[IRENE *stands rigid for a moment, then suddenly making up her mind, hurries into the dressing room emerging with a cloak which she throws about her as she heads for the door, back.*]

JACQUES: [*Barring the way.*] What are you doing?…You're going out?

IRENE: I'm leaving here.

JACQUES: Where are you going?

IRENE: [*Hotly.*] That's my business…I'm going, that's all.

JACQUES: But, Irene—

IRENE: Let me go!

JACQUES: Why do you want to leave?

IRENE: It'll put an end to all this!

JACQUES: You're not in your right senses now!

IRENE: Let me pass!

JACQUES: What shall I say to your father?

IRENE: Whatever you like, I don't care…Let me pass!

JACQUES: No!

IRENE: You've no right to stop me from doing what I want.

JACQUES: I've a right to stop your doing something rash!

IRENE: [*In a torment of terror and despair.*] I've had enough! Enough! I'm twenty-five, free to do as I like without accounting to anyone. Let me pass! Jacques!

JACQUES: Irene, come, calm yourself, I beg of you!

IRENE: Do you realize what my life here will be after, father has spoken to you? No! No! I'll not be questioned any more! I can't stand this being baited by the world! I want to go away!

JACQUES: Irene!

IRENE: After all, what difference does it make to you if I go?

JACQUES: What difference does it make to me?

IRENE: [*In cold fury.*] Yes, —is it any business of yours?

JACQUES: [*After a pause, leaving her.*] You're quite right. Very well, go. [*He comes forward and sits near the table, his head in his hands.* IRENE, *without moving, follows him with her eyes.*] Well, why don't you go? What's keeping you from going to him now? [*A wan smile crosses* IRENE'*s face. She wraps her cloak around her and goes slowly to the door, which she is about to open. He sits up.*] Irene!

IRENE: [*Turning back.*] Yes?

JACQUES: [*After a pause; curtly.*] Stay here!

IRENE: What?

JACQUES: Stay here, I say.

IRENE: I don't understand.

JACQUES: Yes you do, you understand perfectly... Take off your wrap. If your father sees it, he's the one who won't understand.

IRENE: But explain what you—

JACQUES: Do as I say. [MONTCEL *enters at back.* IRENE *hidden by the door, lets her cloak slip off.* MONTCEL *crosses to* JACQUES.]

MONTCEL: Good evening, Jacques.

JACQUES: Good evening, uncle.

MONTCEL: I hope you didn't mind waiting.

JACQUES: Not at all.

MONTCEL: I was going to drop you a line asking you to come in to see me to-morrow, but when I heard you were here with Irene I thought I'd save you the trouble... I wanted to have a chat with you. Shall we go along to my study? [JACQUES *assents.*] I won't keep you long. [*Takes* JACQUES *to door—sees* IRENE—*stops.*] Go ahead, I'll join you. [JACQUES *goes out.* MONTCEL *quickly to* IRENE.] You've already spoken to him, haven't you?

IRENE: What do you mean?

MONTCEL: Well, if he knows—tell me. It will save a lot of useless talk.

IRENE: [*After a moment.*] Yes.

MONTCEL: Well?... What's his answer?

IRENE: He'll tell you himself.

MONTCEL: Good. [*He goes out.* IRENE *remains there, thoughtful, brooding, her face woeful. After a moment, her eyes light on the vase which contains the violets; she is drawn over to them, looks at them, touches them delicately. Then, as if an idea had taken her, she regards her watch, half hesitates and reaches for the telephone. She lifts the receiver with intense anticipation as*

The CURTAIN *falls*

Act Two

Scene: *A study in* JACQUES' *apartment. It has a bookish, comfortable appearance. There are doors at back to the hall, at right to a bedroom and at left to a small salon or reception room. A large desk stands center. A few good-sized chairs and a massive leather divan are placed about.*

It is a month later.

At the rise JACQUES *is discovered seated, musing deeply, his eyes staring ahead. On his lap he has an open snapshot album neglected for the moment.*

A door bell sounds, JACQUES *scowls, regards his watch and, rising, murmurs, "Oh, well!"*

GEORGES, *his man, enters.*

GEORGES: Are you at home, monsieur?
JACQUES: I'm expecting Madame Meillant. It's probably she.
GEORGES: Yes, monsieur. [*He goes out.* JACQUES *places the album in a drawer of desk.* GEORGES *returns.*] It's not Madame Meillant, monsieur; it's Mademoiselle de Montcel.
JACQUES: [*Surprised.*] Mademoiselle de Montcel?
GEORGES: Yes, monsieur.
JACQUES: [*Nervously.*] Have you shown her into the salon?
GEORGES: Yes, monsieur.
JACQUES: Very well. [*He goes toward door which leads to the salon.*] Oh! When Madame Meillant comes tell her—tell her that I telephoned I'd be a bit late. Say that I hope she'll forgive me and ask if she'd mind coming back at four, if that's convenient. [*Looks at his watch.*] That's it, at four.
GEORGES: Very good, monsieur. [*He goes out.* JACQUES *opens door to salon.*]

JACQUES: Do come in—[*Surprised.*] Why, it's—? Well! My man said it was Mademoiselle de Montcel so I thought—

GISELE: [*Entering.*] That it was Irene?

JACQUES: Yes.

GISELE: Oh, I'm so sorry, Jacques.

JACQUES: But not at all—why?

GISELE: Because you must be terribly disappointed!

JACQUES: Not at all, my dear. [*Closes door.*] I'm delighted to see you. A bit surprised, but delighted.

GISELE: You're surprised because you think that a girl of my age shouldn't come alone to a man's apartment, is that it? But I didn't come alone. Mademoiselle Marchand is waiting downstairs in the car.

JACQUES: You've no need to explain. Do sit down!

GISELE: I've just one thing to tell you.

JACQUES: Sit down anyway.

GISELE: [*Sits.*] At first I thought I'd telephone you this morning to ask when I could come, but the phone's in Irene's room and I didn't want her to hear.

JACQUES: I see.

GISELE: So instead I came early to have a better chance of finding you in...[*She hesitates.*] Jacques, perhaps you're going to think that what I'm doing is a bit ridiculous and even uncalled for—but I don't care. It's just this—I've come to tell you that Irene is very unhappy.

JACQUES: Irene?

GISELE: Yes...and you can believe me...I'm saying this only because I'm sure of it. For some time now she's been acting in a very strange, nervous way. Several times it seemed to me that her eyes were rather red. Mademoiselle Marchand had also noticed it. And the other day I went into her room to phone, thinking she'd gone out, and, although she turned her face away, I saw she was crying.

JACQUES: Ah?

GISELE: For Irene to cry means that something's really wrong. I can't bear seeing her wretched! Anything rather than that. I thought it over and decided you didn't know about it and that you should. That's why I've come. So, Jacques—that's all. [*A pause.*] Are you annoyed with me for telling you this?

JACQUES: I'm not annoyed with you at all, my dear,—only I must confess that I don't quite understand why you thought you ought to tell *me* about it!

GISELE: What?

JACQUES: I'm very fond of Irene but I don't see that I —

GISELE: [*Smiling.*] Jacques...papa told me before he left.

JACQUES: [*Surprised and rather annoyed.*] What did he tell you?

GISELE: Oh, don't worry! He swore me to secrecy—and you may be sure I'll never tell a soul. Besides I realize that you both want to think things over, and that you don't feel free to commit yourself definitely just now because of your business troubles...I know all that... [JACQUES *is disturbed and wretched.*]...Are you cross that papa told me?

JACQUES: No, no, it doesn't matter.

GISELE: You see, it would have been difficult for him *not* to say something. It had been arranged that we were to go to Rome with him. Then suddenly plans are changed; we're to remain here—with Mademoiselle Marchand living at the house as chaperon. So papa probably felt obliged to give me *some* explanation. He didn't realize that I had already guessed everything.

JACQUES: What—what had you guessed?

GISELE: Everything! After all, it wasn't so brilliant of me! I knew that Irene wanted to stay in Paris and that papa wouldn't hear of it. Then on top of that, you come to see Irene, you have a talk with papa, and the same evening he announces to Irene that she may remain and that he'll leave me with her. Well, I didn't have to be so awfully bright to understand what all that meant. [*Rises.*] And, Jacques, I was so happy when I *did* understand. I can't begin to tell you how happy!

JACQUES: Really?

GISELE: I'm positive you're just made for one another! Don't you think so too?

JACQUES: Of course, my dear.

GISELE: So now you understand why I came?

JACQUES: I understand.

GISELE: Was it wrong of me to come?

JACQUES: No.

GISELE: And it's true that you had noticed nothing, isn't it?

JACQUES: Nothing.

GISELE: I was sure of it! I said to Mademoiselle Marchand: "If Jacques asked papa to leave Irene in Paris, it's because he loves her, and if he loves her he can't want her to be miserable...or else he hasn't noticed it. And, naturally, if no one does anything it all might go on forever! And it must not go on." [*She takes his hand.*] Must it, Jacques?

JACQUES: No, it mustn't, Gisele dear. Only, don't you see—

GISELE: No, don't tell me. I don't want to know anything. It's none of my business. I've told you what I wanted to say. The rest is your affair. I ask just one thing—never let Irene know I came here, because she'd never forgive me for it. Promise?

JACQUES: I promise.

GISELE: Thank you. [*She lets go his hand.*]

JACQUES: Wait, please don't go yet, do you mind? [*He walks about, thinking, then stops in front of her.*] Do you trust me, Gisele?

GISELE: [*Surprised and a bit worried.*] Why, Jacques, of course!

JACQUES: Enough to believe me without asking for explanations?

GISELE: [*Still anxious.*] Yes, what is it?

JACQUES: You think—and it's natural enough you should—that I could prevent Irene's being unhappy if I wanted to, don't you?

GISELE: Yes.

JACQUES: Well, you're mistaken.

GISELE: What?

JACQUES: I can do nothing for her... or so little...

GISELE: You?

JACQUES: I.

GISELE: Then it's not because of you that she's unhappy?

JACQUES: No.

GISELE: [*Astonished.*] No?...

JACQUES: If it were because of me, believe me she'd not be unhappy long. Of course I can try to do something, for her. It may accomplish nothing, but I can try. Only for that I'll need you.

GISELE: Me?

JACQUES: Yes. I need some information that only you can give me. If I knew of any one else to turn to, I would, but, if you think my questions are indiscreet or if you believe they are prompted by anything but my desire to see Irene happy, don't answer them.

GISELE: What do you want to know?

JACQUES: I'd like to know something about the life she leads, the people she sees.

GISELE: The people she sees? Why *you*, mostly.

JACQUES: Me?

GISELE: Yes.

JACQUES: When does she see me?

GISELE: Well—I don't know. Don't you always have tea together?

JACQUES: Did she tell you that?

GISELE: [*Puzzled.*] I had understood that... I might have been mistaken.

JACQUES: [*After a pause.*] And besides myself, whom does she see?

GISELE: Well, you know, she doesn't tell me a great deal about what she does.

JACQUES: When she goes out, doesn't she ever tell you where she is going?

GISELE: She goes to the studio every day after lunch.

JACQUES: Ah, yes… And at night, does she ever go out?

GISELE: At night? Oh, almost never. She's been once or twice to the theater or a concert, but that's all.

JACQUES: Alone?

GISELE: No, with Monsieur and Madame d'Aiguines.

JACQUES: Oh. [*After a pause.*] She met them in Italy, didn't she?

GISELE: Yes, in Florence, last year.

JACQUES: Do you ever see them?

GISELE: I? Never!

JACQUES: Why?

GISELE: I don't know them.

JACQUES: How is it you've never met them if Irene is so intimate with them?

GISELE: That's no reason. She never suggested my meeting them and I never asked to.

JACQUES: Why? Don't you like them?

GISELE: But I don't know them.

JACQUES: Does she ever speak to you about them?

GISELE: No, never.

JACQUES: And have you never had curiosity enough to ask her questions about them?

GISELE: I never ask Irene questions. When she speaks to me first about some one or something—well and good. But when she doesn't, she doesn't, that's all.

JACQUES: So, you know nothing about the d'Aiguines?

GISELE: Very little. I know that *she* is Polish or Austrian, I don't remember which.

JACQUES: But you know nothing about him?

GISELE: Nothing.

JACQUES: You don't know what he does, whether he has any business?

GISELE: I've no idea.

JACQUES: You don't know either—what he's like?

GISELE: Oh, his looks?

JACQUES: Yes.

GISELE: He's tall, clean shaven—rather smart.

JACQUES: Then you've seen him?

GISELE: Yes.

JACQUES: Where have you seen him?

GISELE: At the front door one evening when he had brought Irene home. I happened to be going in at the same time and saw him. Why?

JACQUES: I went to school with a chap by the name of d'Aiguines. I was wondering if it were the same.

GISELE: Oh, I don't think so. He's quite a bit older you.

JACQUES: Ah? . . . Perhaps he's a cousin, then . . . There are several branches of the family . . . [*Pause.*] Is that the only time you've ever met him?

GISELE: Yes. I heard his voice on the telephone one day when he called up and Irene was out. That's all.

JACQUES: Does he ever come to see her?

GISELE: No, never —

JACQUES: Do you know where they live?

GISELE: Avenue Victor Hugo, but I've forgotten the number. They're in the telephone book.

JACQUES: [*Thoughtful.*] Good.

GISELE: The d'Aiguines interest you as much as that?

JACQUES: Oh! They interest me — because they're friends of Irene, that's all.

GISELE: Is that all you wanted to ask me?

JACQUES: Yes, my dear, thank you. You haven't told me much I didn't already know, as a matter of fact. But our talk hasn't been without value. [*Pause.*] Oh ! — it's understood that Irene must never know about it.

GISELE: I promise you that.

JACQUES: I know I can trust you.

GISELE: [*Hesitatingly.*] Jacques, before I go — I *should* like to — to ask you a question.

JACQUES: Why, certainly.

GISELE: Can't you tell me what you're going to do to help Irene?

JACQUES: No, Gisele. Besides my plan has such a slight chance of success . . .

GISELE: Yes, but you wouldn't attempt it, would you, if you didn't think it might succeed?

JACQUES: Well, let's say the chances are about one in ten.

GISELE: Well, if it does succeed would it — would it mean that you'd get married? Tell me?

JACQUES: No.

GISELE: Ah! [*Pause.*] And yet you love her?

JACQUES: [*Smiling wanly.*] Do you believe so?

GISELE: Oh, come! I've known it for ever so long. You've been in love with her ever since the summer you spent at Montcel.

JACQUES: But that's not enough, you see.

GISELE: You mean that she doesn't love you?

JACQUES: Yes, just that.

GISELE: Are you sure?

JACQUES: Absolutely.

GISELE: What a pity!... [*She hesitates; then realizes there is no more to be said.*] Good-by, Jacques.

JACQUES: Good-by, dear child. [*She looks at him sadly, takes his hand, then with sudden, tender movement, kisses him on both cheeks and exits. He goes with her, enters again a few seconds later, sits at his desk and ponders. Picks up telephone book, looks up a number, then calls.*]

Passy 83-42... Hello, is this Monsieur d'Aiguines' house?... Is Monsieur d'Aiguines at home?... Oh!... well, can you give me his office address? Where?... [*He writes on pad.*] Thank you very much. Do you happen to know until what time he'll be there?... Thank you. [*Hangs up receiver, takes writing-paper and begins to write. After writing a few lines, re-reads what he's written, appears irritated, crumples it up and takes a fresh sheet. When he has finished, he rings, puts letter in envelope, addresses it.* GEORGES *enters.*]

GEORGES: Did you ring, monsieur?

JACQUES: Yes. Jump into a taxi and take this letter to this address. It's a bank. If they tell you that the gentleman is in, deliver the letter and wait for an answer. [*A door bell is heard.*] If he's not in, bring me back the letter and ask if there is a chance of finding him there to-morrow morning. You needn't leave my name—it's not necessary.

GEORGES: Yes, monsieur.

JACQUES: You quite understand?

GEORGES: Yes, monsieur.

JACQUES: See who is at the door.

GEORGES: [*Going toward door, back.*] If it is Madame Meillant, monsieur, what shall I say? [*Bell rings again with insistence.*]

JACQUES: [*Smiling.*] It *is* Madame Meillant—show her in. [GEORGES *goes out, enters a moment later with* FRANÇOISE, *an exceedingly handsome young woman, smartly attired.* GEORGES *leaves.*]

FRANÇOISE: Well, I thought you were going to leave me planted on the doorstep. You must tell Georges to open the door more quickly. One always runs into some one on stairways. [*She moves about, very much at home.*]

JACQUES: I love your plural! [*Lights cigarette at desk.*]

FRANÇOISE: What?

JACQUES: Nothing. It's not Georges' fault, it's mine. I was giving him an order.

FRANÇOISE: Huh, that only makes it worse! [*After pause, turns to him.*] Hullo, dear!

JACQUES: Hullo, Françoise.

FRANÇOISE: Well! After all . . . !

JACQUES: But you don't give me a chance to open my mouth. [*He gives her a light kiss.*]

FRANÇOISE: You're not in a very pleasant mood to-day.

JACQUES: I? Of course, I am.

FRANÇOISE: Why didn't you come to the Van Gartens' last night?

JACQUES: I couldn't get there.

FRANÇOISE: I waited until twelve-thirty for you to come, and I had a beastly headache. At least you might have let me know.

JACQUES: But I told you it wasn't likely I'd be there.

FRANÇOISE: I know. But I'd begged you so hard to at least try to call for me, that I thought surely you'd make a special effort. Apparently the day is past for me to ask that sort of thing.

JACQUES: I'm so sorry, Françoise.

FRANÇOISE: What were you doing that was so entertaining—if I'm not being indiscreet?

JACQUES: I was dining at my brother's house and it was very late when I left.

FRANÇOISE: Couldn't you have told him you were due at a party?

JACQUES: He'd just come back to town. I hadn't seen him for two months.

FRANÇOISE: Evidently that was more amusing than coming to fetch me.

JACQUES: Well, yes. Frankly, you know I hate those parties—

FRANÇOISE: You hate everything I like.

JACQUES: No, I don't, my dear.

FRANÇOISE: You do. It's always like that—I'm beginning to get used to it. [*Pause.*] Only it's possible you made a mistake by not coming last night—

JACQUES: [*His thoughts elsewhere.*] Really?

FRANÇOISE: Oh, I say that, but really everything's of so little interest to you now—

JACQUES: What's of so little interest to me?

FRANÇOISE: Well, for instance, that some one should have paid me—very marked attention.

JACQUES: Some one paid you very marked attention?

FRANÇOISE: Yes—[*Pause.*] Oh, you know well enough that when a woman has been seen frequently with the same man, and then suddenly is noticed arriving and leaving alone, other men begin to take new interest in her. Besides, last night, I had on a very becoming gown —

JACQUES: Which one?

FRANÇOISE: You haven't seen it. I had hesitated before ordering it because of you — imagine that! — I thought you might find it rather *décolleté*. But I'm glad I took it now. It was a terrific success!

JACQUES: I'm so glad, darling!

FRANÇOISE: I knew it was a sensation as soon as I arrived — from the way the women looked at it!

JACQUES: Not by the way the men looked at it?

FRANÇOISE: Yes, but a bit later. Women notice that sort of thing more quickly.

JACQUES: Ah?

FRANÇOISE: Then, too, I think that I was in great form last night.

JACQUES: In spite of the headache?

FRANÇOISE: In spite of the headache. At least I was told so any number of times.

JACQUES: By whom, for instance?

FRANÇOISE: What do you care?

JACQUES: I'm very interested. You don't doubt that, I hope?

FRANÇOISE: Well, let me see ... Several of the men who were there ... your friend Moreuil, by the way, didn't leave my side all evening.

JACQUES: Oh! I thought he was in America?

FRANÇOISE: He's come back — come back, what's more, an amorous devil. He insisted on seeing me to my door, and he was about to suggest coming up with me.

JACQUES: Not really?

FRANÇOISE: I think in fact — between ourselves — that he *did* suggest it.

JACQUES: [*Smiling indifferently.*] Good old Moreuil. [*Puts out cigarette.* FRANÇOISE *is piqued and gives him a glowering look.*] And so, you were saying that he —

FRANÇOISE: [*Rises impatiently.*] Oh! Please! That's enough, isn't it? Let's speak about something else!

JACQUES: As you say.

FRANÇOISE: Listen, Jacques. When I came I'd no idea of making a scene. But it really begins to look as if you were trying to exasperate me! I've stood for a great deal for some time, but this is too much!

JACQUES: All right, let's have it!

FRANÇOISE: I understand well enough that you don't love me any more; that's quite within your rights. But that being the case, why not say it? We've never sworn eternal fidelity, have we? Be frank about it for once—it would be so much better.

JACQUES: But nothing is changed, Françoise.

FRANÇOISE: Ah, you think not, do you?...Well, let me tell you that if you had never shown more ardor than you have to-day I never would have been to you what I have. Ah!...No!...I realize now that I gave in much too soon. You'd have loved me more if I had made you want me longer. I liked you and let you see that I did; so much the worse for me. At least in the beginning I could entertain some illusions about our love! But *now*—!

JACQUES: I give you my word, Françoise, that my feeling for you has not changed in the least.

FRANÇOISE: What does that mean?

JACQUES: Well, that—

FRANÇOISE: That you have never loved me, is that it?

JACQUES: I didn't say that.

FRANÇOISE: But it's what you're thinking. Well, at least you're being frank about it, thank heaven! At last! But if you never loved me why did you ask me to become—to become your—

JACQUES: [*Breaking in quietly.*] I might reply that I never I asked you to.

FRANÇOISE: You never asked me?

JACQUES: No, Françoise.

FRANÇOISE: So! Well, then I—

JACQUES: But don't you remember—

FRANÇOISE: Then I suppose it was I who begged you to become my lover?

JACQUES: No—

FRANÇOISE: Well one of us must have done it—if not you—then it must be I!

JACQUES: Listen, Françoise, let's speak about something else.

FRANÇOISE: No! Not until you've explained what you meant.

JACQUES: Let's pretend that I didn't say anything.

FRANÇOISE: No, no, no! You can't get out of it like that. It would be too easy to insult a person, and then—

JACQUES: How have I insulted you?

FRANÇOISE: Well, if you don't think it insulting to tell a woman who has been your mistress for six months that you never asked her to be, then just what is it?

JACQUES: In that case I offer all kinds of apologies. I simply yielded for the moment to the desire of relating what happened between us. I was wrong. Do forgive me.

FRANÇOISE: Relating what happened between us? You're going back to that?

JACQUES: My dear, try to recall the first talk we had!

FRANÇOISE: Our first talk?

JACQUES: One of the first, if you prefer. It was at Versailles, by the lake. You had telephoned me in the morning to ask if I cared to motor out into the country. We left your car at the entrance of the grounds—if you remember—

FRANÇOISE: I remember, yes.

JACQUES: And you said: "The biggest mistake that women make is to select the same man to make love and to talk about it." I thought that was an amusing idea and I replied, "One can hardly expect to be at the head of one's class in both rhetoric and gymnastics!" You agreed with me and were charming enough to add that I must be at the foot of my class rhetoric! Finally, you said you saw no reason why two people who were physically attracted to each other should not establish an intimacy,—it being thoroughly understood that there would be no trespassing on the domain of sentiment. The idea delighted me, and as it was time for tea I suggested that we return to town and have it at my apartment...which you were good enough to accept...That is exactly how it all happened.

FRANÇOISE: And what has that to do with it?

JACQUES: I always thought that that day we settled the exact relation between us.

FRANÇOISE: [*Shrugging her shoulders.*] As if one meant seriously everything said at such times.

JACQUES: I meant what I said. I only undertook a relation I could abide by. If I had undertaken any other it would have been very unfair to you.

FRANÇOISE: You're being that now, my dear. Do you think that falling in love with me was beneath you?

JACQUES: It's not a question of that!

FRANÇOISE: Strange as it may seem to you, there are many men who feel differently about it.

JACQUES: But I'm aware of that, Françoise! You're a very attractive woman and I know perfectly that there are many men who would like to be in my place. I'm sorry I can't make myself more clear. I only meant to say that at the time of our meeting, I could make no other promises— than those I made—that's all.

FRANÇOISE: Because you were in love with some one else, no doubt...And you still love her, is that it? Say it! Why don't you say it?

JACQUES: That, Françoise, belongs in the domain of sentiment. I have never trespassed on yours, you must admit. Keep off mine.

FRANÇOISE: Do I know her?

JACQUES: Please.

FRANÇOISE: You won't tell me?

JACQUES: There's nothing to tell.

FRANÇOISE: Oh! I'll find out...it can't be very difficult...Who is she?

JACQUES: I assure you, Françoise, that you're wasting your time.

FRANÇOISE: [Searching.] Let's see; a woman that you were already in love with six months ago and who does not love you—

JACQUES: How do you know that she doesn't love me?

FRANÇOISE: That's evident. Else why should you have turned, elsewhere for distraction. That's really all I've been to you—a distraction!

JACQUES: You're mistaken, Françoise.

FRANÇOISE: You're very kind, but don't bother to protest further...I know who she is.

JACQUES: Ah?

FRANÇOISE: The Barentier girl?

JACQUES: Now you have it!

FRANÇOISE: It's not she!

JACQUES: Yes, yes, let's say it is!

FRANÇOISE: Great heavens! You're annoying!

JACQUES: Françoise, please, let's change the subject.

[GEORGES enters.] Pardon me...[To GEORGES.] Well?

GEORGES: I delivered the letter.

JACQUES: Did you see the gentleman?

GEORGES: Yes, monsieur. He didn't write an answer but he asked to say that he was coming here to see you.

JACQUES: Really? When?

GEORGES: Now, monsieur.

JACQUES: What, you mean right away?

GEORGES: Yes, monsieur. He asked if you were at home. I said I thought you were. Then he said he was coming.

JACQUES: [After a pause.] All right...when he rings, ask him to go into the salon.

GEORGES: Yes, monsieur. [Exits.]

FRANÇOISE: Are you expecting some one?

JACQUES: Yes. I hope you'll forgive me, Françoise. It's a man whom I must see about a business matter—a rather important one—concerning my interests in Morocco.

FRANÇOISE: Why, yes, of course.

JACQUES: I wasn't expecting him. Not to-day at least, otherwise—

FRANÇOISE: It doesn't matter at all. [*Goes to divan, gets hat and things.*] As a matter of fact, there was very little left for us to say to each other—wasn't there? [*Pulls hat on.*]

JACQUES: But—I don't know, Françoise.

FRANÇOISE: You see, Jacques, I've only just realized that for the past six months it's I who have given a bit too much both the questions and the answers. So now, I think there's been enough of it and the best thing we can do is put a period at the end of our page. [*He helps her on with her coat.*] Don't you think so too?

JACQUES: Just as you please.

FRANÇOISE: Ah! Well—

JACQUES: What?

FRANÇOISE: Oh, nothing: I feared you might have made some protest—merely as a matter of form. But I see that you've bravely made up your mind—and don't even regard it worth while to protest. Splendid! Let me congratulate you on your resignation—[*Pause.*] What are you thinking?

JACQUES: [*Whose mind is on other things.*] Why—of you and what you've just said...

FRANÇOISE: No, you weren't.

JACQUES: I'm sorry, Françoise. As a matter of fact I was worrying a bit about this coming interview. Do forgive me. Can't we meet again some time soon—perhaps to-morrow?

FRANÇOISE: What for?

JACQUES: I'd like to explain—to attempt to make my position clear.

FRANÇOISE: I assure you, my dear, that I've understood you perfectly! [*She cries a little but controls herself quickly.*]

JACQUES: [*Going toward her.*] Françoise—

FRANÇOISE: Pay no attention to me!—There, it's over. And now let's say good-by to each other sweetly like the two good friends that we are. I shall miss you, Jacques, dear!

JACQUES: Come, Françoise—

FRANÇOISE: Yes, I will. Oh, it's not your fault—you're the sort of man one misses. After all, we have some rather pleasant memories to look back upon, haven't we?

JACQUES: Yes, dear . . . delightful memories.

FRANÇOISE: You see, Jacques, when a woman promises to love you, you mustn't always believe her. But when a woman promises not to, well, then you mustn't, believe her either.

JACQUES: My dear Françoise! . . .

FRANÇOISE: Come, we mustn't weaken now!

JACQUES: But at least, you'll let me write, won't you?

FRANÇOISE: Do! Write me a letter filled with sweetly melancholy thoughts on the way all things come to an end, and send it by the florist with a few of those lovely carnations that I like. I'll wait until they're quite faded before trying to put you out of my thoughts. Good-by. [*She gives him her hand. He kisses it. The bell is heard. He drops her hand and goes up to the door. She follows.*]

JACQUES: Wait a moment, won't you? [GEORGES *enters. To* GEORGES.] Is it the gentleman?

GEORGES: Yes, monsieur.

JACQUES: Very well.

FRANÇOISE: [*Moved.*] Don't forget the carnations. [*He goes out with her. In a moment he reenters and goes to the door of the salon and opens it.*]

JACQUES: [*Talking off.*] Would you mind coming in here, monsieur? [JACQUES *moves a little away from door.* D'AIGUINES *enters past him and turns to* JACQUES *with outstretched hand.*]

D'AIGUINES: How are you, old boy?

JACQUES: Why, it's —

D'AIGUINES: Of course it is! Didn't you know you were writing to me?

JACQUES: Why, no, otherwise —

D'AIGUINES: Otherwise you wouldn't have been so formal, I hope. But didn't my name mean anything to you?

JACQUES: Of course. But I was led to believe that the d'Aiguines I had to deal with was somewhat older.

D'AIGUINES: Somewhat older? Why?

JACQUES: Well, it doesn't matter. I remember you had some cousins. I thought perhaps it might be one of them.

D'AIGUINES: Ah? . . . But what's the reason for —

JACQUES: I'll tell you. [*Pause.*] Do sit down!

D'AIGUINES: [*Puts hat and glove, on desk.*] You're looking at me? . . . You find I've changed, eh? . . . I'm sure you'd hardly have recognized me?

JACQUES: Yes . . . I would have.

D'AIGUINES: Good Lord, it's something like twenty years since we've seen each other. Not since the days when we wore our trousers out sitting

on the same bench at school. Twenty years leave their mark! On some
people at least . . . But you've hardly changed. I'm very glad to see you
again, old chap.

JACQUES: Thanks.

D'AIGUINES: It's strange we shouldn't have met. Of course I haven't been in
France much. What have you been doing? Weren't you in Morocco for
a time?

JACQUES: Yes.

D'AIGUINES: Who was it told me so? [*A pause.*] . . . Ah, yes, I remember; it
was Sicard—you remember him—fat Sicard? I met him one day in
Madrid. We were staying at the same hotel. He had just returned from
Africa, I think, and had seen you there.

JACQUES: Yes.

D'AIGUINES: And now you're living here altogether?

JACQUES: Yes.

D'AIGUINES: Damn funny thing, life. You really didn't know that the
d'Aiguines you were writing to for an appointment was I?

JACQUES: No.

D'AIGUINES: Well, the minute I saw your signature I didn't hesitate. That's
why I came here right away. If Jacques Virieu wanted to see me I
certainly couldn't keep him waiting!

JACQUES: [*Pause.*] Is that the only reason you came here right away?

D'AIGUINES: [*Surprised.*] Good Lord! Since I haven't the least idea what you
have to say to me—

JACQUES: You haven't the least idea?

D'AIGUINES: Why, of course not—no.

JACQUES: Ah . . . ?

D'AIGUINES: Well, look here, you arouse my curiosity! Upon my word, you
sit there looking like a judge! Come, what's it all about?

JACQUES: Whom is it all about, might be better.

D'AIGUINES: Whom? . . . All right, if you prefer it. Well, then, whom is it all
about?

JACQUES: [*Pause.*] About Irene de Montcel.

D'AIGUINES: [*Amazed and annoyed.*] Irene de Montcel?

JACQUES: Yes. [*Pause.*] You seem to begin to understand!

D'AIGUINES: No. What can you have to say to me about Mademoiselle de
Montcel?

JACQUES: You can't guess?

D'AIGUINES: No, I can't!

JACQUES: I'm a distant cousin of hers. But what's more important is that

I've been a friend of hers for a long time. One of her best friends—I might even say her best friend, if you wish.

D'AIGUINES: Well?

JACQUES: You knew that, didn't you?

D'AIGUINES: I didn't even know you were acquainted.

JACQUES: Have you never heard her speak of me?

D'AIGUINES: Never.

JACQUES: She hasn't even spoken of the—rôle that some one was playing for her at the present time?

D'AIGUINES: What rôle?

JACQUES: Don't you know that some one is pretending to Irene's father to be engaged to her, or something of the sort?

D'AIGUINES: Engaged to her?

JACQUES: To ward off her father's suspicions; and to permit her to remain in Paris, yes.

D'AIGUINES: [*Pause.*] She asked you to do that?

JACQUES: Yes.

D'AIGUINES: Did you do it?

JACQUES: Yes. [*Pause.*] You knew nothing about all about that?

D'AIGUINES: I? Why, of course, I didn't!

JACQUES: Really! I had somehow imagined that you would have known about it.

D'AIGUINES: What are you driving at?

JACQUES: I merely wanted to let you know by what right I say what I shall have to say to you about her.

D'AIGUINES: That's all very well—but I've no right to listen to what you may have to say about the young lady. [*Rises.*]

JACQUES: Sit down, please.

D'AIGUINES: [*Disturbed.*] What for? I tell you again that it's something which doesn't concern me.

JACQUES: Steady! Otherwise, I'll be forced to think its something which concerns you deeply.

D'AIGUINES: [*Feelingly.*] What do you mean?

JACQUES: I mean that a suspicion I had before your arrival has become a conviction in the last five minutes.

D'AIGUINES: All right—keep your suspicions to yourself, and allow me to leave?

JACQUES: [*Standing between the door and* D'AIGUINES.] I swear that you'll listen to me!

D'AIGUINES: Good God! Are you crazy?

JACQUES: No.

D'AIGUINES: You insist upon my listening to you?

JACQUES: [*Vehemently.*] Yes!

D'AIGUINES: You're wrong, I tell you!

JACQUES: We'll see as to that.

D'AIGUINES: Very well, I've warned you. Do as you like…

JACQUES: I shan't take long, don't worry. If—contrary to what I think— what I have to say doesn't apply to you, at least you'll know to whom it should be repeated. When a man occupies in a girl's life the place which the person I'm referring to occupies in Irene's life—when he makes her do or lets her do what she has done in order not to be separated from him—he has no valid excuse, none, do you hear, for not marrying her. That is to say, if he's free. If he isn't, then he must take steps to become so, at no matter what cost and at the earliest possible moment. Now you have it.

D'AIGUINES: [*Pause.*] Is that all?

JACQUES: Well, just about. For I shouldn't like to think that the person in question were a man without honor. If that were the case then the duty of a friend is clear; to warn Montcel to protect his daughter. But I hope it won't be necessary to go to that extreme.

D'AIGUINES: Have you quite finished this time?

JACQUES: Yes.

D'AIGUINES: Then, unless I'm crazy I must conclude that you believe me to be Mademoiselle de Montcel's lover or something of the sort. That's it, isn't it?

JACQUES: That is the most likely supposition, yes…

D'AIGUINES: [*Earnestly.*] Well, then look at me and despite the high strung condition you seem to be in, try to see things clearly. I give you my word of honor that you're mistaken. I am not and never have been anything but an acquaintance of hers, do you hear…not even a friend. You can believe me or not, that's your affair. That's all I've got to say. And please understand that if I've taken the trouble of replying to you at all instead of treating you like a lunatic and leaving here without a word, it's solely because of our old friendship.

JACQUES: [*Impressed by* D'AIGUINES' *truthful attitude, but despairing.*] Then… who is it?

D'AIGUINES: How should I know?… *Has* she a lover?

JACQUES Yes.

D'AIGUINES: Did she tell you so?

JACQUES: She let me believe it—which amounts to the same thing.

D'AIGUINES: Not always. You may be too hasty in drawing conclusions.

JACQUES: Well, it's the only possible explanation. If it weren't true, she'd have said so. She couldn't have doubted for a moment that I was convinced of it. I . . .

D'AIGUINES: [*Pause*] Well, in any case, I'm sorry, but I can give you no information. And if you've nothing more to say . . .

JACQUES: You're not going?

D'AIGUINES: I must. I came as soon as I got your note but I'm leaving Paris in a few days and I've a great deal to do.

JACQUES: Don't go, I beg you! You're the only one who can help me find this man and I *must* find him.

D'AIGUINES: But since I know nothing—

JACQUES: That's not possible! You must have some idea, some suspicion. Seeing her constantly . . . knowing the sort of life she leads . . . whom she sees . . .

D'AIGUINES: But you're wrong. I don't see her constantly. Once in a while she goes out with us—but I've much less in common with her than you seem to think—

JACQUES: How can that be? You're almost the only people she ever sees— she spends all her time at your house. You can't help knowing *something*!

D'AIGUINES: [*Coldly, not looking at* JACQUES.] I know nothing.

JACQUES: I don't believe you!

D'AIGUINES: See here! That's quite enough—

JACQUES: I believed you a moment ago, believed you without proof, when you said you were not her lover. You were telling the truth then. Now, you're not, you're lying. You're lying so as not to betray the secret of some one who is probably your friend. That's it, isn't it?

D'AIGUINES: I know nothing.

JACQUES: Listen: just tell me that he's a decent chap and that he'll marry her—and I'll ask you nothing more.

D'AIGUINES: I have nothing to say. I know nothing.

JACQUES: But don't you understand that this poor girl must be saved, that she can't be allowed to go more deeply every day into an affair that is ruining her! . . . And if it were only that! She has already begun to suffer. What's going on? . . . Has she felt that he wants to be rid of her? I don't know. But what I *do* know is that she spends her time locked in her room, sobbing. That's what she has come to!

D'AIGUINES: Oh! . . . [*Gesture.*]

JACQUES: That doesn't worry you, eh? Well it does me! I'd give my life, do you hear, my life, to make her happy.

D'AIGUINES: [*Looks at him in surprise.*] You mean to say you love her?

JACQUES: I am her friend.

D'AIGUINES: Answer me. One doesn't do what you have done out of mere friendship—nor go through with a thing like this pretended engagement. You love her?

JACQUES: Very well, then, I do love her. I've loved her for ten years, and I'll never love anyone else. What of it?

D'AIGUINES: You love her? Is that true?

JACQUES: Yes!

D'AIGUINES: Then for Christ's sake, get away from here! Get away! It doesn't matter where—as far as you and stay away as long as you can! Don't come back until you're cured! That's all I can say!

JACQUES: What do you mean?

D'AIGUINES: I'm giving you some advice, good advice, that's all.

JACQUES: You're going to explain to me exactly what you mean! Aren't you?

D'AIGUINES: [*With hesitation.*] Why—there's nothing to explain—You love this young woman and from what you tell me I gather she loves some one else. That being the case, the best thing to do is clear out. Don't you agree with me?

JACQUES: Clear out and leave her in the hands of some rotter, probably— some rotter who wanted her and so made her believe he'd marry her.

D'AIGUINES: Is she really so simple as that?

JACQUES: A woman is always that the first time she's in love. This is her first experience, I have reasons to know that. If she had loved any one before this, I'd probably have been the man. I adored her and until last year I lived in the hope that some day she'd be my wife. And she would have been, do you hear, if this other man hadn't appeared. I didn't fight against it, there was no use. But since he's been the means of making me unhappy, at least I want him to be the means of making her happy. To do that I must find him.

D'AIGUINES: You can do nothing for her.

JACQUES: How do you know?

D'AIGUINES: No one can do anything for her.

JACQUES: Why? [D'AIGUINES *gestures, but remains silent.*] Ah! You made a slip there! You're not going to keep on pretending that you don't know how things are! You can't keep silent any longer!

D'AIGUINES: Leave her alone! Don't meddle in this, believe me! And don't ask me anything more!

JACQUES: Look here, you don't suppose I'm going to be satisfied with vague warnings that can have only one effect: making me more anxious than ever! I'm not asking for advice, I'm demanding a name!

D'AIGUINES: [*Abruptly.*] The name of her lover? She has no lover! Now, are you satisfied?

JACQUES: What?

D'AIGUINES: It might be better for her if she had one!

JACQUES: I don't understand.

D'AIGUINES: A woman can free herself from a lover—even if he's the worst scoundrel living. She can get over it. Whereas in *her* case—

JACQUES: In her case, what? Finish!

D'AIGUINES: Hers is quite another kind of bondage... And that kind— [*Gesture.*]

JACQUES: Another kind of bondage?

D'AIGUINES: Yes. It is not only a *man* who may be dangerous to a woman... In some cases it can be another woman.

JACQUES: Another *woman*?

D'AIGUINES: Yes.

JACQUES: What are you talking about? You mean to say it's on account of a woman that Irene refused to go with her father to Rome?

D'AIGUINES: Yes.

JACQUES: It's on account of a *woman* that she spends her time crying?

D'AIGUINES: Yes.

JACQUES: What kind of story is this?

D'AIGUINES: The kind of story that often happens—regardless of what men think. The kind of story that people don't believe for the most part, or which makes them smile, half amused and half indulgent.

JACQUES: But it's impossible! Irene is much too well balanced...

D'AIGUINES: What does that prove?

JACQUES: Are you positive of this?

D'AIGUINES: Yes.

JACQUES: Do you—know this woman?

D'AIGUINES: Yes. [*Looks at* JACQUES *quickly, and sees that the latter is not observing him. A great sadness crosses his face.*] I know her.

JACQUES: [*After a moment.*] I am dumbfounded—

D'AIGUINES: And a little relieved... aren't you?

JACQUES: Well, good Lord! After what I had feared!...

D'AIGUINES: So you'd prefer—? [*Pause.*] Well, you're wrong to prefer it!

JACQUES: You'd rather she had a lover?

D'AIGUINES: In your place? Yes! A hundred, a thousand times rather!

JACQUES: Are you mad?

D'AIGUINES: It's you who are mad. If she had a lover I'd say to you:
Patience, my boy, patience and courage. Your cause isn't lost. No man
lasts forever in a woman's life. You love her and she'll come back to
you if you know how to wait... But in this case I say: Don't wait!
There's no use. She'll never return—and if ever your paths should
cross again fly from her, fly from her... do you hear? Otherwise you
are lost! Otherwise you'll spend your existence pursuing a phantom
which you can never overtake. One can never overtake them! They are
shadows. They must be left to dwell alone among themselves in the
kingdom of shadows! Don't go near them... they're a menace! Above
all, never, try to be anything to them, no matter how little—that's
where the danger lies. For, after all, they have some need of us in their
lives... it isn't always easy for a woman to get along. So if a man offers
to help her, to share with her what he has, and to give her his name,
naturally she accepts. What difference can it make to her? So long as
he doesn't exact love, she's not concerned about the rest. Only, can you
imagine the existence of a man if he has the misfortune to love—to
adore a *shadow* near whom he lives? Tell me, can you imagine what
that's like? Take my word for it, old man, it's a rotten life! One's used
up quickly by that game. One gets old in no time—and at thirty-five,
look for yourself, one's hair is gray!

JACQUES: Do you mean—?

D'AIGUINES: Yes. And I hope you'll profit by my example. Understand this:
they are not for us. They must be shunned, left alone. Don't make
my mistake. Don't say, as I said in a situation almost like yours, don't
say: "Oh, it's nothing but a sort of ardent friendship—an affectionate
intimacy... nothing very serious... we know all about that sort of
thing!" No! We don't know *anything* about it! We can't begin to know
what it is. It's mysterious—terrible! Friendship, yes—that's the mask.
Under cover of friendship a woman can enter any household, whenever and however she pleases—at any hour of the day—she can
poison and pillage everything before the man whose home she
destroys is even aware of what's happening to him. When finally he
realizes things it's too late—he is alone! Alone in the face of a secret
alliance of two beings who understand one another because they're
alike, because they're of the same sex, because they're of a different
planet than he, the stranger, the enemy! Ah! If a *man* tries to steal your
woman you can defend yourself, you can fight him on even terms,
you can smash his face in. But in this case—there's nothing to be

done—but *get out* while you still have strength to do it! And that's
what you've got to do!

JACQUES: ...Why don't you get out yourself?

D'AIGUINES: Oh, with me it's different. I can't leave her now. We've been
married eight years. Where would she go?...Besides it's too late. I
couldn't live without her any more. What can I do—I love her?...
[*Pause.*] You've never seen her? [JACQUES *shakes his head.*] You'd understand better if you knew her. She has all the feminine allurements,
every one. As soon as one is near her, one feels—how shall I say it—a
sort of deep charm. Not only I feel it. Every one feels it. But I more
than the rest because I live near her. I really believe she is the most
harmonious being that has ever breathed...Sometimes when I'm away
from her, I have the strength to hate her for all the harm she has done
me...but, with her, I don't struggle. I look at her...I listen to her...I
worship her. You see?

JACQUES: [*Pursuing an idea.*] Tell me...why is Irene suffering?

D'AIGUINES: I don't know. [*Rises.*] You don't suppose I'm confided in, do
you? She is suffering probably, as the weak always do, struggling with a
stronger nature until they give in.

JACQUES: You think Irene is weak?

D'AIGUINES: Compared to the other? Oh, yes. [*Pause.*] She is probably still
struggling.

JACQUES: Ah! [*Pause.*] So that's why she is unhappy? [*Rises.*]

D'AIGUINES: For that reason—or some other. She has many to choose from.

JACQUES: You mean—?

D'AIGUINES: Why shouldn't she suffer? I suffer, don't I?

JACQUES: That's not the same thing.

D'AIGUINES: You think so, do you? Well, on the contrary, I believe it's very
much the same thing. There's only one way to love, you see, and one
way to suffer. It's the same formula for everybody—and in that respect
she and I have been in the same boat for some time. Only she hasn't
got used to it yet—and I have.

JACQUES: I don't quite follow you.

D'AIGUINES: Haven't you heard any mention of a cruise?

JACQUES: A cruise?

D'AIGUINES: Yes. In the Mediterranean...on a yacht, an American yacht?

JACQUES: No. [*Pause.*] Is she to be one of the party?

D'AIGUINES: That's why I'm asking if she spoke of it.

JACQUES: She never speaks to me of anything.

D'AIGUINES: In her place—I'd refuse to go.

JACQUES: You would?

D'AIGUINES: I doubt that she'll be able to refuse. However—that's her affair. What matters most is you. What are you going to do? Will you take my advice and go away for a while?

JACQUES: I don't know yet. I'll think it over.

D'AIGUINES: Don't wait, Jacques. Believe me.

JACQUES: It's not as dangerous for me as you think. I almost never see her.

D'AIGUINES: What difference does that make? When she needs you, she knows where to find you—you've seen that for yourself. That is how one can get caught, even after one has been warned. Remember what I'm telling you.

JACQUES: But where can I go?

D'AIGUINES: Anywhere—so long as it's far away. [*Pause.*] Have you still got your business interests in Morocco?

JACQUES: Yes, but—

D'AIGUINES: Then go back there for a while. At that distance she won't be able to turn to you so easily.

JACQUES: If you knew her as well as I do, you'd realize that, you're needlessly alarmed. She turned to me for help in a moment of frenzy. But she's much too proud to do so again. Besides, I don't see how I could help her any more.

D'AIGUINES: How can you tell? [*Pause.*] If you don't want to go away, then find a woman that is attractive to you, a real woman. See if she can't make you forget the other one.

JACQUES: I've already tried that.

D'AIGUINES: And it didn't succeed? [JACQUES *shakes his head.*] You see my fears were not so exaggerated as you thought. There is nothing for you to do but go away—and without a moment's delay. Now it's up to you. [*Picks up his hat and gloves and offers* JACQUES *his hand. A bell is heard.*] Are you expecting some one?

JACQUES: No.

D'AIGUINES: Well, anyhow, I must be off—good-by, Jacques. [*They shake hands.*]

JACQUES: Thanks . . .

D'AIGUINES: Oh! [*Gesture.*] If only I could have convinced you! [GEORGES *enters.*]

JACQUES: What is it?

GEORGES: Mademoiselle de Montcel would like to know if you can see her.

JACQUES: What!

GEORGES: And I said that I would see if you were in, monsieur.

JACQUES: [*Glances at* D'AIGUINES.] Ask her to wait in the salon, then close the door that gives into the hall.

GEORGES: Very good, monsieur.

JACQUES: It's Mademoiselle Irene?

GEORGES: Yes, monsieur.

JACQUES: Oh! Show Monsieur d'Aiguines out when he leaves. [GEORGES *exits.*] Well! This is an unexpected visit.

D'AIGUINES: Tell me — you've no intention, I hope, of repeating a word of what we've said to Mademoiselle de Montcel, have you?

JACQUES: Do you suppose she'd ever forgive me for knowing?

D'AIGUINES: Right! And now — good luck, old man. Remember — she can never belong to you no matter how you try. They're not for us. [*He exits and* JACQUES *stands a moment in the doorway, then crosses to salon door and opens it.*] Come in!

IRENE: [*Entering.*] You're sure I'm not disturbing you? [*Closes door.*]

JACQUES: Very sure.

IRENE: You'd tell me if I were, wouldn't you?

JACQUES: I'd tell you.

IRENE: Then may I stay? It won't bother you?

JACQUES: It won't bother me.

IRENE: [*She sits on the sofa.*] Were you surprised when you heard it was I?

JACQUES: [*Sitting at his desk and lighting the lamp.*] A little, yes.

IRENE: You wondered what I had come here for, didn't you?

JACQUES: I thought that no doubt there was something you wanted to talk to me about.

IRENE: There is.

JACQUES: Well, I'm listening.

IRENE: [*Smiling.*] Oh, please not like that. Don't speak to me like a lawyer to his client. Be kind, affectionate! . . . Do change that severe look!

JACQUES: Why do you say I have a severe look?

IRENE: You always have a severe look, nowadays.

JACQUES: You're mistaken —

IRENE: Be sweet, Jacques, won't you? Like old times! I'm terribly in need of your sympathy.

JACQUES: Really?

IRENE: Why do you say *really* like that?

JACQUES: For no reason. Go on, continue.

IRENE: Are you surprised I ask you to be kind . . . to be affectionate . . . to me?

JACQUES: I've stopped being surprised by you, my dear —

IRENE: Don't be cruel! . . . I've given you the right to be, I don't forget that!

But just the same I hope you won't be, do you mind? Not to-day, anyway. [*She turns her face away to hide tears.*]

JACQUES: [*More gently.*] What's the matter?

IRENE: Nothing. Pay no attention. [*Pause.*] I want you to tell me something.

JACQUES: What?

IRENE: Since I asked you to—since you agreed to play this part to my father—have you no longer as much affection for me?

JACQUES: Why do you ask me that?

IRENE: Because I must know.

JACQUES: I have as much affection, only—

IRENE: Only?

JACQUES: It is no longer the same affection. I used to admire you. Now, I pity you.

IRENE: [*Pensive, without looking at him.*] And you despise me?

JACQUES: I pity you.

IRENE: You're right...I am to be pitied. But I can still count on you as a friend, can't I?

JACQUES: Yes.

IRENE: I need to believe that, to feel sure of it. You don't know, Jacques, how much you mean to me.

JACQUES: As much as that? [*Rises.*]

IRENE: Please, no sarcasm. You say you pity me. Then prove it.

JACQUES: How?

IRENE: Oh!...By showing me a little tenderness and being a little lenient, that's all.

JACQUES: Aren't you happy?

IRENE: Happy?

JACQUES: Yes.

IRENE: There are times when I wish I were dead.

JACQUES: Well, that *is* a way out, but—

IRENE: You don't believe me?

JACQUES: I hope you're exaggerating—if one had to kill oneself every time he was unhappy—

IRENE: Oh! I'm not thinking of killing myself. It takes courage to die like that. And I haven't even any courage left...I have nothing left...

JACQUES: Yet, you got what you wanted. You had to stay in Paris at any cost. Well, here you are—Oh, talking of that, I meant to tell you that I must write to your father.

IRENE: To father?

JACQUES: Yes. It was understood that I was to let him know as soon as

possible what my intentions were and I promised to do it. He's already
been gone a month and I haven't written yet…It's time I did.

IRENE: Must you?

JACQUES: I'll tell him that the business matters that were worrying me at the
time of his departure are now in such bad shape that I'm in no position to make plans for the future—Does that seem all right to you?

IRENE: Just as you wish.

JACQUES: I'll add that I am going to Morocco to attend directly to my
interests there.

IRENE: [*With great alarm.*] But it isn't true, is it—you're not going away?

JACQUES: Yes, probably.

IRENE: But why? Is it really because of business matters?

JACQUES: No.

IRENE: Well, then?…Oh! You're not going alone?

JACQUES: What do you mean, not alone?

IRENE: Is some one going with you?

JACQUES: No, nobody.

IRENE: Then why must you go?

JACQUES: I need a change. This climate's not agreeing with me. I should
have gone long ago—a year ago when you came back from Italy.
Perhaps I'd have been better by now.

IRENE: It's because of me that you're going.

JACQUES: Good Lord!

IRENE: Is it true?

JACQUES: Don't you think it's about time that I considered my own peace
of mind a little? After all I can't spend my life loving you and beginning to suffer all over again each time I see you.

IRENE: Then you still love me, Jacques? Is it true?

JACQUES: Does that surprise you?

IRENE: After what you must have believed of me lately, I was certain that
was over…that you didn't love me any more. I felt it,—but I hoped it
wasn't true.

JACQUES: You hoped it wasn't true?

IRENE: Yes.

JACQUES: You hoped that I still loved you?

IRENE: Yes.

JACQUES: [*Pause.*] I can't understand you.

IRENE: [*Looking away from him.*] Don't go away, Jacques.

JACQUES: What do you say?

IRENE: Don't go away. [JACQUES *looks at her, stupefied.*]

JACQUES: Ah, yes! You're afraid your father'll send for you when he receives my letter and learns I'm no longer here, eh? Well, I'm sorry, but this time you'll have to manage without me. You can do what you like and how you like, but I shall write to your father to-night.

IRENE: [*Shrugging her shoulders.*] Write all you want to. I don't care!

JACQUES: [*Sarcastically.*] Really!

IRENE: Absolutely, I swear to you!

JACQUES: [*Puzzled.*] Then why don't you want me to go away?

IRENE: Oh!... for no reason at all. [*She rises.*]

JACQUES: Sit down again and answer me.

IRENE: It's no use. Go, go away—since you're in such a hurry to forget me! Go!

JACQUES: Really, Irene, what is this game you're playing now?

IRENE: Please forgive me. I don't know what I'm saying any more. Oh, Jacques, I'm so miserable! [*She falls into a chair and cries.*]

JACQUES: [*Touched, going to her.*] What's the matter?

IRENE: [*Clinging to him.*] You mustn't leave me. I'm so alone, so wretched! Jacques! Only you can save me!

JACQUES: But what do you want me to do?

IRENE: Protect me! Shield me!

JACQUES: Shield you?

IRENE: Yes.

JACQUES: I assure you, Irene, I'm doing my best to understand you, but really—

IRENE: I know, I must seem crazy. Well, I am crazy! You have got to treat me like a crazy person—a sick person—and take care of me, that's all. If you don't come to my rescue right away—it will be too late!

JACQUES: Are you in danger of something?

IRENE: Yes.

JACQUES: An imminent danger?

IRENE: Yes.

JACQUES: Can't you tell me what it is?

IRENE: [*After hesitating.*] It's about a cruise, my going away—and I mustn't go. I don't want to go—if I do, it's all over. I'd be lost!

JACQUES: What is forcing you to go?

IRENE: Ah! I am afraid of myself.

JACQUES: Then why don't you take a train to Rome with Gisele to join your father?

IRENE: I had thought of that... But at the last minute I wouldn't go—I wouldn't have the strength—

JACQUES: Yes, you would! I'll help if you wish.

IRENE: [*Shaking her head.*] Or else I'd come back.

JACQUES: No!

IRENE: You see, there are times in which I can see clearly, such as now, when I am sane and free to use my own mind...But there are other times when I can't, when I don't know what I'm doing. It's like—a prison to which I must return captive, despite myself. I'm—I'm—

JACQUES: Fascinated?

IRENE: Yes! I need some one to watch me, to hold me back. Some one who has understood or guessed certain things—that I can't talk about, that I can never tell!

JACQUES: Is that what you expect of me? How can I restrain you from doing what you want to do? Have I the least influence over you? Have you ever listened to my advice? Please remember that it was only a month ago you rejected it.

IRENE: It's no longer the same.

JACQUES: What is no longer the same?

IRENE: Many things. I will listen to you now. I want to listen to you.

JACQUES: But you won't be able to! You won't be allowed to! What weapons have I to fight with? What can I add to what you yourself have said? You acknowledge that this cruise would be your ruin? What can I add to that? And then do you imagine for one moment that advice from me would hold you back during one of those hours of insensibility you speak of? [IRENE *shakes head.*] You see!...And surely you don't expect me to hold you by force, do you? So, what can I do for you?

IRENE: Everything. You can save me.

JACQUES: How?

IRENE: You are the only one who can save me—

JACQUES: Why?

IRENE: Because you love me—

JACQUES: It's for that very reason that I can do nothing. As soon as I saw you miserable, I'd be useless. You can't take as your trained nurse a man who loves you!

IRENE: Not as a trained nurse—

JACQUES: Well, what then?

IRENE: [*Looking at him.*] Jacques—would you like me to give myself to you?

JACQUES: Irene!

IRENE: Would you?

JACQUES: Don't!

IRENE: Jacques?

JACQUES: So that's it. That's what you've come to offer me?

IRENE: [*Lowering head.*] Yes.

JACQUES: My poor Irene.

IRENE: You don't want me?

JACQUES: [*Faces her.*] But I love you! Don't you understand what that means?

IRENE: Of course —

JACQUES: [*Forcibly.*] You offer me your body, your poor body as a pledge, is that it? You want to soil it with me so that you can tell this woman —

IRENE: [*With a cry.*] Jacques!

JACQUES: [*Still moved.*] Yes, I know! I've guessed it! What of it? I suppose you want to tell her that you've given yourself to a man, so that she'll leave you alone? But as for me, me — it's not your body I want. It's you, all of you, don't you see? Can you give me that — tell me? Can you give that to some one you don't love? For, after all, you don't love me, do you? You don't love me?

IRENE: [*With despair.*] I want so much to love you. [*She bends over and sobs, her head on his breast.*]

JACQUES: [*Distraught.*] Poor child!

IRENE: [*Through her tears.*] You think that I don't know it would mean my happiness? I know only too well that the place I really belong is here against your shoulder. Why won't you let me stay here?

JACQUES: Oh! Irene — what you are asking is too terrible.

IRENE: Why? . . . Perhaps I would learn to love you?

JACQUES: Afterwards, you mean? No, my dear . . .

IRENE: But once you told me that I would.

JACQUES: Ah! Because at that time I thought that only your pride stood between us. I didn't know then all that separates us!

IRENE: But when you will have cured me . . .

JACQUES: Do you really believe that I could?

IRENE: Yes, if you're very kind, very indulgent, if you have a little patience.

JACQUES: But, you see I love you too much for that.

IRENE: Then . . . you refuse me? . . . Is that it, Jacques? . . . What is going to become of me!

JACQUES: What would become of me? I've been hurt enough as it is.

IRENE: But that's over, I won't hurt you any more. How could I hurt you when it will be you who have saved me?

JACQUES: That means nothing. You wouldn't do it on purpose, naturally.

IRENE: Jacques, look at me. Look in my eyes. [*Pause.*] I will give you everything a man can expect from the woman he loves.

JACQUES: [*Disturbed.*] Irene! I have dreamed of that too long.

IRENE: Take me in your arms. I am yours, Jacques, all of me . . .

JACQUES: You don't realize what you're promising.

IRENE: Yes, I do.

JACQUES: There is still time . . . you can still go.

IRENE: I am not afraid.

JACQUES: You really wish it? Are you sure that you do?

IRENE: Yes.

JACQUES: [*Taking her in his arms.*] Irene? . . . Is it true? [*He starts to kiss her on
the mouth. As* IRENE *beholds his face filled with longing, she makes an abrupt
movement of aversion. He lets her go.*] You see?

IRENE: No, no—forgive me! [*This time it is she who offers her lips, to him.
Then, her nerves giving way, she lets her head fall on his shoulder, struggles
with herself a moment, and breaks into tears.*]

JACQUES: [*In despair.*] Irene!

IRENE: No, no!—Pay no attention !—It doesn't mean anything . . . It's all
over! You will keep me with? Always?

JACQUES: I'll try.

The CURTAIN *falls*

Act Three

Scene: *The same as Act Two. A year after.*

JACQUES *is seated alone, smoking and meditating.* GEORGES, *his man, enters at back, bringing a letter which he gives to* JACQUES. *The latter inspects the envelope and seems surprised.*

JACQUES: Who brought this letter?

GEORGES: A maid, monsieur. She is waiting for an answer. [*He walks to back and waits near the door.* JACQUES *opens and reads the letter. After a few moments of thought, he rises, crosses to his desk, takes a sheet of paper and starts writing.*]

JACQUES: For what time did madame order the car?

GEORGES: Three o'clock, monsieur. [JACQUES *looks at watch, finishes letter, slips it into an envelope and hands it to* GEORGES.]

JACQUES: There. [GEORGES *goes out.* JACQUES *again picks up the letter he has received, re-reads it, then carries it to his nose, inhales its scent and smiles.* IRENE *appears at the right.* JACQUES *puts letter in his pocket. Her hat is on and she is ready to go out. She has in her hand a bundle of samples of materials for hangings.*]

IRENE: You didn't tell me which of these samples you preferred. This one — this — or that?

JACQUES: It's for your own room. You'd better choose it yourself.

IRENE: But I want you to like it.

JACQUES: I'll like whichever one you choose.

IRENE: Well, at least you might tell me which one you prefer.

JACQUES: But I approve your choice in advance —

IRENE: Oh! How annoying of you!

JACQUES: Are you going out?

IRENE: Yes, I must go to the decorator's, and to the painter's. Then at three-thirty, I have an appointment at Praxine's studio to have another look at little landscape that I saw the other day. Don't you want to come?

JACQUES: I can't.

IRENE: You'll have to see it some time.

JACQUES: What for?

IRENE: I'm certainly not going to buy a picture as pensive as that without your having seen it.

JACQUES: You don't need my advice. I don't know anything about painting. If you like the picture, buy it, that's all.

IRENE: Can't you really come? I'll pass by here with the car and pick you up. It won't take more than twenty minutes altogether.

JACQUES: I can't, I tell you. I'm waiting for some one.

IRENE: Who?

JACQUES: Oh, just—a caller.

IRENE: At what time?

JACQUES: At half-past three.

IRENE: Will it take long?

JACQUES: That I don't know. [*Telephone rings. He rises, takes up receiver.*] Hullo...yes...who is it please?...Oh! Just a minute. [*To* IRENE.] Praxine wants to speak to you.

IRENE: [*At telephone.*] Hullo...Oh, hullo, how do you do?...Why of course I haven't forgotten...at half-past three, yes...All right! What?...No, he is so sorry, but he has an appointment and won't be able to come. I'll be there. [*She hangs up receiver.*] He asked me to be on time, because he has to leave. [*Pause.*] Well then?

JACQUES: Well then what?

IRENE: May I really buy the picture if I still like it much as I did?

JACQUES: Why, of course.

IRENE: You're a darling. But, you know, I really think it's a good buy. Praxine never gets less than twenty-five thousand francs for his smallest canvases and he's giving me this for fifteen thousand—just because it's I.

JACQUES: That's splendid.

IRENE: I do so hope you'll like it, but I warn you, it's extremely modern. You may think it's horrible—

JACQUES: Of course I won't. What time will you be back?

IRENE: Oh, not late. I have to stop and send some books to Gisele; she writes me she has nothing to read. That's all. I'll be back here for tea.

JACQUES: If by any chance the person I'm expecting should still be here when you return, would you mind not coming in?

IRENE: No, of course not.

JACQUES: I'd rather you didn't meet.

IRENE: Oh! Why not?

JACQUES: I don't think either you or she would enjoy it much.

IRENE: Ah! [*Pause.*] Can't you tell me who it is?

JACQUES: Does it interest you?

IRENE: Well, really!—After what you've just told me.

JACQUES: It's a very charming woman, towards whom I behaved very shabbily.

IRENE: [*Searching in her mind.*] A woman toward whom—Madame Meillant?

JACQUES: Exactly.

IRENE: No? How funny!

JACQUES: Isn't it?

IRENE: She's coming to see you?

JACQUES: I wrote, asking her to call. Whether she'll come or not, I don't know.

IRENE: But why is she coming?

JACQUES: Here. [*He hands her the letter he has just received.*]

IRENE: [*After having read it.*] What are the letters she mentions?

JACQUES: The letters she wrote me while—that she wrote me last year.

IRENE: Hadn't you given them back to her?

JACQUES: No. We left Paris in such a hurry a year ago that I didn't have time, and since our return I haven't given it a thought.

IRENE: [*Smiling.*] Poor thing. [*Gives him back letter.*]

JACQUES: [*Putting it on the desk.*] You don't mind receiving her here?

IRENE: Why no, not at all.

JACQUES: That's what I thought.

IRENE: Why should I mind?

JACQUES: For no reason, that's true.

IRENE: I have perfect confidence in you.

JACQUES: Of course.

IRENE: I suppose you wanted to give her the letters yourself, and you're quite right.

JACQUES: Naturally.

IRENE: [*Looking at him.*] What's the matter?

JACQUES: Nothing.

IRENE: You look annoyed that I should be taking this so amiably.

JACQUES: I? On the contrary, I'm delighted.

IRENE: Would you rather have me jealous?

JACQUES: I repeat that I'm delighted.

IRENE: I have no reason for being jealous, have I?
JACQUES: No! Absolutely—none.
IRENE: Well, then?
JACQUES: Jealousy in your case would certainly be uncalled for.
IRENE: Meaning what?
JACQUES: Simply, that just as jealousy's the most natural thing in the world when one's in love, it becomes meaningless when one isn't, that's all.
IRENE: So—I don't love you?
JACQUES: Of course you don't love me.
IRENE: How absurd!
JACQUES: What is absurd?
IRENE: To say that.
JACQUES: Not at all, why is it?
IRENE: Come now, what are you reproaching me about?
JACQUES: I'm not reproaching you about anything.
IRENE: Have you any fault to find with me?
JACQUES: No. Go along and do your errands. Please!
IRENE: No, let's clear this up. I'd prefer that. [*Removes her coat and puts it on divan.*]
JACQUES: It's so useless.
IRENE: If I've disappointed you in any way, tell me.
JACQUES: In no way.
IRENE: Don't I do all that I can to make you happy?
JACQUES: All that you can.
IRENE: Have I had any other thought than your happiness, since I've been your wife? Has my life had any other purpose? Don't I always ask myself, before doing anything, if you'll be pleased and whether you'll approve?
JACQUES: Even in choosing your bedroom curtains,—quite right.
IRENE: Don't make fun of me, please.
JACQUES: I'm not making fun of you. You're an attentive, devoted and faithful wife. What more can I ask? If all that doesn't make me happy, I must be very hard to please.
IRENE: I don't understand you any more, Jacques.
JACQUES: I know it! That's why all this talk can accomplish nothing.
IRENE: [*Pause.*] Then—then you're not happy?
JACQUES: In any case, it's not your fault. I repeat that I have no reproaches to make.
IRENE: [*Wearily.*] But what can I do, then?
JACQUES: Nothing. There's nothing to be done.

IRENE: Yet you have my every thought. You know that, don't you?

JACQUES: No. I don't know that at all.

IRENE: You don't?

JACQUES: How do you expect me to know what your thoughts are? They're yours. They're no business of mine.

IRENE: But I hide nothing from you. Nothing that might disturb you — I swear it.

JACQUES: As to that — [*A gesture of futility.*]

IRENE: You don't believe me? Well, then, question me. I'd much rather have that.

JACQUES: No, no — no questions! Let's leave in the dark what was meant to be in the dark.

IRENE: No! Since we've come to this, I want you to question me! Perhaps you'll see how unjust you are when you know everything.

JACQUES: Then there are things to know?

IRENE: Only things that can reassure you.

JACQUES: Tell me. I'm listening. [*Pause.*] Have you seen her again?

IRENE: No.

JACQUES: Has she telephoned you?

IRENE: No.

JACQUES: Written?

IRENE: Yes.

JACQUES: When?

IRENE: Shortly after our return to Paris. [*Pause.*] Twice.

JACQUES: Where are the letters?

IRENE: [*Simply.*] I sent them back unopened.

JACQUES: Unopened?

IRENE: Word of honor.

JACQUES: How did you send them back?

IRENE: By the person who brought them.

JACQUES: How docs it happen that I didn't know about it?

IRENE: You weren't in. You had gone out.

JACQUES: Both times?

IRENE: Yes.

JACQUES: They probably waited for me to leave before bringing them!

IRENE: Perhaps. I don't know.

JACQUES: Then you've no idea what she wanted of you?

IRENE: Oh, — to see me again, no doubt.

JACQUES: What makes you think that?

IRENE: I'm just supposing it.

JACQUES: Is that all?

IRENE: No.

JACQUES: What else?

IRENE: A few days after the second letter came her maid spoke to me in the street.

JACQUES: Perfect!

IRENE: It wasn't—she, who had sent her.

JACQUES: [*Ironically.*] Really?

IRENE: No. She was very ill.

JACQUES: [*Same tone.*] Well, well.

IRENE: She'd been ill a long time. She had just had a relapse. All that night she'd been delirious. It seems...that she had asked for me several times...So the maid thought it best to come and tell me.

JACQUES: And then? What did you do?

IRENE: Nothing.

JACQUES: Nothing?

IRENE: [*Shaking her head.*] I merely asked the maid to bring me news of her the next day. The next day the news was better. I told her not to come back.

JACQUES: [*Pause.*] And then?

IRENE: That's all.

JACQUES: Absolutely?

IRENE: Yes.

JACQUES: Why haven't you told me this before?

IRENE: I didn't want to worry you unnecessarily. You're so sensitive, you'd have been agitated despite anything I could say. I decided to wait a few days and then tell you.

JACQUES: Why a few days?

IRENE: She's going to Switzerland for several months to rest. I wanted to wait until she had gone.

JACQUES: Who told you she was going? The maid?

IRENE: Yes. [*Pause.*] Aren't you a little reassured now?

JACQUES: I wasn't worried.

IRENE: You know you can have confidence in me?

JACQUES: But I've always had confidence in you, Irene. I never doubted that when the time came, you would act as you did. You promised when you married me never to see that woman again. I was certain that you never would see her again.

IRENE: Then what's on your mind? Why aren't you happy?

JACQUES: And you, are you happy?

IRENE: I? [*Pause.*] Of course I'm happy.

JACQUES: Oh! Come now!

IRENE: [*Going toward him.*] But really, Jacques! . . . Haven't I everything to make me happy? We have all we need, we get along so well—you're kindness and generosity itself to me. What more can I wish for?

JACQUES: Why do you try to make me believe that nothing is lacking in your life?

IRENE: Because it's true!

JACQUES: No, it's not true!—You're not yet thirty and I'm not thirty-five. Happiness, at our age, doesn't consist in leading a comfortable existence . . . a string of pearls—a couple of cars. It's too soon for that. It's love that's lacking, Irene; you long to love, just as I long to be loved.

IRENE: What do you want me to say? You've convinced yourself that I don't love you—

JACQUES: Ah, if you knew how hard it's been to convince myself of it. The stupidly hopeful stages I went through! I've clung desperately to the substitutes of love—from tenderness and friendship to the most pathetic of all—compliance. On a word or a gesture that I could interpret in terms of my desire I'd regain confidence. Those illusions are gone. I know that I can really mean nothing to you. I'm as incapable of making you happy as of making you unhappy . . . Oh, God! if only I could make you suffer!

IRENE: You can.

JACQUES: How?

IRENE: By continuing to say these silly things!

JACQUES: You know as well as I that they're not silly. Why shut your eyes to it? Listen, do you know why I've made an appointment with Madame Meillant?

IRENE: Why, Jacques?

JACQUES: It was to see the effect it might have on you, whether you would object or seem annoyed. I made you laugh. That's the only result I got.

IRENE: Did you want me to weep?

JACQUES: I wanted to see just how far your indifference went.

IRENE: Is it my fault if I believe in your love for me . . . if I don't fear your being unfaithful?

JACQUES: If you loved me, you would fear it. But the truth is, that it wouldn't matter to you in the least.

IRENE: That's not so!

JACQUES: Oh, yes, it is.

IRENE: It would hurt me a great deal.

JACQUES: Hurt you?

IRENE: Of course.

JACQUES: Tell me just how it would hurt you?

IRENE: How can I tell you that? I don't know.

JACQUES: Well, try to imagine.

IRENE: I'd be very disappointed, very saddened. I'd feel that—that afterwards I would not like to be taken in your arms again as I did before... there.

JACQUES: [*Looking at her mournfully.*] As you did before?

IRENE: Yes.

JACQUES: You really like so much to be in my arms? Tell me!

IRENE: [*Lowering her head.*] Why—yes.

JACQUES: My poor Irene—so you think me blind?

IRENE: [*Pause, then with an effort.*] Have I—have I ever refused you?

JACQUES: You've had a great deal of courage.

IRENE: I thought I made you happy—that was all I wanted.

JACQUES: One can't give happiness so easily as that.

IRENE: I'm sorry.

JACQUES: Love, you see—is something very different.

IRENE: Everything I could give you—I've given. If that doesn't suffice you—

JACQUES: No!

IRENE: Then, look somewhere else, that's all.

JACQUES: You'd like that, wouldn't you? What a deliverance for you that day would be!

IRENE: Oh! Jacques, that will do! [*Pause.*] And anyway, it's getting late and I must be going. [*Gets coat from divan, puts it on and goes toward door.*]

JACQUES: Irene?

IRENE: What?

JACQUES: Come here.

IRENE: What do you want?

JACQUES: Forgive me. I didn't mean—to hurt you. If I have, forgive me.

IRENE: [*Going towards him.*] Why are you so unjust?

JACQUES: Well, you see, I can't get used to it.

IRENE: Used to what? My not loving you? But I do. You are everything that I admire, everything that pleases me, everything that I respect in this world.

JACQUES: [*Dejected.*] Yes, I suppose so.

IRENE: Well, do you think that many wives can say as such of their husbands?

JACQUES: I wasn't asking for as much, either.

IRENE: Do I love anyone else but you? I don't, do I? Well then? . . . If you had been told a year ago that you held the first and only place in my life, wouldn't you have been happy?

JACQUES: Of course.

IRENE: Do you think my feeling for you hasn't grown since I asked you to keep me here? You remember, that day, don't you?

JACQUES: Yes.

IRENE: [*Smiling—comes close to him.*] And at Montcel, three weeks later, the mayor's speech and the little chapel, where it was so cold; you remember that too?

JACQUES: Yes.

IRENE: Do you regret what happened that day?

JACQUES: Do you?

IRENE: No.

JACQUES: That's something anyway.

IRENE: Then—will you kiss me?

JACQUES: You want me to?

IRENE: Yes,—I do. [*He takes her in his arms and holds her there a moment, quietly, looking at her. She leans forward to kiss him, her left arm is raised to clasp him, when her eyes rest on her wrist watch.*] Oh, look! Quarter to four! Can that be the time?

JACQUES: Yes.

IRENE: I had no idea! Oh! what a nuisance. Now I won't have time to go to the decorator's. Hurry, dearest!

JACQUES: What?

IRENE: Aren't you going to kiss me?

JACQUES: [*Drawing away.*] No, you're late already.

IRENE: It doesn't matter.

JACQUES: No, no—run along.

IRENE: Don't be silly! Just because I said . . .

JACQUES: Go on . . . Go—[*He turns his back to her and walks away.*]

IRENE: Great heavens, but you're touchy!

JACQUES: Please go!

IRENE: [*She sighs.*] See you later, then?

JACQUES: Yes. [IRENE *goes toward door. At the door she turns around.*]

IRENE: I hope you won't make love to that woman?

JACQUES: Thank you for thinking of it!

IRENE: You promise me you won't?

JACQUES: Yes, yes, of course. [IRENE *goes out at back.* JACQUES *sits down, thoughtful, a bitter expression on his face. After quite a pause, he sees on the desk the letter* FRANÇOISE *has written, takes it, puts it in his pocket, goes and opens a cabinet and takes out a rather bulky envelope, which he brings to the desk. He empties its contents: letters. He picks one at random and reads it. At that moment a bell is heard. He puts the letters back in the envelope.* GEORGES *enters.*]

GEORGES: Madame Meillant monsieur.

JACQUES: Ask her to come in. [*Puts letters in desk drawer. A moment later* GEORGES *ushers* FRANÇOISE *into the room and retires.*] How are you, Françoise? It was sweet of you to come. [*He kisses her hand.*]

FRANÇOISE: Oh, I only came to get my letters. Don't imagine it was for any other reason.

JACQUES: I'm imagining nothing at all. But I may thank you for having come, mayn't I?

FRANÇOISE: Why didn't you give the maid the letters as I asked in my note? It would have been much simpler.

JACQUES: I preferred their passing directly from my hands into yours. It seemed to me the safest way. And after all, why not say it: I wanted to see you again.

FRANÇOISE: Really? And you didn't ask yourself if *I* wanted to see you?

JACQUES: I ventured to think that if that were too disagreeable you wouldn't come.

FRANÇOISE: I wanted my letters, I've just told you that. You don't seem to realize that I've been waiting for them a year.

JACQUES: They were here and I was circling the world. Unless I were to return especially from Japan to get them—

FRANÇOISE: You could have sent them to me before you left.

JACQUES: I didn't have the time.

FRANÇOISE: You left very hurriedly.

JACQUES: Very. But you weren't anxious about your letters, were you? You knew they were in safekeeping.

FRANÇOISE: Oh, you think so? And suppose your wife had taken a fancy to search your desk?

JACQUES: That's quite unlikely.

FRANÇOISE: Just the same, such things do happen.

JACQUES: Not here.

FRANÇOISE: Then your wife isn't jealous?

JACQUES: Not at all.

FRANÇOISE: You're lucky! She's not in, I hope.

JACQUES: No, she's just gone out.

FRANÇOISE: [*Going to table and regarding picture of* IRENE.] Is this she?

JACQUES: Yes.

FRANÇOISE: My compliments.

JACQUES: Thanks.

FRANÇOISE: Why didn't you tell me the truth the last time I came here?

JACQUES: The truth?

FRANÇOISE: Yes; that you were going to be married. I should have preferred that, you know. It would have been nicer. Besides, at least it was a reason.

JACQUES: I didn't tell you because I didn't know it myself.

FRANÇOISE: You didn't know it?

JACQUES: No.

FRANÇOISE: And three weeks later the papers announced that you were married!

JACQUES: Yes.

FRANÇOISE: You didn't lose much time, then?

JACQUES: Once a thing like that is decided upon...

FRANÇOISE: She's a childhood friend, isn't she?

JACQUES: She's a cousin.

FRANÇOISE: First cousin?

JACQUES: No.

FRANÇOISE: Just as well!—And you've loved each other always, of course?

JACQUES: Well—

FRANÇOISE: Oh, you can tell me now. I really don't know why I'm asking you; it matters to me so little.

JACQUES: Then—

FRANÇOISE: Give me my letters, won't you?

JACQUES: Are you in such a hurry to get them?

FRANÇOISE: Yes.

JACQUES: Why?

FRANÇOISE: Because.

JACQUES: I'm not asking you for mine!

FRANÇOISE: I burned them long ago.

JACQUES: Really?

FRANÇOISE: Besides, for all the letters *you* ever sent—and for all they ever said—

JACQUES: Just the same, it wasn't very nice to burn them.

FRANÇOISE: Why should I have kept them?

JACQUES: To re-read them now and then.

FRANÇOISE: I had other things to do.

JACQUES: Ah?

FRANÇOISE: Jacques—my letters!

JACQUES: Not right away! Wait a bit. We've so many things to say to each other first.

FRANÇOISE: We have absolutely nothing to say. Besides, your wife may come in at any minute, and I'm no more anxious to meet her than she is to meet me.

JACQUES: Sit down. She won't be here for at least an hour. And even then she won't come into this room.

FRANÇOISE: How do you know?

JACQUES: I told her I was expecting you.

FRANÇOISE: You told her that?

JACQUES: Yes.

FRANÇOISE: And she was willing?

JACQUES: Of course.

FRANÇOISE: Well! You have trained her properly!

JACQUES: Now, do sit down and tell me everything.

FRANÇOISE: But I've nothing to tell you. [Sits on divan.]

JACQUES: Oh! Come now! [Draws up chair and sits near her.]

FRANÇOISE: What do you want to know?

JACQUES: With whom are you in love?

FRANÇOISE: That, my dear Jacques, is my—

JACQUES: What do you care? I promise not to tell a soul...Is it Moreuil?

FRANÇOISE: Perhaps.

JACQUES: Seriously? Moreuil? Oh! but he's an awful looking fellow! [He looks at her. She does not falter.] No. You didn't protest. It isn't Moreuil. Then who is it?

FRANÇOISE: Heavens, you're impossible! [She laughs.]

JACQUES: Ah! you're laughing—that's nice.

FRANÇOISE: I'm laughing because you disarm me. But believe me, I've no desire to.

JACQUES: You should laugh. It's very becoming to you. You're lovely when you laugh.

FRANÇOISE: I don't care to be lovely.

JACQUES: What a fib!

FRANÇOISE: Do you think I care a thing about attracting you now?

JACQUES: Oh, I don't say that you care especially about it,—but you'd just as soon I thought you pretty. Well, I find you pretty, very pretty, even prettier than I remembered. Were you as pretty as this before?

FRANÇOISE: Jacques, please give me my letters and let me go.

JACQUES: I'll give them if you tell me with whom you're in love.

FRANÇOISE: I'm in love with no one.

JACQUES: No one?

FRANÇOISE: No!

JACQUES: Is it true?

FRANÇOISE: Oh!... I'd tell you... why not?

JACQUES: [*Thoughtfully, looking at her.*] Françoise?...

FRANÇOISE: What?

JACQUES: If you love no one, won't you — try to love me a little?

FRANÇOISE: You? Ah, no, I should say not!

JACQUES: Why?

FRANÇOISE: No, thank you! That's all over, fortunately.

JACQUES: [*Pause.*] Too bad —

FRANÇOISE: You think so?

JACQUES: Yes, it's too bad... If you had wanted to love me... just a tiny
little bit... I could have loved you so much.

FRANÇOISE: You?

JACQUES: Yes.

FRANÇOISE: You, love? Why, you don't even know what the word means!

JACQUES: Do you believe that?

FRANÇOISE: I know it. For you, love is an amusing pastime. It isn't your
fault; you were born fickle.

JACQUES: I was born faithful, Françoise.

FRANÇOISE: Faithful to whom?

JACQUES: To you, if you wish it.

FRANÇOISE: And your wife, what about her? Are you already dissatisfied
with her? Poor girl! How I pity her!

JACQUES: She isn't to be pitied.

FRANÇOISE: One year! Not even that — eleven months! Eleven months ago
you married her, and already you're looking for an adventure. But then
I was certain how it would turn out.

JACQUES: Really?

FRANÇOISE: When I read your note a while ago, I didn't have a moment's
doubt. From the way in which you asked me to come, I understood
immediately what you wanted.

JACQUES: And you came, just the same?

FRANÇOISE: Because of my letters.

JACQUES: True enough, — pardon me!

FRANÇOISE: But I knew perfectly well that you were thinking much less about returning them to me, than in seeing if I still loved you. I know you, Jacques!

JACQUES: Not so well.

FRANÇOISE: Oh, come now, it's so natural. After that long trip, you came back to Paris, and began getting bored. For a man like you, married life is terribly monotonous, isn't it? A distraction's almost imperative! Only, my dear Jacques, you were wrong in thinking me still available. Your Françoise no longer loves you! And that's that!

JACQUES: [*Pause.*] Well—never mind ... [*He rises.*]

FRANÇOISE: That surprises you, doesn't it?

JACQUES: What?

FRANÇOISE: That one should be able not to love you.

JACQUES: [*Sadly.*] No, it doesn't—it doesn't surprise me in the least, I assure you. It's the way things have been going.

FRANÇOISE: [*After a moment.*] Well, then?

JACQUES: Then nothing. I'm going to give you your letters. That's all. [*He goes to desk, takes out the envelope containing the letters and brings it to* FRANÇOISE.] They are all there.

FRANÇOISE: [*Looking at him.*] What's the matter? [*She takes letters and puts them in her lap.*]

JACQUES: Nothing.

FRANÇOISE: [*She rises and letters fall to floor.*] Why do you look so unhappy, all of a sudden?

JACQUES: Do I?

FRANÇOISE: You're not going to tell me that I've hurt you?

JACQUES: No.

FRANÇOISE: Then what's troubling you?

JACQUES: Nothing, my dear, nothing at all. I'm unhappy because—because we're going to part and will never each other again, that's all.

FRANÇOISE: What do you care?

JACQUES: I shall miss you.

FRANÇOISE: Have you missed me much during the past year?

JACQUES: Perhaps—

FRANÇOISE: What a story! You would have told me!

JACQUES: How?

FRANÇOISE: You could have written me,—I hadn't forbidden you to.

JACQUES: That's true.

FRANÇOISE: Not a line—not even a post card—nothing! And still you expect me to love you. You must admit it would be too stupid of me!

JACQUES: It's never stupid to love…

FRANÇOISE: It is to love you.

JACQUES: That's funny!

FRANÇOISE: What's funny?

JACQUES: How little you know me, my dear Françoise!

FRANÇOISE: Ah?

JACQUES: Really.

FRANÇOISE: Whose fault is that, then?

JACQUES: Oh! It's mine, I realize that.

FRANÇOISE: If you were capable of love, why did you never show it to me? Why did you always belittle the love I had for you? The day may come, Jacques, when you'll be sorry for that.

JACQUES: Be content, my dear, I'm sorry for it already.

FRANÇOISE: No, not yet. You're still too young. But—

JACQUES: You can't imagine how sorry I am, Françoise.

FRANÇOISE: Truly?

JACQUES: Yes.

FRANÇOISE: [*After a pause, looking at him.*] You're without doubt the most bewildering man I've ever known! Things happen when one least expects them, with you—and when it's too late!

JACQUES: Are you sure?

FRANÇOISE: Of what?

JACQUES: That it's too late?

FRANÇOISE: Of course.

JACQUES: Françoise… [*He takes her hand.*]

FRANÇOISE: Don't—

JACQUES: Are you sure that way down, way down in you—there isn't a little flicker—that might be revived by my being very careful?… Tell me?

FRANÇOISE: No! I don't want to!

JACQUES: Too bad.

FRANÇOISE: Where are my letters?

JACQUES: On the floor. [*He picks them up.*]

FRANÇOISE: Give them to me.

JACQUES: Will you do one last thing for me?

FRANÇOISE: What?

JACQUES: Since it's over, since we're going to say good-by and never see each other again,—let me kiss you.

FRANÇOISE: You're silly!

JACQUES: Please. I'd like, just once, to see your eyes again—

FRANÇOISE: My eyes?

JACQUES: Yes. Oh, not as they are now, not your everyday eyes. But the old-time eyes—the eyes I used to know—[*Going toward her.*] I want to see those eyes again—just to see them.

FRANÇOISE: No.

JACQUES: After that, you can go away. I shan't try to hold you, I promise. Grant me that one little happiness. [*He moves to take her in his arms.*]

FRANÇOISE: [*Resisting.*] No, I don't want to!

JACQUES: Please, please let me.

FRANÇOISE: [*Imploring.*] Let me go!

JACQUES: Françoise!—[*He embraces her.*]

FRANÇOISE: Let me go! I implore you! I don't want to—[*More feebly.*] I don't want to—I don't wa—[*Their lips meet. She abandons herself to him. The kiss, a long one, leaves her prostrated, her head thrown back on his shoulder, her eyes closed.*]

JACQUES: [*Looking down at her, in a low voice.*] How beautiful!

FRANÇOISE: [*Quietly, without moving.*] What's beautiful?

JACQUES: A woman!

FRANÇOISE: [*Releasing herself gently.*] I suppose you're happy now? You've had what you wanted? I was almost consoled, I had almost forgotten you . . . And I had to come here to give you the satisfaction of torturing me all over again! . . . I don't know what I'm going to do . . . And I knew what would happen, I *knew*!

JACQUES: [*Smilingly approaching her.*] My sweet Françoise . . .

FRANÇOISE: Oh! no, no, don't come near me, Jacques, please! You wanted to know if you still had your power over me. Now that you've seen that you have, it ought to satisfy you.

JACQUES: Do you really believe that that satisfies me?

FRANÇOISE: You don't want to hurt me all over again, do you?

JACQUES: No, Françoise.

FRANÇOISE: Then give me my letters and let me go!

JACQUES: No.

FRANÇOISE: You won't give them to me?

JACQUES: I'll bring them myself to your house.

FRANÇOISE: No!

JACQUES: In a little while.

FRANÇOISE: You will not!

JACQUES: Will you be there at about five?

FRANÇOISE: No, I will not be there!

JACQUES: [*Tenderly.*] Yes, you will.

FRANÇOISE: But I don't *want* you to come!

JACQUES: [*Taking her by the arm and forcing her to look at him.*] You don't want me to?

FRANÇOISE: [*With less conviction.*] No —

JACQUES: Truly? You don't want me to?

FRANÇOISE: [*In a supplicating tone.*] No.

JACQUES: Françoise —! [*Again he embraces and kisses her.*]

FRANÇOISE: Oh! It's going to begin all over again.

JACQUES: What is?

FRANÇOISE: Everything, as it was before.

JACQUES: Not as it was before.

FRANÇOISE: Oh!

JACQUES: You'll see!

FRANÇOISE: It will be just the same, I know.

JACQUES: No.

FRANÇOISE: Why? What's been changed?

JACQUES: Me.

FRANÇOISE: Do you believe people change?

JACQUES: They learn a little.

FRANÇOISE: [*Smiling.*] While traveling?

JACQUES: Yes, while traveling.

FRANÇOISE: What do they learn?

JACQUES: To love the people of their homeland, the people who speak their language. It's tiresome to talk when one isn't understood. One wearies of it.

FRANÇOISE: [*Surprised, looking at him.*] Poor Jacques!

JACQUES: Don't pity me; I've come back to my own people.

FRANÇOISE: [*Leaning against him; tenderly.*] Oh! Jacques — it's terrifying! I already loved you when you were quite detestable; what will it be like if you start being a darling?

JACQUES: You'll love me a little more, that's all.

FRANÇOISE: [*Nestling against him.*] My dear one . . . I'm happy . . . [*Pause.*]

[*The slam of a door is heard.* JACQUES *listens in surprise.* FRANÇOISE *starts. They separate.*]

FRANÇOISE: What is it?

JACQUES: Probably my wife returning.

FRANÇOISE: [*Nervously.*] Ah! I knew it!

JACQUES: Don't worry, she won't come in. [*They listen a few seconds in silence.*] You see? Does that reassure you? You can go without meeting a soul.

FRANÇOISE: [*Very moved.*] But—you're coming?

JACQUES: Of course I'm coming!

FRANÇOISE: Till you do, my love!

JACQUES: Till I do, my love! [*He opens the door. She goes out, he following her. A few seconds later he reenters followed by* GEORGES.]

GEORGES: Madame asked me to let her know as soon as you were alone, monsieur.

JACQUES: [*Puts letters away. Annoyed.*] Well...go and tell madame. Then bring my hat and my overcoat.

GEORGES: Yes, monsieur. [*He goes out at right to* IRENE*'s room. A moment later* IRENE *enters.*]

JACQUES: Back already?

IRENE: Yes. [*She seems curiously disturbed and unnatural.*]

JACQUES: You weren't gone very long. Well,—what about the painting?

IRENE: What painting?

JACQUES: Praxine's painting—the one you wanted to buy.

IRENE: Oh, yes.

JACQUES: Didn't you bring it back with you?

IRENE: No...Jacques, I'd like to talk with you...May I? [GEORGES *enters from rear door with* JACQUES*' hat and coat.*] Oh, are you going out?

JACQUES: Yes, but I have a few minutes to spare. [*To* GEORGES.] Put them there. [GEORGES *puts hat and coat on arm of divan and goes out.*] What did you want to tell me?

IRENE: I'll wait until you come back.

JACQUES: Please don't.

IRENE: I'd delay you. [*He looks at her and is struck by her appearance.*]

JACQUES: What's the matter with you?

IRENE: Nothing. I'll tell you when you get back.

JACQUES: No. Tell me now.

IRENE: It's not so urgent.

JACQUES: Oh, come, tell me—what is it?

IRENE: ...Jacques, I'd like to go away—to leave Paris.

JACQUES: Leave Paris?

IRENE: Yes.

JACQUES: But what for?

IRENE: I'm just asking you to.

JACQUES: What does it mean? Where do you want to go?

IRENE: We might go for a while to Montcel. Father would be only too happy. He suggested it several times. All we need do is wire the caretaker. He'd meet us at Limoges with a car.

JACQUES: But why do you want to leave Paris? We've hardly been back a month!

IRENE: I know.

JACQUES: Why this whim?

IRENE: It's not a whim.

JACQUES: Explain yourself, then.

IRENE: I hoped — that you'd understand.

JACQUES: That I'd understand?

IRENE: Yes.

JACQUES: No, I don't understand.

IRENE: I mustn't — remain here.

JACQUES: [*Forcibly.*] But why not?

IRENE: [*Trembling all over, her head lowered.*] I've seen her again.

JACQUES: Ah? — [*Pause.*] Where?

IRENE: Praxine's... She knew I was to be there. She was waiting for me.

JACQUES: How did she know?

IRENE: She knows everything.

JACQUES: Then she knows Praxine?

IRENE: She had met him once, in Vienna.

JACQUES: Did you know that?

IRENE: No, of course not.

JACQUES: So — you spoke to her?

IRENE: She spoke to me.

JACQUES: In front of Praxine?

IRENE: No.

JACQUES: What did she say to you?

IRENE: Oh! — I don't remember now.

JACQUES: You don't want to tell me —

IRENE: Really, I don't remember, — I was hardly listening.

JACQUES: She asked to see you again, I suppose?

IRENE: ... Yes.

JACQUES: What did you answer?

IRENE: ... That I didn't want to.

JACQUES: And then?

IRENE: She said — that she would wait.

JACQUES: Until when?

IRENE: ... Until I came.

JACQUES: Isn't she going to Switzerland? [IRENE *shakes her head.*] Or is she cured?

IRENE: She says she doesn't care if she dies.

JACQUES: Don't worry, she won't die. That's the old story.

IRENE: She never lies.

JACQUES: Can't her husband take her away?

IRENE: They're not together any more. She has left him.

JACQUES: Really?

IRENE: [*After a pause.*] Jacques, — is it true that he came to see you a year ago?

JACQUES: Yes. How did she know that?

IRENE: She didn't tell me. [*Pause.*] It was after that, that she left him.

JACQUES: So much the better for him. Is there no one with her who could take her away?

IRENE: [*Shaking her head.*] No one. [*Controlling her feeling.*] She is alone — all alone —

JACQUES: [*After looking at her a while in silence.*] Ah! She's very clever — one must admit that! [IRENE *shrugs her shoulders.*] Mustn't she be clever to be able to upset you like this at your first encounter?

IRENE: How do you know that she wasn't more upset than I!

JACQUES: Of course, that was part of the plan! What surprises me, though, is that seeing you in this condition she should have let you escape, that she didn't attempt to hold you —

IRENE: Do you think — that she didn't try?

JACQUES: Well, then?

IRENE: To get away, I had to promise that I'd go to see her later.

JACQUES: [*Ironically.*] Splendid! [*A slight pause.*] And — do you intend seeing her?

IRENE: You know very well I don't.

JACQUES: Have you the courage not to?

IRENE: Yes.

JACQUES: It will be hard, won't it?

IRENE: [*Barely speaking the word.*] Yes.

JACQUES: How long — will you be able to resist?

IRENE: I don't know. That's why I'm asking to go away.

JACQUES: Well, then, go. Who's preventing you? You don't need me for that, do you?

IRENE: You won't come?

JACQUES: No.

IRENE: Why?

JACQUES: You want to know why? Look at yourself! You're breathless — your eyes are dazed — your hands are trembling — because you've seen her again, that's why! For a year I've been living with a statue and that woman had only to reappear for the statue to come to life, to become a human being capable of suffering and trembling! Well, I give up, Irene, do you understand? I give up! I've loved you more than anything in the world, you know that. I've proved it to you. As long as I hoped that some day you might love me as I loved you, as a man and woman can love each other, with body and soul, I accepted the role of your guardian. But now I've had enough. I resign from a useless and ungrateful task. Protect yourself, if you can. It doesn't interest me any longer. It's over! I'm tired of pursuing a phantom. D'Aiguines knew what he was talking about when he said, "Leave her alone, get out of her way, she isn't for you." He was right—Fortunately, there are women who *are* for us.

IRENE: Madame Meillant, for instance?

JACQUES: Yes.

IRENE: And I've tried so hard.

JACQUES: I didn't ask you to. It was you who came to me.

IRENE: Then you should have turned me away.

JACQUES: You shouldn't have said that you could love me.

IRENE: How did I know? I tried my best to love you! You always speak of what *you* have done! What about me? What about me? What about my feelings,—did you ever know anything about them? Did you ever give them so much as a thought? You loved me, it's true, but in your way.

JACQUES: Were you expecting platonic love from me?

IRENE: I expected a little more tenderness. Is there no spirit in love? Must it be only—*the body*!

JACQUES: Yes, you loathed that, didn't you? Go on, say it, be frank at least! [IRENE *lowers her head, and does not answer.*] But don't bother, don't say it! What for? I've known it for a long time.

IRENE: [*Without looking at him.*] Have you?

JACQUES: You wouldn't have thought so, is that what you mean? Well, you are rid of it now. You can breathe freely at last! I'll never impose my desire again. No more of that drudgery. It's over! Aren't you going to thank me?

IRENE: [*After a moment.*] Have you nothing else to say to me, Jacques?

JACQUES: No, really, I haven't. I think we've said all there is to say! Everything is quite clear, now. You can do what you like—I don't care any more. [*He takes his hat and coat from divan.*] Good night. [*He goes out. She follows him towards the door. As it closes she utters a, half stifled cry. Then she sits down, deep in thought, in a chair, her forehead resting in her hand.* JOSEPHINE, *the maid, enters from* IRENE's *room, carrying some flowers in a box.*]

IRENE: What is it?

JOSEPHINE: Some flowers for you, madame, that have just come. [*She puts the box on the desk and opens it. It contains a large bunch of violets, like those in the first act.*]

IRENE: Who brought them?

JOSEPHINE: The florist, madame.

IRENE: Ah? [*Pause.*] Was there no letter with them?

JOSEPHINE: No, madame, nothing at all.

IRENE: That's all, Josephine, thank you. [JOSEPHINE *goes out.* IRENE *slowly turns and looks at the violets. She walks toward them, lifts them from the box, caresses them. Her eyes become fixed and hard. She turns toward the door through which* JACQUES *went out. She looks at the flowers again, seems to hesitate, then abruptly gets her hat, and rushes out to her room.*]

[*After a few moments the rear door opens and* JACQUES *appears. He closes the door as he enters. He slowly takes off his hat and coat and sits down at his desk, meditating. At that moment the outer door of the apartment is heard to slam.* JACQUES *raises his head.*]

JACQUES: [*He rises, goes to door leading into* IRENE'S *room, opens it, steps in and calls gently.*] Irene? . . . [*Again, louder and anxiously.*] Irene? [*He then reenters, looking surprised, and crosses hurriedly to desk, where he rings bell.* GEORGES *enters.*] Has madame gone out?

GEORGES: Yes, monsieur, just a moment ago.

JACQUES: Oh! [*Pause.*] Did she leave any message?

GEORGES: No, monsieur.

JACQUES: [*After a pause.*] All right, Georges. [*He sits down at desk.*] You can go. [GEORGES *goes toward rear door then seeing hat and overcoat on chair, turns.*]

GEORGES: Shall I take these away, monsieur? [JACQUES, *absorbed in his thoughts, does not hear him. After a few moments, he raises his head and notices* GEORGES *standing there.*]

JACQUES: What?

GEORGES: I was asking monsieur if I should put his hat and coat away?

JACQUES: [*After a pause.*] No. Leave them. I'm going out, too.

The CURTAIN *falls*

The
Children's Hour

Lillian Hellman

Patricia Neal (Karen), Iris Mann (Mary), and Kim Hunter (Martha) in *The Children's Hour*, at the Coronet Theatre, 1952 (revival). (Photo by Eileen Darby. Reprinted with permission from the John Willis Theatre World/Screen World Archive.)

The Children's Hour was first produced on Broadway at Maxine Elliot's Theatre on November 20, 1934. It was produced and directed by Herman Shumlin, and the settings were designed by Aline Bernstein.

Cast
(in order of their appearance)

Peggy Rogers	Eugenia Rawls
Mrs. Lily Mortar	Aline McDermott
Evelyn Munn	Elizabeth Seckel
Helen Burton	Lynne Fisher
Lois Fisher	Jaqueline Rusling
Catherine	Barbara Leeds
Rosalie Wells	Barbara Beals
Mary Tilford	Florence McGee
Karen Wright	Katherine Emery
Martha Dobie	Anne Revere
Doctor Joseph Cardin	Robert Keith
Agatha	Edmonia Nolley
Mrs. Amelia Tilford	Katherine Emmet
A Grocery Boy	Jack Tyler

A note on the text: In 1972, Little, Brown, and Company published a volume by Lillian Hellman entitled *The Collected Plays*, which included a "Publisher's Note" stating "For this edition Miss Hellman has made numerous small revisions and emendations in each of the plays: the texts as given here are henceforth to be regarded as definitive." This version of *The Children's Hour* is taken from that 1972 edition.

for Dashiell Hammett with thanks

Act One
Living Room of the Wright-Dobie School.
Late afternoon in April.

Act Two
Scene I: Living room at Mrs. Tilford's.
   A few hours later.
Scene II: The same. Later that evening.

Act Three
The same as Act One. November.

Act One

Scene: *A room in the Wright-Dobie School for girls, a converted farmhouse about ten miles from the town of Lancet, Massachusetts. It is a comfortable, unpretentious room used as an afternoon study-room and at all other times as the living room.*

A large door left center faces the audience. There is a single door right. Against both back walls are bookcases. A large desk is at right; a table, two sofas, and eight or ten chairs.

It is early in an afternoon in April.

At rise: MRS. LILY MORTAR *is sitting in a large chair right center, with her head back and her eyes closed. She is a plump, florid woman of forty-five with dyed reddish hair. Her dress is too fancy for a classroom.*

Seven girls, from twelve to fourteen years old, are informally grouped on chairs and sofa. Six of them are sewing with no great amount of industry on pieces of white material. One of the others, EVELYN MUNN, *is using her scissors to trim the hair of* ROSALIE, *who sits, nervously, in front of her: she has* ROSALIE's *head bent back at an awkward angle and is enjoying herself.*

The eighth girl, PEGGY ROGERS, *is sitting in a higher chair than the others. She is reading aloud from a book. She is bored and she reads in a singsong, tired voice.*

PEGGY: "It is twice blest; it blesseth him that gives and him that takes: 'tis mightiest in the mightiest; it becomes the throned monarch better than his crown; his sceptre shows the force of temporal power, the attribute to awe and majesty, wherein..." [MRS. MORTAR *suddenly opens her eyes and stares at the haircutting. The children make efforts to warn* EVELYN. PEGGY *raises her voice until she is shouting*] "doth sit the dread and fear of kings; but mercy is above..."

MRS. MORTAR: Evelyn! What are you doing?

EVELYN: [*she lisps*] Uh—nothing, Mrs. Mortar.

MRS. MORTAR: You are certainly doing something. You are ruining the scissors for one thing.

PEGGY: [*loudly*] "But mercy is above. It..."

MRS. MORTAR: Just a moment, Peggy. It is very unfortunate that you girls cannot sit quietly with your sewing and drink in the immortal words of the immortal bard. [*She sighs*] Evelyn, go back to your sewing.

EVELYN: I can't get the hem thtraight. Honeth, I've been trying for three weekth, but I jutht can't do it.

MRS. MORTAR: Helen, please help Evelyn with the hem.

HELEN: [*rises, holding up the garment* EVELYN *has been working on. It is soiled and shapeless and so much has been cut off that it is now hardly large enough for a child of five. Giggling*] She can't ever wear that, Mrs. Mortar.

MRS. MORTAR: [*vaguely*] Well, try to do something with it. Make some handkerchiefs or something. Be clever about it. Women must learn these tricks. [*To* PEGGY] Continue. "Mightiest in the mightiest."

PEGGY: "'Tis mightiest in the mightiest; it becomes the throned monarch better than his crown; his sceptre—his sceptre shows the force of temporal power, the attribute to awe and majesty, wherein—"

LOIS: [*from the back of the room chants softly and monotonously through the previous speech*] Ferebam, ferebas, ferebat, ferebamus, ferebatis, fere— fere—

CATHERINE: [*two seats away, the book propped in front of her*] Fere*bant*.

LOIS: Ferebamus, ferebatis, fere*bant*.

MRS. MORTAR: Who's doing that?

PEGGY: [*the noise ceases. She hurries on*] "Wherein doth sit the dread and fear of kings; but mercy is above this sceptred sway, it is enthroned in the hearts of kings, it is an attribute to God himself—"

MRS. MORTAR: [*sadly*] Peggy, can't you imagine yourself as Portia? Can't you read the lines with some feeling, some pity? [*Dreamily*] Pity. Ah! As Sir Henry said to me many's the time, pity makes the actress. Now, why can't *you* feel pity?

PEGGY: I guess I feel pity.

LOIS: Ferebamus, ferebatis, fere—fere—fere—

CATHERINE: Fere*bant*, stupid.

MRS. MORTAR: How many people in this room are talking? Peggy, read the line again. I'll give you the cue.

PEGGY: What's a cue?

MRS. MORTAR: A cue is a line or word given the actor or actress to remind them of their next speech.

HELEN: [*softly*] To remind *him* or *her.*

ROSALIE: [*a fattish girl with glasses*] Weren't you ever in the movies, Mrs. Mortar?

MRS. MORTAR: I had many offers, my dear. But the cinema is a shallow art. It has no—no—[*Vaguely*] no fourth dimension. Now, Peggy, if you would only try to submerge yourself in this problem. You are pleading for the life of a man. [*She rises and there are faint sighs from the girls, who stare at her with blank, bored faces. She recites with gestures*] "But mercy is above this sceptred sway; it is enthroned in the hearts of kings, it is an attribute to God himself; and earthly power doth then show likest God's when mercy seasons justice."

LOIS: [*almost singing it*] Utor, fruor, fungor, potior, and vescor take the dative.

CATHERINE: Take the *ablative.*

LOIS: Oh, dear. Utor, fruor, fung—

MRS. MORTAR: [*to* LOIS, *with sarcasm*] You have something to tell the class?

LOIS: [*apologetically*] We've got a Latin exam this afternoon.

MRS. MORTAR: And you intend to occupy the sewing and elocution hour learning what should have been learnt yesterday?

CATHERINE: [*wearily*] It takes her more than yesterday to learn it.

MRS. MORTAR: Well, I cannot allow you to interrupt us like this.

CATHERINE: But we're finished sewing.

LOIS: [*admiringly*] I bet you were good at Latin, Mrs. Mortar.

MRS. MORTAR: Long ago, my dear, long ago. Now, take your book over by the window and don't disturb our enjoyment of Shakespeare.
[CATHERINE *and* LOIS *rise, go to window, stand mumbling and gesturing*] Let us go back again. "It is an attribute to—" [*At this point the door opens far enough to let* MARY TILFORD, *clutching a slightly faded bunch of wild flowers, squeeze cautiously in. She is fourteen, neither pretty nor ugly She is an undistinguished-looking girl*] "And earthly power doth then show likest God's when mercy seasons justice. We do pray for mercy, and that same prayer doth teach—"

PEGGY: [*happily*] You've skipped three lines.

MRS. MORTAR: In my entire career I've never missed a line.

PEGGY: But you did skip three lines. [*Goes to* MRS. MORTAR *with book*] See?

MRS. MORTAR: [*seeing* MARY *sidling along wall toward other end of the room, turns to her to avoid* PEGGY *and the book*] Mary!

MARY: Yes, Mrs. Mortar?

MRS. MORTAR: This is a pretty time to be coming to your sewing class I must say. Even if you have no interest in your work you might at least remember that you owe me a little courtesy. Courtesy is breeding. Breeding is an excellent thing. [*Turns to class*] Always remember that.

ROSALIE: Please, Mrs. Mortar, can I write that down?

MRS. MORTAR: Certainly. Suppose you all write it down.

PEGGY: But we wrote it down last week. [MARY *giggles.*]

MRS. MORTAR: Mary, I am still awaiting your explanation. Where have you been?

MARY: I took a walk.

MRS. MORTAR: So you took a walk. And may I ask, young lady, are we in the habit of taking walks when we should be at our classes?

MARY: I am sorry, Mrs. Mortar, I went to get you these flowers. I thought you would like them and I didn't know it would take so long to pick them.

MRS. MORTAR: [*flattered*] Well, well.

MARY: You were telling us last week how much you liked flowers, and I thought that I would bring you some and—

MRS. MORTAR: That was very sweet of you, Mary; I always like thoughtfulness. But you must not allow anything to interfere with your classes. Now run along, dear, and get a vase and some water to put my flowers in. [MARY *turns, sticks out her tongue at* HELEN, *says "A-a-a," and exits left*] You may put that book away, Peggy. I am sure your family need never worry about your going on the stage.

PEGGY: I don't want to go on the stage. I want to be a lighthouse keeper's wife.

MRS. MORTAR: Well, I certainly hope you won't read to him. [*The laughter of the class pleases her.* PEGGY *sits down among the other girls, who are making a great show of doing nothing.* MRS. MORTAR *returns to her chair, puts her head back, closes her eyes.*]

CATHERINE: How much longer, O Cataline, are you going to abuse our patience? [*To* LOIS] Now translate it, and for goodness' sakes try to get it right this time.

MRS. MORTAR: [*for no reason*] "One master passion in the breast, like Aaron's serpent, swallows all the rest." [*She and* LOIS *are murmuring during* KAREN WRIGHT's *entrance.* KAREN *is an attractive woman of twenty-eight, casually pleasant in manner, without sacrifice of warmth or dignity. She smiles at the girls, goes to the desk. With her entrance there is an immediate change in*

the manner of the girls: they are fond of her and they respect her. She gives
Mortar, *whose quotation has reached her, an annoyed look.*]
Lois: "Quo usque tandem *abutere* . . ."
Karen: [*automatically*] "Ab*utere*." [*Opens drawer in desk*] What's happened to your hair, Rosalie?
Rosalie: It got cut. Miss Wright.
Karen: [*smiling*] I can see that. A new style? Looks as though it has holes in it.
Evelyn: [*giggling*] I didn't mean to do it that bad, Mith Wright, but Rothalie'th got funny hair. I thaw a picture in the paper, and I wath trying to do it that way.
Rosalie: [*feels her hair, looks pathetically at* **Karen**] Oh, what shall I do. Miss Wright? [*Gesturing*] It's long here, and it's long here, and it's short here and—
Karen: Come up to my room later and I'll see if I can fix it for you.
Mrs. Mortar: And hereafter we'll have no more haircutting.
Karen: Helen, have you found your bracelet?
Helen: No, I haven't, and I've looked everywhere.
Karen: Have another look. It must be in your room somewhere. [**Mary** *comes in right, with her flowers in a vase.* **Karen** *looks at the flowers in surprise.*]
Mary: Good afternoon, Miss Wright. [*Sits down, looks at* **Karen**, *who is staring hard at the flowers.*]
Karen: Hello, Mary.
Mrs. Mortar: [*fluttering around*] Peggy has been reading Portia for us. [**Peggy** *sighs.*]
Karen: Peggy doesn't like Portia?
Mrs. Mortar: I don't think she quite appreciates it, but—
Karen: [*patting* **Peggy** *on the head*] I don't think I do either. Where'd you get those flowers, Mary?
Mrs. Mortar: She picked them for me. [*Hurriedly*] It made her a little late to class, but she heard me say I loved flowers, and she went to get them for me. [*With a sigh*] The first wildflowers of the season.
Karen: But not the very first, are they, Mary?
Mary: I don't know.
Karen: Where did you get them?
Mary: Near Conway's cornfield, I think.
Karen: It wasn't necessary to go so far. There was a bunch exactly like this in the garbage can this morning.

Mrs. Mortar: [*after a second*] Oh, I can't believe it! What a nasty thing to do! [*To* Mary] And I suppose you have just as fine an excuse for being an hour late to breakfast this morning, and last week — [*To* Karen] I haven't wanted to tell you these things before, but —

Karen: [*hurriedly, as a bell rings off stage*] There's the bell.

Lois: [*walking toward door*] Ad, ab, ante, in, de, inter, con, post, præ [*Looks up at* Karen] I *can't* seem to remember the rest.

Karen: Præ, pro, sub, super. Don't worry, Lois. You'll come out all right. [Lois *smiles, exits.* Mary *attempts to make a quick exit*] Wait a minute, Mary. [*Reluctantly* Mary *turns back as the girls file out.* Karen *moves the small chairs, clearing the room as she talks*] Mary, I've had the feeling — and I don't think I'm wrong — that the girls here are happy; that they like Miss Dobie and me, that they like the school. Do you think that's true?

Mary: Miss Wright, I have to get my Latin book.

Karen: I thought it was true until you came here a year ago. I don't think you're very happy here, and I'd like to find out why. [*Looks at* Mary, *waits for an answer, gets none, shakes her head*] Why, for example, do you find it necessary to lie to us so often?

Mary: [*without looking up*] I'm not lying. I went out walking and I saw the flowers and they looked pretty and I didn't know it was so late.

Karen: [*impatiently*] Stop it, Mary! I'm not interested in hearing that foolish story again. I know you got the flowers out of the garbage can. What I do want to know is why you feel you have to lie out of it.

Mary: I *did* pick the flowers near Conway's. You never believe me. You believe everybody but me. It's always like that. Everything I say you fuss at me about. Everything I do is wrong.

Karen: You know that isn't true. [*Goes to* Mary, *puts her arm around her, waits until the sobbing has stopped*] Look, Mary, look at me. [*Raises* Mary's *face with her hand*] Let's try to understand each other. If you feel that you *have* to take a walk, or that you just *can't* come to class, or that you'd like to go into the village by yourself, come and tell me — I'll try to understand. I don't say that I'll always agree that you should do exactly what you want to do, but I've had feelings like that, too — everybody has — and I won't be unreasonable about yours. But this way, this kind of lying you do, makes everything wrong.

Mary: [*looking steadily at* Karen] I got the flowers near Conway's cornfield.

Karen: [*looks at* Mary, *sighs, moves back toward desk and stands there for a moment*] Well, there doesn't seem to be any other way with you; you'll have to be punished. Take your recreation periods alone for the next

two weeks. No horseback riding and no hockey. Don't leave the
school grounds for any reason whatsoever. Is that clear?

MARY: [*carefully*] Saturday, too?

KAREN: Yes.

MARY: But you said I could go to the boat races.

KAREN: I'm sorry, but you can't go.

MARY: I'll tell my grandmother. I'll tell her how everybody treats me here
and the way I get punished for every little thing I do. I'll tell her, I'll—

MRS. MORTAR: Why, I'd slap her hands!

KAREN: [*turning back from door, ignoring* MRS. MORTAR'*s speech. To* MARY] Go
upstairs, Mary.

MARY: I don't feel well.

KAREN: [*wearily*] Go upstairs now.

MARY: I've got a pain. I've had it all morning. It hurts right here. [*Pointing
vaguely in the direction of her heart*] Really it does.

KAREN: Ask Miss Dobie to give you some hot water and bicarbonate of
soda.

MARY: It's a bad pain. I've never had it before. My heart! It's my heart! It's
stopping or something. I can't breathe. [*She takes a long breath and falls
awkwardly to the floor.*]

KAREN: [*sighs, shakes her head, kneels beside* MARY. To MRS. MORTAR] Ask
Martha to phone Joe.

MRS. MORTAR: [*going out*] Do you think—? Heart trouble is very serious
in a child. [KAREN *picks* MARY *up from the floor and carries her off right.
After a moment* MARTHA DOBIE *enters center. She is about the same age as*
KAREN. *She is a nervous, high-strung woman.*]

KAREN: [*enters right*] Did you get Joe?

MARTHA: [*nodding*] What happened to her? She was perfectly well a few
hours ago.

KAREN: She probably still is. I told her she couldn't go to the boat races
and she had a heart attack. [*Sits down at desk and begins to mark papers*]
She's a problem, that kid. Her latest trick was kidding your aunt out of
a sewing lesson with those faded flowers we threw out. Then she
threatened to go to her grandmother with some tale about being
mistreated.

MARTHA: And, please God, Grandma would believe her and take her away.

KAREN: Which would give the school a swell black eye. But we ought to
do something.

MARTHA: How about having a talk with Mrs. Tilford?

KAREN: [*smiling*] You want to do it? [MARTHA *shakes her head*] I hate to do it. She's been so nice to us. Anyway, it wouldn't do any good. She's too crazy about Mary to see her faults very clearly — and the kid knows it.

MARTHA: How about asking Joe to say something to her? She'd listen to him.

KAREN: That would be admitting that we can't do the job ourselves.

MARTHA: Well, we can't, and we might as well admit it. We've tried every-thing we can think of. She's had more attention than any other three kids put together. And we still haven't the faintest idea what goes on inside her head.

KAREN: She's a strange girl.

MARTHA: That's putting it mildly.

KAREN: [*laughs*] We always talk about her as if she were a grown woman.

MARTHA: It's not so funny. There's something the matter with the kid. That's been true ever since the first day she came. She causes trouble here; she's bad for the other girls. I don't know what it is — it's a feeling I've got that it's wrong somewhere —

KAREN: All right, all right, we'll talk it over with Joe. Now what about our other pet nuisance?

MARTHA: [*laughs*] My aunt the actress? What's she been up to now?

KAREN: Nothing unusual. Last night at dinner she was telling the girls about the time she lost her trunks in Butte, Montana, and how she gave her best performance of Rosalind during a hurricane. Today in the kitchen you could hear her on what Sir Henry said to her.

MARTHA: Wait until she does Hedda Gabler standing on one foot. Sir Henry taught her to do it that way. He said it was a test of great acting.

KAREN: You must have had a gay childhood.

MARTHA: [*bitterly*] Oh, I did. I did, indeed. God, how I used to hate all that —

KAREN: Couldn't we get rid of her soon, Martha? I hate to make it hard on you, but she really ought not to be here.

MARTHA: [*after a moment*] I know.

KAREN: We can scrape up enough money to send her away. Let's do it.

MARTHA: [*goes to her, affectionately pats her head*] You've been very patient about it. I'm sorry and I'll talk to her today. It'll probably be a week or two before she can be ready to leave. Is that all right?

KAREN: Of course. [*Looks at her watch*] Did you get Joe himself on the phone?

MARTHA: He was already on his way. Isn't he always on his way over here?

KAREN: [*laughs*] Well, I'm going to marry him, you know.

MARTHA: [*looking at her*] You haven't talked of marriage for a long time.

KAREN: I've talked of it with Joe.

MARTHA: Then you *are* thinking about it—soon?

KAREN: Perhaps when the term is over. By that time we ought to be out of debt, and the school should be paying for itself.

MARTHA: [*nervously playing with a book on the table*] Then we won't be taking our vacation together?

KAREN: Of course we will. The three of us.

MARTHA: I had been looking forward to someplace by the lake—just you and me—the way we used to at college.

KAREN: [*cheerfully*] Well, now there will be three of us. That'll be fun, too.

MARTHA: [*after a pause*] Why haven't you told me this before?

KAREN: I'm not telling you anything we haven't talked about often.

MARTHA: But you're talking about it as *soon* now.

KAREN: I'm glad to be able to. I've been in love with Joe a long time. [MARTHA, *crosses to window and stands looking out, her back to* KAREN. KAREN *finishes marking papers and rises*] It's a big day for the school. Rosalie's finally put an "l" in could.

MARTHA: [*not turning from window*] You really *are* going to leave, aren't you?

KAREN: I'm not going to leave, and you know it. Why do you say things like that? We agreed a long time ago that my marriage wasn't going to make any difference to the school.

MARTHA: But it will. You know it will. It can't help it.

KAREN: That's nonsense. Joe doesn't want me to give up here.

MARTHA: [*turning from window*] It's been so damned hard building this thing up, slaving and going without things to make ends meet—think of having a winter coat without holes in the lining again!—and now when we're getting on our feet, you're all ready to let it go to hell.

KAREN: This is a silly argument, Martha. Let's quit it. You haven't listened to a word I've said. I'm not getting married tomorrow, and when I do, it's not going to interfere with my work here. You're making something out of nothing.

MARTHA: It's going to be hard going on alone afterward.

KAREN: For God's sake, do you expect me to give up my marriage?

MARTHA: I don't mean that, but it's so—[*Door, center, opens and Doctor* JOSEPH CARDIN *comes in. He is a large, pleasant-looking, carelessly dressed man of about thirty-five.*]

CARDIN: Hello, darling. Hi, Martha. What's the best news?

MARTHA: Hello, Joe.

KAREN: We tried to get you on the phone. Come in and look at your little cousin.

CARDIN: What's the matter with her now?

KAREN: You'd better come and see her. She says she has a pain in her heart. [*Goes out, right.*]

CARDIN: [*stopping to light a cigarette*] Our little Mary pops up in every day's dispatches.

MARTHA: [*impatiently*] Go and see her. Heart attacks are nothing to play with.

CARDIN: [*looks at her*] Never played with one in my life. [*Exits right.*]

[MARTHA *walks around room and finally goes to stare out window.* MRS. MORTAR *enters right.*]

MRS. MORTAR: *I* was asked to leave the room. [MARTHA *pays no attention*] It seems that I'm not wanted in the room during the examination.

MARTHA: [*over her shoulder*] What difference does it make?

MRS. MORTAR: What difference does it make? Why, it was a deliberate snub.

MARTHA: There's very little pleasure in watching a man use a stethoscope.

MRS. MORTAR: Isn't it natural that the child should have me with her? Isn't it natural that an older woman should be present? [*No answer*] Very well, if you are so thick-skinned that you don't resent these things—

MARTHA: What are you talking about? Why, in the name of heaven, should *you* be with her?

MRS. MORTAR: It—it's customary for an older woman to be present during an examination.

MARTHA: [*laughs*] Tell that to Joe. Maybe he'll give you a job as duenna for his office.

MRS. MORTAR: It was I who saved Delia Lampert's life the time she had that heart attack in Buffalo. We almost lost her that time. Poor Delia! We went over to London together. She married Robert Laffonne. Not seven months later he left her and ran away with Eve Cloun, who was playing the Infant Phenomenon in Birmingham—

MARTHA: Console yourself. If you've seen one heart attack, you've seen them all.

MRS. MORTAR: So you don't resent your aunt being snubbed and humiliated?

MARTHA: Oh, Aunt Lily!

MRS. MORTAR: Karen is consistently rude to me, and you know it.

MARTHA: I know that she is very polite to you, and—what's more important—very patient.

MRS. MORTAR: Patient with me? *I*, who have worked my fingers to the bone!

MARTHA: Don't tell yourself that too often, Aunt Lily; you'll come to believe it.

MRS. MORTAR: I *know* it's true. Where could you have gotten a woman of my reputation to give these children voice lessons, elocution lessons? Patient with me! Here I've donated my services—

MARTHA: You are being paid.

MRS. MORTAR: That small thing! I used to earn twice that for one performance.

MARTHA: The gilded days. It was very extravagant of them to pay you so much. [*Suddenly tired of the whole thing*] You're not very happy here, are you, Aunt Lily?

MRS. MORTAR: Satisfied enough, I guess, for a poor relation.

MARTHA: [*makes a motion of distaste*] But you don't like the school or the farm or—

MRS. MORTAR: I told you at the beginning you shouldn't have bought a place like this. Burying yourself on a farm! You'll regret it.

MARTHA: We like it here. [*After a moment*] Aunt Lily, you've talked about London for a long time. Would you like to go over?

MRS. MORTAR: [*with a sigh*] It's been twenty years, and I shall never live to see it again.

MARTHA: Well, you can go any time you like. We can spare the money now, and it will do you a lot of good. You pick out the boat you want and I'll get the passage. [*She has been talking rapidly, anxious to end the whole thing*] Now that's all fixed. You'll have a grand time seeing all your old friends, and if you live sensibly I ought to be able to let you have enough to get along on. [*She begins to gather books, notebooks, and pencils.*]

MRS. MORTAR: [*slowly*] So you want me to leave?

MARTHA: That's not the way to put it. You've wanted to go ever since I can remember.

MRS. MORTAR: You're trying to get rid of me.

MARTHA: That's it. We don't want you around when we dig up the buried treasure.

MRS. MORTAR: So? You're turning me out? At my age! Nice, grateful girl you are.

MARTHA: Oh, my God, how can anybody deal with you? You're going where you want to go, and we'll be better off alone. That suits every-body. You complain about the farm, you complain about the school, you complain about Karen, and now you have what you want and you're still looking for something to complain about.

MRS. MORTAR: [*with dignity*] Please do not raise your voice.

MARTHA: You ought to be glad I don't do worse.

MRS. MORTAR: I absolutely refuse to be shipped off three thousand miles away. I'm not going to England. I shall go back to the stage. I'll write to my agents tomorrow, and as soon as they have something good for me—

MARTHA: The truth is I'd like you to leave soon. The three of us can't live together, and it doesn't make any difference whose fault it is.

MRS. MORTAR: You wish me to go tonight?

MARTHA: Don't act, Aunt Lily. Go as soon as you've found a place you like. I'll put the money in the bank for you tomorrow.

MRS. MORTAR: You think I'd take your money? I'd rather scrub floors first.

MARTHA: You'll change your mind.

MRS. MORTAR: I should have known by this time that the wise thing is to stay out of your way when *he's* in the house.

MARTHA: What are you talking about now?

MRS. MORTAR: Never mind. I should have known better. You always take your spite out on me.

MARTHA: Spite? [*Impatiently*] Oh, don't let's have any more of this today. I'm tired. I've been working since six o'clock this morning.

MRS. MORTAR: Any day that he's in the house is a bad day.

MARTHA: When *who* is in the house?

MRS. MORTAR: Don't think you're fooling me, young lady. I wasn't born yesterday.

MARTHA: Aunt Lily, the amount of disconnected unpleasantness that goes on in your head could keep a psychologist busy for years. Now go take your nap.

MRS. MORTAR: I know what I know. Every time that man comes into this house, you have a fit. It seems like you just can't stand the idea of them being together. God knows what you'll do when they get married. You're jealous of him, that's what it is.

MARTHA: [*her voice is tense and the previous attitude of good-natured irritation is gone*] I'm very fond of Joe, and you know it.

MRS. MORTAR: You're fonder of Karen, and I know that. And it's unnatural, just as unnatural as it can be. You don't like their being together. You were always like that even as a child. If you had a little girl friend, you always got mad when she liked anybody else. Well, you'd better get a beau of your own now—a woman of your age.

MARTHA: The sooner you get out of here the better. You are making me sick and I won't stand for it any longer. I want you to leave—[*At this* *point there is a sound outside the large doors center.* MARTHA *breaks off. After a moment she crosses to the door and opens it.* EVELYN *and* PEGGY *are to be seen on the staircase. For a second she stands still as they stop and look at her. Then, afraid that her anger with her aunt will color anything she might say to the children, she crosses the room again and stands with her back to them.*]

MARTHA: What were you doing outside the door?

EVELYN: [*hurriedly*] We were going upthtairth, Mith Dobie.

PEGGY: We came down to see how Mary was.

MARTHA: And you stopped long enough to see how we were. Did you deliberately listen?

PEGGY: We didn't mean to. We heard voices and we couldn't help —

MRS. MORTAR: [*a social tone*] Eavesdropping is something nice young ladies just don't do.

MARTHA: [*turning to face the children*] Go upstairs now. We'll talk about this later. [*Slowly shuts door as they begin to climb the stairs.*]

MRS. MORTAR: You mean to say you're not going to do anything about that? [*No answer. She laughs nastily*] That's the trouble with these new-fangled notions of discipline and —

MARTHA: [*thoughtfully*] You know, it's really bad having you around children.

MRS. MORTAR: What exactly does that mean?

MARTHA: It means that I don't like them hearing the things you say. Oh, I'll "do something about it," but the truth is that this is their home, and things shouldn't be said in it that they can't hear. When you're at your best, you're not for tender ears.

MRS. MORTAR: So now it's my fault, is it? Just as I said, whenever he's in the house you think you can take it out on me. You've got to have some way to let out steam and — [*Door opens, right, and* CARDIN *comes in.*]

MARTHA: How is Mary? [MRS. MORTAR, *head in air, gives* MARTHA *a malicious half-smile and exits center.*]

MRS. MORTAR: Good day, Joseph.

CARDIN: What's the matter with the Duchess?

MARTHA: Just keeping her hand in, in case Sir Henry's watching her from above. What about Mary?

CARDIN: Nothing. Absolutely nothing.

MARTHA: [*sighs*] I thought so.

CARDIN: I could have managed a better faint than that when I was six years old.

MARTHA: Nothing the matter with her at all?

CARDIN: [*laughs*] No, ma'am, not a thing. Just a little something she thought up.

MARTHA: But it's such a silly thing to do. She knew we'd have you in. [*Sighs*] Maybe she's not so bright. Any idiots in your family, Joe? Any inbreeding?

CARDIN: Don't blame her on me. It's another side of the family. [*Laughs*] You can look at Aunt Amelia and tell: old New England stock, never married out of Boston, still thinks honor is honor and dinner's at eight. Yes, ma'am, we're a proud old breed.

MARTHA: The Jukes were an old family, too. Look, Joe, have you any idea what is the matter with Mary? I mean, has she always been like this?

CARDIN: She's always been a honey. Aunt Amelia's spoiling hasn't helped any, either.

MARTHA: We're reaching the end of our rope with her. This kind of thing—

CARDIN: [*looking at her*] Aren't you taking it too seriously?

MARTHA: [*after a second*] I guess I am. But you stay around kids long enough and you won't know what to take seriously, either. But I do think somebody ought to talk to Mrs. Tilford about her.

CARDIN: You wouldn't be meaning me now, would you, Miss Dobie?

MARTHA: Well, Karen and I were talking about it this afternoon and—

CARDIN: Listen, friend, I'm marrying Karen, but I'm not writing Mary Tilford in the contract. [MARTHA *moves slightly.* CARDIN *takes her by the shoulders and turns her around to face him again. His face is grave, his voice gentle*] Forget Mary for a minute. You and I have got something to fight about. Every time anything's said about marrying—about Karen marrying me—you—I'm fond of you. I always thought you liked me. What is it? I know how fond you are of Karen, but our marriage oughtn't to make a great deal of difference—

MARTHA: [*pushing his hands from her shoulders*] God damn you. I wish—[*She puts her face in her hands.* CARDIN *watches her in silence, mechanically lighting a cigarette. When she takes her hands from her face, she holds them out to him. Contritely*] Joe, please, I'm sorry. I'm a fool, a nasty, bitter—

CARDIN: [*takes her hands in one of his, patting them with his other hand*] Aw, shut up. [*He puts an arm around her, and she leans her head against his lapel. They are standing like that when* KAREN *comes in, right.*]

MARTHA: [*to* KAREN, *as she wipes her eyes*] Your friend's got a nice shoulder to weep on.

KAREN: He's an admirable man in every way. Well, the angel child is now putting her clothes back on.

MARTHA: The angel child's influence is abroad even while she's unconscious. Her roommates were busy listening at the door while Aunt Lily and I were yelling at each other.

KAREN: We'll have to move those girls away from one another. [*A bell rings from the rear of the house.*]

MARTHA: That's my class. I'll send Peggy and Evelyn down. You talk to them.

KAREN: All right. [*As* MARTHA *exits center,* KAREN *goes toward door, right. As she passes* CARDIN *she kisses him*] Mary! [MARY *opens door, comes in, stands buttoning the neck of her dress.*]

CARDIN: [*to* MARY] How's it feel to be back from the grave?

MARY: My heart hurts.

CARDIN: [*laughing. To* KAREN] Science has failed. Try a hairbrush.

MARY: It's *my* heart, and it hurts.

KAREN: Sit down.

MARY: I want to see my grandmother. I want to— [EVELYN *and* PEGGY *timidly enter center.*]

KAREN: Sit down, girls, I want to talk to you.

PEGGY: We're awfully sorry, really. We just didn't think and—

KAREN: I'm sorry too, Peggy. [*Thoughtfully*] You and Evelyn never used to do things like this. We'll have to separate you three.

EVELYN: Ah, Mith Wright, we've been together almotht a year.

KAREN: Peggy, you will move into Lois's room, and Lois will move in with Evelyn. Mary will go in with Rosalie.

MARY: Rosalie hates me.

KAREN: I can't imagine Rosalie hating anyone.

MARY: [*starting to cry*] And it's all because I had a pain. If anybody else was sick they'd be put to bed and petted. You're always mean to me. I get blamed and punished for everything. [*To* CARDIN] I do, Cousin Joe. All the time for everything. [MARY *by now is crying violently and as* KAREN *half moves toward her,* CARDIN, *who has been frowning, picks* MARY *up and puts her down on the couch.*]

CARDIN: You've been unpleasant enough to Miss Wright. Lie here until you've stopped working yourself into a fit. [*Picks up his hat and bag, smiles at* KAREN] I've got to go now. She's not going to hurt herself crying. The next time she faints, I'd wait until she got tired lying on the floor. [*Passing* MARY, *he pats her head. She jerks away from him.*]

KAREN: Wait a minute. I'll walk to the car with you. [*To girls*] Go up now and move your things. Tell Lois to get her stuff ready. [*She and* CARDIN *exit center. A second after the door is closed,* MARY *springs up and throws a cushion at the door.*]

EVELYN: Don't do that. She'll hear you.

MARY: Who cares if she does? [*Kicks table*] And she can hear that, too. [*Small ornament falls off table and breaks on floor.* EVELYN *and* PEGGY *gasp.*]

EVELYN: [*frightened*] Now what are you going to do?

PEGGY: [*stooping down in a vain effort to pick up the pieces*] You'll get the devil now. Dr. Cardin gave it to Miss Wright. I guess it was kind of a lover's gift. People get awfully angry about a lover's gift.

MARY: Oh, leave it alone. She'll never know we did it.

PEGGY: *We* didn't do it. You did it yourself.

MARY: And what will you do if I say *we* did do it? [*Laughs*] Never mind, I'll think of something else. The wind could've knocked it over.

EVELYN: Yeh. She'th going to believe that one.

MARY: Oh, stop worrying about it. I'll get out of it.

EVELYN: Did you really have a pain?

MARY: I fainted, didn't I?

PEGGY: I wish I could faint sometimes. I've never even worn glasses, like Rosalie.

MARY: A lot it'll get you to faint.

EVELYN: What did Mith Wright do to you when the clath left?

MARY: Told me I couldn't go to the boat races.

EVELYN: Whew!

PEGGY: But we'll remember everything that happens and we'll give you all the souvenirs and things.

MARY: I won't let you go if I can't go. But I'll find some way to go. What were *you* doing?

PEGGY: We came down to see what was happening to you, but the doors were closed and we could hear Miss Dobie and Mortar having an awful row. Then Miss Dobie opens the door and there we were.

MARY: And a lot of crawling and crying you both did too, I bet.

EVELYN: We were thort of thorry about lithening. I gueth it wathn't—

MARY: Ah, you're always sorry about everything. What were they saying?

PEGGY: What was who saying?

MARY: Dobie and Mortar, silly.

PEGGY: [*evasively*] Just talking, I guess.

EVELYN: Fighting, you mean.

MARY: About what?

EVELYN: Well, they were talking about Mortar going away to England and—

PEGGY: You know, it really wasn't very nice to've listened, and I think it's worse to tell.

MARY: You do, do you? You just don't tell me and see what happens. [PEGGY *sighs*.]

EVELYN: Mortar got awful thore at that and thaid they juth wanted to get rid of her, and then they thtarted talking about Dr. Cardin.

MARY: What about him?

PEGGY: We'd better get started moving; Miss Wright will be back first thing we know.

MARY: [*fiercely*] Shut up! Go on, Evelyn.

EVELYN: They're going to be married.

MARY: Everybody knows that.

PEGGY: But everybody doesn't know that Miss Dobie doesn't want them to get married. How do you like that? [*The door opens and* ROSALIE WELLS *sticks her head in.*]

ROSALIE: I have a class soon. If you're going to move your things—

MARY: Close that door, you idiot. [ROSALIE *closes door, stands near it*] What do you want?

ROSALIE: I'm trying to tell you. If you're going to move your things—not that I want you in with me—you'd better start right now. Miss Wright's coming in a minute.

MARY: Who cares if she is?

ROSALIE: [*starts for door*] I'm just telling you for your own good.

PEGGY: [*getting up*] We're coming.

MARY: No. Let Rosalie move our things.

ROSALIE: You crazy?

PEGGY: [*nervously*] It's all right. Evelyn and I'll get your things. Come on, Evelyn.

MARY: Trying to get out of telling me, huh? Well, you won't get out of it that way. Sit down and stop being such a sissy. Rosalie, you go on up and move my things and don't say a word about our being down here.

ROSALIE: And who was your French maid yesterday, Mary Tilford?

MARY: [*laughing*] You'll do for today. Now go on, Rosalie, and fix our things.

ROSALIE: You crazy?

MARY: And the next time we go into town, I'll let you wear my gold locket and buckle. You'll like that, won't you Rosalie?

ROSALIE: [*draws back, moves her hands nervously*] I don't know what you're talking about.

MARY: Oh, I'm not talking about anything in particular. You just run along now and remind me the next time to get my buckle and locket for you.

ROSALIE: [*stares at her a moment*] All right, I'll do it this time, but just 'cause I got a good disposition. But don't think you're going to boss me around, Mary Tilford.

MARY: [*smiling*] No, indeed. [ROSALIE *starts for door*] And get the things done neatly, Rosalie. Don't muss my white linen bloomers— [*The door slams as* MARY *laughs.*]

EVELYN: Now what do you think of that? What made her tho agreeable?

MARY: Oh, a little secret we got. Go on, now, what else did they say?

PEGGY: Well, Mortar said that Dobie was jealous of them, and that she was like that when she was a little girl, and that she'd better get herself a beau of her own because it was unnatural, and that she never wanted anybody to like Miss Wright, and that was unnatural. Boy! Did Miss Dobie get sore at that!

EVELYN: Then we didn't hear any more. Peggy dropped a book.

MARY: What'd she mean Dobie was jealous?

PEGGY: What's unnatural?

EVELYN: Un for not. Not natural.

PEGGY: It's funny, because everybody gets married.

MARY: A lot of people don't—they're too ugly.

PEGGY: [*jumps up, claps her hand to her mouth*] Oh, my God! Rosalie'll find that copy of *Mademoiselle de Maupin*. She'll blab like the dickens.

MARY: Ah, she won't say a word.

EVELYN: Who getth the book when we move?

MARY: You can have it. That's what I was doing this morning—finishing it. There's one part in it—

PEGGY: What part? [MARY *laughs.*]

EVELYN: Well, what wath it?

MARY: Wait until you read it.

PEGGY: It's a shame about being moved. I've got to go in with Helen, and she blows her nose all night. Lois told me.

MARY: It was a dirty trick making us move. She just wants to see how much fun she can take away from me. She hates me.

PEGGY: No, she doesn't, Mary. She treats you just like the rest of us— almost better.

MARY: That's right, stick up for your crush. Take her side against mine.

PEGGY: I didn't mean it that way.

EVELYN: [*looks at her watch*] We'd better get upthtairth.

MARY: I'm not going.

PEGGY: Rosalie isn't so bad.

EVELYN: What you going to do about the vathe?

MARY: I don't care about Rosalie and I don't care about the vase. I'm not going to be here.

EVELYN and PEGGY: [*together*] Not going to be here! What do you mean?

MARY: [*calmly*] I'm going home.

PEGGY: Oh, Mary—

EVELYN: You can't do that.

Mary: Can't I? You just watch. [*Begins to walk around the room*] I'm not staying here. I'm going home and tell Grandma I'm not staying anymore. [*Smiles to herself*] I'll tell her I'm not happy. They're scared of Grandma — she helped 'em when they first started, you know — and when she tells 'em something, believe me they'll sit up and listen. They can't get away with treating me like this, and they don't have to think they can.

Peggy: [*appalled*] You just going to walk out like that?

Evelyn: What you going to tell your grandmother?

Mary: Oh, who cares? I'll think of something to tell her. I can always do it better on the spur of the moment.

Peggy: She'll send you right back.

Mary: You let me worry about that. Grandma's very fond of me on account my father was her favorite son. I can manage *her* all right.

Peggy: I don't think you ought to go, really, Mary. It's just going to make an awful lot of trouble.

Evelyn: What'th going to happen about the vathe?

Mary: Say I did it — it doesn't make a bit of difference anymore to me. Now listen, you two got to help. They won't miss me before dinner if you make Rosalie shut the door and keep it shut. Now, I'll go through the field to French's, and then I can get the bus to Homestead.

Evelyn: How you going to get to the thtreetcar?

Mary: Taxi, idiot.

Peggy: How are you going to get out of here in the first place?

Mary: I'm going to walk out. You know where the front door is? Well, I'm going right out that front door.

Evelyn: Gee, I wouldn't have the nerve.

Mary: Of course you wouldn't. You'd let 'em do anything to you they want. Well, they can't do it to me. Who's got any money?

Evelyn: Not me. Not a thent.

Mary: I've got to have at least a dollar for the taxi and a dime for the bus.

Evelyn: And where you going to find it?

Peggy: See? Why don't you just wait until your allowance comes Monday, and then you can go anyplace you want. Maybe by that time —

Mary: I'm going today. *Now.*

Evelyn: You can't *walk* to Lanthet.

Mary: [*goes to* Peggy] You've got money. You've got two dollars and twenty-five cents.

Peggy: I — I —

Mary: Go get it for me.

PEGGY: No! No! I won't get it for you.

EVELYN: You can't have *that* money, Mary—

MARY: Get it for me.

PEGGY: [*her voice is scared*] I won't. I won't. Mamma doesn't send me much allowance—not half as much as the rest of you get—I saved this so long—you took it from me last time—

EVELYN: Ah, she wantth that bithycle tho bad.

PEGGY: I haven't gone to the movies, I haven't had any candy, I haven't had anything the rest of you get all the time. It took me so long to save that and I—

MARY: Go upstairs and get me the money.

PEGGY: [*hysterically, backing away from her*] I won't. I won't. I won't. [MARY *makes a sudden move for her, grabs her left arm, and jerks it back, hard and expertly.* PEGGY *screams softly.* EVELYN *tries to take* MARY'S *arm away. Without releasing her hold on* PEGGY, MARY *slaps* EVELYN'S *face.* EVELYN *begins to cry.*]

MARY: Just say when you've had enough.

PEGGY: [*softly, stiflingly*] All—all right—I'll get it. [MARY *nods her head as the curtain falls.*]

CURTAIN

Act Two

Scene I

Scene: *Living room at* Mrs. Tilford's. *It is a formal room, without being cold or elegant. The furniture is old, but excellent. The exit to the hall is left; glass doors, right, lead to a dining room that cannot be seen.*

At rise: *Stage is empty. Voices are heard in the hall.*

AGATHA: [*offstage*] What are *you* doing here? Well, come on in—don't stand there gaping at me. Have they given you a holiday or did you just decide you'd get a better dinner here? [AGATHA *enters left, followed by* MARY. AGATHA *is a sharp-faced maid, not young, with a querulous voice*] Can't you even say hello?

MARY: Hello, Agatha. You didn't give me a chance. Where's Grandma?

AGATHA: Why aren't you in school? Look at your face and clothes. Where have you been?

MARY: I got a little dirty coming home. I walked part of the way through the woods.

AGATHA: Why didn't you put on your middy blouse and your old brown coat?

MARY: Oh, stop asking me questions. Where's Grandma?

AGATHA: Where ought any clean person be at this time of day? She's taking a bath.

MARY: Is anybody coming for dinner?

AGATHA: She didn't say anything about you coming.

MARY: How could she, stupid? She didn't know.

AGATHA: Then what are you doing here?

MARY: Leave me alone. I don't feel well.

AGATHA: Why don't you feel well? Who ever heard of a person going for a walk in the woods when they didn't feel well?

MARY: Oh, leave me alone. I came home because I was sick.

AGATHA: You look all right.

MARY: But I don't feel all right. I can't even come home without everybody nagging at me.

AGATHA: Don't think you're fooling me, young lady. You might pull the wool over some people's eyes, but—I bet you've been up to something again. [*Stares suspiciously at* MARY] Well, you wait right here till I tell your grandmother. And if you feel so sick, you certainly won't want any dinner. A good dose of rhubarb and soda will fix you up. [*Exits left.*]

[MARY *makes a face in the direction* AGATHA *has gone and stops sniffling. She looks nervously around the room, then goes to a low mirror and tries several experiments with her face in an attempt to make it look sick and haggard.* MRS. TILFORD, *followed by* AGATHA, *enters left.* MRS. TILFORD *is a large, dignified woman in her sixties, with a pleasant, strong face.*]

AGATHA: [*to* MRS. TILFORD, *as she follows her into the room*] Why didn't you put some cold water on your chest? Do you want to catch your death of cold at your age? Did you have to hurry so?

MRS. TILFORD: Mary, what are you doing home? [MARY *rushes to her and buries her head in* MRS. TILFORD'*s dress, crying.* MRS. TILFORD *pats her head, then puts an arm around her and leads her to a sofa.*]

MRS. TILFORD: Never mind, dear; now stop crying and tell me what is the matter.

MARY: [*gradually stops crying, fondling* MRS. TILFORD'*s hand*] It's so good to see you, Grandma. You didn't come to visit me all last week.

MRS. TILFORD: I was coming tomorrow.

MARY: I missed you so. [*Smiling up at* MRS. TILFORD] I was awful homesick.

MRS. TILFORD: I'm glad that's all it was. I was frightened when Agatha said you were not well.

AGATHA: Did I say that? I said she needed a good dose of rhubarb and soda. Most likely she only came home for Wednesday night fudge cake.

MRS. TILFORD: We all get homesick. But how did you get here? Did Miss Karen drive you over?

MARY: I—I walked most of the way, and then a lady gave me a ride and— [*Looks timidly at* MRS. TILFORD.]

AGATHA: Did she have to walk through the woods in her very best coat?

MRS. TILFORD: Mary! Do you mean you left without permission?

MARY: [*nervously*] I ran away, Grandma. They didn't know—

MRS. TILFORD: That was a very bad thing to do, and they'll be worried. Agatha, phone Miss Wright and tell her Mary is here. John will drive her back before dinner.

MARY: [*as* AGATHA *starts toward telephone*] No, Grandma, don't do that. Please don't do that. Please let me stay.

MRS. TILFORD: But, darling, you can't leave school anytime you please.

MARY: Oh, please. Grandma, don't send me back right away. You don't know how they'll punish me.

MRS. TILFORD: I don't think they'll be that angry. Come, you're acting like a foolish little girl.

MARY: [*hysterically, as she sees* AGATHA *about to pick up the telephone*] Grandma! Please! I can't go back! I can't! They'll kill me! They will, Grandma! They'll kill me! [MRS. TILFORD *and* AGATHA *stare at* MARY *in amazement. She puts her head in* MRS. TILFORD'*s lap and sobs.*]

MRS. TILFORD: [*motioning with a hand for* AGATHA *to leave the room*] Never mind phoning now, Agatha.

AGATHA: If you're going to let her—[MRS. TILFORD *repeats the gesture.* AGATHA *exits, right.*]

MRS. TILFORD: Stop crying, Mary.

MARY: It's so nice here. Grandma.

MRS. TILFORD: I'm glad you like being home with me, but at your age you can hardly—What made you say such a terrible thing about Miss Wright and Miss Dobie? You know they wouldn't hurt you.

MARY: Oh, but they would. They—I—[*Breaks off, looks around as if hunting for a clue*] I fainted today!

MRS. TILFORD: Fainted?

MARY: Yes, I did. My heart—I had a pain in my heart. I couldn't help having a pain in my heart, and when I fainted right in class, they called Cousin Joe and he said I didn't. He said it was maybe only that I ate my breakfast too fast and Miss Wright blamed me for it.

MRS. TILFORD: [*relieved*] I'm sure if Joseph said it wasn't serious, it wasn't.

MARY: But I did have a pain in my heart—honest.

MRS. TILFORD: Have you still got it?

MARY: I guess I haven't got it much anymore, but I feel a little weak, and I was so scared of Miss Wright being so mean to me just because I was sick.

MRS. TILFORD: Scared of Karen? Nonsense. It's perfectly possible that you had a pain, but if you had really been sick your Cousin Joseph would certainly have known it. It's not nice to frighten people by pretending to be sick when you aren't.

MARY: I didn't *want* to be sick, but I'm always getting punished for everything.

MRS. TILFORD: [*gently*] You mustn't imagine things like that, child, or you'll
grow up to be a very unhappy woman. I'm not going to scold you
anymore for coming home this time, though I suppose I should. Run
along upstairs and wash your face and change your dress, and after
dinner John will drive you back. Run along.

MARY: [*happily*] I can stay for dinner?

MRS. TILFORD: Yes.

MARY: Maybe I could stay till the first of the week. Saturday's your
birthday and I could be here with you.

MRS. TILFORD: We don't celebrate my birthday, dear. You'll have to go back
to school after dinner.

MARY: But—[*She hesitates, then goes up to* MRS. TILFORD *and puts her arms
around the older woman's neck. Softly*] How much do you love me?

MRS. TILFORD: [*smiling*] As much as all the words in all the books in all the
world.

MARY: Remember when I was little and you used to tell me that right
before I went to sleep? And it was a rule nobody could say another
single word after you finished? You used to say "Wor-rr-ld," and then I
had to shut my eyes tight. I miss you an awful lot. Grandma.

MRS. TILFORD: And I miss you, but I'm afraid my Latin is too rusty—
you'll learn it better in school.

MARY: But couldn't I stay out the rest of this term? After the summer
maybe I won't mind it so much. I'll study hard, honest, and—

MRS. TILFORD: You're an earnest little coaxer, but it's out of the question.
Back you go tonight. [*Gives* MARY *a playful slap*] Let's not have any
more talk about it now, and let's have no more running away from
school ever.

MARY: [*slowly*] Then I really have to go back there tonight?

MRS. TILFORD: Of course.

MARY: You don't love me. You don't care whether they kill me or not.

MRS. TILFORD: Mary.

MARY: You don't! You don't! You don't care what happens to me.

MRS. TILFORD: [*sternly*] But I *do* care that you're talking this way.

MARY: I'm sorry I said that. Grandma. I didn't mean to hurt your feelings.
[*Puts her arms around* MRS. TILFORD*'s neck*] Forgive me?

MRS. TILFORD: What made you talk like that?

MARY: [*in a whisper*] I'm scared, Grandma, I'm scared. They'll do dreadful
things to me.

MRS. TILFORD: Dreadful? Nonsense. They'll punish you for running away.
You deserve to be punished.

MARY: It's not that. It's not anything I do. It never is. They—they just
punish me anyhow, just like they got something against me. I'm afraid
of them. Grandma.

MRS. TILFORD: That's ridiculous. What have they ever done to you that is
so terrible?

MARY: A lot of things—all the time. Miss Wright says I can't go to the
boat races and—[*Realizing the inadequacy of this reply, she breaks off,
hesitates, and finally stammers*] It's—it's after what happened today.

MRS. TILFORD: You mean something else besides your naughtiness in
pretending to faint and then running away?

MARY: I *did* faint. I didn't pretend. They just said that to make me feel bad.
Anyway, it wasn't anything that I did.

MRS. TILFORD: What was it, then?

MARY: I can't tell you.

MRS. TILFORD: Why?

MARY: [*sulkily*] Because you're just going to take their part.

MRS. TILFORD: [*a little annoyed*] Very well. Now run upstairs and get ready
for dinner.

MARY: It was—it was all about Miss Dobie and Mrs. Mortar. They were
talking awful things and Peggy and Evelyn heard them and Miss
Dobie found out, and then they made us move our rooms.

MRS. TILFORD: What has that to do with you? I don't understand a word
you're saying.

MARY: They made us move our rooms. They said we couldn't be together
anymore. They're afraid to have us near them, that's what it is, and
they're taking it out on me. They're scared of you.

MRS. TILFORD: For a little girl you're imagining a lot of big things. Why
should they be scared of me?

MARY: They're afraid you'll find out.

MRS. TILFORD: Find out what?

MARY: [*vaguely*] Things.

MRS. TILFORD: Run along, Mary.

MARY: [*slowly starting for door*] All right. But there're a lot of things.
They have secrets or something, and they're afraid I'll find out and
tell you.

MRS. TILFORD: There's not necessarily anything wrong with people having
secrets.

MARY: But they've got funny ones. Peggy and Evelyn heard Mrs. Mortar telling Miss Dobie that she was jealous of Miss Wright marrying Cousin Joe.

MRS. TILFORD: You shouldn't repeat things like that.

MARY: But that's what she said, Grandma. She said it was unnatural for a girl to feel that way.

MRS. TILFORD: What?

MARY: I'm just telling you what she said. She said there was something funny about it, and that Miss Dobie had always been like that, even when she was a little girl, and that it was unnatural—

MRS. TILFORD: Stop using that silly word, Mary.

MARY: [*vaguely realizing that she is on the right track, hurries on*] But that was the word *she* kept using, Grandma, and then they got mad and told Mrs. Mortar she'd have to get out.

MRS. TILFORD: That was probably not the reason at all.

MARY: [*nodding vigorously*] I bet it was, because honestly. Miss Dobie does get cranky and mean every time Cousin Joe comes, and today I heard her say to him: "God damn you," and then she said she was just a jealous fool and—

MRS. TILFORD: You have picked up some fine words, haven't you, Mary?

MARY: That's just what she said. Grandma, and one time Miss Dobie was crying in Miss Wright's room, and Miss Wright was trying to stop her, and she said that all right, maybe she wouldn't get married right away if—

MRS. TILFORD: How do you know all this?

MARY: We couldn't help hearing because they—I mean Miss Dobie—was talking awful loud, and their room is right next to ours.

MRS. TILFORD: Whose room?

MARY: Miss Wright's room, I mean, and you can just ask Peggy and Evelyn whether we didn't hear. Almost always Miss Dobie comes in after we go to bed and stays a long time. I guess that's why they want to get rid of us—of me—because we hear things. That's why they're making us move our room, and they punish me all the time for—

MRS. TILFORD: For eavesdropping, I should think. [*She has said this mechanically. With nothing definite in her mind, she is making an effort to conceal the fact that* MARY'*s description of the life at school has worried her*] Well, now I think we've had enough gossip, don't you? Dinner's almost ready, and I can't eat with a girl who has such a dirty face.

MARY: [*softly*] I've heard other things, too. I've heard other things. Plenty of other things. Grandma.

MRS. TILFORD: What things?

MARY: Bad things.

MRS. TILFORD: Well, what were they?

MARY: I can't tell you.

MRS. TILFORD: Mary, you're annoying me very much. If you have anything to say, then say it and stop acting silly.

MARY: I mean I can't say it out loud.

MRS. TILFORD: There couldn't possibly be anything so terrible that you couldn't say it out loud. Now either tell the truth or be still.

MARY: Well, a lot of things I don't understand. But it's awful, and sometimes they fight and then they make up, and Miss Dobie cries and Miss Wright gets mad, and then they make up again, and there are funny noises and we get scared.

MRS. TILFORD: Noises? I suppose you girls have a happy time imagining a murder.

MARY: And we've seen things, too. Funny things. [*Sees the impatience of her grandmother*] I'd tell you, but I got to whisper it.

MRS. TILFORD: Why must you whisper it?

MARY: I don't know. I just got to. [*Climbs on the sofa next to* MRS. TILFORD *and begins whispering. At first the whisper is slow and hesitant, but it gradually works up to fast, excited talking. In the middle of it* MRS. TILFORD *stops her.*]

MRS. TILFORD: [*trembling*] Do you know what you're saying? [*Without answering,* MARY *goes back to the whispering until the older woman takes her by the shoulders and turns her around to stare in her face*] Mary! Are you telling me the truth?

MARY: Honest, honest. You just ask Peggy and Evelyn and—[*After a moment* MRS. TILFORD *gets up and begins to pace about the room. She is no longer listening to* MARY, *who keeps up a running fire of conversation*] They know too. And maybe there're other kids who know, but we've always been frightened and so we didn't ask, and one night I was going to go and find out, but I got scared and we went to bed early so we wouldn't hear, but sometimes I couldn't help it, but we never talked about it much, because we thought they'd find out and—Oh, Grandma, don't make me go back to that awful place.

MRS. TILFORD: [*abstractedly*] What? [*Starts to move about again.*]

MARY: Don't make me go back to that place. I just couldn't stand it anymore. Really, Grandma, I'm so unhappy there, and if only I could stay out the rest of the term, why, then—

MRS. TILFORD: [*makes irritated gesture*] Be still a minute. [*After a moment*] You can stay here tonight.

MARY: [*hugging* MRS. TILFORD] You're the nicest, loveliest grandma in all the world. You—you're not mad at me?

MRS. TILFORD: I'm not mad at you. Now get ready for dinner. [MARY *kisses her and runs happily out left.* MRS. TILFORD *stands staring after her for a long moment. Then, very slowly, she puts on her eyeglasses and crosses to the phone. She dials a number*] Is Miss Wright—is Miss Wright in? [*Waits a second, hurriedly puts down the receiver*] Never mind, never mind. [*Dials another number*] Dr. Cardin, please. Mrs. Tilford. [*She remains absolutely motionless while she waits. When she does speak, her voice is low and tense*] Joseph? Joseph? Can you come to see me right away? Yes, I'm perfectly well. No, but it's important, Joseph, very important. I must see you right away. I—I can't tell you over the phone. Can't you come sooner? It's not about Mary's fainting—I said it's not about Mary, Joseph; in one way it's about Mary—[*Suddenly quiet*] But will the hospital take so long? Very well, Joseph, make it as soon as you can. [*Hangs up the receiver, sits for a moment undecided. Then, taking a breath, she dials another number*] Mrs. Munn, please. This is Mrs. Tilford. Miriam? This is Amelia Tilford. Could you come over right away? I want some advice—I want to tell you—Thank you.

CURTAIN

Scene II

Scene: *The same as Scene I. The curtain has been lowered to mark the passing, of a few hours.*

At rise: MARY *is lying on the floor playing with a puzzle.* AGATHA *appears lugging blankets and pillows across the room. Almost at the door, she stops and gives* MARY *an annoyed look.*

AGATHA: And see to it that she doesn't get my good quilt all dirty, and let her wear your green pajamas.
MARY: Who?
AGATHA: Who? Rosalie Wells is coming over to spend the night with you.
MARY: You mean she's going to sleep *here*?
AGATHA: You heard me.
MARY: What for?
AGATHA: Do I know all the crazy things that are happening around here? Mrs. Munn comes over and then they phone Mrs. Wells all the way to New York, three dollars and eighty-five cents and families starving, and Mrs. Wells wanted to know if Rosalie could stay here until tomorrow.
MARY: [*relieved*] Oh. Couldn't Evelyn Munn come instead?
AGATHA: Sure. We'll have the whole town over to entertain you.
MARY: I won't let Rosalie Wells wear my new pajamas.
AGATHA: [*exits as the front doorbell rings*] Don't tell me what you won't do. You'll act like a lady for once in your life. [*Offstage*] Come on in, Rosalie. Just go on in there and make yourself at home. Have you had your dinner?
ROSALIE: [*offstage*] Good evening. Yes'm.
AGATHA: [*offstage*] Hang up your pretty coat. Have you had your bath?
ROSALIE: [*offstage*] Yes, ma'am. This morning.
AGATHA: [*offstage*] Well, you better have another one. [*She is climbing the stairs as* ROSALIE *comes into the room.* MARY, *lying in front of the couch, is hidden from her. Gingerly* ROSALIE *sits down on a chair.*]
MARY: [*softly*] Whooooooo. [ROSALIE *jumps*] Whooooooo. [ROSALIE, *frightened, starts hurriedly for the door.* MARY *sits up, laughs*] You're a goose.
ROSALIE: [*belligerently*] Oh, so it's you. Well, who likes to hear funny noises at night? You could have been a werewolf.
MARY: A werewolf sure wouldn't want you.
ROSALIE: You know everything, don't you? [MARY *laughs.* ROSALIE *comes over, stands staring at puzzle*] Isn't it funny about school?

MARY: What's funny about it?

ROSALIE: Don't act like you can come home every night.

MARY: Maybe I can from now on. [*Rolls over on her back luxuriously*] Maybe I'm never going back.

ROSALIE: Am I going back? I don't want to stay home.

MARY: What'll you give to know?

ROSALIE: Nothing. I'll ask Mamma.

MARY: Will you give me a free T.L. if I tell you?

ROSALIE: [*thinks for a moment*] All right. Lois Fisher told Helen that you were very smart,

MARY: That's an old one. I won't take it.

ROSALIE: You got to take it.

MARY: Nope.

ROSALIE: [*laughs*] You don't know, anyway.

MARY: I know what I heard, and I know Grandma phoned your mother in New York. You're just going to spend the night here.

ROSALIE: But what's happened? Peggy and Helen and Evelyn and Lois went home tonight, too. Do you think somebody's got scarlet fever or something?

MARY: No.

ROSALIE: Do *you* know what it is? How'd you find out? [*No answer*] You're always pretending you know everything. You're just faking. [*Flounces away*] Never mind, don't bother telling me. I think curiosity is very unladylike, anyhow. I have no concern with your silly secrets.

MARY: Suppose I told you that I just may have said that you were in on it?

ROSALIE: In on what?

MARY: The secret. Suppose I told you that I *may have* said that you told me about it?

ROSALIE: Why, Mary Tilford! You can't do a thing like that. I didn't tell you about anything. [MARY *laughs*] Did you tell your grandmother such a thing?

MARY: Maybe.

ROSALIE: Did you?

MARY: Maybe.

ROSALIE: Well, I'm going right up to your grandmother and tell her I didn't tell you anything—whatever it is. You're just trying to get me into trouble and I'm not going to let you. [*Starts for door.*]

MARY: Wait a minute, I'll come with you. I want to tell her about Helen Burton's bracelet.

ROSALIE: [*sits down suddenly*] What about it?

MARY: Just that you stole it.

ROSALIE: Shut up. I didn't do any such thing.

MARY: Yes, you did.

ROSALIE: [*tearfully*] You made it up. You're always making things up.

MARY: You can't call me a fibber, Rosalie Wells. That's a kind of a dare and I won't take a dare. I guess I'll go tell Grandma, anyway. Then she can call the police and they'll come for you and you'll spend the rest of your life in one of those solitary prisons and you'll get older and older, and when you're very old and can't see anymore, they'll let you out maybe and your mother and father will be dead and you won't have anyplace to go and you'll beg on the streets—

ROSALIE: I didn't steal anything. I borrowed the bracelet and was going to put it back as soon as I'd worn it to the movies. I never meant to keep it.

MARY: Nobody'll believe that, least of all the police. You're just a common, ordinary thief. Stop that bawling. You'll have the whole house down here in a minute.

ROSALIE: You won't tell? Say you won't tell.

MARY: Am I a fibber?

ROSALIE: No.

MARY: Then say: "I apologize on my hands and knees."

ROSALIE: I apologize on my hands and knees. Let's play with the puzzle.

MARY: Wait a minute. Say: "From now on I, Rosalie Wells, am the vassal of Mary Tilford and will do and say whatever she tells me under the solemn oath of a knight."

ROSALIE: I won't say that. That's the worst oath there is. [MARY *starts for the door*] Mary! Please don't—

MARY: Will you swear it?

ROSALIE: [*sniffling*] But then you could tell me to do anything.

MARY: And you'd have to do it. Say it quick or I'll—

ROSALIE: [*hurriedly*] From now on, I, Rosalie Wells, am the vassal of Mary Tilford and will do and say whatever she tells me under the solemn oath of a knight. [*She gasps, and sits up straight as* MRS. TILFORD *enters.*]

MARY: Don't forget that.

MRS. TILFORD: Good evening, Rosalie, you're looking very well.

ROSALIE: Good evening, Mrs. Tilford.

MARY: She's getting fatter every day.

MRS. TILFORD: [*abstractedly*] Then it's very becoming. [*Doorbell rings*] That must be Joseph. Mary, take Rosalie into the library. Be sure you're both fast asleep by half past ten. [ROSALIE *starts to exit right, sees* MARY, *stops and hesitates.*]

MARY: Go on, Rosalie [*Waits until* ROSALIE *reluctantly exits*] Grandma.
MRS. TILFORD: Yes?
MARY: Grandma, Cousin Joe'll say I've got to go back. He'll say I really
wasn't—[CARDIN *enters and she runs from the room.*]
CARDIN: Hello, Amelia. [*Looks curiously at the fleeing* MARY] Mary home, eh?
MRS. TILFORD: [*watching* MARY *as she leaves*] Hello, Joseph. Sit down. [*He
sits down, looks at her curiously, waits for her to speak*] Whisky?
CARDIN: Please. How are you feeling? Headaches again?
MRS. TILFORD: [*puts drink on table*] No.
CARDIN: Those are good powders. Bicarbonate of soda and water. Never
hurt anybody yet.
MRS. TILFORD: Yes. How have you been, Joseph? [*Vaguely, sparring for time*] I
haven't seen you the last few weeks. Agatha misses you for Sunday
dinners.
CARDIN: I've been busy. We're getting the results from the mating season
right about now.
MRS. TILFORD: Did I take you away from a patient?
CARDIN: No. I was at the hospital.
MRS. TILFORD: How's it getting on?
CARDIN: Just the same. No money, badly equipped, a lousy laboratory,
everybody growling at everybody else—Amelia, you didn't bring me
here to talk about the hospital. What's the matter with you?
MRS. TILFORD: I—I have something to tell you.
CARDIN: Well, out with it.
MRS. TILFORD: It's a very hard thing to say, Joseph.
CARDIN: Hard for you to say to *me*? [*No answer*] Don't be worried about
Mary. I guessed that she ran home to tell you about her faint. It was
caused by nothing but bad temper and was very clumsily managed, at
that. Amelia, she's a terribly spoilt—
MRS. TILFORD: I heard about the faint. That's not what is worrying me.
CARDIN: [*gently*] Are you in some trouble?
MRS. TILFORD: We all are in trouble. Bad trouble.
CARDIN: We? Me, you mean? Nothing's the matter with me.
MRS. TILFORD: When did you last see Karen?
CARDIN: Today. This afternoon.
MRS. TILFORD: Oh. Not since seven o'clock?
CARDIN: What's happened since seven o'clock?
MRS. TILFORD: Joseph, you've been engaged to Karen for a long time. Are
your plans any more definite than they were a year ago?
CARDIN: You can get ready to buy the wedding present. We'll have the

wedding here, if you don't mind. The smell of clean little girls and boiled linen would worry me.

MRS. TILFORD: Why has Karen decided so suddenly to make it definite?

CARDIN: She has not suddenly decided anything. The school is pretty well on its feet, and now that Mrs. Mortar is leaving—

MRS. TILFORD: I've heard about their putting Mrs. Mortar out.

CARDIN: Putting her out? Well, maybe. But a nice sum for a trip and a promise that a good niece will support you the rest of your life is an enviable way of being put out.

MRS. TILFORD: [slowly] Don't you find it odd, Joseph, that they want so much to get rid of that silly, harmless woman?

CARDIN: I don't know what you're talking about, but it isn't odd at all. Lily Mortar is not a harmless woman, although God knows she's silly enough. She's a tiresome, spoilt old bitch. If you're forming a Mortar Welfare Society, you're wasting your time. [Gets up, puts down his glass] It's not like you to waste your time. Now, what's it that's really on your mind?

MRS. TILFORD: You must not marry Karen.

CARDIN: [shocked, he grins] You're a very impertinent lady. Why must I— [imitates her] not marry Karen?

MRS. TILFORD: Because there's something wrong with Karen—something horrible. [The doorbell is heard to ring loud and long.]

CARDIN: I cannot allow you to say things like that, Amelia.

MRS. TILFORD: I have good reason for saying it. [Breaks off as she hears voices offstage] Who is that?

KAREN: [offstage] Mrs. Tilford, Agatha. Is she in?

AGATHA: [offstage] Yes'm. Come on in.

MRS. TILFORD: I won't have her here.

CARDIN: [angrily] What are you talking about?

MRS. TILFORD: I won't have her here.

CARDIN: Then you don't want me here either. [Turns to face KAREN and MARTHA] Darling, what?—

KAREN: [stops when she sees him, puts her hand over her eyes] Is it a joke, Joe?

MARTHA: [with great force to MRS. TILFORD] We've come to find out what you are doing.

CARDIN: [kissing KAREN] What is it?

KAREN: It's crazy! It's crazy! What did she do it for?

CARDIN: What are you talking about? What do you mean?

MRS. TILFORD: You shouldn't have come here.

CARDIN: What is all this? What's happened?

KAREN: I tried to reach you. Hasn't she told you?

CARDIN: Nobody's told me anything. I haven't heard anything but wild talk. What is it, Karen? [*She starts to speak, then dumbly shakes her head*] What's happened, Martha?

MARTHA: [*violently*] An insane asylum has been let loose. How do we know what's happened?

CARDIN: What was it?

KAREN: We didn't know what it was. Nobody would talk to us, nobody would tell us anything.

MARTHA: I'll tell you, I'll tell you. You see if you can make any sense out of it. At dinnertime Mrs. Munn's chauffeur said that Evelyn must be sent home right away. At half past seven Mrs. Burton arrived to tell us that she wanted Helen's things packed and that she'd wait outside because she didn't want to enter a place like ours. Five minutes later the Wells's butler came for Rosalie.

CARDIN: What was it?

MARTHA: It was a madhouse. People rushing in and out, the children being pushed into cars—

KAREN: Mrs. Rogers finally told us.

CARDIN: What? What?

KAREN: That—that Martha and I are—in love with each other. In love with each other. Mrs. Tilford told them.

CARDIN: [*for a moment stands staring at her incredulously. Then he walks across the room, stares out of the window, and finally turns to* MRS. TILFORD] Did you tell them that?

MRS. TILFORD: Yes.

CARDIN: Are you sick?

MRS. TILFORD: You know I'm not sick.

CARDIN: [*snapping the words out*] Then what did you do it for?

MRS. TILFORD: [*slowly*] Because it's true.

KAREN: [*incredulously*] You think it's true, then?

MARTHA: You fool! You damned, vicious—

KAREN: Do you realize what you're saying?

MRS. TILFORD: I realize it very well. And—

MARTHA: You realize nothing, nothing, nothing.

MRS. TILFORD: And that's why I don't think you should have come here. [*Quietly*] I shall not call you names, and I will not allow you to call me names. I can't trust myself to talk about it with you now or ever.

KAREN: What's she talking about, Joe? What's she mean? What is she trying to do to us? What is everybody doing to us?

MARTHA: [*softly, as though to herself*] Pushed around. We're being pushed around by crazy people. [*Shakes herself slightly*] That's an awful thing. And we're standing here—[CARDIN *puts his arm around* KAREN, *walks with her to the window. They stand there together*] We're standing here taking it. [*Suddenly with violence*] Didn't you know we'd come here? Were we supposed to lie down and grin while you kicked us around with these lies?

MRS. TILFORD: This can't do any of us any good. Miss Dobie.

MARTHA: [*scornfully imitating her*] "This can't do any of us any good." Listen, listen. Try to understand this: you're not playing with paper dolls. We're human beings, see? It's our lives you're fooling with. *Our* lives. That's serious business for us. Can you understand that?

MRS. TILFORD: I can understand that, and I regret it. But you've been playing with children's lives, and that's why I stopped you. [*More calmly*] I know how serious this is for you, how serious it is for all of us.

CARDIN: [*bitterly*] I don't think you do know.

MRS. TILFORD: I wanted to avoid this meeting because it can't do any good. You came here to find out if I made the charge. You've found out. Let's end it there. I'm sorry this had to be done to you, Joseph.

CARDIN: I don't like your sympathy.

MRS. TILFORD: Very well. There's nothing I mean to do, nothing I want to do. There's nothing anybody can do.

CARDIN: [*carefully*] You have already done a terrible thing.

MRS. TILFORD: I have done what I had to do. What they are may be their own business. It becomes a great deal more than that when children are involved.

KAREN: [*wildly*] It's not true. Not a word of it is true; can't you understand that?

MRS. TILFORD: There won't be any punishment for either of you. This— this thing is your own. Go away with it. I don't understand it and I don't want any part of it.

MARTHA: [*slowly*] So you thought we would go away?

MRS. TILFORD: I think that's best for you.

MARTHA: There must be something we can do to you, and, whatever it is, we'll find it.

MRS. TILFORD: That will be very unwise.

KAREN: You are right to be afraid.

MRS. TILFORD: I am not afraid, Karen.

CARDIN: You *are* old—and you *are* irresponsible.

KAREN: [*goes to* MRS. TILFORD] I don't want to have anything to do with your mess, do you hear me? It makes me feel dirty and sick to be forced to say this, but here it is; there isn't a single word of truth in anything you've said. We're standing here defending ourselves—and against what? Against a lie. A great, awful lie.

MRS. TILFORD: I'm sorry that I can't believe that.

KAREN: Damn you!

CARDIN: But you can believe this: they've worked eight long years to save enough money to buy that farm, to start that school. They did without everything that young people ought to have. You wouldn't know about that. That school meant things to them: self-respect, and bread and butter, and honest work. Do you know what it is to try so hard for anything? Well, now it's gone. [*Suddenly hits the side of the table with his hand*] What the hell did you do it for?

MRS. TILFORD: [*softly*] It had to be done.

CARDIN: Righteousness is a great thing.

MRS. TILFORD: [*gently*] I know how you must feel.

CARDIN: You don't know anything about how I feel. And you don't know how they feel, either.

MRS. TILFORD: I've loved you as much as I loved my own boys. I wouldn't have spared them; I couldn't spare you.

CARDIN: [*fiercely*] I believe you.

MARTHA: What is there to do to you? What can we do to you? There must be something—something that makes you feel the way we do tonight. You don't want any part of this, you said. But you'll get a part. More than you bargained for. [*Suddenly*] Listen: are you willing to stand by everything you've said tonight?

MRS. TILFORD: Yes.

MARTHA: All right. That's fine. But don't get the idea we'll let you whisper this lie: you made it and you'll come out with it. Shriek it to your town of Lancet. We'll *make* you shriek it—and we'll make you do it in a courtroom. [*Quietly*] Tomorrow, Mrs. Tilford, you will have a libel suit on your hands.

MRS. TILFORD: That will be very unwise.

KAREN: Very unwise—for you.

MRS. TILFORD: It is you I am thinking of. I am frightened for you. It was wrong of you to brazen it out here tonight; it would be criminally foolish of you to brazen it out in public. That can bring you nothing but pain. You must not be punished any further.

MARTHA: You feel that you are too old to be punished. You believe we should spare you.

MRS. TILFORD: You know that is not what I meant.

CARDIN: [*turns from the window*] So you took a child's word for it?

MARTHA: [*looks at him*] I knew it, too.

KAREN: That is really where you got it? I can't believe — it couldn't be. Why, she's a child.

MARTHA: She's not a child any longer.

KAREN: Oh, my God, it all fits so well now. That girl has hated us for a long time. We never knew why, we never could find out. There didn't seem to be any reason —

MARTHA: There wasn't any reason. She hates everybody and everything.

KAREN: Your Mary's a strange girl, a bad girl. There's something very awful the matter with her.

MRS. TILFORD: I was waiting for you to say that. Miss Wright.

KAREN: I'm telling you the truth. We should have told it to you long ago. [*Stops, sighs*] It's no use.

MARTHA: Where is she? Bring her out here and let us hear what she has to say.

MRS. TILFORD: You cannot see her.

CARDIN: Where is she?

MRS. TILFORD: I won't have that, Joseph.

CARDIN: I'm going to talk to her.

MRS. TILFORD: [*to* KAREN *and* MARTHA] You came here demanding explanations. It was I who should have asked them from you. You attack me, you attack Mary. I've told you I didn't mean you any harm. I still don't. You claim that it isn't true; it may be natural that you should say that, but I *know* that it is true. No matter what you say, you know very well I wouldn't have acted until I was absolutely sure. All I wanted was to get those children away. That has been done. There won't be any talk about it or about you — I'll see to that. You have been in my house long enough. Get out.

KAREN: [*gets up*] The wicked very young, and the wicked very old. Let's go home.

CARDIN: Sit down [*To* MRS. TILFORD] When two people come here with their lives spread on the table for you to cut to pieces, then the only honest thing to do is to give them a chance to come out whole. Are you honest?

MRS. TILFORD: I've always thought so.

CARDIN: Then where is Mary? [*After a moment she moves her head to door, right. Quickly* CARDIN *goes to the door and opens it*] Mary! Come here.

[*After a moment* MARY *appears, stands nervously near door. Her manner is shy and afraid.*]

MRS. TILFORD: [*gently*] Sit down, dear, and don't be afraid.

MARTHA: [*her lips barely moving*] Make her tell the truth.

CARDIN: [*walking about in front of* MARY] Look, everybody lies all the time. Sometimes they have to, sometimes they don't. I've lied for a lot of different reasons, but there was seldom a time when, if I'd been given a second chance, I wouldn't have taken back the lie and told the truth. You're lucky if you ever get that chance. I'm telling you this because I'm about to ask you a question. Before you answer the question, I want to tell you that if you've l—, if you made a mistake, you must take this chance and say so. You won't be punished for it. Do you get all that?

MARY: [*timidly*] Yes, Cousin Joe.

CARDIN:[*grimly*] All right, let's get started. Were you telling your grandmother the truth this afternoon? The exact truth about Miss Wright and Miss Dobie?

MARY: [*without hesitation*] Oh, yes. [KAREN *sighs deeply.* MARTHA, *her fists closed tight, turns her back to the child.* CARDIN *smiles as he looks at* MARY.]

CARDIN: All right, Mary, that was your chance; you passed it up. [*Pulls up a chair, sits down in front of her*] Now let's find out things.

MRS. TILFORD: She's told you. Aren't you through?

CARDIN: Not by a long shot. You've started something and we'll finish it for you. Will you answer some more questions, Mary?

MARY: Yes, Cousin Joe.

MARTHA: Stop that sick, sweet tone. [MRS. TILFORD *half rises;* CARDIN *motions her back.*]

CARDIN: Why don't you like Miss Dobie and Miss Wright?

MARY: Oh, I do like them. They just don't like me. They never have liked me.

CARDIN: How do you know?

MARY: They're always picking on me. They're always punishing me for everything that happens. No matter what happens, it's always me.

CARDIN: Why do you think they do that?

MARY: Because—because they're—because they—[*Stops, turns*] Grandma, I—

CARDIN: All right, we'll skip that one. Did you get punished today?

MARY: Yes, and it was just because Peggy and Evelyn heard them and so they took it out on me.

KAREN: That's a lie.

CARDIN: Sssh. Heard what, Mary?

MARY: Mrs. Mortar told Miss Dobie that there was something funny about her. She said that she had a funny feeling about Miss Wright, and Mrs. Mortar said that was unnatural. That was why we got punished, just because —

KAREN: That was not the reason they got punished.

MRS. TILFORD: [to MARTHA] Miss Dobie?

MARTHA: My aunt is a stupid woman. What she said was unpleasant; it was said to annoy me. It meant nothing more than that.

MARY: And, Cousin Joe, she said every time you came to the school Miss Dobie got jealous, and that she didn't want you to get married.

MARTHA: [to CARDIN] She said that, too. This — this child is taking little things, little family things, and making them have meanings that — [Stops, suddenly regards MARY with a combination of disgust and interest] Where did you learn so much in so little time?

CARDIN: What do you think Mrs. Mortar meant by all that, Mary?

MRS. TILFORD: Stop it, Joseph!

MARY: I don't know, but it was always kind of funny and she always said things like that and all the girls would talk about it when Miss Dobie went and visited Miss Wright late at night —

KAREN: [angrily] And we go to the movies at night and sometimes we read at night and sometimes we drink tea at night. Those are guilty things, too, Mrs. Tilford.

MARY: And there are always funny sounds and we'd stay awake and listen because we couldn't help hearing and I'd get frightened because the sounds were like —

MARTHA: Be still!

KAREN [with violence] No, no. You don't want her still now. What else did you hear?

MARY: Grandma, I —

MRS. TILFORD: [bitterly to CARDIN] You are trying to make her name it.

CARDIN: [ignoring her, speaks to MARY] Go on.

MARY: I don't know; there were just sounds.

CARDIN: But what did you think they were? Why did they frighten you?

MARY: [weakly] I don't know.

CARDIN: [smiles at MRS. TILFORD] She doesn't know.

MARY: [hastily] I saw things, too. One night there was so much noise I thought somebody was sick or something and I looked through the keyhole and they were kissing and saying things and then I got scared because it was different sort of and I —

MARTHA: [*her face distorted, turns to* MRS. TILFORD] That child—that child is sick.

KAREN: Ask her again how she could see us.

CARDIN: How could you see Miss Dobie and Miss Wright?

MARY: I—I—

MRS. TILFORD: Tell him what you whispered to me.

MARY: It was at night and I was leaning down by the keyhole.

KAREN: *There's no keyhole on my door.*

MRS. TILFORD: What?

KAREN: There—is—no—keyhole—on—my—door.

MARY: [*quickly*] It wasn't her room, Grandma, it was the other room, I guess. It was *Miss Dobie's* room. I saw them through the keyhole in Miss Dobie's room.

CARDIN: How did you know anybody was in Miss Dobie's room?

MARY: I told you, I told you. Because we heard them. Everybody heard them—

MARTHA: I share a room with my aunt. It is on the first floor at the other end of the house. It is impossible to hear anything from there. [*To* CARDIN] Tell her to come and see for herself.

MRS. TILFORD: [*her voice shaken*] What is this, Mary? Why did you say you saw through a keyhole? *Can* you hear from your room?—

MARY:[*starts to cry*] Everybody is yelling at me. I don't know what I'm saying with everybody mixing me all up. I did see it! I did see it!

MRS. TILFORD: *What* did you see? *Where* did you see it? I want the truth, now. The truth, whatever it is.

CARDIN: [*gets up, moves his chair back*] We can go home. We are finished here. [*Looks around*] It's not a pleasant place to be.

MRS. TILFORD: [*angrily*] Stop that crying, Mary. Stand up. [MARY *gets up, crying hysterically.* MRS. TILFORD *stands directly in front of her.*]

MRS. TILFORD: *I want the truth.*

MARY: All—all right.

MRS. TILFORD: What is the truth?

MARY: It was Rosalie who saw them. I just said it was me so I wouldn't have to tattle on Rosalie.

CARDIN: [*wearily*] Oh, my God!

MARY: It *was* Rosalie, Grandma, she told us all about it. She said she had read about it in a book and she knew. [*Desperately*] You ask Rosalie. You just ask Rosalie. She'll tell you. We used to talk about it all the time. That's the truth, that's the honest truth. She said it was when the door was open once and she told us all about it. I was just trying to save Rosalie, and everybody jumps on me.

MRS. TILFORD: [*to* CARDIN] Please wait a minute. [*Goes to library door*] Rosalie!

CARDIN: You're giving yourself an awful beating, Amelia, and you deserve whatever you get.

MRS. TILFORD: [*stands waiting for* ROSALIE, *passes her hand over her face*] I don't know. I don't know, anymore. Maybe it's what I do deserve. [*As* ROSALIE, *frightened, appears at the door, making bows to everybody, she takes the child gently by the hand, brings her down center, talking nervously*] I'm sorry to keep you up so late, Rosalie. You must be tired. [*Speaks rapidly*] Mary says there's been a lot of talk in the school lately about Miss Wright and Miss Dobie. Is that true?

ROSALIE: I—I don't know what you mean.

MRS. TILFORD: That things have been said among you girls.

ROSALIE: [*wide-eyed, frightened*] What things? I never—I—I—

KAREN: [*gently*] Don't be frightened.

MRS. TILFORD: What was the talk about, Rosalie?

ROSALIE: [*utterly bewildered*] I don't know what she means, Miss Wright.

KAREN: Rosalie, Mary has told her grandmother that certain things at school have been—er—puzzling you girls. You, particularly.

ROSALIE: History puzzles me. I guess I'm not very good at history, and Helen helps me sometimes, if that—

KAREN: No, that's not what she meant. She says that you told her that you saw certain—certain acts between Miss Dobie and myself. She says that once, when the door was open, you saw us kissing each other in a way that—[*Unable to bear the child's look, she turns her back*] women don't kiss one another.

ROSALIE: Oh, Miss Wright, I didn't, didn't, I didn't. I *never* said such a thing.

MRS. TILFORD: [*grimly*] That's true, my dear?

ROSALIE: I never saw any such thing. Mary always makes things up about me and everybody else. [*Starts to weep in excitement*] I never said any such thing ever. Why I never even could had thought of—

MARY: [*staring at her, speaks very slowly*] Yes, you did, Rosalie. You're just trying to get out of it. I remember just when you said it. I remember it, because it was the day Helen Burton's bracelet was—

ROSALIE: [*stands fascinated and fearful, looking at* MARY] I never did. I—I— you're just—

MARY: It was the day Helen's bracelet was stolen, and nobody knew who

did it, and Helen said that if her mother found out, she'd have the
thief put in jail.

KAREN: [*puzzled, as are the others, by the sudden change in* ROSALIE's *manner*]
There's nothing to cry about. You must help us by telling the truth.
Why, what's the matter, Rosalie?

MARY: Grandma, there's something I've got to tell you that—

ROSALIE: [*with a shrill cry*] Yes. Yes. I did see it. I told Mary. What Mary said
was right. I said it. I said it—[*Throws herself on the couch, weeping
hysterically;* MARTHA *stands leaning against the door;* KAREN, CARDIN, *and*
MRS. TILFORD *are staring at* ROSALIE; MARY *slowly sits down as the curtain
falls.*]

CURTAIN

Act Three

Scene: *The same as Act One. Living room of the school.*

At rise: *the room has changed. It is not dirty, but it is dull and dark and uncared for. The windows are tightly shut, the curtains tightly drawn.* KAREN *is sitting in a large chair, right center, feet flat on floor.* MARTHA *is lying on the couch, her face buried against the pillows, her back to* KAREN. *It is a minute or two after the rise of the curtain before either speaks.*

MARTHA: It's cold in here.
KAREN: Yes.
MARTHA: What time is it?
KAREN: I don't know.
MARTHA: I was hoping it was time for my bath.
KAREN: Take it early today.
MARTHA: [*laughs*] Oh, I couldn't do that. I look forward all day to that bath. It's my last touch with the full life. It makes me feel important to know that there's one thing ahead of me, one thing I've *got* to do. You ought to get yourself something like that. I tell you, at five o'clock every day you comb your hair. How's that? It's better for you, take my word. You wake up in the morning and you say to yourself, the day's not entirely empty, life is rich and full: at five o'clock I'll comb my hair. [*They fall back into silence. A moment later the phone rings. Neither of them pays the slightest attention to it. But the ringing becomes too insistent.* KAREN *rises, takes the receiver off, goes back to her chair and sits down.*]
KAREN: It's raining.
MARTHA: Hungry?
KAREN: No. You?
MARTHA: No, but I'd like to be hungry. Remember how much we used to eat at college?
KAREN: That was ten years ago.

MARTHA: Well, maybe we'll be hungry in another ten years. It's cheaper this way.

KAREN: What's the old thing about time being more nourishing than bread?

MARTHA: Maybe.

KAREN: Joe's late today. What time is it?

MARTHA: [*turns again to lie on her side*] We've been sitting here for eight days asking each other the time. Haven't you heard? There isn't any time anymore.

KAREN: It's been days since we've been out of this house.

MARTHA: Well, we'll have to get off these chairs sooner or later. In a couple of months they'll need dusting.

KAREN: What'll we do when we get off?

MARTHA: God knows.

KAREN: [*almost in a whisper*] It's awful.

MARTHA: Let's not talk about it. [*After a moment*] What about eggs for dinner?

KAREN: All right.

MARTHA: I'll make some potatoes with onions, the way you used to like them.

KAREN: It's a week ago Thursday. It never seemed real until the last day. It seems real enough now, all right. Let's go out.

MARTHA: [*turns over, stares at her*] Where to?

KAREN: We'll take a walk.

MARTHA: Where'll we walk?

KAREN: Why shouldn't we take a walk? We won't see anybody, and suppose we do, what of it? We'll just —

MARTHA: [*slowly gets up*] Come on. We'll go through the park.

KAREN: They might see us. [*They stand looking at each other*] Let's not go. [MARTHA *goes back, lies down again*] We'll go tomorrow.

MARTHA: [*laughs*] Stop kidding yourself.

KAREN: But Joe says we've got to go out. He says that all the people who don't think it's true will begin to wonder if we keep hiding this way.

MARTHA: If it makes you feel better to think there *are* such people, go ahead.

KAREN: He says we ought to go into town and go shopping and act as though —

MARTHA: Shopping? That's a sound idea. There aren't three stores in Lancet that would sell us anything. Hasn't he heard about the ladies' clubs and their meetings and their circulars and their visits and their —

KAREN:[*softly*] Don't tell him.

MARTHA: [*gently*] I won't. [*There are footsteps in the hall and the sound of something being, dragged*] There's our friend. [*A* GROCERY BOY *appears lugging a box. He brings it into the room, stands staring at them, giggles a little. Walks toward* KAREN, *stops, examines her. She sits tense, looking away from him. Without taking his eyes from* KAREN, *he speaks.*]

GROCERY BOY: I knocked on the kitchen door but nobody answered.

MARTHA: You said that yesterday. All right. Thanks. Good-bye.

KAREN: [*unable any longer to stand the stare*] Make him stop it.

GROCERY BOY: Here are the things. [*Giggles, moves toward* MARTHA, *stands looking at her. Suddenly* MARTHA *thrusts her hand in the air.*]

MARTHA: I've got eight fingers, see? I'm a freak.

GROCERY BOY: [*giggling*] There's a car comin' here. [*Starts backing out of door, still looking.*] Good-bye. [*Exits.*]

MARTHA: You still think we should go into town?

KAREN: I don't know. I don't know about anything anymore. [*After a moment*] Martha, Martha, Martha—

MARTHA: [*gently*] What is it, Karen?

KAREN: What are we going to do? It's like that dark hour of the night when half awake you struggle through the black mess you've been dreaming. Then, suddenly, you wake up and you see your own bed or your own nightgown and you know you're back again in a solid world. But now it's all the nightmare; there is no solid world. Oh, Martha, *why* did it happen. *What* happened? What are we doing here like this?

MARTHA: Waiting.

KAREN: For what?

MARTHA: I don't know.

KAREN: We've got to get out of this place. I can't stand it anymore.

MARTHA: You'll be getting married soon. Everything will be all right then.

KAREN: [*vaguely*] Yes.

MARTHA: [*looks up at the tone*] What is it?

KAREN: Nothing.

MARTHA: There mustn't be anything wrong between you and Joe. Never.

KAREN: [*without conviction*] Nothing's wrong. [*As footsteps are heard in the hall, her face lights up*] There's Joe now. [MRS. MORTAR, *small suitcase in hand, stands in the doorway, her face pushed coyly forward.*]

MRS. MORTAR: And here I am. Hello, hello.

MARTHA: [*she has turned over on her back and is staring at her aunt. She speaks to* KAREN] The Duchess, isn't it? Returned at long last. [*Too jovially*]

Come on in. We're delighted to see you. Are you tired from your journey? Is there something I can get you?

MRS. MORTAR: [*surprised*] I'm very glad to see you both, and [*looks around*] I'm very glad to see the old place again. How is everything?

MARTHA: Everything's fine. We're splendid, thank you. You're just in time for tea.

MRS. MORTAR: You know, I should like some tea, if it isn't too much trouble.

MARTHA: No trouble at all. Some small sandwiches and a little brandy?

MRS. MORTAR: [*puzzled*] Why, Martha.

MARTHA: Where the hell have you been?

MRS. MORTAR: Around, around. I had a most interesting time. Things —

MARTHA: Why didn't you answer my telegrams?

MRS. MORTAR: Things have changed in the theater — drastically changed, I might say.

MARTHA: *Why didn't you answer my telegrams?*

MRS. MORTAR: Oh, Martha, there's your temper again.

MARTHA: Answer me and don't bother about my temper.

MRS. MORTAR: [*nervously*] I was moving around a great deal. [*Conversationally*] You know, I think it will throw a very revealing light on the state of the new theater when I tell you that the Lyceum in Rochester now has a toilet backstage.

MARTHA: To hell with the toilet in Rochester. Where were you?

MRS. MORTAR: Moving around, I tell you.

KAREN: What difference does it all make now?

MRS. MORTAR: Karen is quite right. Let bygones be bygones. As I was saying, there's an effete something in the theater now, and that accounts for —

MARTHA: Why did you refuse to come back here and testify for us?

MRS. MORTAR: Why, Martha, I didn't refuse to come back at all. That's the wrong way to look at it. I was on a tour; that's a moral obligation, you know. Now don't let's talk about unpleasant things anymore. I'll go up and unpack a few things; tomorrow's plenty of time to get my trunk.

KAREN: [*laughs*] Things have changed here, you know.

MARTHA: She doesn't know. She expected to walk right up to a comfortable fire and sit down and she very carefully waited until the whole thing was over. [*Leans forward, speaking to* MRS. MORTAR] Listen. Karen Wright and Martha Dobie brought a libel suit against a woman called Tilford because her grandchild had accused them of having what the judge called "sinful sexual knowledge of one another." [MRS. MORTAR *holds up her hand in protest, and* MARTHA, *laughs*] Don't like that, do you? Well, a great part of the defense's case was based on remarks made by Lily Mortar, actress in the toilets of Rochester, against her niece, Martha. And a greater part of the defense's case rested on the telling fact that Mrs. Mortar would not appear in court to deny or explain those remarks. Mrs. Mortar had a moral obligation to the theater. As you probably read in the papers, we lost the case.

MRS. MORTAR: I didn't think of it that way, Martha. It couldn't have done any good for all of us to get mixed up in that unpleasant notoriety— [*Sees* MARTHA's *face. Hastily*] But now that you've explained it, why, I do see it your way, and I'm sorry I didn't come back. But now that I am here, I'm going to stand shoulder to shoulder with you. I know what you've gone through, but the body and heart *do* recover, you know. I'll be here working right along with you and we'll—

MARTHA: There's an eight o'clock train. Get on it.

MRS. MORTAR: Martha.

MARTHA: You've come back to pick the bones dry. There's nothing here for you.

MRS. MORTAR: [*sniffling a little*] How can you talk to me like that?

MARTHA: Because I hate you. I've always hated you.

MRS. MORTAR: [*gently*] God will punish you for that.

MARTHA: He's been doing all right.

MRS. MORTAR: When you wish to apologize, I will be temporarily in my room. [*Starts to exit, almost bumps into* CARDIN, *steps back with dignity*] How do you do?

CARDIN: [*laughs*] Look who's here. A little late, aren't you?

MRS. MORTAR: So it's you. Now. I call *that* loyal. A lot of men wouldn't still be here. They would have felt—

MARTHA: Get out of here.

KAREN: [*opening door*] I'll call you when it's time for your train. [MRS. MORTAR *looks at her, exits.*]

CARDIN: Now, what do you think brought her back?

KAREN: God knows.

MARTHA: I know. She was broke.

CARDIN: [*pats* MARTHA *on the shoulder*] Don't let her worry you this time, Martha. We'll give her some money and get rid of her. [*Pulls* KAREN *to him*] Been out today, darling?

KAREN: We started to go out.

CARDIN: [*shakes his head*] Feel all right? [KAREN *leans over to kiss him. Almost imperceptibly he pulls back.*]

KAREN: Why did you do that?

MARTHA: Karen.

CARDIN: Do what?

KAREN: Draw back that way.

CARDIN: [*laughs, kisses her*] If we sit around here much longer, we'll all be bats. I sold my place today to Foster.

KAREN: You did what?

CARDIN: We're getting married this week. Then we're going away—all three of us.

KAREN: You can't leave here. I won't have you do this for me. What about the hospital and—

CARDIN: Shut up, darling, it's all fixed. We're going to Vienna and we're going quick. Fischer wrote that I can have my old place back.

KAREN: No! No! I'm not going to let you.

CARDIN: It's already done. Fischer can't pay me much, but it'll be enough for the three of us. Plenty if we live cheap.

MARTHA: I couldn't go with you, Joe.

CARDIN: Nonsense, Martha, we're all going. We're going to have fun again.

KAREN: [*slowly*] You don't want to go back to Vienna?

CARDIN: No.

KAREN: Then why?

CARDIN: Look: I don't want to go to Vienna; I'd rather have stayed here. But then you don't want to go to Vienna—you'd rather have stayed here. Well, to hell with that. We *can't* stay here, and Vienna offers enough to eat and sleep and drink beer on. Now don't object any more, please, darling. All right?

KAREN: All right.

MARTHA: I can't go. It's better for all of us if I don't.

CARDIN: [*puts his arm around her*] Not now. You stay with us now. Later on, if you want it that way. All right?

MARTHA: [*smiles*] All right.

CARDIN: Swell. I'll buy you good coffee cakes and take you both to Ischl for a honeymoon.

MARTHA: [*picking up grocery box, she starts for door*] A big coffee cake with a lot of raisins. It would be nice to like something again. [*Exits.*]

CARDIN: [*with a slightly forced heartiness*] I'll be going back with a pretty girl who belongs to me. I'll show you off all over the place—to Dr. Engelhardt, and the nurse at the desk, and to the fat gal in the cake shop, and to Fischer. [*Laughs*] The last time I saw him was at the railroad station. He took me back of the baggage car. [*With an imitation of an accent*] "Joseph" he said, "you'll be a good doctor; I would trust you to cut up my Minna. But you're not a great doctor, and you never will be. Go back where you were born and take care of your sick. Leave the fancy work to the others." I came home.

KAREN: You'll be coming home again someday.

CARDIN: Let's not talk about it. [*After a moment*] You'll need some clothes?

KAREN: A few. Oh, your Dr. Fischer was so right. This is where you belong.

CARDIN: I need an overcoat and a suit. You'll need a lot of things—heavy things. It's cold there now, much colder than you'd expect—

KAREN: I've done this to you. I've taken you away from everything you want.

CARDIN: But it's lovely in the mountains, and that's where we'll go for a month.

KAREN: They—*they've* done it. They've taken away every chance we had. Everything we wanted, everything we were going to be.

CARDIN: And we've got to stop talking like that. [*Takes her by the shoulder*] We've got a chance. But it's just one chance, and if we miss it we're done for. It means that we've got to start putting the whole business behind us now. *Now*, Karen. What you've done, you've done—and that's that.

KAREN: What *I've* done?

CARDIN: [*impatiently*] What's been done to you.

KAREN. What did you mean? [*When there is no answer*] What did you mean when you said: "What you've done"?

CARDIN: [*shouting*] Nothing. Nothing. [*Then very quietly*] Karen, there are a lot of people in this world who've had bad trouble in their lives. We're three of those people. We could sit around the rest of our lives and exist on that trouble, until in the end we had nothing else and we'd want nothing else. That's something I'm not coming to and I'm not going to let you come to.

KAREN: I know. I'm sorry. [*After a moment*] Joe, can we have a baby right away?

CARDIN: [*vaguely*] Yes, I guess so. Although we won't have much money now.

KAREN: You used to want one right away. You always said that was the way you wanted it. There's some reason for your changing.

CARDIN: My God, we *can't* go on like this. Everything I say to you is made to mean something else. We don't talk like people anymore. Oh, let's get out of here as fast as we can.

KAREN: [*as though she is finishing the sentence for him*] And every word will have a new meaning. You think we'll be able to run away from that?

Woman, child, love, lawyer—no words that we can use in safety anymore. [*Laughs*] Sick, high-tragic people. That's what we'll be.

CARDIN: [*gently*] No, we won't, darling. Love is casual—that's the way it
should be. We must find that out all over again. We must learn again to
live and love like other people.

KAREN: It won't work.

CARDIN: What?

KAREN: The two of us together.

CARDIN: [*sharply*] Stop talking like that.

KAREN: It's true. [*Suddenly*] I want you to say it now.

CARDIN: I don't know what you're talking about.

KAREN: Yes, you do. We've both known for a long time. I knew surely the
day we lost the case. I was watching your face in court. It was
ashamed—and sad at being ashamed. Say it now, Joe. Ask it now.

CARDIN: I have nothing to ask. Nothing—[*Quickly*] All right. Is it—was it
ever—

KAREN: [*puts her hand over his mouth*] No. Martha and I have never touched
each other. [*Pulls his head down on her shoulder*] That's all right, darling.
I'm glad you asked. I'm not mad a bit, really.

CARDIN: I'm sorry, Karen, I'm sorry. I didn't mean to hurt you, I—

KAREN: I know. You wanted to wait until it was all over, you really never
wanted to ask at all. You didn't know for sure; you thought there might
be just a little truth in it all. [*With great feeling*] You've been good to me
and loyal. You're a fine man. [*Afraid of tears, she pats him, walks away*]
Now go and sit down, Joe. I have things to say. They're all mixed up
and I must get them clear.

CARDIN: Don't let's talk any more. Let's forget and go ahead.

KAREN: [*puzzled*] Go ahead?

CARDIN: Yes, Karen.

KAREN: You believe me, then?

CARDIN: Of course I believe you. I only had to hear you say it.

KAREN: No, no, no. That isn't the way things work. Maybe you believe me.
I'd never know whether you did or not. You'd never know whether
you did, either. We couldn't do it that way. Can't you see what would
happen? We'd be hounded by it all our lives. I'd be frightened, always,
and in the end my own fright would make me—would make me hate
you. [*Sees slight movement he makes*] Yes, it would; I know it would. I'd
hate you for what I thought I'd done to you. And I'd hate myself, too.
It would grow and grow until we'd be ruined by it. [*Sees him about to
speak*] Ah, Joe, you've seen all that yourself. You knew it first.

CARDIN: [*softly*] I didn't mean it that way; I don't now.

KAREN: [*smiles*] You're still trying to spare me, still trying to tell yourself that we might be all right again. But we won't be all right. Not ever, ever, ever. I don't know all the reasons why. Look, I'm standing here. I haven't changed. [*Holds out her hands*] My hands look just the same, my face is the same, even my dress is old. We're in a room we've been in so many times before; you're sitting where you always sit; it's nearly time for dinner. I'm like everybody else. I can have all the things that everybody has. I can have you and I can go to the market, and we can go to the movies, and people will talk to me and—[*Suddenly notices the pain in his face*] Oh, I'm sorry. I mustn't talk like that. That couldn't be true anymore.

CARDIN: It could be, Karen. We'll make it be like that.

KAREN: No. That's only what we'd like to have had. It's what we can't have now. Go home, darling.

CARDIN: [*with force*] Don't talk like that. No matter what it is, we can't leave each other. I can't leave you—

KAREN: Joe, Joe. Let's do it now and quick; it will be too hard later on.

CARDIN: No, no, no. We love each other. [*His voice breaks*] I'd give anything not to have asked questions, Karen.

KAREN: It had to be asked sooner or later—and answered. You're a good man—the best I'll ever know—and you've been better to me than— But it's no good now, for either of us; you can see that.

CARDIN: It can be. You say I helped you. Help me now; help me to be strong and good enough to—[*Goes toward her with his arms out*] Karen!

KAREN: [*drawing back*] No, Joe! [*Then, as he stops*] Will you do something for me?

CARDIN: No. I won't—

KAREN: Will you—will you go away for two days—a day—and think this all over by yourself—away from me and love and pity? Will you? And then decide.

CARDIN: [*after a long pause*] Yes, if you want, but it won't make any difference. We will—

KAREN: Don't say anything. Please go now. [*She sits down, smiles, closes her eyes. For a moment he stands looking at her, then slowly puts on his hat*] And all my heart goes with you.

CARDIN: [*at door, leaving*] I'll be coming back. [*Exits, slowly, reluctantly, closing door.*]

KAREN: [*a moment after he has gone*] No, you won't. Never, darling. [*Stays as she is until* MARTHA *enters right.*]

MARTHA: [*goes to lamp, lights it*] It gets dark so early now. [*Sits down, stretches, laughs*] Cooking always makes me feel better. Well, I guess we'll have to give the Duchess some dinner. When the hawks descend, you've got to feed 'em. Where's Joe? [*No answer*] Where's Joe?

KAREN: Gone.

MARTHA: A patient? Will he be back in time for dinner?

KAREN: No.

MARTHA: [*watching her*] We'll save dinner for him, then. Karen! What's the matter?

KAREN: He won't be back anymore.

MARTHA: [*slowly and carefully*] You mean he won't be back anymore tonight.

KAREN: He won't be back at all.

MARTHA: [*quickly, walks to* KAREN] What happened? [KAREN *shakes her head*] What happened, Karen?

KAREN: He thought that we had been lovers.

MARTHA: [*tensely*] I don't believe you. [*Wearily* KAREN *turns her head away.*]

KAREN: All right.

MARTHA: [*automatically*] I don't believe it. He's never said a word all these months, all during the trial— [*Suddenly grabs* KAREN *by the shoulder, shakes her*] Didn't you tell him? For God's sake, didn't you tell him it wasn't true?

KAREN: Yes.

MARTHA: He didn't believe you?

KAREN: I guess he believed me.

MARTHA: [*angrily*] Then what have you done?

KAREN: What had to be done.

MARTHA: It's all wrong. It's silly. He'll be back in a little while and you'll clear it all up— [*Realizes why that can't be, covers her mouth with her hand*] Oh, God, I wanted that for you so much.

KAREN: Don't. I feel sick to my stomach.

MARTHA: [*goes to couch opposite* KAREN, *puts her head in her arms*] What's happened to us? What's really happened to us?

KAREN: I don't know. I want to be sleepy. I want to go to sleep.

MARTHA: Go back to Joe. He's strong; he'll understand. It's too much for you this way.

KAREN: [*irritably*] Stop talking about it. Let's pack and get out of here. Let's take the train in the morning.

MARTHA: The train to where?

KAREN: I don't know. Someplace; anyplace.

MARTHA: A job? Money?

KAREN: In a big place we could get something to do.

MARTHA: They'd know about us. We've been famous.

KAREN: A small town, then.

MARTHA: They'd know more about us.

KAREN: [*as a child would say it*] Isn't there anywhere to go?

MARTHA: No. We're bad people. We'll sit. We'll be sitting the rest of our
lives wandering what's happened to us. You think this scene is strange?
Well, get used to it; we'll be here for a long time. [*Suddenly pinches*
KAREN *on the arm*] Let's pinch each other sometimes. We can tell
whether we're still living.

KAREN: [*shivers, listlessly gets up, starts making a fire in the fireplace*] But this isn't
a new sin they tell us we've done. Other people aren't destroyed by it.

MARTHA: They are the people who believe in it, who want it, who've
chosen it. We aren't like that. We don't love each other. [*Suddenly stops,
crosses to fireplace, stands looking abstractedly at* KAREN. *Speaks casually*] I
don't love you. We've been very close to each other, of course. I've
loved you like a friend the way thousands of women feel about other
women.

KAREN: [*only half listening*] Yes.

MARTHA: Certainly that doesn't mean anything. There's nothing wrong
about that. It's perfectly natural that I should be fond of you, that I
should—

KAREN: [*listlessly*] Why are you saying all this to me?

MARTHA: Because I love you.

KAREN: [*vaguely*] Yes, of course.

MARTHA: I love you that way—maybe the way they said I loved you. I don't
know. [*Waits, gets no answer, kneels down next to* KAREN] Listen to me!

KAREN: What?

MARTHA: *I have loved you the way they said.*

KAREN: You're crazy.

MARTHA: There's always been something wrong. Always—as long as I can
remember. But I never knew it until all this happened.

KAREN: [*for the first time looks up*] Stop it!

MARTHA: You're afraid of hearing it; I'm more afraid than you.

KAREN: [*puts her hands over her ears*] I won't listen to you.

MARTHA: Take your hands down. [*Leans over, pulls* KAREN'*s hands away*]
You've got to know it. I can't keep it any longer. I've got to tell you
how guilty I am.

KAREN: [*deliberately*] You are guilty of nothing.

MARTHA: I've been telling myself that since the night we heard the child

231

say it; I've been praying I could convince myself of it. I can't, I can't any longer. It's there. I don't know how, I don't know why. But I did love you. I do love you. I resented your marriage; maybe because I wanted you; maybe I wanted you all along; maybe I couldn't call it by a name; maybe it's been there ever since I first knew you—

KAREN: [*tensely*] It's a lie. You're telling me a lie. We never thought of each other that way.

MARTHA: [*bitterly*] No, of course *you* didn't. But who says I didn't? I never felt that way about anybody but you. I've never loved a man—[*Stops. Softly*] I never knew why before. Maybe it's that.

KAREN: [*carefully*] You are tired and sick.

MARTHA: [*as though she were talking to herself*] It's funny; it's all mixed up. There's something in you, and you don't know it and you don't do anything about it. Suddenly a child gets bored and lies—and there you are, seeing it for the first time. [*Closes her eyes*] I don't know. It all seems to come back to *me*. In some way I've ruined your life. I've ruined my own. I didn't even *know*. [*Smiles*] There's a big difference between us now, Karen. I feel all dirty and—[*Puts out her hand, touches* KAREN'*s head*] I can't stay with you anymore, darling.

KAREN: [*in a shaken, uncertain tone*] All this isn't true. You've never said it; we'll forget it by tomorrow—

MARTHA: Tomorrow? Karen, we would have had to invent a new language, as children do, without words like tomorrow.

KAREN: [*crying*] Go and lie down, Martha. You'll feel better. [MARTHA *looks around the room, slowly, carefully. She is very quiet. Exits right, stands at door for a second looking at* KAREN, *then slowly shuts the door behind her.* KAREN *sits alone without moving. There is no sound in the house until, a few minutes after* MARTHA'*s exit, a shot is heard. The sound of the shot should not be too loud or too strong. For a few seconds after the noise has died out,* KAREN *does not move. Then, suddenly, she springs from the chair, crosses the room, pulls open door, right. Almost at the same moment footsteps are heard on the staircase.*]

MRS. MORTAR: What was that? Where is it? [*Enters door center, frightened, aimlessly moving about*] Karen! Martha! Where are you? I heard a shot. What was—[*Stops as she sees* KAREN *reappear, right. Walks toward her, still talking. Stops when she sees* KAREN'*s face*] What—what is it? [KAREN *moves her hands, shakes her head slightly, passes* MRS. MORTAR, *and goes toward window.* MRS. MORTAR *stares at her for a moment, rushes past her through door right. Left alone,* KAREN *leans against the window.* MRS. MORTAR *reenters crying. After a minute*] What shall we do? What shall we do?

KAREN: [*in a toneless voice*] Nothing.

Mrs. Mortar: We've got to get a doctor—right away. [*Goes to phone, nervously, fumblingly starts to dial.*]

Karen: [*without turning*] There isn't any use.

Mrs. Mortar: We've got to do something. Oh, it's awful. Poor Martha. I don't know what we can do—[*Puts phone down collapses in chair, sobs quietly*] You think she's dea—

Karen: Yes.

Mrs. Mortar: Poor, poor Martha. I can't realize it's true Oh how could she—she was so—I don't know what—[*Looks up, still crying, surprised*] I'm—I'm frightened.

Karen: Don't cry.

Mrs. Mortar: I can't help it. How can I help it? [*Gradually the sobs cease and she sits rocking herself*] I'll never forgive myself for the last words I said to her. But I was good to her, Karen, and you know God will excuse me for that once. I always tried to do everything I could. [*Suddenly*] Suicide's a sin. [*No answer. Timidly*] Shouldn't we call somebody to—

Karen: In a little while.

Mrs. Mortar: She shouldn't have done it, she shouldn't have done it. It was because of all this awful business. She would have got a job and started all over again—she was just worried and sick and—

Karen: That isn't the reason she did it.

Mrs. Mortar: What—why—?

Karen: [*wearily*] What difference does it make now?

Mrs. Mortar: [*reproachfully*] You're not crying.

Karen: No.

Mrs. Mortar: What will happen to me? I haven't anything. Poor Martha—

Karen: She was very good to you; she was good to us all.

Mrs. Mortar: Oh, I know she was, Karen, and I was good to her too. I did everything I could. I—I haven't any place to go. [*After a few seconds of silence*] I'm afraid. It seems so queer—in the next room. [*Shivers.*]

Karen: Don't be afraid.

Mrs. Mortar: It's different for you. You're young. [*The doorbell rings.* **Mrs. Mortar** *jumps.* **Karen** *doesn't move. It rings again.*]

Mrs. Mortar: [*nervously*] Who is it? [*The bell rings again*] Shall I answer it? [**Karen** *shrugs*] I think we'd better [*Exits through center doors. Returns in a minute followed by* **Agatha**, *who stands in the door*] It's a woman. [*No answer*] It's a woman to see you, **Karen**. [*Getting no answer, she turns to* **Agatha**] You can't come in now; we've had a—we've had trouble here.

Agatha: Miss Karen, I've *got* to speak to you.

Karen: [*turns slowly, mechanically*] Agatha.

AGATHA: [*goes to* KAREN] Please, Miss Karen. We've tried so hard to get you. I been phoning here all the time. Trying to get you. Phoning and phoning. Please, please let her come in. Just for a minute. Miss Karen. Please —

MRS. MORTAR: Who wants to come in here?

AGATHA: Mrs. Tilford. [*Looks at* KAREN] Don't you feel well? [KAREN *shakes her head*] You ain't mad at *me*?

MRS. MORTAR: That woman can't come in here. She caused all —

KAREN: I'm not mad at you, Agatha.

AGATHA: Can I — can I get you something?

KAREN: No.

AGATHA: You poor child. You look like you got a pain. [*Hesitates, takes* KAREN's *hands*] I only came cause she's so bad off. She's got to see you, Miss Karen, she's just got to. She's been sittin' outside in the car, hoping you'd come out. She can't get Dr. Joe. He — he won't talk to her anymore. I wouldn't a come — I always been on your side — but she's sick. If only you could see her, you'd let her come for just a minute.

KAREN: I couldn't do that, Agatha.

AGATHA: I don't blame you. But I had to tell you. She's old. It's going to kill her.

KAREN: [*bitterly*] Kill her? Where is Mrs. Tilford?

AGATHA: Outside.

KAREN: All right.

AGATHA: [*presses* KAREN's *arm*] You always been a good girl. [*Hurriedly exits.*]

MRS. MORTAR: You going to allow that woman to come in here? With Martha lying there? How can you be so feelingless? [*She starts to cry*] I won't stay and see it. I won't have anything to do with it. I'll never let that woman — [*Rushes sobbing from the room.*]

[*A second after,* MRS. TILFORD *appears in the doorway. Her face, her walk, her voice have* changed.]

MRS. TILFORD: Karen, let me come in. [*Without turning,* KAREN *bows her head.* MRS. TILFORD *enters stands staring at the floor.*]

KAREN: Why have you come here?

MRS. TILFORD: I had to come. [*Stretches out her hand to* KAREN, *who does not turn. She drops her hand*] I know now; I know it wasn't true.

KAREN: What?

MRS. TILFORD: [*carefully*] I know it wasn't true, Karen.

KAREN: [*stares at her, shudders*] You know it wasn't true? I don't care what you know. It doesn't matter anymore. If that's what you had to say, you've said it. Go away.

MRS. TILFORD: [*puts her hand to her throat*] I've *got* to tell you.

KAREN: I don't want to hear you.

MRS. TILFORD: Last Tuesday Mrs. Wells found a bracelet in Rosalie's room. The bracelet had been hidden for several months. We found out that Rosalie had taken the bracelet from another girl, and that Mary — [*Closes her eyes*] that Mary knew that and used it to force Rosalie into saying that she had seen you and Miss Dobie together. I—I've talked to Mary. I've found out. [KAREN *suddenly begins to laugh, high and sharp*] Don't do that, Karen. I have only a little more to say. I've tried to say it to you for six days. I've talked to Judge Potter. He will make all arrangements. There will be a public apology and an explanation. The damage suit will be paid to you in full and—and any more that you will be kind enough to take from me. I—I must see that you won't suffer anymore.

KAREN: We're not going to suffer anymore. Martha is dead.

[MRS. TILFORD *gasps, shakes her head as though to shake off the truth, and covers her face.* KAREN *watches her for a minute*] So you've come here to relieve your conscience? Well, I won't be your confessor. It's choking you, is it? [*Violently*] And you want to stop the choking, don't you? You've done a wrong and you have to right that wrong or you can't rest your head again. You want to be "just," don't you, and you wanted us to help you be just? You've come to the wrong place for help. You want to be a "good" woman again, don't you? [*Bitterly*] Oh, I know. You told us that night you had to do what you did. Now you "have" to do this. A public apology and money paid, and you can sleep again and eat again. That done and there'll be peace for you. You're old, and the old are callous. Ten, fifteen years left for you. But what of me? It's a whole life for me. A whole God-damned life. [*Suddenly quiet, points to door, right*] And what of her?

MRS. TILFORD: [*she is crying*] You are still living.

KAREN: Yes. I guess so.

MRS. TILFORD: [*with a tremendous effort to control herself*] I didn't come here to relieve myself. I swear to God I didn't. I came to try—to try anything. I knew there wasn't any relief for me, Karen, and that there never would be again. [*Tensely*] But what I am or why I came doesn't matter. The only thing that matters is you and—You, now.

KAREN: There's nothing for me.

MRS. TILFORD: Oh, let's try to make something for you. You're young and I—I can help you.

KAREN: [*smiles*] You can help me?

MRS. TILFORD: [*with great feeling*] Take whatever I can give you. Take it for yourself and use it for yourself. It won't bring me peace, if that's what's worrying you. [*Smiles*] Those ten or fifteen years you talk about! They will be bad years.

KAREN: I'm tired, Mrs. Tilford. You will have a hard time ahead, won't you?

MRS. TILFORD: Yes.

KAREN: Mary?

MRS. TILFORD: I don't know.

KAREN: You can send her away.

MRS. TILFORD: No. I could never do that. Whatever she does, it must be to me and no one else. She's—she's—

KAREN: Yes. Your very own, to live with the rest of your life. [*For a moment she watches* MRS. TILFORD'*s face*] It's over for me now, but it will never end for you. She's harmed us both, but she's harmed you more, I guess. [*Sits down beside* MRS. TILFORD] I'm sorry.

MRS. TILFORD: [*clings to her*] Then you'll try for yourself.

KAREN: All right.

MRS. TILFORD: You and Joe.

KAREN: No. We're not together anymore.

MRS. TILFORD: [*looks up at her*] Did I do that, too?

KAREN: I don't think anyone did anything, anymore.

MRS. TILFORD: [*makes a half-movement to rise*] I'll go to him right away.

KAREN: No, it's better now the way it is.

MRS. TILFORD: But he must know what I know, Karen. You must go back to him.

KAREN: [*smiles*] No, not anymore.

MRS. TILFORD: You must, you must—[*Sees her face, hesitates*] Perhaps later, Karen?

KAREN: Perhaps.

MRS. TILFORD: [*after a moment in which they both sit silent*] Come away from here now, Karen. [KAREN *shakes her head*] You can't stay with—[*Moves her hand toward door, right.*]

KAREN: When she is buried, then I will go.

MRS. TILFORD: You'll be all right?

KAREN: I'll be all right, I suppose. Good-bye, now. [*They both rise.* MRS. TILFORD *speaks, pleadingly.*]

MRS. TILFORD: You'll let me help you? You'll let me try?

KAREN: Yes, if it will make you feel better.

MRS. TILFORD: [*with great feeling*] Oh, yes, oh, yes. Karen. [KAREN *walks toward the window.*]

KAREN: [*suddenly*] Is it nice out?

MRS. TILFORD: It's been cold. [KAREN *opens the window slightly, sits on the ledge.*]

KAREN: It feels very good.

MRS. TILFORD: You'll write me sometime?

KAREN: If I ever have anything to say. Good-bye, now.

MRS. TILFORD: Good-bye, my dear. [KAREN *smiles as* MRS. TILFORD *exits. She does not turn, but a minute later she raises her hand.*]

KAREN: Good-bye.

CURTAIN

Oscar Wilde

Leslie and Sewell Stokes

Preface

I **t will probably be within the general recollection** that when, about eighteen months ago, Mr. Norman Marshall proposed to put on at the Gate Theatre an English version of Monsieur Maurice Rostand's play about Oscar Wilde, I intervened and objected to the production. My objection, as I explained to Mr. Marshall in an interview I had with him at the time in my flat at Hove, was not because I considered then, any more than I do now, that a play dealing with more or less contemporary facts and persons may not rightly be presented on the stage, but simply because Monsieur Rostand's play was a travesty of the truth and a deliberate misrepresentation of well-known and often-recorded facts. It is sufficient to point out that the whole idea of Rostand's play was based on the false assumption that I had never seen or spoken to Oscar Wilde again after he came out of prison. This is, of course, so far from being the truth that it is well known, or notorious if one prefers the word, that I resumed my friendship with Wilde which, on my side at least, had never been interrupted, immediately after his release, that I wrote to him a number of letters and received a number of letters in reply while he was at Bernaval for three months after he came out of prison, that I then invited him to stay as my guest at my villa in Posilippo (Naples), where he remained for several months with me, that I left him there in possession of my villa, and after giving him a sum of money, only because my mother threatened to stop my allowance if I continued to reside in the same house with him, and that thereafter in Paris for three years, right up to the time of his death, I saw him constantly (often daily for months at a time), that I continually supplied him with money, and that when he died I paid for his funeral and was the principal mourner at the church of Saint Germain des Près, and at the cemetery at Bagneux. Naturally I objected violently to the production of a play which was based on what I can only describe as a deliberate perversion of the truth, and it did not take me ten minutes to convince Mr. Marshall that, quite apart from the legal aspect of the matter, it would be impossible for him as an honorable man to be a party to any such production.

Mr. Marshall entirely agreed as soon as he had grasped the facts and after I had shown him a number of Wilde's letters written to me from Bernaval. He at once stopped the rehearsals and issued notices to the Press that the production was canceled.

At that time I told Mr. Marshall that if, and when, he cared to produce another play which did not falsify the story, I would not raise any objection to its production, and I pointed out that Monsieur Rostand, whatever may have been his motives (possibly he was only ignorant and had not taken the trouble to verify the facts), had merely succeeded in completely destroying what was and is, in truth, a very dramatic and romantic story.

Accordingly, when Mr. Marshall and Mr. Sewell Stokes visited me at Hove a few months ago and showed me the present play, I agreed at once to its performance, with a few minor alterations in the text. As it stands it represents an historically true story, allowing, of course, for dramatic license.

For example, when Wilde came out of prison he left England the same day and never returned. The house in Tite Street was no longer his, and his furniture and goods had all been seized and sold under distraint to satisfy his creditors, within a week or two of his arrest.

To place the second act of the play in Tite Street is therefore, of course, incorrect, but I think it is a legitimate piece of dramatic arrangement.

Again the scenes at Algiers and in Paris while not pretending to be exact reproductions of actual scenes are sufficiently close to the truth to be accepted without objection. I could have wished that poor Wilde had not been shown in the last act drunk on the stage. On the other hand, it is idle to deny that he was drunk, on occasions, at that period of his life, and if Byron and Browning and Shakespeare can be shown on the stage, why not Oscar Wilde?

I did not see the play myself, because I felt that it would be too painful for me, devoted as I still am and always shall be to the memory of this brilliant and wonderful man, and conscious as I am and always shall be of my own failings (though not in the direction of any unkindness or disloyalty to

Wilde) to witness it. But as I have been asked to write a preface for the present publication, I can say that I regard the play as truthful and dramatic in a high degree, and I am glad to know from the evidence of numerous people who witnessed it that it aroused great sympathy for a man whom I consider to have been cruelly and unjustly treated and whose brilliant genius, if he had not been condemned by an ungrateful country to prison and resulting early death, would have enriched the English stage with many more masterpieces of dramatic art. Wilde was at his best a fine poet and a master of prose, and he was also the author of what I consider to be, apart from Shakespeare, the finest comedy ever written in the English language. If his fellow countrymen had treated him in a more Christian spirit, he would have written half a dozen more comedies as good. Let England bear the responsibility for what she did to him.

"From the beginning when was ought but stones for English prophets?"

— Alfred Douglas
St. Ann's Court, Hove.

John Carol (Charlie Parker) and Robert Morley (Oscar Wilde) in *Oscar Wilde*, at the Fulton Theatre, 1938. (Photograph reprinted with permission from the Billy Rose Theatre Collection, The New York Public Library for the Performing Arts, Astor, Lenox, and Tilden Foundations.)

Oscar Wilde was first presented on Broadway at the Fulton Theatre on October 10, 1938. It was produced and directed by Norman Marshall, and the settings and costumes were designed by Raymond Sovey.

Cast
(In order of appearance)

Lord Alfred Douglas	John Buckmaster
Louis Dijon	Edward Trevor
An Arab Boy	Richard Charlton
Oscar Wilde	Robert Morley
An Hotel Waiter	Kenneth Treseder
Eustace	Wyman Kane
A Waiter	Reginald Malcolm
Frank Harris	Harold Young
Charlie Parker	John Carol
A Butler	Colin Hunter
Allen	Arthur Gould-Porter
Sir Edward Clarke, Q.C.	J.W. Austin
Mr. Justice Henn Collins	Frederick Graham
Clerk of the Court	Lewis Dayton
Mr. E.H. Carson, Q.C.	Mark Dignam
The Solicitor-General	Gordon Richards
Mr. Justice Wills	Oswald Yorke
A Waiter	Jean Del Val

For Norman Marshall and Robert Morley
to whom the authors owe more than
they care to admit.

Authors' note

The authors particularly wish to express their gratitude to Lord Alfred Douglas for his kindness in permitting them to portray him on the stage, and also for his help in checking the authenticity of several facts contained in this play. In addition they wish to acknowledge the various works on which they have drawn for information, especially, the following: *Wilde: Three Times Tried* (Ferrestone Press, 1912); *Letters to the Sphinx*, Ada Leverson (Duckworth, 1930); *Oscar Wilde: His Life and Confessions* by Frank Harris; *Oscar Wilde* by Andre Gide; *Poems in Prose* by Oscar Wilde (Paris, 1905); *The Complete Works of Oscar Wilde* (Collins).

Act One

Scene I: The terrace of an Hotel in Algiers.
Scene II: A Private Room at a Restaurant.
Scene III: Wilde's study, Tite Street, Chelsea.

Act Two

Scene I: The Queensberry Trial. The old Court at the Old Bailey.
    [*The curtain is lowered once to denote a lapse of time*]
Scene II: The Wilde Trial. Another view of the Court.
    [*The curtain is lowered twice to denote lapse of time.*]

Act Three

Scene I: Wilde's study, Tite Street.
Scene II: A Café in Paris.

Act One

Scene I

Scene: *The terrace of an hotel in Algiers. There are two or three wicker chairs, and tables. The entrance to the hotel is on the left. Beyond the stone balustrade at the back is a deep blue sky, against which a palm-tree spreads itself decoratively.*

When the curtain rises a native orchestra is playing not far away, and its music is heard at intervals throughout the scene.

LORD ALFRED DOUGLAS, *a startlingly good-looking, golden-haired young man of twenty-four, is lounging in a chair and writing.*

From the right enters an ARAB PORTER, *carrying a large suitcase. He is closely followed by* LOUIS DIJON, *an elegant young Frenchman.*

LORD ALFRED *puts his pencil down and closes his eyes.*

PORTER: [*Putting down the case at the hotel entrance*] This hotel very nice. Very quiet. What Monsieur wants, yes?

DIJON: It looks all right. Tell me, are there any other tourists staying here?

PORTER: [*Hoping to please*] Yes, many tourists stay here. Very nice hotel.

DIJON: Then I shall certainly have to find somewhere else. [*Explaining, with emphasis*] I do not like tourists. [*He turns, and for the first time sees* LORD ALFRED] Un moment! [*In a loud whisper*] Isn't that gentleman Lord Alfred Douglas?

PORTER: Yes. He stays in the hotel with friend—*big* gentleman.

DIJON: Oh. I think I will stay here. [*The* PORTER *and* DIJON *go into the hotel.* LORD ALFRED *immediately turns to look after them. He smiles; then slowly lights a cigarette. Taking up the Ms. on which he has been working, he reads softly to himself, making one or two corrections with a pencil. Looking up from the paper, he recites aloud.*]

LORD ALFRED: "Pipe unto him with pipes and flute with flutes,
Woo him with flowers and spices odorous,
Let singing boys with lips mellifluous
Make madrigals and lull his ears with lutes."

DIJON: [*Who has appeared in time to hear the last two lines*] But that is enchanting. Is it your own?

LORD ALFRED: It is. And who may you be?

DIJON: I am Louis Dijon. You are Lord Alfred Douglas, I believe. We met in London, about a year ago, at Lady Brandon's house.

LORD ALFRED: Why, of course. [*Shaking hands*] How are you?

DIJON: When we met you told me that you wrote poetry. I remember, too, that you were brought to the house by Mr. Oscar Wilde.

LORD ALFRED: Your memory is a little at fault there. It was I who brought Oscar Wilde to the house. He is staying with me here now.

DIJON: Yes, I've just seen your name in the hotel register. And how is dear Oscar?

LORD ALFRED: You know him, then?

DIJON: Not intimately. But we've met several times. And he has always been perfectly charming to me.

LORD ALFRED: That is not at all surprising.

DIJON: Why do you say that?

LORD ALFRED: Oscar is always charming to young men—particularly young men with good looks.

DIJON: [*Bowing*] Thank you, Lord Alfred!

LORD ALFRED: And how is Lady Brandon? I haven't seen her lately.

DIJON: She continues to entertain as lavishly as ever.

LORD ALFRED: Her dinners are always rather tiresome, don't you think? She treats her guests exactly as an auctioneer treats his goods. She tells one everything about them except what one wants to know.

DIJON: Poor Lady Brandon! Aren't you being a little hard on her?

LORD ALFRED: My dear fellow, you can't expect me to admire her. She tried to found a *salon*, and only succeeded in opening a restaurant.

DIJON: Is that one of Oscar's sayings?

LORD ALFRED: It is what *I* say. The disadvantage of being Oscar's great friend is that all one's best remarks are believed to be his. I have a little wit of my own, I hope.

DIJON: I am sorry, Lord Alfred.

LORD ALFRED: Call me just Alfred. [*Smiling*] And do sit down, please.

DIJON: [*Sitting*] Thank you. Are you making a long stay in Algiers?

LORD ALFRED: That depends entirely upon Oscar. He ought to return to

London for the rehearsals of his new play. But at present he seems to be enjoying himself far too much to want to leave this town. He finds it full of attractions.

DIJON: What is his new play like? You've read it, of course?

LORD ALFRED: It's a farce, called "The Importance of Being Earnest." I think it is really one of the best things Oscar has done.

DIJON: I shall make a point of being in London for the *première*.

LORD ALFRED: You don't live in London?

DIJON: No, in Paris. Oscar is very popular there, too. Everybody talks about him.

LORD ALFRED: And what do they say?

DIJON: Opinions are divided. Some say that he is nothing more than a dandy who smokes gold-tipped cigarettes and walks about the streets with a sunflower in his hand. But he is more generally regarded as the most amusing and successful man in England.

LORD ALFRED: Sometimes I think perhaps he is too successful. It makes me a little afraid of what may happen.

DIJON: How do you mean — afraid?

LORD ALFRED: Oh, I don't know. You see, Oscar has reached that stage when he believes he can do no wrong. Sometimes he is positively reckless.

DIJON: He has the reputation of being wonderfully wicked.

LORD ALFRED: And that pleases him. He is always declaring that his pleasure is to amuse the mob, frighten the middle-classes, and fascinate the aristocrats.

DIJON: Well, he does all three superbly. Where is he now?

LORD ALFRED: Somewhere in the town, I expect. He spends most of the day walking about the streets surrounded by a crowd of Arab boys — throwing them money, and joking with them. He imagines himself a king distributing largesse among his subjects. He should be back any moment now.

DIJON: Perhaps I had better leave you for the time being. Oscar might like to find you alone when he returns.

LORD ALFRED: My dear Louis, your presence will be a delightful surprise for him. Oscar and I have known each other long enough not to be jealous of another's company. In fact, Oscar is only jealous of my poems, which happen to be rather better than his own. You must certainly dine with us tonight.

DIJON: That is most kind of you. I shall be charmed. [OSCAR WILDE'*s voice can be heard off, admonishing a crowd of Arab boys who have followed him, and whose voices can also be distinguished. He enters with his back to the audience, throwing few coins to the crowd.*]

WILDE: That is sufficient . . . Off with you now! Run along home! [*He turns and faces* LORD ALFRED *and* DIJON. WILDE *is over six feet in height, broad and rather stout. He evidently pays a great deal of attention to his personal appearance. His hair is waved; his clothes fit him a little too tightly; he wears a large green scarab ring on one finger. Most people dislike him at first, but they are quickly won over by his charm of manner, his exceptionally fine speaking voice, his genial gaiety and vivacity of expression.*]

WILDE: What is this picture I behold? [*Looking from one to the other*] Hylas and Hyacinthus have returned to earth! The flower of Grecian boyhood is here to welcome my homecoming. Too wonderful! [*Moving forward*] How are you, my dear Louis? This is indeed a delightful surprise. [*He offers a limp hand for* LOUIS *to shake.*]

DIJON: [*Shaking hands*] How are you, Oscar?

WILDE: You are looking younger than ever. [*Drawing back a little*] But I am not sure that I like your lips, they are quite straight, like the lips of a man who has never told a lie. You must learn to lie, so that your lips may become beautiful and curved like the lips of an antique mask.

LORD ALFRED: Will you stop acting, Oscar?

WILDE: But I like acting. It is so much more real than real life. [*Suddenly remembering*] Let me introduce you. Louis Dijon. [*Turning to* LORD ALFRED; *and emphasizing the title*] *Lord* Alfred Douglas.

LORD ALFRED: We have already met. And Louis is aware of my title. [*Smiling at this little thrust,* WILDE *playfully flicks* LORD ALFRED'S *cheek with his finger*] What have you been doing with yourself all day, Oscar?

WILDE: Demoralizing the town, dear boy. I find the Arabs too attractive. [*To* DIJON] Don't tell me, Louis, that you have come to this lovely spot to work?

DIJON: I had thought of starting to write a new novel here. I came from Paris for that purpose.

WILDE: Oh, but really you must do nothing of the sort. In such heavenly surroundings as these, your duty is to plunge madly into amusement. I do — all the time.

DIJON: But are you doing no work?

WILDE: I am fleeing from art. Have you never noticed how the sun detests thought? The sun always causes thought to withdraw itself and take refuge in the shade. Thought dwelt in Egypt originally, but the sun conquered Egypt; then it lived for a long time in Greece; and the sun conquered Greece; then in Italy and then in France. Nowadays all thought is driven as far back as Norway and Russia, places where the sun never goes. The sun is jealous of art.

LORD ALFRED: Nevertheless, I managed to write a very good poem while you were playing in the sun.

WILDE: Busy little Bosie! [*To* DIJON] He will spend his time writing pretty verses. I can't think why.

LORD ALFRED: Have you any objection, Oscar?

WILDE: You know I haven't, Bosie. [*Looking at him with affection*] I am always telling you that it doesn't matter in the least *what* you do, since you happen to be a charming and graceful young man, related to everyone in the peerage, who does whatever he wants to do in a charming and graceful manner.

LORD ALFRED: Then why do you blame me for working?

WILDE: It is only of your looks I am thinking, dear boy. Real beauty ends where an intellectual expression begins. The moment one sits down to think, one becomes all nose, or all forehead, or something horrid. Look at the successful men in any of the professions. How perfectly hideous they are! Except, of course, in the Church. But then in the Church they don't think. A bishop keeps on saying at the age of eighty what he was told when he was a boy of eighteen, and as a natural consequence he always looks absolutely delightful.

LORD ALFRED: You harp too much on my good looks, Oscar.

WILDE Not at all. While it is considered in England almost criminal for a man to speak of good looks either in himself or in another man, good looks are half the battle in society.

LORD ALFRED: All the same, I shall continue to write poetry.

WILDE: Of course. You should publish one of those slim volumes that are so much in vogue. Bring out a book that is all margin; full of beautiful unwritten thoughts, and bound in some Nile-green skin, powdered with gilt stars. It must be dedicated to me; and Aubrey Beardsley shall illustrate the unwritten text.

LORD ALFRED: Aubrey has a superb line, but he doesn't know where to draw it.

WILDE: Really, Bosie. I would not have been ashamed to say that myself.

LORD ALFRED: Thank you, Oscar! The book is a marvelous idea. There must be five hundred signed copies for particular friends, six for the general public, and one for America.

WILDE: Be an angel, Bosie, and fetch me my cigarettes from my room. I am too fatigued to mount the stairs. [*Until now* WILDE *has been standing, with one leg resting on a chair. He now sits down.*]

LORD ALFRED: [*Rising*] Where shall I find them?

WILDE: In my room, by the bed. I am *always* tidy. Which reminds me, Bosie, that you are *not*. How often have I told you never to leave letters lying about? On the table in your room this morning I found several that I wrote to you over a year ago, at Oxford. Why do you not destroy them?

LORD ALFRED: You know very well, Oscar, that you would be perfectly furious if I did. [*To* DIJON] Oscar regards his letters as masterpieces.

WILDE: Some of them are! But the point is that people in our position cannot afford to leave letters about for anybody to read. It is not always — safe.

LORD ALFRED: It's strange to hear you talk of safety, Oscar. [*He goes into the hotel.*]

WILDE: [*To* DIJON] I am absolutely devoted to Bosie. But sometimes I feel that I have given away my whole soul to someone who treats it as if it were a flower to put in his coat.

DIJON: You must not think such things, Oscar. Even I can see how fond of you Lord Alfred really is.

WILDE: [*Gratefully patting his hand*] Thank you, dear boy. [*Smiling, and with a return to his assured mood*] I think, perhaps, that Bosie will always be fond of me — if only because I represent to him all the sins he will never have the courage to commit. [*A* WAITER *enters with letters.*]

WAITER: [*To* WILDE] The post has just arrived, sir.

WILDE: [*Taking the letters*] Thank you. [*Looking up from the letters*] You might bring us three of those inspiring new drinks you mix in the bar. What is it they're called . . . cocktails.

WAITER: Certainly, sir. [*He goes out.*]

WILDE: [*To* DIJON] Such a fascinating drink. Like a synthesis of sins. [*Starting to open the letters*] Will you excuse me?

DIJON: Of course.

WILDE [*Glancing at the first letter*] From Frank Harris, the journalist. Do you know him?

DIJON: I think I have met him in London.

WILDE: Possibly you have. Frank is asked to all the best houses — once. [*Opening another letter, he reads it with a smile of affectionate amusement*] From Charlie Parker. You will not have met him. He is a groom, or something. But a dear lad. His spelling is too amusing.

DIJON: A groom did you say?

WILDE: Yes. I have some quite odd friends, you know. But all of them are charming in their way. Where youth is concerned, I make no social distinctions. [*Laughs to himself.* LORD ALFRED *returns.*]

Lord Alfred: Here are your cigarettes, Oscar. Is there a letter for me?

Wilde: One from your dear father, Bosie. Judging by the handwriting on the envelope, I should say he is in a temper about something.

Lord Alfred: [*Crossly*] What does he want, I wonder? [*He opens the letter and reads it.*]

Wilde: [*To* Dijon] Can I offer you one of my perfumed cigarettes? A cigarette is the perfect type of a perfect pleasure. It is exquisite, and it leaves one unsatisfied. What more can one want? [*He lights* Dijon*'s cigarette, and they smoke for a few seconds in silence, while* Lord Alfred, *whose expression has darkened, reads his letter.*]

Lord Alfred: [*Rising from his chair in anger*] But this is monstrous. My father must be mad. He *is* mad.

Wilde: Is something the matter, Bosie?

Lord Alfred: You would not believe what my father has put in this letter.

Wilde: I can believe anything, provided it is quite incredible.

Lord Alfred: Then listen to this.

Wilde: [*Turning to* Dijon] Forgive these domestic interludes. They will occur.

Dijon: Would you rather I left you?

Lord Alfred: There is no need for you to go, Louis. The whole world knows that I have a madman for a father. [*He reads the letter in a tone one imagines the writer would have used had he spoken the words*] "Alfred. It is extremely painful to me to have to write to you in the strain I must; but understand that I strongly disapprove of your intimacy with this man Wilde. It must either cease or I will disown you and stop all money supplies. I am not going to try and analyze this intimacy, and I make no charge; but to my mind to pose as a thing is as bad as to be it. No wonder people are talking as they are. If I catch you again with that man I will make a public scandal in a way you little dream of; it is already a suppressed one. I prefer an open one, and at any rate I shall not be blamed for allowing such a state of things to go on. Unless this acquaintance ceases at once, I shall carry out my threat. Your disgusted so-called father—Queensberry."

Wilde: [*After a pause*] It is perfectly monstrous the way people say things against one behind one's back that are absolutely and entirely true.

Lord Alfred: He's insufferable! He's always hated me since I was a child. What are we going to do about it, Oscar? We must put a stop to these insults.

Wilde: At the moment I'm not sure that we can do anything.

LORD ALFRED: We must return to London at once. Meanwhile I shall send him a telegram. That will at least make him angry.

WILDE: I think he is already quite angry. What will you say?

LORD ALFRED: I shall think of something. [*He goes out. WILDE gets up from his chair, and paces slowly about, smoking. He is upset, but not too much so.*]

DIJON: I am sorry this has happened, Oscar.

WILDE: Oh, it is really nothing to worry about. The Marquis of Queensberry has been persecuting me for some time. Bosie is right, you know; his father is a little mad.

DIJON: Madmen can be very dangerous. Surely it would be better to remain out of England until the scandal has died down?

WILDE: I think I must return to London.

DIJON: But if you do, what will happen? Do you know the risk you are running?

WILDE: [*Significantly*] It is best never to know. My friends are extraordinary. They are always begging me to be careful. But that would be a backward step. I must go on as far as possible. [*Confidentially*] I cannot go much farther. Something is bound to happen.

DIJON: But for the sake of your own happiness...

WILDE: I don't want happiness, only pleasure.

DIJON: I am afraid I don't understand.

WILDE: Some things in my life nobody understands but myself. Even Bosie does not share all my secrets. Would you like to know the great drama of my life? It is that I put my genius into life, and only my talent into my work. Writing bores me so.

DIJON: Is that true?

WILDE: [*Smiling*] Nothing is ever quite true! [*The WAITER brings in the drinks, places them on a table, and goes out again. As he goes out he passes LORD ALFRED, who returns with a smile of satisfaction on his face.*]

LORD ALFRED: Well, I've sent my telegram.

WILDE: What did you put?

LORD ALFRED: I put "What a funny little man you are." [*All three laugh at the joke. They take up their glasses.*]

DIJON: May I propose a toast? To Oscar Wilde. A lord of language. And a king of life! [*He drains his glass, then breaks it on the table and throws away the stem. The other two gaze at him, a little bewildered by his sudden enthusiasm.*]

WILDE: [*Bowing*] Thank you, Louis, for that sweet gesture. I hope you may never have cause to regret it.

CURTAIN

Scene II

Scene: *A private room at a restaurant. A supper table is set for two on the one side of the stage, and there is a settee on the other side. The orchestra in the restaurant downstairs is playing when the curtain rises, and is heard at intervals during the scene.*

A WAITER *ushers into the room* EUSTACE, *a young dandy who wears a satin-lined cloak over his evening-clothes, a green carnation in his buttonhole, and carries a cane.*

WAITER: Excuse me, sir, but are you the young gentleman Mr. Wilde is expecting to supper?

EUSTACE: No. But I wish to see Mr. Wilde for a moment, so I will wait until he comes.

WAITER: Very good, sir. [*He goes out.* EUSTACE *looks at his face closely in a mirror which hangs on the wall. He licks a finger and smoothes down each eyebrow, tidies his hair, then makes a grotesque grin and examines his teeth. While he is still at the mirror the door is opened by the* WAITER *to admit* LOUIS DIJON, *who is also in evening dress, and wears a green carnation. The* WAITER *goes out.*]

DIJON: Eustace!

EUSTACE: My dear Louis! [*They shake hands.*]

DIJON: How are you? I caught sight of you at the theater, but there was such a tremendous crush, I couldn't get near you.

EUSTACE: So you, Louis, are the honored guest whom Oscar has chosen to sup with him after his victorious first-night? Congratulations!

DIJON: [*Surprised*] Oscar has not invited me to supper. I heard he was coming on here, so I called in to tell him how much I enjoyed his play.

EUSTACE: I did the same. [*Looking toward the table*] Then for whom is the nocturnal feast? [*They both gaze at the table in wonder.*]

DIJON: I haven't the slightest idea.

EUSTACE: This is most intriguing. If we wait long enough we may learn who is the new favorite.

DIJON: And you enjoyed "The Importance of Being Earnest"?

EUSTACE: I thought it was too marvelous. Altogether a perfectly divine evening.

DIJON: There can be no doubt about the importance of being Oscar Wilde. Simply *everybody* was at the theater tonight, despite the rain and the bitter wind.

EUSTACE: I am sure to catch cold. I left the tassel off my cane.

DIJON: Even George Alexander couldn't help being good in the play.

EUSTACE: And what a performance Oscar himself gave. Coming to the front of the box at the end, and solemnly informing the audience that Mr. Wilde was not in the house! Oscar's too marvelous.

DIJON: There's nobody like him.

EUSTACE: He's had a new triumph tonight.

DIJON: There was a solid block of carriages from the Haymarket to St. James's; and people who'd been standing for hours in the rain cheered him as he went into the theater.

EUSTACE: I've never seen anything like it. But did you hear what the Marquis of Queensberry did? He arrived at the theater with a large bouquet, only to find that the police had orders not to admit him.

DIJON: Queensberry with a bouquet for Oscar? You're not serious.

EUSTACE: It was a bouquet composed of carrots, turnips, and cauliflowers! Queensberry is a perfectly dreadful person, and utterly mad. He's furious about Oscar's friendship with Bosie, and he'll stop at nothing to get his revenge. One of these days, unless I'm much mistaken, he'll expose Oscar. When that happens, we shall all have to look out for ourselves.

DIJON: A man's private life ought to be his own affair.

EUSTACE: Life would be very much easier if it were. But Oscar is more than a trifle indiscreet. I believe he takes a positive delight in shocking the Philistines.

DIJON: Yes, he can be absurdly reckless.

EUSTACE: And invariably he is.

DIJON: I don't see why, just because Oscar and Bosie choose to go about together, the whole town should fling mud at them. England may be a country of hypocrites, but surely things are not as bad as all that?

EUSTACE: It's not merely his friendship with Bosie. That's the least part of it.

DIJON: Then what...?

EUSTACE: If Oscar chose all his friends from the pages of Debrett, it would not matter so much. But he goes farther afield than that. And one can hardly blame people, when they see him treating a stable-lad to champagne at the Café Royal, for thinking it a little—well odd.

DIJON: [_Thoughtfully_] Does he really make his pleasures so obvious?

EUSTACE: He does. That's why so many of his friends are afraid for him. There's one young groom he goes about with who paints his face as if he were Sarah Bernhardt. I use a little color myself, but there are limits. [LORD ALFRED _comes in. He is also in evening dress, but does not wear a green carnation. He looks worried._]

LORD ALFRED: Have either of you seen Oscar since he left the theater? I've missed him.

DIJON: He hasn't arrived yet, Alfred; but [*Pointing to the table*] your supper awaits you.

EUSTACE: So you are the mysterious guest. *What* a disappointment!

LORD ALFRED: I'm not having supper here, but there's something I must talk to Oscar about. I suppose you know how my father tried to insult us?

EUSTACE: The bouquet of vegetables? Disgraceful!

LORD ALFRED: [*Passionately*] I won't tolerate it! I'm of age and my own master. My father has disowned me at least a dozen times, and has no right over me either legally or morally. I shall go where I like and with whom I choose.

DIJON: If I were you, Alfred, I should try to reason with your father.

LORD ALFRED: One can't reason with a madman, and he's quite mad. If Oscar were to prosecute him in the criminal courts for libel, he'd get seven years' penal servitude. I want to avoid that for the sake of the family. But if he tries to assault me, as he's threatened to, I shall defend myself with a revolver. And if I shoot him, or if Oscar does, we should be completely justified, because we should be acting in self-defense against a violent and dangerous rough. [*There is a noise outside, then the door bursts open, and* WILDE *enters. He wears a cloak, a green carnation, and carries a cane and white gloves. He is flushed with success, but appears a little surprised at finding the room occupied.*]

DIJON and EUSTACE: Oscar! Oscar! [*They rush to help him off with his things.*]

DIJON: The play was superb, magnificent! Quite the most amusing thing you've ever written.

EUSTACE: Too divinely witty, Oscar. I simply *loved* every word of it!

WILDE: Wasn't it a *delightful* play? So amusing. I can't remember *when* I've laughed so much.

DIJON: You're a second Congreve.

EUSTACE: Only infinitely more amusing.

WILDE: [*With his arms round their shoulders*] Thank you, dear boys; thank you a thousand times. [*He sees* LORD ALFRED, *who has been impatiently standing apart*] But why is Bosie looking so somber? Did he not have a wonderful evening, too?

LORD ALFRED: I want to talk to you, Oscar. Alone.

DIJON: [*To* WILDE, *taking* EUSTACE'S *arm*] We're just going. We only came to offer our congratulations.

EUSTACE: Yes, we are leaving you. [*Glances at the table*] To your little romance!

DIJON: Good night, Alfred.

EUSTACE: Good night, Bosie.

LORD ALFRED: Good night. [EUSTACE *and* DIJON *go out.*]

WILDE: [*As they leave*] Good night, dear boys. Tonight I am in love with all the world!

LORD ALFRED: All the world is not in love with you, Oscar. You have as many enemies as friends.

WILDE: I beg of you, Bosie, let us not talk of enemies tonight. Do not spoil my hour of triumph. You heard them at the theater, cheering me as if I had been a king. [*Drawing himself up*] I feel like a king! Not even your father can touch me now.

LORD ALFRED: I know my father better than you do, Oscar. He will stop at nothing, to ruin you. If we don't do something to silence him, at once, we shall have only ourselves to blame. Oh, I wish you'd be reasonable, and face the facts.

WILDE: [*Puts his hand on* LORD ALFRED'*s shoulder*] Tonight, Bosie, I wish to face only one fact; to forget the ugliness of the world, and surrender myself entirely to the pleasures that are my reward for creating beauty. Leave me, now, Bosie — please. In the morning, I promise you, we will discuss these tedious matters together. Please, Bosie . . .

LORD ALFRED: [*Giving in*] Very well, Oscar. I will leave you.

WILDE: Thank you. I knew you would understand.

LORD ALFRED: Good night, Oscar.

WILDE: Good night, my dear. [LORD ALFRED *goes. As the door closes* WILDE *goes to the mirror and arranges his hair, tie, etc. There is a sharp knock at the door. He turns with a smile on his face*] Come in! [FRANK HARRIS *comes quickly into the room. He is a determined, loud-voiced little man, with a big mustache curled upward at the ends. Seeing him,* WILDE'*s smile almost fades.*]

HARRIS: Ah! There you are, Oscar! I was having supper in the restaurant downstairs, and they told me you were up here. I must have a word with you.

WILDE: You must excuse me, Frank. I am expecting to supper a guest who is already late. Can't what you have to say to me wait?

HARRIS: My dear fellow, I want to speak to you seriously. Very seriously indeed! Don't frown like that. You make it so much more difficult for me.

WILDE: Frank, what is it you have to say? [*Impatiently*] I hope it is not about myself.

HARRIS: It is about yourself, and I must say it to you. It is entirely for your own sake that I am speaking. I think it right that you should know that the most scandalous things are being said against you, all over London.

WILDE: I don't wish to hear anything about them. I love scandals about other people, but scandals about myself don't interest me. They haven't the charm of novelty. [*Takes an olive from the table and eats it.*]

HARRIS: Surely, you don't want people to talk of you as something vile and degraded? I know that you have the security of your position, and your wealth, and all that kind of thing. But in these matters position and wealth are not everything. Mind you, *I* don't believe a word of these rumors. I treat them as what they are—malicious lies, manufactured by those who are jealous of your success.

WILDE: [*Offering the dish of olives to* HARRIS] Have an olive?

HARRIS: [*Irritably*] No, thank you! You must be more careful in your behavior, Oscar. Avoid giving these enemies of yours a chance to gossip.

WILDE: And how would you have me do that, Frank?

HARRIS: By being more careful of the company you keep; and less extravagant in the theories you are always propounding.

WILDE: What theories?

HARRIS: Oh, your theories about life; your theories about pleasure. All your theories, in fact.

WILDE: Pleasure is the only thing worth having a theory about.

HARRIS: I'm no prude, as you very well know, but…

WILDE: [*Holding his olive stone*] Tell me, what do you do with the stones? My dear Frank, medieval art is charming, but medieval emotions are out of date. Believe me, no civilized man ever regrets a pleasure, and no uncivilized man ever knows what a pleasure is. One must be in harmony with one's self. One's own life, that is the important thing.

HARRIS: [*Earnestly*] If one lives one's own life, one may have to pay a terrible price for doing so.

WILDE: [*Lightly*] Yes, we are over-charged for everything nowadays. I should fancy that the real tragedy of the poor is that they can afford nothing but self-denial. Beautiful sins, like beautiful pleasures, are the privilege of the rich.

HARRIS: You don't believe half of what you say, Oscar; you know you don't. You are much better than you pretend to be. [*There is a knock at the door.*]

WILDE: Come in! [CHARLES PARKER *is ushered in by the* WAITER. *He is a cockney lad, not yet out of his teens, flashily dressed, with his hair plastered in a lovelock on his forehead. He is obviously ill at ease in the surroundings in which he finds himself, but is anxious to make himself pleasant. The* WAITER *goes out.*]

WILDE: [*With a gracious smile*] Charlie Parker, at last!

PARKER: Good evening, sir.

HARRIS: [*Quickly*] I must be going, Oscar.

WILDE: Good night then, Frank. We must continue our little discussion some other time.

HARRIS: I'll call at your house during the week, Good night. [HARRIS *goes, at the same time glancing suspiciously at* PARKER.]

WILDE: [*Looking at* PARKER *and taking out his cigarette case*] Cigarette, Charlie?

PARKER: Ta!

WILDE: Let me take your hat and coat, Charlie, [WILDE *takes the hat and coat and* PARKER *lights his cigarette*] Sit down, Charlie, and make yourself at home.

PARKER: Thank you, sir.

WILDE: How many times have I told you that you must not call me "sir"? My name is Oscar.

PARKER: Thank you, Mr. Oscar.

WILDE: Just "Oscar" will do.

PARKER: All right — [*Smiling*] — Oscar.

WILDE: That's better. And now, Charlie, you must have some supper. [*They sit at the table, and during the following scene drink and eat liberally.* PARKER'*s table manners leave something to be desired.*]

PARKER: [*Putting out his cigarette*] Nice fags, these. [*He has only smoked half the cigarette, so he puts the stub behind his ear.*]

WILDE: I'm *so* glad you like them. I will give you some — and a silver cigarette-case to put them in. When you came into the room just now, I decided to give you a present.

PARKER: [*With his mouth full*] Thanks, Oscar. You're very kind.

WILDE: Well, you know, people are often very kind to me. *You* are. When my friend Mr. Taylor first spoke to me about you, he said you were a good boy, and now I know that he was perfectly right.

PARKER: [*Sitting back and holding his knife and fork vertically*] My dad don't think I'm good! He turned me outer the house. Said I 'adn't got no principles. [*He smiles.*]

WILDE: I think that your father and I would never agree. [*Confidentially*] You see, I happen to like people better than principles. And I like people with no principles better than anything else in the world! [*After a pause*] Has anybody ever told you, Charlie, what a nice face you have?

PARKER: Yes, I think Mr. Taylor said something of that sort to me.

WILDE: And what else did Mr. Taylor say to you?

PARKER: [*After a pause for mastication*] He said you — [*He finds that a further pause is necessary for mastication*] — he said you was a very nice gentleman. And he told me that you did a bit of writin'.

WILDE: I write books and plays. Do you ever go to the theater, or read?

PARKER: I've been to the Old Mo' once or twice, to see Marie Lloyd and Charlie Coburn. I'm not much of a one for readin', really, though I like a bit of Dickens now and again. Are your books like his?

WILDE: Not exactly.

PARKER: Dickens ain't so dusty.

WILDE: No, indeed. One must have a heart of stone to read the death of Little Nell without laughing.

PARKER: [*Seriously*] I don't remember that one.

WILDE: Now, Charlie, you must tell me about yourself. It would interest me enormously to know what you do with your time.

PARKER: I don't know as I do much with my time.

WILDE: And what do you think about life?

PARKER: I don't know as I think so very much about life, either.

WILDE: So much the better. There are only two kinds of people who are really fascinating — those who know absolutely everything, and those who know absolutely nothing. [PARKER *looks rather bewildered*] Dear boy, don't look so tragic. The secret of remaining young is never to have an emotion that is unbecoming. [PARKER *smiles*] That's better! Let me fill your glass. [WILDE *fills both glasses and they drink.*]

PARKER: [*Smacking his lips*] This stuff's all right.

WILDE: [*Regarding him with admiration*] How inspiring you are, Charlie! You remind me of a youth in Ancient Greece. [*He takes a decoration of leaves from the dish of fruit and places it on* PARKER'*s head, having first removed the cigarette-end from behind his ear*] And with this to wear, you will look like a young victor, crowned at the Olympic Games.

PARKER: [*Amused*] Did Greek boys wear things like this in their 'air?

WILDE: Often they wore nothing else.

PARKER: Do you mean to say they was niked?

WILDE: Divinely nude. Clothed only in sunshine and beauty.

PARKER: [*He gets up from the table and goes to look at himself in the mirror*] Blimey! Don't I look funny? [*He turns from the mirror to find that* WILDE *is standing close beside him, and is watching his face intently*] Who's looking tragic now?

WILDE: [*Slowly*] I was thinking — thinking of The Pleasure that Abideth for a Moment. Sit down, Charlie, and I will tell you a story. [*They sit on the settee*] Once there was an artist and there came into his soul the desire to fashion an image of The Pleasure that Abideth for a Moment. And he went forth into the world to look for bronze. For he could only think in bronze. But all the bronze in the whole world had disappeared; nor anywhere in the whole world was there any bronze to be found, save only the bronze of the image of The Sorrow that Endureth for Ever. Now this image the artist had himself, with his own hands, fashioned, and had set it on the tomb of the one thing he had loved in life. On the tomb of the dead thing he had most loved had he set this image of his own fashioning that it might serve as a sign of the love of man that dieth not, and a symbol of the sorrow of man that endureth for ever. And in the whole world there was no other bronze save the bronze of this image. And out of the bronze of the image of The Sorrow that Endureth for Ever he fashioned an image of The Pleasure that Abideth for a Moment.

PARKER: Was you ever a play-actor? [*Goes to the table and finishes the food on his plate.*]

WILDE: [*Shocked*] No! What put such an idea into your head, Charlie?

PARKER: Well, you talk like one.

WILDE: Lots of people act well, but very few people talk well, which shows that talking is much the more difficult of the two.

PARKER: Is it?

WILDE: Yes, I suppose so.

PARKER: I wish I'd seen your play tonight. A pal of mine who was up in the gallery told me it was a proper scream. Said 'e didn't arf laugh.

WILDE: The first act is ingenious, the second beautiful, the third abominably clever. You shall see it whenever you like, Charlie. I will arrange for you to be given one of the best seats.

PARKER: Thanks, Oscar. You're a sport. D'you think I'll understand the play?

WILDE: Why not, dear boy?

PARKER: [*Confidentially*] Between you and me, I ain't 'ad much edgecation.

WILDE: Really, Charlie, I should never have guessed. Shall we be going? [*They collect their things. The orchestra plays "You Should See Me Dance the Polka"*] Delicious tune! [*He dances a few steps.* PARKER *takes his arm and sings the song as they dance out of the room.*]

CURTAIN

Scene III

Scene: *The study of* WILDE's *house in Chelsea. It is a small room with a window in the left wall looking on to the street. Door leading to hall in back center. Fireplace right. The walls are lined with books. A desk is placed in front of the window. One or two comfortable chairs are about.*

When the curtain rises the stage is in darkness. A knocking at the front door is heard, followed by the sound of voices in the hall and the door closing.

The study door is then opened by a BUTLER *carrying a lighted lamp, which he places on the desk. He is followed by* FRANK HARRIS, *who wears a heavy overcoat and carries his silk hat.*

HARRIS: But I insist upon seeing your master!

BUTLER: I am sorry, sir, but my master's instructions were that on *no* account was he to be disturbed. No matter *who* called, he said.

HARRIS: Isn't it unusual for him to retire so early? [*Looking at his watch*] Why, it's scarcely past midnight.

BUTLER: The master has had a busy day. If I may say so, sir, he seemed a bit worried this evening, and he did mention that he needed a good night's rest.

HARRIS: Yes. Yes. Your master has worries—business worries, you understand. It is about them that I particularly wish to see him. So, my good man, please tell him at once that Mr. Frank Harris is here.

BUTLER: I'm afraid, sir, that I cannot very well... [WILDE, *wearing an elaborate dressing-gown, enters at this moment. He is smoking a cigarette.*]

WILDE: Good evening, Frank! [*To the* BUTLER] You need not wait up, Charles. Nobody else is likely to call.

BUTLER: Thank you, sir. Good night, sir.

WILDE: Good night, Charles. [BUTLER *goes out.*]

HARRIS: I have been trying to get hold of you all day, Oscar. What is this I hear about Queensberry making a scandal at the club?

WILDE: So you have heard? All London seems to have heard. It is not a pretty story, Frank.

HARRIS: What happened exactly? Already there are several versions floating about. But I have come to you to hear the right one.

WILDE: It is not a story you can publish in the "Saturday," Frank. Need we discuss it? To tell you the truth, I am rather weary of the whole business.

HARRIS: [*Extravagantly*] I come, not as a journalist, but as your friend, Oscar, to help you if I can.

WILDE: That is good of you, Frank. But I have put the matter in the hands of my solicitors. I am charging Queensberry with criminal libel.

HARRIS: [*Vehemently*] You intend to do that?

WILDE: What else would you have me do? Queensberry called at my club today with a card addressed to: "Oscar Wilde, posing as sodomite," and handed it to the porter. It was delivered to me later in an envelope. That is sufficient evidence for me to act upon.

HARRIS: [*Gently for once*] But is it wise to act at all, Oscar?

WILDE: It is time somebody shut this madman's mouth. For Bosie's sake, as well as for my own, I feel that it is the right thing—the only thing—to do.

HARRIS: I am not thinking of Lord Alfred, but of you, Oscar. If this is only a family feud between father and son, you cannot afford to get yourself mixed up in it.

WILDE: Frank, I am sure your advice is well meant, but I have already decided what to do.

HARRIS: Oscar, I don't think you realize what is being said about you.

WILDE: I realize how people chatter in England. The middle-classes air their moral prejudices over their gross dinner-tables, and whisper about what they call the profligacies of their betters, in order to try and pretend that they are in smart society, and on intimate terms with people they slander. In this country it is enough for a man to have distinction and brains for every common tongue to wag against him. You forget that we are in the native land of the hypocrite.

HARRIS: [*Excitedly*] That is just what I am remembering when I ask you to think before taking a rash step that you may afterwards regret. Instead of being careful, you go out of your way to shock the very public who would jump at an opportunity to bring about your downfall. Why do you behave so recklessly, Oscar?

WILDE: Do I?

HARRIS: You know very well that you do. For one thing, you are singularly careless in your choice of associates. You think nothing of being seen in public with the oddest people. That lad I saw you at supper with the other night . . .

WILDE: Charlie Parker? An altogether charming person. I found his youthful company most stimulating.

HARRIS: Naturally, Oscar, I have never believed a word of the things that are said against you. I know that as a writer you must familiarize yourself with every type of mind, and for that reason go into every sort of company. But there are others who think differently. And when they see you, as you were, the other night, treating a working lad to champagne, and plying him with rich food, they immediately start slandering you.

WILDE: [*Wistfully*] But Charlie Parker is a friend of mine.

HARRIS: [*Impatiently*] A friend! Really, Oscar…

WILDE: Yes, a friend. I choose my friends for their good looks, my acquaintances for their good characters, and my enemies for their good intellects.

HARRIS: [*Hopelessly*] You are quite incorrigible, Oscar. Yet it is impossible to be angry with you.

WILDE: Then don't be angry with me, Frank.

HARRIS: I repeat, though, that you are seriously misguided in your determination to prosecute Queensberry. You would do better to ignore him, instead of making his accusations public property; turning them into a scandal for a dirty-minded world to lick its lips over.

WILDE: I am quite indifferent to the world's opinion. Let it think what it likes of me.

HARRIS: [*Suddenly recollecting*] I heard something the other day about a strange letter that was sent to Beerbohm Tree, anonymously. I believe it concerned you, Oscar.

WILDE: [*Smiling*] Journalists seem always to be hearing something, but seldom the truth.

HARRIS: I had my information on the best authority.

WILDE: I am sure you did, Frank. It would not surprise me if one day you wrote the story of my life.

HARRIS: Who knows? I may!

WILDE: Oh, I hope not. Every man should be his own Boswell. It is always Judas who writes the biography.

HARRIS: [*After laughing uncomfortably*] Well, what about this letter to Tree?

WILDE: How persistent you are! But I will tell you exactly what happened. [*After a pause*] A *copy* of a letter I wrote to Bosie was sent anonymously to Tree, who showed it to me, saying he thought it dangerous. I laughed at the idea. A little later a man came to me with some more of my letters which he said he had found in an old suit of clothes Bosie had given him. I gave the man some money for them, but I noticed afterwards that the original of the letter sent to Tree was not amongst them. That is all I know.

HARRIS: And where do you suppose the original of that letter is?

WILDE: I haven't the slightest idea.

HARRIS: Does it occur to you that some blackmailer may be awaiting his opportunity to sell it?

WILDE: I should think that is very probable.

HARRIS: And if it should fall into the hands of the defense at the Queensberry trial, what will you do?

WILDE: I shall not mind in the least. It is a perfectly harmless and beautifully written letter. In fact, I think I shall insist upon its being used for the prosecution. That will make it utterly useless for the defense.

HARRIS: Since you're determined to bring this absurd case, I have nothing more to say. I came to warn you, Oscar, and I have done what I can. I am sorry you won't listen to me.

WILDE: Believe me, Frank, I appreciate your intentions. But Bosie and I have decided that what we are doing is for the best.

HARRIS: Then good night, Oscar. [*He goes out.* WILDE *rises and puts out a lamp by the sofa. He then crosses the stage, and is about to put out the lamp on the desk, when the* BUTLER *enters.*]

BUTLER: Excuse me, sir.

WILDE: I thought I told you not to wait up, Charles. What is it?

BUTLER: A person called to see you, sir. He was very insistent, sir. I asked him to wait in the kitchen until Mr. Harris had gone.

WILDE: What's his name?

BUTLER: He wouldn't give his name. [*Lowering his eyes*] I think it would be wise to see him.

WILDE: Oh, very well. [*The* BUTLER *leaves and returns in a moment to usher in* ALLEN, *a cunning youth, shabbily dressed. The* BUTLER *goes out, and* ALLEN, *after watching him go, crosses slowly to* WILDE.]

WILDE: This is an absurd hour to call upon anybody.

ALLEN: I waited till the other gentleman had gone. I wanted to see you alone.

WILDE: Well, what is it you wish to see me about?

ALLEN: I've got a letter of yours here with me.

WILDE: Indeed? I don't remember ever having written to you.

ALLEN: Oh, the letter ain't written to me. [*Grinning*] I 'aven't got rose-leaf lips, *or* a slim-gilt soul!

WILDE: I suppose you have come about my beautiful letter to Lord Alfred Douglas.

ALLEN: You're right. I 'ave.

WILDE: If you had not been so foolish as to send a copy of it to

Mr. Beerbohm Tree, I would gladly have paid you a very large sum of money for the letter, as I consider it to be a work of art.

ALLEN: A very curious construction can be put on that letter.

WILDE: Art is rarely intelligible to the criminal classes.

ALLEN: A man offered me sixty pounds for it.

WILDE: If you take my advice you will go to that man and sell my letter to him for sixty pounds. I myself have never received so large a sum for any prose work of that length; but I am glad to find that there is someone in England who considers a letter of mine worth sixty pounds.

ALLEN: [*Slightly taken aback*] Trouble is, the man's out of town just now.

WILDE: He is sure to come back. It will undoubtedly pay you to wait until he does.

ALLEN: [*Changing his attitude*] Fact is, I'm broke to the wide. I 'aven't a penny. I've been trying to find you for a long time.

WILDE: I'm afraid I cannot guarantee your cab expenses, but I shall be happy to give you half a sovereign for your trouble. [*Gives it to* ALLEN, *who takes it without a word, and goes to the door*] By the way, it may interest you to know that the letter is a prose poem, and will shortly be published as a sonnet in a delightful magazine. I will send you a copy of it. [ALLEN *turns back into the room and holds out the letter.*]

ALLEN: You can 'ave it.

WILDE: [*Not taking it*] Why do you give it to me?

ALLEN: It's no good trying to rent you. You only laugh at me.

WILDE: [*Taking the letter*] Very well, I will accept it. [*Seeing how soiled it is*] I think it quite unpardonable that better care was not taken of this original manuscript of mine.

ALLEN: I'm sorry, but it's been in so many hands.

WILDE: Well, we'll say no more about it. [*As they leave the room*] I am afraid you are leading a wonderfully wicked life.

ALLEN: There's good and bad in everyone of us.

WILDE: You are a born philosopher! [*They go out. The sound of their "Good nights" is heard, and the closing of the front door.* WILDE *comes wearily into the room and sits at the desk. He glances at the letter in his hand and reads:*]

WILDE: "My own boy . . . It is a marvel that those red rose-leaf lips of yours should be made no less for music of song than for madness of kisses . . . " [*He turns the letter over*] What a mess they've made of it!

CURTAIN

Act Two

Scene I

Scene: *The Old Court at the Old Bailey. The dock is not visible to the audience in this scene.*

Sir Edward Clarke, Mr. E. H. Carson *and* Mr. Justice Henn Collins *are in Court.*

Clarke: The libel charged against the Defendant was published in the form of a visiting card left by Lord Queensberry at the club to which Mr. Wilde belongs. On that card his lordship wrote: "Oscar Wilde, posing as sodomite."

The accusation contained in those words does not suggest guilt of the actual offense, but that Mr. Wilde appears to be, or desires to appear to be, a person guilty of or inclined to the commission of the gravest offense.

The defendant by his plea has raised a much graver issue. In that plea there is a series of allegations, mentioning the names at several persons and impugning Mr. Wilde's conduct with those persons.

Between eighteen ninety-two and eighteen ninety-four, Mr. Wilde became aware that certain statements were being made against his character. A man named Allen called on Mr. Wilde, and said he possessed a letter which Mr. Wilde had written to Lord Alfred Douglas, and asked Mr. Wilde to give him something for it. Mr. Wilde absolutely and peremptorily refused. He sent Allen away, giving him ten shillings for himself. But before he left, Allen said he so much appreciated Mr. Wilde's kindness that he was willing to return the letter, and he did so.

Mr. Wilde looks upon this letter as a sort of prose poem. Here it is:

"My own Boy,

"Your sonnet is quite lovely, and it is a marvel that those red rose-leaf lips of yours should have been made no less for music of song than for madness of kisses. Your slim-gilt soul walks between passion and poetry. I know Hyacinthus, whom Apollo loved so madly, was you in Greek days.

"Why are you alone in London, and when do you go to Salisbury? Do go there to cool your hands in the gray twilight of Gothic things, and come here whenever you like. It is a lovely place—it only lacks you; but go to Salisbury first.

"Always, with undying love,

"Yours,

Oscar."

The words of that letter may appear extravagant to those who are in the habit of writing commercial correspondence; but Mr. Wilde is prepared to produce it anywhere as the expression of a poetical feeling, and with no relation whatever to the hateful suggestions put to it in the plea in this case.

There are two counts at the end of the plea which are extremely curious. It is said that Mr. Wilde has published a certain indecent and immoral work with the title of "The Picture of Dorian Gray." And, secondly, that in December, eighteen ninety-four, was published a certain immoral work in the form of "The Chameleon," and that Mr. Wilde had contributed to it under the title of "Phrases and Philosophies for the Use of the Young."

Those are two very gross allegations. Directly Mr. Wilde saw a story in "The Chameleon," called "The Priest and the Acolyte," he communicated with the editor, and upon Mr. Wilde's insistence the magazine was withdrawn. The volume called "The Picture of Dorian Gray" is one that can be bought on any bookstall in London. It has been published five years. My learned friend has the task of satisfying you that the excuses made by the defendant are true. [WILDE *is called to the witness-box. He wears a tight-fitting frock-coat of a dark material, a collar with wide points, and a black tie. His hair is banked on the top of his head and carefully parted down the center. His manner is confident, and he leans over the rail in front of him toying with a pair of gloves, while answering questions. He retains his equanimity until he makes the fatal slip when* **CARSON** *is cross-examining him about Walter Grainger.*]

CLARKE: Are you the prosecutor in this case?
WILDE: I am.
CLARKE: Are you a dramatist and author?
WILDE: I believe I am well known in that capacity.
THE JUDGE: Only answer the questions, please.
CLARKE: How old are you?
WILDE: Thirty-nine.
CLARKE: In eighteen ninety-two, did you make the acquaintance of Lord Alfred Douglas?
WILDE: Yes.
CLARKE: When did you meet Lord Queensberry?
WILDE: In November, eighteen ninety-two.
CLARKE: When did you see him again?
WILDE: In eighteen ninety-four. On both occasions I was lunching with Lord Alfred Douglas at the Café Royal, when Lord Queensberry joined us.
CLARKE: Shortly after the second meeting, did you become aware that he was making suggestions with regard to your character and behavior?
WILDE: Yes. At the end of June, eighteen ninety-four, Lord Queensberry called upon me at my house; not by appointment. The interview took place in the library. Lord Queensberry was standing by the window. I walked over to the fireplace, and he said to me, "Sit down." I said to him, "I do not allow anyone to talk to me like that in my house or anywhere else. I suppose you have come to apologize for the statements you have been making about me." Lord Queensberry repeated several lies he had heard about Lord Alfred Douglas and myself. Then I asked, "Lord Queensberry, do you seriously believe these lies?" He said, "I do not say you are it, but you look it..." [*Laughter in Court.*]
THE JUDGE: I shall have the court cleared, if I hear the slightest disturbance again.
WILDE: "...but you look it, and you pose as it, which is just as bad." Then I told Lord Queensberry to leave my house.
CLARKE: Before you sent your contribution to "The Chameleon," had you anything to do with the preparation of that magazine?
WILDE: Nothing whatever.
CLARKE: Did you approve of the story "The Priest and the Acolyte"?
WILDE: I thought it bad and indecent, and I thoroughly disapproved of it.

CLARKE: Your attention has been called to the plea and to the names of the persons with whom your conduct is impugned. Is there any truth in these allegations?

WILDE: There is no truth whatever in anyone of them. [CARSON *cross-examines.*]

CARSON: You stated that your age was thirty-nine. I think you are over forty. You were born on October the sixteenth, eighteen fifty-four?

WILDE: I had no wish to pose as being young. I am thirty-nine to forty.

CARSON: But being born in eighteen fifty-four makes you more than forty?

WILDE: Ah! Very well.

CARSON: How old was Lord Alfred Douglas when you first knew him?

WILDE: Between twenty and twenty-one years of age.

CARSON: There were two poems by Lord Alfred Douglas in "The Chameleon" in which your article appeared?

WILDE: There were. I thought them exceedingly beautiful poems.

CARSON: Did you think they made any improper suggestions?

WILDE: No, none whatever.

CARSON: You read "The Priest and the Acolyte"?

WILDE: Yes.

CARSON: You have no doubt whatever that *that* was an immoral story?

WILDE: It was worse—it was badly written.

CARSON: Wasn't the story that of an acolyte who was discovered by the rector in the priest's room, and a scandal arose?

WILDE: I have read it only once and nothing would induce me to read it again.

CARSON: Do you think the story blasphemous?

WILDE: I think it violated every artistic canon of beauty.

CARSON: That is not an answer.

WILDE: It is the only one I can give.

CARSON: I want to see the position you *pose* in. Did you think the story blasphemous?

WILDE: It filled me with disgust. The end was wrong.

CARSON: Answer the question, sir. Did you or did you not consider the story blasphemous?

WILDE: I did not consider the story blasphemous. I thought it disgusting.

CARSON: I am satisfied with that. As regards your own works, you *pose* as not being concerned with morality or immorality?

WILDE: I do not know whether you use the word "pose" in any particular sense.

CARSON: It is a favorite word of your own.

WILDE: Is it? I have no pose in this matter. In writing a play or a book, I am concerned entirely with literature — that is, with art. I aim not at doing good or evil, but in trying to make a thing that will have some quality of beauty.

CARSON: Listen, sir. Here is one of the "Phrases and Philosophies for the Use of the Young," which you contributed to "The Chameleon": "Wickedness is a myth invented by good people to account for the curious attractiveness of others." You think that is true?

WILDE: I rarely think that anything I write is true.

CARSON: Did you say "rarely"?

WILDE: I might have said "never."

CARSON: "Religions die when they are proved to be true." Do you think that was a safe axiom to put forward for the philosophy of the young?

WILDE: Most stimulating.

CARSON: "If one tells the truth, one is sure, sooner or later, to be found out?"

WILDE: That is a pleasing paradox.

CARSON: Is it good for the young?

WILDE: Anything is good that stimulates thought at whatever age.

CARSON: Whether moral or immoral?

WILDE: There is no such thing as morality or immorality in thought. There is immoral emotion.

CARSON: "Pleasure is the only thing one should live for?"

WILDE: I think that the realization of one's self is the prime aim of life, and to realize one's self through pleasure is finer than to do so through pain. I am, on that point, entirely on the side of the ancients — the Greeks. It is a pagan idea.

CARSON: "There is something tragic about the enormous number of young men there are in England at the present moment who start life with perfect profiles, and end by adopting some useful profession?"

WILDE: I should think the young have enough sense of humor.

CARSON: You think that is humorous?

WILDE: An amusing play upon words.

CARSON: This is in your introduction to "Dorian Gray": "There is no such thing as a moral or immoral book. Books are well written or badly written." That expresses your view?

WILDE: My view on art, yes.

CARSON: Here is a passage from the book. The artist is speaking to Dorian Gray. "From the moment I met you, your personality had the most extraordinary influence over me. I quite admit that I adored you madly." Have you ever adored a young man madly?

WILDE: No, not madly; I prefer love — that is a higher form.

CARSON: Never mind that. Let us keep down to the level we are at now.

WILDE: I have never given adoration to anybody but myself.

CARSON: I suppose you think that a very smart thing?

WILDE: Not at all.

CARSON: Then you have never had that feeling?

WILDE: No. The whole idea was borrowed from Shakespeare, I regret to say — yes, from Shakespeare's sonnets.

CARSON: "I have adored you extravagantly?"

WILDE: Do you mean financially?

CARSON: Oh, yes, financially. Do you think we are talking about finance?

WILDE: I don't know what you are talking about.

CARSON: Don't you? Well, I hope I shall make myself very plain before I have done. Where was Lord Alfred Douglas staying when you wrote that letter which my learned friend read in court just now?

WILDE: At the Savoy; I was at Torquay.

CARSON: Why should a man of your age address a boy nearly twenty years younger as "My own boy"?

WILDE: I was fond of him.

CARSON: Did you adore him?

WILDE: No, but I have always been fond of him. I think it is a beautiful letter. It is a poem, I was not writing an ordinary letter. You might as well cross-examine me as to whether "King Lear" or a sonnet of Shakespeare was proper.

CARSON: Suppose a man who was not an artist had written this letter?

WILDE: A man who was not an artist could not have written that letter.

CARSON: "Your slim-gilt soul walks between passion and poetry." Is that a beautiful phrase?

WILDE: Not as you read it, Mr. Carson.

CARSON: I do not profess to be an artist; and when I hear you give evidence, I am glad I am not.

CLARKE: [*Rising*] I don't think my friend should talk like that. [*To* WILDE] Pray, do not criticize my friend's reading again.

CARSON: Is not this a very exceptional letter?

WILDE: I should say it is unique.

CARSON: Have you often written letters in the same style as this?

WILDE: I don't repeat myself in style.

CARSON: Here is another letter which I believe you also wrote to Lord Alfred Douglas. Will you read it?

WILDE: No; I decline. I don't see why I should.

CARSON: Then I will.

"Dearest of all boys,

"Your letter was delightful, red and yellow wine to me; but I am sad and out of sorts. I must see you soon. You are the divine thing I want, the thing of grace and beauty. Why are you not here, my dear, my wonderful boy?

"Your own Oscar."

Is that an ordinary letter?

WILDE: Everything I write is extraordinary. It was a tender expression of my great admiration for Lord Alfred Douglas. It was not, like the other, a prose poem.

CARSON: How long have you known Wood?

WILDE: I think I met him at the end of January, eighteen ninety-three.

CARSON: Who was Wood?

WILDE: He had no occupation. He was looking for a situation.

CARSON: The first time you met Wood, did you take him to supper in a private room at a restaurant?

WILDE: Yes. I had been asked to be kind to him.

CARSON: How much money did you give Wood on that occasion?

WILDE: Two pounds.

CARSON: Why?

WILDE: Because I had been asked to be kind to him.

CARSON: I suggest that you had another reason for giving him money?

WILDE: It is perfectly untrue.

CARSON: Did you consider that he had come to levy blackmail?

WILDE: I did; and I determined to face it.

CARSON: And the way you faced it was by giving him fifteen pounds to go to America?

WILDE: No. I gave him the money after he had told me the pitiful tale about himself; foolishly perhaps, but out of pure kindness.

CARSON: Had you a farewell lunch at a restaurant?

WILDE: Yes.

CARSON: In a private room?

WILDE: Yes.

CARSON: Did Wood call you Oscar?

WILDE: Yes.

CARSON: What did you call Wood?

WILDE: His name is Alfred.

CARSON: Didn't you call him "Alf"?

WILDE: I never use abbreviations.

CARSON: When you were staying at the Albemarle Hotel in eighteen ninety-two, did you become fond of your publisher's office-boy?

WILDE: That is not the proper form for the question to be addressed to me. I deny that that was the position held by Mr. Edward Shelley, to whom you are referring.

CARSON: What age was *Mister* Shelley?

WILDE: About twenty. I met him when arranging for the publication of my books.

CARSON: Did you ask him to dine with you at the Albemarle Hotel?

WILDE: Yes.

CARSON: Was that for the purpose of having an intellectual treat?

WILDE: Well, for him, yes.

CARSON: On that occasion, did you have a room leading into a bedroom?

WILDE: Yes.

CARSON: Did you become intimate with a young man named Alphonse Conway at Worthing?

WILDE: Yes.

CARSON: He sold newspapers at the kiosk on the pier?

WILDE: This is the first I have heard of his connection with literature.

CARSON: Did you take the lad to Brighton and provide him with a suit of blue serge?

WILDE: Yes.

CARSON: And a straw hat with a band of red and blue?

WILDE: That, I am afraid, was his own unfortunate selection.

CARSON: Have you been to afternoon tea-parties at Alfred Taylor's rooms in Little College Street?

WILDE: Certainly.

CARSON: Did you get Taylor to arrange dinners at which you could meet young men?

WILDE: No.

CARSON: But you have dined with young men?

WILDE: Often.

CARSON: Always in a private room?

WILDE: Generally. I prefer it.

CARSON: Now, did you not know that Taylor was notorious for introducing young men to older men?

WILDE: I never heard that in my life. He has introduced young men to me.

CARSON: How many?

WILDE: About five.

CARSON: Have you given money to them?

WILDE: Yes, I think to all five—money and presents.

CARSON: Did they give you anything?

WILDE: Me? Me? No!

CARSON: Among these five, did Taylor introduce you to Charles Parker?

WILDE: Yes.

CARSON: You became friendly with him?

WILDE: Yes.

CARSON: Did you know that he was a groom out of employment?

WILDE: No.

CARSON: How old was he?

WILDE: Really, I do not keep a census.

CARSON: Never mind about a census. Tell me how old he was.

WILDE: About twenty.

CARSON: How much money did you give Parker?

WILDE: During the time I have known him, I should think about four or five pounds.

CARSON: Why? For what?

WILDE: Because he was poor and I liked him. What better reason could I have?

CARSON: Did you invite Parker and his brother to dinner?

WILDE: Yes.

CARSON: Did you know that one Parker was a groom, and the other a gentleman's valet?

WILDE: I did not know it, but if I had, I should not have cared. I have a passion to civilize the community.

CARSON: Was there plenty of champagne?

WILDE: Well, I did not press wine upon them.

CARSON: You did not stint them?

WILDE: What gentleman would stint his guests?

CARSON: What gentleman would stint the valet and the groom?

CLARKE: [*Jumping to his feet*] I object!

THE JUDGE: I cannot allow that objection.

CARSON: Do you drink champagne yourself?

WILDE: Yes; iced champagne is a favorite drink of mine—strictly against my doctor's orders.

CARSON: Never mind your doctor's orders, sir.

WILDE: I never do.

CARSON: How many times did Charles Parker have tea with you at your rooms in St. James's Place?

WILDE: Five or six times.

CARSON: What did he do all the time?

WILDE: What did he do? Why, he drank his tea, smoked cigarettes, and, I hope, enjoyed himself.

CARSON: What was there in common between this young man and yourself? What attraction had he for you?

WILDE: I delight in the society of people much younger than myself. I like those who may be called idle and careless. I recognize no social distinctions of any kind; and to me youth, the mere fact of youth, is so wonderful that I would rather talk to a young man for half an hour than be even — well, cross-examined in court by an eminent Irish Queen's Counsel.

CARSON: When did you first meet Fred Atkins?

WILDE: In October, eighteen ninety-two.

CARSON: You called him Fred and he called you Oscar?

WILDE: I have a passion for being addressed by my Christian name.

CARSON: You took him to Paris?

WILDE: Yes.

CARSON: When you were in Paris, did you suggest that he should have his hair curled?

WILDE: I should have been very angry if he had had his hair curled. It would have been most unbecoming.

CARSON: Did Taylor introduce you to a man named Ernest Scarfe?

WILDE: Yes.

CARSON: Did you give him any money?

WILDE: Never.

CARSON: Did you give him any presents?

WILDE: Yes, a cigarette case. It is my custom to present cigarette cases.

CARSON: When did you first know Sidney Mavor?

WILDE: In September, eighteen ninety-two.

CARSON: Did you give him anything?

WILDE: I don't think I even gave him a cigarette case.

CARSON: On October the third, did you not order Thornhill's in Bond Street to send him one of the value of four pounds, eleven shillings and sixpence?

WILDE: Well, if it is there, perhaps I did.

CARSON: Why did you give him a cigarette case when you had known him only a month?

WILDE: I give what presents I like to anybody I like. I found pleasure in his society.

CARSON: Did you find pleasure in his society when he stayed with you at the Albemarle Hotel for the night?

WILDE: Yes, in the evening, and at breakfast.

CARSON: Do you know Walter Grainger?

WILDE: Yes.

CARSON: Have you dined with him?

WILDE: Never. He was a servant at a house in Oxford where Lord Alfred Douglas had rooms.

CARSON: Did you ever kiss him?

WILDE: Oh, dear, no. He was a peculiarly plain boy. He was, unfortunately, extremely ugly. I pitied him for it.

CARSON: Was that the reason why you did not kiss him?

WILDE: Mr. Carson, you are pertinently insolent.

CARSON: Did you say that in support of your statement that you never kissed him?

WILDE: No. It is a childish question.

CARSON: Did you ever put that forward as a reason why you never kissed the boy?

WILDE: Not at all.

CARSON: Why, sir, did you mention that the boy was extremely ugly?

WILDE: For this reason: If I were asked why I did not kiss a doormat, I should say because I do not like to kiss door-mats. I do not know why I mentioned that he was ugly, except that I was stung by your insolent question.

CARSON: Why did you mention his ugliness?

WILDE: It is ridiculous to imagine that any such thing could have occurred under any circumstances.

CARSON: Then why did you mention his ugliness, I ask you?

WILDE: You insulted me by an insulting question.

CARSON: Was that a reason why you should say the boy was ugly? [WILDE's *unfinished replies are incoherent and almost inaudible.*]

WILDE: It was the reason why...that...

CARSON: Why did you say he was ugly?

WILDE: Because you said...because I wasn't...

CARSON: Why did you add that?

WILDE: I was...I was...

CARSON: Why? Why?

WILDE: You sting me and insult me and try to unnerve me; and at times one says things flippantly when one ought to speak more seriously. I admit it.

CARSON: Then you said it flippantly?

WILDE: Oh, yes, it was a flippant answer.

CARSON: That is my last question. [*The curtain falls. When it rises again, CARSON is opening the case for the defense, and addressing the jury. WILDE is not in court.*]

CARSON: [*Speaking as the curtain rises*] I hope I have sufficiently demonstrated to the jury already that Lord Queensberry was absolutely justified in bringing to a climax the connection of Mr. Oscar Wilde and Lord Alfred Douglas.

I am not here to say that anything has ever happened between Lord Alfred Douglas and Mr. Oscar Wilde. God forbid! But everything shows that the young man is in a dangerous position.

There is a startling similarity in all the cases that have been raised against Mr. Wilde. In each we find no equality in age, education, or position with Wilde. But on the other hand there is a curious similarity in the ages of the young men themselves.

Who are these young men? There is Wood. Of his history Mr. Wilde has told you that he knew nothing. Who was Parker? Mr. Wilde professed the same ignorance as to that youth. Who was Scarfe? Exactly in the same way Mr. Wilde knew nothing about him.

Parker will be called to tell his unfortunate story. If Mr. Wilde wanted to assist Parker, was it doing the lad a good turn to take him to a restaurant and prime him with champagne and a good dinner? Parker will tell you that when he dined with Mr. Wilde he had whiskies and sodas and iced champagne—that iced champagne in which Mr. Wilde indulged, contrary to his doctor's orders.

CLARKE: [*Rising*] May I claim your lordship's indulgence while I interpose to make a statement? [CARSON *resumes his seat.*]

CLARKE: Those who represent Mr. Wilde in this case cannot conceal from themselves that the judgment that might be formed on the literary questions might not improbably induce the jury to say that Lord Queensberry in using the word "posing" was using a word for which there was sufficient justification to entitle him to be relieved of a criminal charge in respect of his statement. And I, and my learned friends associated with me in this matter, have to look forward to this—that a verdict, given to the defendant on that part of the case, might be interpreted outside as a conclusive finding with regard to all parts of the case.

We feel that we cannot resist a verdict of "Not Guilty"—having regard to the word "posing." I trust that this may make an end of the case.

CARSON: [*Rising*] If there is a plea of Not Guilty, a plea which involves that the defendant has succeeded in his plea of justification, I am satisfied. Of course, the verdict will be that the plea of justification is proved, and that the words were published for the public benefit.

THE JUDGE: I shall have to tell the jury that justification was proved; and that it was true in substance and fact that the prosecutor had "posed as a sodomite." [*To the jury*] Your verdict will be—Not Guilty.

CURTAIN

Scene II

Scene: *The Old Court at the Old Bailey. A different view of the court. The dock, in which* WILDE *stands, is now visible to the audience.*

Others in court: The SOLICITOR-GENERAL, SIR EDWARD CLARKE, *and* THE JUDGE.

When the curtain rises the SOLICITOR-GENERAL *is concluding his opening speech for the prosecution.*

SOLICITOR-GENERAL: Gentlemen, it has been necessary for me to go through the case in detail, because I must assume, as you are an entirely fresh jury, that you are totally ignorant of all the facts previously elucidated. I have endeavored to limit myself to a plain and simple statement of testimony which the prosecution is in a position to call before you. In conclusion, I can only invite your very earnest and careful attention to the evidence, for it is upon this evidence that the defendant must be judged. Call Charles Parker. [CHARLES PARKER *called to the witness-box. He gives his evidence with impudent self-assurance and does not appear to be in the least ashamed of the incidents which he relates.*]

SOLICITOR-GENERAL: What is your name?

PARKER: Charles Parker.

SOLICITOR-GENERAL: How old are you?

PARKER: Nineteen.

SOLICITOR-GENERAL: You have been employed as a groom?

PARKER: Yes.

SOLICITOR-GENERAL: Were you out of employment in March, eighteen ninety-three?

PARKER: Yes.

SOLICITOR-GENERAL: Without means?

PARKER: Not absolutely.

SOLICITOR-GENERAL: Did you go with your brother one evening to the St. James's restaurant?

PARKER: Yes.

SOLICITOR-GENERAL: And a man spoke to you?

PARKER: Yes; Taylor spoke to us.

SOLICITOR-GENERAL: What did he say?

PARKER: He offered us drinks.

SOLICITOR-GENERAL: What happened then?

PARKER: He spoke about men.

SOLICITOR-GENERAL: In what way?

PARKER: I think he asked us if we ever went out with men. He said there was some good money to be made in that way.

SOLICITOR-GENERAL: Did he mention any names?

PARKER: He mentioned Mr. Wilde and said he would like to introduce him to us.

SOLICITOR-GENERAL: For what purpose?

PARKER: He said he was a good man.

SOLICITOR-GENERAL: But for what purpose?

PARKER: He meant he was a good man for money.

SOLICITOR-GENERAL: But did he say why he wanted to introduce Wilde to you?

PARKER: Because he liked meeting boys.

SOLICITOR-GENERAL: Later, did you go by appointment to Taylor's rooms in Little College Street?

PARKER: Yes.

SOLICITOR-GENERAL: What passed there?

PARKER: I forget.

SOLICITOR-GENERAL: Think now; you went there by appointment and you saw Taylor. What passed?

PARKER: I forget.

SOLICITOR-GENERAL: What was said?

PARKER: Oh—he said he had arranged to introduce us to Mr. Wilde that evening at a restaurant.

SOLICITOR-GENERAL: Did you go?

PARKER: Yes.

SOLICITOR-GENERAL: What happened?

PARKER: We were shown upstairs into a private room with a table laid for four. After a while Mr. Wilde came in. Then we all sat down to dinner. Mr. Wilde sat on my left.

SOLICITOR-GENERAL: Was it a good dinner?

PARKER: Yes. The table was lighted with pink-shaded candles.

SOLICITOR-GENERAL: What did you have to drink?

PARKER: Champagne, and brandy and coffee afterwards.

SOLICITOR-GENERAL: Did you see who paid for the dinner?

PARKER: I saw Mr. Wilde write out a check.

SOLICITOR-GENERAL: Now, after dinner, did Mr. Wilde say anything to you?

PARKER: Yes. He said, "This is the boy for me." Then he asked me to go back to his hotel with him.

SOLICITOR-GENERAL: Did you go?

PARKER: Yes. We went in a hansom.

SOLICITOR-GENERAL: What happened at the hotel?

PARKER: First of all, we went up to a sitting-room on the second floor, and Mr. Wilde ordered some more drink — whisky and soda.

SOLICITOR-GENERAL: After the waiter who brought it had gone, what did Wilde say to you?

PARKER: He asked me to stay with him. And I did. I was there about two hours. Before I left Mr. Wilde gave me two pounds and told me to come again next week.

SOLICITOR-GENERAL: Did you go?

PARKER: Yes. He gave me three pounds the second time.

SOLICITOR-GENERAL: Did you see Wilde at other places?

PARKER: Yes, from time to time. He took me to the Crystal Palace, and to the Pavilion — we had a box there. We dined at restaurants, and I went to his rooms in St. James's Place seven or eight times. And once he visited me at my room in Chelsea. He kept his cab waiting. After that there was some unpleasantness with my landlady, so I left.

SOLICITOR-GENERAL: When did you last see Wilde?

PARKER: About nine months ago. He drove past me in Trafalgar Square and stopped his cab. We shook hands, and he said, "You're looking as pretty as ever." [*Laughs.*]

SOLICITOR-GENERAL: Until Taylor introduced you to Wilde, had you ever been mixed up with this kind of thing before?

PARKER: No, never. And I've given it up now. I've joined the army. [*The curtain falls. When it rises again,* WILDE *is in the witness-box, being cross-examined by the* SOLICITOR-GENERAL. WILDE *looks haggard and worn. His hair is untidy. He gives his answers wearily.*]

SOLICITOR-GENERAL: [*Speaking as the curtain rises*] Why did you go to Taylor's rooms?

WILDE: Because I used to meet amusing people there.

SOLICITOR-GENERAL: A rather curious establishment, wasn't it?

WILDE: I didn't think so.

SOLICITOR-GENERAL: Did you notice that no one could see in through the windows?

WILDE: No; I didn't notice that.

SOLICITOR-GENERAL: Did it strike you that this place was at all peculiar?

WILDE: Not at all.

SOLICITOR-GENERAL: Not the sort of street you would usually visit in? Rather a rough neighborhood?

WILDE: [*With a momentary flash of the old humor*] Perhaps—it was very near the Houses of Parliament.

SOLICITOR-GENERAL: You have given away a large number of cigarette cases?

WILDE: Yes. I have a great fancy for giving cigarette cases.

SOLICITOR-GENERAL: To young men?

WILDE: Yes.

SOLICITOR-GENERAL: Was the conversation of these young men literary?

WILDE: No: but the fact that I had written a successful play seemed to them very wonderful, and I was gratified by their admiration.

SOLICITOR-GENERAL: The admiration of these boys?

WILDE: Yes. I am fond of praise. I like to be made much of.

SOLICITOR-GENERAL: By these boys?

WILDE: Yes.

SOLICITOR-GENERAL: You like bright boys?

WILDE: I like bright boys.

SOLICITOR-GENERAL: Did you not pause to consider whether it would be of the slightest service to lads in their position to be entertained in such style by a man in your position?

WILDE: No. They enjoyed it as schoolboys would enjoy a treat. It was something they did not get every day.

SOLICITOR-GENERAL: You looked on them as schoolboys?

WILDE: They were amused by the little luxuries at the restaurants I took them to. The pink lampshades and so forth.

SOLICITOR-GENERAL: When you wrote letters to Lord Alfred Douglas, why did you choose the words "My own boy" as a mode of address?

WILDE: It was a fantastic, extravagant way of writing. It does not seem to me to be a question of whether a thing is right or proper, but of literary expression.

SOLICITOR-GENERAL: I did not use the words proper or right. Was it decent?

WILDE: Oh, decent? Of course; there is nothing indecent in it.

SOLICITOR-GENERAL: Do you think that was a decent way for a man of your age to address a man of his?

WILDE: It was a beautiful way for an artist to address a young man of culture and charm. Decency does not enter into it.

SOLICITOR-GENERAL: Doesn't it? Do you know the meaning of the word?

WILDE: Yes.

SOLICITOR-GENERAL: Did Lord Alfred Douglas read you his poem, "Two Loves"?

WILDE: Yes.

SOLICITOR-GENERAL: It contains these lines:
"I am true love, I fill
The hearts of boy and girl with mutual flame."
Then sighing said the other, "Have thy will,
I am the love that dare not speak its name."

Was that poem explained to you?

WILDE: I think it is clear.

SOLICITOR-GENERAL: There is no question as to what it means?

WILDE: Most certainly not.

SOLICITOR-GENERAL: Is it not clear that the love described relates to natural and unnatural love?

WILDE: No.

SOLICITOR-GENERAL: What is "The love that dare not speak its name"?

WILDE: The love that dare not speak its name in this century is such a great affection of an elder for a younger man as there was between David and Jonathan, such as Plato made the very basis of his philosophy, and such as you find in the sonnets of Michael Angelo and Shakespeare. It is that deep, spiritual affection that is as pure as it is perfect. It dictates and pervades great works of art like those of Shakespeare and Michael Angelo, and those two letters of mine, such as they are. It is in this century misunderstood, so much misunderstood that it may be described as "The love that dare not speak its name," and on account of it I am placed where I am now. It is beautiful, it is fine, it is the noblest form of affection. There is nothing unnatural about it. It is intellectual, and it repeatedly exists between an elder and a younger man, when the elder man has intellect, and the younger man has all the joy, hope and glamour of life before him. But that it should be so the world does not understand. [*The curtain falls. When it rises again,* WILDE *is in the dock.*]

THE JUDGE: Oscar Wilde, the crime of which you have been convicted is so bad that one has to put stern restraint upon one's self to prevent one's self from describing, in language which I would rather not use, the sentiments which must rise to the breast of every man of honor who has heard the details of these two terrible trials. That the jury have arrived at a correct verdict in this case I cannot persuade myself to entertain a shadow of doubt; and I hope, at all events, that those who sometimes imagine that a judge is half-hearted in the cause of decency and morality because he takes care no prejudice shall enter into the case, may see that this is consistent with the utmost sense of indignation at the horrible charges brought home to you.

It is no use for me to address you. People who can do these things must be dead to all sense of shame, and one cannot hope to produce any effect upon them. It is the worst case I have ever tried. That you, Wilde, have been the center of a circle of extensive corruption of the most hideous kind among young men, it is impossible to doubt.

I shall, under the circumstances, be expected to pass the severest sentence that the law allows. In my judgment it is totally inadequate for such a case as this.

The sentence of this court is that you be imprisoned and kept to hard labor for two years.

CURTAIN

Act Three

Scene I

Scene: *The study of Wilde's House in Chelsea. The room is seen in the light of early morning. Dust-sheets cover most of the furniture.*

EUSTACE is arranging flowers in a vase on the desk, and DIJON is watching him. They wear overcoats, as the room is cold.

EUSTACE: [*Standing back from the flowers*] There! I think that makes the room a little less somber. We want it to look as gay as possible.

DIJON: These dust-sheets aren't very gay. Hadn't we better remove them?

EUSTACE: Yes, we had better. They look too ghostly. [*As they talk they remove the dust-sheets, folding them with the proficiency of chambermaids.*]

DIJON: Is Oscar coming by himself?

EUSTACE: No. Frank Harris has gone to the prison to meet him. They should be here quite soon.

DIJON: Harris has behaved very well. He went several times to Reading to see Oscar.

EUSTACE: I can't help feeling that Harris did it more out of journalism than friendship. No doubt he'll publish the whole story some day.

DIJON: Perhaps. [*After a pause*] Where do you think Oscar will go? To France?

EUSTACE: If he does, he'll find simply heaps of his friends there. On the day after he was sentenced the continental express was packed with people who thought it advisable to leave England for a while.

DIJON: How do you know?

EUSTACE: My dear, I was on it myself.

DIJON: In France we were very shocked when Oscar was sent to prison. The newspapers said, "This is how the English behave to their poets."

EUSTACE: The American papers said, "This is how the English poets behave."

DIJON: I feel that this reunion is going to be rather awkward.

EUSTACE: That will depend upon Oscar. He used always to manage any situation with marvelous tact.

DIJON: In the old days, yes. But it won't be too easy for him — taking up the threads again. By the way, where is Bosie?

EUSTACE: He's abroad. Somewhere in Italy, I think.

DIJON: I thought he would have been the first to welcome his friend home.

EUSTACE: That is because you don't know what has been going on since Oscar went away. The disciples — as his so-called friends style themselves — have decided to keep him and Bosie apart. They say Bosie is a bad influence on Oscar. Really, of course, they're desperately jealous of the friendship. And now they think their master's body should belong entirely to them.

DIJON: You talk as if Oscar were dead.

EUSTACE: It's a wonder he isn't, after what he's been through. [*The front-door is heard closing*] What's that?

DIJON: It must be Oscar. [*After a moment* WILDE *comes in with the dignity of a king returning from exile. He is smoking, and wears a flower in his buttonhole.*]

EUSTACE *and* DIJON: Oscar!

WILDE: Louis! Eustace! [*To* EUSTACE] How marvelous of you to know exactly the right tie to wear at eight o'clock in the morning to meet a friend who has been — away.

DIJON: It's wonderful to see you again, Oscar; and looking so well, too.

WILDE: Thank you, dear boy. It is charming of you both to be here to welcome me at such an early hour. You can't possibly have got up. You must have sat up.

DIJON: [*Laughing*] Oscar!

WILDE: But you must not call me Oscar. I have chosen a new name for my new life. A beautiful name — because it is going to be a beautiful new life. Sebastian Melmoth.

EUSTACE: Oh, it's a divine name, Oscar! I mean — Sebastian. [FRANK HARRIS *comes in.*]

HARRIS: I shan't be more than a few minutes, Oscar. The place is quite near and the cab's waiting. I shall deliver your note myself, and bring back an answer.

WILDE: Thank you, Frank. I shall be perfectly happy here with my friends until you return. I do hope there will be no difficulty about my admission.

HARRIS: You must not worry. [*He goes out.*]

WILDE: [*Walking up and down, as he does throughout the scene*] For a while, to collect my thoughts, I am going into a Catholic retreat. At least, I have written to ask them if they will receive me at once. I should like to remain there for quite six months.

DIJON: [*Surprised*] You are going to shut yourself away again—of your own free will?

EUSTACE: That doesn't sound like you, Oscar. You were always so fond of life.

WILDE: You forget—prison has completely changed me. I am Sebastian Melmoth now. My life is like a work of art. An artist never begins the same work twice, or else it shows that he has not succeeded. My life before prison was as successful as possible. Now all that is finished and done with.

DIJON: But you are going to write again?

EUSTACE: You must write a new play. In Paris!

WILDE: I don't want to show myself until I have written a new play. So I must hide while I am writing it. The public is so dreadful that it knows a man only by the last thing he has done. If I were to go to Paris now, people would see in me only the convict. [*After a pause*] Scandals used to lend charm, or at least interest, to a man. Now they crush him.

DIJON: You must not think about prison any more.

EUSTACE: Forget it, Sebastian.

WILDE: Even if I could forget what was done to me there, I could never forget the others. During the first six months I was dreadfully unhappy—so utterly miserable that I wanted to kill myself. But what prevented me from doing so was looking at *the others*, and seeing that they were as unhappy as I was, and feeling sorry for them. It's a wonderful thing—pity. I never knew.

EUSTACE: You were allowed to read while you were . . . away?

WILDE: Yes, I have been reading. The governor was a charming man, and most considerate to me. You cannot imagine how much good it did me in prison that "Salome" was being played in Paris just then. In prison it had been entirely forgotten that I was a literary person; but when they saw that my play was a success in Paris, they said to one another, "Well, but this is strange; he has talent, then." And from that moment they let me have all the books I wanted. At first I couldn't think what to ask for. And suddenly I thought of Dante. His "Inferno." I could read that. You see—I was in hell too.

DIJON: Poor Oscar.

EUSTACE: It must have been dreadful for you.

WILDE: It was—dreadful [*in his story-telling voice*] One day a warder came into my cell. "Take off your boots," he said. Of course I began to obey him, then I asked: "What is it? Why must I take off my boots?" He would not answer me. As soon as he had my boots, he said: "Come out of your cell." "Why?" I asked again. I was frightened. What had I done? I could not guess; but then I was often punished for nothing. As soon as we were in the corridor he ordered me to stand with my face to the wall, and went away. There I stood in my stocking feet waiting. The cold chilled me through; I began standing first on one foot and then on the other, racking my brains as to what they were going to do to me, wondering why I was being punished like this, and how long it would last. After what seemed an eternity, I heard him coming back. I did not dare to move or even look. He came up to me; stopped by me for a moment; my heart stopped; he threw down a pair of boots beside me, and said: "Go to your cell and put those on," and I went into my cell shaking. That's the way they give you a new pair of boots in prison. That's the way they are kind to you.

DIJON: Everybody will be kind to you now, Oscar. In future you will be always amongst friends. You need never feel lonely again. [WILDE *makes no response*] Where is Bosie?

WILDE: He is in Italy, I think. [*Regretfully*] It seems we are not allowed to see each other. His mother threatens to cut off his allowance if he tries to see me, and my friends say they cannot help me if I go to him.

EUSTACE: Why should you be kept apart? I'm sure Bosie wants to see you as much as you want to see him.

WILDE: I am sure, too. It is jealousy on the part of certain people—that is all. But we shall come together again, I know. Bosie would never desert me.

DIJON: [*Encouragingly*] You will see him directly you come out of your retreat.

WILDE: I hope so. [*Purposely changing the subject*] Do you know one of the punishments that happen to people who have been "away"? They are not allowed to read "The Daily Chronicle"! Coming along I begged to be allowed to read it in the train. "No!" Then I suggested I might be allowed to read it upside down. This they consented to allow, and I read all the way "The Daily Chronicle" upside down, and never enjoyed it so much. [*They laugh. Enter* FRANK HARRIS. *It is impossible to tell from his manner if the news he brings is good or bad.*]

WILDE: [*Seeing* HARRIS] Oh, Frank, you are soon back. What did they say?

HARRIS: They said nothing to me, Oscar; but gave me this note for you. [*Holds it out.*]

WILDE: [*Is about to take it, but changes his mind*] No, you open it, and tell me what is in it, Frank. [HARRIS *opens and reads the note to himself*] Well, Frank, what do they say? Are we to start at once?

HARRIS: [*Avoiding a direct answer*] It seems, Oscar, that these matters take some time to decide. They would need—some months—in which to think it over.

WILDE: [*Takes the letter and crumples it in his hand*] They won't receive me. Even they won't receive me. [*He sinks into a chair*] I thought my punishment was ended. It has just begun . . . [*He buries his face in his hands and sobs.*]

CURTAIN

Scene II

Scene: *Outside a Paris café.*

An orchestra is playing inside the café. One or two tables are placed on either side of the café entrance, which is in the center. A WAITER *is cleaning one of the tables when* FRANK HARRIS *comes out of the café and looks up and down the street.*

WAITER: Is monsieur looking for somebody?

HARRIS: I had expected to meet a gentleman here. But he is either late, or has forgotten the appointment.

WAITER: An English gentleman, monsieur?

HARRIS: Yes. Man by the name of Melmoth, know him at all?

WAITER: [*Shaking his head*] I have not heard the name. [*Pause*] At first, when you said English gentleman, I thought you meant Monsieur Oscar Wilde. Excuse my mistake. He often meets his friends here.

HARRIS: [*Embarrassed*] Really? Then you know him?

WAITER: I know him very well. [*Smiling*] Too well! Perhaps that is why he does not come here this evening.

HARRIS: I don't follow. Speak plainly, man.

WAITER: Monsieur Wilde drinks much. But he has not much money. Because of what he owes me, he stays away. When he can pay, he will come back.

HARRIS: [*Shocked*] Mr. Wilde owes *you* money?

WAITER: But yes. For myself, I do not mind. Mr. Wilde is a nice gentleman. But I have a wife, and three little ...

HARRIS: [*Taking out his purse*] How much is the debt?

WAITER: [*After calculation*] Twenty francs.

HARRIS: [*Holding out the money*] The debt is paid!

WAITER: Many thanks, monsieur.

HARRIS: [*Brushing the thanks aside*] How is Mr. Wilde these days? I have not seen him for some months.

WAITER: He is always the same. He talks. And he drinks. He is a nice gentleman. But some people—the English tourists—do not like to see him here. When he sits down, they get up and go.

HARRIS: Indeed! And what does Mr. Wilde do then?

WAITER: He does not mind. So long as he can pay for something to drink, he is quite happy I think.

HARRIS: Yes, yes. Bring me a bock.

WAITER: Certainly, monsieur. [*Exit.* HARRIS *has just sat down, when*

LORD ALFRED DOUGLAS *enters from the right. As he is about to sit at another table he notices* HARRIS *and goes over to him.*]

LORD ALFRED: That's curious, Harris, meeting you here!

HARRIS:[*Distantly*] May I ask, Lord Alfred Douglas, why my presence here should seem curious to you?

LORD ALFRED: Because I came here to look for somebody you know. [*Pause*] I came to look for Oscar.

HARRIS: Indeed!

LORD ALFRED: Is that very surprising?

HARRIS: [*Dramatically*] When Oscar came out of prison there were familiar faces to greet him. The faces of his *friends*. I do not remember yours amongst them, Lord Alfred.

LORD ALFRED: How could I have been there? You know quite well why it was impossible for me to be present.

HARRIS: I have been told several stories by friends of Oscar's.

LORD ALFRED: Friends of Oscar's. I've no doubt you've been told a lot of lies. I can hear the shrill little voices — denouncing me as the man who left a friend in his hour of need. But Oscar won't tell you that. It is for his sake that we are not living under the same roof now. The allowance made him by his wife carries with it the condition that we shall not do that. But we meet each other constantly. You wouldn't know of our meetings. What business is it of yours, or anybody else?

HARRIS: Strictly speaking, I suppose it is not my business. But, unfortunately, circumstances have made your friendship with Oscar a piece of public property. It will remain that now, I'm afraid.

LORD ALFRED: You're right there. A friendship is something between two people which belongs only to them. It cannot be understood by others. Nor have others the right to try and understand it. People won't leave Oscar and me alone. When he came out of prison he stayed with me at my villa in Naples and we could have remained there perfectly happy, if his family and mine hadn't separated us. But of course they had to interfere. Lately, though, I've come into some money and I'm able to help Oscar. I have always been his friend and I shall remain his friend so long as he needs me.

HARRIS: [*Changing his attitude*] Well spoken, young man. Oscar has need of friends to stand by him. He knows he can count on me.

LORD ALFRED: Are you meeting Oscar here?

HARRIS: Yes, by appointment. We have some business to discuss. [*Looking at his watch*] He's very late.

LORD ALFRED: I won't interrupt you then.

HARRIS: But isn't *your* business with Oscar important?

LORD ALFRED: Not important. Oscar still loves talking, to me, and I still love listening to him. He talks as wonderfully as ever. And tonight I have a surprise for him — a present.

HARRIS: Tell me, in confidence, how badly is Oscar in need of money?

LORD ALFRED: So long as I'm alive he'll be provided for. I have made up my mind on that. But Oscar was always extravagant, and after what he has suffered it is a pleasure for me to give him what luxuries I can. A horse of mine has won a race this afternoon. That is why there is a special present for Oscar. I will leave you now, and return later.

HARRIS: Shall I tell him you've been here?

LORD ALFRED: Please say nothing. But if your business with him won't take too long, I'll look in again later.

HARRIS: I shan't keep him long. It's just a little matter of business that... [*Seeing* OSCAR *in the distance*] Why, that is Oscar, getting out of the cab. He's grown much stouter. [LORD ALFRED *glances in the direction indicated, then goes quickly out. The* WAITER *brings* HARRIS' *drink.*]

WAITER: Your bock, monsieur. [*Enter* WILDE.]

HARRIS: Ah, here you are at last, Melmoth.

WILDE: My dear Frank!

HARRIS: What will you drink?

WAITER: Absinthe, monsieur? [WILDE *nods and the* WAITER *goes into the cafe.*]

HARRIS: I have settled your little account with the waiter, Melmoth.

WILDE: That is very kind of you, Frank. But please do not call me Melmoth. Oscar Wilde is not a name of which to be ashamed.

HARRIS: I thought you preferred to be known as Melmoth now.

WILDE: I only use that name to spare the blushes of the postman. To my friends, and to posterity, I am always Oscar Wilde. Tell me, Frank, how do you think I am looking?

HARRIS: Oh, very well, Oscar; very well, indeed.

WILDE: Honestly, Frank?

HARRIS: No. To be honest, I think you looked far better when you came out of prison.

WILDE: [*Reproachfully*] You always say what you think.

HARRIS: [*Pompously*] I hope I do. To say what we think is the nearest we mortals can attain to truth.

WILDE: Truth can be dangerous and so cruel. We should never tell people the truth. It is kinder to tell them the little lies which they would like to believe. That is the highest form of charity.

HARRIS: I have a great deal to discuss with you, Oscar. And I haven't much time.

WILDE: I am sorry I am so late, Frank. But what could you expect? In your letter you told me you wanted to see me on business. Now if you had said pleasure … [*The* WAITER *brings* WILDE'S *drink.*]

WAITER: Absinthe, monsieur. [*He pours the absinthe out and puts the perforated spoon on the glass.* WILDE *removes the spoon and pours water into the glass.*]

WILDE: But, even then, I fear I should have been late today. You see, today is Thursday.

HARRIS: What has that got to do with it?

WILDE: Thursday is the one day of the week for which I live. You don't know, Frank, what a great romantic passion is.

HARRIS: Is that what you are suffering from?

WILDE: The suffering hasn't begun yet. That comes … afterwards. Such an ugly word — afterwards. Do you remember once in the summer you wired me from Calais to meet you at Maire's restaurant and I was very late?

HARRIS: You're always late, Oscar.

WILDE: I drove up to the restaurant, in time, and I was just getting out of the cab when a little soldier passed, and our eyes met. He had great dark eyes and an exquisite olive-dark face — a Florentine bronze, Frank, by a great master. I got out hypnotized and followed him down the boulevard as in a dream. I overtook him and asked him to come and have a drink; and he said to me in his quaint French way: *"Ce n'est pas de refus!"* [*He beckons to the* WAITER, *who brings the absinthe bottle and refills* WILDE'S *glass.*]

We went into a café, and we began to talk. I was in a hurry to meet you, but I had to make friends with him first. He began by telling me all about his mother, Frank — [*Smiling*] — yes, his mother. But at last I got from him that he was always free on Thursdays. And I found out that the thing he desired most in the world was a bicycle; he talked of nickel-plated handle-bars — and finally I told him it might be arranged. He was very grateful, and so we made a rendezvous for the next Thursday, and I came on at once to dine with you.

HARRIS: Good heavens! A soldier, a nickel-plated bicycle, and a great romantic passion!

WILDE: If I had said a brooch, or a necklace, or some trinket which would have cost ten times as much, you would have found it quite natural.

HARRIS: Yes; but I don't think I'd have introduced the necklace the first evening, if there had been any romance in the affair. And as for a nickel-plated bicycle. [*He laughs.*]

WILDE: Only the handle-bars were nickel-plated. He comes to see me on it! Rides to and fro from the barracks. You have no idea how intelligent he is. I lend him books, and his mind is opening like a flower. Once, when you were in Paris, you asked me to a dinner-party one Thursday night—you always seem to choose Thursday, Frank.

HARRIS: [*Laughingly*] I'll remember to make it another day next time!

WILDE: Don't laugh at me; I am quite serious. I told him I had to go and dine with you. He didn't mind. He was glad when I said that I had an English editor for a friend, glad that I should have someone to talk to about London and the people I used to know. If it had been a woman, she would have been jealous of my past. He asked me if he might come and leave his bicycle outside and look through the window of the restaurant, just to see us at dinner. He would be so happy to see me in dress-clothes talking to gentlemen and ladies. He came, but I never saw him. The next time we met he told me all about it; how he had picked you out from my description; he was delightful about it all. Such unselfish devotion... [HARRIS *looks at* WILDE *for a moment with tolerant amusement.*]

HARRIS: Oscar, have you been writing anything lately?

WILDE: Oh, Frank, I cannot. You know my rooms; how can I write in such miserable poverty? [*He beckons to the* WAITER, *who again replenishes his glass.*]

HARRIS: You could easily gain thousands, and live like a prince again. Why not make the effort?

WILDE: If I had pleasant, sunny rooms, I'd try... It's harder than you think.

HARRIS: Nonsense, it's easy for you. Your punishment has made your name known in every country in the world. A book of yours would sell like wildfire; a play would draw in any capital.

WILDE: When I take up my pen all the past comes back. I cannot bear the thoughts... did you know that when I was arrested the police let the reporters come to the cell and stare at me? As if I had been a monster on show.

HARRIS: I think it would be finer, instead of taking the punishment lying down, to trample it under your feet, and make it a rung of the ladder. That is what you were going to do when you came out of prison.

WILDE: That talk about reformation, Frank, was all nonsense. No one ever really reforms or changes. I am what I always was.

HARRIS: The only thing that will ever make you write is absolute, blank poverty. That's the sharpest spur of all—necessity.

WILDE: You don't know me. I would kill myself.

HARRIS: Suicide is the natural end of the world-weary. You love life as much as you ever did.

WILDE: Yes, that's true. Life delights me, still. The people passing on the boulevards, the play of the sunshine in the trees; the noise, the quick movement of the cabs, the costumes of the *cochers* and *sergents-de-ville*; workers and beggars, pimps and prostitutes—all please me to the soul, charm me—and if you would only let me talk instead of bothering me to write, I should be quite happy. Why should I write any more? I have done enough for fame.

HARRIS: You ought to work, Oscar. After all, why should anyone help you, if you will not help yourself?

WILDE: I was born to sing the joy and pride of life, the pleasure of living, the delight in everything beautiful in this most beautiful world, and they took me and tortured me till I learned pity and sorrow. Now I cannot sing the joy, because I know the suffering, and I was never made to sing of suffering.

HARRIS: We must get down to business.

WILDE: Ah . . . business . . .

HARRIS: It is not going to be pleasant.

WILDE: Business never is.

HARRIS: I wrote and told you that I had sold the play "Mr. and Mrs. Daventry" to Mrs. Patrick Campbell.

WILDE: Really, Frank, I never thought you would take my scenario; you had no right to touch it!

HARRIS: But, Oscar, you refused to write the play yourself, or to collaborate with me, and you accepted my £50 for the story.

WILDE: No man could write a play on another's scenario! *C'est ridicule.*

HARRIS: I told you that if I made anything out of the play, I would send you some more money.

WILDE: It is sure to be a failure. Plays cannot be written by amateurs. It's quite absurd of you, Frank, who hardly ever go to the theater, to think you can write a successful play straight off. [*Complete change of tone*] You ought to get a good sum down in advance of royalties from Mrs. Patrick Campbell, and at once send me half of it.

HARRIS: You have already had £50, Oscar. And immediately the play was announced Mrs. Brown Potter wrote to tell me that she paid you £100 for this scenario some years ago. Is it true?

WILDE: I am a dramatist and you are not. How can you meddle with my scenario! *C'est ridicule!*

HARRIS: And now it appears that Horace Sedger, Beerbohm Tree, George Alexander, Ada Rehan and Olga Nethersole have all bought the same scenario! What does it mean, Oscar?

WILDE: It means that you have deprived me of a steady income.

HARRIS: What?

WILDE: I was just about to start selling that play to the French managers, and when I had exhausted them, I should have tried the German managers. Now your interference has ruined everything! Therefore, you owe me more than you will ever get from the play, which in any case is bound to fall flat!

HARRIS: Oscar, I don't know what to say! We have been friends...

WILDE: [*Almost in tears*] I thought you were my friend. When you gave me that paltry £50 I thought you were taking the scenario as a — as a formality. So that it shouldn't seem like charity. In order not to hurt my feelings.

HARRIS: I don't think I need ever have any fear of hurting your feelings. You are obviously not in a condition to discuss the matter any further at present. [*He turns to go.*]

WILDE: Frank!

HARRIS: What is it?

WILDE: The waiter... the drinks... [HARRIS *gives the* WAITER *a coin and goes. With a sigh of relief,* WILDE *opens his newspaper. The* WAITER *is sprinkling the sawdust with water.* LORD ALFRED *appears and watches* WILDE, *who does not see him.*]

WILDE: [*After looking at the* WAITER *for a few moments*] What beautiful flowers you are watering. Tulips, lilies, and roses... [*The* WAITER *looks mystified*] Don't you see them?

WAITER: Yes, monsieur; they are beautiful flowers. [WILDE *pushes his empty glass across the table to the* WAITER, *who refills it.*]

WILDE: Beautiful flowers! [LORD ALFRED *remains in the background looking at* WILDE.]

WILDE: [*Holding the glass*] Absinthe... it helps you to see things as you wish they were. Then you see them as they are not. Finally, you see them as they really are. And that is the most horrible thing in the world. [*The* WAITER *goes into the café.* LORD ALFRED *comes up to* WILDE's *table. Seeing him*] Things as you wish they were.

LORD ALFRED: Oscar. [LORD ALFRED *sits at the table.*]

WILDE: Sh! This is a dream. I am telling one of my stories, and all the stars have come out to listen.

When Jesus returned to Nazareth, Nazareth was so changed that He no longer recognized His own city.

The Nazareth where He had lived was full of lamentations and tears; this city was filled with outbursts of laughter and song...

In the street He saw a woman whose face and raiment were painted and whose feet were shod with pearls, and behind her came slowly, as a hunter, a young man who wore a cloak of two colors. The face of the woman was the face of an idol, and the eyes of the young man were bright with lust. And Jesus followed swiftly, and touched the hand of the young man, and said to him: "Why do you look at this woman in such-wise?" And the young man turned round, and recognized Him, and said: "But I was blind once and you gave me my sight. At what else should I look?"

And Jesus ran forward and touched the painted raiment of the woman, and said to her: "Is there no other way in which to walk save the way of sin?" And the woman turned round and recognized Him, and laughed, and said: "But you forgave me my sins, and the way is a pleasant way."

When Jesus had passed out of the city, He saw, seated by the roadside, a young man who was weeping. He went towards him, touched the long locks of his hair, and said to him: "Why are you weeping?" The young man looked up, recognized Him, and made answer: "But I was dead once, and you raised me from the dead. What else should I do but weep?" [*He makes an attempt to get up, finds that he is too unsteady, and sinks back into his chair. He speaks without looking at* LORD ALFRED.]

I perceive that I am drunk! I find that alcohol, taken persistently, and in sufficiently large quantities, produces all the effects of intoxication! [*After a pause*] I have had my hand on the moon. What is the use of trying to rise a little way from the ground! [WILDE *is apparently no longer conscious of* LORD ALFRED'*s presence.* LORD ALFRED *goes to the door of the café and beckons to the* WAITER, *who comes out.*]

LORD ALFRED: [*Gives the* WAITER *a roll of notes*] When I have gone, I want you to give this to Mr. Wilde. It's some money I won on a horse for him this afternoon.

WAITER: [*Glances at the notes, very respectfully*] Certainly, monsieur. [LORD ALFRED *goes. The* WAITER *looks after him, and at the notes in his hand.* WILDE *beckons to the* WAITER]

WILDE: Will you ask the orchestra to play something gay?

WAITER: Something gay? Yes, monsieur. [*He goes into the café. The orchestra plays "See Me Dance the Polka," the tune which was played at the end of the scene when* WILDE *dined with* CHARLIE PARKER. *As he hears it,* WILDE *bursts into a horrible laugh, which ceases abruptly as the* WAITER *returns.*]

WAITER: The gentleman who was here asked me to give monsieur this — your winnings from the race. [*Gives him the notes.*]

WILDE: [*Looks at the notes; then he turns to the chair in which* LORD ALFRED *has been sitting and speaks as though he is still there*]

Thank you, Bosie. Thank you.

CURTAIN

The Immoralist

Ruth and Augustus Goetz

Adapted from the book by Andre Gide

James Dean (Bachir) and Louis Jourdan (Michel) in *The Immoralist*, at the Royale Theater, 1954. (Photo by Frank Donato. Reprinted with permission from the John Willis Theatre World/Screen World Archive.)

The Immoralist was first produced on Broadway at the Royale Theatre on Monday, February 8, 1954. It was produced by Billy Rose and directed by Daniel Mann. The settings were designed by George Jenkins, the costumes were designed by Motley, and the lighting was designed by Abe Feder.

Cast

Marcelline . . . . Geraldine Page
Dr. Robert . . . . John Heldebrand
Bocage . . . . Charles Dingle
Michel . . . . Louis Jourdan
Bachir . . . . James Dean
Dr. Garrin . . . . Paul Huber
Sidma . . . . Adelaide Klein
Moktir . . . . David J. Stewart

(In the present version two characters have been added — the shepherd boys **Akur** and **Dolit**.)

Manager: Irving Cooper
Press: Bill Doll, Robert Ullman
Stage Managers: Lucia Victor, Richard Grayson, Vivian Matalon
Photographer: Frank Donato

A note on the text: The Immoralist was successfully revived as the first production at the Bouwerie Lane Theatre on November 7, 1963, in a production starring Frank Langella and Marcie Huhert. In this subsequent production, details and omissions in the original production nine years earlier were replaced by the authors, most notably the orchard scene with two Arab boys tossing a ball in the background. The unexpurgated version follows.

Act One
Scene I. Normandy, France, November, 1900.
Scene II. Biskra, North Africa, two months later.

Act Two
Scene I. Biskra, the following week.
Scene II. Biskra, February.
Scene III. Biskra, late spring.
Scene IV. Biskra, summer.

Act Three
Scene I. Biskra, the next day.
Scene II. Normandy, that autumn.

Act One

Scene I

The study of a country house in Normandy, France, about 1900. Before the curtain rises, we hear the sound of church bells. Now we see a room furnished with a center table, some chairs and a desk. R. there is a large French window onto an outer court-yard. U. L. there is a door from the central hall of the house. It is late afternoon of a grey, autumn day. There is a pause, then MARCELLINE *enters. She is a slim young woman in her twenties, modestly dressed, and fittingly for a funeral. She removes a black lace veil which has been draped over her head in lieu of a hat, and she puts a small bouquet of flowers on the table.*

Now DOCTOR ROBERT *enters. He is a man in his thirties, dressed severely, who carries a medical bag in his gloved hands. He watches* MARCELLINE *as she gets a vase and puts the flowers in it. Now he puts down his medical bag and removes his gloves.*

DR. ROBERT: I don't think you should be as free in this house, as you have been. [*He reaches for his card case.*] I think we should leave cards and go. [MARCELLINE *is busy with the flowers and does not answer.*] Couldn't I just add your name to mine? [*Takes a card out.*] I can cross mine out and just write — [*Now he is writing.*] Our deepest sympathy — Doctor Robert and sister . . . [*A pause while he finishes.*]

MARCELLINE: Robert, this is probably the loneliest moment of Michel's life and I would like to be with him.

ROBERT: [*He looks at her perplexed.*] Marcelline, Michel has never spoken to me about you.

MARCELLINE: Why should he?

ROBERT: Well — it's proper, that's why — it might be that because you are an orphan he thinks you are completely independent. But you *are* under my roof, and I am the nominal head of the family.

MARCELLINE: Michel could not consider marrying while his father was alive.

309

ROBERT: Other young men have.

MARCELLINE: Michel is not other young men, Robert.

ROBERT: No, that's true. He has reached a certain eminence as an historian—

MARCELLINE: [*Correcting him.*] Archeologist, Robert.

ROBERT: He has outdistanced his father certainly—I was never able to read the old professor's books, and I must say I've found Michel's interesting—[*He indicates the one on the table.*] Is this the new one?

MARCELLINE: [*Looks at it.*] Yes . . . that's three years work. He and his father gathered most of that material in Greece.

ROBERT: I remember that trip. Michel came home with quite a cough.

MARCELLINE: Are you uneasy about his health, Robert? Is that why you discourage me?

ROBERT: I am not discouraging you. I believe you are sincere in your devotion to him. I don't understand it, but I have had to accept it.

MARCELLINE: What is difficult to understand? He is learned, he is considerate, he is gentle—

ROBERT: Those are good qualities, if he was up for Holy orders but he isn't. You're talking of a man you want for a husband.

MARCELLINE: Will you let me lead my own life, Robert? Michel and I grew up together and he is the only person I have ever felt safe with.

ROBERT: I don't quite understand that.

MARCELLINE: I don't expect you to. There is a great difference between you and me.

ROBERT: And between you and the other young ladies of the village.

MARCELLINE: I have heard you and your friends discuss the other young ladies of the village—as if you were at a live stock sale. How fat they are or how thin they are or if they have good legs—but never what they think or feel!

ROBERT: Marriage is not all poetry and walks in the garden, Marcie.

MARCELLINE: Don't you tell me what marriage is. I have my own picture of it.

ROBERT: Yes, I know—sickness and health, better or worse—all of the words.

MARCELLINE: Yes . . . the sharing of everything.

ROBERT: You'd better find out first whether he wants to do all this sharing. You're not getting any younger.

MARCELLINE: That's what I mean—you always permit yourself to say the thing that might hurt, but Michel does not. [ROBERT *is sorry—he tries to retreat a little.*]

ROBERT: I don't know Michel. I wish I did.

MARCELLINE: That is your fault.

ROBERT: They were away the better part of every year. [*He uses his fingers to make his points.*] As a child he was in boarding school—until the year he came home so suddenly. After that he and his father were always together, the father tutoring, the boy with a book in his hand wherever they went. How could anyone know them? People around here thought he was crazy to coddle the boy as he did.

MARCELLINE: Michel loved his father very dearly.

ROBERT: Marcelline, I have been in constant attendance here during the old man's illness. I saw something of this love you speak of—and I say most of it was fear!

MARCELLINE: Fear of what?

ROBERT: [*Puzzled.*] I don't know … the father was afraid to let Michel out of his sight—Michel was afraid to stir from the old man's side. And this is no child—he is a grown man, and perfectly well able to take care of himself.

MARCELLINE: You have never liked him—

ROBERT: He is an eccentric, and I don't like eccentrics! [*Before* MARCELLINE *can answer him,* BOCAGE *comes in from the hallway. He is a stout, middle-aged man in the modest black suit of the upper peasantry. He has a pleasant, self-confident manner.*]

BOCAGE: Hello, Miss Marcelline.

MARCELLINE: Hello, Bocage.

BOCAGE: That was a fine service—I saw people today I haven't seen in twenty years. I've put your horse under cover, Doctor. It looks as if it might rain. [*He goes to the French windows and peers out.*] I hope Michel doesn't get caught in it. He said he wanted to walk home from the cemetery. If he gets a chill he will have that cough again.

MARCELLINE: Has he an umbrella?

ROBERT: We need rain—

BOCAGE: Yes, some of the fields are getting dry. [*He comes away from the window.*] But you've got a nice stand of rye, Doctor. I walked your upper field the other day.

ROBERT: That's the seed you told me to buy. It ought to be good—at that price … Will you stay on here and manage, Bocage?

BOCAGE: Yes, the old professor left me my stone cottage and the two fields around it.

ROBERT: Well, that's fine—Tell Michel we were here, will you Bocage?

BOCAGE: Oh, you musn't go! Let me get you something. Some Calvados.

ROBERT: No thanks, we really — [*But* BOCAGE *has exited and it is too late. Annoyed at* MARCELLINE's *composure.*] How long are you going to sit there?

MARCELLINE: Until Michel comes.

ROBERT: [*With bite.*] Wouldn't it be more proper if *he* came to see *you?*

MARCELLINE: Yes, Robert, it would — Now will you please sit down and be patient? Michel will be here soon. [*He stands over her waiting for her to rise.*]

ROBERT: Have a little pride, Marcelline!

MARCELLINE: [*Quietly.*] I have a great deal of pride, Robert.

ROBERT: Well, nobody in the village thinks you have! Let him cover over and see us — Let him act like every other man who's courting a girl! [MICHEL *enters through the French windows. He might well have heard the last line. He is a fine looking young man, dressed in a dark suit with a mourning band around his arm. He comes into the room and turns to* MARCELLINE.]

MICHEL: Hello, Marcie . . . I'm so glad you're here. Hello, Doctor. [MARCELLINE *rises immediately.*]

ROBERT: Our deepest sympathy on your very great loss, Michel! —

MARCELLINE: Are you all right, Michel?

MICHEL: Yes —

MARCELLINE: We waited in the carriage. We thought we could bring you home.

MICHEL: I walked across the fields . . . What did you think of it?

ROBERT: Very impressive service —

MARCELLINE: [*Warmly.*] It is always awful, Michel, no matter how it is done.

MICHEL: I wish I could have carried him into the woods and buried him myself. [*A pause.*] But you are not allowed to do that, are you?

ROBERT: Even if you were, people would still want to pay their respects.

MICHEL: It amazes me how people gather at funerals. The dead one is gone, so it must be the survivor who interests them. How will he act? What will he do? They stand watching and they weigh the sorrow — Is it small, medium or great? I wish I could have satisfied them. I wanted to fulfill what they expected of me — but I didn't know how. [*There is an embarrassed silence, while* MICHEL *attempts to recover himself. Realizing that they are both still standing:*] Marcelline, will you sit down? Robert?

ROBERT: [*Moving again toward door.*] We just came by for an instant — [*But* MARCELLINE *sits down.* ROBERT *is left standing.* MICHEL *looks at him.*]

MICHEL: Do you have calls to make, Robert?

ROBERT: No. [*But he doesn't sit.*]

MICHEL: [*To* MARCELLINE. *Sitting beside her.*] I looked for you, but I couldn't see you among the others.

MARCELLINE: [*Sweetly.*] I am glad you looked—

ROBERT: [*Clears his throat.*] Bocage says your father left him the stone cottage. Were there any other bequests?

MICHEL: I don't know, Robert.

ROBERT: Have you made any plans?

MICHEL: About what?

ROBERT: Well, about what you're going to do?

MICHEL: No, Robert.

ROBERT: I suppose you will travel?

MICHEL: I don't know.

MARCELLINE: [*To* ROBERT.] You ask so many questions!

MICHEL: That's all right, Marcie. [*To* ROBERT.] I have been invited to lecture at the Royal Society in London. Or I can join an expedition to North Africa. You're right, Robert, I should be making plans.

ROBERT: [*To* MARCELLINE.] Our countryside isn't very stimulating for an archaeologist. [*To* MICHEL.] Is it?

MARCELLINE: This is Michel's home, Robert.

ROBERT: Yes, but he isn't like the rest of us—tied down by a profession or a business. You're free—now. [MICHEL *coughs.*] I mean, you are free to do what you want to do. Besides you ought to go some place to get rid of that cough.

MICHEL: Where do you suggest I go, Robert? And how long should I stay away?

ROBERT: You know more about that than I do. [*He rises.*] Come, Marcelline, I've got patients to see.

MARCELLINE: Robert means—just a couple of weeks, for a rest.

MICHEL: I know what Robert means. [*Now* BOCAGE *enters from the hall, carrying two glasses and a decanter.*]

BOCAGE: Michel, my boy, I guess you need this more than any of us.

MICHEL: [*Taking glass.*] I'm all right, Bocage.

BOCAGE: [*Offering tray to* DR. ROBERT.] Doctor?

ROBERT: [*To* BOCAGE.] I'm sorry but we've got to get on our way.

BOCAGE: Oh, the cook's sliced up a platter of ham and there's some fresh bread coming in—

ROBERT: Some other time, Bocage.

BOCAGE: [*Coaxing.*] You'll stay for supper, won't you, Miss?

MICHEL: Robert wants Miss Marcelline to go with him.

ROBERT: Yes—good day. [*He exits.*]

MARCELLINE: [*Hesitates at the door.*] Shall I stay, Michel?

MICHEL: [*Comes to her.*] I want you to, but you had better do as he says. [*She looks at him and leaves.* BOCAGE *and* MICHEL *are left alone.* BOCAGE *watches him a moment.*]

BOCAGE: She likes you. [*No answer.*] And *she* doesn't keep it a secret... She likes you very much.

MICHEL: [*He turns to* BOCAGE.] I like her very much.

BOCAGE: Well, then, this is the time to count your blessings! [*He goes to the desk and takes out a ledger book.*] And there are other blessings—this place, your work—Do you know our fruit crop was the largest picking in my twenty-six years here? And the new seedlings have all taken root—[*He opens the ledger, puts on his glasses, but looks at* MICHEL.]

MICHEL: Bocage, sit with me—I always thought I was alone—more alone than anyone else. But it wasn't true. I had him. I never knew it would be like this.

BOCAGE: [*Puts aside the ledger.*] This will pass, Michel, believe me. I've had sorrow in my life—and when I was your age. I lost my wife—and... and my child. [*He pours himself a drink.*] But, you live—[*He puts down the bottle.*] This is a good home. You can be very happy in time. And you don't need a lot of people around you. The more people you have, the more demands they make.

MICHEL: [*Remembering.*] Yes, particularly people who love you. How greedy they are of your time. How they ask you to stay by them five minutes longer, or tell one more story, or take one last turn around the garden. [*There is a silence between them.* BOCAGE *pours himself another drink.*]

BOCAGE: You miss your father very much—but he was a very selfish man. Especially the last few months... [*He gulps his drink.*]

MICHEL: [*Quietly.*] I don't think so. He was as he had always been—

BOCAGE: He was better when he was with you. But between times he did things he didn't know he was doing.

MICHEL: There were no between times. He was never irrational, Bocage.

BOCAGE: [*Angrily.*] He was wrong—!

MICHEL: Wrong about what?

BOCAGE: [*Pouring another drink.*] About many things—many things...

MICHEL: Bocage—[*Points to the glass.*]—before you fortify yourself to a point where you've forgotten what you want to tell me, come over and sit down. [BOCAGE *looks at him mutely and puts down the glass.*]

BOCAGE: Michel—

MICHEL: [*Waits for him to sit down.*] Yes?

BOCAGE: I tried to tell him... that I wouldn't be responsible... But he was a stubborn old man and he wouldn't listen…Even the day before he died I tried to explain to him—I tried to make him understand how it would look! [*Rising.*] I don't know how to tell you this.

MICHEL: [*Gently. Rising to* BOCAGE's *side.*] Start where it is hardest and then it will get easier as you go along.

BOCAGE: You mustn't be angry with me, Michel. When all's said and done, I'm just a hired hand. There is very little you can say to a man after you've taken his wages all your life.

MICHEL: [*Now he is sympathetic.*] Bocage, you can say anything to me. You couldn't make me angry, not even by trying.

BOCAGE: [*Looks up at him and now takes the plunge.*] There is a will…

MICHEL: You mean my father made a Will? [BOCAGE *nods his head yes.*] Well…

BOCAGE: Three weeks ago when you decided not to go to England. You walked into the village to mail your letter and he and I were alone here. He made me write it down word by word, and then I had to be his witness and sign after him. But now if that will were to disappear, who'd be the wiser?

MICHEL: Well, now that you've told me, I'd be the wiser. Where is it, Bocage?

BOCAGE: [*Averts his eyes.*] I don't know.

MICHEL: [*Rises and goes to the desk.*] If I am to share my inheritance with the Sisters of Mercy or the village orphanage, I can bear it. [*At the desk he opens some compartments.*]

BOCAGE: [*Rises and pleads with him.*] There are no other heirs, Michel. You know that! And my little cottage you will give me whether you see the will or no! Let it be! Don't read it! He was a sick old man—

MICHEL: Yes, he was. And he was my father whom I loved. He has left me a last message and you are asking me not to read it—not to pay any attention to it. [*With authority. He points to the desk.*] Now find it for me! Immediately—

BOCAGE: [*His hand reaches tremblingly for another ledger.*] You will say to me why didn't I destroy it myself and never let you know it was here. But I could not do that. I, too, have an obligation to him.

MICHEL: Give it to me, please. [*He holds out his hand.*]

BOCAGE: [*Opens the ledger, exposes the paper, but before be hands it over, he speaks very solemnly and humbly.*] I swear to you…I will never lift a hand to carry out what he asks. [MICHEL *snatches the will, opens it and reads it. Then with some surprise:*]

MICHEL: He just wants his debts paid, and his bequests to you and the village taken care of—[*He turns back to the will.*] "I then leave every-thing I possess to my only beloved son—"

BOCAGE: In trust—

MICHEL: [*Smiles.*] And you are to be the trustee?

BOCAGE: Not only me...

MICHEL: [*Turns back to the will.*]—"should Bocage fail to qualify, my attorneys in Paris—" [*To* BOCAGE.] This is a favor to me, Bocage. It relieves me of a burden. I don't want to be concerned with the business of the estate and he knew that.

BOCAGE: That's right—[*He holds out his hand for the paper.*] Give it to me.

MICHEL: [*Holds on to the paper and looks at* BOCAGE *puzzled. Then be resumes reading.*] "The propriety of my son's behavior shall be the sole condi-tion of his enjoying his inheritance. And I appoint the same Bocage as full guardian over him, with power to pay or to withhold all income as it may accrue. Should Bocage fail to exercise his judgment or be unable to do so by illness or death, then I direct my lawyers to assume this guardianship—" [MICHEL *stops reading, there is a pause, then be speaks very quietly.*] What does he mean? "The propriety of my behavior...?"

BOCAGE: I don't know.

MICHEL: You must know.

BOCAGE: I don't, I tell you! It's an old man's craziness—

MICHEL: [*Looking at the will again.*] "Should Bocage fail—" [*He searches* BOCAGE*'s face.*] It is some stranger in Paris who will pass on my conduct?

BOCAGE: [*Placating.*] You know how it is with kidney trouble—his mind wandered...

MICHEL: What has my conduct been but to do my work, to write my books, to conduct myself as a man? [*Brokenly.*] When did I ever disappoint him?

BOCAGE: He was a moral man.

MICHEL: And what am I? What propriety have I ever neglected? What restraint have I ever escaped from?

BOCAGE: He was full of fear, Michel. And a frightened man is a foolish man.

MICHEL: Frightened? Of what? Of me?

BOCAGE: *For* you, my boy. In all these years, since that terrible time when you came home from school—he never dared to ask you the questions he wanted to. [*Points to the document.*] So he's arranged to have me ask them.

MICHEL: Then ask them!

BOCAGE: [*Puts his hand on his arm.*] I don't have to. Whatever sin you committed—God knows you paid for it.

MICHEL: I was eleven years old!...tormented and full of problems...when you are eleven you are not very good at problems. And I solved mine vilely—I know that!

BOCAGE: If it had been anything else—like stealing or lying—the school would not have expelled you. But this was a sin of the flesh, an offense against yourself and the other boy—it frightened your father! He never forgot it.

MICHEL: *He* never forgot it! Do you think I did? That morning as the teachers packed my boxes, they threw my clothing in as if it were infected. Then they walked me through the courtyard at the recess so that everybody could watch me leave. I was alone on earth. At that moment they cut me away from other human beings. I have never been able to make my way back...not even to my father. [*In torment he crumples up the paper.*] What did he want of me that I didn't give him? [*There is a pause, then he continues more calmly.*] The more I tried to appease him, the less he trusted me. In the end he believed that I must always be guilty of the things he suspected. Otherwise why had I tried so hard to please him?

BOCAGE: Let me burn it, Michel.

MICHEL. No, don't burn it. I will always keep it. It will remind me that not even he could love me.

BOCAGE: He was a stupid old man! No one should withhold forgiveness!

MICHEL. [*Savagely.*] I don't care any more whether he withheld it or gave it—whether he believed in me or hated me. He is a dead man now and I am through with the dead. I've got to get out of here! I've got to be where he can no longer reach me. I'm going now—tonight!

BOCAGE: Don't go away like this. Stay until you have got over it. Otherwise you will not come back.

MICHEL: You are right. I will never come back! Never! Never!

BOCAGE: Don't go among strangers, Michel. You are liked and trusted here..

MICHEL: Don't lie to me! Even you see in me what he saw.

BOCAGE: Michel! No!

MICHEL: You do! And more terrible than that—they all do!

BOCAGE: You must never believe that! [*Outside there is the sound of a bell. It rings twice.*]

MICHEL: How can I believe anything else? That is his legacy to me. [*The bell rings again. He puts will on table.*] I don't want to see neighbors,

Bocage! [BOCAGE *hesitates, then exits to the outer door. Now* MICHEL *is left alone. He snatches off mourning band—tosses it on table, starts to ball.*]

MARCELLINE: [*off stage*] Michel! [*She enters followed by* BOCAGE.]

MARCELLINE: Michel—I came back to apologize for Robert.

MICHEL: It doesn't matter, Marcie.

BOCAGE: You came back just in time, Miss. Michel wants to leave here.

MARCELLINE: [*To* MICHEL.] Because of what Robert said?

MICHEL: No.

MARCELLINE: Where would you go?

MICHEL: As far away as I can get.

BOCAGE: [*Quickly.*] Maybe just for the winter—

MICHEL: I don't think so.

MARCELLINE: For how long?

MICHEL: I don't know.

MARCELLINE: Is it to finish up some work?

BOCAGE: [*Quickly.*] Yes.

MARCELLINE: Will you be back by spring?

MICHEL: No, Marcie.

MARCELLINE: [*In alarm.*] Do you mean you might be gone for—for a long time?

MICHEL: Yes, Marcie—I think so.

MARCELLINE: Bocage, will you leave us alone? I can ask you to do that, can't I? You're my friend. [*To* MICHEL.] I have a great favor to ask of you.

MICHEL: Can't Bocage hear it? He should. He should hear everything.

MARCELLINE: Very well, I don't care who hears. I was going to wait until spring—But now there may be no spring.

MICHEL: What is it, Marcelline?

MARCELLINE: I want to marry you, Michel. I formally ask your hand in marriage. I have half the money my parents left Robert and me, and I have been careful with it. It isn't much, but I will be no expense to you. [*The two men listen to her in silence.*] When I would sit with your father, he made me understand how important your work was. I will never interfere with it, Michel.

MICHEL: [*To* BOCAGE.] Will you leave us alone, Bocage?

BOCAGE: [*Picking up will from table, backing to hall.*] He will tell you he is unworthy, Miss Marcelline. But you know better than that—[BOCAGE *exits. Left alone, there is a pause. Then* MICHEL *goes to* MARCELLINE.]

MICHEL: Marcelline, you are a dear friend—[*Then with effort.*] My only friend—and you are full of pity for me—[*She shakes her head no.*] You don't really mean this.

MARCELLINE: I do mean it.

MICHEL: Look at me!

MARCELLINE: I am looking at you.

MICHEL: Do you see me...?

MARCELLINE: I have never seen anyone else.

MICHEL. You were very fond of my father. But you are not bound by any promise he might have extracted from you, Marcelline. I release you from it.

MARCELLINE: He never asked me to promise him anything.

MICHEL: But he told you what would please him. And that is what you are trying to do. [*Then with vehemence.*] I know! I did it myself.

MARCELLINE: Your father liked me. I told him I loved you to get his help. But he never helped me. He said to me once I should try to stop loving you. He said you would never return it. Maybe he was right — here you are going away without a thought of me!

MICHEL: He was wrong about everything!

MARCELLINE: [*Very surprised.*] Michel —!

MICHEL: *You* are the only good thought I carry away from this place!

MARCELLINE: Don't take thoughts, Michel. Take me —

MICHEL: Why did he tell you such a thing! How could he —?

MARCELLINE: [*Smiles.*] It didn't matter very much, Michel. I have loved you since I was fourteen — every minute of every day. I loved you when you were here, and when you were away. And I will always love you!

MICHEL: Me...?

MARCELLINE: Why is it so hard for you to believe that?

MICHEL: Because no one ever has —

MARCELLINE: Michel, you've never let them — [*Pause.*] Even now, you won't let me.

MICHEL: [*Despairing.*] Marcie, I don't know what to say to you —

MARCELLINE: I don't expect you to love me as I love you.

MICHEL: Let me come for you when I can say to you the things you are saying to me.

MARCELLINE: [*Sadly.*] You won't. If I were with you, you would turn to me in time. I know it.

MICHEL: [*Anguished.*] You deserve better than me!

MARCELLINE: For me, there is no better. [*She turns to leave. There is a pause.*]

MICHEL: Marcelline, this has been one of the most terrible days of my life. I keep hearing my father. If I cannot be responsible for myself, how can I be for you?

MARCELLINE: I didn't come to you for that. I don't need another guardian.

You said you were going away, so I thought I ought to tell you the truth. Goodbye. [*She starts out.*]

MICHEL: Wait! You are all I have! I have no one else!

MARCELLINE: [*She smiles a little, confidently.*] Then take me . . . You will love me . . .

MICHEL: [*Frustrated.*] But—I cannot live here! I must go away from this place!

MARCELLINE: I would go wherever you say.

MICHEL: But I mean now !—Tonight !

MARCELLINE: Yes . . . I know.

MICHEL: You mean you would go with me?

MARCELLINE: [*Indicating herself as she is.*] As I am, Michel.

MICHEL: [*Calls out.*] Bocage! [*He goes to her.*] Marcie, I will love you . . . I know I will!

MARCELLINE: [*Smiling at him.*] Of course you will. [BOCAGE *enters.*]

MICHEL: Bocage, we are going away together!

BOCAGE: What?

MICHEL: We are going to be married tonight! Away from this place—in another town, surrounded by strangers, away from this, away from all of it—!

BOCAGE: Tonight?

MICHEL: In a few hours! As fast and as far as we can go!

BOCAGE: The finest girl in our village—I am almost as happy as he is, Miss. You do this house great honor.

MICHEL: [*Goes to her.*] She does *me* great honor . . .

The CURTAIN *falls*

Scene II

Their house in Biskra. A dividing wall marks off an inner room from a terrace. In the room we see a bed, two night tables and a chair. There is a doorway to the hall in back hung with beaded portieres, and a narrow window-door that connects with the terrace.

It is night and at the rise MARCELLINE *and* MICHEL *are on the terrace together. They are both in dressing gowns and night apparel. He is relaxing in a deck chair while she leans against the wall, peering through a single eyeglass at the sky.*

MARCELLINE: There is a small star to one side of the cluster. What's that?
MICHEL: That could be one finger of the Heavenly Twins. Do you see them?
MARCELLINE: No . . .
MICHEL: [*Takes glass, looks through it, stands, finds star.*] Let me show you. [*He motions her to him and moves away from the glass, trying to hold it in position while she steps up to look.*] Here. Do you see their outspread arms?
MARCELLINE: Yes! Yes! That's the first time! We never see them back home. [*He coughs a little, going L. to sit on wall.*]
MICHEL: The sky in Normandy is so dull and cold.
MARCELLINE: But here in Africa it's brilliant—it's exciting. [*With this she has crossed to sit on wall U. next to* MICHEL—*solicitously.*]
MICHEL: You delight in everything—
MARCELLINE: [*Scanning Heavens with glass.*] I like every place we've been. I liked Genoa, and Naples, and Carthage—[*Taking down glass.*]—no, I didn't like Carthage. You coughed too much there. [*With real expectancy.*] I know I will like Biskra very much. [*A pause.*] If anyone had told me two months ago that I would be living in the Sahara desert with you—[*She laughs, then he laughs with her.*]
MICHEL: If anyone had told me two months ago that my life could be like this—[*He laughs lightly again—she puts glass in its case from tabouret—he crosses to sit again in deck chair, saying:*] We must go to El Sidi Okba.
MARCELLINE: What's that?
MICHEL: [*Sitting into deck chair—head back—relaxed.*] The most ancient tomb in the Arab world. I want to show it to you. Maybe you can charm the priests while I take off a rubbing of the inscription.
MARCELLINE: [*Coming above him.*] Let's not do that right away. We just got here. Let us rest and be comfortable for the first few days.
MICHEL: Whatever you want—
MARCELLINE: [*gently stroking his face and head.*] Are you sleepy?

MICHEL: No—

MARCELLINE: Are you going to sit up very long?

MICHEL: For a while. The desert air makes me feel easier.

MARCELLINE: Shall I sit with you?

MICHEL: No, you're tired.

MARCELLINE: I'm not terribly tired...

MICHEL: You must be. It was a long train ride. [*A pause—she kisses his fore-head and crosses to go into bedroom, but he speaks and she turns to listen. He sits up.*] Tomorrow we will shop the bazaar and see everything in the village. I'll buy you a good parasol, and we'll walk out into the desert. We'll do a lot of things tomorrow. [*He reaches out, takes her hand, kisses it.*] Have a good sleep. [*He stretches back again—she goes into bedroom.*]

MARCELLINE: Yes—[*She looks all about the room, turns the bed down with real delight.*] This is the first night we haven't been in a hotel...I like it. It's private. It's like nothing I ever saw before, but at the same time it's a little like our home—[*Pause—no answer—she goes to door, looks at him—he turns head to smile lightly at her.*]—isn't it?

MICHEL: Yes. [*She looks at him, but he says nothing more. She goes back in, sits on bed, D. side. He coughs—bending forward with the spasm—she listens—it's over and he feels a chill, goes into bedroom.*] Can you spare the shawl?

MARCELLINE: You don't have to sleep out there.

MICHEL: Marcelline—dearest—you know it's only because of this cough that I leave you to yourself.

MARCELLINE: [*Rising with shawl from D. R. chair and putting it around his neck as he stands at foot of bed.*] Yes. Now that we are married, I have the thing I have wanted most in my life.

MICHEL: We have so many things we enjoy. [*A pause.*]

MARCELLINE: One night you will look at me and say—"Heavens, you look pretty tonight—"

MICHEL: [*Pause.*] Heavens, you look pretty tonight...[*She embraces him hungrily—the move to break the embrace seems to come from him—they sit slowly on end of bed.*]

MARCELLINE: [*Speaks with difficulty.*] Michel...married people say things to one another. I want to say something to you. I will never say it again. And I shall forget it as soon as you tell me. What did other women do?

MICHEL: [*A beat.*] There were no other women. [*Pause.*]

MARCELLINE: Are we frightened, Michel? Is that what is wrong with us?

MICHEL: Yes.

MARCELLINE: They teach us all the arts, except how to make you love me.

MICHEL: [*Rising to stand above bed.*] It isn't you, it is me! And it has nothing to do with love. [*Kneeling on U. L. corner of bed, taking hold of her shoulders.*] I never loved you more than I do right this minute!... But I am stopped!

MARCELLINE: [*Timidly.*] I wonder if you think I will be afraid, or shocked—I won't be, Michel. To be a good animal is sometimes very beautiful... [MICHEL *turns away from her.* MARCELLINE *sees his deep distress.*] If we had had a courtship like the other young people of the village, we wouldn't be so afraid of each other now. We'd be more at ease. I've loved you a long time, and I can wait a little longer—

MICHEL: [*Castigating himself.*] Wait for what? A magical moment that never comes!

MARCELLINE: It is enough for me that we are together—

MICHEL: [*Desperately.*] We are not together! Not like people who love each other!

MARCELLINE: [*Comforting him.*] We will be...

MICHEL: [*With increasing pain.*] Will be! I should be holding you in my arms *now.* We are young, and we are on our wedding trip! There must be some way for me to feel what all men feel at such times!

MARCELLINE: [*Pause, then quietly.*] Maybe not, my darling.

MICHEL: Maybe not—?

MARCELLINE: Haven't you thought of it, Michel?

MICHEL: Thought of what?

MARCELLINE: [*She speaks quietly and with great fortitude.*] Sometimes people marry, and live together, and *never* feel desire.

MICHEL: But it would be like the loneliness of my childhood.

MARCELLINE: [*Trying to comfort him.*] We would have each other's comfort and companionship—we would not be lonely... It is a possibility that I have had to accept—

MICHEL: *What* possibility?

MARCELLINE: That you cannot live with me. That—that you are physically unable...

MICHEL: [*Looks at her for a long moment, then he understands.*] Do you think I would have married you if that were so?... It is not true...!

MARCELLINE: [*Puzzled.*] Are you sure?

MICHEL: Of course, yes.

MARCELLINE: You told me you had never been with a woman—

MICHEL: I have not. [*There is a pause between them.*]

MARCELLINE: Then how can you know?

MICHEL: You mustn't think that! It is not true!

MARCELLINE: I would rather think that—than that while I have been next to you—[*She covers her eyes.*] You have wanted someone else.

MICHEL: [*He takes her hands away from her face, and with sincerity.*] Marcelline, it is you I want—There has never been another woman—only you!

MARCELLINE: [*Desperately.*] But...but I cannot understand it! If you love me, and you are physically able—why have we lived this way? Why... [*She has put her two hands on his two shoulders, and he and she are looking into each other's eyes.*] Am I ugly to you?...Is that it?...Do I repel you? [*She puts her face in her hands and weeps.*]

MICHEL: Marcelline, you must not believe that! Anything is better than that I let you believe it. It isn't true—it isn't the reason!

MARCELLINE: [*Looks up at him.*] Even now you don't want me. I can see it in your eyes.

MICHEL: [*Resolutely.*] I do! I do! [*He looks at her, takes her in his arms and kisses her. Her arms go around his neck and she clings to him passionately, but almost immediately he must hold her away from him as he starts to cough. Now, as the coughing becomes a spasm, he releases her, and she stands watching him with growing concern.*]

MARCELLINE: Michel, what can I get you? [*He cannot answer, as he turns away from her and bends over the bed to ease himself.*] Michel—darling— where's the medicine? [*He helplessly points to the washstand. She gets it quickly, but now he has covered his face. She bends over him, then looks around wildly.*] Help—help!

MICHEL: [*In a final effort he gasps out.*] Don't look! [*Now with a great groan he delivers himself up to the hemorrhage which ends all questions.*]

MARCELLINE: [*Holding on to him.*] Help! Oh, won't somebody help... Somebody, please!

The CURTAIN *falls*

Act Two

Scene I
Scene: *House in Biskra, middle morning, a week later.*

At rise: MARCELLINE *is straightening up the bedroom. She is in shirtwaist and skirt. An Arab boy,* BACHIR, *is squatting bidden in the hallway. She calls.*

MARCELLINE: Bachir! [*He doesn't answer—she goes out on terrace, calls down road.*] Bachir!

BACHIR: [*Quickly appearing from hall.*] Yes, Madame?

MARCELLINE: [*Nervously.*] Why don't you answer me?

BACHIR: I am here, Madame.

MARCELLINE: Well, just don't sit there! Do things! [*Sees broom leaning against wall, picks it up and hands it to* BACHIR.] Sweep the terrace! Make it clean!

BACHIR: Yes, Madame.

MARCELLINE: Have you ever worked in a house before?

BACHIR: Oh, yes, Madame.

MARCELLINE: I doubt it. I'm going to the Barracks Hospital to get my husband and when I get back I want to see everything just as spick and span.

BACHIR: Master is better today?

MARCELLINE: Yes, my husband is getting better. [*At this moment* DR. GARRIN *enters from the street and looks over the wall.*]

GARRIN: Good morning! [MARCELLINE *staggers at seeing him.*]

MARCELLINE: What is it, Doctor? What is it? [*She covers her mouth to keep from screaming.*]

GARRIN: Now, now—he's all right—Don't always expect the worst, my dear lady. He's all right. They've got him dressed and I'm on my way to the hospital to get him now.

MARCELLINE: I'll go with you.

GARRIN: I would rather you would not. I want to tell you about him.

MARCELLINE: How is he?

GARRIN: He's very low in spirits. Now it might be the atmosphere of the Barracks hospital. God knows, it's a miserable place. But this illness has taken a lot out of him—taken the fight out of him. And you've got to put it back.

MARCELLINE: I will do my best.

GARRIN: [*Smiles.*] I'm sure you will. I took the liberty of finding a house-woman for you.

MARCELLINE: Oh?

GARRIN: I would have brought her along, but you had better see her. And do it now, before she goes to the washing stones. Her name is Sidma. She lives in that clay hut just down the road.

MARCELLINE: We'll go for Michel first.

GARRIN: Better get the woman first. It is important for you to have help here. I will go for your husband, and I will have him here by the time you get back.

MARCELLINE: [*She hesitates.*] Doctor—I have been wanting to ask you something...Before the hemorrhage last week, my husband must have had fever.

GARRIN: Undoubtedly.

MARCELLINE: Perhaps for many weeks?

GARRIN: I would say so.

MARCELLINE: So that would account for any weakness—any physical weakness, I mean?

GARRIN: It might.

MARCELLINE: Yes—that's what I have been thinking. [*She would exit but has a last order.*] Bachir—arrange the netting.

GARRIN: I don't want him to get right into bed, Madame. I want him to sit in the sun. It's the best cure I know.

MARCELLINE: [*To* BACHIR.] Very well, then, fix the chair. [*Going off.*] Did you say her name is Sidma?

GARRIN: Yes.

MARCELLINE: Thank you. [*She exits.* GARRIN, *on the terrace, looks down at* BACHIR.]

GARRIN: Haven't I seen you before?

BACHIR: No, sir.

GARRIN: Didn't I treat you for a head wound not long ago?

BACHIR: No, sir.

GARRIN: Why, they caught you with some of the soldiers in the barracks, didn't they?

BACHIR: Oh, no, sir.

GARRIN: [*Takes* BACHIR's *hat off and separates his hair to see the scar.*] Of course, I never forget a face. Stay away from the barracks, or the next time they'll put you in jail.

MICHEL: [*Calls from offstage L.*] Marcelline! [*Now* MICHEL *comes along the wall. He is weak.* GARRIN *goes to him.*]

GARRIN: On your own steam, eh? Well, well, well—[*He goes outside the wall and takes* MICHEL's *arm.*] I was just coming down to get you.

MICHEL: [*Calls out.*] Marcelline!

GARRIN: She's gone off to get a cleaning woman—I insisted on it—[*As he leads him through the gate.*] She's going to spend every minute she can with you—

BACHIR: Welcome home—sir. [*Now that* MICHEL *is inside the gate,* BACHIR *salutes him Arab fashion.*] Madame and I were just coming to the hospital for you.

MICHEL: [*To* DOCTOR.] I couldn't stay there another minute. Bachir, go to the hospital later and get the handbag with the clothes that you brought me last week.

BACHIR: It is done!

MICHEL: I couldn't carry it...

GARRIN: [*To* BACHIR.] Go get him a blanket, or something—[BACHIR *turns into the hall,* MICHEL *starts for bedroom door.*] Now, you just sit out here—and forget you're ill—and think about what you're going to do when your strength comes back.

MICHEL: When will Marcelline be back?

GARRIN: Very soon.

MICHEL: [*Sitting in deck chair.*] I'm exhausted.

GARRIN: Of course you are—that was quite a trick, getting here on your own feet. That ought to give you some confidence.

MICHEL: Doctor, the two soldiers that carried me to the hospital—I'd like to give them something, but I didn't see them today—[*Takes the money out of his pocket and gives it to the Doctor.*] Will you give it to them?

GARRIN: That's very nice. [*He takes the money.* BACHIR *comes out with shawl from across foot of bed, he drapes it over back of deck chair. To* BACHIR.] Is there any food back there?

BACHIR: Food? A feast, sir—Madame burned all her fingers cooking it.

GARRIN: Go get it. [*To* MICHEL.] If you can eat a little it will do you good.

MICHEL: Yes, I will try.

GARRIN: [*Puts his hand on* MICHEL's *shoulder.*] You know, your wife's had a very anxious time of it this past week—so let her see a little light in

your face. If she sees you low in your mind, it will be hard for her to
help you.

MICHEL: Thank you, doctor.

GARRIN: I've got to be getting along. I'll be by tomorrow morning. [*He
exits.* MICHEL *leans back exhausted*—BACHIR *comes out with a tray of food.*]

BACHIR: Sir—did that doctor tell you anything about me, sir?

MICHEL: Why, is there something to tell?

BACHIR: Oh, no, sir. He is a good doctor. Are you hungry?

MICHEL: No.

BACHIR: [*In fake despair.*] Oh. [*Indicates covered bowl.*] I brought it too soon!
What a shame!

MICHEL: [*Bored.*] Just eat it, if you want it.

BACHIR: [*Happy now, gets the bowl and squats down near* MICHEL *and starts to
gobble the food.*]

MICHEL [*Watching* BACHIR *with some amusement.*] You eat too quickly.

BACHIR: You want a little?

MICHEL: No.

BACHIR: This is very good for me. I was in the quarter last night and I was
the strongest boy of all.

MICHEL: [*Smiles.*] Why do you have to be the strongest boy of all?

BACHIR: [*Pauses—then he smiles.*] It is safer that way, in the quarter—
[*Finishes a mouthful.*] But soon the warm season will come and I can
spend the nights in the orchards.

MICHEL: The orchards?

BACHIR: Yes, sir—the trees are filled with fruit; dates, figs, oranges, everything grows in the orchards. Many boys tend the crops, the earth, the
goats. They are very beautiful, those places.

MICHEL: Where are they?

BACHIR: Which one, sir?

MICHEL: I don't know—the one you seem so poetic about.

BACHIR: They are all out there beyond the walls. It is always green and cool
and they live like a thousand years ago.

MICHEL: [*Interested.*] And do whole families live there?

BACHIR: There are no families. Only men and boys. Beautiful men . . . they
live without women.

MICHEL: [*Shocked.*] Oh—[*Coldly*] That is not very interesting.

BACHIR: You asked me, sir.

MICHEL: You misunderstood me! [*Turns away.*] And you eat disgustingly,
Bachir!

BACHIR: [*Smiles.*] Yes, sir. I think so. I am very healthy and disgusting. [*Now*

MARCELLINE *and* SIDMA *appear at the house gate.* SIDMA *is a native woman.* MARCELLINE's *immediate reaction on seeing* MICHEL *is to cry and run to him.* BACHIR *exits with tray, but not until* SIDMA *has had a chance to recognize him and register a slight look of disapproval.*]

MARCELLINE: Michel! [*He turns quickly in his chair and rises.*] Michel! My darling! [*They embrace.*] I wanted to go for you, but the Doctor said no. He said—

MICHEL: I know. It's all right.

MARCELLINE: But I wanted to be here when you came home.

MICHEL: [*Smiles.*] You must not worry—I am better.

MARCELLINE: Of course you are, my dearest. I'm glad you're home. I'm going to take care of you. You're going to be *much* better. [*Remembering, turns to* SIDMA.] Sidma—[*She opens the gate for* SIDMA *who enters as she speaks.*] She's so nice, Michel, and she's going to take care of us. Sidma, this is my husband.

MICHEL: How do you do? [*He nods and sits again.*]

MARCELLINE: I'll show her where the things are, then I'll come right back and sit with you. [*She goes into the bedroom, followed by* SIDMA.] This is our bedroom, Sidma, it needs a thorough cleaning.

SIDMA: Yes, Madame.

MARCELLINE: And you'll find a lot of laundry to do at the bottom of the closet.

SIDMA: Yes, Madame. [*Nods toward the terrace.*] That boy—does he work here?

MARCELLINE: Yes, Sidma, he's been running errands for me.

SIDMA: No good.

MARCELLINE: [*Laughs.*] Yes, you're right.

SIDMA: No, Madame—Inside no good.

MARCELLINE: What?

SIDMA: Many boys like him in Biskra—come from all over—look for rich tourist to charm—make their fortune.

MARCELLINE: I—I don't know what you mean.

SIDMA: You very nice people. This boy bad all through. Be careful. [*Changing subject.*] Shall I wash in kitchen, Madame? [MARCELLINE *is deep in her thoughts.*] Where, Madame?

MARCELLINE: [*Comes out of it.*] Oh, I'll show you. [*She exits, followed by* SIDMA. BACHIR *re-enters from hall, having hidden between terrace and doorway to bedroom.*]

BACHIR: [*Picks up scissors out of sewing basket on wall. He holds them up, snaps them, enjoys their gleam.*] These are good scissors. One could make a jewel of them. They shine. [*Pause.*] Many interesting places in Biskra—

I will take you, sir. [*He twirls the scissors.*] Many cafes, bazaars, night places — I know them all. With money you can buy anything that pleases you... Anything at all.

MICHEL: [*Turns his head away.*] I don't want to listen to any more of that, Bachir.

BACHIR: Yes, sir.

MICHEL: And if you go on with it I will have Madame send you away.

BACHIR: Yes, sir. [MICHEL *turns away from him.* BACHIR *watches him a moment, puts down scissors, rises, then servily.*] Can I get you a cool drink, sir?

MICHEL: No.

BACHIR: A cigarette?

MICHEL: No.

BACHIR: A pillow?

MICHEL: No. Nothing.

BACHIR: Then maybe I amuse you, sir. I dance for you — [*He takes scissors from tabouret where he had put them down, and snips them in a rhythm, then slips the scissors in his burnoose and continues the rhythm by snapping his fingers and he dances sensuously with his arms extended into the air.*]

MICHEL: [*Is intrigued at first, then suddenly feels he must withdraw from it and rises from his chair as be speaks:*] Stop that! Stop that, immediately! [BACHIR *doesn't stop and* MICHEL *is turned away from him as* MARCELLINE *appears at the doorway in the hall. They exchange a look as if agreeing that the dance is silly and* MICHEL *goes up to lean against the low wall.*]

BACHIR: [*Turns in his dance and now sees* MARCELLINE *and stops abruptly, lowering hands to head.*] I was amusing my gentleman. [*He exits through gate and around behind the house quickly.*]

MICHEL: [*Making an effort to cover the situation.*] Marcelline, as soon as I am able — I will take you away from here — we must move on.

MARCELLINE: Oh, I am so glad you don't like it! When Dr. Garrin said you were low in spirits, my heart sank. I thought — now he will want to stay out of sheer weakness.

MICHEL: I am not weak!

MARCELLINE: Of course not! And if you feel a little tired, it's because of this heat and the sunlight — Also, the people are trying. They are so strange. They don't like each other — they don't trust each other. Even Sidma — she says things and you don't know what it's for — or what she means — [*Troubled she picks up her sewing basket.*] Biskra is a very confusing place. Don't you think so, Michel?

MICHEL: No.

MARCELLINE: [*Wifely.*] Well, perhaps not. Perhaps I think so because you've been away in that awful hospital. Once you're a married woman you only feel safe when your husband is by your side. [BACHIR *enters quietly from hall.*]

BACHIR: [*Humbly.*] I am sorry Madame—I was so glad my gentleman came back—I was too lively. [MARCELLINE *now takes a square of linen out of her sewing basket and folds it. Now she looks in the basket.*]

MARCELLINE: Have you seen my scissors, Bachir?

BACHIR: [*Pause.*] No, Madame.

MARCELLINE: I had them right here—look for them, please. [BACHIR *does, with one eye on* MICHEL.]

BACHIR: I do not see them, Madame. [MICHEL, *troubled, starts to bedroom door.*] Maybe the doctor took them by mistake, Madame.

MARCELLINE: [*After a pause.*] Did he, Michel?

MICHEL: [*Stopping with hand on door, then speaks with difficulty.*] I didn't notice. [*He exits to bedroom.* MARCELLINE *looks once more in her sewing basket as* BACHIR *smiles.*]

The CURTAIN *falls*

Scene II

An orchard outside Biskra, brilliant mid-day light. Two date palms throw spots of dense shade, there is a broken bit of white-washed wall, and a goat lies on its side, half-hidden behind the trees. A shepherd stands in the shade holding a primitive flute or recorder in his hand. He plays two simple notes on it, but he stops when MICHEL enters from the other side of the wall. He is weak, and perspiring, and he drags a shawl on the ground behind him. As be touches the wall, he clings to it, wearily, and looks around.

MICHEL: Hello . . .

SHEPHERD: Good day, sir.

MICHEL: I am looking for the orchards.

SHEPHERD: Whose, sir?

MICHEL: I don't know. [*He throws himself on the ground and wipes the sweat from his face and neck as the shepherd watches him.*]

SHEPHERD: My master will be honored if you sit in the shade of his magnificent date tree.

MICHEL: I am too tired to move.

SHEPHERD: [*Goes to him.*] Let me assist. [*He puts an arm under MICHEL's arm and supports him to the tree's shade. They are silent during this, but MICHEL sighs with relief once he is there.*] Is it not cool, sir?

MICHEL: Yes. Thank you.

SHEPHERD: Seven pails of water on this tree every night. You can see why it is so cooling.

MICHEL: It is very empty here. I thought there would be people — and games.

SHEPHERD: It is only a date orchard, sir.

MICHEL: [*Disappointed.*] It has taken me a long time to be able to walk here —

SHEPHERD: Do you live in Biskra, sir?

MICHEL: Yes. I live near the public gardens.

SHEPHERD: That is not very far.

MICHEL: I have been ill.

SHEPHERD: Will you buy some of our goat's milk, sir? It is very good for you.

MICHEL: Are the goats clean?

SHEPHERD: They are, sir. A cup is only five sous. [*Earnestly.*] It is a good investment, sir.

MICHEL: [*Laughing.*] Very well, I will invest. [*The shepherd blows two notes on his flute, then two more.*] Is that to announce my purchase?

SHEPHERD: No, sir, we keep some clean cups at our well. [*Now two young shepherd boys appear from another part of the orchard. The first shepherd says a few words in Arabic and they squat immediately beside the goat. While one pets the animal, the other, out of our sight, milks her.*]

MICHEL: Who are they?

SHEPHERD: They assist me.

MICHEL: [*Smiles.*] What is your name?

SHEPHERD: Moktir, the shepherd.

MICHEL: And theirs?

MOKTIR: [*Pointing.*] He is Akur. He is Dolit. Five sous, please.

MICHEL: [*Takes some coins out of his pocket.*] If I give you more will you divide it with them?

MOKTIR: If you want them to have money, sir, you had better give it to them yourself.

MICHEL: You are very honest—for a master.

MOKTIR: I am not their master. I am only my own. [AKUR *brings a small cup of milk to* MOKTIR, *who indicates that he must give it to* MICHEL.]

MICHEL: [*Handing him a coin.*] Thank you, Akur. [*He takes a sip.*] It is delicious. [DOLIT *comes close now.*]

MOKTIR: He helped Akur, sir.

MICHEL: Yes, so I saw. [*He holds out a coin to* DOLIT *who takes it quickly and steps back.*]

MOKTIR: He is from a tribe in the desert, sir. He cannot speak French to thank you.

MICHEL: [*Drinking.*] I see.

MOKTIR: We are going to teach him if he stays.

MICHEL: Where are your homes?

MOKTIR: Some in Biskra. The men in the orchards come from many places.

MICHEL: [*Looking around.*] But you have no shelter. Where do you go at night?

MOKTIR: We have the trees to lie under.

MICHEL: And your families…?

MOKTIR: Are you from the Government, sir?

MICHEL: No.

MOKTIR: I know you are not police because you are weak and sickly. Police are always healthy.

MICHEL: [*Smiles.*] I am just a tourist.

MOKTIR: Sometimes at night we have music and the tourists come out from the town. They stand at the wall, laughing and making fun…

MICHEL: I hope I'm not that kind of tourist. But maybe that's because I am ill...

MOKTIR: Biskra will make you well, sir.

MICHEL: Perhaps.

MOKTIR: You should drink our goat's milk every day.

MICHEL: [*Smiles.*] I hope I can afford it.

MOKTIR: Tomorrow I will try to manage with just one assistant.

MICHEL: Tomorrow I may not be able to come—

MOKTIR: The air is pure under our trees, sir.

MICHEL: Are you inviting me to return?

MOKTIR: We are open to all. We welcome anyone who is at ease here...
[*Now he takes his goatherd's pipe from his belt and plays a weird, high tune on it. It is like the music we associate with a snake charmer. As he plays, holding the pipe in one hand, he reaches up into the tree and plucks a spray of dates. He gives it to* MICHEL *who accepts it, and nods his thanks. Now* MOKTIR *stops playing.*] See how easily you breathe here, sir.

MICHEL: Yes, I do... It's like a landscape in a dream, so effortless, so green.
[*He picks a date off the stem and puts it to his mouth, then stops before eating it.*] How do you know I did not breathe easily before?

MOKTIR: You said you were ill.

MICHEL: It might have been my legs or my belly. How did you know it was my lungs?

MOKTIR: This is a small community—

MICHEL: But we know no one in it. [AKUR, *followed by* DOLIT, *re-enters.*]

AKUR: Is there a stray? I heard your pipe. I thought one had gone off.

MOKTIR: No—I was playing to amuse.

MICHEL: Would the sound of the pipe stop them from running off?

MOKTIR: They don't run off. But the music tells them where we are. [*Now* AKUR, *up back, shows a small rubber ball to* DOLIT.]

AKUR: *Oui?*

DOLIT: [*Nods his head.*] *Si.* [*Now* AKUR *and* DOLIT, *in back of the trees, stand across from one another, and slowly, regularly, like finely coordinated athletes, throw the ball back and forth between them. It should be like the throwing in baseball practice, of two men in our country.*]

MICHEL: [*Watching them.*] How well they are matched.

MOKTIR: They should not play here. The flock is at the other end of the pasture.

MICHEL: You watch over all the animals, the fruit, the shepherds.

MOKTIR: It is my uncle's property.

MICHEL: What kind of man is he?

MOKTIR: Here in the orchards, we are all the same... Arab, Nubian, Frenchman, Jew — we are all the same. [*They are silent, watching the two men throw the ball.*]

MICHEL: How freely they move —

MOKTIR: They are not so free, for they are very poor. But one freedom they have — they have no shame.

MICHEL: You have not always been here.

MOKTIR: I once taught at the University of Fez.

MICHEL: [*Shocked.*] Surely that was a better life — !

MOKTIR: [*Smiles.*] I needed that one freedom. [*He nods toward the two who are playing.*] The one they have. [DOLIT *misses a catch and goes off to retrieve the ball.* AKUR *stands still waiting for him.*]

MICHEL: I should go back. [*He leans his head against the tree trunk.*] But it is so — easy here.

MOKTIR: When you are stronger, sir, you must bring your learned books with you. It might please you to sit here.

MICHEL: I don't read any more. I am too ill.

MOKTIR: When you are stronger, you will write again.

MICHEL: Will I? About what?

MOKTIR: [*Surprised.*] About the excavations — about the dead cities out in the desert, sir.

MICHEL: You know all about me.

MOKTIR: [*Bowing.*] Yes, sir.

MICHEL: And you expected me...

MOKTIR: [*Shrugs.*] It is simple, sir. Bachir comes here in the evenings when he has finished his house service. [*Now he looks anxiously off to where* DOLIT *has gone.*] I must see to the animals. They are moving too far... [MICHEL *sits watching the ball-players.* DOLIT *is out of sight, but* AKUR *we can see.* MICHEL'S *head turns in rhythm, as they throw and catch. Now slowly he rises from his place, and removes his coat. He goes to where he is in line to join the game, his back to us. Now he signals to* AKUR *to let him catch one, and he does so, from* DOLIT'S *off-stage throw.* MICHEL *then throws to* AKUR, AKUR *throws to* DOLIT, DOLIT *again throws to* MICHEL, *who catches it.* MOKTIR *re-enters and stands watching the game, and* MICHEL *sees him.*]

MICHEL: [*Apologetic.*] I'm not very good at it — I never enjoyed this when I was a boy. I preferred books.

MOKTIR: There is a line in one book you must know. It is by Aristippus. [*Quoting.*] The art of life lies in taking pleasures as they pass. [MICHEL *returns the ball to* DOLIT.] And the keenest pleasures are not intellectual... Nor are they always moral. [MICHEL *stares at* MOKTIR, *then picks up his coat and starts to leave the garden, as:*]

The CURTAIN *falls*

Scene III

Scene: *Their house in Biskra, a few weeks later. The terrace is bathed in brilliant late afternoon light, which turns to dusk as the scene progresses. There is a tabouret and some chairs, and the invalid chair which* MICHEL *used before is no longer there.*

At rise: SIDMA *is arranging some silverware on the table.* BACHIR *is sprawled on the ground near the house.*

SIDMA: [*Calling out to* BACHIR *who seems to sleep.*] Go to the cook-shop now—

BACHIR: [*Lazily.*] I am no slave.

SIDMA: [*Exasperated.*] You can see for yourself it's almost sundown! Go to the cook-shop!

BACHIR: [*Not moving.*] Later—

SIDMA: [*Comes close, threatening him.*] Not later! Now! I have ordered a special pudding of rice for them and I want it while it's hot!

BACHIR: [*Mocking her as he rises.*] A special pudding of rice—! Well, well, we are so lordly. We are so French! Stop pretending you are their old nursie! I know them longer than you do! I saved his life. It isn't the slop you feed him that has made him fat and healthy—

SIDMA: [*Indignant.*] If you don't bring me that pudding I will tell the garrison police where they can find you!

BACHIR: Old nursie! [*She comes toward him, hand upraised.*] Old sow—! [*And he runs out.* SIDMA *goes back to the table to finish her work, when* MARCELLINE *appears, wearily bowed under her parasol. That is all she carries. A moment later* MICHEL *appears behind her. He has all their day's needs on his head—a campstool, books, a cushion—Arab-fashion, and he balances all this with his one hand. He stands erect and handsome.*]

MARCELLINE: [*Tired, she lowers the parasol.*] We're here, Sidma. [*Closing it.*] After a nice long walk inside a bake-oven . . . [*She sinks exhaustedly into one of the chairs.*]

MICHEL: [*Unloading his burden.*] Get Madame a cool drink, Sidma.

SIDMA: Yes, sir. [*She turns to leave but* MARCELLINE *speaks:*]

MARCELLINE: A glass of wine, Sidma, so I have the strength to wash my face. [SIDMA *nods and leaves.*]

MICHEL: [*Concerned, he looks down at her.*] So tired—?

MARCELLINE: Yes . . . [*She plays with her parasol.*] And you carried the stool, and the books and the box—and you're not tired at all.

MICHEL: I feel pleasantly used up. No more than that.

MARCELLINE: Each day we walk farther and farther out of the town, away from the trees and the shade.

MICHEL: Moktir says the oasis used to be far wider. He says the sands blow in closer each year.

MARCELLINE: Then we'll be walking in the desert soon. [*She goes into the house, and lets her shawl and parasol fall on the bed.* MICHEL *watches her apprehensively.*]

MICHEL: To-morrow it might be better if we went to the orchard in the late afternoon. I could try to work here if you would prefer it.

MARCELLINE: [*Picking up the water jug.*] I didn't say I would prefer anything, Michel.

MICHEL: Well, if I stay here in the mornings, will you come out there with me for the rest of the day?

MARCELLINE: Why must I do that? Moktir is more helpful than I.

MICHEL: You are *very* helpful.

MARCELLINE: [*Standing in his path.*] Oh, Michel, you keep saying that. And I don't believe it. When I sit with you and Moktir, I feel completely unnecessary.

MICHEL: That's not true.

MARCELLINE: Well, I feel it anyway. [MICHEL *goes out to terrace, sits left of table. She crosses to table upstage of bed, pours water in basin, puts down the jug.*] You keep trying to make a place for me in your work—as if to reassure me. But I'm not envious of your work, or your learning! I am proud of it. [*She returns to basin.*]

MICHEL: If I leave you here, you will be lonely and you will tire of this place.

MARCELLINE: [*Tossing down towel, taking up blouse, comes to doorway putting on blouse.*] I am tired of it now. Look at it. It's sun-baked and dirty. There's no life here!

MICHEL: Marcie, there has been more living here than any place on earth.

MARCELLINE: I know that—historically I know it. There were pictures in my school books and now I've seen it. But the people aren't living— they are just staying in a place they know, like farm animals. They breathe, they eat, they sleep—that's all.

MICHEL: Those are wonderful things in themselves, Marcie.

MARCELLINE: [*Quietly.*] There are other things. [SIDMA *comes with a wine carafe.* MARCELLINE *sits at the table.*] Would you like a glass of wine, Michel? It's Chateau Neuf. [*She pours herself a glass.*]

MICHEL: [*Turning away.*] It's too hot for wine—Besides, it doesn't go very well with rice.

MARCELLINE: It goes well with me—[*She drinks.*] It reminds me of Bocage.

MICHEL: You want to go home—

MARCELLINE: I want to do anything you want to do. But we seem to be settling here, and it frightens me. We are not Arabs. We can't be content with the life they lead.

MICHEL: [*Turns to her.*] Marcie, give me time! For the first time in my life I am at ease among a people. They live without ambition, without judgment, without standards—

MARCELLINE: That's right, Michel! And so they are lying and deceitful and bad!

MICHEL: No, Marcie... They are only different.

MARCELLINE: [*Her hand on his arm.*] You see no faults in anyone.

MICHEL: This is how you help... when you reassure me.

MARCELLINE: I need to be assured now—[*She finishes her drink.*] We've been living each day as if the next would never come, but they have come and you have got well. Now I must know whether you will ever *want* me, whether there is a future for us anywhere. Since we have been married you have never wanted us to be separated, not for a day—not for an hour—and yet you have never wanted us to be *one*.

MICHEL: [*Painfully.*] You say 'wanting' as if wanting were deliberate. But it isn't like that—[*She looks at him and starts to exit into the house. Then she stops.*]

MARCELLINE: I could live with you anywhere, without comfort, without children—But I cannot live with your denial of me. It makes me feel half dead! [*She puts her hands over her face and leaves the terrace blindly for the bedroom. We see her in the darkened portion of the house, where she goes to lie on the bed, her head in her arms. MICHEL looks after her, then rises as if to join her but stops as he hears BACHIR just behind him. BACHIR has entered from the other side of the wall, carrying the pudding. It is in a pot, wrapped in a cloth. He comes to the tabouret and puts it down immediately.*]

BACHIR: I was long because they tried to give me something stale—but I would not accept it. I made them cook it fresh.

MICHEL: [*Abstracted.*] Take it to Sidma.

BACHIR: But it is hot, sir. You should eat it now. Shall I call Madame?

MICHEL: No! Go to the kitchen.

BACHIR: Madame is not well?

MICHEL: She is tired—

BACHIR: [*Slyly.*] She tires herself, sir. Always with you — like a nurse. Or a policeman.

MICHEL: [*Sharply.*] Go away, Bachir.

BACHIR: Are you angry at me?

MICHEL: I am neither angry or anything! Just do your work, Bachir! Go back to the village — go anywhere!

BACHIR: [*Outraged.*] But it is evening. I have not eaten!

MICHEL: Then take the food with you! But get out!

BACHIR: [*Cagily.*] You have had a fight, eh?

MICHEL: Madame and I will eat later. She is resting — get out!

BACHIR: I don't mean her. You have had a fight with Moktir, maybe?

MICHEL: [*Turns away from the door.*] What —

BACHIR: When Moktir is in good humor, you are — When he is not, you are not. The fight will end. He is very clever — he will not break off. It is too profitable. You are a rich foreigner.

MICHEL: [*Comes toward him.*] Moktir is an educated man — he has given me the shelter of the orchards in which to work . . . He is a friend!

BACHIR: [*Smiles.*] You need not talk like that with me — With Madame, yes. Not with me —

MICHEL: [*Outraged.*] Get out of here! [*A second thought, he pulls money out of his pocket.*] I want you to leave this house immediately! [*Puts money on table beside rice pot.*]

BACHIR: [*Quiet with astonishment.*] What, sir? You dismiss me?

MICHEL: Yes, Bachir, right now!

BACHIR: It is impossible. How can you do that, sir? I am he who brought the doctor to you. I am the one who told you about the orchards. I coaxed you to stay in Biskra —

MICHEL: I was ill. I wanted this climate!

BACHIR: [*Mock surprise.*] This climate? You mean the climate of the orchards, sir. The first time I saw you with Madame — the day you took this house — I knew what you were — I am never fooled — I can smell it! [MICHEL *reaches out for* BACHIR's *throat.* BACHIR *grabs his hands.*]

MICHEL: How dare you! [*He grabs him.*]

BACHIR: Don't! I will not tell her! I promise you! [MICHEL *flings him to the ground.*]

MICHEL: Get out!

BACHIR: It is no secret — [*He stands up.*] Maybe not even to her — [*He exits quickly away from the house. His laughter can be heard in the distance.*] It is no secret! [MARCELLINE *roused by the noise, gets off the bed.*]

MICHEL: [*Going to her.*] Marcelline... [*He comes to her.*] Will you lie
with me?
MARCELLINE: What?
MICHEL: [*He takes her in his arms.*] I want you now...
MARCELLINE: Yes... Oh, my dearest... [*He embraces her desperately. They sink
to the bed, as total blackness envelops the room.*]

The CURTAIN *falls*

Scene IV
The house in Biskra some months later.

It is mid-morning. There is a moment's pause and SIDMA *enters from the direction of the town carrying a full market bag. She puts the bag on the table, looks at the change in her hand, and then mentally adds up her purchases. She takes out a bottle of wine and looks at it. Now she goes towards the bedroom door, speaking as she reaches it:*

SIDMA: Sidma home, Madame — [*No answer. She looks in bedroom and then comes to the other door leading to the kitchen and calls down the hall.*] Sidma home, Madame!

MARCELLINE: [*Off stage.*] Yes, Sidma.

SIDMA: I pay wine shop. [*She hurries to* MARCELLINE *in the kitchen. She talks to her as she exits.*] Eat soon, Madame. Sidma cook... eat soon. [*She is out of sight. Now* MICHEL *enters from the direction of the gardens. Followed by* MOKTIR.]

MOKTIR: [*Continuing a discussion.*] I will continue on.

MICHEL: I'll only be a moment. I have three more chapters that I must mail to Paris, that's all.

MOKTIR: I will go on ahead. I am uncomfortable here.

MICHEL: I know.

MOKTIR: If she comes, I will leave.

MICHEL: You need not.

MOKTIR: It is not for *her* sake that I don't want to be here, it is for my own... and yours.

MICHEL: Moktir, let me find my own way! No preachments, for God's sake! No advice! [*He calls out.*] Sidma! Will you come here...? [*Back to* MOKTIR.] You don't really understand my situation —

MOKTIR: [*Gravely.*] And you don't understand your wife's.

MICHEL: That's not true! She knows perfectly well that I am away during the day because I work on my book. But at night I come back here — I always come back!

MOKTIR: When she is asleep — when you won't have to face her.

MICHEL: [*Wretchedly.*] That part is true enough, God knows... I almost wish someone would tell her. Sometimes I think — perhaps she knows already.

MOKTIR: If she knew she would be gone.

MICHEL: [*Appalled.*] Marcelline wouldn't leave me! She knows that I need her. I couldn't live without her —

MOKTIR: You live without her now.

MICHEL: But she's here! She's my wife—! [*Frustrated.*] You don't know about us—I love her!

MOKTIR: Your love is pity.

MICHEL I don't care what it is—if *she* finds it sufficient then it's good enough!

MOKTIR: Can you lead two lives?

MICHEL: [*Bitterly.*] Who does not?

MOKTIR: Michel, you should tell her the truth.

MICHEL: I cannot! It would be as if I were glad of the truth and I am not.

MOKTIR: No one is glad... But you aren't honest, Michel. You have listened to your body and accepted what it told you. You pretend that what you are is only pleasure-deep, no more important to your wife than if you drank too much or gambled. That isn't true. It would be better for your wife if you were vicious, but you aren't. You are simply different—

MICHEL: But that is what I cannot tell her! It would mean that everything she hoped for is denied forever!

MOKTIR: Well—isn't it?

MICHEL: No! There's a way for us to live and enjoy what we have and not be miserable for what we haven't! [SIDMA *enters from the back of the house.*] When does Madame get back from the Bazaar?

SIDMA: [*Shrugs.*] Who can tell?

MICHEL: [*Impatient.*] She goes each morning, Sidma, you must know—

SIDMA: Madame stays away different times. Like you, sir. [*And she exits back to the house.*]

MOKTIR: If you want to find her, you might look in the wine shop.

MICHEL: The wine shop?

MOKTIR: I believe she buys there quite frequently.

MICHEL: [*Angrily.*] *I* don't believe it!

MOKTIR: Then you should see for yourself and prove me wrong.

MICHEL: [*Fearful.*] Moktir, if it's true you should have told me—

MOKTIR: It is not the kind of thing one likes to tell—

MICHEL: [*Apprehensive.*] Come—I must find her—[*He exits quickly.* MOKTIR *follows.* SIDMA *steps out of hallway and looks to be certain that they are out of sight, then turns and calls into house.*]

SIDMA: He is gone—[*Suddenly there is the sound of a chair falling over, off R.* SIDMA, *alarmed, exits down hall.*] Madame! Madame!

MARCELLINE: [*Appears behind the beaded portieres. She is very quiet, moves very deliberately, and talks very slowly throughout the scene. She wears a lace blouse, but it is unbuttoned and askew, its ends out of her skirt and the ties banging loosely down her back. She comes through the doorway and turns to* SIDMA *who has followed her.*] Do you know what time it is? [*Without waiting for an answer she turns and crosses down to sit on D. edge of bed, but it's more like losing her balance than just sitting. She notices the freshly ironed lace petticoats on the bed.*] I would like to wash a pair of gloves.

SIDMA: I wash, Madame.

MARCELLINE: [*Almost crying.*] No, no, I have to do these myself... [*She picks up the petticoats and cradles them in her lap, blurrily examining them.*] I can iron better than that. Not now, I can't. But I used to. I would do my brother's shirts. And my summer dresses. Do you know what knife pleats are? I can do them, too. And ruffles, tiny little ruffles. I always had a summer dress with ruffles... Always.

SIDMA: [*Helping* MARCELLINE *up from bed, taking her in direction of hall.*] Madame eat good now.

MARCELLINE: [*As they get in line with terrace door, she breaks away from* SIDMA.] I'm not hungry. [*She goes out onto the terrace. She stands in the sun for a moment, then goes and looks idly at* MICHEL'S *work.*] It's always the same. Pages and pages about dead people. [*She picks up the wine carafe and looks at it, but it is empty. She puts it down.*] The sun is hot—[*She opens her rumpled collar.*] Bring out the cards, Sidma!

SIDMA: [*Comes to door and protests.*] No, must work, Madame!

MARCELLINE: Please, Sidma, please—[*She begs like a child.*] Let's have a card party, here in the garden. I wish we had a chestnut tree. [*She looks up, and sees no tree.*] Well—it doesn't matter. Get the cards... [SIDMA, *in the room, takes a pack of cards from a small shelf near the door and comes onto the terrace.* MARCELLINE *tears up two pages of* MICHEL'S *work and throws them into the box, gathers up his pencils and scatters them on the floor near the box, and sits down where he sat.*] Right here. This is a lovely place. I'm sick of playing on the floor. Why should I? We'll sit here, like ladies. [*They sit at the table,* MARCELLINE *facing us. She takes the cards from* SIDMA *and shuffles.*] The one with the highest score will win a prize. I have a manicuring set. If you win I will give it to you. And if I win—well, I'll just keep it. [*She breaks down and sobs hysterically into her arm.*]

SIDMA: [*Rises.*] Must work.

MARCELLINE: [*Lifting her head.*] No... no. You stay there. Let me get you a glass of wine. Then I'll explain the whole thing. We can have a nice game. Please, Sidma, please—please—please. Sidma. [*Sitting down.*] Yes, Madame. [MARCELLINE *goes to the carafe and picks it up, while* SIDMA *looks at the pack of cards. Disappointed,* MARCELLINE *puts the bottle down.*]

MARCELLINE: I'm so sorry, Sidma, but there isn't any left. You must remind me later, to get some. Some Chablis, perhaps. It's hot out here—it's so terribly hot—[*Her hand knocks some cards to the floor.*]

SIDMA: [*Helping* MARCELLINE *to door, but she slumps to the terrace floor.*] Madame must eat—must eat. [SIDMA *goes into bedroom to prepare damp cloth.*]

MARCELLINE: After we finish our game, Sidma. I must see if I can win at something! [*She sees the cards on the floor.*] You dropped your cards, Sidma! [*She falls to the floor and picks them up.*] I won't look at them—see, I'm covering my eyes. [MICHEL *and* MOKTIR *appear on the other side of the wall. They stand and watch for a second.*] I'll pick them up and put them into your hand, and you play them the way you did before.

MICHEL: What is it, Marcelline?

MARCELLINE: [*On the floor, she turns to see him.*] Oh . . . Sidma dropped her cards.

MICHEL: Then let her pick them up.

MARCELLINE: She doesn't want to. She wants to cook . . . And I want to finish our game. [*She is trying to get off the ground, first by holding onto a chair, then by grabbing at a table leg.*] But it was hot out here, and there are no refreshments to offer . . . [*She tries to get up from the uneven balance of one knee and one foot placed flat, but still cannot manage it.* MICHEL *tries to help her but she brushes him aside.*] You cannot expect people to sit with you, if you have nothing to offer. [MICHEL *goes to her again, but she takes his hands off her shoulders, deliberately. Now she screams hysterically.*] Sidma! Sidma! Sidma! Sidma! [SIDMA *comes to her.*] Help me, Sidma. I'm drunk [SIDMA *enters from bedroom, takes her under the arms and brings her into the house. They go to the bed, and* MARCELLINE *mutters incoherently as* SIDMA *puts her to bed.*]

MOKTIR: [*Comes onto the terrace.*] You have not deceived her. You have deceived yourself.

MICHEL: I have to help her! [MOKTIR *starts out.*] Don't go! Help me, Moktir!

MOKTIR: It is dishonor to live two lives. I return to my own life. I deceive no one. I corrupt no one. Do you think that because I am what I am I have no morality? Do you think that because you have come to our life, you will be able to live without any?

MICHEL: I must help her!

MOKTIR: Your power to help her is not great. You hide behind her. You use her. The only way you could help her is to spare her what is coming—you should bear that alone!

MICHEL: No! No! I will not be alone! I cannot lose her! I cannot live as you do!

MOKTIR: [*Gravely.*] You harm us all. [*He exits.* MICHEL *goes to the bed. She stirs, for the first time since* SIDMA *left her.*]

MICHEL: Marcelline —

MARCELLINE: Yes. [*She turns her head away from him.*]

MICHEL: I want to talk to you.

MARCELLINE: It was a dizzy spell — from the heat.

MICHEL: Cover your eyes, and listen to me.

MARCELLINE: Are you going to scold me?

MICHEL: I have to tell you the truth. I have to tell you everything. You will not understand it, just as I cannot. But if you know about me, you will not destroy yourself any more.

MARCELLINE: [*Puts her feet on the ground to rise.*] I am drunk. Thank God, I am drunk.

MICHEL: [*Comes to her and takes her by the arms.*] I am everything you fear I am.

MARCELLINE: [*Almost screams.*] How dare you tell me the truth? How dare you?

MICHEL: [*Holding on to her.*] I want to help you! I want to be as good to you now as you were to me! [*She struggles to get away from him, but he holds on.*] I am going to take you to Tunis and put you on the boat for home.

MARCELLINE: No! I won't go!

MICHEL: If you live with me here in Biskra on my terms you will try to die. And if I live with you in Normandy I will do the same thing.

MARCELLINE: It's not true.

MICHEL: It is true, Marcie. We both know it.

MARCELLINE: What will I say? What will I tell people?

MICHEL: Don't spare me! Tell the truth. See that no one ever makes our mistake again!

MARCELLINE: [*Pleading.*] I don't care about others. I just care about you and me.

MICHEL: Listen to me, Marcie! You must go home hating me! For your own sake you must see me as I am.

MARCELLINE: [*Pulls away from him.*] Don't . . . don't . . . don't . . . [*She backs away from him.*]

MICHEL: [*Following her.*] You must understand me! [MARCELLINE *is trying to escape the words, but he follows her.*] I will say it everywhere! I will write it! I will speak it!

MARCELLINE: Don't, Michel…don't!

MICHEL: [*Against her loud protests.*] I will never be silent again! Whoever knows me will know that about me first. Whoever hears of me will hear that before anything! If there is an ounce of energy within me, I will say what I am like! This one thing I can do! I can speak out! [*He raises his head in defiance as the Curtain starts down.*]

The CURTAIN *falls*

Act Three

Scene I

The house in Biskra.
The next morning.

MARCELLINE, *dressed in her black suit, with her hat in her lap, her pocketbook and small travelling bag next to her, is sitting upright on the edge of the bed.* SIDMA *is on her knees, an open Gladstone bag in front of her, and a small pile of* MARCELLINE's *clothes next to her. She is packing them carefully.*

SIDMA: Is all wash, Madame. Clean. [*No response from* MARCELLINE. *Then with hesitation.*] Sidma could go with Madame. I leave here—no trouble.
MARCELLINE: No, Sidma—thank you.
SIDMA: Long ride Tunis. I go there, too.
MARCELLINE: No.
SIDMA: [*Simply.*] Yes, Madame. [*She would pack the black spyglass but* MARCELLINE *stops her.*]
MARCELLINE: I don't want that! There's nothing to look at, at home. Leave it here—for him!
SIDMA: Yes, Madame. [*Puts spyglass to one side.*]
MARCELLINE: Could you bring me something?
SIDMA: Yes, Madame.
MARCELLINE: Is there any wine?
SIDMA: [*Hesitates.*]—No, Madame. [MICHEL *comes from the back of the house into the bedroom. He is fully dressed in his European clothes. He studies* MARCELLINE *for a moment, then looks down at* SIDMA *packing.*]
MICHEL: Get Madame some coffee.
SIDMA: Yes, sir. [SIDMA *rises and exits into the other part of the house.* MICHEL *leans over and carefully packs the few remaining things—after a moment's silence between them* MICHEL *speaks.*]

MICHEL: I'll try to get the back bench in the diligence, so you can stretch out.

MARCELLINE: Are you coming with me?

MICHEL: Of course I am! And I will stay with you until you get on the boat!

MARCELLINE: I feel as if I would never get that far—

MICHEL: [*Trying to comfort her.*] Soon you will be home. You will have my mother's room. There is a view of the woods from the windows. You will watch the seasons, the birds. And you will have many friends around you.

MARCELLINE: Will you write to me?

MICHEL: I will write to you all the time. And when my book is finished—

MARCELLINE: [*Interrupting.*] Don't send it to me . . . [MARCELLINE *rises from the bed.*] I need some air . . . [*He goes to her to steady her, but she holds him off.*] I'll sit outside until we're ready. [*She starts to the terrace, then turns to him.*] Michel, could I have something with my coffee? I am shaking— I feel ill.

MICHEL: [*Very gently.*] The wine won't help, Marcie. [*She looks at him and leaves the room. She comes onto the terrace and sits down on the edge of the deck chair.* MICHEL *goes back to the suitcase and is busy closing it, while* SIDMA *goes to* MARCELLINE *on the terrace with a cup of coffee.*]

SIDMA: Hot coffee, Madame.

MARCELLINE: You remember Doctor Garrin?

SIDMA: Yes, Madame . . .

MARCELLINE: Get him for me! Get him immediately!

SIDMA: Yes, Madame.

MARCELLINE: Say nothing. [SIDMA *exits as* MICHEL *comes out.*]

MICHEL: [*He goes out onto the terrace.*] I will cable Robert that if he cannot meet you in Marseilles he should send Bocage.

MARCELLINE: For God's sake, don't do that! I want to crawl back, without anyone seeing me! I can't answer their questions yet, Michel! Please don't make me!

MICHEL: [*Gently.*] There will be no questions. I have written to Robert and told him everything.

MARCELLINE: Oh, Michel, why did you do that?

MICHEL: So that he can take the proper steps to free you.

MARCELLINE: Free me! For what? You are free! But I am sent home—not wanted!

MICHEL: I will attend to the tickets. [*He leaves the terrace, comes into the bedroom briefly, and leaves by the back hall. On the terrace,* MARCELLINE *leans against the wall for support—begins to cry. As she is turned away from the wall,* BACHIR *appears over the wall.*]

BACHIR: Good morning, Madame. [MARCELLINE *tenses, but doesn't turn to him—crosses and picks up coffee cup.*] Have you hired another houseboy?

MARCELLINE: Why, are you still out of work?

BACHIR: I have never worked harder. I have been in jail. Where's Michel?

MARCELLINE: My husband has gone to the ticket company.

BACHIR: Which one?

MARCELLINE: I don't know.

BACHIR: [*Smiles.*] Maybe that is what he told you…

MARCELLINE: [*A pause.*] Go away.

BACHIR: I need money, Madame. Badly. I have trouble with these police in Biskra. I want to get out.

MARCELLINE: Is that why you want Michel? To get money?

BACHIR: [*Shrugs.*] Yes, Madame, he has money.

MARCELLINE: I promise you he has none for you.

BACHIR: [*Looks at her, and changes tactics.*] Madame used to like me.

MARCELLINE: I still like you. That is a fault with me. What people are does not change what I feel about them.

BACHIR: Madame looks old.

MARCELLINE: Yes, I know.

BACHIR: I could tell Madame such things… terrible things! Madame would be shocked! And when Michel did not behave Madame would know ways to threaten him… of course, he is a friend of mine and I would have to have money to tell these things about him. Then I could go away and not see him and not feel ashamed.

MARCELLINE: [*Revolted.*] You are corrupt into your veins!

BACHIR: I must have money.

MARCELLINE: I won't give you money!

BACHIR: I can sign a complaint against him!

MARCELLINE: And I will sign a complaint against you!

BACHIR: Ah, Madame, they do not care about me—or any native. It is the Europeans who pay quickly—they have something to lose.

MARCELLINE: I will tell the police you are a thieving houseboy. And you will go back to jail for that!

BACHIR: [*His whole manner changes.*] Madame—help me! Help me! They beat me. I have waited to get free and come to you—You are the only person I can turn to!

MARCELLINE: [*Indicates the room.*] Go in there and bring me my purse. [BACHIR *darts into the room, looks around and sees it.*] Bring it to me unopened. [BACHIR *finds the bag on the U. bedside table, picks it up and opens it.*] Bachir, I might give you more than you dare to steal— [BACHIR *thinks a moment, closes the bag, and rejoins her on the terrace. He brings her the purse.*]

BACHIR: You have not much money.

MARCELLINE: I have enough to buy you a ticket to the next town... [*She gives him some.*]

BACHIR: Are you leaving Biskra?

MARCELLINE: I am going home.

BACHIR: Michel stays?

MARCELLINE: My *husband* stays...

BACHIR: [*Hands her back the money.*] Thank you, Madame. You are very kind.

MARCELLINE: [*Looks at it.*] You would rather blackmail him.

BACHIR: [*Simply.*] It will pay better—

MARCELLINE: Poor Michel.

BACHIR: He will have it everywhere, Madame. It might as well be Bachir who profits—[*Doctor* GARRIN *appears, ushered in from hall by* SIDMA *who turns and departs as* GARRIN *speaks*]

GARRIN: [*Going out to the terrace.*] Good morning, Madame. How have you been?

MARCELLINE: How do you do, Doctor. [*To* BACHIR.] Leave us.

BACHIR: May I wait in there?

MARCELLINE: No.

BACHIR: I will be in the kitchen, Doctor. In case you wish to send me for medicine. [*He shouts into the house.*] Poor Madame. She looks very old. [*He exits.*]

GARRIN: [*Sitting down on the foot of her chair.*] It is a long time since you sent for me. I've seen your husband from time to time, at a distance. Seems to have made a good recovery.

MARCELLINE: He grew strong and well here. He's been working on a book.

GARRIN: Good! [*Watching her closely.*] Would you like to tell me why you sent for me?

MARCELLINE: I cannot eat or sleep—I want you to give me something to quiet me.

GARRIN: [*Extracts his stethoscope.*] Have you any fever?

MARCELLINE: No... that is, I don't know. Maybe I have. My heart beats so loud sometimes, it deafens me! Give me something, Doctor!

GARRIN: Let me see if I can find out what you need.

MARCELLINE: I need to sleep from here to Normandy!

GARRIN: Have you any pains?

MARCELLINE: Yes! Here—[*She puts her hand on her chest.*]

GARRIN: [*Adjusting the stethoscope.*] Unbutton your blouse... Now where is this pain?

MARCELLINE: Here. [*She puts her hand on her waist. He listens. Talking as he auscults her chest and back.*] Lately I have found that a little wine after dinner helped me. But Michel took it away from me. He said it was bad for me and I have had to do without it! And I cannot sleep now. And I cannot breathe either. I am afraid. [*He listens now to the region near her waist.*] I am hot with fright. That is how I feel all the time.

GARRIN: [*Removing the stethoscope from his ears.*] I don't think I have confused you with another patient. Did you tell me, Madame, that your brother was a doctor?

MARCELLINE: Yes, Robert—

GARRIN: [*Smiles.*] You are remarkably inaccurate for a young lady from a medical family.

MARCELLINE: [*Faltering.*] How do you mean? What I've told you is true! I haven't imagined this—it's real!

GARRIN: I am sure it is. And the palpitation you feel in your heart is real. But there are two hearts, Madame. And two palpitations. [*He rises.*] I would imagine you to be about four and a half months with child. [*She is speechless. He puts the stethoscope away and takes out a pad.*] Your house woman told me you are going home; you will be in good care very soon.

MARCELLINE: A child?

GARRIN: I can give you a tonic to take until your doctor at home, or your brother, suggests something better. [*Apologetically.*] We have not the latest medicines here. You know—colonial doctors are always a few years behind the home country. [*He briefly examines her eyeballs by pulling down the lower lid.*] Yes, you are somewhat out of condition— anemic perhaps. Your child will fix you up. Usually the year after a pregnancy is a woman's best year of health.

MARCELLINE: [*Apprehensively.*] My husband will be back here soon, Doctor.

GARRIN: [*Quickly.*] Good. [*Laughs.*] Perhaps we can share a glass of wine, on the news.

MARCELLINE: I wish you would not tell him. I would like to tell him.

GARRIN: [*Sits down.*] Very well—you tell him and I'll enjoy it—

MARCELLINE: [*Frustrated.*] No, please—I—I don't want him to worry—I don't want him to change his—[*With difficulty.*] plans. He can't—[*She lowers her eyes.* **GARRIN** *goes to her.*]

GARRIN: [*Puts a hand on her shoulder.*] Now, now—you do it just the way you

want to do it—I won't mention it. [*Then kindly.*] You will feel easier
once you're home—[*Reassuring.*] My wife is native, of course, but I see
with her that a new baby is like a trip to the highlands—[MICHEL *enters
at the gate.* GARRIN *seeing him breaks off speaking to her.*] How do you do—
MICHEL: Hello, Doctor. [*Anxiously.*] Is anything wrong?
MARCELLINE: Dr. Garrin heard we were leaving—he has come by to wish
us a good journey.
GARRIN: [*Smiles.*] Oh, you'll...have that! [*He circles around* MICHEL.] Well,
you are a fine specimen! Africa has been good to you. Restored your
health, and your wife tells me you're writing a book here.
MICHEL: [*Disturbed.*] You know, Doctor, my wife has not been very well—
GARRIN: [*Smiles broadly.*] She will be. Just give her four or five months—
[*He picks up his bag, turns to* MARCELLINE.] You might break up your
trip at Poitiers, Madame. [*To* MICHEL.] You know I come from
Poitiers—so naturally I always tell people to stop off there and see it.
But I haven't seen it myself for sixteen years. [*He sees that no small-talk
is forthcoming.*] Well, good day to you both. [*To* MARCELLINE.] I would
like to hear from you sometimes—
MARCELLINE: Yes, Doctor. [*He leaves. They are alone.*]
MICHEL: He has never come to see us in all those months. Why did he
come today?
MARCELLINE: I sent for him.
MICHEL: Why? [*A long pause.*]
MARCELLINE: I wanted something to make me sleep.
MICHEL: Marcelline, if you are afraid to travel alone, I can take you to
Marseilles.
MARCELLINE: And return me to the soil from which I came?
MICHEL: I will take you home. I will take you to the door, if you want me to.
MARCELLINE: No, Michel...I am afraid I would try to hold you.
MICHEL: You would not want to—even if you could—[MARCELLINE *sits
down and folds her arms across her body.*]
MARCELLINE: I do want to—and I could—But I won't... [*Now* SIDMA
comes to the terrace.]
SIDMA: [*Calls out from the hallway.*] Time, Madame. You go now. [*Enters.*]
MARCELLINE: Yes, Sidma. [*Rises and she puts on her hat. Now* SIDMA *goes into
the bedroom to get the other bag.* MICHEL *picks up* MARCELLINE'S *handbag,
and as she starts to leave, he follows.* SIDMA *comes out on the terrace with the
suitcase. All three are going to the gate as:*]

The CURTAIN *falls*

Scene II

The house in Normandy, six weeks later. The lamps are lit, it is after the evening meal. Dr. Robert *is seated on the couch, holding a demitasse of coffee. There is a pause, then he rises, goes to the table as* Bocage *enters.*

Robert: It was a very nice supper, Bocage. [*No answer.*] Isn't Marcelline going to have her coffee in here with me?
Bocage: No, Robert.
Robert: Then I'll join her—
Bocage: You've talked to her enough, Robert.
Robert: [*Surprised.*] What's this, Bocage?
Bocage: I'm sorry I have to say this to you, Robert, but your sister would like you to leave now, and so would I.
Robert: Oh?
Bocage: She cannot bear the way you speak about Michel.
Robert: Oh, she can't?
Bocage: You pick at her and pick at her. What good does it do? She's got all she can do to hold herself together as it is.
Robert: Naturally *you* defend him! You helped to bring him up—you and that crazy father. A fine example, he is. So unnatural, so degraded he doesn't even come near her after he's made her pregnant! [*Shakes his finger.*] I was right about him from the beginning and you know it!
Bocage: You take too much pleasure in being right. You've spread it all over the village—how right you are. Don't you realize your sister's got to live here? And pretty soon her child with her! Let her keep her head up—because that's what she's got to do. In spite of all the whispering—
Robert: Since when have you become so tolerant?
Bocage: There are a lot of things going on in the world I don't understand. I don't understand you, either. A fine young doctor in a pressed suit— and half the bordellos in Trouville would close up if it weren't for you.
Robert: [*Enraged.*] You're an old man, Bocage, and you take advantage of it!
Bocage: [*At the desk.*] Your sister wants to pay you for your visits. Since she's been home you've been here at least three times a week for six weeks. She'd like to pay you and be done with it. What does she owe you?
Robert: I'll let her know when I have the stomach to come back into the house. [*He exits. There is a pause and* Marcelline *enters.*]
Marcelline: [*At the door.*] Bocage, I'm going to bed.
Bocage: Yes, Miss Marcie.
Marcelline: Did you tell him?

BOCAGE: Yes.

MARCELLINE: Thank you. [*Pause.*] You have a sister in Rouen, haven't you, Bocage?

BOCAGE: Yes.

MARCELLINE: I would like you to write to her for the name of the best doctor there—someone especially good with babies.

BOCAGE: Rouen is far away, Miss.

MARCELLINE: Not too far—you and I could go there a month before I'm due. We'd be away from these people—and Robert. It would be better for me, and it would be much better for the baby.

BOCAGE: You mustn't worry so about the child—

MARCELLINE: Don't say that, Bocage! He must have every chance! That's one thing I can do—!

BOCAGE: [*Reassuring.*] I will write to her tonight. And you're going to have a fine baby with all your character and quality.

MARCELLINE: Yes . . . and his father's. [*Pause.*]

BOCAGE: Have a good night's rest. [*Turns back to his ledger.*]

MARCELLINE: [*About to leave.*] I will—Good night.

BOCAGE: Good night. [*She exits.* BOCAGE *locks up the desk, closes the inkwell, and would turn down the light when he hears a sound. Now* MICHEL *enters by way of the French windows. The two men see each other,* BOCAGE *unbelieving.*] Michel? [*Then joyfully.*] Michel, my boy!

MICHEL: Bocage, I had to see you! [*He lays a small package on the table.*]

BOCAGE: Why do you come in like a thief? This is your home!

MICHEL: I went to the front door, but saw Robert leaving . . . I only want to talk to you. Will you let me?

BOCAGE: Of course! Of course! Tell me everything—[*Catches himself.*] I mean, anything you want! [*Anxiously.*] Are you well, my boy?

MICHEL: [*Looks around.*] I never thought I'd see this place again.

BOCAGE: Nothing here has changed. All in order—all waiting for you! I've had dreams about your coming back like this—to make everything all right again!

MICHEL: [*Ignores this.*] How are you, Bocage?

BOCAGE: A little older—but no wiser, Michel.

MICHEL: [*Hesitant.*] Do you know—everything that happened?

BOCAGE: [*Ironical.*] Doctor Robert is full of information, and Marcelline and I have talked . . . I have sat here night after night wondering what I could have done.

MICHEL: You could have done nothing.

BOCAGE: If I hadn't shown you your father's letter—

MICHEL: That didn't change anything. It only hurried it.

BOCAGE: You might not have left here.

MICHEL: [*Realistic.*] You've known me all my life. You know perfectly well I'd have left sooner or later, in search of myself. And eventually I'd have found—what I did find.

BOCAGE: [*Flinches.*] I—I don't want to think about that. I want to think of good things, things for the future. Have you come back to stay?

MICHEL: Stay here? How can I? I came back because my fears for Marcelline haunt me. How is she? I keep wondering about her—will she ever recover from what I've done to her? Is she all right, Bocage?

BOCAGE: She is, my boy. She's doing nicely—

MICHEL: [*Interrupts him.*] I should have held back the truth perhaps, but there it was like a trap between us! I had to make her see it so that she might save herself…

BOCAGE: [*Pleading.*] Michel, take your losses on all that, and start anew. Scholars can do that as well as farmers! You could stay and start again. You have a tie here now—

MICHEL: What tie? If you knew all the truth about me, even you would put me out!

BOCAGE: [*Pained.*] No, no! That couldn't be true!

MICHEL: [*Savagely.*] I have scavenged through the back streets of every town from Tunis to Paris! I've been exploited by those who are like me, and shunned by those who are not… There is no loneliness like that!…

BOCAGE: [*Not wanting to hear.*] Spare me, my boy—

MICHEL: [*Desperate.*] It's Marcelline I wanted to spare! If I could tell her that I didn't invent this, that it existed before we did, and that the marriage was my failure—none of it hers! [*Anxiously.*] Tell me about her.

BOCAGE: She is living as best she can.

MICHEL: Does she talk about us?

BOCAGE: She tries not to. [*At this moment we hear* ROBERT's *voice loud and angry, outside in the hall.*]

ROBERT: Marcelline! Marcelline! I know he's here! I saw him! [*He enters the room carrying a wrap for* MARCELLINE.] I will not let her stay under the same roof with him!

MICHEL: This is Marcelline's home…

ROBERT: I have nothing to discuss with you!

BOCAGE: This is her home; roof, deed and crops. She's the one to decide if she stays.

ROBERT: She can come back when he's gone! [MARCELLINE *enters, and is instantly aware of* MICHEL.]

MARCELLINE: Michel—
ROBERT: [*Tries to put the wrap on her shoulders but she evades him.*] You are leaving this house with me.
MICHEL: Robert—how noisy you are! [*To* MARCELLINE.] I will leave, Marcelline. But I hope you will stay here—always.
ROBERT: [*Outraged.*] I don't want her near you for even a minute! And if you value your skin you'll be off before morning! [*Takes a step toward him.*] I have your letter here—the one from Biskra—and I'll hold it over your head the rest of your life! And if you ever try to come back here after her child is born—I'll post it on the church door! [*There is a dead silence while* MICHEL *grasps what he has said.*]
MICHEL: [*Crosses to* MARCELLINE.] Child?...
MARCELLINE: Yes. Yours and mine. [*Heartbroken.*] The fruit of the marriage—Isn't that what they say—?
MICHEL: I would like to talk to you—alone.
MARCELLINE: [*Indicates the door.*] Please, Robert, go away.
ROBERT: [*Protests.*] What if you need me?
MARCELLINE: [*Sharply.*] I need only myself! [ROBERT *leaves, followed by* BOCAGE. *There is a moment while* MICHEL *and* MARCELLINE *look at each other.*]
MICHEL: How you must hate me—not to have told me! [MARCELLINE *is silent.*] Are you all right?
MARCELLINE: Yes.
MICHEL: Did you know this in Biskra?
MARCELLINE: Yes. Doctor Garrin told me—the day I left.
MICHEL: [*Appalled.*] You don't think I would have let you go, if I had known?
MARCELLINE: Yes, I do. If you don't want a woman—you don't want anything that comes from her!
MICHEL: Will you listen to me?
MARCELLINE: How can I? All I hear is Bachir's laughter—[*In her despair she turns away from him.*]
MICHEL: [*He stands so that she must face him.*] Marcelline, punish me for what I did, but not for what I am. What I did was terrible enough—to lie to myself for so many years and to marry you, still lying...But what I am—is the very same person you loved so long. I am your friend, from childhood. I am your companion of those first months of the marriage. And the night you held me in your arms—I could have been a murderer and you would still have loved me!
MARCELLINE: [*Her resistance to him melts, as the memory overtakes her.*] That was

the whole trouble. From the very beginning, in this room, I forced more love on you than you could give back. It turned you away from me—

MICHEL: [*Firmly.*] It did not turn me… If *I* won't lie to you, you mustn't lie to yourself. We both know what really happened.

MARCELLINE: [*Angrily.*] You and the truth—! You love it more than you ever loved me!

MICHEL: I didn't love it when I married you, Marcelline. And I didn't love you enough to need it—to search for it. But now we can't do without it.

MARCELLINE: You mean you love me now? I don't believe you. You found what you loved in Biskra!

MICHEL: If I had, would I be here?

MARCELLINE: You might be! Maybe you are homesick! Or lonely—

MICHEL: For neighbors like Robert—who'd jail me if they could?

MARCELLINE: Maybe you feel guilty about the baby!

MICHEL: Even if I had known, I could never feel guilty about that. A child is a great gift, another chance at life for both of us.

MARCELLINE: [*In torment.*] A child of ours? You with your boys and me with my bottle—what chance has he?

MICHEL: [*Sad and worried.*] None—if you don't want him…

MARCELLINE: Want! Want! That's all you think about, Michel. Well, I wanted you—but did it mean anything? Did it make you want me back? Why should it be different with a child? You have to have something rare to give to people—even babies! I don't know what it is—because I don't have it!

MICHEL: [*Protesting.*] You'll be a dear, tender mother—as good to a child as you were to me!

MARCELLINE: [*Wearily.*] And as useless? One failure like that is enough—

MICHEL: [*Anxious.*] Where was the failure? Not in *you*, Marcie! I forbid you to think of it! Or to turn away from this baby because you fear it!

MARCELLINE: [*Ironically.*] Can *you* help whom *you* turn away from—?

[*Before* MICHEL *can respond to this*, BOCAGE *enters.*]

BOCAGE: Your brother's gone home, Miss. Full of threats and bluster. [*To* MICHEL.] He'll sleep some of it off with the brandy. [*Looks from one to the other.*] Would you like to show Michel the changes we made? [*She does not answer.*] We have turned the end of the dining room into a sun-porch for Miss Marcelline and later—the baby. [*No answer from* MICHEL.] We had a good year with our apples and our oats, Michel. [*Eagerly.*] I could show you the account book—[*But* MICHEL *stops him.*]

MICHEL: No, Bocage.

BOCAGE: Your room is in order, Michel...ready for use.

MICHEL: [*Shakes his head.*] It's Marcelline's home. She will decide who lives in it.

BOCAGE: [*Looks at her, but she does not answer his unspoken question.*] Miss... ask him to stay. We need him.

MARCELLINE: I needed him before, Bocage, and I didn't have him.

BOCAGE: Have you forgotten what you said to me this evening? I was to write to Rouen for the best doctor. And you would move there to wait your time, because the child must have every chance! And so he must, Miss. But once he's born, a child's two parents are his best chance. I know Michel, I know how he will be —

MARCELLINE: [*She looks* BOCAGE *in the eye.*] Different from Biskra?

BOCAGE: Each will answer that in his own way, Miss. Your brother would say no. I would say yes. [*Looks at* MICHEL.] I don't know that Michel can answer. He won't know — except day by day. You are the only one who can look into the future, Miss. You and the child — [*Turns to leave.*] If you want me to call a hack from the village, I'll be in the kitchen — [*He exits.*]

MICHEL: [*Goes to her.*] If anything I did — were to harm the child — what would you do, Marcelline?

MARCELLINE: [*Quietly.*] I would kill you.

MICHEL: [*He is both satisfied and amused.*] And a minute ago you said you didn't want it! You dismiss Robert as your doctor because he's not as good as he should be. And you will kill me, if I'm not — You say you have nothing rare enough to give your baby, but you are rare enough, my dearest, if you will fight for him! That's all you have to do, Marcie. Fight me, or Robert, or the village, but for God's sake be *his* ally when no one else is!

MARCELLINE: [*Looking at him.*] That's a reproach. You want me to fight for you, too. But you won't even lie a little to make it easier.

MICHEL: I love you, Marcelline, and I would love the young creature who came from us — But you cannot make me give you a promise that is beyond my power to give...[*He picks up from the table the slender package he has put there on entering.*] I brought you back the little telescope you used to enjoy —

MARCELLINE: [*She does not accept it.*] I won't use it...I can't understand *this* world, let alone the ones in the sky.

MICHEL: [*Puts it down on the table again.*] No one understands. We try to learn — [*He starts to leave.*] Goodbye.

MARCELLINE: [*Cries out in her unhappiness.*] How can you leave me like this?

MICHEL: How can you let me go?

MARCELLINE: Then help me! Tell me how to accept it or to ignore it—To say to myself this is only a fraction of him!

MICHEL: If I said it you'd have contempt for me. But if you ever reach a place where you believe it—I will come home.

MARCELLINE: How would we live together? Think of the things we can never say to one another, the questions we can never ask!

MICHEL: There are many kinds of marriages, Marcelline, and people sacrifice many things to hold on to them... [*She goes to the table and looks down at the eyeglass.*]

MARCELLINE: My greatest joys I owe to you—and also my greatest sorrows. The best—and the most bitter.

MICHEL: [*Smiles.*] If that were so, I'd be like all husbands—everywhere.

MARCELLINE: [*Picks up the telescope.*] Put this away, Michel. [*She hands it to him. He takes it.*] When you're here with me, we'll use it. When you are away I want you to know that I will not spy on other doorsteps to see where you have gone...

MICHEL: We must promise nothing—except to like each other as we are. Will you sit here with me as you used to?

MARCELLINE: You want me to look at you as I used to—and to accept all of you.

MICHEL: That's what our child will want.

MARCELLINE: I can do it for him!

MICHEL: Can you? Can I? [*Sadly.*] And what will happen to him if we don't? [*They look at each other, and now she puts out her hand to comfort him.*]

MARCELLINE: We must learn, Michel. A good way will be to practise on each other... [*As she sits down to talk with him.*]

The CURTAIN *falls*

The
Killing of
Sister George

Frank Marcus

Eileen Atkins (Alice), Beryl Reid (June) and Lally Bowers (Mercy) in *The Killing of Sister George*, at the Belasco Theatre, 1965. (Photograph reprinted with permission from the John Willis Theatre World/Screen World Archive.)

The Killing of Sister George was first presented in London at the Duke of York's Theatre on June 17, 1965. It was produced by Michael Codron in association with Bernard Delfont, and directed by Val May. The production was designed by Catherine Browne.

Cast

Alice "Childie" McNaught . . . . Eileen Atkins
June Buckridge (Sister George) . . . . Beryl Reid
Mrs. Mercy Croft . . . . Lally Bowers
Madame Xenia . . . . Margaret Courtenay

The Killing of Sister George was first produced in the United States at the Belasco Theatre on Broadway on Wednesday, October 5, 1966. It was produced by Helen Bonfils and Morton Gottlieb, by arrangement with Michael Codron in association with Bernard Delfont. It was directed by Val May. The foreign production was designed by Catherine Browne, and the American production was supervised by William Rittman. The costumes were supervised by Jane Greenwood.

Cast

Alice "Childie" McNaught . . . . Eileen Atkins
June Buckridge (Sister George) . . . . Beryl Reid
Mrs. Mercy Croft . . . . Lally Bowers
Madame Xenia . . . . Polly Rowles

STANDBYS   Paddy Croft
                                            Anne Murray

General Manager: Richard Seader
Press: Dorothy Ross, Richard O'Brien, Michael Gershman, Jane Friedman
Stage Managers: Warren Crane, Anne Murray

The action takes place in the living room of June Buckridge's flat on Devonshire Street, in London's West End.

Act One
A Tuesday afternoon in late September.

Act Two
Scene I: A week later, 4 A.M.
Scene II: Late afternoon of the same day.

Act Three
Two weeks later. Morning.

Time: *The present.*

Act One

Scene: *The living-room of a London West End flat. A Tuesday afternoon in late September.*

Down R is a wide arch showing part of a small entrance hall which leads to the front door of the flat. The fireplace is R, above the arch, and is fitted with an electric fire. Up RC, facing the audience, under a sloping ceiling, is a window with a narrow window-seat, overlooking roofs. Up L is a low, wide rostrum, reached by two long steps, which forms a wide corridor leading off up L to the bathroom. In the back wall of the corridor, facing the audience, is the bedroom door. There is a banister rail along the right side of the rostrum. In the wall L is a serving hatch, which when open shows a glimpse of kitchen shelves. The door to the kitchen is down L, below the hatch. The furniture, an incongruous mixture of antique, nineteen-thirtyish and modern, looks expensive but ill-assorted. Down R is a small table with a single chair in front of it. On the wall over the table is a two-way speaker on an extending arm. Above the arch R there is a whatnot with Victorian china ornaments on its shelves. In front of the whatnot, facing L, is a small tub armchair. Above the fireplace is a long bookcase and there is a canterbury against the wall R of the window. A bureau-type radiogram is L of the window. A low coffee-table stands L of the bedroom door, on the rostrum. A long side-board is underneath the serving hatch L and a small occasional table and an upright chair are down L, below the kitchen door. A sofa with a table behind it is RC. There is a telephone on the table. A circular, pedestal table is LC with chairs R and L of it. A pouffe is down RC. The hall is furnished with a small table and an umbrella vase. At night the room is lit by a standard lamp up R and table-lamps down R and L. There is a light switch below the fireplace.

Before the CURTAIN *rises, as the house-lights fade, the 'Applehurst Theme', a cheerful folk-dance tune, is heard.*

When the CURTAIN *rises, the music fades. The room is empty. The front door is heard to slam off R.* JUNE BUCKRIDGE *enters from the hall. She is a rotund, middle-aged woman, wearing a belted white mackintosh. She carries a leather brief-case and string gloves. She is very agitated.*

ALICE: [*off in the kitchen; calling*] George? George, is that you? [JUNE *shows exasperation at the sound of* ALICE'*s voice, throws her gloves and brief-case on to the sofa and goes to the table behind it. She opens a cigar box on the table, finds it empty and throws it violently on to the floor up C, then moves to the fireplace.* ALICE 'CHILDIE' MCNAUGHT, *in the kitchen, opens the hatch and looks into the room. She is a girl-woman in her thirties, looking deceptively young. She conveys an impression of pallor: her hair, eyes and complexion are all very light. She is wearing a sweater and jeans, with a plastic apron and orange rubber gloves*]

[*Surprised*] George, what on earth...? [JUNE *takes a cheroot from a box on the mantelpiece, reaches for the lighter, finds a doll in long clothes in the way and throws it into the fender*]

George! What are you doing at home at this time of the afternoon? [JUNE *lights her cheroot and moves down R of the sofa*]

JUNE: [*after a pause*] They are going to murder me.
ALICE: What...?
JUNE: [*moving LC*] I've suspected it for some time.
ALICE: What...?
JUNE: Kindly close that hatch. [*She moves to R of the table LC and removes her coat*]

[ALICE *quickly closes the hatch and comes into the room by the kitchen door L. She carries a tea cloth*]

ALICE: George, I don't understand what you're saying—what are you talking about? [JUNE *puts her cheroot on the rim of the ashtray on the table LC*]
JUNE: [*brutally*] Shut up! You know nothing. [*She moves RC, below the sofa*]

[ALICE, *silenced, watches* JUNE'*s nervous pacing*]

That Australian bitch, that Sheila, let it out.

ALICE: [*sitting R of the table LC*] The one who used to be a lady cricketer?
JUNE: [*with disgust*] Yes, that's her—the lolloping great trollop! [*She removes her coat*]
ALICE: So, what did she say?

JUNE: [*very excited*] It was during the tea-break; she handed me my cup of tea and said, 'I trust you're in good health', she said with a sly wink.

ALICE: There's nothing wrong with that.

JUNE: [*tossing her coat into the armchair R*] I knew what she meant. I got the message all right. [*She moves up RC*]

ALICE: [*rising, crossing and picking up* JUNE'S *coat*] It might have been quite innocuous. [*She follows to R of* JUNE]

JUNE: Innocuous! [*She raps the table behind the sofa*] They are trying to kill me and you call that innocuous. Somebody's leaked it to her — another Australian probably. The place is rampant with them: they're multiplying like rabbits. [*She goes to the table LC and picks up her cheroot*]

ALICE: You're imagining things.

JUNE: No, no, not rabbits — opossums. Those dreary little pests.

ALICE: [*moving above the sofa*] Well, anyway, what did you *do*?

JUNE: [*moving to the sideboard*] I left.

ALICE: [*moving to L of the sofa; alarmed*] You walked out of the rehearsal? [*She removes her rubber gloves*]

JUNE: [*subdued*] I wasn't going to let some illiterate bitch wink at me. [*She picks up a bottle of gin and a glass and takes them to the table LC*]

ALICE: [*biting her lip*] They won't like it. [*She crosses to the arch R*]

JUNE: I've given six years devoted service to this programme.

ALICE: You said yourself: they don't like contract artists to have tantrums. [ALICE *exits to the hall and deposits the coat, the tea-cloth and her rubber gloves*]

JUNE: [*excitedly*] They have no right to do this to me. I'm a senior member of the cast. [ALICE *re-enters from the hall*]

If they wanted to — [*she swallows*] write me out — [*she pours a drink*] they should have asked me to come to the office in a proper manner. [*She returns the bottle of gin to the sideboard, replacing it with a bang*]

[ALICE *picks up a doll from the pouffe then sits on the pouffe and hugs the doll*]

ALICE: Nobody wants to write you out. It's unthinkable. *Applehurst* couldn't survive without you.

JUNE: [*sitting R of the table LC*] Don't you be too sure. *Applehurst* is more than a village, you know — it's a community, it's a way of life. It doesn't depend on individuals. [*In a country accent*] There's many a stone in that churchyard...

ALICE: You talk as if it was real. [JUNE *leans forward and raises her voice*]

JUNE: [*in her own voice*] It is real to millions. It stands for the traditional values to English life—common sense—tenacity—our rural heritage...

ALICE: Oh, belt up!

JUNE: You're getting above yourself, missy.

ALICE: You *are* the serial. It would be nothing without you.

JUNE: Stranger things have happened. Only the other day Ronnie said to me: 'There'll have to be some changes, you know.'

ALICE: He probably meant the story line.

JUNE: No—no—it's the axe again. We're losing listeners, and they're looking for a scapegoat. It's over a year since old Mrs. Prescott was kicked by a horse. [*She drinks*]

ALICE: Yes, and look at the rumpus there was over that. And she was only a minor character.

JUNE: She had her following.

ALICE: She hardly had a line to say from one week to the next.

JUNE: What about the time I nursed her back to health, when she had concussion?

ALICE: That was exceptional.

JUNE: No, no, no. She had nice little bits and pieces here and there. When she found that stray dog, and the village adopted it... [*A dark thought occurs to her*] Until it was run over by a tractor. [*She shudders*]

ALICE: There's no comparison. Mrs. Prescott...

JUNE: [*rising and shouting*] Mrs. Prescott had a following. [*She leaves her drink on the table*]

ALICE: [*shrugging*] All right—Mrs. Prescott had a following.

JUNE: [*moving down L*] The subject is now closed.

ALICE: [*after a pause*] But she *was* expendable.

JUNE: [*crossing to* ALICE; *angrily*] Are you trying to aggravate me? Are you deliberately trying to annoy me?

ALICE: [*loudly*] You're the most popular character in it. [*She rises*]

JUNE: Don't screech at me. It's an ugly, grating sound.

ALICE: Well, look at your ratings.

JUNE: They are down. Four percent last week—I'm slipping. Now do you understand? [*She moves C*]

ALICE: [*after a pause*] You still get the most fan mail, don't you? [*Still holding the doll, she goes to the small table down R and takes a threaded needle from the work-basket*]

JUNE: [*sitting R of the table LC*] Only just. Ginger, the publican, is close on my heels. Ever since he had that win on the Premium Bonds, and gave the money to Farmer Bromley, so that they wouldn't turn his place into a broiler house…

ALICE: [*moving RC*] What about young Rosie?

JUNE: [*conspiratorially*] Aha! [ALICE *looks puzzled*]

She's preggers.

ALICE: No! [*She sits on the pouffe*] You mean the actress…?

JUNE: No, the character, blockhead! We reckon that'll bring back some listeners.

ALICE: [*intrigued*] Who was responsible? [*She sews the skirt of Emmeline, the doll*]

JUNE: We haven't been told yet. I think it was Lennie, her steady. If so it'll be absolutely splendid. They can get married—everybody loves a wedding. But Arthur thinks it was Roy.

ALICE: Who's Roy?

JUNE: That soldier—stationed at the army camp at Oakmead. He took her to that dance, remember?

ALICE: [*concerned*] What's she going to do—about the baby?

JUNE: Well, she confides in me—in the next installment. Comes to me in tears; wants to get rid of it. [*She sighs*] Don't know what the younger generation's coming to.

ALICE: What do you tell her?

JUNE: What *don't* I tell her? [*She puts out her cheroot in the ashtray on the table LC*] I give her a dressing-down she won't forget in a hurry. [*She rises, moves to L of* ALICE *and speaks in her country accent*] Where is he? Mr. Clever Lad? Show me where he is so's I can tear some strips off him, the fine young fellow. Just don't you aggravate yourself, my dear—leave it to me. Just you tell me who it was, my dear. Just you tell me who it was.

ALICE: And does she tell you?

JUNE: No. [*She pauses, crosses to R of the table LC and sits*] But I'll wheedle it out of her, never fear. Just give me three installments, that's all. [*She picks up her drink*]

ALICE: [*tensely*] They shouldn't talk about—things like that.

JUNE: [*happier now*] It's nice, though, the way they come to me with their troubles. Oh, they know they'll get straight talking from me. [*In her country accent*] No lard ever passed my lips. No, sir, fine words butter no parsnips.

ALICE: What *are* you talking about?

JUNE: [*putting down her glass and leaning forward*] They *need* me. Get that into your thick head. *Applehurst* needs a District Nurse. Who'd deliver the babies, who'd look after the old folk, I'd like to know.

ALICE: Exactly. [*She finishes her sewing, rises, leaves the doll on the pouffe and crosses to* JUNE] Nobody's suggesting...

JUNE: What do you mean—nobody's suggesting? Why did that woman enquire after my health? Why did she wink at me, eh?

ALICE: Perhaps she fancies you. [*She gives a slight snigger and crosses to R*]

JUNE: This is no time for jesting.

ALICE: [*replacing the needle in the work-basket*] How do I know why she winked at you? Perhaps she's got a nervous twitch. [*She tidies the things in the work-basket*]

JUNE: [*picking up her glass, rising and moving down C*] She's Australian, dunce! They're extroverts, not neurotic townsfolk, like us. They come from the bloody bush.

ALICE: [*becoming exasperated*] Well, I don't know why she winked at you.

JUNE: Oh, shut up! Silly bitch! [*She moves to L of the table behind the sofa, puts down her glass, picks up a framed certificate and reads*] 'And in recognition of your devoted work and care for the old and sick, we name the Geriatric Ward the Sister George Ward.' [*She replaces the certificate*]

[ALICE *applauds slowly and ironically*]

Take care, Childie, you're trailing your coat...

ALICE: [*giggling*] You're the bull. [*She moves to the pouffe, kneels on it with one knee and puts the doll's clothes straight*]

JUNE: [*dangerously*] We're very cocky all of a sudden.

ALICE: [*mock innocently*] Who—me?

JUNE: Yes, you. [*She moves C*] And what the hell are you doing at home on a Tuesday afternoon? Why aren't you at work?

ALICE: Mr. Katz gave us the day off. It's a Jewish holiday.

JUNE: [*suspiciously*] Oh, really! What holiday?

ALICE: I don't know. The Feast of the Contamination, or something.

JUNE: You seem to have more holidays than work days lately.

ALICE: [*picking up the doll and moving to the fireplace*] Not my fault.

JUNE: [*still suspicious*] He hasn't been having another 'go' at you, your Mr. Katz, has he?

ALICE: [*moving to the table behind the sofa and putting the doll on it; primly*] Certainly not.

JUNE: I bet he has.

ALICE: He hasn't. I'd tell you.

JUNE: I wonder. [*Self-pityingly*] Nobody tells me anything.

ALICE: That's because you always make such a stupid fuss about things. [*She sits on the right arm of the sofa and puts her feet on the fender*]

JUNE: All right, then, I won't make a fuss. [*She moves to L of the sofa*] Come on, tell me.

ALICE: There's nothing to tell.

JUNE: [*venomously*] You expect me to believe that after what happened last time?

ALICE: Nothing happened.

JUNE: A four-inch tear and three buttons off your blouse and you call that nothing.

ALICE: [*angrily*] I told you. I got it caught in the Gestetner.

JUNE: Don't lie to me, Childie.

ALICE: [*rising and moving above the sofa*] I'm not lying. [*She crosses towards the kitchen door*]

[JUNE *intercepts* ALICE, *grasps her arm and turns her to face her*]

JUNE: Then why are you avoiding my eyes?

ALICE: Because — because . . . Oh! [*She throws off* JUNE's *hand*] You're impossible, George. [ALICE *runs up the two steps and exits up L to the bathroom*]

JUNE: [*calling*] Don't throw tantrums with me, young lady. [*She leans over the banister and roars*] Come out! Come out this instant.

ALICE: [*off L calling*] I shan't. [JUNE *turns, picks up Emmeline the doll from the table behind the sofa, moves up LC and calls towards the bathroom*]

JUNE: Can you hear me, Childie? I've got Emmeline here, your favorite doll. [*Softly but clearly*] And if you don't come out of the bathroom at once — I'm going to pull Emmeline's head off. [ALICE, *tear-stained, rushes in up L, tears the doll out of* JUNE's *hand and hugs it*]

ALICE: Monster! [*She moves down C*]

JUNE: [*moving to L of* ALICE] There, that's better. [*She pauses*] And now: apologize.

ALICE: What for?

JUNE: For causing me unnecessary aggravation.

ALICE: I'm sorry.

JUNE: [*crossing to R of* ALICE] You don't sound it.

ALICE: Look, George, I know that you're worried and everything, but that's no reason . . .

JUNE: Don't answer back. Don't be cheeky.

ALICE: Look, George . . .

JUNE: Has Mr. Katz 'had a go' at you?

ALICE: [*screaming*] No!

JUNE: Don't screech at me. Apologize this instant, or there'll be severe chastisement.

ALICE: I'm sorry.

JUNE: That's better. Now, down on your knees.

ALICE: Must I?

JUNE: Yes. Come on. [ALICE, *still hugging the doll, goes on her knees*]

Show your contrition.

ALICE: How?

JUNE: You must eat the butt of my cigar.

ALICE: I couldn't; it would make me sick.

JUNE: [*standing over* ALICE] Are you arguing with me?

ALICE: O.K. Hand it over. [JUNE *crosses to the table LC, picks up the ashtray and holds it out to* ALICE, *who takes the cigar butt. This is actually a piece of chocolate previously concealed in the ashtray*]

JUNE: Good girl. Now eat it.

ALICE: Can I take the ash off?

JUNE: You may take the ash off, but you must eat the paper. [ALICE, *with an expression of extreme distaste, eats the butt*]

ALICE: Ooh, it tastes vile.

JUNE: Good. [*The telephone rings*]

That'll teach you to be rude. [ALICE *jumps to her feet, rushes to the telephone, lifts the receiver, sits on the sofa at the right end of it, with her feet up and speaks with her mouth full*]

ALICE: [*into the telephone*] Hello ... Miss June Buckridge? ... One moment, please.

JUNE: [*moving above the sofa; apprehensively*] Who is it?

ALICE: Don't know.

JUNE: [*moving to R of the sofa*] Why didn't you ask, fathead? [*She takes the receiver from* ALICE. *Into the telephone*] Hello, this is June Buckridge. Who wants her? ... Yes, of course ... Yes, I'll hold on ... [*She puts her hand over the mouthpiece. To* ALICE] God Almighty, Childie, it's the B.B.C.

ALICE: [*trembling*] Oh, Lord, I hope it's nothing serious.

JUNE: [*into the telephone*] Hello? ... Hello, Mrs. Mercy, dear ... No, of *course* not ... Quite ... Quite ... Yes, I—there was something I wanted to talk to you about ... Perhaps we'd better have a man-to-man ... You have something to say to *me*? ... No, I'm not doing anything at the moment... Well, I'd rather not come back to Broadcasting House today... Yes, yes, that's a *splendid* idea... *Love* to see you... That's right: Devonshire Street—top floor. You press the bell, and one of those 'I speak your weight' machines answers... [*With a rather forced laugh*] Yes, you know the kind of thing. [*She intones in a deep voice*] 'You are thirteen stone two.'... No, no, of course not—I wasn't implying that you were... Yes, that'll be absolutely lovely... *Any* time... 'Bye. [*She replaces the receiver and wipes her brow*] She's coming round. She'll be here in a minute. Oh, God, I'm for it. [*She crosses to L of the sofa*]

ALICE: [*putting the doll on the table behind the sofa*] Who was it? [JUNE *goes to the table LC, takes a cigar from the box and lights it with the lighter*]

JUNE: The Assistant Head—Mrs. Mercy Croft.

ALICE: The one who has that weekly spot on *Woman's Hour*?

JUNE: 'Ask Mrs. Mercy.' Yes, that's her.

ALICE: [*rising*] But she sounds awfully nice on the radio—at least her advice is sort of—sensible.

JUNE: [*pacing nervously down L*] She *is* nice. [*She tries to convince herself*] Mrs. Mercy is a *nice woman.*

ALICE: [*crossing to LC*] Well, then.

JUNE: [*crossing below* ALICE *to the fireplace*] She's coming to see me, you understand? First she asked to see me in her office, now she's asking to see me.

ALICE: [*after a pause*] Did she seem friendly?

JUNE: [*tensely*] Yep.

ALICE: It'll be a good thing to clear the air.

JUNE: [*moving to R of* ALICE] You don't know what you're talking about. She wants to see me on an urgent matter. We must brace ourselves for the worst.

ALICE: Will she expect some tea?

JUNE: Tea, oh, God, yes! [*She turns* ALICE *round and gives her a push towards the sideboard*] You must make her something special—at the double. [ALICE *clears everything from the table LC on to the sideboard*]

ALICE: There's that piece of Dundee cake that mother sent. [*She takes a lace tablecloth from the sideboard cupboard and spreads it on the table LC*]

JUNE: [*pacing R*] That'll be absolutely first class. [*She paces to LC*] And make her some of those Scotch scones of yours. And when you're serving the stuff, try to make a good impression, look cheerful, keep your shoulders back. And if she speaks to you don't open your mouth about things you don't understand.

ALICE: I can quite easily go out. [*She gets three teaspoons and three knives from the sideboard drawer and puts them on the table, then takes three cups, saucers and small plates from the sideboard cupboard and puts them on the table*]

JUNE: What, and leave me to pour out and all that pansy stuff. Not likely. [*She crosses to the fireplace*] You'll stay here and do some work.

ALICE: [*setting out the china, etc.*] Look, George, try not to show her how worried you are. You always get sort of—aggressive when you're nervous.

JUNE: [*moving C*] Go on. Back to the kitchen where you belong. [*She roughly tidies the cushions on the sofa*]

ALICE: I wish you'd do relaxing exercises or something. [ALICE *exits to the kitchen*]

JUNE: [*shouting after* ALICE] I'll do relaxing exercises on your behind in a minute. [*She collects her brief-case and puts it on the floor R of the radiogram*] Now then. [*She picks up two framed certificates from the top of the radiogram and reads*] 'Personality of the Year.' I'll put that in a prominent position. [*She puts the certificate on the mantelpiece and reads the second certificate*] 'The English Village Preservation Society.' [*She puts the certificate on the right end of the table behind the sofa, then goes to the radiogram and moves a third framed certificate into a better position*] 'The Variety Club of Great Britain.' [*She moves a silver cup along the top of the radiogram*] 'The Association of British Nursing Sisters.' [*She moves another cup along and then picks up a silver statuette, faces front, holds out the statuette and reads its inscription*] 'Miss Humanity'—[*she pauses*] 'nominated by the* Daily Mirror.' [*She places the statuette on the left end of the table behind the sofa and turns to the radiogram*] There's something missing. [*She calls*] Alice.

ALICE: [*off; calling*] I'm busy.

JUNE: [*moving down C; imperiously*] Come here. I want you. [ALICE *enters from the kitchen, carrying a washing-up mop*]

ALICE: What is it *now*? You're always interrupting.

JUNE: [*pointing to the trophies*] There's one missing.

ALICE: I haven't touched anything.

JUNE: [*moving to R of the table LC*] There's one missing, isn't there? Go on—*have a look*. I want to hear you tell me, in your own words, which one is missing.

ALICE: [*without looking*] I don't know.

JUNE: [*softly, but with deadly emphasis*] Where is the Honorary 'Stag'?

ALICE: [*uncertainly*] What...?

JUNE: [*in the same tone*] What have you done with it? [ALICE *is silent*]

I'll give you ten seconds to confess. [*She waits, breathing heavily*]

ALICE: Let me get on with the tea. She'll be here in a minute.

JUNE: You've destroyed it, haven't you? [*She pauses*] Where is the Honorary 'Stag'?

ALICE: [*after a pause*] I threw it away.

JUNE: [*moving to* ALICE] You—*what?*

ALICE: [*slightly hysterically*] I *hated* it. A cut-off stag's head, impaled on a pike. You had no right to keep such abominations in the house—you know I like animals.

JUNE: When did you—throw it away?

ALICE: [*looking at* JUNE] Last night. [*There is a pause.* JUNE *sits R of the table LC,* ALICE *sits L of it*]

JUNE: You know it meant a lot to me—to be nominated Honorary 'Stag'.

ALICE: [*very contrite*] I'll get it back; I'll get another.

JUNE: [*tragically*] Too late.

ALICE: I'll phone up the Town Hall—the Borough Litter Disposal Unit...

JUNE: [*tragically*] You mean the dustman, don't you? Why can't you bloody well say so? [*There is a long ring from the front door buzzer*]

It's her. [*She stubs out her cigar on a tea plate*]

[ALICE *rises*]

[*She rises and crosses to the speaker R*] It's the bitch, the cow, the plague spot, the embossed carbuncle. [*She pulls out the extending arm of the speaker and speaks into it*] Hello, Mrs. Mercy, dear... Yes, we're expecting you... Top floor. [*She pushes the speaker back against the wall and crosses to C*] Don't stand there, gawping. Blow your nose. Pull your sweater straight: you look disgusting. [*She tweaks* ALICE'*s sweater down like an angry mother*] Now, remember: be polite and keep mum. [*She moves R.*] I'll speak to you later. [*She pauses*] Where the hell has she got to?

ALICE: Maybe she got stuck in the lift.

JUNE: [*aghast*] Oh, my God, I forgot to close the lift gates.

ALICE: [*moving R of the table LC*] I'll do it.

JUNE: [*in a hoarse whisper*] Don't—it's too late. [*The front door bell rings*]

She'll either walk, or...

ALICE: [*suddenly scared*] Let's not open the door. [JUNE *throws* ALICE *a glance expressing contempt and strides out through the arch R*]

JUNE: [*off R*] Oh, hello, Mrs. Mercy. [*The front door is heard to close*] I'm so

377

sorry—I forgot to tell you that the lift was out of order. [MRS. MERCY CROFT *enters through the arch R. She is a well-groomed lady of indeterminate age, gracious of manner and freezingly polite. She is wearing a navy blue two-piece suit, matching hat and accessories, and a discreet double string of pearls round her neck. She carries a brief-case*]

MERCY: [*as she enters; cheerfully*] Not at all—I never use the lift. [*She sees* ALICE] Oh? [*She moves C*]

[JUNE *enters through the arch*]

JUNE: [*moving RC*] This is Miss Alice McNaught—Mrs. Mercy Croft.
MERCY: [*smiling but not shaking hands*] How do you do? [*She turns to* JUNE] Yes, I always say: we get far too little exercise these days. If we walked upstairs instead of using lifts, those extra inches would disappear.
ALICE: [*the mop behind her back; trying to be helpful*] I sometimes walk…
MERCY: *You* don't need to lose any weight, my dear.
JUNE: [*at* ALICE] Alice was just preparing the tea.
MERCY: Oh, that *is* nice. [*She smiles politely at* ALICE]

[JUNE, *while* MERCY *is looking away, makes a furious gesture to* ALICE *to go into the kitchen*]

I do hope I haven't put you to any trouble—inviting myself out of the blue.

JUNE and ALICE: [*together*] Rubbish! Not at all. [ALICE *exits to the kitchen*]
MERCY: May I look round? [*She moves up C*] I *adore* looking at other people's flats—they do reflect their occupiers' personalities in an uncannily accurate way. [JUNE *moves to the fireplace*]

[*She looks around*] To be perfectly honest, I imagined your home to be—different.

JUNE: Really?
MERCY: [*indicating the ornaments on the bookcase*] This charming Victoriana— the dolls—somehow…
JUNE: [*slightly embarrassed*] They're Miss McNaught's.
MERCY: Oh, of course, that would explain it. They just weren't *you*. I didn't know…
JUNE: [*rather sheepishly*] Yes, I have a flat-mate.
MERCY: [*sympathetically*] How nice. It's so important to have—companion-ship—especially when one's an artist.

JUNE: [*moving down R and indicating the brasses on the wall*] These are mine—
I collect horse brasses.

MERCY: How useful. [*She moves to the window*] May I look out from your
window? [JUNE *moves up R of the sofa*]

I love overlooking things. I've always adored heights. In my
young days, my husband and I often used to go mountaineering—
in the Austrian Alps for preference. [*She looks out of the window
and gives a sudden yell of delight*] Ah! There's B.H.! You can see
Broadcasting House from your window—isn't that—*super*! To
have that reassuring presence brooding over you, seeing that
you don't get into mischief. [JUNE *laughs nervously*. ALICE *raises
the hatch L and leans through*]

ALICE: Ready in a minute.

MERCY: Oh—good.

JUNE: Kindly close that hatch. [ALICE *withdraws and slams the hatch down*]

Sometimes I have the insuperable desire to decapitate her. [*She laughs*]

MERCY: [*moving to L of the sofa*] Oh, poor Miss McNaught. I do like your
settee cover—a homely pattern. I love a floral design—I know it's
old-fashioned, but...

JUNE: Childie—Miss McNaught—made them.

MERCY: [*putting her brief-case, handbag and gloves on the table behind the sofa*]
Really. How clever of her—they're beautifully fitted. You're fortunate
to have such a handy companion.

JUNE: [*moving down R; in her country accent*] Yes, she's good with the needle,
I'll say that for her.

MERCY: [*lightly*] That was Sister George speaking.

JUNE: [*in her own voice; self-consciously*] One can't help slipping.

MERCY: [*moving below the sofa*] But you *are* Sister George far more than
Miss June Buckridge to all of us at B.H.

JUNE: Jolly nice of you to say so. [*She indicates to* MERCY *to sit on the sofa*]

[MERCY *sits on the sofa, at the left end of it.* JUNE *sits in the armchair
R, with her knees apart*]

MERCY: Thank you. You have made the part completely your own. It was
obvious—even at the first auditions. I remember it quite clearly,
although it must be—oh...

JUNE: Almost six years ago. I was scared stiff.

MERCY: How charming! One can't imagine you scared stiff.

JUNE: I don't mind actual physical danger. You know, I almost like it. I was in the A.T.S. during the war.

MERCY: Lovely!

JUNE: None of that sissy ENSA stuff for yours truly.

MERCY: It wasn't that bad. [*There is a slight pause.* JUNE's *smile fades*] As a matter of fact, I did a bit of organizing for ENSA myself.

JUNE: I'm sorry. No offence meant.

MERCY: None taken. [*She reaches over the back of the sofa and gets her brief-case*] Now, Miss Buckridge—or may I call you Sister George, like everybody else?

JUNE: Certainly.

MERCY: As you know, I hold a monthly 'surgery' in my office, when I welcome people to come to me with their problems. I've always made it a rule to be approachable. But in certain cases, involving matters of special importance, I prefer to visit the subjects in their own homes, so that we can talk more easily, without any duress. That's why I'm here today.

JUNE: [*in her country accent*] Ah, well, a farmer's footsteps are the best manure. [*She laughs*]

MERCY: Quite. But there is rather a serious matter I wish to discuss with you.

JUNE: I see. [ALICE *enters from the kitchen, carrying a tray of tea. She has removed her apron*]

ALICE: Sorry I took so long. [*She puts the tray on the table LC*]

MERCY: [*slightly annoyed at the interruption, but politely*] Ah, lovely! [*She rises. To* JUNE] We'll continue our little chat after tea.

ALICE: If you'd rather...

JUNE: [*rising and moving RC*] You can speak quite freely, Mrs. Mercy. Miss McNaught and I have no secrets from each other.

MERCY: Oh. Well, let's all have tea first. [ALICE *moves the chair L of the table LC and places it above the table*]

[*She moves above the table LC*] I say, what delicious-looking scones. [ALICE *moves the chair down L and places it L of the table*]

ALICE: They're Scotch scones. [*She goes to the hatch, opens it and collects a plate with a lump of Dundee cake with four small slices of cake arranged beside it. She leaves the hatch open and puts the plate on the table LC*]

JUNE: They're Childie's speciality. Copied from a recipe of her grand-mother's. [*She sits R of the table*]

[MERCY *sits above the table, and* ALICE *sits* L *of it*]

MERCY: They look delish! May I try one?

ALICE: Help yourself. [*She puts the plate of scones in front of* MERCY] Here's the jam. [*She passes the jam-pot to* MERCY]

MERCY: [*taking a scone and spreading it with jam*] They're what we used to call 'Girdle Scones'.

JUNE: [*mocking* MERCY'*s inflection*] Or 'Drop Scones'.

ALICE: It's frightfully important not to get the girdle too hot, or the outside of the scones will brown before the inside is cooked.

MERCY: They're a lovely even colour. [ALICE *pours tea for* MERCY *and herself but not for* JUNE]

ALICE: [*very animated*] I always cool them in a towel.

MERCY: Do you?

ALICE: Yes, and I wait till the bubbles rise to the surface before I turn them over.

MERCY: They're very successful.

ALICE: I use half a level teaspoon of bicarbonate of soda—

MERCY: Now you're giving away trade secrets.

ALICE: —and one level teaspoonful of cream of tartar—

JUNE: Shut up! [*There is a moment's silence*]

ALICE: —eight ounces of flour—

JUNE: [*exploding*] Shut up!

ALICE: [*softly but firmly*] —and one egg.

JUNE: Shut up! [*She picks up the lump of Dundee cake and hurls it at* ALICE]

[ALICE *ducks. The cake flies to pieces against the sideboard. There is a pause during which* MERCY *continues to eat unperturbed*]

MERCY: Now then, girls!

ALICE: [*after a pause*] She hates me to talk about food. [*Confidentially*] She's a wee bit overwrought.

JUNE: [*rising*] Overwrought my arse! [*She stumps over to the fireplace, takes a cheroot from the box on the mantelpiece, and lights it*]

ALICE: [*chiding*] Now that wasn't nice—that was not a nice thing to say.

MERCY: [*smiling indulgently*] I expect she picked it up in the army.

ALICE: She swears like a trooper.

MERCY: But she has a heart of gold.

ALICE: Once, she got into such a temper, that I wrote a poem about it.

JUNE: [*moving below the sofa; bitterly*] Yes, she fancies herself as a poetess. Goes to the City Lit. every Wednesday night, to learn about metre and things.

MERCY: What a nice hobby.

JUNE: As a poetess, she makes a very good cook.

MERCY: It's still a question of mixing the right ingredients to make a tasty whole.

ALICE: That night she came back in a raging temper—

JUNE: [*moving C*] Thank you very much, we've all stopped listening.

ALICE: [*ignoring* JUNE]—I wrote this poem. It began:
'Fierce as the wind
Blows the rampaging termagant...' [JUNE *prowls furiously RC*]

MERCY: Very expressive. [*To* JUNE] And how did you like being compared to the wind? [JUNE *blows a raspberry. There is a pause.* MERCY *drinks her tea*]

ALICE: [*passing the plate of cake*] Slice of cake, Mrs. Mercy? [JUNE *sits R of the table*]

MERCY: [*taking a slice of cake*] Just a teeny one. I mustn't be greedy. [*She spreads the cake with jam*]

[ALICE *takes a piece of cake*]

JUNE: Her mother made it. [*She continues smoking and uses her plate as an ashtray*]

MERCY: You can always tell if it's home-baked; it tastes quite different.

JUNE: [*laughing*] You'd be amazed if you knew what old Mother McNaught put into it.

MERCY: I'm not even going to ask.

JUNE: I'm delighted to hear it. [*She laughs*]

MERCY: [*enjoying herself*] Oh, dear, this is just like a dormitory feast—all this girlish banter. [*To* JUNE] I bet you were a terror at school. [*She eats her cake*]

JUNE: I was captain of the hockey team and a keen disciplinarian—God help the girl I caught—[*in her country accent*] making me an apple-pie bed. [*She chuckles*]

MERCY: Ah, there's Sister George again. It's wonderful how over the years the character's *evolved*.

ALICE: Who first thought of putting her on a Moped?

JUNE: That was because of the sound effects. As long as I was on the old bike, listeners never knew whether I was static or mobile.

MERCY: It's a unique sound—Sister George on her Moped, whizzing through the countryside, singing snatches of hymns. [*She drinks her tea*]

JUNE: I got into a terrible row the other day because I sang a hymn which sounded like '*On the good ship Venus...*'

MERCY: A traditional air?

JUNE: I've found it safer to stick to hymns. Once I tried a pop song, and d'you know — hundreds of letters came in protesting.

MERCY: We learn from experience. But we don't want *Applehurst* falling behind the times.

JUNE: No. [*She looks away. Worried*] No, of course not.

MERCY: But we must constantly examine criticism, and if it's constructive, we must act on it. Ruthlessly.

JUNE: What sort of criticism?

MERCY: Oh, nothing in *particular*. At least . . .

JUNE: But *what*?

MERCY: Well, that, I'm afraid, brings me — [*she rises*] to the unpleasant part of my business.

ALICE: Oh, dear!

MERCY: But first, would you show me to the little girls' room?

JUNE: [*rising*] Alice — show Mrs. Mercy to the . . .

ALICE: [*rising and moving up L*] This way, Mrs. Mercy. [ALICE *exits up L. MERCY follows her off*]

JUNE: [*muttering*] 'Little girls' . . .' [*She moves to the table behind the sofa, stubs out her cigar in the ashtray on it, and looks off up L*]

ALICE: [*off*] It's that door there. [JUNE *sees* MERCY's *brief-case on the sofa, looks off L, hurriedly picks up the brief-case, crosses to the armchair R and opens the case.* ALICE *enters up L and stands at the top of the steps*]

[*Aghast*] What are you doing?

JUNE: [*turning*] Shh! Keep a look-out. [*She rummages in the case*]

ALICE: [*moving up C*] You can't, you mustn't.

JUNE: [*taking a folder from the case*] My own personal file.

ALICE: [*in an hysterical whisper*] Put it back! [JUNE *searches in the folder, takes an envelope from it and reads the inscription*]

JUNE: 'Sister George. Confidential.' [*The sound of a water cistern flushing is heard off L*]

ALICE: She's coming. [JUNE *quickly replaces the folder in the brief-case, moves up R of the sofa, closes the brief-case and puts it on the sofa. She realizes too late that she has still got the envelope in her hand, so quickly hides it behind a cushion at the right end of the sofa. She then picks up the doll Emmeline from the table behind the sofa*]

JUNE: So Emmeline said: 'I don't want any drop scones today, thank you very much.' [MERCY *enters up L and crosses below the sofa.* JUNE *and* ALICE *stand rigid with suspense*]

MERCY: I got on the scales, to see if I've put on any weight. [*She picks up her brief-case*]

JUNE: [*indicating the tea table*] I don't suppose... [*Meaning 'you would like any more tea?'*]

MERCY: [*sitting on the sofa*] Now, then...

ALICE: I'll make myself scarce. [ALICE *exits to the kitchen*]

MERCY: Please sit down. [JUNE *sits in the armchair R*]

You won't hold it against me if I speak quite plainly?

JUNE: Please do.

MERCY: It's my unpleasant duty to haul you over the coals and administer a severe reprimand.

JUNE: [*with no apology in her tone*] Oh?

MERCY: Believe me. Sister George, I'd much rather let bygones be bygones...

JUNE: [*in her country accent*] Let sleeping dogs lie.

MERCY: Precisely. But I must remind you of the little chat we had just about a year ago, after that unfortunate incident in the Club — involving a lady colleague of mine.

JUNE: [*in her country accent*] Well, we don't want to rake over old embers.

MERCY: I don't intend to. But in the light of recent events, it's difficult to forget an incident as vivid as the pouring of a glass of beer over the Assistant Head of Talks. I had hoped one black mark — [*she opens her brief-case*] would have been enough for you, but this morning — [*she takes out a clip-board and removes a sheet of paper from it*] I received this memo from the Director of Religious Broadcasting. [*She hands the paper to* JUNE] I should like to have your comments. [*She puts the brief-case beside her on the sofa, but holds the clip-board on her knee*]

[JUNE *reads the paper then jumps up violently*]

JUNE: [*excitedly*] It's a lie! It's an utter, bloody lie!

MERCY: [*firmly*] Please calm yourself, Miss Buckridge. Kindly hand me back the paper.

JUNE: [*handing the paper to* MERCY] It's — preposterous! [*She moves up R of the sofa*]

MERCY: [*looking at the paper as she replaces it on the clip-board*] I take it you don't deny that you were drinking in *The Bells* on the night of the nineteenth?

JUNE: [*turning at the fireplace*] How the hell should I know? [*She crosses to C and calls*] Alice! Come here. [ALICE *enters from the kitchen, wide-eyed and worried*]

ALICE: You want me?

JUNE: Where was I on the night of the nineteenth?

MERCY: I'm sorry to involve you in this, Miss McNaught. [*She rises*]

ALICE: [*quietly*] That was a Wednesday: I was at the City Lit.

JUNE: You would be. [*She moves to L of* MERCY] All right; I possibly was drinking at *The Bells* on the night in question, having a few pints with the boys. There's no crime in that, is there?

MERCY: Miss Buckridge, according to this letter — [*she refers to the second paper on her clip-board*] from the Mother Superior of the Convent of the Sacred Heart of Jesus, you boarded a taxi which had stopped at the traffic lights at Langham Place...

JUNE: I thought it was empty.

MERCY: [*reading*] 'A taxi bearing as passengers two novitiate nuns from Ireland who had just arrived at King's Cross Station.'

JUNE: How was I to know?

MERCY: You boarded this taxi in a state of advanced inebriation — [*she looks at* JUNE] and — [*she consults the paper*] proceeded to assault the two nuns, subjecting them to actual physical violence.

ALICE: [*moving below the table LC*] You didn't really!

JUNE: No, no, no, of course not. I'd had a few pints — I saw this cab, got in — and there were these two black things — screaming blue murder.

MERCY: Why didn't you get out again?

JUNE: Well, I'd had a very nasty shock myself. What with their screaming and flapping about — I thought they were bats, vampire bats. It was they who attacked me. I remember getting all entangled in their skirts and petticoats and things — the taxi driver had to pull me free.

MERCY: A deplorable anecdote. [*She refers to the paper*] According to the Mother Superior, one of the nuns required medical treatment for shock, and is still under sedation. [*She pauses*] She thought it was the devil. [*She moves to the sofa, sits on it at the right end and replaces the clip-board in her brief-case*]

ALICE: George, how could you!

JUNE: [*moving to R of* ALICE] Don't you start on me. Back to the kitchen. Washing up. Presto!

ALICE: [*firmly*] No, I'm staying here. [*She sits L of the table LC*] This concerns me, too.

JUNE: [*moving up C*] It was all a ghastly mistake.

MERCY: No doubt, but it'll take some explaining.

JUNE: Fancy reporting it to the Director of Religious Broadcasting. What a nasty thing to do for a holy woman. [*She moves to L of the sofa*]

MERCY: The Mother Superior is responsible for the nuns in her charge.

JUNE: [*leaning over the left arm of the sofa to* MERCY] Then she should jolly well teach them how to behave in public. I got the fright of my life, in there. Those nuns were like *mice*—albino mice—with teeny little white faces and weeny little red eyes. And they were vicious, too. They scratched and they bit. [*She bares her arm*] Look—you can still see the tooth marks—do you see that? I've a good mind to make a counter-complaint to the Mother Superior. [*She moves up R of the table LC*] They deserve to be scourged in their cells.

MERCY: [*wearily*] I can hardly put through a report to the Controller, informing him of your allegation that you were bitten by two nuns.

JUNE: No, well, you could say...

MERCY: Let's be practical, Sister George—we're concerned with retaining the trust and respect of the public. Now people are perfectly well aware that artists frequently work under great emotional stress. We do all we can to gloss over minor disciplinary offences, but we simply cannot tolerate this sort of behavior. It's things like this which make people resent paying more for their wireless licenses. Thousands of pounds spent on public relations—[*she rises and moves RC*] and you jeopardize it all with your reckless and foolish behavior. Really, Sister George, we have every reason to be very, very angry with you. [JUNE, *beaten, sits wearily R of the table LC*]

JUNE: What do you want me to *do*?

MERCY: [*moving to R of* JUNE] You must write a letter immediately to the Mother Superior, apologizing sincerely for your behaviour, and I suggest you offer a small donation for some charity connected with the Convent. Then you must send a copy of your letter to the Director of Religious Broadcasting, with a covering note from you, couched in suitable terms.

JUNE: You mean: humbling myself?

ALICE: [*rising and moving above the table LC*] Don't worry, Mrs. Mercy, I'll see she does it and I'll make quite sure she doesn't get into any mischief in the future.

MERCY: There speaks a true friend. [*To* JUNE] You're very lucky to have someone like Miss McNaught to rely on. Treasure her. [*She crosses to R of the sofa, then moves above it and collects her gloves, handbag and brief-case*]

JUNE: [*bitterly*] I'll treasure her all right. [ALICE *moves to the sofa, sits on the left arm of it and puts her feet on the seat*]

ALICE: I'll see to it that the letters are written and sent off right away.

MERCY: [*moving down RC and putting on her gloves*] Good. That's what I like to hear. [*To* JUNE] I'll leave you in Miss McNaught's expert charge.

JUNE: What about *Applehurst?*

MERCY: [*non-committally*] That's another, rather more complex problem.

JUNE: [*rising and moving to L of* MERCY] But—has anything been decided about the future?

MERCY: I'm afraid I can't say anything about that at the moment.

JUNE: [*moving down L*] It comes as a bit of a shock to me, you know, all this.

MERCY: [*moving C*] It comes as a bit of a shock to me, too, I assure you, particularly as I understand that you often open church bazaars. [JUNE *turns slowly to face* MERCY]

ALICE: [*rising and moving to R of* MERCY] I'll look after her. I'll keep her away from convents.

MERCY: You keep her on a tight rein, and all will be well.

ALICE: I'm sure it will. Between us we'll keep her in order.

MERCY: [*jocularly*] She won't stand a chance, will she? [ALICE *moves down R, and keeps a steady look on* JUNE *throughout the next passage*]

JUNE: [*moving to L of* MERCY] Look here—I'm sorry—you know—if I've been a bad boy. [MERCY *turns her charm on* JUNE *and shakes hands with her*]

MERCY: Well, good-bye, dear Sister George. Keep your chin up. Things are never as bad as they seem.

JUNE: [*in her country accent; listlessly*] Every cloud has a silver lining.

MERCY: That's the spirit. And—[*she whispers confidentially*] no more walk-outs at rehearsals, eh? If you have any complaints please come and see me about them.

JUNE: [*in her country accent*] Well, it's the creaking gate that gets oiled.

MERCY: [*reflecting for a moment*] A somewhat unfortunate simile. [JUNE *looks at* MERCY]

[*She turns to* ALICE] So nice to have met you.

ALICE: [*moving to R of* MERCY] Nice to have met *you*, Mrs. Mercy. [MERCY *crosses to the arch R*]

[*She follows to L of* MERCY] What's the subject of your talk tomorrow? Is it a secret, or are you allowed to tell?

MERCY: It's family planning this week and foundation garments next.

[MERCY *and* ALICE *exit to the arch.* JUNE *moves* RC *and looks nervously after them*]

ALICE: [*off*] Good-bye. [*The front door is heard to close.* JUNE *turns away quickly to* LC. ALICE *enters* R *and stands in the archway* R]

[*She gives* JUNE *a meaningful look*] Well!

JUNE: [*alarmed*] Did she say anything? Did she drop any hints behind my back?

ALICE: [*moving above the sofa; sarcastically*] No. Just general comments—you know—about—[*angrily*] nuns in taxis. [*She collects* JUNE's *gin glass from the table behind the sofa*]

JUNE: What do you mean?

ALICE: [*crossing to the sideboard*] Nuns. You know—N-U-N-S. Brides of Christ. [*She bangs the glass down on to the tray on the sideboard*]

JUNE: [*moving C*] Oh, I see what's biting you.

ALICE: [*moving above the table LC; in an outburst*] How could you! How could you make such an exhibition of yourself? [*She stacks the crockery on to the tray*]

JUNE: [*trying to laugh* ALICE *out of it*] Oh, come on, be your age. Don't be so bloody—squeamish.

ALICE: [*primly*] I think you owe me some sort of explanation.

JUNE: [*chuckling*] When I think of all those petticoats... [*She waves her arms*]

ALICE: It's the sort of thing you used to do when I first knew you. In that club in Notting Hill Gate. I remember how you used to go clomping about, without a bra, hitting girls over the head. [*She picks up the tray and puts it through the hatch*]

JUNE: Kindly keep your foul-mouthed recollections to yourself. [ALICE *returns to the table LC*]

In my young days...

ALICE: [*collecting the jam and plates*] Your young days were spent in a cul-de-sac in Aldershot, with the Band of Hope on one side and the Foot Clinic on the other. You told me so yourself. [*She puts the jam and plates through the hatch*]

JUNE: [*angrily*] How dare you! [*She moves to the sofa and sits on it at the right end*] This is a respectable house—and I'll thank you to remember who's paying the rent.

ALICE: [*folding the tablecloth*] Not much longer, perhaps.

JUNE: They wouldn't dare get rid of me because of this—of this trivial incident.

ALICE: [*imitating* JUNE's *country accent*] We none of us know what the future may hold for us. [*She puts the tablecloth in the sideboard cupboard*]

JUNE: [*after a pause*] Childie, I'm worried. I say, do me a favor. [ALICE *reaches through the kitchen door and collects a dust-pan and brush*]

ALICE: What? [*She goes to the sideboard and brushes up the remains of the cake thrown by* JUNE]

JUNE: Go and ask Madame Xenia to come up. She's an expert on the future.

ALICE: Oh, I can't. She's probably got a client.

JUNE: Maybe she's between appointments. Go on.

ALICE: [*kneeling and sweeping up crumbs L of the table LC*] I can't just *barge* in . . .

JUNE: Well, it wouldn't be the first time. Remember when I was bitten by that Lakeland Terrier and you thought I had rabies. She can always tell us what's going to happen. Go on.

ALICE: [*rising; exasperated*] Ohhh! [*She returns the dust-pan and brush to the kitchen*]

JUNE: [*rising and moving C*] This is an emergency. Extreme measures must be taken. Go and get her at once.

ALICE: I can't. She hates my guts.

JUNE: Madame Xenia? Why?

ALICE: She thinks I'm after her lodger. [JUNE *looks menacing*]

It's complete fantasy.

JUNE: [*in her country accent; ominously*] There's no smoke without fire.

ALICE: Just like the last one you scared off.

JUNE: [*in her own voice*] I could see which way the wind was blowing. I soon nipped that in the bud.

ALICE: I only helped him with his homework. He was a mere boy.

JUNE: [*decisively*] There is nothing mere about boys. Now go and fetch her at once and watch your step.

ALICE: You've always got to have someone to do your dirty work. [*She trails off and crosses to* R *with the slummocky walk typical of all her movements throughout the play*]

JUNE: Thanks — you're a pal. [ALICE *exits through the arch R*]

[*She moves to L of the table behind the sofa, picks up the framed certificate and reads it*] '. . . and in recognition of your devoted work and care for the old and sick.' [*She replaces the certificate, moves to R of the sofa, remembers the envelope and takes it from behind the cushion. She is tempted, does not dare to open it, replaces it behind the cushion and crosses to C*]

ALICE: [*off R*] I'm so sorry to drag you away.

XENIA: [*off R*] That's all right. I know. I know. [MADAME XENIA *enters through the arch R. She is a hawk-faced, elderly woman of foreign origin, hennaed and hung with beads. She carries a little evening bag with a pack of playing cards in it.* ALICE *follows her on*] George! George? Darling? What's the matter?

ALICE: [*moving down R*] Madame was in the middle of a consultation with a client.

JUNE: Oh, I *am* sorry.

XENIA: [*crossing to R of* JUNE *and embracing her*] Never mind. You are my friend. [*She holds* JUNE *at arm's length*] Always you come first. Now — [*she pats* JUNE'*s arm*] darling, what's the matter?

JUNE: Madame Xenia, I'm worried out of my wits. It's the B.B.C. They're driving me mad.

XENIA: [*crossing above* JUNE *to the table LC*] They will suffer for it. I will put curses on them. [*She sits above the table LC. To* JUNE; *professionally*] Sit down; make yourself at home.

JUNE: Thanks. [*She sits R of the table LC*]

XENIA: Oh, I'm sorry, I forgot. I always say it to people to make them relax. Right. Would you draw the curtains, please? [*She takes the cards from her bag*]

JUNE: [*rising*] Certainly. [*She goes to the window and closes the curtains*]

XENIA: [*to* ALICE] And you: will you please sit facing the East.

ALICE: [*looking around*] Which way's the East?

XENIA: [*pointing L*] There. Towards Great Portland Street. [*She shuffles the cards*]

ALICE: [*sitting on the pouffe and facing L*] Yes, of course. [JUNE *moves C*]

XENIA: [*looking at* JUNE] I require a personal possession from you — [JUNE *looks startled*]

—to hold in my hand. To connect with your vibrations. Anything — a piece of jewellery . . .

JUNE: [*sheepishly*] I don't wear jewellery. Will a hankie do? [*She takes a handkerchief from her pocket then resumes her seat R of the table*]

XENIA: [*taking* JUNE'*s handkerchief*] Beautiful. Now to work. First a warning. Next week will be tough for Sagittarians — Mars is in conjunction with Venus, and I don't have to tell you what that means. [*She puts the cards on the table*] Cut the cards.

JUNE: [*cutting the cards*] All right?

XENIA: Again. [JUNE *cuts again*]

And once more, just for luck. [JUNE *cuts again*]

ALICE: As the bishop said to the actress. [XENIA *turns up one card from each little pile*]

JUNE: [*to* ALICE; *sternly*] We can dispense with observations from the East.

XENIA: [*scrutinizing the cards*] A short journey to see a friend; a pleasant surprise; unexpected money. [*She turns up another card*] The Queen of Spades—a woman in black you do not like?

ALICE: The Mother Superior?

JUNE: Shut up!

XENIA: Whoever it is—keep out of her way—she's no good to you.

JUNE: [*stuttering*] What—what is she going to do?

XENIA: [*consulting the cards*] She's inviting you to a big do.

JUNE: [*incredulously*] The Mother Superior? [ALICE *giggles and* JUNE *laughs with her*]

XENIA: I see lots of people, lots of drink, dancing…

ALICE: [*lightly*] I know! It's not the convent—it's the drag ball at Richmond.

XENIA: [*continuing with the cards*] Maybe. A slight emotional upset. [JUNE *and* XENIA *look at* ALICE]

Nothing serious. [*She looks at the cards*] You hear of a broken romantic association. You catch a cold—a very bad cold.

JUNE: [*alarmed*] When?

XENIA: [*thoughtfully*] Maybe it's because I'm holding your handkerchief. Forget the cold. [*She returns the handkerchief to* JUNE] What else? [*She looks at the cards*]

JUNE: My career.

XENIA: I can see a red-headed man.

JUNE: [*turning to* ALICE] Ginger the publican. [*To* XENIA] What's he doing?

XENIA: I'm afraid it's not very clear. Ah! I see a letter—a very important letter.

ALICE: [*suddenly remembering*] The envelope!

JUNE: [*panic-stricken*] The envelope.

ALICE and JUNE: [*together*] The envelope! [ALICE *rises and runs to the sofa.* JUNE *jumps up*]

XENIA: [*helpfully*] It could be a postcard.

ALICE: [*snatching the letter from behind the cushion*] Here it is. [*To* JUNE] Do you want to open it?

JUNE: [*anguished*] No.

ALICE: Let's send it back to her—tell her she must have dropped it out of her bag.

JUNE: [*crossing to* ALICE] No, no. It's fallen into our hands—we'd better read it.

XENIA: [*rising and crossing to* JUNE] May I see the envelope?

JUNE: Yes, of course. [*She gives the envelope to* XENIA]

[XENIA *steps mysteriously down C and holds the envelope to her cheek*]

Do you—do you get any—vibrations?

XENIA: [*carefully*] Mmm. It's difficult to say. It could mean one of two things.

JUNE: [*squaring her shoulders*] Give it to me. I'm going to open it. [*She takes the envelope from* XENIA, *crosses down LC and opens it*] What must be, must be. [*She glances at the contents and collapses on to the chair L of the table LC*] Oh, my God! [*She drops the letter to the floor*]

[ALICE *rushes and kneels L of* JUNE. XENIA *kneels and picks up the letter*]

ALICE: George! What's the matter? George! [JUNE *remains impassive.* XENIA *reads the letter*]

[*To* Xenia] What does it say?

XENIA: [*reading*] 'Memo from Audience Research. Latest Popularity Ratings.' [*She rises slowly*] 'Sister George sixty-four point five per cent. Ginger Kopkins sixty-eight.' [ALICE *collapses, sitting back on her heels*]

JUNE: That's the weapon they've been waiting for. [*She rises*] Now they'll kill me. [JUNE *rushes towards the bedroom door up C as—*

the CURTAIN *quickly falls*]

Act Two

Scene I
Scene: *The same. A week later. 4 a.m.*

Before the CURTAIN *rises, as the house-lights fade, the 'Applehurst Theme' is heard.*

When the CURTAIN *rises, the music fades. By the light of the table-lamp on the side-board and shafts of light from the archway R,* JUNE *can be discerned sitting R of the table LC, her head in her arms. She is wearing a dressing-gown over pyjamas. On the table beside her is a bottle of gin, a tumbler, a press-cutting book and her spectacles. The window curtains are open and show a faint blue light outside. After a few moments,* JUNE *is roused from her torpor by the sound of an alarm clock in the bed-room up LC.*

JUNE: [*looking up; startled*] What...? It must be morning. I must have dropped off. [*She calls*] Alice! Childie! Rise and shine—that's if you persist in this ridiculous enterprise. Childie! [*The sound of the alarm ceases*]

I'm in the living-room. [*She drops her head on to her arms*]

[ALICE *enters quietly from the bedroom. She is dressed only in a black brassiere and pants and carries a bundle of clothing. She puts the clothes on the sofa, moves quietly and mischievously to R of* JUNE, *and attacks her, pinching and punching her right arm*]

ALICE: Pinch, punch, first of the month. [JUNE, *very startled, jumps up and clutches the back of her chair*]
JUNE: Are you out of your mind?
ALICE: [*retreating RC; squashed*] It's the first of the month—October.
JUNE: You could have given me a heart attack.

ALICE: Sorry. [*She goes to the switch below the fireplace and switches on the table-lamp R and the standard lamp*]
JUNE: [*collapsing on to the chair R of the table LC*] Gawd Almighty! What's the time?
ALICE: [*glancing at the clock on the mantelpiece*] Ten to four. [*She takes her slippers from the pile of clothes, and puts them on*]
JUNE: When are you supposed to get there?
ALICE: There's no rush; the gang gets there at about five. Have you made out your list?
JUNE: No.
ALICE: [*annoyed*] Well, why didn't you? You are a nuisance. Are you sure you don't want me to try for *Swan Lake*? [*She takes a pullover from the sofa and puts it on*]
JUNE: Positive. I can't stand those bloody little cygnets prancing about in their tu-tus.
ALICE: All right, all right. Nobody's forcing you.
JUNE: [*rising and stretching*] My sympathy's entirely with Von Rothbart. [*She moves to the sideboard*]
ALICE: I'll just try for *Giselle*, then.
JUNE: Yeah, you try. [*She takes a box of cheroots from the sideboard cupboard*] And *Petrushka*—don't forget *Petrushka*.
ALICE: You told me last night you didn't want to see *Petrushka*.
JUNE: [*moving to the table LC*] Did I? Well, I changed my mind. [*She puts the box on the table*]

[ALICE, *exasperated, goes to the mantelpiece and collects a Covent Garden brochure and a pencil*]

ALICE: Oh, you are a nuisance! I'd put a tick against *Petrushka* and then I crossed it out, and now I've got to put a tick again. [*She kneels above the pouffe, puts the brochure on it and looks through it*] And now I can't find it.
JUNE: [*sitting R of the table LC*] You're annoying me, you know. Stop getting so—so het-up about your bloody ballet. [*She pours a drink for herself*]
ALICE: It's all very well for you to talk—you'll be sitting at home. There's a big queue, and if you don't know what to ask for...
JUNE: You've got plenty of time to decide what to ask for. You're only queueing for queue tickets now. [*She drinks*]
ALICE: I know. But we've all got our lists. [*She rises, moves to the fireplace and studies the brochure*] Anyway, there's no certainty that we get what we ask for: you only get so many for Fonteyn and Nureyev.
JUNE: In that case, why make a list?

ALICE: [*on the brink of hysteria*] You've got to ask for it first, even if you don't get it.

JUNE: You'll get something you're *not* asking for in a minute.

ALICE: [*turning to the mantelpiece and writing on the brochure*] Anyway, it wouldn't have hurt you to come with me. You're up.

JUNE: I wouldn't be seen dead with that mob. What a collection! [ALICE *puts the brochure and pencil on the mantelpiece and crosses to* JUNE]

ALICE: There's nothing wrong with them. They're very nice, the regulars. I've known some of them for fifteen years. Do you know — there's a woman there who follows Anya Linden everywhere.

JUNE: *Everywhere?*

ALICE: [*crossing to the hatch*] Oh, shut up!

JUNE: Anyway, I did come with you one day — remember? Never again. All that gossip and name-dropping... [ALICE *reaches through the hatch and switches on the electric kettle, then puts a spoonful of instant coffee from a tin into a mug standing on the hatch shelf*]

ALICE: The only reason you didn't like it was because you were embarrassed by the lorry-driver. [*She picks up a knapsack from the floor L and puts it on the table LC*]

JUNE: What lorry-driver?

ALICE: The one that called at you 'That's a nice pair of headlamps'.

JUNE: I had totally forgotten. Besides, he was paying me a compliment — unlike the gentleman in Soho, who suggested that you should wear a pair of sun-glasses for a brassiere.

ALICE: [*taking a packet of potato crisps from the hatch shelf*] Don't be disgusting!

JUNE: [*jeering*] You're my flat mate in more senses than one. [*She pours herself a gin*]

[*There is a pause.* ALICE *puts the crisps in the knapsack*]

ALICE: George, don't drink any more.

JUNE: [*dangerously*] Mind your own business.

ALICE: Night after night I find you sitting up — with a bottle of gin and that old press-cutting book. And then you wonder why you're tired.

JUNE: I can't sleep.

ALICE: You don't even try. [*She picks up the knapsack and crosses to the sofa*] You must try to relax — unwind.

JUNE: [*imitating; caustically*] Relax — unwind! It's easy for you to talk. [ALICE *puts her office skirt and slip into the knapsack*]

ALICE: You've been impossible ever since that day Mrs. Mercy came to tea.

JUNE: Well, I'm more impossible since I ran into her again yesterday.
ALICE: Where? [*She drops the knapsack to the floor*]
JUNE: At B.H.
ALICE: Was she friendly? [*She sits on the sofa*]
JUNE: She smiled at me — with the same expression as my old cat Tiddles had when she used to look in the goldfish bowl. Until one Sunday my parents and I came home from church, and there on the table lay the five goldfish — [*she demonstrates on the table*] all neatly laid out, like sardines.
ALICE: Did she — say anything to you?
JUNE: [*rising*] I'll show you what she did. Get up. Go on, stand up. I'll show you what she did. [*She moves RC*]

[ALICE *rises and moves to R of* JUNE] You're me. I was just coming out from the studio on my way to the canteen, when I turned a corner rather sharply, and ran slap bang into her. Go on — bump into me.

ALICE: [*peevishly shifting from foot to foot*] Oh, I don't want to do that.
JUNE: Don't be so soppy. *Bump into me.* [ALICE *turns her back to the audience and feebly pushes her right shoulder against* JUNE'S *left shoulder*]

Oh, God help us! No, properly, daftie!

ALICE: [*shifting from foot to foot*] I've got to go in a minute. [*She moves to the fireplace*]
JUNE: [*moving below the table LC*] You'll wait till I've bloody well finished with you. Now then: you're coming down the corridor. [*She claps her hands and gives an imperious gesture*] Start! [ALICE *takes a run, bumps into* JUNE *and floors her. The light increases a little for dawn effect.* JUNE *rises.* ALICE *watches with a slightly malicious smile*]

[*As* MERCY] Oh, it's you. [*She surveys* ALICE *with* MERCY'S *half-smile*] Chin up, Sister George. [*She pats* ALICE'S *arm and crosses below her to R*] Chin up, indeed, the lousy old cow. You noticed the way she patted my arm — as if to say 'Sorry, it can't be helped'.

ALICE: You're imagining things again.
JUNE: [*moving down R*] She's been avoiding me, I tell you, and I know why.
ALICE: She was probably in a hurry to get somewhere. A committee meeting or something. [*She moves RC*]
JUNE: They've had that. And I found out what happened.
ALICE: [*alarmed*] What?

JUNE: [*sitting on the chair down R*] I'm to be written out of next Tuesday's
episode.
ALICE: What?
JUNE: Are you deaf? I said . . .
ALICE: I heard. So what? It's happened before. Every time you go on
holiday.
JUNE: But I'm not going on holiday, am I? [ALICE *is silent*]

Sister George is confined to bed with a bad cold.

ALICE: Oh, now, that in itself . . . [JUNE *rises, moves above the arch R and turns
away*]
JUNE: That in itself could mean a dress rehearsal for my extinction.
ALICE: [*sitting on the pouffe*] Nothing of the sort.
JUNE: They want to see what it sounds like without me. If I am
expendable.
ALICE: What about the following episodes?
JUNE: [*grimly*] We shall know soon. The new scripts are due in the post this
morning. I can see what is going to happen. [*She moves down R and
wraps her dressing-gown tightly around her*] That cold's going to get
worse — I can feel it in my bones. It'll turn to bronchitis, then
pneumonia, and before I know where I am I shall be out like a light.
[*She sits in the chair down R*]
ALICE: [*only half-convinced*] You are making a mountain out of a molehill.
You've missed episodes before — it's nothing to lose sleep over.
JUNE: That's what you think. [*She blows her nose*] Anyway, I'm not the only
one.
ALICE: What do you mean?
JUNE: Did you know that you talk in your sleep?
ALICE: I don't.
JUNE: You do. I heard you. Last night and distinctly again tonight. You woke
me up.
ALICE: [*nervously*] What did I say?
JUNE: You were tossing about, and mumbling something. And then out it
came, loud and clear.
ALICE: [*unconvinced*] What?
JUNE: [*leaning back with arms spread out; in a plaintive high-pitched voice*] 'Take
me!'
ALICE: You're lying!
JUNE: [*as before*] 'Take me, Isidore!'
ALICE: [*rising and moving to* JUNE] That's a filthy lie, and you know it.

JUNE: The 'Isidore' wasn't any too distinct: it might have been some other name.

ALICE: [*moving C*] I don't believe a word of this.

JUNE: [*more in sorrow than in anger*] You're having an affair with someone, aren't you?

ALICE: [*looking back over her left shoulder*] I wish I were.

JUNE: [*after a pause; crushed*] That was very — unkind.

ALICE: Well, you asked for it. Always nagging me. Even if I did shout 'Take me' in my sleep — and I am not aware of it...

JUNE: You couldn't be, of course, because you were asleep at the time.

ALICE: [*moving above the table LC*] All right: even if I did, it might have meant 'take me for a walk' — or — [*brightly*] 'take me to the ballet'.

JUNE: A likely story. [ALICE *goes to the hatch, switches off the kettle then pours hot water on to the coffee in the mug*]

ALICE: You always put the nastiest interpretation on things.

JUNE: [*rising and moving RC*] In nine cases out of ten I'm right. Are you making yourself some breakfast before you go? [*She moves C*]

ALICE: Just a cup of coffee. I usually have a hot pie later on with the gang. In one of the workmen's cafés. [*She picks up her coffee and sits L of the table LC*] It's ever such fun, really. You get the ballet crowd and the night shift from the market all mixing together.

JUNE: Sounds scintillating.

ALICE: It's ever so lively. [JUNE *sits R of the table LC*]

Why don't you get dressed and come? They'd be thrilled to see you, and everyone would ask you for your autograph.

JUNE: [*in a high-pitched tone*] 'Take me!'

ALICE: Oh, George!

JUNE: No, you run along and enjoy yourself. Leave me here — waiting for the new scripts to arrive.

ALICE: I don't know what's the matter with you just lately. You've become really — morbid. You used to be such fun.

JUNE: What are you talking about? We're going to that fancy dress ball tonight, aren't we? I bet it'll be you who'll be pale and wan tonight — after getting up at this unearthly hour.

ALICE: [*rising and moving to the sideboard*] I'm glad you said that. I must take my iron pills. [*She collects a small bottle of pills from the sideboard*] They help to keep me awake. [*She shakes out a pill, swallows it and replaces the cap on the bottle*]

JUNE: Let me see them.

ALICE: What for?
JUNE: [*emphatically*] Let me see them.
ALICE: [*handing the bottle to* JUNE] All right. [*She sits L of the table LC*]
JUNE: [*examining the bottle*] Why doesn't it say what they are? [ALICE *looks nonplussed*]

There's no name on the label.

ALICE: I don't know.
JUNE: [*scrutinizing the label*] All it says—[*she has difficulty in deciphering the writing*] is—'One to be taken every day, as prescribed.' [*She sniffs the bottle*] I don't believe these are iron pills at all. They're those birth pills. [*She bangs the bottle down on to the table*]
ALICE: Oh, really! [*She picks up the bottle*] Dr Kunjaghari gave them to me. Why don't you go and ask him?
JUNE: [*viciously*] Because I don't trust Dr Kunjaghari, that's why. He's a quack. He's like those Indians who come to the door in turbans, flogging brass bangles for rheumatism.
ALICE: Perhaps you'd like to have them chemically analysed?
JUNE: It would shake you if I did, wouldn't it?
ALICE: [*rising and putting the pills on the sideboard*] You can do what you like—you'd only make yourself look ridiculous. [*She crosses to the sofa and sorts through the pile of clothing. Contemptuously*] Like that time you rang up at the office, pretending to be Mrs. Katz.
JUNE: Well, it served its purpose—it gave him a fright.
ALICE: It very nearly got me the sack. He knew it was you.
JUNE: He couldn't prove it.
ALICE: He's a solicitor—he could prove anything. Can't find my socks. [*She picks up the knapsack, puts it on the armchair R and rummages inside*]
JUNE: I say—[*she looks benignly at* ALICE] seeing you in black pants reminds me of the A.T.S. We had to wear regulation black woolen pants. We used to refer to them as our black-outs. One day, a chap came to talk to us on the subject 'What not to do with our black-outs down'. He couldn't understand why we kept giggling.
ALICE: [*bringing out a pair of long white socks*] Found them. [*She sits on the pouffe, kicks off her slippers and puts on the socks*]
JUNE: [*after a pause*] Your legs are unusually white—luminous white. Loooo-minous white. I don't think I've ever seen such white legs.
ALICE: They don't get much sun on them.
JUNE: There's something uniquely touching about white legs—especially when they are loo-minous white. You're pale altogether, you know.

You're anemic—you ought to take iron pills. [ALICE *throws* JUNE *a meaningful glance and puts on her slippers*]

I mean proper pills—not that muck. [*She pours herself another gin*]

ALICE: Haven't you had enough? [*She rises, crosses to the sofa, kicks off her slippers and picks up her slacks from the pile of clothing*]

JUNE: [*quickly*] No. [*She raises her glass and chuckles*] To absent friends. Your health, albino mice.

ALICE: [*putting on her slacks; with a smile*] You *are* naughty.

JUNE: Say that again.

ALICE: What?

JUNE: [*pouring another drink*] What you just said.

ALICE: You *are* naughty?

JUNE: That's it. The same inflection. Takes me back years.

ALICE: Oh. You mean…

JUNE: When we first met—in Mrs. Goodbody's tastefully furnished bed-sitters. D'you know for weeks I watched you come and go—and never said a word to you.

ALICE: [*collecting a windcheater from the sofa and putting it on*] You were different then—you hadn't become famous.

JUNE: Every morning I used to watch you go to work. Punctually at ten past nine every morning. You were always in a rush.

ALICE: [*fastening the windcheater*] I had to get on the underground at twenty past.

JUNE: Often you were in such a hurry you would fall over the doorstep; or, if it had been raining, you'd come slithering out, shouting 'oops!' [ALICE *picks up her shoes, scarf and woolen cap and puts the scarf and cap in the knapsack*]

ALICE: I had no idea you were watching me. [*She sits in the armchair R*]

JUNE: One night, I went into the bathroom just after you'd had a bath. The mirror was all steamed up, and the bath mat was moist and glistening where you'd stood on it. There was a smell of talcum powder and bath crystals—it was like an enchanted wood. I stood quite still on that mat—in your footsteps—and I saw that you'd left your comb behind. It was a small pink plastic comb, and it had your hairs in it. I kept that comb as a souvenir. And all this time I'd never spoken a word to you.

ALICE: [*after a pause*] You soon made up for it. [*She puts on her shoes*]

JUNE: That night your boy friend saw you home, I knew I'd have to strike quickly. [ALICE *rises, picks up the knapsack, puts it on the pouffe, then kneels on the floor above the pouffe*]

ALICE: That was Roger. He wanted to marry me.

JUNE: [*bitterly*] That's what they all said—and you fell for it, silly goose.

ALICE: [*pulling out the cap and scarf and putting them on the floor L of the pouffe*] Some of them meant it; Roger meant it.

JUNE: What are you talking about; Roger was already married.

ALICE: [*adamantly*] He still meant it. I liked Roger; he had a ginger moustache.

JUNE: What a lot of rubbish. His moustache was ginger because he used to singe it with his cigarettes—you told me so yourself. You said that every time he kissed you it tasted all burnt and beery. [*She drinks*]

ALICE: [*after a pause*] I might have had babies. [*There is a long pause*]

JUNE: [*quietly*] You haven't been lonely, exactly. [ALICE *picks up the cap, rises, goes to the fireplace, looks in the mirror and puts the cap on. It is a babyish knitted cap which fastens under her chin*]

ALICE: [*changing the subject*] There's a performance of *Petrushka* on the nineteenth. I might try for that.

JUNE: [*rising; suddenly*] Shh! Shh! [*She pauses and listens*] Was that the post?

ALICE: At this time in the morning? It won't be here for hours yet. You really ought to go to bed. [*There is a pause*]

JUNE: [*crossing below the table LC to L of it; seriously*] What am I going to do? They're driving me round the bend.

ALICE: You're driving yourself round the bend. [*She crosses to C*] Why don't you go to bed?

JUNE: [*sitting L of the table LC; desperately*] Because I *can't* sleep.

ALICE: [*moving above the table LC*] Shall I get you some hot milk?

JUNE: Urghh!

ALICE: You'll catch cold, you know, sitting up like this.

JUNE: I've already got a cold.

ALICE: [*moving above* JUNE *to L of her*] Well, keep your throat covered up, then. [*She arranges* JUNE's *collar*] Put your dressing-gown on properly. It's time we got you a new dressing-gown—this collar is all frayed. I'll put some new braid on it tomorrow. There, better?

JUNE: Thanks.

ALICE: [*moving above the table LC and indicating the gin bottle*] Shall I put this away?

JUNE: [*picking up the bottle*] No, I just want to hold it for a moment. [*She hugs the bottle*]

ALICE: [*moving C and looking at the clock*] I ought to be going—it's half past four. [*She turns to* JUNE. *Worried*] Will you be all right? [*She moves to R of the table LC and faces* JUNE *across it*]

JUNE: Childie, they won't do it, will they? They *can't*, after all I've done for them.

ALICE: Of *course* they won't, George. You must stop brooding about it. You'll make yourself ill. [*She sits R of the table LC*] Why don't you go to bed and try and sleep it off? You can set the alarm to wake you for rehearsal tomorrow.

JUNE: There's no rehearsal tomorrow.

ALICE: That's good, then. You can get a nice long rest. [*She pauses a moment, then rises and moves R*] Now George, I've got to go.

JUNE: [*looking yearningly across at* ALICE] No, wait a minute.

ALICE: Oh, George, they'll be waiting for me. [*She picks up the knapsack and puts it on*] I'll be at the back of the queue.

JUNE: [*rising and moving C*] You can't go like *that*, you know.

ALICE: Like what?

JUNE: [*pointing to the knapsack*] You're not going on a hike, you know. Mind you, donkeys are best for loading.

ALICE: There's only a change of clothing in it, to take to the office. And a few provisions. [*She backs towards the arch R and puts on her scarf*] Please, may I go now?

JUNE: Did you speak?

ALICE: Yes, I said 'May I go now?'

JUNE: [*considering the request*] Not before you have made your obeisances to me in the proper manner.

ALICE: [*alarmed*] What do you mean? [JUNE *breathes heavily and alcoholically for a few moments*]

JUNE: You must kiss the hem of my garment. [*With an imperious gesture*] On your knees. Go on! Down, boy, down! [*She snaps her fingers and motions* ALICE *down stage*]

[ALICE *removes her knapsack and shrugs*]

ALICE: Oh, all right. [*She goes on her knees down R of the pouffe*]

JUNE: [*moving to L of* ALICE] Now repeat after me: 'I hereby solemnly swear—'

ALICE: [*mechanically*] 'I hereby solemnly swear—'

JUNE: '—that I will not allow—'

ALICE: '—that I will not allow—'

JUNE: '—anyone whooomsoever—'

ALICE: '—anyone—[*she imitates* JUNE] whoomsoever—'

JUNE: '—including Mr. Katz, gratification of his fleshly instincts with me today or at any other time.'

ALICE: [*quickly*] All right, all right, I swear. [*She kisses the hem of* JUNE'*s dressing-gown*]

JUNE: [*making sweeping gestures over* ALICE'*s head*] Mind you remember, or may the curse of Satan fall on your head.

ALICE: [*rising and quickly reiterating*] That's one *Giselle*, one *Petrushka*, and no *Lac*—right?

JUNE: [*with enormous effort*] *Rien de 'Lac de Cygnes'. C'est juste.* [*She holds on to* ALICE'*s scarf. With maudlin affection*] *Mon petit chou.*

ALICE: All right, all right, George, let go. Let go.

JUNE: [*still with affection*] What's this? [*She looks at the scarf*]

ALICE: What?

JUNE: This isn't yours, is it? [*She jerks the scarf away from* ALICE *and looks suspiciously at it*] Where did you get it?

ALICE: Oh, come on now, give it back to me.

JUNE: [*moving C and looking at the label on the scarf*] Who is J.V. S. Partridge?

ALICE: A young Liberal. Satisfied? [*She makes a grab for the scarf*]

[JUNE *jerks the scarf out of* ALICE'*s reach*]

JUNE: Far, far from satisfied. How long have you been entangled with this—youth?

ALICE: He's not a youth. He's forty-six.

JUNE: Bit long in the tooth for a young Liberal, isn't he? [*Fiercely*] Who is he?

ALICE: [*shifting from foot to foot*] The chap from downstairs, daftie. Madame Xenia's lodger. [*She crosses behind* JUNE *to L of her and makes a grab for the scarf*]

JUNE: [*jerking the scarf out of* ALICE'*s reach*] Ah—I thought there was some monkey business going on there.

ALICE: There is not. I've only ever seen him twice.

JUNE: How did you get his scarf, then?

ALICE: [*after a pause; sheepishly*] I pinched it off the hall-stand.

JUNE: D'you expect me to believe that?

ALICE: [*shaken, but sincerely*] Look, George, I've never even spoken to him. It's nothing.

JUNE: That's what you said when you went off with that estate agent for a weekend in Birmingham.

ALICE: [*moving L*] That was five years ago.

JUNE: It happened once—it can happen again.

ALICE: [*looking away*] Nothing happened.

JUNE: [*suspiciously*] Oh?

ALICE: [*rounding on* JUNE; *almost screaming*] Nothing!

JUNE: Well, *nothing's* going to happen now because I forbid you to speak to him.

ALICE: You must be raving mad. He's a neighbour, there's no harm in being friendly.

JUNE: [*shouting*] I forbid you to speak to him, do you hear?

ALICE: I'll flipping well speak to him if I want to — why shouldn't I?

JUNE: [*venomously*] You fancy him, don't you? [*She shouts*] Don't you?

ALICE: He seems perfectly agreeable. [JUNE's *face is contorted with suspicion*]

Yes, I do fancy him — he's a dish. [JUNE *steps threateningly towards* ALICE]

[*She shrinks back against the sideboard*] Don't you touch me — you've no right to...

JUNE: I've got every right.

ALICE: I'm not married to you, you know. [*There is a long pause then* JUNE *hands the scarf to* ALICE *and moves up C*]

[*In a low voice*] I'm sorry, George, but you asked for it.

JUNE: You'd better get along, you'll be late. [*She moves C*]

[ALICE *crosses to R, picks up the knapsack, but does not put it on*]

ALICE: Look after yourself. Don't forget the party tonight. [ALICE *makes a kissing motion to* JUNE, *but* JUNE *has turned away and does not see it.* ALICE *exits through the arch R.* JUNE *wanders up C, turns and surveys the room for a few moments, swaying slightly. She moves to the chair R of the table LC with her arms out*]

JUNE: [*in her country accent*] Ah, there's my beautiful bike. [*She pats the back of the chair*] 'Morning, old friend. We'll have you started up in no time. [*She turns the chair and places it C with the back to the audience, stands L of it, looks after* ALICE *for a moment, then makes a starting movement with her foot, and a purring noise to indicate the start of the engine*] Prrrrm! Prrrrrrrrrrrr! [*She sits astride the chair and grasps the back as handlebars*] Prrr! Prrr! 'Bye, Jean, 'bye, Rosie. Tell your dad to mind his gammy leg. [*She sways the chair from side to side*] Prrr! Prrrrr! Prrrrr! [*She sings*] 'Oh God, our help in ages past —' Prrr — prrr — prrr — 'our hope for years to come.' Prrr — prrr! 'Morning, Ginger, 'morning, Vicar, my word you're up early. Prrr — prrr! Yes, first call old Mrs Hinch. Prrrr — prrrr! [*She sings*] 'Be Thou our guard while troubles last —' Prrrr — prrrr! 'And our eternal —' — prrr — 'home...'

The CURTAIN *quickly falls*

Scene II

Scene: The same. Late afternoon of the same day.

Before the CURTAIN *rises, as the house-lights fade, the 'Applehurst Theme' is heard.*

When the CURTAIN *rises, the music fades. The chairs have been replaced. The hatch is cleared and closed. Through the window can be seen the pink rays of sunset, which spill into the room. It is late afternoon and becomes darker as the scene progresses. The room is empty. Laughter and shrieks can be heard off in the bedroom.*

JUNE: [*off; imperiously*] Pull yourself together. Try again, and this time do it properly.

ALICE: [*off*] I can't promise I'll get it right. [*There is more laughter, then the well-known signature tune of Laurel and Hardy is heard, laboriously played on the penny whistle.*

JUNE *enters from the bedroom, in the costume of Hardy, and carrying a carpet bag.*

ALICE *follows* JUNE *on, dressed as Laurel and playing the whistle. They march on in step to the tune, down the steps from the rostrum and across down R.* JUNE *halts abruptly, which makes* ALICE *bump into her.* ALICE *blows the whistle in* JUNE's *ear.* JUNE *drops the bag on to her toe and nurses her foot*]

JUNE: [*imitating Hardy*] And what, may I ask, is the meaning of that? [*She strikes* ALICE's *upstage arm with her bowler hat*]

ALICE: [*as Laurel*] Nothing, Olly. I was just playing — a tune.

JUNE: May I suggest that you stop playing — a tune — and get on with the next bit. A-one, a-two ... [ALICE *and* JUNE, *side by side, do a soft-shoe dance routine, dancing across and down L*]

BOTH: [*singing*] 'By the light — dum da dum da dum da dum — of the silvery moon — dum da dum — ' [*They reverse and dance to RC*] 'I used to — rum dum da dum da dum da dum — with my honey and — la da da. By the light...' [JUNE *turns to L to reverse again.* ALICE *bumps into her*]

JUNE: What was the meaning of that?

ALICE: [*imitating Laurel and starting to cry*] Nothing, Olly, I was only — practising.

JUNE: [*turning away and fluttering her tie*] Oh, fiddlesticks! [*She moves R and bends to pick up the bag*]

ALICE: [*following* JUNE] Did you say 'fiddlesticks'? [*She jabs the whistle into* JUNE's *behind*]

JUNE: [*straightening up and forgetting her impersonation*] Ouch, that hurt! [*She rubs her behind*]

ALICE: [*moving C; giggling*] Sorry, Olly. [JUNE *follows* ALICE *and gives her a great swipe with the bowler hat on her upstage arm*]

[*As herself*] That hurt!

JUNE: Sorry, Stan.

ALICE: That's not in it. [JUNE, *in the best Hardy manner, dusts her hands and crosses above* ALICE *to L of her*]

JUNE: Let that be a lesson to you. [*She turns away down L, beaming*]

ALICE: [*singing the Laurel and Hardy tune*] Boop-a-doo, boop-a-doo ... [*She follows* JUNE *and rams the whistle against her*]

[JUNE *seizes the whistle*] No, no, be careful, it's Miss Broadbent's.

JUNE: [*only half acting*] A very useful instrument. [*She hits* ALICE *over the head with the whistle*]

[ALICE *squares up to* JUNE, *making sounds of frustrated rage and boxing movements with her hands*]

ALICE: You, oh ... [*She backs C*]

JUNE: That's not Laurel, daftie, that's the Three Stooges.

ALICE: [*moving down C, taking off her hat and scratching her head*] Sorry, Olly. [*Brightly*] Olly.

JUNE: Yep?

ALICE: Give me your hat.

JUNE: What for, Stan?

ALICE: I just want to look at something. [*She puts her own hat on*]

JUNE: [*thrusting her hat at* ALICE] O.K., Stan. [ALICE *bends over the bowler and spits into it slowly, then puts the hat on* JUNE's *head again, giving it a little tap.* JUNE *makes no protest while this is going on, but watches coldly*]

[*As herself*] What was that supposed to be?

ALICE: [*as herself; backing RC*] I don't know. Just an idea. Horse-play, you know. We're celebrating because you're back in the series, aren't we?

JUNE: [*with an evil glint in her eye*] Just because the scriptwriters have cured my cold, there's no need to go raving bloody mad, you know.

ALICE: I thought it was funny.

JUNE: You thought it was funny?

ALICE: Yes, I thought it was funny.

JUNE: You thought it was funny. [*As Hardy*] Stan.

ALICE: [*as Laurel*] Yes, Olly?

JUNE: Give me your hat.

ALICE: What for, Olly?

JUNE: I just want to look at something. [ALICE *gives* JUNE *her hat*]

[*She points up R*] Look up there, Stan. [ALICE *obediently looks up R.* JUNE *goes to the table LC, squirts soda water from a syphon into* ALICE'S *hat then returns to L of* ALICE]

ALICE: [*staring upwards*] There's nothing up there, Olly.

JUNE: Try this, then, Stan. [*She empties the water over* ALICE *as she puts the hat on* ALICE's *head*]

ALICE: [*as herself*] Oh! You fool—now you've spoilt my costume. [*She hits* JUNE]

JUNE: [*keeping* ALICE *at arm's length*] Steady, now. Steady.

ALICE: What was the point of that? [*She hits* JUNE, *feebly*]

JUNE: Just an idea. Horseplay, you know. [*She does Hardy's slightly reeling turn round towards L and puts the whistle on the table LC*]

ALICE: [*crossing towards the arch R and brushing herself*] You are rotten. I'm all wet. Now I'll have to change my things.

JUNE: [*moving C*] Don't be so soppy, woman. A drop of water never did anybody any harm.

ALICE: Oh, didn't it? All right. [*She takes the flowers from the vase on the table down R and moves menacingly towards* JUNE *with the vase of water*]

JUNE: [*laughing and backing to the table LC*] Don't! No! No! No!

ALICE: Take your punishment like a man.

JUNE: [*shouting*] All right. [*She takes off her hat and stands like a martyr with arms outstretched and squared shoulders, eyes shut*] Go on—what are you waiting for? [ALICE *quickly pulls out* JUNE's *trousers by the waist and makes to pour the water inside. Both burst into shrieks of laughter and struggle with the vase*]

No! No! No! [*They are helpless with laughter, then they straighten up and* ALICE *returns the vase to the table down R*]

ALICE: Never mind.

JUNE: [*gasping and putting on her hat*] You're like marshmallow. [*The door bell rings off R*]

ALICE: It's Madame Xenia, come to fetch us. She's early. [*She picks up the carpet bag, moves up C and stops, hesitantly*]

JUNE: Well, don't stand and gape. Open the door. [ALICE *gives the bag to* JUNE, *who turns her round and shoves her towards the arch R, giving her a good-humoured kick*]

ALICE: [*imitating the Laurel and Hardy whistle and still giggling happily*] Doo-do-doo, doo-do-doo…[ALICE *exits through the arch.* JUNE *puts the carpet bag on the floor L of the sofa*]

JUNE: I must get it right this time. [*She moves down LC, closes her eyes and winds her tie, twiddling it round, like Hardy, and turning from side to side*]

ALICE: [*off R*] Oh! Oh, I'm sorry—we were expecting…[MERCY *enters through the arch, looking back in bewilderment at* ALICE. ALICE *follows* MERCY *on and stands down R*]

MERCY: [*moving RC*] I'm so sorry to intrude. I do hope it's not inconvenient. [*She turns and looks startled on seeing* JUNE]

JUNE: [*taken aback*] Not at all. I'm sorry, we were just…

MERCY: Playing charades?

ALICE: As a matter of fact we were just getting ready to go out—to a fancy dress ball.

JUNE: [*overlapping*] Ball—fancy.

MERCY: Oh, I'll come back another time when it's more convenient. [*She moves C*] Perhaps Miss Buckridge could come to see me tomorrow morning, before the rehearsal?

JUNE: We're not in a rush. We can talk now. Would you have a drink?

MERCY: No, thank you. [JUNE *takes the tray of drinks from the table LC and puts it on the sideboard*]

ALICE: [*moving RC; cordially*] Won't you sit down, Mrs. Mercy?

MERCY: [*moving to the table LC*] Thank you, dear. I know it's most remiss of me, turning up unexpectedly like this. [*She sits R of the table*] Actually, I've come straight from a meeting—I felt I had to see you personally. [*She puts her handbag on the table and removes her gloves*]

ALICE: [*anxiously*] The nuns?

MERCY: Oh, didn't the office tell you? We had a most charming communication from the Mother Superior. All is forgiven. But there's still the little matter of the charity.

JUNE: What charity?

ALICE: The donation you promised to give to the convent.

JUNE: Oh, that.

MERCY: It's only obliquely mentioned in the letter.

JUNE: [*with a wry smile*] I didn't expect her to forget about it. [*To* ALICE] Remind me to send her a cheque tomorrow. [*She moves to the table down L*] It'll help keep their Irish novices in hair shirts. [*She picks up a cigar box from the table*]

[ALICE *moves to the fireplace and makes a note on a notepad on the mantelpiece*]

MERCY: Very nice of you, Miss Buckridge. I'm relieved to see the matter settled.

JUNE: [*moving and proffering the box to* MERCY] May I offer you a small cigar?

MERCY: Oh, no—no, thank you. I gave up smoking years ago.

JUNE: You don't mind if I smoke?

MERCY: Well . . .

ALICE: [*moving RC*] You smoke far too much.

JUNE: [*with a mock bow*] Thank you for your touching concern. [*She returns the box to the table down L, without taking a cigar, then moves below the chair L of the table*]

MERCY: [*after a pause*] Well, now, Miss Buckridge, I'm afraid I have some bad news for you. [*The lights dim a little for dusk effect*]

JUNE: Bad news?

MERCY: You're the first to be told. It's only just been decided; or rather, it's only just received the official stamp of approval.

ALICE: [*terrified*] You can't mean . . .

JUNE: Be quiet, Childie.

MERCY: Yes. I'm sorry, Miss Buckridge: it's the end of Sister George. [*There is a stunned pause.* JUNE *sinks into the chair L of the table LC*]

ALICE: [*suddenly shouting*] But why? Why?

MERCY: Believe me, dear Miss Buckridge, the decision is no reflection on your ability as an actress. You created a character that has become a nation-wide favourite.

ALICE: [*still incredulous*] But why kill her?

MERCY: Why do some of our nearest and dearest have to die? Because that's life. [ALICE *moves slowly to the pouffe and sits on it, facing L*]

In *Applehurst* we try to re-create the flavour of life, as it is lived in hundreds of English villages.

ALICE: But she's the most popular character in it.

MERCY: [*slightly uncomfortable*] I know. The B.B.C. took that into considera-tion. They felt—and I must say I concurred—that only some dramatic event, something that would get into the news headlines, could save *Applehurst*. We felt that in their grief, robbed of one of their greatest favourites, listeners would return again to *Applehurst* with a new loyalty, with a . . .

JUNE: [*interrupting dully*] How?

MERCY: [*quietly*] It's not for another fortnight. It's scheduled for the twelfth.

JUNE: But how?

MERCY: [*smiling benignly*] It's just an ordinary morning in Applehurst. The chaffinch on Sister George's window-sill wakes her up as usual and is rewarded with its daily saucerful of crumbs.

JUNE: [*under her breath, automatically, in her country accent*] Hello, dicky. [*She sits, staring downwards, very subdued*]

MERCY: [*brightly*] Up the road, in the Old Mill Farm, young Jimmy Bromley, the scamp, wakes up with a cough and doesn't want to go to school. 'We'd better get Sister George in,' says his mother—and he's up in a jiffy. Meanwhile, punctual to the minute, Sister George finishes her breakfast and packs a basketful of preserves and cottage cheese for old Mrs. Hinch, in bed with bronchitis. On with her bonnet and cape, and off she goes, striding purposefully through the autumn leaves—sound effects here—to the bicycle shed. The bolts are pushed back, and the door creaks open, and there stands her prized possession—the Moped.

JUNE: [*in her country accent; quietly*] 'Morning, old friend.

MERCY: Whiz—pop—the engine starts—and away she goes. Pop-pop-pop-pop-pop-pop-pop-pop . . . 'Hurry up, Jimmy, you'll be late for school,' she calls out. 'Tell Mrs. Pemberton to give you plenty of homework to keep you out of mischief.' 'I will,' the boy calls back—adding as she drives out of earshot—'I don't think.'

JUNE: [*in her country accent*] Cheeky little beggar!

MERCY: A chorus of greetings follows her as she heads for the open country—the wind billowing in her cape—and bursts, as usual, into a snatch of her favourite hymn; 'Oh God, our help in ages past.' Honk-honk answers her hooter in a merry descant as she turns into Oakmead Road, and then—*bang!* Collision with a ten-ton truck.

JUNE: [*very quietly*] Oh, my God! [*She puts her hand over her eyes for a moment*]

ALICE. Is it—is it . . . ?

MERCY: Instantaneous. Never regains consciousness.

ALICE: [*weeping*] You can't, you can't . . .

MERCY: It so happens that your death will coincide with Road Safety Week: a cause which we know has been close to you for many years.

JUNE: [*recovering slightly*] I've never ridden carelessly. [*She rises and moves above her chair*] I protest.

MERCY: [*anxious to placate her*] I know, I know. We're taking great care to establish it's the lorry-driver's fault.

JUNE: [*pacing up L and turning; unconvinced*] But even so—a ten-ton truck...[*She paces down LC*]

MERCY: I'm sorry, but there it is.

JUNE: [*with dignity*] I think I have a right to a say in my own mode of death.

MERCY: [*kindly*] Now, do leave it to us, dear Miss Buckridge. Leave it to the B.B.C. We know best. We've had experience in these matters.

JUNE: [*crossing above* MERCY *to* C] If I could have been killed in the course of duty—from some infection, perhaps. [*With a sudden idea*] An epidemic! That's it—I could go to nurse a patient somewhere up in the hills, someone suffering from some unspeakable disease...

MERCY: I'm sorry, Miss Buckridge, the scripts have been typed.

JUNE: But they could be altered.

MERCY: I'm afraid they've been officially approved.

JUNE: [*moving down R*] Then I shall take this to a higher authority.

ALICE: [*rising and moving to L of* JUNE] Yes, don't let them treat you like this. You've still got your public behind you: they won't let them kill you off.

MERCY: [*rising and facing* JUNE *and* ALICE; *annoyed*] I'm surprised at your attitude, Miss McNaught: I thought you'd be more sensible. I came here of my own volition, as a gesture of courtesy to a valued and trusted colleague.

ALICE: But—it's not fair.

JUNE: Shut up, Childie!

ALICE: I won't shut up.

MERCY: I was going to say that I'm sure the B.B.C. will want to find some other outlet for Miss Buckridge's talents.

JUNE: I'm still not satisfied about the—accident.

MERCY: [*hard*] I'm afraid that decision is final. [JUNE *subsides on to the chair down R. There is a pause*]

ALICE: [*to* JUNE] Do you think you ought to lie down? You look awful. [*To* MERCY] She hasn't been sleeping well lately. [*She puts an arm around* JUNE's *shoulders*]

MERCY: [*crossing slowly to* C] Oh, I'm sorry to hear that.

JUNE: [*after a pause*] Will I be buried in the churchyard?

MERCY: [*moving to the pouffe and sitting on it; cheerfully*] Oh, it'll be done in style. Don't you worry your head about that. There's some talk of a special memorial broadcast, with contributions from all sorts of famous people—but I shouldn't really be talking about that, as everything's still in the planning stage.

JUNE: Would I be in it? In the memorial broadcast, I mean?

MERCY: Naturally. There will be lots of recorded extracts of Sister George.
JUNE: No, I meant: would I be able to tell the people how the character developed?
MERCY: Oh, no! That would spoil the illusion.
JUNE: But you said the B.B.C. wanted to use me again.
MERCY: Yes, but not as Sister George.
JUNE: [*on the brink of hysteria*] What's wrong with Sister George?
MERCY: Nothing, dear Miss Buckridge. She'll be dead, that's all. [*There is a pause.* JUNE's *head droops.* ALICE *gently helps* JUNE *to her feet*]
ALICE: Come on, George, come and lie down. [*She leads* JUNE *up C*] Come on—come on.
MERCY: [*rising*] In due course, I hope to discuss ideas for a new series with you. We'll do something really exciting; I'm sure of it. [JUNE *halts C and turns to* MERCY. ALICE *takes her arm away from* JUNE's *shoulders and stands R of her*]
JUNE: [*with dignity; quietly*] Mrs. Mercy: I would like to thank you for coming here personally today to tell me of the—the decision. I don't really feel up to discussing ideas for a new series at the moment.
MERCY: Of course you don't.
JUNE: Please don't go. Childie—Miss McNaught—will make you a cup of tea, or something. I'll have to go and lie down—[*she moves above the table LC*] for a bit, I think. [*She picks up the bottle of gin from the sideboard and turns to* MERCY] I'll put this away, in the—[*she pauses*] cabinet. [*She moves towards the bedroom door*]
ALICE: [*moving to R of the steps*] Will you be all right, George?
JUNE: [*stopping and turning*] What did you say?
ALICE: I said: Will you be all right?
JUNE: You called me 'George' then, didn't you. You'll have to get out of that habit. [JUNE *exits to the bedroom and is heard to bolt the door. There is a pause*]
MERCY: [*moving C*] I really don't think I should stay any longer.
ALICE: [*moving to L of* MERCY] Please stay, Mrs. Mercy. I'd like you to.
MERCY: Well, of course—if I can be of any assistance . . .
ALICE: Just to have someone to talk to . . .
MERCY: [*crossing to the armchair R*] I expect things haven't been easy for you—recently. [*She sits*]

[ALICE *crosses to RC*]

ALICE: [*with an anxious look at the bedroom door; quietly*] She's been impossible. Life's been absolute hell. You've no idea.

MERCY: I thought as much.

ALICE: Night after night I found her sitting up, drinking. Said she couldn't go to sleep with worry.

MERCY: Did she keep you awake? [ALICE *moves to the sofa, sits, takes off her bowler hat and puts it on the seat beside her*]

ALICE: Some nights she made such a din—you know, reciting and things—that the neighbours complained.

MERCY: I had no idea it was as bad as that.

ALICE: It's been—diabolical.

MERCY: I do feel sorry for you.

ALICE: When she gets anxious, or nervous, or anything, she has to take it out on somebody. Who do you think bears the brunt? Yours truly.

MERCY: I'm amazed you put up with it.

ALICE: I have no alternative.

MERCY: Oh, come, surely there must be lots of openings for a girl with your qualifications.

ALICE: I've been with George for seven years.

MERCY: Seven years—as long as that.

ALICE: Yes, she was quite unknown when we first met.

MERCY: I expect she was easier to get on with in those days.

ALICE: She was always very jealous: wouldn't let anyone come near me.

MERCY: What a shame. Particularly as it's so important for someone with literary ability to have contact with a lot of people.

ALICE: How did you know that I...?

MERCY: You mentioned your interest in poetry last time we met—you attend classes, I believe?

ALICE: Yes, every Wednesday.

MERCY: I'd like to read your poems, if I may.

ALICE: Would you? Would you, really? [*She rises and moves up LC*] Shall I get them now?

MERCY: [*rising and moving RC*] No, we'd better not disturb Miss Buckridge now. Give me a ring at the B.B.C. and my secretary will fix an appointment.

ALICE: [*moving to L of* MERCY] Oh, thank you. It's really awfully kind of you—to take such an interest.

MERCY: Have you ever thought of writing for the radio?

ALICE: It had occurred to me. You know: sometimes one hears such tripe, and one thinks... [*She hastily puts a hand over her mouth*]

MERCY: [*with mock reproof*] I know what you were going to say.

ALICE: Sorry.

MERCY: Never mind. We all feel the same way at times. Anyway, I'm not responsible for *all* the programmes.

ALICE: I'm sure yours are by far the best.

MERCY: [*very pleased*] Flattery.

ALICE: No, honestly. Years ago, before I knew you had anything to do with *Applehurst*, I listened to your talks on the wireless about people's problems, and honestly, they were really — understanding.

MERCY: [*touched*] I'm so glad. [*She crosses below* ALICE *to the table LC and collects her bag and gloves*] You've got a little problem on *your* hands — [*she looks towards the bedroom door*] and no mistake.

ALICE: A big problem.

MERCY: What are we going to do?

ALICE: [*moving C*] Don't know.

MERCY: [*after a pause; quietly sympathetic*] Is she always so — difficult?

ALICE: Difficult! She gets very violent — especially after she's had a few pints. You've no idea the things she gets up to.

MERCY: [*sitting L of the table LC*] Really?

ALICE: Oh, yes. [*She looks round a little wildly, then turns quickly to R of the table LC and sits, facing* MERCY] Mrs. Mercy: I'm scared. I'm scared of what will happen.

MERCY: Now don't be silly. Nothing will happen. You've been living through a difficult few weeks, that's all. It was the uncertainty that made her nervous. Now that she knows the worst she'll be much more bearable, you'll see.

ALICE: You don't know George. I don't know how I'm going to survive the next two weeks.

MERCY: [*putting on her gloves*] I'll do what I can to help.

ALICE: [*after a pause*] I hope she won't get in a rage and murder me.

MERCY: [*startled*] Are you serious?

ALICE: Dead serious. When she gets into a temper, she's capable of anything.

MERCY: Has she ever — attacked you?

ALICE: Often. It happens all the time.

MERCY: But this is *outrageous*.

ALICE: She beats me, you know. She hits me with anything that comes into her hand.

MERCY: [*with sudden sharpness*] But why do you put up with it?

ALICE: [*after a pause*] I have nowhere else to go.

MERCY: Surely there's somewhere . . .

ALICE: I couldn't face living alone. Not any more.

MERCY: [*overcome*] My poor child. This is terrible. [*She rises, glances at the bedroom door then moves above the table and leans over to* ALICE] Look, if there's any more trouble—with George, I mean, don't hesitate to give me a ring. Please regard me as your friend.

ALICE: [*seizing* MERCY's *hand*] Oh, you are kind, Mrs. Mercy.

MERCY: And we must find somewhere for you to go.

ALICE: [*gratefully*] Would you? Would you really?

MERCY: [*patting* ALICE's *hand*] Leave it to me. [*She moves to the table behind the sofa and looks around. After a pause*] How pretty this room looks in the evening sunlight. All these charming dolls. [*She picks up the doll Emmeline from the table behind the sofa*]

ALICE: That one's my favourite. Her name is 'Emmeline'.

MERCY: [*shaking the doll by the hand*] Hello, Emmeline. [*There is a pause.* ALICE *rises and moves up LC*]

ALICE: Do you think I ought to go and see if George is all right?

MERCY: [*speaking in a childish voice to the doll*] I should leave her where she is—the naughty woman.

ALICE: [*moving C*] I haven't even offered you a cup of tea.

MERCY: We haven't time for a cup of tea. We have to go. [*To the doll*] Good-bye, little Emmeline. [*She replaces the doll on the table then moves towards the arch R*]

ALICE: I wish you could stay.

MERCY: [*stopping and turning*] So do I. But I'm glad we had a chance to have a little chat. Now remember what I told you: if there's any more trouble, get straight on the telephone to me. [ALICE *picks up her bowler hat from the sofa and puts it on*]

That's the spirit.

ALICE: [*moving below the sofa; in a Laurel voice*] Gee, I'm frightened.

MERCY: Don't let her bully you.

ALICE: [*in a Laurel voice*] She's a devil when roused.

MERCY: Good-bye, dear. Must run. Have fun. [MERCY *exits through the arch R*]

ALICE: [*mechanically*] Must run—have fun. [*She looks towards the bedroom, undecided, picks up the whistle from the table LC and goes to the bedroom door, playing the Laurel and Hardy signature tune. She calls*] George. [*She knocks on the door and tries the handle but the door is bolted. She calls*] George, are you all right? [*She taps on the door with the whistle and chants*] Geor-orge. [*She suddenly angrily kicks the door and shouts*] George! [*She pauses, then runs to the table LC, slams down the whistle on to the table and throws the bowler hat on to the sofa. Rapidly and intensely*] What am I going to do?

The CURTAIN *quickly falls*

Interlude

At the end of the interval the house-lights go out, leaving the footlights lighting the CURTAIN, *and the following recording is heard on the front-of-house speakers.*

There is the sound of SISTER GEORGE'S *Moped, a background of country noises, the twittering of birds, mooing and neighing, etc.*

SISTER GEORGE: [*singing*] 'Oh God, our help in ages past, our hope for years to come, our shelter from the stormy blast and our eternal home.' [*The singing fades out. The monotonous sound is heard of the engine of a heavy lorry*]

BILL: [*in a thick North Country accent*] You awake, Fred?

FRED: [*grunting something unintelligible*] Oh, ay...

BILL: Won't do to fall asleep now. We're nearly there.

FRED: [*in a thick North Country accent*] I'm not up to it any more—this all-night driving.

BILL: There's the turning coming up now—don't miss it.

SISTER GEORGE: [*approaching; singing*] 'Oh God, our help in ages past...' [*There is a sound of acceleration and changing of gears from the lorry*]

FRED: Let's get there fast—I'm hungry.

BILL: [*shouting*] Look out. [*There is a screeching of brakes, followed by an explosion*]

[*Near hysteria*] We hit her! Fred, we hit her! [*The lorry cab door is heard to slam*]

FRED: It weren't my fault. I braked...

BILL: Is she...? My God, she looks bad. [*He calls*] Hey, there! [*The sound of heavy footsteps is heard, coming nearer*]

FARMER BROMLEY: [*in a country accent*] What happened?

BILL: Bike came round the corner, oh—fast.

FRED: I tried to brake. It weren't my fault.

FARMER BROMLEY: [*panting*] I always did say it's a dangerous crossing. Is she—is she badly...? Holy Saints! It's—it's Sister George!

FRED: It *were*.

The 'Applehurst Theme' swells up and plays cheerfully.

Act Three

Scene: *The same. Two weeks later. Morning.*

Before the CURTAIN *rises, as the house-lights fade, the 'Applehurst Theme' is heard.*

When the CURTAIN *rises, the music fades. It is a sunny October morning. There is an abundance of flowers everywhere, including a large yellow wreath on the window-seat, a bouquet on the table behind the sofa, a pink and red wreath R of the radiogram, and a white wreath R of the banisters. On the table LC there are piles of telegrams and a transistor tape-recorder.* XENIA, *discreetly dressed in mauve, is sitting R of the table LC, listening to* SISTER GEORGE's *accident on the tape-recorder. As the 'Applehurst Theme' swells up and fades,* XENIA *switches off the transistor and wipes her eyes.*

XENIA: [*overcome*] Oi oi oi—poor George! [*The front door bell rings*]

[*She rises*] All right, all right, I come. [XENIA *exits through the arch R*]

[*Off*] Yes, I will take them, but I don't know where I am going to put them. [XENIA *re-enters through the arch, carrying a wreath, a bouquet, and a large cross of yellow roses*]

Soon we shall not be able to move. [*She puts the wreath and bouquet on the sofa, and leans the cross against the left end of the sofa*]

[*The telephone rings*]

[*She moves to the telephone and lifts the receiver*] They are mad. I told them we were not accepting any more calls. [*Into the telephone*] You are mad. I told you we were not accepting any more calls...A message from whom?...The girls of your Exchange?...Yes, I will convey it... Very nice of you...Charming. Miss Buckridge will be very touched...Who am I?...Never you mind—I am her temporary secretary...No, I have nothing to do with *Applehurst*...No, I am not the old gypsy woman who stole a pig. You are beginning to make me very upset. I will not speak to you any more. And no more calls, if you please. [*She replaces the receiver*] Stupid nit! [*She crosses to the fireplace*]

[ALICE *enters from the bedroom, rubbing her eyes and yawning. She wears baby doll pyjamas*]

ALICE: What time is it?

XENIA: [*with a black look*] Half past ten. [*She picks up the wreath and bouquet from the sofa*]

ALICE: Heavens—I'm going to be late for the funeral [*She nearly trips over the yellow cross leaning against the sofa*] Oh, not more flowers—I shall never find my things. [*She kneels, looks under the sofa, finds one slipper and puts it on*]

[XENIA *takes the wreath and bouquet and leans them against the upstage end of the bookcase*]

XENIA: [*pointedly*] I have been working already two hours.

ALICE: Where's George?

XENIA: [*crossing to L of the sofa*] Out—gone. I don't know where. I am very worried.

ALICE: [*standing below the sofa*] Gone? When?

XENIA: Since early this morning. I came up with two wreaths and some lilies—she took one look, rushed into the lift, slammed the gate in my face and went down like a captain on a sinking ship—but not saluting—swearing.

ALICE: [*sitting in the armchair R*] I hope she is not going to do something awful.

XENIA: I think she could not stand to be in the flat another moment with all this. [*She looks round at the flowers and picks up the yellow cross*] She felt claustrophobia—I must get out. [*She moves to the sideboard*] It has been terrible for her since the accident—nothing but the telephone—letters—reporters. [*She places the yellow cross against the centre of the sideboard*]

ALICE: She ought never to have listened to the accident—it was dreadful.

XENIA: [*moving above the table LC*] Oi oi oi, I just listened to the tape again—that beautiful hymn—the screeching brakes—then—[*she puts her hands to her face*] crash, bang, wallop!

ALICE: [*covering her ears*] Don't!

XENIA: It was like a gas-works blowing up—horrible. [*She shudders*] I cried again.

ALICE: [*rising*] Ought we to ring up the police or something? [XENIA *picks up the tape-recorder, goes up L and puts it down just off up L*]

XENIA: No. We must wait. And work. Everything must be right for her when she comes back. [ALICE *goes to the sofa, puts the cushions at the left end and flops on to it, lying with her head L*]

ALICE: I feel so exhausted—I think it's the strain.

XENIA: [*moving to L of the sofa*] Nonsense—it was the farewell party last night. You have no stamina. You are a—what you call it—a milksop. [*She moves to R of the radiogram and picks up a pink and red wreath*]

ALICE: I've probably caught a cold. George stuffed a peach Melba down the back of my dress. Really, she's getting worse and worse.

XENIA: [*moving to L of the sofa and reading the card on the wreath*] Listen to this. 'Unforgotten, from the patients and staff of the Sister George Geriatrics Ward.' Beautiful! I could cry. [*She crosses to the sideboard*]

ALICE: She'll like that.

XENIA: [*placing the wreath against the wall above the sideboard*] All wreaths against the wall. There. All beautifully organized.

ALICE: Honestly, Madame Xenia, you're a brick.

XENIA: [*moving to L of the table LC; suspiciously*] Why do you say that?

ALICE: It's an expression: a friend, a help.

XENIA: I see. [*She makes a note in a notebook on the table LC*] But I promised George I would take charge today and I hold my promise.

ALICE: [*rising and moving C*] Could I look at some of the telegrams?

XENIA: If you're very careful and don't get them mixed up. [*She points to three piles of opened telegrams*] Those are personal, those are official and those are doubtful.

ALICE: Let's look at some of the doubtfuls. [*She picks up a telegram*]

XENIA: [*sitting wearily L of the table LC*] What I would like more than anything is a nice cup of tea.

ALICE: [*moving C and reading the telegram*] Oh, *no*!

XENIA: What?

ALICE: [*bitterly*] Trust her to get in on the act. [*She crumples the telegram and moves R*]

XENIA: [*chiding*] You must not do this.

ALICE: [*very red in the face*] How dare she send telegrams after all these years?

XENIA: From what person?

ALICE: [*reading*] 'Heartfelt condolences. Love Liz.'

XENIA: Liz?

ALICE: A friend of George's. Before my time.

XENIA: Aha!

ALICE: [*moving L of the sofa*] An absolute cow. Kept writing sarcastic little notes at first; things like 'hope you are divinely happy' and 'hope this finds you as it leaves me—guess how'. [*She sits on the left arm of the sofa*]

XENIA: [*quietly*] What I would like more than anything is a nice cup of tea.

ALICE: Anyway, she stole a fountain pen and a camera off George.

XENIA: [*clicking her teeth*] Tut-tut. [*She opens a telegram from the pile of unopened ones on the table*]

ALICE: 'Heartfelt condolences'—she's mocking her.

XENIA: [*changing the subject*] Listen to this. Here is a nice one from my old friend the Baroness. [*She reads*] 'Shall be thinking of you today. Best wishes for a triumphant funeral. Love Augusta.' She specially put off her hairdresser so that she can listen to the funeral this morning. And she only met George once—at my Hallowe'en party last year.

ALICE: Which one was the Baroness?

XENIA: She came as Julius Caesar. At least that's what we *thought* she was meant to be. [*ALICE rises, moves R and looks off through the arch*]

ALICE: I hope George isn't going to be late.

XENIA: I think it is a mistake for her to listen today. Psychologically it is a mistake.

ALICE: [*wandering to the window*] Oh, I don't know. She can't just play a character for six years and miss her own exit.

XENIA: But it will upset her. [*She makes a note on the pad*]

[*ALICE picks up an orange, circular wreath from the window-seat and takes it down L of the sofa*]

ALICE: All her old friends will be there—people she's worked with for years. There'll be tributes paid. [*She sits on the left arm of the sofa*] There'll be a proper service. I mean to say: there's a right way and a wrong way of doing things. [*She stretches one bare leg through the middle of the wreath*]

XENIA: [*shrugging*] I do not understand you.

ALICE: Maybe in your country, people…

XENIA: [*flaring up*] What do you mean: in my country? We had state funerals which could have taught you something: twenty-eight horses with black plumes, ha!

ALICE: [*bitchily*] Well, you had a lot of practice, didn't you? All those assassinations.

XENIA: Assassinations?

ALICE: Shooting people.

XENIA: Of course we shoot people we don't like. You send them to the House of Lords—what's the difference?

ALICE: [*rising*] Anyway, if you expect the B.B.C. to lay on twenty-eight horses with black plumes, you're in for a disappointment. [*She throws the wreath upstage against the bottom of the radio-gram and moves above the table LC*]

XENIA: [*jumping up; furious*] Do you want me to go? [*She crosses towards the arch R*] Immediately I go downstairs.

ALICE: [*moving to L of* XENIA] No, no.

XENIA: [*stopping and turning*] You can explain my absence to George when she comes back. If she comes back. [*She turns to go*]

ALICE: [*running to* XENIA] No! Madame Xenia, please stay—I didn't mean to be rude. [XENIA *stops and turns*]

It's my nerves, I'm so worried about George—supposing she's really cracked up and thrown herself under a bus or something—what am I going to do?

XENIA: [*after a pause*] No, it is not a bus. [*Mysteriously*] I read the cards this morning—it is something to do with the head.

ALICE: [*moving down RC*] The *head!* Oh, no, I can't bear it. [*The sound is heard of a door handle rattling off R*]

XENIA: Shhh! There's somebody at the door.

ALICE: George!

XENIA: Look cheerful—she must see happy faces. [*The sound is heard of a door closing off R.* XENIA *moves to the fireplace*]

ALICE: [*rushing towards the kitchen door L*] She'll kill me if she sees me walking about like this.

JUNE: [*off R; shouting*] Open the windows and let the sunshine in. [ALICE *realizes it is too late to escape, grabs the cross of yellow roses by the sideboard and tries to hide behind it, staying down L*]

XENIA: [*apprehensively*] We are here, my darling. [JUNE *sails in through the arch R, wearing an extravagant orange chiffon hat with her tweed suit and carrying a picnic basket*]

JUNE: [*as she enters*] It's glorious out. [*She crosses to C and turns to* XENIA] Darling—how sweet of you to hold the fort—I do hope you weren't pestered too much. [ALICE'*s wreath rustles*]

[*She turns and sees* ALICE] Oh God, down in the forest something stirred. [*She puts the basket on the table LC*]

XENIA: [*moving C*] George, we were so worried—where have you been?

JUNE: [*opening the basket*] Shopping. I picked up this marvellous Christmas Gift hamper packed full of goodies. And two bottles of Veuve Cliquot 'fifty-three. [*She takes two bottles from the basket and puts them on the table*]

XENIA: But—what for?

JUNE: I've decided to skip the funeral and have a celebration.

XENIA: Celebration?

JUNE: Yes, more a coming-out party, really.

XENIA: But who is coming out?

JUNE: *I* am.

XENIA: [*looking at* JUNE's *hat*] I see you bought something else, as well.

JUNE: Do you like it?

XENIA: It is *charming!* Where did you find it?

JUNE: That little shop on the corner. Saw it in the window and couldn't resist it.

XENIA: You were absolutely right. It does something for you.

JUNE: Do you think so?

XENIA: It makes you look so young. Like eighteen years. [JUNE *and* XENIA *laugh happily.* ALICE *sniggers sarcastically*]

JUNE: [*turning on* ALICE *and moving below the table LC*] What are you laughing at? And why aren't you dressed yet? You look positively indecent.

ALICE: [*putting the yellow cross on the floor down L*] I overslept. I had a bit of a hangover.

JUNE: [*incredulously*] A hangover? After two glasses of shandy?

ALICE: I mixed it a bit.

JUNE: What with—ginger ale? [JUNE *and* XENIA *laugh together at this.* ALICE *does not reply*]

[*She moves down LC*] Do you think it proper to entertain visitors in this—this unseemly attire?

XENIA: [*placatingly*] Oh, please—please.

JUNE: Did you make Madame Xenia a cup of tea?

XENIA: It really wasn't necessary.

JUNE: [*to* ALICE] What's the matter with you?

ALICE: Don't know.

JUNE: You should have been out and about for the last three hours. Did you do your exercises?

ALICE: [*defiantly*] No.

JUNE: [*moving to L of* XENIA] Oh, God help us, she takes a Keep Fit course, you know: knee bends, running on the spot, bicycling on her back. To judge by her condition it's been singularly ineffective [*She moves to R of* ALICE] I want a cup of tea *now*. And one for Madame Xenia. And get dressed. And look sharpish about it. [*She claps her hands*] *Avanti!*

ALICE: [*after a pause; looking straight at* JUNE] I think your hat is a mistake.

JUNE: [*thundering*] *What?* [ALICE *does not reply*]

This day will end in tears.

ALICE: [*shouting*] They won't be my tears. [ALICE *runs out to the kitchen*]

JUNE: [*moving up L of the table LC*] The baggage! The little baggage.

XENIA: [*moving R of the table LC*] She is upset.

JUNE: [*rounding on* XENIA] She has no business to be upset: it's *my* funeral. [*She crosses to the sofa*]

XENIA: [*putting one champagne bottle back into the basket and fastening the clasp*] She's taking it hard. Some people . . .

JUNE: Oh, some people are no good in a crisis. I've seen it over and over again during the war.

XENIA: Ah, the war. I was an air raid warden.

JUNE: [*sitting on the sofa*] I was in the Army. Attached to the Commandos. It was tough, but by God it was rewarding.

XENIA: [*picking up the basket and putting it on the floor above the sideboard*] It's lucky for her she wasn't old enough.

JUNE: Childie in the Army? That'd be a giggle. She'd have collapsed under the weight of her forage cap. [*She laughs*]

XENIA: [*picking up the red and pink wreath*] Would you like to go through the latest tributes? [*She crosses to L of the sofa*]

JUNE: If it's absolutely necessary.

XENIA: Look at this—from the patients and staff of the Sister George Geriatrics Ward. In that hospital your name will never die.

JUNE: [*firmly*] *Her* name.

XENIA: Her name, your name: it's the same thing.

JUNE: No, it's not. George and I have parted company. And do you know, I'm glad to be free of the silly bitch.

XENIA: What?

JUNE: Honestly.

XENIA: George, what are you saying?

JUNE: I'm saying that my name is *June*. June Buckridge. I'm endeavouring to memorize it.

XENIA: [*laughing*] You are incredible! [*She replaces the wreath against the wall above the sideboard*]

[ALICE *enters from the kitchen, carrying a tray of tea for two, with the crumpled telegram on a side plate. She puts the tray on the table LC and takes the telegram on the plate to* JUNE. XENIA *sits L of the table LC and pours a cup of tea for herself*]

ALICE: I'm afraid one of the telegrams got crumpled up. You'd better read it.

JUNE: What telegram?

ALICE: Here. [*She holds out the plate*] Will there be any reply, Modom?

[JUNE *takes the telegram and reads it*]

JUNE: Liz—I don't believe it.

ALICE: I thought you'd be pleased. [*She moves to R of the table LC*]

XENIA: [*attempting to mediate*] It's always nice to hear from old friends.

ALICE: [*moving above the table LC and singing to the tune of 'Auld Lang Syne'*] La *la* la la, la *la* la la... Sugar, Madame Xenia? [*She angrily pushes the sugar bowl towards* XENIA]

XENIA: No, thank you. I take it neat.

JUNE: [*reminiscing*] She was a thoroughbred, you know, Liz: nervy, stringy, temperamental. I remember I used to tease her because her hair grew down her neck, like a thin mane, between her shoulder-blades. [ALICE *bangs the plate down on the table LC and runs off into the bedroom, slamming the door violently behind her*]

[*She laughs*] Ho, I knew that would annoy her.

XENIA: She got out of bed with the left foot this morning.

JUNE: Her behaviour recently has left much to be desired. I may have to speak to her mother about it.

XENIA: She has her mother here?

JUNE: No, no, no. In Glasgow. Inoffensive old soul. Bakes cakes; minds her own business—but a terrific mumbler. Can't understand a word she says. [*She mumbles inaudibly in a high-pitched refined Scottish accent*] Ooo noo noo noo. You're far too decent, you're may guest, would you no' like a cup of tea and a hot pay about fave and twenty past fave. [*She laughs*]

XENIA: [*laughing*] Oh, you are a scream!

JUNE: [*rising and moving to R of the table LC*] Well, come on—let's open the champers. [*She looks at the flowers*] Then we can clear out some of the foliage. [*The door bell rings off R*]

XENIA: [*rising and crossing R*] I go. Soon we shall need a greenhouse.

JUNE: I say, thanks awfully for helping me out today, Madame Xenia.
XENIA: But you are my friend. For you I do anything. [*The door bell rings off R*]

Perhaps this one is from Buckingham Palace. [XENIA *laughs and exits through the arch*]

JUNE. And about time, too. They've been slacking. [*She untwists the wire of the champagne cork*]
XENIA: [*off*] Oh. Did you want to see Miss Buckridge? [MERCY *enters through the arch. She is dressed in mourning with a small black hat. She carries a sheaf of lilies.*
XENIA *follows her on. As* MERCY *reaches C,* JUNE *opens the champagne with a pop. Froth pours out.* JUNE *puts one hand over the mouth of the bottle and turns to ask for glasses*]
JUNE: Have you got...? [*She sees* MERCY]
MERCY: I do hope I'm not disturbing you.
JUNE: [*surprised*] Mrs. Mercy! No, of course not. [*She puts the bottle on the table LC and wipes her hand on her skirt*]
MERCY: [*handing the bouquet to* JUNE] Dear Sister George — for you — a little tribute — from all of us in Admin. at B.H.
JUNE: [*nonplussed*] Oh. Thanks. Extremely decent of you. I — appreciate the thought. [*To* XENIA] Would you be an angel, Madame, and put them in water? [*She hands the bouquet in front of* MERCY *to* XENIA] Oh, I'm terribly sorry: do you know each other? This is Madame Xenia — Mrs. Mercy Croft. [XENIA *throws the bouquet into the armchair R then bears down on* MERCY]
XENIA: What? *The* Mrs. Mercy? [*She embraces* MERCY]
JUNE: Of course. Didn't you know?
XENIA: [*to* MERCY] But I love you, my dear. [*She holds* MERCY *at arm's length for a few moments then again embraces her*] I *adore* you.
MERCY: [*clamped in the embrace*] Have I had the pleasure...?
XENIA: [*releasing her*] You don't know me from Adam, my darling, but for twenty years I have listened to you — every single week.
JUNE: How nice. [*She picks up the bottle of champagne, goes to the sideboard and pours herself a glass of champagne*]
MERCY: [*overlapping*] Charming! [JUNE *drinks*]
XENIA: [*quite overcome*] I am — I cannot tell you — your advice is a hundred per cent. A hundred and twenty per cent. One senses — you have a heart, you have suffered...
MERCY: Well, we all have our ups and downs.

427

XENIA: But you have had more downs than ups. [*She pauses briefly*] Am I right?

MERCY: I shouldn't like... [*She retreats above the sofa and puts her handbag and gloves on the table behind the sofa*]

XENIA: Of course I am. I knew at once. Ask George here. [*She moves up C. To* JUNE] Am I ever wrong?

JUNE: Never. She is quite infallible. You see, Madame Xenia is a clairvoyant.

XENIA: A psychometrist.

JUNE: Oh, sorry. [*She sits L of the table and reads the notes on the pad*]

XENIA: [*moving to L of* MERCY] I write a syndicated column every week: star forecasts — hack work, but what the hell, one's got to live.

MERCY: [*moving R to avoid* XENIA] I'm afraid I don't really believe in that kind of...

XENIA: [*pointing at* MERCY; *quickly*] Be careful what you do on the tenth. [MERCY *pauses R of the sofa*]

There's treachery around you. [*She moves to L of* MERCY] Don't sign any important document before full moon.

MERCY: [*moving to the fireplace*] I'm obliged to you, but really...

XENIA: [*following* MERCY *and pointing at her*] There's news from abroad...

MERCY: [*crossing to C; to* JUNE] I thought you'd be all alone this morning. That's why I came.

JUNE: Very kind of you. [XENIA *crosses to R of* MERCY *and taps her on the shoulder*]

XENIA: You're inclined to suffer from digestive disorders. Don't worry, it's nothing serious. [MERCY *turns to* JUNE]

JUNE: [*apologetically*] Madame is helping me out today.

XENIA: [*tapping* MERCY'*s shoulder*] A tall man doesn't like you. Avoid him.

MERCY: It would be somewhat difficult in my job to...

XENIA: An old association will be broken. Never mind: there are plenty of birds in the sky.

MERCY: [*icily*] I think you mean fish in the sea.

XENIA: [*to herself*] Interesting. [*She crosses to the armchair R and picks up the bouquet*] Must be born under Pisces. [*Cheerfully*] Oh, well, I'll get some water for the flowers. [XENIA *exits through the arch R*]

JUNE: She's been marvellous today: done all the organizing.

MERCY: Isn't your friend — er — Miss...?

JUNE: Miss McNaught? She's not up yet. I'm afraid she's no good at times like these. No backbone. Ballast.

MERCY: [wandering up C and inspecting the flowers] What beautiful tributes. May I read some? I adore inscriptions.

JUNE: There's a whole lot more in the bathroom. As soon as Childie's
dressed she can take them all and dump them on the Cenotaph.

MERCY: But you can't do that. They're for *you*. [*She moves down C.
Seriously*] Do you know the entire *Applehurst* company turned up for
the recording today in black? It was quite spontaneous.

JUNE: [*annoyed*] They must be bonkers. I can just see old Mrs. Hinch. She
must have looked like 'Keep Death Off the Roads'. [*She sees* MERCY'*s
black suit*] Oh, I do beg your pardon.

MERCY: We felt we couldn't let her go without some mark of respect. After
all, she has been with us for—how long?

JUNE: [*looking away; with assumed toughness*] Six perishing years.

MERCY: Oh, come now—you know you enjoyed every minute of it.

JUNE: [*getting exasperated*] Yes, but it's over—I just want to forget it.

MERCY: I don't think your public will let you. [*She moves to R of the sofa
and indicates the wreaths*] You can see how much you meant to them.
[*She moves above the sofa*]

[JUNE, *trying to escape, rises, removes her hat and puts it on the table LC*]

JUNE: Actually, I was just on the point of changing.

MERCY: For the funeral?

JUNE: For the broadcast. [XENIA *enters through the arch, brandishing a large,
hideous, ornate vase which bears* MERCY'*s flowers*]

XENIA: [*crossing to R of the table LC*] All right?

JUNE: [*sitting in the chair L of the table LC*] Wasn't there something a little
more—conservative?

XENIA: I can put them in a milk bottle, if you like. Or perhaps you'd prefer
a bottle of gin? [*She moves up C and puts the vase on the radio shelf.
Piqued*] It is good to have one's hard work appreciated. Getting up
early in the morning...

JUNE: [*interrupting and overlapping*] Madame Xenia—I'm eternally grateful.
You've been a brick.

XENIA: Yes, so I've been told before.

MERCY: [*picking up a bouquet from the table behind the sofa*] What a charming
message. [*She reads*]
'Ever-present, spirit-like
Harken! The familiar sound:
Sister George, astride her bike,
In the happy hunting-ground.' [JUNE *mutters under her breath*]

XENIA: [*moving down RC*] Well, happy hunting, Sister George.

JUNE: You're off, then, are you, dear?

XENIA: I'm afraid my client is waiting. The moment you need me, just stamp on the floor. [*She moves to the arch R*]

JUNE: I shall be absolutely all right. [*Suddenly*] I say. [XENIA *stops and turns*]

If any more flowers come, shove them in the coal-shed. [MERCY *moves to R of the banister and picks up a wreath*]

XENIA: Leave everything to me. I am your friend.

MERCY: [*reading the label on the wreath*] 'Fare thee well. Go in peace, good woman.'

XENIA: I can take a hint. [XENIA, *her nose in the air, strides out through the arch*]

JUNE: [*blowing a kiss after* XENIA] Thank you, darling.

MERCY: [*moving down C*] You do have a lot of friends, don't you?

JUNE: I hope so. I like to think . . .

MERCY: [*moving to R of the table LC*] Loneliness is the great scourge of our time.

JUNE: Too true.

MERCY: I had visions of you, sitting by your set, alone with your grief.

JUNE: With Miss McNaught, actually, but it comes to the same thing. [*She laughs*]

MERCY: Frankly, I'm amazed you're taking it like this.

JUNE: Like what?

MERCY: So calmly. [*She sits R of the table LC*] Cheerfully.

JUNE: The uncertainty was the worst. Once that was over . . .

MERCY: You have a very strong character. [*She pauses*] Will you go on listening to the programme now?

JUNE: I don't know. I hadn't really thought. Probably not. I mean — it might be rather — distressing — you know, hearing all the old voices going on without me.

MERCY: Isn't that rather a selfish attitude to take?

JUNE: Selfish?

MERCY: You died to save the series — surely you'll want to take an interest in its fortunes?

JUNE: Well . . .

MERCY: I think the next few episodes will be particularly fascinating. [*She warms to the subject*] Your death means an enormous re-adjustment to the whole community. It will take them weeks, even months, to get over the shock. But eventually the gap must be filled; new leaders will arise . . .

JUNE: Leaders? What new leaders? Who?

MERCY: [*confidentially*] Well, it's not really ready for release yet, but between you and me — I believe Ginger . . .

JUNE: [*rising; horrified*] Ginger? [*In her country accent*] He couldn't lead a cow down Buttercup Hill, couldn't Ginger. [*She crosses above the table to R of* MERCY] He's weak. Weak as the rotten apples that fall off a tree.

MERCY: Ginger will be our new anti-hero.

JUNE: [*turning to face* MERCY] An anti-hero in *Applehurst*?

MERCY: Contemporary appeal, Sister George. *Applehurst* is facing up to the fact that the old values have become outdated.

JUNE: [*crossing to the armchair R and sitting*] I wonder how old Mrs. Hinch is going to take that.

MERCY: [*quickly*] Not very well, I'm afraid. She passes away.

JUNE: [*aghast*] *What?*

MERCY: It's due the second week in December.

JUNE: How?

MERCY: It'll be a cold winter in Applehurst. She gets up in the middle of the night to let the cat in.

JUNE: And . . .

MERCY: Bronchitis. Gone in two days.

JUNE: [*rising and crossing to* MERCY; *angrily*] But you can't do this — after all the care I've taken of that woman. Why, I've nursed her from gout to gastro-enteritis over the last six years.

MERCY: That's neither here nor there.

JUNE: I could have saved her — [*she moves to the fireplace*] just like old Mr. Burns last winter. He's three years older, and — [*she turns to face* MERCY] look at him now, fit as a fiddle. At least he was . . .

MERCY: I'm afraid he's due for a stroke next Friday.

JUNE: [*moving to R of* MERCY] But why this carnage, why all this slaughter?

MERCY: [*rising and facing* JUNE] We live in a violent world, Miss Buckridge, surrounded by death and destruction. It's the policy of the B.B.C. to face up to reality.

JUNE: Who's going to look after the — survivors?

MERCY: Nurse Lawrence.

JUNE: *What!*

MERCY: Yes, she arrives from the District Hospital tomorrow to take over from you. [*She moves down L*]

JUNE: But she's a probationer. She couldn't put a dressing on a — salad. [*She moves R*] They won't stand for that, you know.

MERCY: On the contrary, Nurse Lawrence wins the trust and affection of the village, and becomes known, rather charmingly, I think, as 'Sister Larry'.

JUNE: *Sister Larry!* You're going to make this ill-bred, uneducated little slut...

MERCY: [*moving RC; shouting*] Contemporary appeal, Sister George. People like that *do* exist—and in positions of power and influence: flawed, credible characters like Ginger, Nurse Lawrence, Rosie...

JUNE: [*squaring up to* MERCY] What about Rosie?

MERCY: She's pregnant.

JUNE: I know that. And as she's not married, either, that's about as flawed and credible as you can get.

MERCY: She's going to marry her boy friend—Lennie.

JUNE: Oh, good. Good. [*She moves to the armchair R*] I'm glad. I'm glad about that—glad. [*She sits*]

[*There is a pause*]

MERCY: [*sitting on the sofa*] Mind you, it's not his baby.

JUNE: Eh?

MERCY: It's Roy's, from the army camp at Oakmead. She tells Lennie, makes a full confession; he forgives her, and they live happily ever after.

JUNE: [*leaning over the arm of the chair*] Pardon me while I vomit. [ALICE *enters from the bedroom. She is wearing a gaily coloured dress*]

ALICE: [*moving R of the table LC*] Oh, hello.

MERCY: [*cordially*] Hello, dear. I was wondering where you were.

ALICE: I didn't go to work today.

MERCY: No, of course not.

ALICE: [*sweetly*] Can I make you a cup of tea, Mrs. Mercy?

MERCY: I'd *adore* a cup of tea. [*She rises, goes to the table behind the sofa, takes a mirror from her handbag and looks in it*]

[ALICE *opens the hatch*]

JUNE: [*bitterly*] Mrs. Mercy's come over with the charming news that I'm to be replaced by Nurse Lawrence.

ALICE: [*picking up the tea tray*] Nurse Lawrence—Nurse Lawrence? Do I know her?

JUNE: Don't be irritating. Of course you know her. That interfering busy-body from Oakmead.

ALICE: [*with indifference*] Oh, her. [*She puts the tea tray through the hatch*]

JUNE: Yes, *her.*

ALICE: Anyway, it's not really your concern any more what happens in *Applehurst.* You're out of it. [*She moves to the table LC and tidies the telegrams*]

JUNE: [*rising and crossing to R of the table LC*] Can't you understand? Can't you understand anything? I built it up: I made it what it is. It's not *nice* to see one's life work ruined. [ALICE *moves to the sideboard and tidies up*]

MERCY: [*moving to the fireplace*] I have got one piece of cheering news for you, if you can bear to hear it.

JUNE: I can bear it. [*She sits R of the table LC*] Pour me out a glass of gin, Childie, while you're over at the sideboard. [ALICE *pours a gin, hands it to* JUNE *and stands L of the table with the bottle in her hand*]

[*She drinks*] You were saying, Mrs. Mercy?

MERCY: It concerns your future.

JUNE: [*putting down her glass, rising and crossing to* MERCY] My future, yes. You are quite right: we must talk of the future. Is there still time?

MERCY: There's still nearly an hour to go.

JUNE: Did you want to stay for the—the . . . ?

MERCY: Broadcast?

JUNE: The funeral. Yes.

MERCY: No, I have to get back to B.H. We're having a little party, you know. Perhaps 'party' isn't quite the right word.

JUNE: A wake?

MERCY: I suppose one could call it that. That's why—[*she leads* JUNE *down R*] I want a quick word with you, Miss Buckridge. Mrs. Coote has promised to come. You know Mrs. Coote, don't you? She's in charge of *Toddler Time.*

JUNE: Yes, of course I know her: a charming woman.

MERCY: Well, dear, she's very anxious to have you.

JUNE: Really? [MERCY *moves the chair down R near to the pouffe and sits.* JUNE *sits on the pouffe, facing* MERCY]

MERCY: What I'm telling you now is strictly off the cuff. Everything's still in the planning stage. I thought I'd nip over and tell you that there's a ray of sunshine on the horizon.

JUNE: I'm all ears. [ALICE *puts the bottle on the table, exits to the kitchen and removes the tray from the hatch*]

MERCY: [*confidentially*] Well, dear, as you probably know, *Toddler Time* has been—what shall we say—a wee bit disappointing. Audience research figures—this is strictly *entre nous*, you understand—

JUNE: Yes, yes, of course.

433

MERCY:—show a slight, but perceptible slide. Mrs. Coote, I may tell you, is worried out of her mind. She hasn't slept a wink for three weeks.

JUNE: [*looking away*] Poor love.

MERCY: The script-writers are running round in circles—one of them's had a nervous breakdown: the one who wrote the series about Tiddlywink, the Cockerel, which, as you know, was withdrawn after only three installments. Anyway, to cut a long story short, there's been some agonizing reappraisal over *Toddler Time*. A completely new approach has been decided on.

JUNE: Don't tell me—marauding gollywogs, drunk teddy bears, and pregnant bunnies. [ALICE *enters from the kitchen with a tray of tea for one which she puts on the table LC*]

MERCY: [*smiling enigmatically*] Not quite, dear. [ALICE *sits L of the table LC*]

But we're preparing an absolutely super new adventure series, in which we've all got loads of confidence, which will combine exciting narrative with a modern outlook—and you're being considered for the title role.

JUNE: What's it called?

MERCY: 'The World of Clarabelle Cow.' [*There is a pause.* JUNE *rises and moves C*]

JUNE. Am I to understand that this—this character is a cow?

MERCY: A very human one, I assure you: full of little foibles and prejudices.

JUNE: [*slowly*] A—flawed—credible—cow?

MERCY: Credible in human terms, certainly. Otherwise the children wouldn't believe in her. Children are very discerning.

ALICE: Ought to be fun.

JUNE: [*moving to L of the sofa*] I don't think I could have understood you correctly. I don't believe I really grasped the meaning of your words.

MERCY: I thought I made myself perfectly clear.

ALICE: Oh, don't be dense, George.

JUNE: [*to* ALICE] Shut up! [*She moves to R of the table LC and turns to* MERCY] Am I to take it that you have come here today—the day of the funeral of Sister George—to offer me the part of a cow?

MERCY: We must be practical, dear. None of us can afford to be out of work for too long.

JUNE: Pour me out another gin, Childie, will you? [ALICE *refills* JUNE*'s glass*]

[*To* MERCY] You're not serious, are you? You're joking, aren't you?

MERCY: [*rising*] We don't joke about these things at the B.B.C., Miss Buckridge.

ALICE: [*rising*] It's jolly nice of Mrs. Mercy to come over specially to tell you. [*She moves up C*]

MERCY: [*crossing to R of* JUNE] I thought it was a brilliant idea of Mrs. Coote's.

JUNE: [*shouting and tearing her hair*] I can't stand it! [*She crosses to the window*] I'm going mad! [XENIA *enters through the arch R carrying a cross of white chrysanthemums*]

XENIA: One more for luck.

JUNE: [*tonelessly*] Who from?

XENIA: [*reading the inscription*] 'I never thought I'd survive you. Mrs. Ethel Hinch.'

MERCY: She doesn't know yet.

JUNE: [*crossing to* XENIA; *distracted*] She's going to die, Madame Xenia—in two months' time. They're going to murder her, too. An old lady of eighty-five, who's never done anyone the slightest harm. [MERCY *moves below the table LC*]

XENIA: How terrible! [*She puts the cross in the chair RC*] Are you sure?

JUNE: [*to* MERCY; *wildly*] Murderess! [JUNE *lunges at* MERCY. ALICE *and* XENIA *move quickly to* JUNE *and restrain her.* XENIA *grabs* JUNE *by her right arm and shoulder and* ALICE *grabs* JUNE's *left arm*]

ALICE: George!   MERCY: Really, Miss Buckridge. Restrain yourself.

JUNE: Is your blood lust sated? How many other victims are you going to claim?

MERCY: [*shrilly*] Control yourself!

ALICE: George, you're drunk!

XENIA: My darling is upset. She's had a shock. [JUNE *throws off the constraining arms and moves slowly to* MERCY, *making a great effort to control herself.* ALICE *stands C.* XENIA *is RC.* MERCY, *a little frightened, is below the table LC*]

JUNE: [*after a pause*] With reference to *Toddler Time*, would you thank Mrs. Coote for her kind interest—

MERCY: There's no need for you to decide today.

JUNE: —and tell her I cannot possibly accept the part in question.

MERCY: Very well. I'll tell her. [*The buzzer R sounds.* XENIA *goes to the speaker, pulls it out and listens*]

ALICE: [*moving to R of* JUNE] Don't be silly, George. You can't afford to turn down…

JUNE: I'm not playing the part of a cow.

XENIA: A cow? What cow?

JUNE: [*frantically*] I'm not playing the part of a cow!

MERCY: I've taken your point, Miss Buckridge.

XENIA: [*turning to* JUNE] There are two nuns, to see Sister George.

JUNE: No! *No!* [JUNE, *groaning with dismay, rushes off up L*]

XENIA: [*to* MERCY] Nuns before noon is a good omen.

MERCY: [*moving C*] I'll take your word for it.

ALICE: [*moving up L*] I'd better see what she's doing. [ALICE *exits up L*]

> [*Off; calling*] George: what are you doing? [MERCY *moves up C. The sound of running bath water is heard off L*]

XENIA: [*into the speaker*] I'm sorry, Sister George is getting ready for her funeral. [*She pushes the speaker back to the wall*]

> [ALICE *enters up L*]

ALICE: She appears to be running a bath.

XENIA: [*moving RC*] Shall I go and speak to her?

MERCY: She won't do anything silly, will she?

XENIA: [*to* ALICE] See if she's all right. [ALICE *exits up L*]

> [*She sits on the sofa*] I'm so worried.

MERCY: [*moving above the sofa*] There was bound to be a reaction. [*She moves R of the sofa*]

ALICE: [*off; calling*] George! [*She pauses*] I can't hear what you're saying. Turn the bloody taps off!

JUNE: [*calling*] Leave me alone!

XENIA: Oi, oi, oi! [*The sound of the water ceases.*]

ALICE *enters up L*]

ALICE: [*as she enters*] Says she wants to be left alone. [MERCY *moves to the fireplace*]

XENIA: How did she sound?

ALICE: Like a walrus.

XENIA: Thank God she is herself again. [*She rises and moves to the arch R*] Oi, oi, what a morning! [XENIA *exits through the arch. There is a pause. MERCY, at the fireplace and* ALICE *up L, face each other for a few moments, then* MERCY *extends her arms.* ALICE *runs into* MERCY's *arms, lays her head on* MERCY's *shoulder and bursts into tears.* MERCY *gently puts her arms around* ALICE]

MERCY: My poor child. There, there.

ALICE: I can't stand it any more.

MERCY: I know, I know. You've been under a terrible strain.

ALICE: [*breaking from* MERCY] You've no idea, Mrs. Mercy.
MERCY: I can imagine.
ALICE: She's been *terrible!*
MERCY: Hush, dear. She'll hear you. [*She leads* ALICE *to the sofa*]

[ALICE *sits on the sofa.* MERCY *sits R of* ALICE]

ALICE: I was praying you'd come.
MERCY: I wasn't going to leave you alone with her today. [*She smiles*]
Besides — I had promised.
ALICE: Oh, I know, but I knew how busy you were.
MERCY: First things first.
ALICE: I knew I could rely on you. I felt it the first time I met you.
MERCY: And I felt I was speaking to a proud and sensitive person, whose
personality was being systematically crushed.
ALICE: [*turning away*] Don't!
MERCY: And with a definite literary talent.
ALICE: [*turning*] Honestly? Do you really think so?
MERCY: I'm being quite objective.
ALICE: Gosh! Wouldn't it be marvellous!
MERCY: What, dear?
ALICE: If I could do some work for you — writing, I mean.
MERCY: We shall see what transpires. I'll certainly give you all the help I can.
ALICE: Oh, you are nice.
MERCY: And the other offer still stands.
ALICE: [*looking away*] Yes, well — I think I've almost definitely decided. I'm
sorry to be so vague.
MERCY: [*after a pause*] Not at all. [*She rises and moves up R of the sofa*]
ALICE: It's a bit of a wrench, you know. I've been working for Mr. Katz for
nearly four years. I'd have to give him a month's notice.
MERCY: [*moving above the sofa*] There's no rush. I told you I'd keep the job
open for a fortnight.
ALICE: And then there's George.
MERCY: [*with a glance up L*] Yes.
ALICE: I mean: I don't know how she'd take it.
MERCY: [*moving to L of the sofa*] You have told her, of course?
ALICE: God, no! She'd have murdered me. [MERCY *crosses to the table LC,
stands with her back to the audience and pours a cup of tea*]
MERCY: In view of what happened today, I think we were very wise.
ALICE: If she suspected I'd been to see you behind her back . . .

MERCY: There was no reason why you shouldn't. You're perfectly entitled...

ALICE: Oh, I *know*. But she's so possessive. I'm never allowed anywhere near the B.B.C. I'm kept a guilty secret.

MERCY: She's shackled you to her. [*She sits R of the table LC*] Anyway, you wouldn't be working for the B.B.C. You'd be working for me as my own private secretary, in my London flat.

ALICE: [*rising and crossing to R of* MERCY] It sounds absolutely super. I'm sorry I'm being so slow about making up my mind.

MERCY: A thought has just occurred to me: if you're in any kind of trouble—you know, with George—you can always camp down at the flat. There's a divan...

ALICE: Oh, that'd be *wonderful!*

MERCY: It could serve as your temporary H.Q. It's not luxurious, mind. [*She drinks her tea*]

ALICE: Never mind that. It would be an escape—if necessary.

MERCY: That's what I thought. I only ever stay there myself if I've been kept late at a story conference, or something like that. I find it useful. I suppose it's a place for me to escape, too.

ALICE: [*after a pause*] We'd be like prisoners on the run. [*There is a pause.* MERCY *drinks then puts down her cup*]

MERCY: Do you really think you can escape?

ALICE: [*after a pause*] I don't know. [*She moves up C and glances off L*]

MERCY: It's very difficult for you.

ALICE: [*moving up R*] It's been so long, so many years. [*She picks up Emmeline from the table behind the sofa*]

MERCY: It's hard to break the routine.

ALICE: It's the little things one misses most.

MERCY: [*smiling*] You could bring your dolls.

ALICE: [*moving to the armchair R and hugging Emmeline*] I couldn't go anywhere without them. I even take them on holiday—and then I'm terrified they'll get lost or stolen. Sometimes George hides them—it's her idea of a joke.

MERCY: A very cruel joke. [ALICE, *still holding the doll, runs to* MERCY *and kneels R of her*]

ALICE: Don't let her get at me, Mrs. Mercy. Stay here—don't go away. [*She clutches* MERCY'S *knees*]

MERCY: I can't stay here all day, dear.

ALICE: Please don't leave me. I'm terrified of what she will do.

MERCY: Calm yourself, Alice. No one's going to hurt you. Here, put your head on my shoulder. [ALICE *lays her head on* MERCY*'s shoulder*]

Close your eyes. Relax. My goodness, you're trembling like a leaf. [*She strokes* ALICE*'s hair*]

ALICE: [*with her eyes shut*] That's nice.

MERCY: You're my little girl. You're going to be—my little girl. [JUNE *enters up L. She is wearing her bath robe*]

JUNE: What a touching sight.

ALICE: George! [*Panic-stricken, she rises, runs R and shrinks against the armchair*]

[JUNE *crosses to* ALICE, *snatches the doll from her and turns to* MERCY]

JUNE: I always did say she had nice hair. I always said that for her.

ALICE: George, you don't understand.

JUNE: [*to the doll*] Did you hear what your mummy said, Emmeline? She said I don't understand. Did you see what your mummy was doing with that strange lady?

MERCY: She was overwrought, Miss Buckridge. [*She rises*] I tried to comfort her. [ALICE *edges down R*]

JUNE: How absolutely sweet of you. And how well you have succeeded. [ALICE *is trembling from head to toe*]

MERCY: I hope you don't think…

JUNE: [*to* ALICE; *sweetly*] Come here, I want to talk to you. Come on, I want to talk to you. [ALICE *looks terrified*]

Don't be fright, I'm not going to hurt you.

ALICE: Why can't you tell me in front of Mrs. Mercy?

JUNE: [*feigning gaucheness*] Well, you know, boy's talk…

MERCY: Would you rather I left?

JUNE: [*turning to* MERCY] Oh, no, no. Whatever could have given you that idea? [*She moves to* ALICE *and grabs her arm*] Come here, I want to whisper to you. [*She whispers to* ALICE]

ALICE: [*breaking from* JUNE; *shouting*] No! [JUNE *grabs* ALICE *again and whispers to her*]

No, I'm not going to do it. [*She runs down L*]

JUNE: [*slapping the doll on her thigh to punctuate her line*] Yes or no, Childie? Yes or no?

ALICE: [*frantically*] No, no, *no!*

MERCY: [*white with indignation*] What are you asking her to do, Sister George?

JUNE: The suitable treatment. The punishment that fits the crime.

ALICE: She wants me to drink her bath water.

MERCY: [*astounded*] Her bath water?

ALICE: To humiliate me.

MERCY: But this is preposterous! I've never heard of such an obscene suggestion.

JUNE: [*moving to R of* MERCY] You're shut off from the world, Mrs. Mercy. 'Ask Mrs Mercy—all your problems answered.' 'Dear Mrs. Mercy, what shall I do? My flat-mate is nasty to me and wants to punish me by making me drink her bath water. By the time you reply to this— glug, glug, glug—it may be too late—glug—and I might have drowned.'

MERCY: [*to* ALICE] I strongly advise you to leave this house at once.

JUNE: [*to* ALICE] Well, you've had the benefit of Mrs. Mercy's expert advice. Are you going to take it?

ALICE: I'm sorry, George, I can't stay with you any longer.

MERCY: Very sensible.

JUNE: [*crossing below* MERCY *to R of* ALICE] Did you hear what your mummy said, Emmeline? She said she's going to leave us. [*She raises the doll over her head as if to hit* ALICE]

MERCY: I wish you wouldn't . . .

JUNE: [*dangerously*] You keep out of this. This is between Alice and myself.

ALICE: [*pleading*] Let me have Emmeline.

JUNE: [*pointing the doll at* ALICE] Glug, glug to you.

MERCY: I don't know how you can be so cruel. The poor child . . .

JUNE: [*moving above the table LC*] 'The poor child'! As you're going to see quite a lot of 'the poor child' in the near future, I'd better put you in the picture about her.

ALICE: George, don't! George, please!

JUNE: 'The poor child' likes to pretend she's a baby, but have a look at her; go on, have a close. look at her. [ALICE *bursts into tears and sinks on to the chair down L*]

MERCY: [*crossing quickly to* ALICE] Can't you see you're upsetting the child. [*She puts her arm protectively around* ALICE]

JUNE: [*shouting*] The child? The child is a woman—she's thirty-four. [ALICE *sobs loudly*]

She's old enough to have a grandchild.

MERCY: Oh, really, now you're exaggerating.

JUNE: [*to* ALICE] Am I? *Am I?*

ALICE: [*whimpering*] Don't, George—don't.

JUNE: [*moving down C; with disgust*] Look at you: whimpering and pleading. Have you no backbone, can't you stand up like a man?

ALICE: [*sobbing*] I can't—help it.

JUNE: [*imitating her savagely*] 'I can't help it.' She'll never be any different—feckless, self-indulgent. [*She throws the doll on to the sofa and moves up C*]

ALICE: [*jumping up and running towards the bedroom door*] I'm going. I'm packing my bag. [JUNE *intercepts* ALICE, *grabs her by the arm and drags her C*]

JUNE: Come back here.

MERCY: Let her go. Let her go.

JUNE: [*to* MERCY] You've got yourself a prize packet there, and no mistake.

ALICE: [*screaming*] Let me go! [*She wrenches herself free and collapses on the floor down C, weeping*]

JUNE: [*after a pause; looking down at* ALICE] She had an illegitimate child when she was eighteen. [ALICE *weakly covers her ears*]

She gave it away—to strangers. She's got a daughter of sixteen. [ALICE *sobs*]

Do what you like—you make me sick. [*She sits R of the table, takes a drink of gin and remains sitting, not looking at the others, until the end of the scene*]

[*There is a pause.* ALICE *cries despairingly.* MERCY *moves to L of* ALICE *and looks down at her*]

MERCY: Stop crying. [ALICE'*s sobs subside*]

Get up, quickly. [ALICE *rises and stands R of* MERCY, *her head down*]

Go and pack. You needn't take everything now. Go along, hurry. I'll wait for you here. [ALICE *exits to the bedroom*]

[*She turns to* JUNE] I'm sorry, Miss Buckridge, about all this. It'll be all for the best, you'll see. I do hope you're not bearing me any grudge. [JUNE *shakes her head*]

Oh, good, good. Sometimes it's best to make a clean break—it's painful, but that's the advice I always give in my programme. Which reminds me—[*she looks at her watch*] it's about time for the broadcast. Shall I switch it on? [*She moves to the radiogram and switches it on, then collects her handbag and gloves and puts her gloves on*] Let it give you strength, Miss Buckridge. Remember: Sister George was killed, not because she was hated, but because she was loved. [ALICE *enters from the bedroom. She carries a mackintosh and a small suitcase*]

[*She moves to R of* JUNE] If you study anthropology, you'll discover that in primitive societies it was always the best-loved member of the community who was selected as the sacrificial victim. They felt that by killing him the goodness and strength of the victim would pass into them. It was both a purge and a re-dedication. What you are about to hear is the purge and—

[*The slow tolling of a bell sounds softly from the radio*]

—re-dedication of *Applehurst*. Good-bye, Sister George. [*She crosses to the arch R and looks back*]

[ALICE *crosses to the sofa, picks up the doll Emmeline, moves to R of the sofa, hesitates and looks back at* JUNE]

ALICE: I think she's right in what she said, George—Mrs. Mercy, I mean. I love you, too, that's why I've got to leave you. You do understand, don't you? I mean... [*She weeps and looks almost impatiently at* MERCY] All right, Mrs. Mercy, I'm coming. [MERCY *exits through the arch R*] Good-bye, George, and—you know—thanks for everything. [ALICE *exits through the arch R.* JUNE, *who has not looked up, remains sitting R of the table. An* ANNOUNCER'*s voice is heard from the radio, backed up by the tolling bell*]

ANNOUNCER: [*through the radio*] *Applehurst*, a chronicle of an English village. This is a sad day for *Applehurst*. The church bell is tolling for the funeral of Sister George, the well-beloved District Nurse, whose forthright, practical no-nonsense manner had endeared her to the community, but death—[*Very soft music, a slow and minor variation on the 'Applehurst Theme' is heard over the* ANNOUNCER'*s voice and continues softly to the end of the scene*]

—comes to the best of us, and the picturesque village of Applehurst is today swathed in mourning.

JUNE: [*a very plaintive sound*] Moo! [*Louder*] Moo! *Moo!* [*A heartrending sound*]

The music increases in volume as—

the CURTAIN *falls*

The Boys
in the Band

Mart Crowley

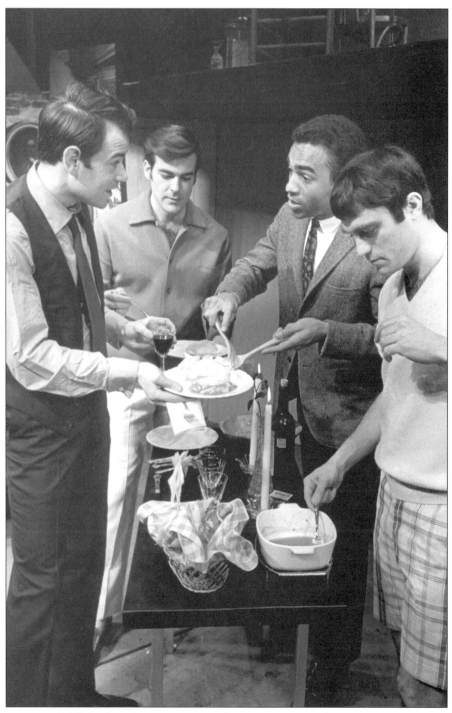

Laurence Luckinbill (Hank), Keith Prentice (Larry), Reuben Greene (Bernard), and Cliff Gorman (Emory) in *The Boys in the Band*, at Theater Four, 1968. (Photograph reprinted with permission from the John Willis Theatre World/Screen World Archive.)

The Boys in the Band was first presented Off-Broadway at Theater Four on Sunday, April 14, 1968. It was produced by Richard Barr and Charles Woodward, and directed by Robert Moore. It was designed by Peter Harvey, and the Administrative Director was Barry Plaxen. The General Manager was Michael Kasdan, the press agents were David Rothenberg and Lawrence Schneider, and the stage managers were Charles Kindl and Richard Foltz. The photographer was Friedman–Abeles.

Cast

Michael . . . . Kenneth Nelson
Donald . . . . Frederick Combs
Emory . . . . Cliff Gorman
Larry . . . . Keith Prentice
Hank . . . . Laurence Luckinbill
Bernard . . . . Reuben Greene
Cowboy . . . . Robert La Tourneaux
Alan . . . . Peter White
Harold . . . . Leonard Frey

UNDERSTUDIES:
Donald, Larry, Cowboy . . . . William Leet
Michael . . . . Eric James
Hank, Alan . . . . Jered Mickey
Bernard . . . . Bob Broadway
Harold, Emory . . . . Page Johnson

The play is divided into two acts. The action is continuous and occurs one evening within the time necessary to perform the play.

Description of Characters

MICHAEL: *Thirty, average face, smartly groomed.*

DONALD: *Twenty-eight, medium blond, wholesome American good looks.*

EMORY: *Thirty-three, small, frail, very plain.*

LARRY: *Twenty-nine with a starkly simple sense of individual style and color in his clothes. Dark eyes, dark hair, extremely handsome.*

HANK: *Thirty-two, tall, solid, athletic, attractive.*

BERNARD: *Twenty-eight, Negro, tall, gaunt, nice-looking, dressed in Ivy-League clothes.*

COWBOY: *Twenty-two, light blond, muscle-bound, too pretty.*

HAROLD: *Thirty-two, dark, lean, strong limbs, unusual semitic face.*

ALAN: *Thirty, aristocratic Anglo-Saxon features.*

Act One

There is no curtain. The LIGHTS *come up on a smartly appointed duplex apartment in the East Fifties, New York, consisting of a living room and, on a higher level, a bedroom. Bossa nova* MUSIC *blasts from a Phonograph.* MICHAEL, *wearing a robe, enters from the kitchen, carrying a Scotch liquor bottle and one red rose in a vase. He crosses to set Scotch on the bar, moves to the Left table to place vase. He crosses to sofa and sits and starts ribbon on package. The front door* BUZZER *sounds.* MICHAEL *stops tying package, goes to door, pushes button to release outside building door and opens apartment door and turns off* PHONOGRAPH *as* DONALD *enters.* DONALD *is dressed in khakis and a Lacoste shirt, carrying an airlines zipper bag and a stack of books.* DONALD *drops his books on sofa.*

MICHAEL: Donald! You're about a day and a half early!

DONALD: The doctor cancelled! [DONALD *puts zipper bag at top of stairs.*]

MICHAEL: Cancelled! How'd you get inside? [*Looks out front door.*]

DONALD: The street door was open. [*As he comes back to sofa to pick up books and* MICHAEL *closes door.*]

MICHAEL: You wanna drink?

DONALD: [*Deposits his books on bar and sits Right end of sofa.*] Not until I've had my shower. I want something to work-out today—I want to try to relax and enjoy *something.*

MICHAEL: [*Comes to Left end of sofa.*] You in a blue funk because of the doctor?

DONALD: [*Returning.*] Christ, no. I was depressed long before I got *there.*

MICHAEL: Why'd the prick cancel?

DONALD: A virus or something. He looked awful.

MICHAEL: [*Goes to desk for shopping bag and returns to Left of sofa.*] Well, this'll pick you up. I went shopping today and bought all kind of goodies— Sandalwood Soap...

DONALD: [*Removing his sox and shoes.*] I feel better already.

MICHAEL: [*Producing articles.*]—Your very own toothbrush because I'm sick to death of your using mine.

DONALD: How do you think *I* feel.

MICHAEL: [*Holds up a cylindrical can and crosses to Right end of sofa.*] And, also for you...something called "Control." Notice nowhere is it called hair spray—just simply, "Control." And the words, "For Men," are written about thirty-seven times all over the goddamn can!

DONALD: It's called Butch Assurance.

MICHAEL: Well, it's *still* hair spray—no matter if they call it *"Balls"! [Goes above sofa, picks up bag and goes to step landing.*] It's all going on your very own shelf which is to be labeled: Donald's Saturday Night Douche Kit. [*Shouting over shoulder as he takes bag to bathroom on second level.*] By the way, are you spending the night?

DONALD: [*Shouting.*] Nope. I'm driving back. I still get very itchy when I'm in this town too long. I'm not that well yet.

MICHAEL: [*Enters from bath and crosses to landing and sits on railing.*] That's what you say every weekend.

DONALD: Maybe after about ten more years of analysis I'll he able to stay one night.

MICHAEL: Maybe after about ten more years of analysis you'll be able to move back to town permanently.

DONALD: If I live that long.

MICHAEL: You will. If you don't kill yourself on the Long Island Expressway some early Sunday morning. I'll never know how you can tank-up on martinis and make it back to the Hamptons in one piece.

DONALD: [*Rises with shoes and socks and crosses to* MICHAEL.] Believe me, it's easier than getting here. Ever had an anxiety attack at sixty miles an hour? Well, tonight I was beside myself to get to the doctor—and just as I finally make it, rush in, throw myself on the couch and vomit-out how depressed I am, he says, "Donald, I have to cancel tonight—I'm just too sick." [*Starts to bathroom.*]

MICHAEL: Why didn't you tell him you're sicker than he is.

DONALD: He already knows *that*. [*Picks up bag and goes to bath where he leaves bag, shoes and socks.*]

MICHAEL: Why didn't the prick call you and cancel? Suppose you'd driven all this way for nothing.

DONALD: [*Enters from bath to Right of bed.*] Why do you keep calling him a prick?

MICHAEL: Whoever heard of an analyst having a session with a patient for two hours on Saturday evening.

DONALD: He simply prefers to take Mondays off. [*Removing his shirt.*]

MICHAEL: Works late on Saturday and takes Monday off—what is he, a psychiatrist or a hairdresser?

DONALD: Actually, he's both. He shrinks my head and combs me out. [MICHAEL *enters bedroom and crosses to hair drier.*] Besides, I had to come in town to a birthday party anyway. Right? [*Sits on bed.*]

MICHAEL: You had to remind me. If there's one thing I'm not ready for, it's five screaming queens singing Happy Birthday: [*Winding up cord on drier and exits bath.*]

DONALD: Who's coming?

MICHAEL: [*Putting pants on in bath.*] They're really all Harold's friends. It's *his* birthday and I want everything to be just the way he'd want it. I don't want to have to listen to him kvetch about how nobody ever does anything for anybody but themself.

DONALD: Himself.

MICHAEL: I think you know everybody anyway—[*He enters from bath and crosses to* DONALD.] they're the same old tired fairies you've seen around since the day one. Actually, there'll be seven counting Harold and you and me.

DONALD: Are you calling me a screaming queen or a tired fairy?

MICHAEL: Oh, I beg your pardon—six tired screaming fairy queens and one anxious queer. [*Removes slippers and deposits Left side of bed.*]

DONALD: You don't think Harold'll mind my being here, do you? Technically, I'm *your* friend, not his.

MICHAEL: [*Crossing to bed table for comb.*] If she doesn't like it, she can twirl on it. Listen, I'll be out of your way in just a second. I've only got one more thing to do. [*He goes to mirror.*]

DONALD: Surgery, so early in the evening?

MICHAEL: [*Turns to* DONALD.] Sunt! That's French, with a cedilla. I've just got to comb my hair for the thirty-seventh time. Hair—that's singular. My hair, without exaggeration, is clearly falling on the floor. And *fast*, baby!

DONALD: You're totally paranoid. You've got plenty of hair.

MICHAEL: What you see before you is a masterpiece of deception. My hairline starts about here. [*Indicates his crown.*] All this is just tortured forward.

DONALD: Well, I hope for your sake, no strong wind comes up.

MICHAEL: If one does. I'll be in terrible trouble. I will then have a bald head and shoulder-length fringe. [*He runs his fingers through his hair, holds it away from his scalp, dips the top of his head so that* DONALD *can see.* DONALD *is silent.*] Not good, huh?

DONALD: Not the greatest.

MICHAEL: It's called, "getting old" — Well, one thing you can say for masturbation — you certainly don't have to look your best. [*He slips out of the robe, flings it at* DONALD. DONALD *laughs, takes the robe, exits to the bath.* MICHAEL *takes a sweater from bed table and pulls it on.*] What are you so depressed about? I mean, other than the usual *everything*. [*At mirror checking hair.*]

DONALD: [*Reluctantly.*] Michael, I really don't want to get into it.

MICHAEL: Well, if you're not going to tell me how can we have a conversation *in depth* — a warm, rewarding, meaningful friendship? [*Sits on bench and puts on shoes.*]

DONALD: Up yours!

MICHAEL: [*Southern accent.*] Why, Cap'n Butler, how you talk! [DONALD *crosses to* MICHAEL *holding a glass of water with* MICHAEL'*s robe on and no pants.* MICHAEL *looks up.*]

DONALD: It's just that today I finally realized that I was *raised* to be a failure. I was *groomed* for it. [*Takes a pill.*]

MICHAEL: You know, there was a time when you could have said that to me and I wouldn't have known what the hell you were talking about.

DONALD: Naturally, it all goes back to Evelyn and Walt. [*Sits bedroom chair.*]

MICHAEL: Naturally. When doesn't it go back to Mom and Pop. Unfortunately, we all had an Evelyn and a Walt. The Crumbs! Don't you love that word — crumb? Oh, I love it! It's a real Barbara Stanwyck word. [*He rises. A la Stanwyck's frozen-lipped Brooklyn accent:*] "Cau'll me a keab, you kr-rumm."

DONALD: Well, I see all vestiges of sanity for this evening are now officially shot-to-hell.

MICHAEL: [*Goes to* DONALD.] Oh, Donald, you're so serious tonight! You're fun-starved, baby, and I'm eating for two! [*Sings.*] "Forget your troubles, c'mon get happy! You better chase all your blues away. Shout, 'Hallelujah!' c'mon get happy..." ★ [MICHAEL *does a few Garland poses. Sees* DONALD *isn't buying it.*] — what's more boring than a queen doing a Judy Garland imitation?

DONALD: [*Rises.*] A queen doing a Bette Davis imitation. [*Exits to bath, leaving glass.*]

★ GET HAPPY, by Harold Arlen and Ted Koehler. © 1929 (Renewed) Warner Bros. Inc. Rights for extended renewal term in U.S. controlled by Warner Bros. Inc. and S.A. Music Company. All rights outside U.S. controlled by Warner Bros. Inc. All rights reserved. Used by permission WARNER BROS. PUBLICATIONS U.S. INC. Miami, FL 33014

MICHAEL: [*Goes to chair, sits and buffs shoes with mitt.*] Meanwhile—back at the Evelyn and Walt Syndrome.

DONALD: [*Crosses to* MICHAEL.] America's Square Peg and America's Round Hole.

MICHAEL: Christ, how sick analysts must get of hearing how mommy and daddy made their darlin' into a fairy.

DONALD: It's beyond just that now. Today I finally began to see how some of the other pieces of the puzzle relate to them. — Like why I never finished anything I started in my life . . . my neurotic compulsion to not succeed. I've realized it was always when I failed that Evelyn loved me the most—because it displeased Walt who wanted perfection. And when I fell short of the mark she was only too happy to make up for it with her love. [*Sits on bed.*] So I began to identify failing with winning my mother's love. And I began to fail on purpose to get it. I didn't finish Cornell—I couldn't keep a job in this town. I simply retreated to a room over a garage and scrubbing floors in order to keep alive. Failure is the only thing with which I feel at home. Because it is what I was taught at home.

MICHAEL: Killer whales. Killer whales is what they are. How many whales could a killer whale kill?

DONALD: A lot especially if they get them when they are babies. [*Pause.* MICHAEL *suddenly tears off his sweater, throws it in the air, letting, it land where it may, goes to Left of bed and whips another sweater out pulls it on as he starts for the living room.* DONALD *follows.*] Hey! Where're you going? [*Stops on landing.*]

MICHAEL: [*Finishes putting sweater on at bar.*] To make drinks! I think we need about thirty-seven!

DONALD: Where'd you get *that* sweater?

MICHAEL: This clever little shop on the right bank called *Hermes*.

DONALD: I work my ass off for forty-five lousy dollars a week *scrubbing* floors and you waltz around throwing cashmere sweaters on them.

MICHAEL: The one on the floor in the bedroom is vicuna.

DONALD: I *beg* your pardon.

MICHAEL: You could get a job doing something else. Nobody holds a gun to your head to be a char-woman. That is, how you say, your neurosis.

DONALD: [*Sits on landing.*] Gee, and I thought it's why I was born.

MICHAEL: [*Goes to desk for scotch tape.*] Besides, just because I *wear* expensive clothes doesn't necessarily mean they're paid for.

DONALD: That is, how you say, *your* neurosis.

MICHAEL: [*Crosses to Center.*] I'm a spoiled brat so what do I know about being mature. The only thing mature means to me is *Victor* Mature who was in all those pictures with Betty Grable. [*Sings a la Grable.*] "I can't begin to tell you, how much you mean to me . . ." Betty sang that in 1945. [*Crosses to coffee table and puts tape by gift package.*] '45? — '43. No, '43 was "Coney Island" which was re-made in '50 as "Wabash Avenue." Yes, "Dolly Sisters" was in '45. [*Crosses to desk for scissors and bow.*]

DONALD: How did I manage to miss these momentous events in the American Cinema? I can understand people having an affinity for stage — but movies are such garbage, who can take them seriously?

MICHAEL: [*He is back to Center.*] Well, I'm sorry if your sense of art is offended. Odd as it may seem there was no Shubert Theatre in Hot Coffee, Mississippi! [*Crosses to sofa, sits and finishes ribbon tying.*]

DONALD: However — thanks to the silver screen, your neurosis has got style. [*Rises, crosses to* MICHAEL.] It takes a certain flair to squander one's unemployment check at Pavillion.

MICHAEL: What's so snappy about being head over heels in debt. The only thing smart about it is the ingenious ways I dodge the bill collectors. [DONALD *helps* MICHAEL *to tie a knot with the use of his finger.*]

DONALD: Yeah. Come to think of it, you're the type that gives faggots a bad name.

MICHAEL: And you, Donald, *you* are a credit to the homosexual. A reliable, hard-working, floor-scrubbing, bill-paying fag who don't owe nothin' to nobody. [*Cuts off excess ribbon.*]

DONALD: *I* am a model fairy.

MICHAEL: [*Puffs up bow.*] You think it's just nifty how I've always flitted from Beverly Hills to Rome to Acapulco to Amsterdam — [DONALD *slowly goes above sofa, looks at phono and then to bar where he leans to listen.*] picking up a lot of one-night stands and a lot of custom-made duds along the trail, but I'm here to tell you that the only place in all those miles — the only place I've ever been *happy* — was on the goddamn plane. Bored with Scandinavia, try Greece. Fed up with dark meat, try light. Hate tequila, what about slivovitz? Tired of boys, what about girls? — or how about boys and girls mixed and in what combination? [DONALD *laughs and sits in Down Right chair.*] And if you're sick of people, what about poppers? Or pot or pills or the hard stuff. And can you think of anything else the bad baby would like to indulge his spoiled-rotten, stupid empty, boring, selfish, self-centered self in? [*Makes a scotch tape loop.*] Is that what you think has style, Donald? Huh? Is that what you think you've missed out on — my hysterical escapes from country to country, party to party, bar to bar, bed to bed,

hangover to hangover, and all of it, hand to mouth! [*Tape to package.*]
Run, charge, run, buy, borrow, make, spend, run, squander, beg, run,
run, run, waste, waste, *waste!* [*Bow to tape.*] And why? And why? [*Leans
back on sofa.*]

DONALD: Why, Michael? Why?

MICHAEL: I really don't want to get into it.

DONALD: Then how can we have a conversation in depth?

MICHAEL: Oh, you know it all by heart anyway. Same song, second verse.
Because my Evelyn refused to let me grow up. She was determined to
keep me a child forever and she did one helluva job of it. And my Walt
stood by and let her do it. [*A beat.*] What you see before you is a
thirty-year-old infant. And it was all done in the name of love—what
she labeled love and probably sincerely believed to be love, when what
she was really doing was feeding her own need—satisfying her own
loneliness. [*Picks up cut-off ribbon and puts in ashtray.*] She bathed me in
the same tub with her until I grew too big for the two of us to fit and
she made me sleep in the same bed with her until I was fourteen years
old—until I finally flatly refused to spend one more night there. And
do you know until this day she still says, "I don't care if you're seventy
years old, you'll always be my baby." [*Rises and crosses to DONALD.*] And
can I tell you how that drives me mad! Will that bitch never understand that what I'll always *be* is her son—but that I haven't been her
baby for twenty-five years! [*Picks up scissors and tape from coffee table and
takes up to desk.*] And don't get me wrong. I know it's easy to cop out
and blame Evelyn and Walt and say it was *their* fault. That we were
simply the helpless put-upon victims. But I've dropped enough dough
on the couch to know that in the end, you are responsible for yourself. [*Crosses to finished package on coffee table and picks up.*] And I
guess—I'm not sure—but I want to believe it—that in their own
pathetic, dangerous way, they just loved us too much. [*A beat.*] Finis.
Applause. [*DONALD hesitates, walks over to MICHAEL, puts his arms around
him and holds him. It is a totally warm and caring gesture.*] There's nothing
quite as good as feeling sorry for yourself, is there?

DONALD: Nothing.

MICHAEL: [*A la Bette Davis.*] I adore cheap sentiment. [*Breaks away to steps,
putting gift on fourth step.*] Okay, I'm taking orders for drinks. What'll
it be?

DONALD: [*As going up stairs to bath.*] An extra-dry-Beefeater-martini-on-
the-rocks-with-a-twist.

MICHAEL: Coming up. [*DONALD exits to bath. MICHAEL starts to bar to make*

DONALD'*s drink and notices there is no ice, so exits to kitchen singing* "*Acapulco.*" *As he exits, the telephone rings on an empty Stage. Momentarily,* MICHAEL *returns, carrying an ice bucket in one hand and a tray of cracked crab in the other. He puts crab on coffee table and answers phone on desk.*] Backstage, "New Moon" [*A beat.*] Alan? Alan! My God, I don't believe it. How *are* you? Where *are* you? In town! Great! When'd you get in? Is Fran with you? Oh. What? No. [*Crosses to bar with phone and ice, sets ice on bar.*] No, I'm tied-up tonight. No, tonight's no good for me. — You mean, *now?* [*Empties ashtray on coffee table to waste can under bar.*] Well, Alan, ole boy, it's a friend's birthday and I'm having a few people. — No, you wouldn't exactly call it a birthday party — well, yes, actually, I guess you would. I mean, what else would you call it? A *wake*, maybe. [*Ashtray back to coffee table.*] I'm sorry I can't ask you to join us — but — well, kiddo, it just wouldn't work out. — No, it's not place cards or anything. It's just that — well, I'd hate to see you for just ten minutes and Alan? Alan? What's the matter? — Are you — are you crying? — Oh, Alan, what's wrong? — Alan, listen, come on over. No, no, it's perfectly all right. Well, just hurry up. I mean, just come on by and have a drink, okay? Alan . . . are you all right? Okay. Yeah. Same old address. Yeah. Bye. [*He sits on stool and slowly hangs up, stares blankly into space.*]

[DONALD *appears, bathed and changed. He strikes a pose on landing.*]

DONALD: Well. Am I stunning?

MICHAEL: [*He looks up. Tonelessly.*] You're absolutely stunning. — You look like shit, but I'm absolutely stunned.

DONALD: [*Crestfallen, goes to bar.*] Your grapes are, how you say, sour.

MICHAEL: Listen, you won't believe what just happened.

DONALD: Where's my drink?

MICHAEL: I didn't make it — I've been on the phone. [DONALD *makes himself a martini.*] My old roommate from Georgetown just called.

DONALD: Alan what's-his-name?

MICHAEL: McCarthy. He's up here from Washington on business or something and he's on his way over here.

DONALD: Well I hope he knows the lyrics to Happy Birthday.

MICHAEL: [*Rises with phone.*] Listen, asshole, what am I going to do? He's *straight.* And *Square City!* [*"Top Drawer" accent through clenched teeth.*] I mean he's rally vury proper. Auffully good family.

DONALD: [*Same accent.*] That's so important.

MICHAEL: [*Regular speech.*] I mean his family looks down on people in the theatre—so whatta you think he'll feel about the freak show we've got booked for dinner? [*Returns phone to desk and crosses to Left end of sofa.*]

DONALD: [*Sipping his drink.*] Christ, is that good. [*Sits in Down Right chair.*]

MICHAEL: Want some cracked crab?

DONALD: Not just yet. Why'd you invite him over?

MICHAEL: I didn't. He invited himself. He said he had to see me tonight. Immediately. He absolutely lost his spring on the phone—started crying. [*Crosses to* DONALD.]

DONALD: Maybe he's feeling sorry for himself too.

MICHAEL: Great heaves and sobs. Really boo-hoo-hoo-time—and that's not his style at all. I mean he's so pulled together he wouldn't show any emotion if he were in a plane crash. What am I going to do? [*Gets a glass and ice at bar.*]

DONALD: What the hell do you care what he thinks?

MICHAEL: Well, I don't really.

DONALD: Or are you suddenly ashamed of your friends?

MICHAEL: Donald, you are the only person I know of whom I am truly ashamed. Some people do have different standards from yours and mine, you know. And if we don't acknowledge them, we're just as narrow-minded and backward as we think they are.

DONALD: You know what you are, Michael? You're a real person.

MICHAEL: Thank you and fuck you. [MICHAEL *points to crab.*] Want some?

DONALD: No, thanks. [MICHAEL *crosses to bar and opens club soda.*] How could you ever have been friends with a bore like that?

MICHAEL: Believe it or not there was a time in my life when I didn't go around *announcing* that I was a faggot.

DONALD: That must have been before speech replaced sign language. [*Goes to other side of ottoman.*]

MICHAEL: [*Crosses to Right end of sofa with glass.*] Don't give me any static on that score. I didn't come out until I left college.

DONALD: It seems to me that the first time we tricked we met in a gay bar on Third Avenue during your junior year.

MICHAEL: Cunt.

DONALD: I thought you'd never say it.

MICHAEL: Sure you don't want any cracked crab?

DONALD: *Not yet! If you don't mind!*

MICHAEL: Well, it can only be getting colder. [*Puts glass on coffee table and picks up crab and leaves it on Left table.*] What time is it?

DONALD: I don't know. Early. [*Goes to bar.*]

MICHAEL: Where the hell is Alan? [*Goes to coffee table for glass.*]
DONALD: Do you want some more club soda? [*Picking up soda bottle.*]
MICHAEL: What?
DONALD: There's nothing but club soda in that glass. It's not gin — like mine. You want some more?
MICHAEL: No. [*Puts glass on coffee table and goes to desk for cigarettes.*]
DONALD: I've been watching you for several Saturdays now. You've actually stopped drinking, haven't you?
MICHAEL: And smoking too. [*Opening cigarettes at Up Left end of sofa.*]
DONALD: And smoking too. How long's it been?
MICHAEL: Five weeks.
DONALD: That's amazing.
MICHAEL: I've found God. [*Goes to waste can with wrappings.*]
DONALD: [*Crosses above sofa to ottoman.*] It is amazing — for you.
MICHAEL: Or is God dead?
DONALD: [*Sits on ottoman.*] Yes, thank God. And don't get panicky just because I'm paying you a compliment. I can tell the difference.
MICHAEL: [*Crosses to Right end coffee table.*] You always said that I held my liquor better than anybody you ever saw.
DONALD: I could always tell when you were getting high — one way.
MICHAEL: I'd get hostile.
DONALD: You seem happier or something now — and that shows.
MICHAEL: [*Quietly.*] Thanks. [*Puts opened cigarettes on coffee table and exits to kitchen for beer tub.*]
DONALD: What made you stop — the analyst?
MICHAEL: [*Offstage.*] He certainly had a lot to do with it. [*Returns from kitchen and puts beer tub under bar.*] Mainly, I just didn't think I could survive another hangover, that's all. I don't think I could get through that morning-after ick attack.
DONALD: Morning-after what?
MICHAEL: Icks! Anxiety! Guilt! Unfathomable guilt — either real or imagined — from that split second your eyes pop open and you say, "Oh, my God, what did I do last night!" and ZAP, Total Recall! [*Picks up two ashtrays from bar.*]
DONALD: Tell me about it!
MICHAEL: [*Goes to Left table leaving an ashtray.*] Then, the coffee, aspirin, alka-seltzer, darvon, deprisal, and a quick call to I.A. — Ick's Anonymous.
DONALD: "Good morning, I.A."

MICHAEL: [*Crosses in.*] "Hi! Was I too bad last night? Did I do anything wrong? I didn't do anything terrible, did I?"

DONALD: [*Laughing.*] How many times! How many times!

MICHAEL: [*Takes ashtray to desk.*] And from then on, that struggle to live til lunch when you have a double Bloody Mary — that is, if you've *waited* until lunch — and then you're half-pissed again and useless for the rest of the afternoon. And the only sure cure is to go to bed for about thirty-seven hours but who ever does that. Instead, you hang on til cocktail time, and by then you're ready for what the night holds-which hopefully is another party where the whole goddam cycle starts over! [*Crosses to Right end of coffee table.*] Well, I've been on that merry-go-round long enough and I either had to get off or die of centrifugal force.

DONALD: And just how does a clear head *stack up* with the dull fog of alcohol?

MICHAEL: Well, all those things you've always heard are true. Nothing can compare with the experience of one's faculties functioning at their maximum natural capacity. The only thing is . . . I'd *kill* for a drink. [*The* BUZZER *sounds.*]

DONALD: Joe College has finally arrived.

MICHAEL: [*He puts his drink on coffee table and goes to door and presses the wall panel button.*] Suddenly, I have such an ick! [*Crosses back to* DONALD.] Now listen, Donald . . .

DONALD: [*Rises. Quick.*] Michael, don't insult me by giving me any lecture on acceptable social behavior. I promise to sit with my legs spread apart and keep my voice in a deep register.

MICHAEL: Donald, you are a real *card-carrying cunt.* [*The apartment door* BUZZES. MICHAEL *goes to door and opens it and* DONALD *goes to base of steps.*]

EMORY: [*Offstage.*] ALL RIGHT THIS IS A RAID! EVERYBODY'S UNDER ARREST! [EMORY *is in Bermuda shorts and a sweater. He enters and gives* MICHAEL *a kiss on the cheek, refers to dish:* EMORY *carries a covered dish.*] Hello, darlin'! Connie Casserole. Oh, Mary, don't ask.

MICHAEL: Hello, Emory. Put it in the kitchen. [EMORY *spots* DONALD *and goes to him.*]

EMORY: Who is this exotic woman over here? [HANK *enters first, then* LARRY. LARRY *has on a shirt and pants.* HANK *is in a suit and tie.* LARRY *and* HANK *carry birthday gifts.*]

MICHAEL: Hi, Hank. Larry. [*They say, "Hi," shake hands, enter.* HANK *crosses to*

Right end of coffee table and LARRY *goes above sofa.* MICHAEL *looks out in the hall, comes back into the room, closes the door.*]

DONALD: Hi, Emory.

EMORY: My dear, I thought you had perished! Where have you been hiding your classically chiseled features?

DONALD: [*To* EMORY.] I don't live in the city any more.

MICHAEL: [*To* LARRY *and* HANK *re: the gifts.*] Here, I'll take those. Where's yours, Emory?

EMORY: It's arriving later. [EMORY *exits to the kitchen.*]

[LARRY *and* DONALD's *eyes have met.* HANK *has handed* MICHAEL *his gift.* LARRY *is too preoccupied.*]

HANK: Larry! Larry!

LARRY: What!

HANK: Give Michael the gift!

LARRY: Oh. Here. [LARRY *crosses, gives gift to* MICHAEL *who puts box on third step and leans poster against step pillar. To* HANK.] Louder. So my mother in Philadelphia can hear you.

HANK: Well, you were just standing there in a trance.

MICHAEL: [*To* LARRY *and* HANK.] You both know Donald, don't you?

DONALD: Sure. Nice to see you. [*To* HANK.] Hi.

HANK: [*Shaking hands.*] Nice to meet you. [*Continues crosses to Down Left chair.*]

MICHAEL: Oh, I thought you'd met.

DONALD: Well...

LARRY: We haven't exactly met but we've...Hi. [*Crosses to* HANK.]

DONALD: Hi. [*Crosses and sits Down Right chair.*]

HANK: But you've what?

LARRY: ...Seen...each other before.

MICHAEL: Well, *that* sounds murky. [EMORY *re-enters from kitchen crossing to* MICHAEL *at Center.*]

HANK: You've never met but you've seen each other.

LARRY: What was wrong with the way *I* said it.

HANK: Where?

EMORY: [*Loud aside to* MICHAEL.] I think they're going to have their first fight.

LARRY: [*Leans on landing.*] The first one since we got out of the taxi.

MICHAEL: [*Re:* EMORY.] Where'd you find this trash?

LARRY: Downstairs leaning against a lamppost.

EMORY: With an orchid behind my ear and big wet lips painted over the lipline.

MICHAEL: Just like Maria Montez.

DONALD: Oh, *please!*

EMORY: [*Crossing to* DONALD.] What have you got against Maria?—she was a good woman. [*Crosses above sofa.*]

MICHAEL: Listen, everybody, this old college friend of mine is in town and he's stopping by for a fast drink on his way to dinner somewhere. But, listen, he's straight. [*Crosses to* EMORY.]

LARRY: *Straight!* If it's the one I met he's about as straight as the Yellow Brick Road.

MICHAEL: [*Crosses in.*] No, you met Justin Stuart.

[EMORY *exits kitchen Up Center.*]

HANK: I don't remember meeting anybody named Justin Stuart.

LARRY: Of course you don't, dope. *I* met him.

MICHAEL: Well, this is someone else.

DONALD: Alan McCarthy. A very close total stranger.

MICHAEL: It's not that I care what he would think of me, really—it's just that *he's* not ready for it. And he never will be. You understand that, don't you, Hank? [EMORY *enters Up Center and crosses to landing.*]

HANK: Oh, sure.

LARRY: You honestly think he doesn't know about you?

MICHAEL: If there's the slightest suspicion, he's never let-on one bit.

EMORY: What's he had, a lobotomy? [*He continues to bath for a Kleenex picking up the vicuna sweater from floor enroute and putting it on the bed.*]

MICHAEL: I was super careful when I was in college and I still am whenever I see him. I don't know why, but I am.

DONALD: Tilt.

MICHAEL: [*Crosses to Center.*] You may think it was a crock of shit, Donald, but to him I'm sure we were close friends. The closest. To pop that balloon now just wouldn't be fair to him. Isn't that right? [*Looks to* LARRY.]

LARRY: Whatever's fair. [LARRY *gives* HANK *a look and* HANK *goes around staircase looking over apartment, ending up at Center.*]

MICHAEL: Well, of course. And if that's phony of me, Donald, then that's phony of me and make something of it.

DONALD: I pass.

MICHAEL: [*Crosses to* DONALD.] Well, even you have to admit it's much simpler to deal with the world according to its rules and then go right ahead and do what you damn well please. You do understand *that,* don't you?

DONALD: Now that you've put it in layman's terms.

MICHAEL: I was just like Alan when I was in college. Very large in the dating department. Wore nothing but those constipated Ivy League clothes and those ten-pound cordovan shoes. [*To* HANK.] No offense.

HANK: Quite all right. [*Goes to bar.*]

[EMORY *enters from bath and comes down steps.*]

MICHAEL: I butched-it-up quite a bit. And I didn't think I was lying to myself. I really thought I was straight. [*Goes to steps.*]

EMORY: Who do you have to fuck to get a drink around here? [*Stops on steps.*]

MICHAEL: Will you light somewhere? [EMORY *sits on steps.*] Or I thought I thought I was straight. I know I didn't come out til after I'd graduated.

DONALD: What about all those weekends up from school?

MICHAEL: [*Crosses in.*] I still wasn't out. I was still in the "Christ-Was-I-Drunk-Last-Night Syndrome."

LARRY: The *what?*

MICHAEL: [*Crosses Center.*] The Christ-Was-I-Drunk-Last-Night Syndrome. You know, when you made it with some guy in school and the next day when you had to face each other there was always a lot of shit-kicking crap about, "Man, was I drunk last night! Christ, I don't remember a thing!"

DONALD: You were just guilty because you were Catholic, that's all.

MICHAEL: [*Crosses to Left end coffee table.*] That's not true. The Christ-Was-I-Drunk-Last-Night Syndrome knows no religion. It has to do with immaturity. Although I will admit there's a high percentage of it among Mormons.

EMORY: Trollop.

MICHAEL: [*Crosses to Left table.*] Somehow, we all managed to justify our actions in those days. I later found out that even Justin Stuart, my closest friend—

DONALD: Other than Alan McCarthy.

MICHAEL: [*A look to* DONALD.]—was doing the same thing. Only Justin was going to Boston on weekends.

LARRY: [*To* HANK.] Sound familiar? [*Crosses to* HANK, *motions* HANK *to give him the cigarettes.*]

MICHAEL: [*Takes crab to coffee table.*] Yes, long before Justin or I or God-only-knows how many others *came out,* we used to get drunk and "horse-around" a bit. You see, in the Christ-Was-I-Drunk-Last-Night Syndrome, you really *are* drunk. That part of it is true. It's just that you also *do remember everything.* Oh God, I use to have to get loaded to go in a gay bar!

DONALD: Well, times certainly have changed.

MICHAEL: They *have.* Lately I've gotten to despise the bars. Everybody just standing around and standing around—it's like one eternal intermission.

HANK: [*To* LARRY.] Sound familiar?

EMORY: I can't stand the bars either. All that cat-and-mouse business—you hang around *staring* at each other all night and wind-up going home alone.

MICHAEL: And pissed.

LARRY: [*Goes to sofa.*] A lot of guys have to get loaded to have sex. [*Quick look to* HANK *who is unamused.*] So I've been told. [*Sits sofa, Right end.*]

MICHAEL: [*Crosses to* DONALD.] If you remember, Donald, the first time we made it I was so drunk I could hardly stand up.

DONALD: You were so drunk you could hardly get-it-up.

MICHAEL: [*Mock innocence.*] Christ, I was so drunk I don't remember.

DONALD: Bullshit, you remember.

MICHAEL: [*Sings to* DONALD.] "Just friends, lovers no more..."

EMORY: You may as well be. Everybody thinks you are anyway.

DONALD: We never *were*—*really.*

MICHAEL: We didn't have time to be—we got to know each other too fast. [*The door* BUZZER *sounds.*] Oh, Jesus, it's Alan! [LARRY, HANK, *and* DONALD *uncross their legs.*] Now, please everybody, do me a favor and cool-it for the few minutes he's here. [*Goes to door and pushes panel button.*]

EMORY: [*Rises and goes to Left end sofa.*] Anything for a sis, Mary.

MICHAEL: [*Crosses to* EMORY.] That's *exactly* what I'm talking about, Emory. No *camping!*

EMORY: Sorry. [*Sits Left end sofa. Deep, deep voice to* DONALD.] Think the Giants are gonna win the pennant this year?

DONALD: [*Deep, deep voice.*] Fuckin' A, Mac. [*Rises and goes to Left of steps.*]

[MICHAEL *goes to the door, opens it to reveal* BERNARD, *dressed in a shirt and tie and a Brooks Brothers jacket. He carries a birthday gift and two bottles of red wine.*]

EMORY: [*Big scream.*] Oh, it's only another queen!

BERNARD: And it ain't the Red one, either.

EMORY: It's the queen of spades! [BERNARD *enters.* MICHAEL *looks out in the hall.*]

MICHAEL: Bernard, is the downstairs door open? [*Closing door.*]

BERNARD: It was, but I closed it.

MICHAEL: Good. [BERNARD *starts to put wine on bar. Re: the two bottles of red wine.*] I'll take those. You can put your present with the others. [BERNARD *hands him the wine. The* PHONE *rings.*]

BERNARD: Hi, Larry. Hi, Hank. [*Crossing below coffee table to steps.*]

MICHAEL: Christ of the Andes! Donald, will you bartend, please? [MICHAEL *gives* DONALD *the wine bottles, goes to the phone.* DONALD *puts wine on Left table as* BERNARD *puts gift on steps.*]

BERNARD: Hello, Donald. Good to see you.

MICHAEL: [*Into phone.*] Hello?

DONALD: Bernard.

MICHAEL: Alan?

EMORY: Hi, Bernardette. Anybody ever tell you you'd look divine in a hammock, surrounded by louvres and ceiling fans and lots and lots of lush tropical ferns?

BERNARD: [*To* EMORY.] You're *such* a fag. You take the cake. [BERNARD *and* DONALD *ad-lib Left of steps.*]

EMORY: Oh, what *about* the cake—whose job was that?

LARRY: Mine. I ordered one to be delivered.

EMORY: How many candles did you say put on it—eighty?

MICHAEL: . . . What? Wait a minute. There's too much noise. Let me go to another phone. [*He presses the hold button, hangs up, dashes toward stairs.*]

LARRY: [*Rises and goes above sofa.*] Michael, did the cake come?

MICHAEL: No.

DONALD: [*To* MICHAEL.] What's up?

MICHAEL: Do I know?

LARRY: Jesus, I'd better call. Okay if I use the private line?

MICHAEL: [*Going upstairs.*] Sure. Go ahead. [*Stops dead on stairs, turns.*] Listen, everybody, there's some cracked crab there. Help yourselves. [DONALD *shakes his head.* MICHAEL *continues up the stairs to the bedroom.* LARRY *crosses to the phone, presses the free line button, picks up receiver, dials Information.* HANK *rises and sits Right end sofa for crab.*]

DONALD: Is everybody ready for a drink? [*Goes to bar.*]

EMORY: [*Flipping up his sweater and rising.*] *Ready!* I'll be your topless cocktail waitress.

BERNARD: Please spare us the sight of your sagging tits.

EMORY: [*To* HANK, LARRY.] What're you having, kids?

MICHAEL: [*Having picked up the bedside phone.*] Yes, Alan...

LARRY: Vodka and tonic. [*Into phone.*] Could I have the number for the Marseilles Bakery in Manhattan.

EMORY: [*Crosses to* HANK *above sofa.*] A vod and ton and a...

HANK: Is there any beer?

EMORY: Beer! Who drinks beer before dinner?

BERNARD: Beer drinkers.

DONALD: That's telling him.

MICHAEL: ... No, Alan, don't be silly. What's there to apologize for?

EMORY: Truck drivers do. Or... or wall-paperers. Not school teachers. They have sherry.

HANK: This one has beer.

EMORY: Well, maybe school teachers in public schools. [*To* LARRY.] How can a sensitive artist like you live with an insensitive bull like that?

LARRY: [*Hanging up the phone and re-dialing.*] I can't.

BERNARD: Emory, you'd live with Hank in a minute, if he'd ask you. In fifty-eight seconds. Lord knows, you're *sss*ensitive.

EMORY: [*Crosses to Center.*] Why don't you have a piece of watermelon and hush-up!

MICHAEL: ... Alan, don't be ridiculous.

DONALD: [*Giving beer can to* HANK.] Here you go, Hank.

HANK: Thanks.

LARRY: Shit. They don't answer.

DONALD: [*Handing* BERNARD'*s beer to* EMORY *who takes it to* BERNARD.] What're you having, Emory?

BERNARD: A Pink Lady.

EMORY: A vodka martini on-the-rocks, please. [*Slaps* BERNARD'*s outstretched hand, hands him the beer and goes to Left table, looks at wine.*]

LARRY: [*Hangs up.*] Well, let's just hope. [DONALD *hands* LARRY *his drink.* DONALD *returns to the bar to make* EMORY'*s drink.* LARRY *sit on steps and* BERNARD *goes above sofa.*]

MICHAEL: Lunch tomorrow will be great. One o'clock — the Oak Room at the Plaza okay? Fine.

BERNARD: [*To* DONALD.] Donald, read any new libraries lately?

DONALD: One or three. I did the complete works of Doris Lessing this week. I've been depressed.

MICHAEL: Alan, forget it, will you? Bye, bye. [MICHAEL *hangs up.*]

DONALD: You must not work in Circulation any more.

BERNARD: Oh, I'm still there — every day.

DONALD: Well, since I moved, I only come in on Saturday evenings.

[DONALD *moves his stack of books off the bar and goes to making a pitcher of vodka martinis.*]

HANK: Looks like you stock-up for the week. [MICHAEL *crosses to steps landing.*]

BERNARD: Are you kidding?—that'll last him two days.

EMORY: It would last *me* two years. I still haven't finished "Atlas Shrugged" which I started in 1912.

MICHAEL: [*To* DONALD.] Well, he's not coming.

DONALD: It's just as well now.

BERNARD: Some people eat, some people drink, and some take dope.

DONALD: I read.

MICHAEL; And read and read and read. It's a wonder your eyes don't turn back in your head at the sight of a dust jacket.

HANK: Well, at least, he's a constructive escapist.

MICHAEL: Yeah, what do I do?—take planes. No, I don't do that any more. Because I don't have the *money* to do that any more. I go to the baths. That's about it.

EMORY: I'm about to do both. I'm flying to the West Coast—

BERNARD: You still have that act with a donkey in Tijuana? [MICHAEL *decides on change of sweater. Goes to bedroom for a red one.*]

EMORY: [*Crosses to* BERNARD.] I'm going to San Francisco on a well-earned vacation.

LARRY: No shopping?

EMORY: [*Sits Left end sofa.*] Oh, I'll look for a few things for a couple of clients but I've been so busy lately, I really couldn't care less if I never saw another piece of fabric or another stick of furniture as long as I live. I'm going to the Club Baths and I'm not coming out til they announce the departure of TWA one week later. [DONALD *pours* EMORY *a glass and refills his glass from pitcher.*]

BERNARD: [*To* EMORY.] You'll never learn to stay out of the baths, will you. [*Crosses Center to* LARRY.] The last time Emily was taking the vapors, this big hairy number strolled in. Emory said, "I'm just resting," and the big hairy number said, "I'm just *ar*resting!" It was the vice! [*Goes to Down Right chair.*]

EMORY: You have to tell everything, don't you.

DONALD: [*Crosses to give* EMORY *his drink.*] Here you go, Emory.

EMORY: Thanks, sonny. You live with your parents?

DONALD: Yeah. But it's all right—they're gay. [EMORY *roars, slaps him on the knee.* HANK *gets up, moves away to phonograph. To* MICHAEL.] What happened to Alan?

MICHAEL: He suddenly got terrible icks about having broken down on the phone. Kept apologizing over and over. Did a big about-face and reverted to the old Alan right before my very eyes.

DONALD: Ears.

MICHAEL: Ears. Well, the cracked crab obviously did not work out. [*He starts to take away the tray on coffee table.*]

EMORY: Just put-that down if you don't want your hand slapped. I'm about to have some.

MICHAEL: It's really very good. [*Gives* DONALD *a look.*] I don't know why everyone has such an aversion to it. [*Picking up his glass from coffee table.*]

DONALD: Sometimes you remind me of the Chinese water torture. I take that back. Sometimes you remind me of the *relentless* Chinese water torture. [*Sits on high stool with his drink.*]

MICHAEL: Bitch. [*Goes to bar to refill glass.*]

[HANK *has put on some* MUSIC.]

BERNARD: Yeah, baby, let's hear that sound.

EMORY: A drum beat and their eyes sparkle like Cartier's. [BERNARD *starts to snap his fingers and move in time with the music.*]

HANK: [*Crosses in above sofa.*] Michael, I wonder where Harold is?

EMORY: Yeah, where is the frozen fruit?

MICHAEL: [*To* DONALD.] Emory refers to Harold as the frozen fruit because of his former profession as an ice skater.

EMORY: She used to be the Vera Hruba Ralston of the Borscht Circuit. [MICHAEL *and* BERNARD *dance.* LARRY *is dancing alone.* HANK *goes to* LARRY *but doesn't dance and* HANK *goes back to desk.*]

BERNARD: [*To* MICHAEL.] If your mother could see you now she'd have a stroke.

MICHAEL: Got a camera on you?

LARRY: Let's go, Miss Montez! [EMORY *goes to* LARRY *to dance. As* EMORY *gets to* LARRY *the door* BUZZER *sounds.*]

EMORY: [*Lets out a yelp.*] Oh my God, it's Lilly Law! Everybody three feet apart! [MICHAEL *goes to the panel button and presses it and opens the door and looks out.* HANK *turns off the* PHONOGRAPH. EMORY *quickly sits on sofa.* BERNARD *quickly sits in Down Right chair.* LARRY *quickly sits on steps.*]

BERNARD: It's probably Harold now.

MICHAEL: [*He leans back in the room.*] No, it's the delivery boy from the bakery.

LARRY: Thank God. [MICHAEL *goes out into the hall,* HANK *goes to door and looks out.*]

EMORY: [*Loudly.*] Ask him if he's got any hot cross buns!

HANK: [*Crosses to* EMORY.] Come on, Emory, knock it off.

BERNARD: You can take her anywhere but out.

EMORY: [*To* HANK.] You remind me of an old maid schoolteacher.

HANK: You remind me of a chicken wing. [*Goes to phonograph.*]

EMORY: I'm sure you meant that as a compliment. [HANK *turns the* MUSIC *on.*]

MICHAEL: [*In hall.*] Thank you, good night. [MICHAEL *returns with a cake box, closes the door, and takes it into the kitchen.*]

LARRY: [*Goes to Left table.*] Hey, Bernard, you remember that thing we used to do on Fire Island? [LARRY *starts to do a kind of "Madison."*]

BERNARD: [*Rises and crosses in.*] That was "in" so far back I think I've forgotten.

EMORY: I remember. [*Goes to* LARRY *and starts doing the steps.* LARRY *and* BERNARD *start to follow.* BERNARD *crosses to* EMORY.]

LARRY: Well, show us.

MICHAEL: [*He enters from the kitchen, falls in line with them.*] Well, if it isn't the Geriatrics Rockettes. [*Now* ALL *are doing practically a precision routine.* DONALD *comes to above sofa, sips his drink, and watches in fascination.* HANK *goes to sofa and sits. At a point in the dance the door* BUZZER *sounds. No one seems to hear it.* HANK *turns toward the door, hesitates. He looks toward* MICHAEL *who is now deeply involved in the intricacies of the dance. No one, it seems, has heard it but* HANK. *He goes to the door, opens it wide to reveal* ALAN. *He is dressed in black-tie. The* DANCERS *continue, turning and slapping their knees and heels and laughing with abandon as* ALAN *goes to Right end of coffee table. Suddenly,* MICHAEL *looks up, stops dead.* HANK *goes to the* RECORD PLAYER, *turns it off abruptly.* EMORY, LARRY, *and* BERNARD *scatter as though they were not dancing.* BERNARD *walks out of dance up steps.* LARRY *goes around step unit and* EMORY *sits in Down Left chair. At ottoman.*] I thought you said you weren't coming.

ALAN: I . . . well, I'm sorry . . .

MICHAEL: [*Forced lightly.*] We were just—acting silly . . .

ALAN: Actually, when I called I was in a phone booth around the corner. My dinner party is not far from here. And . . .

MICHAEL: Emory was just showing us this . . . silly dance.

ALAN: . . . well, then I walked past and your downstairs door was open and . . .

MICHAEL: This is Emory. [EMORY *curtsies and sits on steps between* BERNARD's *legs.* MICHAEL *glares at him.* HANK *closes door and goes to Down Right chair.*] Everybody, this is Alan McCarthy. Counterclockwise, Alan:

Larry, Emory, Bernard, Donald, and Hank. [ALL *mumble "Hello," "Hi,"*
and LARRY *moves in to steps near* EMORY *and* BERNARD *as introduced.*]

HANK: Nice to meet you.

ALAN: Good to meet you. [*Shaking hands with* HANK.]

MICHAEL: Would you like a drink?

ALAN: Thanks, no. I . . . I can't stay . . . long . . . really.

MICHAEL: Well, you're here now, so stay. What would you like?

ALAN: Do you have any rye?

MICHAEL: I'm afraid I don't drink it any more. You'll have to settle for gin
or scotch or vodka.

DONALD: Or beer.

ALAN: Scotch, please. [MICHAEL *starts for bar.*]

DONALD: I'll get it. [*Goes to bar.*]

HANK: Guess I'm the only beer drinker.

ALAN: [*Looking around* GROUP.] Whose . . . birthday . . . is it?

LARRY: Harold's.

ALAN: [*Looking from face to face.*] Harold?

BERNARD: He's not here yet.

EMORY: She's never been on time — [BERNARD *nudges* EMORY *with his knee.*
MICHAEL *shoots* EMORY *a withering glance.*] He's never been on time in
his —

MICHAEL: [*Crosses to* ALAN.] Alan's from Washington. We went to college
together. Georgetown.

EMORY: Well, isn't that fascinating?

DONALD: [*He hands* ALAN *his drink.*] If that's too strong, I'll put some
water in it.

ALAN: It looks fine. Thanks. [DONALD *goes to desk.*]

HANK: Are you in the government?

ALAN: No. I'm a lawyer. What . . . what do you do?

HANK: I teach school.

ALAN: Oh. I would have taken you for an athlete of some sort. You look
like you might play sports . . . of some sort.

HANK: Well, I'm no professional but I was on the basketball team in college
and I play quite a bit of tennis.

ALAN: I play tennis too.

HANK: Great game.

ALAN: Yes. Great. [*A beat. Silence as* LARRY, BERNARD *and* EMORY *look bored.*]
What . . . do you teach?

HANK: Math.

ALAN: Math?
HANK: Yes.
ALAN: Math. Well.
EMORY: Kinda makes you want to rush out and buy a slide rule, doesn't it?
MICHAEL: [*Pulling* EMORY *to his feet.*] Emory. I'm going to need some help with dinner and you're elected.
EMORY: I'm *always* elected.
BERNARD: You're a natural born domestic.
EMORY: Said the African queen! You come on too—you can fan me while I make the salad dressing.
MICHAEL: [*Glaring: phony smile.*] RIGHT THIS WAY, EMORY! [MICHAEL *pushes* EMORY *and* BERNARD *to kitchen. They exit and he follows. The muffled sound of* MICHAEL'*s voice can be heard.*] You son-of-a-bitch!
EMORY: [*Offstage.*] What the hell do you want from me?
HANK: Why don't we all sit down? [*Sits Left end sofa.*]
ALAN: Sure. [*Sits Right end of sofa.*]

[HANK *and* ALAN *come to sit on the couch.* LARRY *at steps as* DONALD *goes to steps and sits on third step.*]

LARRY: Hi.
DONALD: Hi.
ALAN: I really feel terrible—barging in on you fellows this way.
LARRY: [*To* DONALD.] How've you been?
DONALD: Fine, thanks.
HANK: [*To* ALAN.] Oh, that's okay.
DONALD: [*To* LARRY.] And you?
LARRY: Oh . . . just fine.
ALAN: [*To* HANK.] You're married? [MICHAEL *enters from the kitchen.*]
HANK: What?
ALAN: I see you're married. [*He points to* HANK'*s wedding band.*]
HANK: Oh.
MICHAEL: Yes. Hank's married.
ALAN: You have any kids?
HANK: Yes. Two. A boy nine, and a girl seven. You should see my boy play tennis—really puts his dad to shame. [HANK *looks toward* DONALD.]
DONALD: I better get some ice. [*He exits to kitchen with ice bucket.*]
ALAN: [*To* HANK.] I have two kids too. Both girls.
HANK: Great.
MICHAEL: How *are* the girls, Alan? [*Sits ottoman.*]

ALAN: Oh, just sensational. [*Shakes his head.*] They're something, those kids. God, I'm nuts about them.

HANK: How long have you been married?

ALAN: Nine years. Can you believe it, Mickey?

MICHAEL: No.

ALAN: Mickey used to go with my wife when we were all in school.

MICHAEL: Can you believe that?

ALAN: [*To* HANK.] You live in the city?

LARRY: Yes, we do. [LARRY *comes over to couch next to* HANK.]

ALAN: Oh.

HANK: I'm in the process of getting a divorce. Larry and I are—roommates.

MICHAEL: Yes.

ALAN: Oh. I'm sorry. Oh, I mean—

HANK: I understand.

ALAN: [*Gets up.*] I...I...I think I'd like another drink...if I may.

MICHAEL: [*Rises.*] Of course. What was it?

ALAN: I'll do it...if I may. [*He goes to the bar. Suddenly, there is a loud Offstage* CRASH. ALAN *jumps, looks toward kitchen.*] What was that? [DONALD *enters with the ice bucket.*]

MICHAEL: Excuse me. Testy temperament out in the kitch! [MICHAEL *exits Up Center to kitchen.* ALAN *continues nervously picking-up and putting-down bottles, searching for the scotch.*]

HANK: [*To* LARRY.] Larry, where do you know that guy from?

LARRY: What guy? [DONALD *is crossing below coffee table with ice bucket to above* ALAN *at the bar.*]

HANK: That guy.

LARRY: I don't know. Around. The bars. [*Goes to Left table.*]

DONALD: Can I help you, Alan?

ALAN: I...I can't seem to find the scotch.

DONALD: You've got it in your hand.

ALAN: Oh. Of course. How...stupid of me. [DONALD *watches* ALAN *jumble with the scotch bottle and glass.*]

DONALD: Why don't you let me do that?

ALAN: [*Gratefully hands him both.*] Thanks.

DONALD: Was it water or soda?

ALAN: Just make it straight—over ice. [MICHAEL *enters crossing to Left end sofa.*]

MICHAEL: You see, Alan, I told you it wasn't a good time to talk. But we—

ALAN: [*At Right end of sofa.*] It doesn't matter. I'll just finish this and go. [DONALD *gives* ALAN *his drink. He takes a long swallow.*]

LARRY: [*Crosses to ottoman and sits.*] Where can Harold be?

MICHAEL: Oh, he's always late. You know how neurotic he is about going out in public. It takes him hours to get ready.

LARRY: Why *is* that? [EMORY *breezes in via above steps from kitchen, carrying a stack of plates which he places on Left table and picks up two wine bottles.*]

EMORY: Why is what?

LARRY: Why does Harold spend hours getting ready before he can go out?

EMORY: Because she's a sick lady, that's why. [*Exits kitchen via Up Center with two wine bottles.*]

[ALAN *finishes his drink.*]

MICHAEL: Alan, as I was about to say, we can go in the bedroom and talk.

ALAN: It really doesn't matter.

MICHAEL: Come on. Bring your drink.

ALAN: I . . . I've finished it.

MICHAEL: Well, make another and come on. [DONALD *picks up the scotch bottle and pours into the glass* ALAN *has in his hand.* MICHAEL *has started for the stairs.*]

ALAN: [*To* DONALD.] Thanks.

DONALD: Don't mention it. [*Picks up club soda bottle and exits kitchen.*]

ALAN: [*To* HANK.] Excuse us. We'll be down in a minute. [*Goes to steps.*]

HANK: Sure. Sure.

LARRY: Oh, he'll still be here. [*Rises and crosses to bar leaving glass at bar.* ALAN *turns at bottom of steps and* MICHAEL *indicates steps.*]

MICHAEL: This way, Alan. [ALAN *and* MICHAEL *linger on landing a bit looking out window.*]

HANK: [*To* LARRY.] What was *that* supposed to mean?

LARRY: What was what supposed to mean?

HANK: You know.

LARRY: You want another beer?

HANK: No. You're jealous, aren't you? [HANK *starts to laugh.* LARRY *doesn't like it.* DONALD *enters from kitchen via Upstage of stairs with his drink.* ALAN *and* MICHAEL *go to bedroom.*]

LARRY: I'm Larry— *You're* jealous. [*Crosses to* DONALD.] Hey, Donald, where've you been hanging out these days? I haven't seen you in a long time. [LARRY *sits on steps with* DONALD *standing in front of* LARRY *talking quietly.* HANK *exits into the kitchen.*]

ALAN: [*To* MICHAEL.] This is a marvelous apartment.

MICHAEL: It's too expensive. I work to pay rent.

ALAN: What are you doing these days?

MICHAEL: Nothing.

ALAN: Aren't you writing any more?

MICHAEL: I haven't looked at a typewriter since I sold the very very wonderful, very very marvelous *screenplay* which never got produced.

ALAN: [*Crosses to* MICHAEL.] That's right, the last time I saw you, you were on your way to California. Or was it Europe?

MICHAEL: Hollywood. Which is not in Europe nor does it have anything whatsoever to do with California.

ALAN: [*Crosses to pillar.*] I've never been there but I would imagine it's awful. Everyone must be terribly cheap.

MICHAEL: No, not everyone. Alan, I want to try to explain this evening...

ALAN: What's there to explain? [*Crosses to chair.*] Sometimes you just can't invite everybody to every party and some people take it personally. But I'm not one of them. I should apologize for inviting myself.

MICHAEL: [*Sits bench.*] That's not exactly what I meant.

ALAN: Your friends all seem like very nice guys. That Hank is really a very attractive fellow.

MICHAEL: ... Yes. He is.

ALAN: We have a lot in common. What's his roommate's name?

MICHAEL: Larry.

ALAN: ... What does *he* do?

MICHAEL: He's a commercial artist.

ALAN: I liked Donald too. The only one I didn't care too much for was — what's his name — Emory?

MICHAEL: Yes. Emory.

ALAN: [*Puts drink on Upstage table.*] I just can't stand that kind of talk. It just grates on me.

MICHAEL: What kind of talk, Alan?

ALAN: [*Crosses to* MICHAEL.] Oh, you know. His brand of humor, I guess.

MICHAEL: He can be really quite funny sometimes.

ALAN: I suppose so. If you find that sort of thing amusing. He just seems like such a goddamn little pansy. [*Silence. A pause. He steps away.*] I'm sorry I said that. I didn't mean to say that. That's such an awful thing to say about *anyone*. But you know what I mean, Michael — you have to admit he *is* effeminate.

MICHAEL: He is a bit.

ALAN: A bit! He's like a ... a butterfly in heat! I mean there's no wonder he was trying to teach you all a dance. He *probably* wanted to dance *with* you! [*Crosses to* MICHAEL.] Oh, come on, man, you know me—you know how I feel—your private life is your own affair. [*Sits bed chair.*]

MICHAEL: [*Icy.*] No. I *don't* know that-about-you.

ALAN: I couldn't care less what people do—as long as they don't do it in public—or—or try to force their ways on the whole damned world.

MICHAEL: Alan, what was it you were crying about on the telephone?

ALAN: Oh, I feel like such a fool about that. I could shoot myself for letting myself act that way. I'm so embarrassed I could die.

MICHAEL: But Alan, if you were genuinely upset—that's nothing to be embarrassed about.

ALAN: All I can say is—please accept my apology for making such an ass of myself.

MICHAEL: You must have been upset or you wouldn't have said you were and that you wanted to see me—*had* to see me and had to talk to me.

ALAN: Can you forget it? Just pretend it never happened. I know *I* have. Okay?

MICHAEL: Is something wrong between you and Fran?

ALAN: Listen, I've really got to go. [*Rises and crosses Left of* MICHAEL.]

MICHAEL: [*Rises, counters Right to chair.*] Why are you in New York?

ALAN: I'm dreadfully late for dinner.

MICHAEL: *Whose* dinner? Where are you going?

ALAN: Is this the loo?

MICHAEL: Yes.

ALAN: Excuse me. [*He quickly goes into the bathroom.*]

[MICHAEL *remains silent, stares into space; sits on bed. Downstairs,* EMORY *pops in from the kitchen to discover* DONALD *and* LARRY *in quiet, intimate conversation.*]

EMORY: What's-going-on-in-here-oh-Mary-don't-ask! [*He puts napkin holder on the table at Left.*]

[HANK *enters, carrying a bottle of red wine, from kitchen and goes to bar for corkscrew. He looks toward* LARRY *and* DONALD. DONALD *sees him.*]

DONALD: Hank, why don't you come and join us?

HANK: That's an interesting suggestion. Whose idea is that?

DONALD: Mine.

LARRY: [*To* HANK.] He means in a conversation. [BERNARD *enters from the kitchen, carrying two wine glasses, without sport coat on.*]

EMORY: [*To* BERNARD.] Where're the rest of the wine glasses? [*Catching* BERNARD *at Center.*]

BERNARD: Ahz workin' as fas' as ah can! [*A la Butterfly McQueen.*]

EMORY: They have to be told everything. Can't let 'em out of your sight. [EMORY *takes the two wine glasses and puts on the Left table, then exits to kitchen via Upstage of stairs. BERNARD goes to bar for two more wine glasses. DONALD leaves LARRY's side and goes to the coffee table, helps himself to the cracked crab as he sits on sofa. HANK crosses to Left of LARRY with wine bottle and corkscrew. Upstairs, MICHAEL gets up off the bed and goes down the stairs to the landing.*]

HANK: I thought maybe you were abiding by the agreement.

LARRY: We have no agreement.

HANK: We *did*.

LARRY: *You* did. I never agreed to anything! [LARRY *rises and goes above sofa and sits Down Right chair. HANK takes wine to Left table, finishes uncorking and sits in Down Left chair. DONALD looks up to see MICHAEL on landing and raises a crab claw toward him.*]

DONALD: To your health.

MICHAEL: Up yours.

DONALD: Up my health?

BERNARD: Where's the gent?

MICHAEL: [*Coming down stairs.*] In the gents' room. If you can all hang on for five more minutes, he's about to leave. [*The* DOOR *buzzes.* MICHAEL *crosses to it.*]

LARRY: Well, at last! [MICHAEL *opens the door to reveal a muscle-bound young* MAN, *wearing boots, tight levis, a calico neckerchief, and a cowboy hat. Around his wrist there is a large card tied with a string.*]

COWBOY: [*Singing fast.*]
"Happy birthday to you,
Happy birthday to you,
Happy birthday, dear Harold.
Happy birthday to you." [*And with that, he gives* MICHAEL *a big kiss on the lips.* EMORY *enters from kitchen.*]

MICHAEL: Who the hell are you?

EMORY: She's Harold's present from me and she's *early!*

[*Quick to* COWBOY.] And that's not even Harold, you *idiot!* [*He pushes* COWBOY *Down Left Center as* MICHAEL *closes the door and crosses to Right end of sofa.*]

COWBOY: You said whoever answered the door.

EMORY: But *not until midnight!* [*Quickly to* GROUP.] He's supposed to be a *midnight cowboy!*

475

DONALD: He *is* a midnight cowboy.

MICHAEL: He looks right out of a William Inge play to me.

EMORY: [*To* COWBOY.] ... Not until midnight and you're supposed to sing to the right person, for Chrissake! I *told* you Harold has very, very, tight, tight, black curly hair. [*Referring to* MICHAEL.] This number's practically bald!

MICHAEL: Thank you and fuck you.

BERNARD: It's a good thing *I* didn't open the door.

EMORY: Not that tight and not that black.

COWBOY: I forgot. Besides, I wanted to get to the bars by midnight.

MICHAEL: He's a class act all the way around.

EMORY: What do you mean—get to the bars! Sweetie, I paid you for the whole night, remember?

COWBOY: I hurt my back doing my exercises and I wanted to get to bed early tonight.

BERNARD: Are you ready for this one?

LARRY: [*To* COWBOY.] That's too bad, what happened?

COWBOY: I lost my grip doing my chin-ups and I fell on my heels and twisted my back.

EMORY: You shouldn't *wear* heels when you do chin-ups.

COWBOY: [*Oblivious.*] I shouldn't do chin-ups—I got a weak grip to begin with.

EMORY: A weak grip. In my day it used to be called a limp wrist.

BERNARD: Who can remember that far back?

MICHAEL: [*To* LARRY.] Who was it that always used to say, "You show me Oscar Wilde in a cowboy suit, and I'll show you a gay caballero."

DONALD: I don't know. Who *was* it who always used to say that?

MICHAEL: I don't know. Somebody. [*Crosses above sofa.*]

LARRY: [*To* COWBOY.] What does your card say?

COWBOY: [*Holds up his wrist crossing to* LARRY.] Here. You read it...

LARRY: [*Rises. Reading card.*] "Dear Harold, bang, bang, you're alive. But roll-over and play dead. Happy Birthday, Emory." [ALAN *enters from bath and comes down the stairs.*]

BERNARD: Ah, sheer poetry, Emmy.

LARRY: And in your usual good taste. [*Sits chair.*]

MICHAEL: Yes, so conservative of you to resist a sign in Times Square.

EMORY: [*Glancing toward stairs.*] Cheese it! Here comes the socialite nun. [*Goes to high stool and sits.*]

MICHAEL: Goddammit, Emory! [*Crosses to* EMORY.]

ALAN: [*On bottom step.*] Well, I'm off.... Thanks, Michael, for the drink.

MICHAEL: You're entirely welcome, Alan. See you tomorrow?

ALAN: . . . No. No, I think I'm going to be awfully busy. I may even go back to Washington.

EMORY: Got a heavy date in La Fayette Square?

ALAN: What?

HANK: Emory.

EMORY: Forget it.

ALAN: [*Sees* COWBOY *and crosses Down Left Center.*] Are you . . . Harold?

EMORY: No, he's not Harold. He's *for* Harold. [*Silence.* ALAN *lets it pass. Turns to* HANK *and crosses to him.* MICHAEL *gets on first step, glaring at* EMORY.]

ALAN: Goodbye, Hank. It was nice to meet you.

HANK: [*Rises.*] Same here. [*They shake hands.*]

ALAN: If you're ever in Washington — I'd like you to meet my wife.

HANK: Good. [ALAN *starts for the door, crossing Up Center.*]

LARRY: That'd be fun, wouldn't it, Hank?

EMORY: Yeah, they'd love to meet him — *her*. I have such a problem with pronouns.

ALAN: [*Quick, to* EMORY.] How many esses are there in the word pronoun?

EMORY: How'd you like to kiss my ass — that's got two or more *essessss* in it!

ALAN: How'd you like to blow me!

EMORY: What's the matter with your *wife*, she got lockjaw?

ALAN: [*Lashes out.*] Faggot, Fairy, pansy . . . [*Lunges at* EMORY, *grabs him, pulls him off stool to floor and attacks him fiercely.*] queer, cocksucker! I'll kill you, you goddamn little mincing, swish! You goddamn freak! FREAK! FREAK! [*Pandemonium!* EVERYONE *overlaps words.* ALAN *has quickly beaten* EMORY *to the floor before anyone has recovered from the surprise, and reacted to move.*]

EMORY: Oh, my God, somebody help me! Bernard! He's killing me! [BERNARD *and* HANK *rush forward.* EMORY *is screaming.*]

HANK: Alan! ALAN! *Alan!* [*Pulls* ALAN *off* EMORY *via above sofa and gets* ALAN *Down Right on floor.*]

EMORY: Get him off me! Get him off me! Oh, my God, he's broken my nose! I'm BLEEDING TO DEATH! [BERNARD *quickly bends over* EMORY, *puts his arm around him and lifts him to Down Left where* EMORY *falls to the floor.*]

BERNARD: Somebody get some ice! And a cloth! [LARRY *runs to the bar, grabs the bar towel and the ice bucket, rushes to put it on the floor beside* BERNARD *and* EMORY. BERNARD *quickly wraps some ice in the towel, holds it to* EMORY'*s mouth.*]

EMORY: Oh, my face!

BERNARD: He busted your lip, that's all. It'll be all right. [HANK *has gotten*

ALAN *down on the floor on the opposite side of the room.* ALAN *relinquishes the struggle.* MICHAEL *is still standing on the first step, immobile.*]

DONALD: [*Rises. To* COWBOY.] Would you mind waiting over there with the gifts? [*The front door* BUZZER *sounds.* DONALD *has crossed to high stool, which is the gift-wrapped packages area, and indicates for the* COWBOY *to sit there and* DONALD *continues to move to answer the door, opens it to reveal* HAROLD.] Well, Harold! Happy Birthday. [HAROLD *is entering the room getting near* COWBOY *at Center but too busy taking in the room to see him.*] You're just in time for the floor show which, as you see, is on the floor. [*To* COWBOY.] Hey, you, *this* is Harold! [HAROLD *looks at* COWBOY — COWBOY *rises and sings.*]

COWBOY:
"Happy birthday to you,
Happy birthday to you,
Happy birthday, dear Harold.
Happy birthday to you." [*And he gives* HAROLD *a big kiss.*]

[DONALD *has gone to the phonograph and turns on* MUSIC *as* COWBOY *finishes singing.* HAROLD *breaks away from* COWBOY, *reads the card, begins to laugh, continues to laugh.* MICHAEL, *as* COWBOY *finishes singing, walks to the bar, pours a glass of gin, raises it to his lips as the* LIGHTS *dim out to a* SPOT *pointing up* MICHAEL's *first drink.* DONALD *watches silently as* HAROLD *continues to laugh and* SPOT *dims to black.*]

CURTAIN

Act Two

A moment later. HAROLD *is still laughing.* MICHAEL, *still at the bar, lowers his glass, turns to* DONALD, *indicates for him to cut* PHONOGRAPH *which he does.*

MICHAEL: What's so fucking funny?

HAROLD: [*Unintimidated.*] Life. Life is a god-damn laff-riot. You remember life.

MICHAEL: *You're stoned.*

LARRY: Happy Birthday, Harold.

MICHAEL: [*To* HAROLD.] You're stoned and you're late! You were supposed to arrive at this location at approximately eight-thirty dash nine o'clock!

HAROLD: What I *am*, Michael, is a thirty-two year old, ugly, pock-marked Jew Fairy — and if it takes me a while to pull myself together and if I smoke a little grass before I can get up the nerve to show my face to the world, it's nobody's god-damn business but my own. [*Instant switch to chatty tone.*] And how are *you* this evening? [HANK *lifts* ALAN *to the sofa and both sit.* COWBOY *sits on fourth step of stairs.* MICHAEL *turns away from* HAROLD, *pours himself another drink.* DONALD *watches.*]

EMORY: Happy Birthday, Hallie. [*Now wearing a bloody sweater.*]

HAROLD: What happened to *you?*

EMORY: [*Groans.*] Don't ask!

HAROLD: Your lips are turning blue — you look like you been rimming a snowman. [LARRY *rises and returns ice bucket to bar and sits Down Right chair.*]

EMORY: [*Indicating* ALAN.] That piss-elegant kooze hit me! [BERNARD *helps* EMORY *up from the floor to sit him in Down Left chair.* HAROLD *looks toward the sofa.* ALAN *has slumped forward with hands over his ears.*]

MICHAEL: Careful, Emory, that kind of talk just makes him s'nervous.

HAROLD: [*crosses to Left end sofa to* ALAN.] Who is she? Who was she? Who does she hope to be?

EMORY: Who knows, who cares!

HANK: His name is Alan McCarthy.

MICHAEL: Do forgive me for not formally introducing you.

HAROLD: [*Sarcastically to* MICHAEL.] Not the famous college *chum.*

MICHAEL: [*Takes an ice cube from ice bucket, throws it up and catches it.*] Do a figure eight on that. [*Puts ice in his glass.*]

HAROLD: Well, well, well. I finally get to meet dear ole Alan after all these years. And in black-tie too. Is this my surprise from you, Michael?

LARRY: I think Alan is the one who got the surprise.

DONALD: And, if you'll notice, he's absolutely speechless. [*Crosses to above sofa.*]

EMORY: I *hope* she's in *shock!* She's a beast!

COWBOY: [*Indicating* ALAN.] Is it his birthday too?

EMORY: [*Indicates* COWBOY *to* HAROLD. *Rises and brings* COWBOY *to Down Left Center.*] That's your surprise.

LARRY: Speaking of beasts. [BERNARD *sits in Down Right chair.*]

EMORY: From me to you, darlin'. How do you like it?

HAROLD: [*Crosses to* COWBOY.] Oh, I suppose he has an interesting face and body — but it turns me right off because he can't talk intelligently about art.

EMORY: Yeah, ain't it a shame? [COWBOY *goes to ottoman and sits.*]

HAROLD: I could never *love* anyone like that. [*Going to* EMORY.]

EMORY: Never. *Who could?*

HAROLD: *I* could and *you* could, that's who could! Oh, Mary, she's *gorgeous!*

EMORY: She may be dumb, but she's all yours!

HAROLD: In affairs of the heart there are no rules! Where'd you ever find him? [*Crossing to* COWBOY.]

EMORY: Rae knew where.

MICHAEL: [*To* DONALD.] Rae is Rae Clark. That's R.A.E. She's Emory's dike friend who sings at a place in the Village. She wears pin-striped suits and bills herself, "Miss Rae Clark — Songs Tailored To Your Taste." [COWBOY *picks up crab tray and investigates.*]

EMORY: Rae's a fabulous chanteuse. I adore the way she does "Down In The Depths On The Ninetieth Floor."

MICHAEL: The faggot national anthem. [*Exits to the kitchen with soda glass.*]

HAROLD: [*To* EMORY.] All I can say is thank God for Miss Rae Clark. [*Goes to* EMORY.] I think my present is a super surprise! I'm so thrilled to get it I'd kiss you but I don't want to get blood all over me.

EMORY: Ohhh, look at my sweater! [BERNARD *rises and goes to* EMORY.]

HAROLD: Wait'll you see your face.

BERNARD: Come on, Emory, let's clean you up. Happy Birthday, Harold. [*Follows* EMORY *upstairs.*]

HAROLD: [*Smiles.*] Thanks, love. [*Goes to Left table.*]

[MICHAEL *enters from kitchen.*]

EMORY: My sweater is ruined!

MICHAEL: Take one of mine in the bedroom.

DONALD: The one on the floor is vicuna. [COWBOY *rises and exits to kitchen with cracked crab.*]

BERNARD: [*To* EMORY.] You'll feel better after I bathe your face. [BERNARD *and* EMORY *exit to bath.*]

HAROLD: Just another birthday party with the folks.

MICHAEL: [*He has a wine bottle and a green crystal white wine glass. Going to* HAROLD.] Here's a cold bottle of Puilly-Fuisse I bought especially for you, kiddo. [*Pours a glass.*]

HAROLD: Pussycat, all is forgiven. You can stay. [*Takes glass.*] No. You can stay, but not all is forgiven. Cheers. [*Sits Down Left chair.*]

MICHAEL: I didn't want it this way, Hallie. [*Puts wine bottle on Left table.*]

[DONALD *crosses to Left of stairs.*]

HAROLD: [*Indicating* ALAN.] Who asked Mr. Right to celebrate my birthday?

DONALD: There are no accidents.

HAROLD: [*Referring to* DONALD.] And who asked *him?*

MICHAEL: *Guilty again.*

HAROLD: Always got to have your crutch, haven't you.

DONALD: I'm *not* leaving.

HAROLD: Nobody ever thinks completely of somebody else. They always please themselves, they always cheat, if only a little bit.

LARRY: [*Referring to* ALAN.] Why is he sitting there with his hands over his ears?

DONALD: I think he has an ick. [DONALD *looks at* MICHAEL — MICHAEL *returns it, steely and goes above sofa.*]

HANK: [*To* ALAN.] Can I get you a drink?

LARRY: How can he hear you, dummy, with his hands over his ears?

HAROLD: He can hear every word. In fact, he wouldn't miss a word if it killed him. [ALAN *removes his hands from his ears.*] What'd I tell you?

ALAN: [*Rises.*] I ... I ... feel sick. I think ... I'm going to ... throw up.

HANK: This way. [*Rises and takes* ALAN *to landing of stairs.*]

HAROLD: Say that again and I won't have to take my appetite depressant. [BERNARD *and* EMORY *come out of the bath.*]

BERNARD: There. Feel better?

EMORY: Oh, Mary, what would I do without you? [EMORY *looks at himself in the mirror.*] I am not ready for my close-up, Mr. De Mille. Nor will I be for the next two weeks. [BERNARD *picks up* MICHAEL'S *sweater.*]

ALAN: I'm going to throw up! Let me go! Let me go! [*He tears loose of* HANK, *bolts up the remainder of the stairs to bath.* HANK *follows.*]

[EMORY *lets out a scream as* ALAN *rushes toward him.*]

EMORY: Oh, my God, he's after me again! [EMORY *jumps over bed.*]

HANK: He's sick.

BERNARD: Yeah, sick in the head. Here, Emory, put this on. [*Going to* EMORY *with vicuna sweater.*]

EMORY: [*Sits on bench.*] Oh, Mary, take me home. My nerves can't stand any more of this tonight. [EMORY *takes the sweater from* BERNARD, *starts to put it on.*]

[*Downstairs, at same time,* HAROLD *flamboyantly takes out a cigarette, takes a match from a striker and crosses to Center of sofa.*]

HAROLD: TURNING ON! [*With that, he strikes the match and lights up. Through a strained throat.*] Anybody care to join me? [*He waves the cigarette in a slow pass.*]

[COWBOY *enters from kitchen.*]

MICHAEL: Many thanks, no.

DONALD: No, thank you.

HAROLD: [*To* COWBOY.] How about you, Tex?

COWBOY: Yeah. [*Sits ottoman with pot cigarette.*]

MICHAEL: I find the sound of the ritual alone, utterly humiliating. [*He turns away.*]

[EMORY *and* BERNARD *come downstairs.*]

LARRY: I hate the smell poppers leave on your fingers.

HAROLD: Why don't you get up and wash your hands? [EMORY *is on bottom step and* BERNARD *is on landing.*]

EMORY: Michael, I left the casserole in the oven. You can take it out any time.

MICHAEL: You're not going. [*Picks up gin.*]

EMORY: I couldn't eat now anyway.

HAROLD: Well, *I'm* absolutely ravenous, I'm going to eat until I have a fat attack.

MICHAEL: [*To* EMORY.] I said, you're *not going.* [*Crosses to Right end of sofa with gin.*]
HAROLD: [*To* MICHAEL.] Having a cocktail this evening, are we? In my honor?
EMORY: It's your favorite dinner, Hallie. I made it myself.
BERNARD: *Who* fixed the casserole?
EMORY: Well; *I* made the sauce!
BERNARD: Well, *I* made the salad!
LARRY: Girls, please.
MICHAEL: Please *what!* [*Returns gin to bar.*]
HAROLD: Beware the hostile fag. When he's sober he's dangerous, when he drinks, he's lethal.
MICHAEL: [*Referring to* HAROLD.] Attention must *not* be paid. [*Paces to above sofa.*]
HAROLD: I'm starved, Em, I'm ready for some of your Alice B. Toklas's opium baked Lasagna.
EMORY: Are you really? Oh, that makes me so pleased maybe I'll just serve it before I leave. [EMORY *exits kitchen.*]
MICHAEL: *You're not leaving.* [*Crosses to desk.*]
BERNARD: I'll help. [*Starts for kitchen.*]
LARRY: [*Rises and exits kitchen.*] I better help too. We don't need a nosebleed in the Lasagna.
BERNARD: When the sauce is on it you wouldn't be able to tell the difference anyway. [*Exits kitchen.*]
MICHAEL: [*Proclamation.*] Nobody's going anywhere! [*Goes to high stool and puts in front of front door.*]
HAROLD: You are going to have schmertz tomorrow you wouldn't believe.
MICHAEL: [*Crosses to bar for drink.*] May I kiss the hem of your schemata, Doctor Freud?
COWBOY: What are you two talking about? I don't understand. [HANK *enters from bath and comes to landing.*]
DONALD: [*Crossing above sofa.*] He's working through his Oedipus Complex, sugar. With a machete.
COWBOY: Huh?
HANK: Michael, is there any air spray? [*On landing.*]
HAROLD: Hair spray! You're supposed to be holding his head, not doing his hair.
HANK: *Air* spray, not *hair* spray. [DONALD *goes to bar, pours drink out of martini pitcher.*]

MICHAEL: [*Crosses below coffee table to steps with his drink.*] There's a can of floral spray right on top of the john.

HANK: Thanks. [HANK *goes back upstairs leaving his suit coat on bedroom bench as he exits into the bath.*]

HAROLD: [*To* MICHAEL.] Aren't you going to say, "If it was a snake, it would have bitten you."

MICHAEL: [*Indicating* COWBOY.] That is something only your friend would say.

HAROLD: [*To* MICHAEL.] I am turning-on and you are just turning. [MICHAEL *and* HAROLD *look at each other for a beat*—MICHAEL *decides to break to Left of stairs. To* DONALD.] I keep my grass in the medicine cabinet. In a Band-Aid box. Somebody told me it's the safest place. If the cops arrive you can always lock yourself in the bathroom and flush it down the john. [HAROLD *has removed his eye glasses.*]

DONALD: [*Takes* HAROLD's *glasses and puts them on Upstage end of bar.*] Very cagey.

HAROLD: It makes more sense than where I *was* keeping it—in an oregano jar in the spice rack. I kept forgetting and accidentally turning my hateful mother on with the salad. [*A beat.*] But I think she liked it. No matter what meal she comes over for—even if it's breakfast—she says, "Let's have a salad!" [HAROLD *looks to* MICHAEL, *and* MICHAEL *goes to Down Left chair and sits as* COWBOY *rises and crosses to* MICHAEL.]

COWBOY: [*To* MICHAEL.] Why do you say, I would say, "If it was a snake it would have bitten you"? I think that's what I *would* have said.

MICHAEL: Of course you would have, baby. That's the kind of remark your pint-size brain thinks of. You are definitely the type who still moves his lips when he reads and who sits in a steam room and says things like, "Hot enough for you?"

COWBOY: I never use the steam room when I go to the gym. It's bad after a work-out. It flattens you down.

MICHAEL: Just after you've broken your back to blow yourself up like a poisoned dog.

COWBOY: Yeah. [*Crosses to ottoman and sits.*]

[DONALD *goes to Down Right chair and sits.*]

MICHAEL: You're right, Harold. Not only can he not talk intelligently about art, he can't even follow from one sentence to the next.

HAROLD: But *he's beautiful.* He has *unnatural,* natural beauty. Not that that means anything.

MICHAEL: It doesn't mean *everything.*

HAROLD: Keep telling yourself that as your hair drops out in handfuls. [*Rises and crosses to* MICHAEL.] Not that it's not *natural* for one's hair to recede as one reaches seniority. Not that those wonderful lines that have begun creasing our countenances don't make all the difference in the world because they add so much *character.*

MICHAEL: Faggots are worse than women about their age. They think their lives are over at thirty. Physical beauty is not that god-damned important!

HAROLD: Of course not. How could it be?—it's only in the eye of the beholder.

MICHAEL: And it's only skin deep—don't forget that one.

HAROLD: Oh, no, I haven't forgotten that one at all. It's only skin deep and it's *transitory* too. It's *terribly* transitory. [*Crosses to* COWBOY.] I mean, how long does it last?—thirty or forty or fifty years at the most—depending on how well you take care of yourself. And not counting, of course, that you might die before it runs out anyway. Yes, it's too bad about this poor boy's face. It's tragic, He's absolutely cursed! [COWBOY *looks to* HAROLD.] How can *his* beauty ever compare with *my* soul? And although I have never seen my soul, I understand from my mother's rabbi that it's a knock-out. [*Crosses to left table.*] I, however, cannot seem to locate it for a gander. And if I could, I'd sell it in a flash for some skin-deep, transitory, meaningless beauty! [*Picks up wine bottle and glass.*]

MICHAEL: [*Makes sign of the cross with his drink in hand.*] Forgive him, Father, for he know not what he do. [*He rises and crosses to pillar at Center.*]

[*Upstairs,* ALAN *walks weakly into bedroom and lies down on bed.*]

HAROLD: Michael, you kill me. You don't know what side of the fence you're on. [LARRY *enters from kitchen via stair passage with silverware to Left table.*] If somebody says something pro-religion, you're against them. [LARRY *gives two clicks of silverware which makes* HAROLD *move out of way to stairs as* LARRY *puts silver on table.*] If somebody denies God, you're against *them.* One might say that you have some problem in that area. You can't live with it and you can't live without it. [EMORY *enters from kitchen via Up Center carrying the hot casserole with pot holders, crossing to* MICHAEL, *who has arm up leaning on pillar blocking* EMORY's *passage.*]

EMORY: Hot stuff! Comin' through! [LARRY *crosses to sofa and sits.*]

MICHAEL: [*To* EMORY.] One could murder you with very little effort. [*Lets arm down so* EMORY *can pass and put casserole on Left table.*]

HAROLD: [*To* MICHAEL.] You hang onto that great insurance policy called The Church.

MICHAEL: [*Crossing above sofa.*] That's right. I believe in God and if it turns out that there really isn't one, okay. Nothing lost. But if it turns out that there *is*—I'm covered. [BERNARD *enters carrying a salad bowl from kitchen Up Center and puts on Left table.*]

EMORY: [*To* MICHAEL.] Harriet Hypocrite, that's who you are.

MICHAEL: [*Going to bar.*] Right. I'm one of those truly rotten Catholics who gets drunk, sins all night and goes to Mass the next morning. [EMORY *and* BERNARD *move Left table out from wall.*]

EMORY: Gilda Guilt. It depends on what you think sin is.

MICHAEL: Would you just shut-up your god-damn minty mouth and get back in the god-damn kitchen!

EMORY: Say anything you want—*just don't hit me!* [*He exits into kitchen with pot holders via Up Center.*]

MICHAEL: Actually, I suppose Emory has a point—I only go to confession before I get on a plane.

BERNARD: Do you think God's power only exists at thirty thousand feet? [*Lights candles.*]

[HANK *enters from bath, retrieves his coat.*]

MICHAEL: It must. On the ground I *am* God. In the air, I'm just one more scared son-of-a-bitch.

BERNARD: I'm scared on the ground. [HANK *hits bedroom* LIGHT SWITCH *and comes down steps to sofa.*]

COWBOY: Me too. That is, when I'm not high on pot or up on acid. [BERNARD *pours wine.*]

LARRY: [*To* HANK.] Well, is it bigger than a breadstick?

HANK: [*Ignores last remark, to* MICHAEL.] He's lying down for a minute. [*Lowers sleeves and puts on coat.*]

HAROLD: How does the bathroom smell?

HANK: Better.

MICHAEL: Before it smelled like somebody puked. Now it smells like somebody puked in a gardenia patch. [EMORY *enters from kitchen via Up Center with rolls going to Left table.*]

LARRY: And how does the big hero feel?

HANK: Lay off, will you.

EMORY: *Dinner is served!*

HAROLD: [*He comes to the buffet table, puts down wine and glass and picks up plate, fork and napkin.*] Emory, it looks absolutely fabulous.

EMORY: I'd make somebody a good wife. [DONALD *rises and notes* MICHAEL *pouring another gin as he puts ice in his own drink.* EMORY *serves pasta,*

BERNARD *serves the salad.* HANK, *with coat on, goes to* Left *table, followed by* LARRY.] I could cook and do an apartment and entertain... [He grabs a long-stem rose from an arrangement on the table, clenches it between his teeth, snaps his fingers and strikes a pose.] Kiss me quick, I'm Carmen! [HAROLD *just looks at him blankly and goes to* Down Right *chair and sits.* EMORY *takes the flower out of his mouth.*] One really needs castanets for that sort of thing. [DONALD *crosses to* COWBOY *indicating for him to get in food line at* Left *table.*]

MICHAEL: And a getaway car. [HANK *comes up to* EMORY.]

EMORY: What would you like, big boy?

LARRY: Alan McCarthy, and don't hold the mayo.

EMORY: I can't keep up with you two—[*Indicating* HANK, *then* LARRY.] I thought you were mad at him—now he's bitchin' you. What gives? [HANK *takes his food and wine to sofa and sits.*]

LARRY: Never mind.

COWBOY: [*He comes over to the table.*] What is it?

LARRY: Lasagna.

COWBOY: [*To* DONALD.] It looks like spaghetti and meatballs sorta flattened out.

DONALD: It's been in the steam room.

COWBOY: It has? [LARRY *crosses to ottoman and sits with his food.*]

MICHAEL: [*Contemptuously.*] It looks like spaghetti and meatballs sorta flattened out. Ah, yes, Harold—truly enviable. [COWBOY *goes to stairs and sits on third step with his food.*]

HAROLD: As opposed to you who knows so much about haute cuisine. Raconteur, gourmet, troll.

COWBOY: It's good.

HAROLD: [*Quick.*] You like it, eat it.

MICHAEL: Stuff your mouth so that you can't say anything. [DONALD *takes a plate.*]

HAROLD: Turning. [MICHAEL *crosses via above sofa to* DONALD *at stairs.*]

BERNARD: [*To* DONALD.] Wine?

DONALD: No thanks. [*Crosses to* MICHAEL *at stairs with his drink and food.*]

[BERNARD *hands* EMORY *a plate, which* EMORY *puts food on.*]

MICHAEL: Aw, go on, kiddo, force yourself. Have a little vin ordinaire to wash down all that depressed pasta. [DONALD *passes by and sits on high stool at door as* MICHAEL *goes to* Left *table.*]

HAROLD: Somelier, connoisseur, pig. [EMORY *hands* BERNARD *a plate he has served with food.*]

BERNARD: [*To* EMORY.] Aren't you going to have any?

EMORY: No. My lip hurts too much to eat. [BERNARD *sits Down Left chair with his plate.*]

MICHAEL: [*Crosses to table, picks up knife.*] I hear if you puts a knife under de bed it cuts de pain.

HAROLD: [*To* MICHAEL.] I hear if you put a knife under your chin it cuts your throat.

EMORY: Anybody going to take a plate up to Alan?

MICHAEL: The punching bag has now dissolved into Flo Nightingale.

LARRY: Hank?

HANK I don't think he'd have any appetite. [MICHAEL *raps the knife on a wine bottle.*]

MICHAEL: Ladies and gentlemen.... Correction: Ladies and ladies, I would like to announce that you have just eaten Sebastian Veneble. [*Puts knife on table.*]

COWBOY: Just eaten *what?*

MICHAEL: [*Goes to* COWBOY.] Not *what*, stupid, *who*. A character in a play. A fairy who was eaten alive. I mean the chop-chop variety.

COWBOY: Jesus. [*Puts plate down on steps.*]

[MICHAEL *crosses to sofa.*]

HANK: Did Edward Albee write that play?

MICHAEL: No. Tennessee Williams.

HANK: Oh, yeah.

MICHAEL: Albee wrote "Who's Afraid of Virginia Woolf?"

LARRY: Dummy.

HANK: I know that. I just thought maybe he wrote that other one too.

LARRY: Well, you made a mistake.

HANK: So I made a mistake.

LARRY: That's right, you made a mistake.

HANK: What's the difference? You can't add. [BERNARD *laughs.*]

COWBOY: Edward who?

MICHAEL: [*To* EMORY.] How much did you pay for him?

EMORY: He was a steal.

MICHAEL: He's a ham sandwich—fifty cents any time of the day or night. [*Crosses to bar via below coffee table.*]

[DONALD *rises, crosses to Left table with plate.*]

HAROLD: King of the Pig People. [MICHAEL *gives him a look.*]

EMORY: [*To* DONALD.] Would you like some more?

DONALD: No, thank you, Emory. It was very good.

EMORY: Did you like it?

COWBOY: I'm not a steal. I cost twenty dollars. [DONALD *returns to stool*. BERNARD *returns his plate to* EMORY.]

EMORY: More?

BERNARD: [*Nods negatively.*] It was delicious—even if I did make it myself.

EMORY: Isn't anybody having seconds? [EMORY *bends over to whisper "cake" to* BERNARD. BERNARD *goes to* COWBOY *and beckons him to follow him out to the kitchen.* COWBOY *exits with his plate to kitchen.*]

HAROLD: I'm having seconds and thirds and maybe even fifths. [*He rises and crosses to* EMORY.] I'm absolutely desperate to keep the weight up.

MICHAEL: [*Parodying* HAROLD.] You're *absolutely* paranoid about *absolutely* everything.

HAROLD: Oh, yeah, well, why don't you *not* tell me about it? [*Returns to his chair.*]

MICHAEL: [*Crosses above sofa.*] You starve yourself all day; living on coffee and cottage cheese so that you can gorge yourself at one meal. Then you feel guilty and moan and groan about how fat you are and how ugly you are when the truth is you're no fatter or thinner than you ever are.

EMORY: Polly Paranoia. [EMORY *moves to the coffee table to take* HANK's *empty plate.*]

HANK: Just great, Emory. Thanks.

EMORY: Connie Casserole, no-trouble-at-all-oh-Mary, D.A. [*Takes* HANK's *plate to Left table, and* LARRY *follows* EMORY *with his plate.*]

MICHAEL: [*Crossing to* HAROLD.] . . . And this pathological lateness. It's downright *crazy.*

HAROLD: Turning. [EMORY *exits into kitchen via stairs with dirty plates.*]

MICHAEL: Standing before a bathroom mirror for hours and hours before you can walk out on the street. And looking no different after Christ knows how many applications of Christ knows how many ointments and salves and creams and masks. [LARRY *nods to* HANK *to help put table back to wall, which* HANK *is slow to respond to.*]

HAROLD: I've got bad skin, what can I tell you?

MICHAEL: Who wouldn't after they deliberately take a pair of tweezers and *deliberately* mutilate their pores—no wonder you've got holes in your face after the hack-job you've done on yourself year in and year out! [HANK *rises with wine glass and goes to Left table.*]

HAROLD: [*Coolly but definitely.*] You hateful sow. [LARRY *and* HANK *move table to wall.* LARRY *sits down Left chair,* HANK *sits on steps.*]

MICHAEL: Yes, you've got scars on your face—but they're not that bad and if you'd leave yourself alone you wouldn't have any more than you've already awarded yourself.

HAROLD: You'd really like me to compliment you now for being so honest, wouldn't you? For being my best friend who will tell me what even my best friends won't tell me. Slut!

MICHAEL: And the pills! [*Announcement to* GROUP.] Harold has been gathering, saving and storing up barbiturates for the last year like a god-damn squirrel. Hundreds of nembutals, hundreds of seconals. All in preparation for and anticipation of the long winter of his death. [*Crossing via above coffee table to bar to pour another gin.*] But I tell you right now, Harold. When the time comes, you'll never have the guts. It's not always like it happens in plays, not all faggots bump themselves off at the end of the story.

HAROLD: [*Rises, taking plate to Left table.*] What you say may be true. Time will undoubtedly tell. But, in the meantime, you've left out one detail— the cosmetics and astringents are *paid* for, the bathroom is *paid* for, the tweezers are *paid* for, and the pills are *paid for!* [*Throws napkin on floor.*]

[EMORY *darts to the* LIGHT SWITCH, *plunges the room into* DARKNESS, *except for the light from the tapers on the buffet table, and begins to sing, "Happy Birthday." Immediately, the* COWBOY *enters carrying a cake ablaze with candles and goes to* HAROLD. BERNARD *follows* COWBOY *with his sport coat on.* EVERYONE *has now joined in: "Happy Birthday, dear Harold, Happy Birthday to you." This is followed by a round of applause as* HAROLD *sits on sofa.*]

EMORY: Blowout your candles, Mary, and make a wish!

MICHAEL: Blowout your candles, *Laura.* [*The* COWBOY *has brought cake over in front of* HAROLD. *He blows out the candles. More applause.*]

EMORY: Awwww, she's thirty-two years young! [*The* LIGHTS *are restored.*]

HAROLD: Oh, my God! [*The* COWBOY *takes the cake to the Left table.*]

HANK: [*Hands his sweater gift to* HAROLD *and goes above Center of sofa.*] Now, you have to open your gifts. [LARRY *has come over to the stairs during the singing and now is gathering all the gifts and takes them to* HAROLD.]

HAROLD: Oh, do I have to open them here?

LARRY: Open this one first. [*Handing* HAROLD *the poster gift and taking* HANK's *gift back from* HAROLD *as* LARRY *sits next to* HAROLD *on sofa.*]

EMORY: Of course you've got to open them here. Where does she think she's gonna open them? [*He is crossing above sofa when he sees the card on tile floor by tile pillar and retrieves it.*]

HAROLD: [*Begins to rip the paper from poster gift.*] Where's the card?

EMORY: Here. [*Hands card to* HAROLD *as he sits on ottoman.*]

HAROLD: Oh. From Larry. [ALL *groan "aahhh" as* HAROLD *finishes tearing off the tissue paper. While* HAROLD *is tearing paper* MICHAEL *gets cigarettes from coffee table and lights up one at the bar, which* DONALD *takes note of.*] It's heaven! I just love it, Larry.

COWBOY: What is it? [*Crossing to steps.*]

HAROLD: It's the deed to Boardwalk. [HAROLD *holds up a graphic design: a large-scale "Deed to Boardwalk," like those used in a Monopoly game.* LARRY *puts ripped-off tissue from gift under sofa.*]

EMORY: Oh, gay pop art!

DONALD: [*To* LARRY.] It's sensational. Did you do it? [*At Right end of sofa.*]

LARRY: Yes.

HAROLD: Oh, it's super, Larry. It goes up the minute I get home. [HAROLD *gives* LARRY *a kiss on the cheek as he hands "Boardwalk" to* EMORY.]

COWBOY: [*To* HAROLD.] I don't get it—you cruise Atlantic City or something?

MICHAEL: Will somebody get him out of here! [*Sits in Down Right chair.*]

[HAROLD *has opened another gift, takes the card from inside. The gift is a sweater.* EMORY *leans "Boardwalk" at Left End sofa.*]

HAROLD: Oh, what a nifty sweater! Thank you, Hank.

HANK: [*At above Center sofa.*] You can take it back and pick out another one if you want to.

HAROLD: I think this one is just nifty. [HAROLD *gives sweater to* LARRY *with a look "ugly" as* LARRY *gives him the pad box and* LARRY *puts sweater box on floor next to "Boardwalk."*]

BERNARD: Who wants cake? [*At Right end of sofa.*]

EMORY: Everybody? [*Rises and goes to cake on buffet table.*]

[COWBOY *sits on ottoman.*]

DONALD: None for me.

MICHAEL: I'd just like to sleep on mine, thank you.

HAROLD: [*He has opened another gift, suddenly laughs aloud.*] Oh, Bernard! How divine! Look, everybody! Bejewelled knee-pads! [*He holds up a pair of basketball knee-pads with sequin initials.*]

BERNARD: Monogrammed!

EMORY: [*Crossing to* HAROLD.] Bernard, you're a camp! Let me see. [HAROLD *hands pads to* EMORY. HAROLD *gives* LARRY *pad box and* LARRY *gives him* MICHAEL'S *gift.*]

MICHAEL: Y'all heard of Gloria De Haven and Billy De Wolfe, well, dis here is Rosemary De Camp!

BERNARD: Who?

EMORY: I never miss a Rosemary De Camp picture.

HANK: I've never heard of her.

COWBOY: Me neither.

HANK: Not all of us spent their childhood in a movie house, Michael. Some of us played baseball.

DONALD: And mowed the lawn.

EMORY: Well, *I* know who Rosemary De Camp is.

MICHAEL: You would. It's a cinch you wouldn't recognize a baseball or a lawnmower.

HAROLD: [*He has opened his last gift. He is silent.*] Thank you, Michael.

MICHAEL: What? [*Turns to see the gift.*] Oh. [*Rises, goes to bar and puts out cigarette.*] You're welcome. [*Gets his drink.*]

LARRY: What is it, Harold?

HAROLD: It's a photograph of him in a silver frame. And there's an inscription engraved and the date.

BERNARD: What's it say?

HAROLD: Just . . . something personal. [*Gives* LARRY *the gift.*]

MICHAEL: [*Turns round from the bar.*] Well, Bernard, what do you say we have a little music to liven things up! [LARRY *hands* HANK *the sweater box and* HANK *pulls out the desk chair and puts it on the seat and lingers Up Center.* LARRY *also hands* DONALD *"Boardwalk" which he puts on desk chair and then goes to Down Left chair and sits.*]

BERNARD: Okay. [*Goes to Phonograph.*]

EMORY: Yeah, I feel like dancing.

MICHAEL: [*Crosses above sofa.*] How about something good and ethnic, Emory?—one of your specialties like a military toe-tap with sparklers.

EMORY: [*Puts pads in box on coffee table and picks up his drink.*] I don't do that at birthdays—only on the Fourth of July. [BERNARD *puts on* RECORD *and crosses to bar.* EMORY *goes to* BERNARD, *picking up* HAROLD's *napkin from floor and puts in waste can and then joins* BERNARD *and starts to dance slowly.* HAROLD *lights a pot cigarette.* ALAN, *in second floor bedroom, rises from bed and comes downstairs to landing.* LARRY *has taken the remaining gifts to the desk chair. Gives* HANK *a look before turning to* MICHAEL.]

LARRY: Come on, Michael.

MICHAEL: I can only lead.

LARRY: I can follow. [LARRY *and* MICHAEL *start to dance above sofa.* HANK *exits into kitchen.* EMORY *gets pot cigarette from* HAROLD *while still dancing and shares it with* BERNARD.]

HAROLD: [*Rises and goes to* COWBOY.] Come on, Tex, you're on. [COWBOY *gets to his feet, but he is a washout as a dancing partner. He just stands still.* HAROLD *even tries to let him lead, but no good and so gives up.*] Later. [HAROLD *takes out another cigarette and a match as he crosses Left and catches sight of someone over by the stairs landing, walks over to* ALAN *and strikes a match.*] Wanna dance? [*Lights his cigarette.*]

EMORY: [*Sees* ALAN, *pronounces the following name: "E-von."*] Uh- oh, Ivan the terrible is back.

MICHAEL: [*Turns to* ALAN.] Oh, hello, Alan, Feel better? This is where you came in, isn't it? [ALAN *starts to cross down steps breaking away and giving* LARRY *his drink to hold.*] Excuse me, Larry.... [ALAN *has reached the third step as* MICHAEL *intercepts, blocking* ALAN *with his foot.*] As they say in the Deep South, don't rush off in the heat of the day.

HAROLD: Revolution complete.

MICHAEL: ... You missed the cake—and you missed the opening of the gifts—but you're still in luck. You're just in time for a party game.... Hey, everybody! Game time! [MICHAEL *indicates to* BERNARD *to turn phonograph off, which he does.* LARRY *takes* MICHAEL'S *drink to bar and sits on high stool at door.*]

HAROLD: Why don't you just let him go, Michael? [*He crosses to Down Right chair and sits indicating to* COWBOY *to come over to him.* COWBOY *goes to* HAROLD *and sits on a cushion by* HAROLD'S *chair on the floor, where he removes his hat, card and kerchief.*]

MICHAEL: [*Crossing to Left of* ALAN.] He can go if he wants to—but not before we play a game. [ALAN *starts to move,* MICHAEL *catches him gently by the sleeve and tugs* ALAN *to sit.* ALAN *sits on third step.*]

EMORY: What's it going to be—movie star gin? [*Sits on sofa.*]

MICHAEL: That's too faggy for Alan to play—he wouldn't be any good at it.

BERNARD: [*Crosses to pillar and leans.*] What about Likes and Dislikes? [HANK *enters from kitchen and crosses Up Right near* LARRY.]

MICHAEL: [*Crosses to Left end sofa.*] It's too much trouble to find enough pencils, and besides, Emory always puts down the same thing. He dislikes artificial fruit and flowers and coffee grinders made into lamps—and he likes Mabel Mercer, poodles, and "All about Eve"—the screenplay of which he will then recite *verbatim.*

EMORY: I put down other things sometimes.

MICHAEL: Like a tan out of season?

EMORY: I just always put down little "Chi-Chi" because I adore her so much.

MICHAEL: If one is of the masculine gender, a poodle is the *insignia* of one's deviation. [*Goes to desk for pad and pencil.*]

BERNARD: [*Crosses in to* EMORY.] You know why old ladies like poodles — because they go down on them.

EMORY: *They do not.* [*Gives* BERNARD *a swat as* BERNARD *returns to pillar.*]

LARRY: We could play B For Botticelli.

MICHAEL: [*Crosses to Right end sofa.*] We *could* play *Spin* The Botticelli, but we're not going to.

HAROLD: What would you like to play, Michael — The Truth Game?

MICHAEL: [*He chuckles to himself.*] Cute, Hallie.

HAROLD: Or do you want to play Murder? You all remember that one, don't you?

MICHAEL: [*To* HAROLD.] Very, very cute.

DONALD: [*Rises and crosses to stairs, leaning on landing.*] As I recall, they're quite similar. The rules are the same in both — you kill somebody.

MICHAEL: [*Crosses to steps.*] In affairs of the heart, there are no rules. Isn't that right, Harold?

HAROLD: That's what I always say.

MICHAEL: Well, that's the name of the game. The Affairs Of The Heart.

COWBOY: I've never heard of that one.

MICHAEL: [*To* COWBOY.] Of course you've never heard of it — I just made It up, baby doll. [*To* ALL.] Affairs Of The Heart is a combination of both the Truth Game and Murder — with a new twist.

HAROLD: I can hardly wait to find out what that is.

ALAN: Mickey, I'm leaving. [*He starts to move, ending up Down Center.*]

MICHAEL: [*Firmly, flatly.*] Stay where you are.

HAROLD: Michael, let him go.

MICHAEL: [*Crosses to* ALAN.] He really doesn't *want* to. If he did, he'd have left a long time ago — or he wouldn't have come here in the first place.

ALAN: [*Holding his forehead.*] . . . Mickey, I don't feel well.

MICHAEL: [*Low tone but distinctly articulate.*] My name is Michael. I am called Michael. You must never call anyone called Michael, Mickey. Those of us who are named Michael are very nervous about it. If you don't believe it — try it.

ALAN: I'm sorry. I can't think. [*Starts to go.*]

MICHAEL: [*Stops* ALAN *by stepping in his way.*] You can think. What you can't do — is leave. It's like watching an accident on the highway — you can't look at it and you can't look away.

ALAN: I . . . feel . . . weak . . .

MICHAEL: You are weak. Much weaker than I think you realize. [ALAN *crosses to Down Left chair and sits.*] Now! Who's going to play with Alan and me? Everyone?

HAROLD: I have no intention of playing.

DONALD: Nor do I.

MICHAEL: Well, not everyone is a participant in life. There are always those who stand on the sidelines and watch.

LARRY: What's the game?

MICHAEL: [*Goes to desk and brings phone to Left end sofa.*] Simply this: We all have to call on the telephone the *one person* we truly believed we have loved.

HANK: [*Crosses in to above sofa.*] I'm not playing.

LARRY: Oh, yes you are.

HANK: [*Turns to* LARRY.] You'd like for me to play, wouldn't you?

LARRY: You bet I would. I'd like to know who you'd call after all the fancy speeches I've heard lately. Who would you call? Would you call me?

MICHAEL: [*To* BERNARD.] Sounds like there's, how you say, trouble in paradise.

HAROLD: If there isn't, I think you'll be able to stir up some.

HANK: [*Crosses to* LARRY.] And who would *you* call? Don't think I think for one minute it would be me. Or that one call would do it. You'd have to make several, wouldn't you? About three long distance and God-only-knows how many locals. [*Crosses below coffee table to Left table.*]

COWBOY: I'm glad I don't have to pay the bill.

MICHAEL: Quiet!

HAROLD: [*To* COWBOY.] Oh, don't worry, Michael won't pay it either.

MICHAEL: Now, here's how it works.

LARRY: I thought you said there were no rules.

MICHAEL: [*Crosses to* LARRY.] That's right. In Affairs Of The Heart, there are no rules. This is the god-damn point system! [*Crosses to Center.* DONALD *goes to steps and sits fourth step,* HANK *takes* DONALD'*s place at landing.*] If you make the call, you get one point. If the person you are calling answers, you get two more points—if somebody else answers, you get only one. If there's no answer at all, you're screwed.

DONALD: You're screwed if you make the call.

HAROLD: You're a *fool*—if you screw yourself.

MICHAEL: . . . When you get the person whom you are calling on the line—if you tell them who you are, you get two points, And then—if you tell them that you *love* them—you get a bonus of five more points!

HAROLD: Hateful.

MICHAEL: Therefore you can get as many as ten points and as few as one.

HAROLD: You can get as few as none — if you know how to work it.

MICHAEL: The one with the highest score wins.

ALAN: Hank. Let's get out of here.

EMORY: Well, now. Did you hear that!

MICHAEL: Just the two of you together. The pals . . . the guys . . . the buddie-buddies . . . the he-men.

EMORY: I think Larry might have something to say about that.

BERNARD: Emory.

MICHAEL: [*Re: last remark.*] The duenna speaks. So who's playing? Excluding Cowboy, who, as a gift, is neuter. And, of course, la voyeurs. Emory? [*A beat.*] Bernard?

BERNARD: I don't think I want to play.

MICHAEL: Why, Bernard! Where's your fun-loving spirit?

BERNARD: I don't think this game is fun. [*Goes to ottoman and sits.*]

HAROLD: It's absolutely hateful.

ALAN: [*Rises.*] Hank, leave with me.

HANK: You don't understand, Alan. I can't. You can . . . but I can't.

ALAN: Why, Hank? Why can't you?

LARRY: [*To* HANK.] If he doesn't understand, why don't you explain it to him?

MICHAEL: *I'll* explain it.

HAROLD: I had a feeling you might.

MICHAEL: [*Puts phone on sofa.*] Although I doubt that it'll make any difference. That type refuses to understand that which they do not wish to accept. They reject certain facts. And Alan is decidedly from The Ostrich School of Reality. [*A beat.*] Alan . . . Larry and Hank are lovers. Not just roommates, *bed*-mates. *Lovers.*

ALAN: Michael! [*Turns away.*]

MICHAEL: No man's still got *a roommate* when he's over thirty years old. If they're not lovers, they're sisters. [ALAN *sits Down Left chair.*]

LARRY: Hank is the one who's over thirty.

MICHAEL: [*Crosses to Center.*] Well, you're pushing it!

ALAN: . . . Hank?

HANK: [*Turns to* ALAN.] Yes, Alan. Larry is my lover.

ALAN: But you're married. [MICHAEL, LARRY, EMORY, *and the* COWBOY *are sent into instant gales of laughter.*]

HAROLD: I think you said the wrong thing.

MICHAEL: Don't you love that quaint little idea?—if a man is married, then he is automatically heterosexual. [*A beat.*] Alan—Hank swings both ways—with a decided preference. [*A beat.*] Now. Who makes the first call? Emory?

EMORY: You go, Bernard.

BERNARD: I don't want to.

EMORY: I don't want to either. I don't want to at all.

DONALD: [*To himself.*] There are no accidents.

MICHAEL: Then, may I say, on your way home I hope you *will* yourself over an embankment.

EMORY: [*To* BERNARD.] Go on. Call up Peter Dahlbeck. That's who you'd like to call, isn't it?

MICHAEL: [*Crosses to* EMORY *above sofa.*] Who is Peter Dahlbeck?

EMORY: The boy in Detroit whose family Bernard's mother has been a laundress for since he was a pickaninny.

BERNARD: I worked for them too—after school and every summer.

EMORY: It's always been a large order of Hero Worship.

BERNARD: I think I've loved him all my life. But he never knew I was alive. Besides, he's straight.

COWBOY: So nothing ever happened between you?

EMORY: Oh, they finally made it—in the pool house one night after a drunken swimming party.

LARRY: With the right wine and the right music there're damn few that aren't curious.

MICHAEL: [*To* DONALD.] Sounds like there's a lot of Lady Chatterley in Mr. Dahlbeck, wouldn't you say, Donald?

DONALD: I've never been an O'Hara fan myself.

BERNARD: . . . And afterwards, we went swimming in the nude in the dark with only the moon reflecting on the water.

DONALD: Nor Thomas Merton.

BERNARD: It was beautiful.

MICHAEL: How romantic. And then the next morning you took him his coffee and alka-seltzer on a tray.

BERNARD: It was in the afternoon. I remember I was worried sick all morning about having to face him. But he pretended like nothing at all had happened.

MICHAEL: [*Looks at* DONALD.] Christ, he must have been so drunk he didn't remember a thing.

BERNARD: Yeah. I was sure relieved.

MICHAEL: Odd how that works. [*Put phone on coffee table.*] And now, for ten points, get that liar on the phone. [*A beat.* BERNARD *picks up the phone, dials.*]

LARRY: You *know* the number?

BERNARD: Sure. He's back in Grosse Pointe, living at home. He just got separated from his third wife. [ALL *watch* BERNARD *as he puts the receiver to his ear, waits. A beat. He hangs up quickly.*]

EMORY: D.A. or B.Y.?

COWBOY: What?

EMORY: D.A. or B.Y. That's operator lingo. It means—"Doesn't Answer" or "Busy."

MICHAEL: He didn't even give it time to find out. [*Coaxing.*] Go ahead, Bernard. Pick up the phone and dial. You'll think of something.—You know you want to call him. You know that, don't you? Well,—go ahead. [BERNARD *starts dialing.*] Your curiosity has got the best of you now. So...go on, call him. [BERNARD *lets it ring this time.*]

HAROLD: Hateful.

BERNARD: ...Hello?

MICHAEL: One point. [*He efficiently takes note on the pad.*]

[HANK *crosses to the Onstage landing area.*]

BERNARD: Who's speaking? Oh...Mrs. Dahlbeck.

MICHAEL: [*Taking note.*] One point.

BERNARD: ...It's Bernard.—Francine's boy.

EMORY: *Son*, not *boy*.

BERNARD: ...How are you?—Good. Good. Oh, just fine, thank you.— Mrs. Dahlbeck, is...Peter—at home?—Oh. Oh, I see.

MICHAEL: [*Crosses up to desk and back to* BERNARD.] Shhhhiiii...

BERNARD: ...Oh, no. No, it's nothing important. I just wanted to...to tell him...that...to tell him I...

MICHAEL: [*Prompting flatly.*] I love him. That I've always loved him.

BERNARD: ...that I was sorry to hear about him and his wife.

MICHAEL: No points! [*Crosses above sofa.*]

BERNARD: ...My mother wrote me.—Yes. It is. It really is.—Well. Would you just tell him I called and said...that I was—just—very, very sorry to hear and I...hope—they can get everything straightened out.—Yes. Yes. Well, good night.—Goodbye. [*He hangs up slowly.* MICHAEL *draws a definite line across his pad, makes a definite period.*]

MICHAEL: Two points total. Terrible. Next!

EMORY: Are you all right, Bernard?

BERNARD: [*Almost to himself.*] Why did I call? Why did I do that?
LARRY: [*To* BERNARD.] Where was he?
BERNARD: Out on a date. [*Hangs up phone and goes to Left table.*]
MICHAEL: Come on, Emory. Punch in. [*Turns Phone toward* EMORY.]

[DONALD *rises, goes to high stool and sits.* EMORY *picks up the phone, dials information.* LARRY *rises and crosses Right side of sofa. A beat.*]

EMORY: Could I have the number, please—in the Bronx—for a Delbert Botts.
LARRY: *A* Delbert Botts! How many can there be! [*Sits sofa.*]
BERNARD: Oh, I wish I hadn't called now.
EMORY: . . . No, the residence number, please. [*Grabs pencil from* MICHAEL'*s hand. He writes on the white, plastic phonecase. Into phone.*] . . . Thank you. [*And he indignantly slams down the receiver.*] I do wish information would stop calling me, "Ma'am"!
MICHAEL: By all means, scribble all over the telephone. [*He snatches the pencil from* EMORY'*s hands.*]
EMORY: It comes off with a little spit. [*Picks up his drink from coffee table.*]
MICHAEL: [*To* ALAN.] Like a lot of things.
LARRY: Who the hell is Delbert Botts?
EMORY: The one person I have always loved. [*To* MICHAEL.] That's who you said to call, isn't it?
MICHAEL: That's right, Emory board.
LARRY: How could you love anybody with a name like that?
MICHAEL: Yes, Emory, you couldn't love anybody with a name like that. It wouldn't look good on a place card. Isn't that right, Alan? [ALAN *is silent.*]
EMORY: I admit his name is not so good—but he is absolutely beautiful—At least, he was when I was in high school. Of course, I haven't seen him since and he was about seven years older than I even then.
MICHAEL: [*Goes to bar, pours gin.*] Christ, you better call him quick before he dies.
EMORY: I've loved him ever since the first day I laid eyes on him which was when I was in the fifth grade and he was a senior.—Then, he went away to college and by the time he got out I was in high school, and he had become a dentist.
MICHAEL: [*With incredulous disgust.*] A *dentist!* [*Crosses above sofa with drink, leaving pad and pencil on bar.*]
EMORY: Yes. Delbert Botts, D.D.S. And he opened his office in a bank

building. [*Gives empty glass to* LARRY, *who hands it to* DONALD, *who refills it from martini pitcher.*]

HAROLD: And you went and had every tooth in your head pulled out, right?

EMORY: No. I just had my teeth cleaned, that's all. [*Gets his drink handed back.*]

[DONALD *decides to make a scotch for* ALAN.]

BERNARD: [To *himself.*] Oh, I shouldn't have called.

MICHAEL: [*To* BERNARD.] Will you shut-up, Bernard! And take your boring, sleep-making icks somewhere else. *Go!* [BERNARD *takes the red wine bottle and glass and moves to the desk via above stair passage.* MICHAEL *crosses to Center.*]

EMORY: I remember I looked right into his eyes the whole time and I kept wanting to bite his fingers.

HAROLD: Well, it's absolutely mind boggling. [DONALD *takes* ALAN *a scotch.*]

MICHAEL: Phyllis Phallic.

HAROLD: It absolutely boggles the mind. [ALAN *takes the drink.*]

MICHAEL: [*Re:* DONALD's *action.*] Sara Samaritan. [DONALD, *with his own drink, sits on landing.*]

EMORY: ...I told him I was having my teeth cleaned for the Junior-Senior Prom for which I was in charge of decorations. I told him it was a celestial theme and I was cutting stars out of tin foil and making clouds out of chicken wire and angel's hair. [*A beat.*] He couldn't have been less impressed.

COWBOY: I got angel's hair down my shirt once at Christmastime. Gosh, did it itch!

EMORY: ...I told him I was going to burn incense in pots so that white fog would hover over the dance floor and it would look like heaven—just like I'd seen it in a Rita Hayworth movie.—I can't remember the title.

MICHAEL: The picture was called "Down To Earth." Any *kid* knows that.

COWBOY: ...And it made little tiny cuts in the creases of my fingers. Man, did they sting! It would be terrible if you got that stuff in your...I'll be quiet. [MICHAEL *goes to bar, leaves glass and picks up pad and pencil.*]

EMORY: He was engaged to this stupid-ass girl named Loraine whose mother was truly Supercunt.

MICHAEL: Don't digress. [*Crosses above sofa.*]

EMORY: Well, anyway, I was a wreck. I mean a total mess. I couldn't eat, sleep, stand up, sit down, nothing. I could hardly cut out silver stars or finish the clouds for the Prom. So I called him on the telephone and asked if I could see him alone.

HAROLD: Clearly not the coolest of moves.

EMORY: He said okay and told me to come by his house. — I was so nervous this time — my hands were shaking and my voice was unsteady. I couldn't look at him — I just stared straight in space and blurted out why I'd come. — I told him . . . I wanted him to be my friend. I said that I never knew anyone who I could talk to and tell everything to and trust. I asked him if he would be my friend.

COWBOY: You poor bastard.

MICHAEL: SHHHHHHH!

BERNARD: What'd he say? [*Crossing to pillar Center with wine glass.*]

EMORY: He said he would be glad to be my friend. And anytime I ever wanted to see him or call him — to just call him and he'd see me. And he shook my trembling wet hand and I left on a cloud.

MICHAEL: One of the ones you made yourself.

EMORY: And the next day I went out and bought him a gold-plated cigarette lighter and had his initials monogrammed on it and wrote a card that said, "From your friend, Emory."

HAROLD: Seventeen years old and already big with the gifts.

COWBOY: Yeah. And cards too.

EMORY: . . . And then the night of the Prom I found out.

BERNARD: Found out what?

EMORY: I heard two girls I knew giggling together. They were standing behind some god-damn corrugated cardboard Greek columns I had borrowed from a department store and had draped with yards and yards of god-damn cheesecloth. Oh, Mary, it takes a fairy to make something pretty.

MICHAEL: *Don't digress.*

EMORY: This girl who was telling the story said she had heard it from her mother — and her mother had heard it from Loraine's mother. You see, Loraine and her mother were not beside the point. Obviously, Del had told Loraine about my calling and about the gift. [*A beat.*] Pretty soon everybody at the dance had heard about it and they were all laughing and making jokes. Everybody knew I had a crush on Doctor Delbert Botts and that I had asked him to be my friend. [*A beat.*] What they didn't know was that I *loved* him. And that I would go on loving him years after they had all forgotten my funny secret. [*Pause.*]

HAROLD: Well, I for one, need an insulin injection.

MICHAEL: *Call him.*

BERNARD: [*Takes glass to desk and goes to* EMORY.] Don't, Emory.

MICHAEL: Since when are you telling him what to do!

EMORY: [*To* BERNARD.] What do I care—I'm pissed! I'll do anything. Three times.

BERNARD: Don't. *Please!* [*Squats Left of* EMORY.]

MICHAEL: I said call him.

BERNARD: Don't! You'll be sorry. Take my word for it.

EMORY: What have I got to lose?

BERNARD: Your dignity. That's what you've got to lose.

MICHAEL: [*Crosses to Left table and deposits pad and pencil.*] Well, *that's* a knee-slapper! I love *your* telling him about dignity when you allow him to degrade you constantly by Uncle Tom-ing you to death.

BERNARD: [*Rises and crosses to Center.*] He can do it, Michael. *I* can do it. But *you can't* do it.

MICHAEL: Isn't that discrimination?

BERNARD: I don't like it from him and I don't like it from me—but I do it to myself and I let him do it. I let him do it because it's the only thing that, to him, makes him my equal. We both got the short end of the stick— but I got a hell of a lot more than he did and he knows it. So, I let him Uncle Tom me just so he can tell himself he's not a complete loser.

MICHAEL: How very considerate.

BERNARD: It's his defense. You have your defense, Michael. But it's indescribable. [EMORY *quietly licks his finger and begins to rub the number off the telephone case.*]

MICHAEL: [*To* BERNARD.] Y'all want to hear a little polite parlor jest from the liberal Deep South?—Do you know why *Nigras* have such big lips? Because they're always going, "p-p-p-p-a-a-a-hl" [*The labial noise is exasperating with lazy disgust.* BERNARD *sits on second step.*]

DONALD: Christ, Michael!

MICHAEL: I can do without your god-damn spit all over my telephone, you nellie coward. [*Grabs Phone from* EMORY *but* EMORY *manages to keep it from the tug of war.*]

EMORY: I may be nellie, but I'm no coward. [MICHAEL *lets go of phone and goes up Right corner to compose himself. Starts to dial.*] Bernard, forgive me. I'm sorry. I won't ever say those things to you again. [BERNARD *rises and goes to desk and wine.*] B.Y.

MICHAEL: [*Crosses above sofa.*] It's busy?

EMORY: [*Nods.*] Loraine is probably talking to her mother. Oh, yes, Delbert married Loraine.

MICHAEL: I'm sorry, you'll have to forfeit your turn. We can't wait. [*He takes the Phone from* EMORY's *lap and puts it in* LARRY's *lap.* LARRY *takes phone and starts to dial.*]

HAROLD: [*To* LARRY.] Well, you're not wasting any time.

HANK: Who are you calling?

LARRY: Charlie. [EMORY *jerks the phone out of* LARRY*'s hands.*]

EMORY: I refuse to forfeit my turn! It's *my turn* and I'm taking it! [*Rises, backs up into* MICHAEL*'s arms with phone.*]

MICHAEL: That's the spirit, Emory! *Hit that iceberg—don't miss it! Hit it! God-damnit!* I want a smash of a finale! [MICHAEL *pushes* EMORY *to floor between ottoman and coffee table.*]

EMORY: Oh, God, I'm drunk.

MICHAEL: A falling-down-drunk-nellie-queen.

HAROLD: Well, that's the pot calling the kettle beige!

MICHAEL: [*Snapping, to* HAROLD.] *I am not drunk!* You cannot tell that I am drunk!—Donald! I'm not drunk! Am I!

DONALD: *I'm* drunk.

EMORY: So am I. I am a *major drunk.*

MICHAEL: [*To* EMORY.] Shut up and dial! [*Goes to Left table for pad and pencil.*]

EMORY: [*Dialing.*] I am a major drunk of this or any other season.

DONALD: [*To* MICHAEL.] Don't you mean, shut up and *deal?*

EMORY: . . . It's ringing. It is no longer B.Y.—Hello?

MICHAEL: [*Taking note.*] One point.

EMORY: . . . Who's speaking? Who? . . . Doctor Delbert Botts?

MICHAEL: Two points.

EMORY: Oh, Del, is this really you?—Oh, nobody. You don't know me. You wouldn't remember me. I'm . . . just a friend. A falling-down drunken friend. Hello? Hello? Hello? [*He lowers the receiver.*] He hung up. [EMORY *hangs up the telephone.*]

MICHAEL: Three points total. You're winning.

EMORY: He said I must have the wrong party. [BERNARD *exits kitchen Up Center.*]

HAROLD: [*Rises.*] He's right. We have the wrong party. We should be somewhere else.

EMORY: [*Rises, taking drink from coffee table, going to* HAROLD.] It's your party, Harold. Aren't you having a good time?

HAROLD: Simply fabulous. And what about you? Are you having a good time, Emory? Are you having as good a time as you thought you would? [*Puts* EMORY *in Down Right chair.*]

[LARRY *takes the phone.*]

MICHAEL: If you're bored, Harold, we could sing Happy Birthday again— to the tune of Havah Nagelah.

HAROLD: Not for all the tea in Mexico. [*Crosses Up Center to desk where he lights up a cigarette.*]

[LARRY *starts to dial.*]

HANK: My turn now. [*Crossing to* LARRY.]
LARRY: It's my turn to call Charlie.
HANK: No. Let me.
LARRY: Are you going to call Charlie?
MICHAEL: [*Crosses to Left of steps.*] The score is three to two. Emory's favor.
ALAN: Don't, Hank. Don't you see — Bernard was right.
HANK: [*Firmly to* ALAN.] I want to. [He holds out his hand for the phone.] Larry?
LARRY: [*Gives him the phone.*] Be my eager guest.
COWBOY: [*To* LARRY.] Is he going to call Charlie for you? [HANK *starts to dial as he sits on sofa.* HAROLD *comes to bar.*]
LARRY: Charlie is all the people I cheat on Hank with.
DONALD: With whom I cheat on Hank.
MICHAEL: The butcher, the baker, the candlestick maker.
LARRY: Right! I love 'em all. And what Hank refuses to understand — is that I've, got to *have* 'em all. I am *not* the marrying kind, and I never will be.
HAROLD: Gypsy feet. [*Crosses to Right end sofa.*]
LARRY: [*Step in to* HANK.] Who are you calling?
MICHAEL: Jealous?
LARRY: Curious as hell!
MICHAEL: And a little jealous too.
LARRY: Who are you calling?
MICHAEL: Did it ever occur to you that Hank might be doing the same thing behind your back that you do behind his?
LARRY: I wish to Christ he would. It'd make life a hell of a lot easier. Who are you calling? [*Sits ottoman.*]
HAROLD: Whoever it is, they're not sitting on top of the telephone. [*Sits sofa Right end.*]
HANK: Hello?
COWBOY: They must have been in the tub.
MICHAEL: [*Snaps at* COWBOY.] Eighty-six! [*Crossing above sofa.* BERNARD *enters, uncorking another bottle of wine and sits on desk. Taking note.*] One point.
HANK: . . . I'd like to leave a message.
MICHAEL: Not in. One point.

HANK: Would you say that Hank called. — Yes, it is. Oh, good evening, how are you?

LARRY: Who the hell *is* that? [*Grabs for phone but* HANK *keeps phone and transfers it to other ear.*]

HANK: . . . Yes, that's right—the message is for my roommate, Larry. Just say that I called and . . .

LARRY: It's our answering service! [*Rising and going Up Center to pillar.*]

HANK: . . . and said . . . I love you.

MICHAEL: [*Crosses to Right end sofa.*] Five points! You said it! You get five god-damn points for saying it!

ALAN: [*Rises and crosses in.*] Hank! . . . Are you crazy?

HANK: [*Into phone.*] . . . No. You didn't hear me incorrectly. That's what I said. The message is for Larry and it's from me, Hank, and it is just as I said—I . . . love . . . you. Thanks. [*He hangs up and rises.*]

MICHAEL: Seven points total! Hank, you're ahead, baby. You're way, way ahead of everybody!

ALAN: Why, Hank? Why did you do that?

HANK: Because I do love him. And I don't care who knows it.

ALAN: Don't say that.

HANK: Why not? It's the truth.

ALAN: I can't believe you.

HANK: [*Crossing to* ALAN.] I left my wife and family for Larry.

ALAN: I'm really not interested in hearing about it. [*Turns back to chair.*]

MICHAEL: Sure you are. Go ahead, Hankola, tell him all about it.

ALAN: No! I don't want to hear it. It's disgusting! [*Sits in same chair.*]

HANK: Some men do it for another woman.

ALAN: Well, I could understand *that*. That's *normal*.

HANK: It just doesn't always work out that way. No matter how you might want it to. And God knows, Alan, nobody ever wanted it more than I did. I really and truly felt that I was in love with my wife when I married her. It wasn't altogether my trying to prove something to myself. I did love her and she loved me. But . . . there was always that something there.

DONALD: You mean your attraction to your own sex.

HANK: Yes.

ALAN: Always?

HANK: I don't know. I suppose so. [*Goes to Left table.*]

EMORY: I've known what I was since I was four years old.

MICHAEL: Everybody's always known it about *you*, Emory.

DONALD: [*Rises and sits stool at door.*] I've always known it about myself too.

HANK: [*Crosses to Left of steps.*] I don't know when it was that I started admitting it to myself. For so long I either labeled it something else or denied it completely.

MICHAEL: Christ-was-I-drunk-last-night.

HANK: And then there came a time when I just couldn't lie to myself any more... I thought about it but I never did anything about it. — I think the first time was during my wife's last pregnancy. We lived near Hartford — in the country. She and the kids still live there. — Well, anyway, there was a teachers' meeting here in New York. She didn't feel up to the trip and I came alone. And that day on the train I began to think about it and think about it and think about it. I thought of nothing else the whole trip. And within fifteen minutes after I had arrived I had picked up a guy in the men's room of Grand Central Station.

ALAN: [*Quietly.*] Jesus.

HANK: I'd never done anything like that in my life and I was scared to death. But he turned out to be a nice fellow. I've never seen him again and it's funny I can't even remember his name any more. [*A beat.*] Anyway. After that, it got easier.

HAROLD: Practice makes perfect.

HANK: And then... sometime later... not very long after, Larry was in Hartford and we met at a party my wife and I had gone in town for.

EMORY: And your real troubles began.

HANK: That was two years ago.

LARRY: Why am I always the god-damn villain in the piece! If I'm not thought of as a happy home wrecker, I'm an impossible son-of-a-bitch to live with!

HAROLD: Guilt turns to hostility. Isn't that right, Michael?

MICHAEL: Go stick your tweezers in your cheek.

LARRY: I'm fed up to the teeth with everybody feeling so god-damn sorry for poor shat-upon Hank.

EMORY: Aw, Larry, everybody knows you're Frida Fickle.

LARRY: [*Rises.*] I've never made any promises and I never intend to. It's my right to lead my sex life without answering to *anybody* — Hank included! — And if those terms are not acceptable, then we must not live together. — Numerous relations is a part of the way I am! [*Crosses to bar.*]

[MICHAEL *rises and takes Center Stage.*]

EMORY: You don't have to be gay to be a wanton.

LARRY: By the way I am, I don't mean being gay—I mean my sexual appetite. And I don't think of myself as a wanton. Emory, you are the most promiscuous person I know. [*Crosses Up Center.*]

EMORY: I am not promiscuous at all!

MICHAEL: [*Crosses to bar to pour another gin.*] Not by choice, by design. Why would anybody want to go to bed with a flaming little sissy like you?

BERNARD: Michael! [*Crosses in to Pillar with wine bottle and glass.*]

MICHAEL: [*To EMORY.*] Who'd make a pass at you?—I'll tell you who—nobody. Except maybe some fugitive from the Braille Institute.

BERNARD: [*To EMORY.*] Why do you let him talk to you that way?

HAROLD: Physical beauty is not everything.

MICHAEL: Thank you, Quasimodo. [*Crossing above sofa with drink and pad.*]

LARRY: [*Crosses to Center.*] What do you think it's like living with the god-damn gestapo! I can't breathe without getting the third degree!

MICHAEL: Larry, it's your turn to call. [*Sits on sofa back.*]

LARRY: [Steps to Right.] I can't take all that let's-be-faithful-and-never-look-at-another-person-routine. It just doesn't work.—If you want to promise that, fine. Then do it and stick to it. But if you *have* to promise it—as far as I'm concerned—nothing finishes a relationship faster. [*Crosses to steps to* HANK.]

HAROLD: Give me librium or give me meth.

BERNARD: [*Intoxicated now.*] Yeah, freedom, baby! Freedom!

LARRY: [*Crosses Center.*] You gotta have it! It can't work any other way. And the ones who swear their undying fidelity are lying. Most of them, anyway—ninety percent of them. They cheat on each other constantly and lie through their teeth. I'm sorry, I can't be like that and it drives Hank up the wall.

HANK: There is that ten percent.

LARRY: The only way it stands a chance is with some sort of an understanding.

HANK: I've tried to go along with that.

LARRY: Aw, *come on!*

HANK: I agreed to an agreement.

LARRY: Your agreement.

MICHAEL: What agreement? [*Stands up.*]

LARRY: A menage.

HAROLD: The lover's agreement.

LARRY: Look, I know a lot of people think it's the answer. They don't consider it cheating. But it's not my style.

HANK: Well, *I* certainly didn't want it.

LARRY: Then who suggested it?

HANK: It was a compromise.

LARRY: Exactly.

HANK: And you agreed.

LARRY: I didn't agree to anything. You agreed to your own proposal and *informed me* that I agreed. [HANK *goes to sofa and sits.*]

COWBOY: I don't understand. What's a me . . . menaa . . .

MICHAEL: A menage a trois, baby. Two's company — three's a menage.

HANK: Well, it works for some.

LARRY: Well, I'm not one for group therapy. I'm sorry, I can't relate to anyone or anything that way. I'm old-fashioned — I like 'em all, but I like 'em one at a time!

MICHAEL: [*To* LARRY.] Did you like Donald as a single side attraction? [*Pause.* DONALD *rises, crosses to Right end sofa.*]

LARRY: Yes. I did.

DONALD: So did I, Larry.

LARRY: [*To* DONALD *re:* MICHAEL.] Did you tell him?

DONALD: No.

MICHAEL: [*Crosses to* LARRY.] It was perfectly obvious from the moment you walked in the door. What was this big song and dance about having seen each other but never having met?

DONALD: It was true. We saw each other in the baths and went to bed together but we never spoke a word and never knew each other's names.

EMORY: You had better luck than I do. If I don't get arrested, my trick announces upon departure that he's been exposed to hepatitis!

MICHAEL: In spring a young man's fancy turns to a fancy young man. [*Goes to Left table and puts drink, pad and pencil down.*]

LARRY: [*Crosses to* HANK.] Don't look at me like that. You've been playing footsie with the Blue Book all night.

DONALD: I think he only wanted to show you what's good for the gander is good for the gander.

HANK: That's right. [DONALD *returns to his stool.*]

LARRY: [*To* HANK.] I suppose you'd like the three of us to have a go at it.

HANK: At least it'd be together.

LARRY: That point eludes me. [*Crosses Left of steps.*]

HANK: What kind of an understanding do you *want!*

LARRY: Respect — for each other's freedom. With no need to lie or pretend. [*Crosses to* HANK *and kneels.*] In my own way, Hank, I love you, but you've got to understand that even though I do want to go on living with you, sometimes there may be others. I don't want to flaunt it in your face. If it happens I know I'll never mention it. But if you ask me, I'll tell you. I don't want to hurt you but I won't lie to you if you want to know anything about me.

BERNARD: He gets points.

MICHAEL: What?

BERNARD: He said it—he said, "I love you," to Hank—he gets the bonus.

MICHAEL: He didn't call him.

DONALD: He called him. He just didn't use the telephone.

MICHAEL: Then he doesn't get any points.

BERNARD: He gets five points!

MICHAEL: He didn't use the telephone—he doesn't get a god-damn thing! [LARRY *goes to the phone, picks up the receiver, looks at the number of the second line, dials. A beat. The* PHONE *rings.*]

LARRY: It's for you, Hank. Why don't you take it upstairs? [*The phone continues to ring.* HANK *gets up, goes up the stairs to the bedroom. Pause. He presses the second line button, picks up the receiver.* EVERYONE *downstairs is silent.*]

HANK: Hello?

BERNARD: One point.

LARRY: Hello, Hank.

BERNARD: Two points.

LARRY: . . . This is Larry.

BERNARD: Two more points!

LARRY: . . . For what it's worth, I love you.

BERNARD: Five points bonus!

HANK: I'll . . . I'll try.

LARRY: I will too. [*He hangs up.* HANK *hangs up.*]

BERNARD: That's ten points total! [*Rises and comes down steps to Up Center.*]

EMORY: Larry's the winner! [*Rises and stretches.*]

[DONALD *rises and pulls high stool to right of desk and gets up Right Center.* COWBOY *rises and puts cushion under bar and sits Right end of sofa.* EMORY *continues via below coffee table to stairs.*]

HAROLD: [*Rises.*] Well, that wasn't as much fun as I thought it would be. [ALAN *rises and crosses to Left table.*]

MICHAEL: THE GAME ISN'T OVER YET! [*Meets* EMORY an*d pushes him Up Center.*]—Your turn, Alan. [*Goes to* ALAN.] PICK UP THE PHONE, BUSTER! [*Grabs* ALAN'*s arm and swings him to below ottoman.*]

EMORY: [*Crosses to* MICHAEL.] Michael, don't!

MICHAEL: STAY OUT OF THIS! [*Pushes* EMORY *Left.*]

EMORY: You don't have to, Alan. You don't have to.

ALAN: Emory . . . I'm sorry for what I did before. [*A beat.*]

EMORY: . . . Oh, forget it.

MICHAEL: Forgive us our trespasses. Christ, now you're both joined at the goddamn hip! [*Forcing* EMORY *to sit in Down Left chair by crossing in on* EMORY.] You can decorate his home, Emory—and he can get you out of jail the next time he's arrested on a morals charge. [MICHAEL *turns to* ALAN *as* ALAN *turns Upstage. A beat.*] Who are you going to call, Alan? [*No response.*] Can't remember anyone? Well, maybe you need a minute to think. Is that it? [*No response.* ALAN *sits ottoman.*]

HAROLD: [*Crosses to Left table.*] I believe this will be the final round.

COWBOY: Michael, aren't you going to call anyone?

HAROLD: How could he?—He's never loved anyone.

MICHAEL: [*Sings the classic vaudeville walk-off to* HAROLD.]
"No matter how you figger,
It's tough to be a nigger,
But it's tougher
To be a Jeeeew-ooouu-oo!" [*Turns to* HAROLD *and flicks* HAROLD's scarf.*]

DONALD: My God, Michael, you're a charming host.

HAROLD: Michael doesn't have charm, Donald. Michael has counter-charm. [LARRY *crosses to the stairs.*]

MICHAEL: Going somewhere?

LARRY: [*He stops, turns to* MICHAEL.] Yes. Excuse me.

MICHAEL: You're going to miss the end of the game.

LARRY: [*Pauses on stairs.*] You can tell me how it comes out.

MICHAEL: I never reveal an ending. And no one will be re-seated during the climactic revelation.

LARRY: With any luck I won't be back until it's all over. [*He turns, continues up the stairs.* LARRY *exits Left from second floor escape.*]

MICHAEL: [*Crosses to* ALAN.] What do you suppose is going on up there? Hmmm, Alan? What do you imagine Larry and Hank are doing? Hmmmmm? Shooting marbles?

EMORY: Whatever they're doing, they're not hurting anyone.

HAROLD: And they're minding their own business.

MICHAEL: [*Crosses to* HAROLD.] And you mind yours, Harold. I'm warning you! [*A beat.*]

HAROLD: [*Coolly.*] Are you now? Are you warning me? Me? I'm Harold. I'm the one person you don't warn Michael. Because you and I are a match. — And we tread very softly with each other because we both play each other's game too well. Oh, I know this game you're playing. I know it very well. And I *play* it very well. — You play it very well too. But you know what? I'm the only one that's better at it than you are. I can beat you at it. So don't push me. I'm warning *you*. [*A beat.* MICHAEL *starts to laugh.*]

MICHAEL: You're funny, Hallie. A laff-riot. Isn't he funny, Alan? Or, as you might say, isn't he amusing? He's an amusing faggot, isn't he? Or, as you might say, freak. — That's what you called Emory, wasn't it? A freak? A pansy? My, what an antiquated vocabulary you have. I'm surprised you didn't say sodomite or pedarist. [*A beat.*] You'd better let me bring you up to date. — Now it's not so new but it might be new to you — [*A beat.*] Have you heard the term, "closet queen"? Do you know what that means? Do you know what it means to be "in the closet"? [BERNARD *goes to front of landing and collapses to floor.*]

EMORY: Don't, Michael. It won't help anything to explain what it means.

MICHAEL: [*Crosses to* EMORY.] He already knows. He knows very, very well what a closet queen is. Don't you, Alan?

ALAN: Michael, if you are insinuating that I am homosexual, I can only say that you are mistaken.

MICHAEL: Am I? [*A beat.*] What about Justin Stuart?

ALAN: . . . What about . . . Justin Stuart?

MICHAEL: [*Crosses to Phone above sofa.*] You were in love with him, that's what about him. And *that* is who you are going to call. [*Slams Phone from sofa Center to Left end.*]

ALAN: Justin and I were very good friends. That is all. Unfortunately, we had a parting of the ways and that was the end of the friendship. We have not spoken for years. I most certainly will not call him now. [*Rises and crosses to Left end of sofa.*]

MICHAEL: [*Crosses Right end sofa.*] According to Justin, the friendship was quite passionate.

ALAN: What do you mean?

MICHAEL: I mean that you slept with him in college. Several times.

ALAN: That's not true!

MICHAEL: Several times. Once that's youth. Twice, a phase maybe. Several times, *you like it!*

ALAN: That's NOT TRUE!

MICHAEL: Yes, it is true. Because Justin Stuart *is* homosexual. He comes to New York on occasion. He calls me. I've taken him to parties.

Larry's "had" him once. *I* have slept with Justin. And he has told me all about *you.*

ALAN: Then he told you a lie.

MICHAEL: You were obsessed with Justin. That's all you talked about morning, noon, and night. You started doing it about Hank upstairs tonight. — What an attractive fellow he is and all that transparent crap.

ALAN: He *is* an attractive fellow. What's wrong with saying so?

MICHAEL: Would you like to join him and Larry right now?

ALAN: I said he was attractive. That's all.

MICHAEL: How many times do you have to say it? How many times did you have to say it about Justin? — what a good tennis player he was — what a good dancer he was — what a good body he had — what good taste he had — how bright he was — how amusing he was — how the girls were all mad for him — what close friends you were. [*Crosses Right end coffee table.*]

ALAN: We were very close . . . very good friends. *That's all!* [*Crosses to* MICHAEL.]

MICHAEL: It was *obvious* — and when you did it around *Fran* it was downright embarrassing. Even she must have had her doubts about you.

ALAN: *Justin . . . lied.* If he told you that, he lied. It is a lie. A vicious lie. He'd say anything about me now to get even. He could never get over the fact that *I* dropped *him.* But I had to. I had to because he told me about himself . . . he told me that he wanted me to be his lover. And I told him that he made me sick . . . I told him I pitied him. [*Sits sofa.*]

MICHAEL: You ended the friendship, Alan, because you couldn't face the truth about yourself. [*Crosses to Left end sofa.*] You could go along, sleeping with Justin as long as he lied to himself and you lied to yourself and you both dated girls and labeled yourselves men and called yourselves just fond friends. But Justin finally had to be honest about the truth, and you couldn't take it. [MICHAEL *goes to the desk, and gets address book.*] You couldn't take it and so you destroyed the friendship and your friend along with it. [*Crosses to* ALAN.]

ALAN: No!

MICHAEL: Justin could never understand what he'd done wrong to make you drop him. He blamed himself.

ALAN: No!

MICHAEL: He did until he eventually found out who he was and what he was.

ALAN: No!

MICHAEL: But to this day, he still remembers the treatment—the scars he got from you. [*He puts address book in front of* ALAN *on coffee table.*]
ALAN: NO!
MICHAEL: Pick up this phone and call Justin. Call him and apologize and tell him what you should have told him twelve years ago. [*He picks up the phone, shoves it at* ALAN.]
ALAN: No! HE LIED! *Not a word is true!*
MICHAEL: Call him! [ALAN *won't take it.*] All right then, *I'll dial!*
HAROLD: You're so helpful. [MICHAEL *starts to dial.*]
ALAN: Give it to me. [*Clicking off dialing.* MICHAEL *hands* ALAN *the receiver.* ALAN *takes it, releases cradle button, starts to dial.* EVERYONE *is watching in silent attention.* ALAN *finishes dialing, lifts the receiver to his ear.*] . . . Hello?
MICHAEL: One point.
ALAN: . . . It's . . . it's Alan.
MICHAEL: Two points.
ALAN: . . . Yes, yes, it's *me.*
MICHAEL: Is it Justin?
ALAN: . . . You sound surprised.
MICHAEL: I should hope to think so—after twelve years! Two more points.
ALAN: No, I'm in New York. Yes. I won't explain now . . . I . . . I just called to tell you . . .
MICHAEL: THAT I LOVE YOU, GOD-DAMNIT! *I love you!*
ALAN: I love you.
MICHAEL: FIVE BONUS POINTS. TEN POINTS TOTAL! JACKPOT!
ALAN: I love you and I beg you to forgive me.
MICHAEL: Give me that! [*He snatches the phone from* ALAN.] Justin! Did you hear what that son-of-a-bitch said! [*A beat.* MICHAEL *is speechless for a moment.*] Fran. [*A beat.* MICHAEL *sits on sofa.*] Fran, of course, I expected it to be you! How are you? . . . Me too . . . Yes, he told me everything . . . Oh, don't thank *me, please!* I'll put him back on. My love to the kids. [MICHAEL *lowers his hand with the receiver and* ALAN *takes the receiver as* MICHAEL *stares front.*]
ALAN: . . . Darling? I'll take the first plane I can get.—Yes. I'm sorry too. Yes . . . I love you very much. [*He hangs up, stands up, crosses to the door, stops. He turns around, surveys the* GROUP.] Thank you, Michael. [*He opens the door and exits.*]

[*Silence.* MICHAEL *brings hands to face and sinks face into seat of sofa.*]

COWBOY: Who won?

DONALD: It was a tie.

HAROLD: [HAROLD *crosses to* MICHAEL. *Calmly, coldly, clinically.*] Now it is my turn. And ready or not, Michael, here goes. [*A beat.*] You are a sad and pathetic man. You're a homosexual and you don't want to be. But there is nothing you can do to change it. — Not all your prayers to your God, not all the analysis you can buy in all the years you've got left to live. You may very well one day be able to know a heterosexual life if you want it desperately enough — if you pursue it with the fervor with which you annihilate — but you will always be homo-sexual as well. Always, Michael. Always. Until the day you die. [*He turns, goes toward* EMORY.] Oh, friends, thanks for the nifty party and the super gift. [*He looks toward the* COWBOY.] It's just what I needed. [EMORY *smiles.* HAROLD *spots* BERNARD *sitting on the floor, head bowed.*] . . . Bernard, thank you. [*No response. To* EMORY:] Will you get him home?

EMORY: Don't worry about her. I'll take care of everything. [HAROLD *turns, passes* DONALD *who is sitting on steps and goes to Up Center.*]

HAROLD: Donald, good to see you.

DONALD: Good night, Harold. See you again sometime.

HAROLD: Yeah. How about a year from Shevuoth? [*Goes to desk chair and gathers gifts and goes to* COWBOY.] Come on, Tex. Let's go to my place. [*The* COWBOY *gets up.*] Are you good in bed?

COWBOY: Well . . . I'm not like the average hustler you'd meet. I try to show a little affection — it keeps me from feeling like such a whore. [HAROLD *gives* COWBOY *the gifts.* COWBOY *takes gifts, goes to door and opens it.*]

HAROLD: [*Picks up his eye glasses from bar.*] Oh, Michael . . . thanks for the laughs. Call you tomorrow. [*No response.* HAROLD *and the* COWBOY *exit.*]

EMORY: Come on, Bernard. Time to go home. [EMORY, *frail as he is, manages to pull* BERNARD*'s arm around his neck, gets him on his feet.*]

BERNARD: [*Practically inaudible mumble.*] Why did I call? Why?

EMORY: Oh, Mary, you're a heavy mother. [*Takes* BERNARD *to Left end of sofa.*] Thank you, Michael. Good night, Donald.

DONALD: Goodbye, Emory.

BERNARD: Why . . . [*As* EMORY *crosses to door with* BERNARD.]

EMORY: It's all right, Bernard. Everything's all right. I'm going to make you some coffee and everything's going to be all right. [EMORY *virtually carries* BERNARD *out.* DONALD *closes the door.* MICHAEL *slides to floor and begins a low moan that increases in volume — almost like a siren — to a blood-curdling shriek. He slams his open hands on floor.*]

MICHAEL: [*In desperate panic.*] Donald! Donald! DONALD! *Donald!* [DONALD *puts down his drink, rushes to* MICHAEL. MICHAEL *is now white with fear and tears are bursting from his eyes. He begins to gasp his words.*] Oh, no! No! What have I done! Oh, my God, what have I done! [MICHAEL *starts to writhe.* DONALD *grabs him, cradles him in his arms.*]

DONALD: Michael! Michael!

MICHAEL: [*Tears pouring forth.*] Oh, no! No! It's beginning! The anxiety! Oh, No! No! I feel it! I know it's going to happen. Donald!! Donald! Don't leave. Please! Please! Oh, my God, what have I done! Oh Jesus, I can't handle it. I won't make it!

DONALD: [*Physically subduing him.*] Michael! Michael! Stop it! Stop it! I'll give you a Valium—I've got some in my pocket!

MICHAEL: [*Hysterical.*] No! No! Pills and alcohol—I'll die!

DONALD: I'm not going to give you the whole bottle! Come on, let go of me!

MICHAEL: [*Clutching him.*] No!

DONALD: Let go of me long enough for me to get my hand in my pocket!

MICHAEL: Don't leave! [*As he loosens his grip he crumbles to the floor.*]

[MICHAEL *quiets a bit, as* DONALD *gets a pill from his pocket.*]

DONALD: Here. [*Putting pill in* MICHAEL*'s hand as he pulls* MICHAEL*'s head and arms up from floor.*]

MICHAEL: [*Sobbing.*] I don't have any water to swallow it with!

DONALD: Well, if you'll wait one god-damn minute, I'll get you some! [*He goes to the bar, gets a glass of water.* MICHAEL *collapses, his head on the sofa seat.* DONALD *returns with glass.*] Your water, Your Majesty. [*A beat.* DONALD *puts glass in* MICHAEL*'s hand as he pulls* MICHAEL*'s head up.*] Michael, stop that god-damn crying and take this pill! [MICHAEL *puts the pill into his mouth amid choking sobs, takes the water, washes it down, returns the glass to* DONALD *which* DONALD *returns to bar.*]

MICHAEL: [*Sitting on sofa.*] I'm like Ole Man River—tired of livin' and scared o' dyin'. [DONALD *helps* MICHAEL *to sit sofa and also sits down.* MICHAEL *collapses into his arms, sobbing.*]

DONALD: Shhhhh. Shhhhh. Michael. Shhhhh. Michael. Michael. [DONALD *rocks him back and forth. He quiets.*]

MICHAEL: . . . If we . . . if we could just . . . learn not to hate ourselves so much. That's it, you know. If we could just not hate ourselves just quite so very very much.

DONALD: Yes, I know. I know. [*A beat.*] Inconceivable as it may be, you used to be worse than you are now. Maybe with a lot more work you can help yourself some more — if you try. [MICHAEL *straightens up, dries his eyes in his handkerchief.*]

MICHAEL: Who was it that used to always say, "You show me a happy homosexual, and I'll show you a gay corpse."

DONALD: I don't know. Who was it who always used to say that?

MICHAEL: [*Pulls away so* DONALD'*s arm is free from him.*] And how dare you come on with that holier-than-thou attitude with me! — "A lot more work," "if I try," indeed! You've got a long row to hoe before you're perfect, you know.

DONALD: I never said I didn't.

MICHAEL: And while we're on the subject — I think your analyst is a quack. [MICHAEL *blows his nose.*]

DONALD: Earlier you said he was a prick.

MICHAEL: That's right. He's a prick quack. Or a quack prick, whichever you prefer. [DONALD *gets up from the sofa, goes to bar and pours a brandy.*]

DONALD: [*Heaving a sigh.*] Harold was right. You'll never change.

MICHAEL: Come back, Donald. Come back, Shane. [*Catching himself at a movie imitation.*]

DONALD: I'll come back when you have another anxiety attack.

MICHAEL: I need you. Just like Mickey Mouse needs Minnie Mouse — just like Donald Duck needs . . . Minnie Duck — Mickey needs Donnie.

DONALD: My name is Donald. I am called Donald. You must never call anyone called Donald, Donnie.

MICHAEL: [*Grabs his head, moans and rises, going Left of steps.*] Ohhhhh . . . icks! Icks! Terrible icks! Tomorrow is going to be "Bad Day at Black Rock." A day of nerves, nerves, and more nerves! [MICHAEL *surveys the room.*] Do you suppose there's any possibility of just burning this room? [*Goes to candles and puts them out.*]

[*A beat.*]

DONALD: Why do you think he stayed, Michael? Why do you think he took all of that from you?

MICHAEL: There are no accidents. He was begging to get killed. He begged for somebody to let him have it and he got what he wanted.

DONALD: He could have been telling the truth — Justin could have lied. [*Crossing to sofa.*]

MICHAEL: Who knows? What time is it?

DONALD: It seems like it's day after tomorrow. [*Sits sofa.*]

[MICHAEL *goes toward kitchen glancing Off Left to clock. He comes back to pillar and gets his raincoat.*]

MICHAEL: It's early. [*Leans wearily on pillar.*]

DONALD: What does life *hold?* Where're you going?

MICHAEL: The bedroom is occupado and I don't want to go to sleep anyway until I try to walk-off some of this booze. If I went to sleep like this, when I wake up they'd have to put me in a padded cell — not that that's where I don't belong. [*A beat.*] And there's a midnight mass at St. Malachy's that all the show people go to. I think I'll walk over there and catch it.

DONALD: [*Raises his glass.*] Well, pray for me.

MICHAEL: [*Indicates bedroom.*] Maybe they'll be gone by the time I get back.

DONALD: [*Rises and goes to bar.*] Well, *I* will be — just as soon as I knock off this bottle of brandy. [*Pours brandy to his snifter.*]

MICHAEL: Will I see you next Saturday?

DONALD: [*Turns to* MICHAEL.] Unless you have other plans. [MICHAEL *shakes his head "no."*] Michael, did he ever tell you why he was crying on the phone — what it was he *had* to tell you?

MICHAEL: No. It must have been that he'd left Fran. — Or maybe it was something else and he changed his mind.

DONALD: Maybe so. [*A beat.*] I wonder why he left her.

MICHAEL: [*Wearily.*] . . . As my father said to me when he died in my arms, "I don't understand any of it. I never did." [*A beat.* DONALD *goes to his stack of books, selects one, sits Down Right chair.*] Turn out the lights when you leave, will you? [DONALD *nods.* MICHAEL *goes to the door, opens it and exits closing door behind him as*:]

Lights fade out

The End

Bent

Martin Sherman

Michael Gross (Greta), David Marshall Grant (Rudy), and Richard Gere (Max) in *Bent*, at the New Apollo Theatre, 1979. (Photo by James Hamilton. Reprinted with permission from the John Willis Theatre World/Screen World Archive.)

Michael York (Max) and Jeffrey DeMunn (Horst) in *Bent*, at the New Apollo Theatre, 1980. (Photo by Jody Caravaglia. Reprinted with permission from the John Willis Theatre World/Screen World Archive.)

Bent was originally presented at London's Royal Court Theatre on May 3, 1979. It was produced by Eddie Kulukundis by arrangement with Jack Schlissel. It was directed by Robert Chetwyn, designed by Alan Tagg, and the lighting was by Robert Bryan. The music was by Andy Roberts, the sound was by John Del'Nero, and the assistant director was Antonia Bird. The stage manager was Chloe Wright, the deputy stage manager was Simon Hall, the assistant stage manager was David Lockwood, the costume supervisor was Francis Roe, and the production photographer was John Haynes. BENT IS BASED ON FACT. *Bent* was originally given a staged reading at the 1978 National Playwrights Conference of the Eugene O'Neill Memorial Theater.

Cast

Max	Ian McKellen
Rudy	Jeff Rawle
Wolf	Simon Shepherd
Lieutenant	Haydn Wood
2nd Lieutenant	Jeremy Arnold
Greta	Ken Shorter
Freddie	Richard Gale
Horst	Tom Bell
Guard on train	Haydn Wood
Officer	Gregory Martyn
Corporal	John Francis
Captain	Peter Cellier

Bent was first presented in the U.S. on Broadway at the New Apollo Theatre on Sunday, December 2, 1979. It was produced by Jack Schlissel and Steven Steinlauf. It was directed by Robert Allan Ackerman, the settings were by Santo Loquasto, and the lighting was by Arden Fingerhut. The costumes were by Robert Wojewodski, the music was by Stanley Silverman, and the co-producers were Lee Minskoff and Patty Grubman. Special effects were by Randy McAndrews, the production associate was Gilbert Wang, the wardrobe was by Clarence Sims, and the production assistants were Karen Gromis and Marjorie Ornston. The general manager was Jay Kingwall, the company manager was Al Isaac, the press was by Jeffrey Richards, Warren Knowlton, Alan Eichler, Marjorie Ornston, Robert Ganshaw, Helen Stern, and Karen Gromis, and the stage managers were Robert Bennett and Donald Walters The photographer was James Hamilton.

Cast

Max	Richard Gere
Rudy	David Marshall Grant
Wolf	James Remar
Guard	Kai Wulff
Guard	Philip Kraus
Greta	Michael Gross
Uncle Freddie	George Hall
Officer	Bryan E. Clark
Guard	John Snyder
Horst	David Dukes
Captain	Ron Randell

UNDERSTUDIES:

Max, Officer, Capt., Uncle Freddie	David Davies
Horst	Gregory Salata
Rudy	James Remar
Greta	John Snyder
Wolf	Kai Wulff
Guards	Michael Morrows

For Alan Pope and Peter Whitman

Act One

Scene I

The living room of an apartment. Small. Sparse furniture. A table with plants. A door on left leads to the outside hall. Nearby is an exit to the kitchen. At right, an exit to the bedroom, and nearby an exit to the bathroom.

MAX enters. He is thirty-four. He wears a bathrobe. He is very hung-over. He stares into space.

MAX: Oh God! [*Goes into bathroom—pause—then offstage, from bathroom*] Oh God! [MAX *returns to the living room and sits down.* RUDY *enters. He is thirty. He wears a bathrobe. He also wears glasses. He carries a cup.*]

RUDY: Here. [*Hands* MAX *the cup;* MAX *stares and doesn't take it.*] Here. Coffee!

MAX: [*Takes the cup.*] Thanks. [*They kiss.* MAX *sips the coffee.*]

RUDY: It's late. It's almost three. We really slept. I missed class. I hate to dance when I miss class. Bad for the muscles. And there's no place to warm up at the club. I hate that nightclub anyhow. The floor's no good. It's cement. You shouldn't dance on cement. It kills my ankle. They've covered it with wood. Last night, before the show, I pounded on the wood—real hard—and I could hear the cement. I'm going to complain. I really am. [*He goes into the kitchen.*]

MAX: [*Sits in silence and stares.*] Oh God. [RUDY *returns from the kitchen with a pitcher of water and waters the plants.*]

RUDY: The plants are dying. The light's bad in this apartment. I wish we had a decent place. I wish one of your deals would come through again. Oh, listen to me, wanting a bigger place. Rosen's gonna be knocking on our door any minute now, you know that, wanting his rent. We're three weeks overdue. He always comes on a Sunday. He only cares about money. What's three weeks? He can wait. Well, at least

I got the new job. I'll get paid on Thursday. If Greta keeps the club open. Business stinks. Well, I guess it means I can't complain about the cement, huh? The thing is, I don't want to dance with a bad ankle. More coffee? [MAX *shakes his head yes.* RUDY *goes into the kitchen.* MAX *stares into space. He puts his hand on his head and takes a deep breath, then closes his eyes.*]

MAX: One. Two. Three. Four. Five. [*Opens his eyes, takes another deep breath.*] Six. Seven. Eight. Nine. Ten. [RUDY *returns from kitchen and hands* MAX *another cup of coffee.* RUDY *resumes watering the plants.* MAX *watches him for a moment.*]

MAX: O.K. Tell me.

RUDY: What?

MAX: You know.

RUDY: No.

MAX: Come on.

RUDY: I *don't* know. Listen, do you think I should ask Lena for the rent money? She's such a good person. No feeling for music, though. Which is crazy, she's got such a good line. Perfect legs. Teddy wants to do a dance for her in total silence. You think that's a good idea? There's no place to do it, though. There's no work. Lena lost that touring job. So she must be broke. So she can't lend us the money. Want some food?

MAX: Just tell me.

RUDY: What?

MAX: Must really be bad.

RUDY: What must?

MAX: That's why you won't tell me.

RUDY: Tell you what?

MAX: Don't play games.

RUDY: I'm not playing anything.

MAX: I'll hate myself, won't I? [*Silence.*] Won't I?

RUDY: I'll make some breakfast.

MAX: Was I really rotten?

RUDY: Eggs and cheese.

MAX: I don't want eggs.

RUDY: Well, we're lucky to have them. I stole them from the club. They don't need eggs. People go there to drink. And see a terrific show. Oh boy, that's funny, 'cause that show stinks. You know, I'm so embarrassed, I have to think of other things while I'm dancing. I have to think of grocery lists, they can tell, out there, that you're not thinking about straw hats or water lilies—I mean, it really shows;

particularly when it's grocery lists. Your face looks real depressed, when you can't afford groceries . . .

MAX: [*Rises and puts his hand on* RUDY'*s mouth.*] Stop it. [RUDY *tries to speak.*] Stop it! [*They struggle; he keeps his hand over* RUDY'*s mouth.*] I want to know what I did. [*Releases him.*]

RUDY: [*Smiles.*] I love you. [*Goes into kitchen.*]

MAX: Rudy! Your plants! I'll pull the little bastards out unless you tell me. [RUDY *comes back in.* MAX *stands over the plants.*]

RUDY: No you won't.

MAX: Like to bet. I did last month.

RUDY: You killed one. That was mean.

MAX: I'll do it again.

RUDY: Don't touch them. You have to be nice to plants. They can hear you and everything. [*To the plants*] He's sorry. He didn't mean it. He's just hung-over.

MAX: What did I do? [*Silence.*]

RUDY: Nothing much.

MAX: I can't remember a thing. And when I can't remember, it means . . .

RUDY: It doesn't mean anything. You drank a lot. That's all. The usual.

MAX: How'd I get this? [*Pulls his robe off his shoulder, shows a mark on his skin.*]

RUDY: What's that?

MAX: Ouch! Don't touch it.

RUDY: I want to see it.

MAX: So *look.* You don't have to touch.

RUDY: What is it?

MAX: What does it look like? A big black and blue mark. There's another one here. [*Shows a mark on his arm.*]

RUDY: Oh.

MAX: How did I get them?

RUDY: You fell.

MAX: How?

RUDY: Someone pushed you.

MAX: Who?

RUDY: Some guy.

MAX: What guy?

RUDY: Nicky's friend.

MAX: Who's Nicky?

RUDY: One of the waiters at the club.

MAX: Which one?

Rudy: The redhead.

Max: I don't remember him.

Rudy: He's a little fat.

Max: Why'd the guy push me?

Rudy: You asked Nicky to come home with us.

Max: I did?

Rudy: Yeah.

Max: But he's *fat.*

Rudy: Only a little.

Max: A threesome with a fat person?

Rudy: Not a threesome. A twelvesome. You asked *all* the waiters. All at the same time, too. You were standing on a table, making a general offer.

Max: Oh. Then what?

Rudy: Nicky's friend pushed you off the table.

Max: And...

Rudy: You landed on the floor, on top of some guy in leather.

Max: What was he doing on the floor?

Rudy: I don't know.

Max: Was Greta mad?

Rudy: Greta wasn't *happy.* [*Pause.*] It was late. Most everyone was gone. And you were very drunk. People like you drunk. [*Pause.*] I'll make some food.

Max: I don't want food. Why didn't you stop me?

Rudy: How can I stop you.

Max: Don't let me drink.

Rudy: Oh. Sure. When you're depressed?

Max: Was I depressed?

Rudy: Of course.

Max: I don't remember why.

Rudy: Then drinking worked, didn't it? [*Returns to kitchen.*]

[*A blond man, in his early twenties, enters, bleary-eyed, from the bedroom. He is naked.*]

Blond Man: Good morning. [*He stumbles into the bathroom.*]

Max: Rudy!

Rudy: [*Coming out of kitchen.*] What?

Max: Who was that?

Rudy: Who was what?

Max: *That!* That person!

Rudy: Oh. Yeah. Him. Blond?

Max: Yes.

Rudy: And big?

Max: Yes.

Rudy: That's the one you fell on.

Max: The guy in leather?

Rudy: Yes. You brought him home. [*Goes into kitchen.*]

Max: Rudy! Your plants!

Rudy: [*Returns from kitchen.*] You brought him home, that's all. He got you going. All that leather, all those chains. You called him your own little storm trooper. You insulted all his friends. They left. I don't know why they didn't beat you up, but they didn't. They left. And you brought him home.

Max: And we had a threesome?

Rudy: Maybe the two of you had a threesome. Max, there is no such thing. You pick guys up. You think you're doing it for me, too. You're not. I don't like it. You and the other guy always end up ignoring me anyhow. Besides, last night, you and your own little storm trooper began to get rough with each other, and I know pain is very chic just now, but I don't like it, 'cause pain hurts, so I went to sleep. [*Takes* Max's *coffee cup, pours it onto the plants.*] Here, Walter, have some coffee.

Max: Walter?

Rudy: I'm naming the plants. They're my friends. [Rudy *goes into the kitchen. The* Blond Man *comes out of the bathroom, wearing a towel. He grins at* Max.]

Max: Rudy!

Rudy: [*Returns from kitchen; looks at the* Blond.] Oh. There's a bathrobe in there—in the bedroom. [*The* Blond Man *goes into the bedroom. A pause.*]

Max: I'm sorry.

Rudy: It's O.K.

Max: I'm a rotten person. Why am I so rotten? Why do I do these things? He's gorgeous, though, isn't he? I don't remember anything. I don't remember what we did in bed. Why don't I ever remember?

Rudy: You were drunk. And high on coke.

Max: That too?

Rudy: Yeah.

Max: Whose coke?

Rudy: Anna's.

Max: I don't remember.

Rudy: You made arrangements to pick up a shipment to sell.

Max: A *shipment?*
Rudy: Yeah.
Max: Christ! When?
Rudy: I don't know.
Max: That can be a lot of rent money.
Rudy: Anna will remember.
Max: Right. Hey — rent money. Maybe . . . do you think . . .
Rudy: What?
Max: We can ask him.
Rudy: Who?
Max: *Him.*
Rudy: You're kidding.
Max: Why not?
Rudy: We don't know him.
Max: I slept with him. I think. I wonder what it was like.
Rudy: You picked him up, one night, and you're going to ask him to loan you the rent money?
Max: Well, you know how I am.
Rudy: Yeah.
Max: I can talk people into things.
Rudy: *Yeah.*
Max: I can try.
Rudy: It won't work. He thinks you're rich.
Max: Rich?
Rudy: You told him you were rich.
Max: Terrific.
Rudy: And Polish.
Max: Polish?
Rudy: You had an accent. [**Rudy** *laughs and returns to the kitchen. The* **Blond Man** *walks out, in a short bathrobe. He stands and looks at* **Max**. *An embarrassed silence.*]
Max: Hi.
Man: Hi. The robe is short. I look silly.
Max: You look O.K.
Man: Yes? You too. [*Goes to* **Max** *and kisses him, then starts to pull* **Max**'*s robe off, and bites* **Max** *on the chest.*] Ummm . . .
Max: Hey. Not now.
Man: Later, then.
Max: Yes.
Man: In the country.

MAX: The country?
MAN: Your voice is different.
MAX: Oh?
MAN: You don't have an accent.
MAX: Only when I'm drunk.
MAN: Oh.
MAX: Last night—was it good?
MAN: What do you think?
MAX: I'm asking.
MAN: Do you have to ask?
RUDY: [*Comes in with a cup of coffee.*] Some coffee?
MAN: Yes. Thank you. [*RUDY hands him the cup. A silence.*] This place...
MAX: Yes?
MAN: It's really... [*Stops—silence.*]
MAX: Small?
MAN: Yes. Exactly.
MAX: I guess it is.
MAN: You people are strange, keeping places like this in town. I don't meet people like you too much. But you interest me, your kind.
MAX: Listen...
MAN: Oh, look, it doesn't matter, who you are, who I am. I'm on vacation. *That* matters. The country will be nice.
MAX: What's the country?
MAN: The house. Your house. Your country house.
MAX: [*To* RUDY] My country house?
RUDY: Oh. That. I forgot to tell you about that. We're driving there this afternoon.
MAX: To our country house?
RUDY: *Your* country house.
MAX: How do we get there?
RUDY: Car.
MAX: Mine?
RUDY: Right.
MAX: Why don't we stay here?
MAN: Don't make jokes. You promised me two days in the country.
MAX: Your name.
MAN: Yes?
MAX: I forgot your name.
MAN: Wolf.
MAX: Wolf? Good name.

WOLF: I didn't forget yours.

MAX: Look, Wolf, I don't have a car.

WOLF: Sure you do.

MAX: No.

WOLF: You showed me. On the street. Pointed it out.

MAX: Did I? It wasn't mine.

WOLF: Not yours?

MAX: No. I don't have a house in the country, either.

WOLF: Of course you do. You told me all about it.

MAX: I was joking.

WOLF: I don't like jokes. You don't want me with you, is that it? Maybe I'm not good enough for you. Not rich enough. My father made watches. That's not so wonderful. Is it, Baron? [*Pause.*]

MAX: Baron?

RUDY: Don't look at me. That one I didn't know about.

MAX: Baron. [*Begins to laugh.*]

[*There is a loud knock at the front door.*]

RUDY: Rosen!

MAX: Shit!

WOLF: You like to laugh at me, Baron? [*The knocking continues.*]

MAX: Listen, Wolf darling, you're really very sweet and very pretty and I like you a lot, but you see, I'm not too terrific, because I have a habit of getting drunk and stoned and grand and making things up. Believe me, I'm not a baron. There is no country house. There is no money. I don't have *any* money. Sometimes I do. Sometimes I sell cocaine, sometimes I find people to invest in business deals, sometimes . . . well, I scrounge, see, and I'm good at it, and in a few weeks I will have some money again. But right now, nothing. Rudy and I can't pay our rent. This rent. Right here. This lousy apartment. That's all we have. And that man knocking at our door is our landlord. And he's going to throw us out. Because we can't pay our rent. Out into the streets, Wolf, the streets. Filled with filth, vermin. And lice. And . . . urine! Urine! Unless someone can help us out. Unless someone gives us a hand. *That's* the truth. Look, you don't believe me, I'll show you. Right out there we have, just like in the movies, the greedy landlord. [*Puts his hand on the door-knob.*] Fanfare please.

[**RUDY** *simulates a trumpet call.*]

MAX: Here he is, the one and only, Abraham Rosen!

[MAX *swings the door open with a flourish. Two men are standing out-side—a Gestapo* CAPTAIN *and an* OFFICER *in full Nazi uniform—both holding guns.* MAX *shuts the door.*]

MAX: That's not Rosen! [*The door is kicked open. The* CAPTAIN *points to* WOLF.]

CAPTAIN: Him!

WOLF: No! [WOLF *throws the coffee cup at the* CAPTAIN *and runs into the bath-room. The* CAPTAIN *and the* OFFICER *run after him.* RUDY *starts toward the bathroom;* MAX *pulls him back.*]

MAX: Idiot! Run!

[MAX *grabs* RUDY *and they run out the front door. The lights black out on the left side of the stage. A shot rings out in the bathroom.* WOLF *screams. The lights rise on the left side of the stage, as* GRETA *enters.*

GRETA *is a man dressed as a woman. He wears a silver dress, high green leather boots, and a top hat and carries a silver cane. He is both elegant and bizarre.*

The CAPTAIN *watches as the* OFFICER *drags* WOLF *out of the bath-room.* WOLF *is bleeding, but still alive. He looks up at the* CAPTAIN *and crawls slowly toward him.*]

WOLF: Bastard!

CAPTAIN: Wolfgang Granz, we have an order for your arrest. You resisted. Too bad.

[*The* CAPTAIN *grabs* WOLF *by the neck, takes out a knife, and slits his throat.* GRETA *tugs at a rope above him and pulls down a trapeze. He thrusts himself up onto the trapeze bar and sits there.*

A projection in the center of the stage reads:

BERLIN—1934

Lights out on the apartment. Full spotlight on GRETA.]

Scene II

GRETA *sits on the trapeze. He sings in a smoky, seductive voice.*

GRETA: Streets of Berlin,
I must leave you soon,
Ah!
Will you forget me?
Was I ever really here?

Find me a bar
On the cobblestoned streets
Where the boys are pretty.
I cannot love
For more than one day
But one day is enough in this city.

Find me a boy
With two ocean-blue eyes
And show him no pity.
Take out his eyes,
He never need see
How they eat you alive in this city.

Streets of Berlin,
Will you miss me?
Streets of Berlin,
Do you care?
Streets of Berlin,
Will you cry out
If I vanish
Into thin air?

GRETA: [*Spotlight dims. Lights rise on* GRETA'S *Club. The stage is to the left.* GRETA'S *dressing room is on the right—a chair facing a mirror, and a screen to change behind.* GRETA *enters the dressing room. The lights fade on the rest of his club.*] My heroes! Where are you?

[MAX *and* RUDY *come from behind the screen. They are dressed in trousers and shirts, pieces of nightclub costumes.* GRETA *looks at them.*]

GRETA: Schmucks!

[MAX *sits on a stool, lost in thought.* GRETA *sits in the chair, adjusting his costume in the mirror.*]

GRETA: I'm getting rid of all the rough songs. Who am I kidding? I'm getting rid of the club. Well — maybe. Maybe not. I'll turn it into something else. We'll see.

RUDY: Is it safe?

GRETA: What?

RUDY: For us to go home?

GRETA: You fucking queers, don't you have any brains at all? No, it's not safe.

RUDY: I want to go home.

GRETA: You can't. You can't go anyplace.

RUDY: I have to get my plants.

GRETA: Oh, Jesus! Forget your plants. You can't go home. You certainly can't stay here. And you can't contact friends, so don't try to see Lena, she's a good kid, you'll get her into a lot of trouble. You understand? You have to leave Berlin.

RUDY: Why? I live here, I work here.

GRETA: No, you don't. You're fired.

RUDY: I *don't* understand. What did we do? Why should we leave?

GRETA: Don't leave. Stay. Be *dead* schmucks. Who gives a damn? I don't.

MAX: [*Looks up.*] Who was he?

GRETA: Who was who?

MAX: The blond?

GRETA: Wolfgang Granz.

MAX: What's that mean?

GRETA: He was Karl Ernst's boyfriend.

MAX: Who's Karl Ernst?

GRETA: What kind of world do you live in? Aren't you guys ever curious about what's going on?

MAX: Greta, don't lecture. Who's Karl Ernst?

GRETA: Von Helldorf's deputy. You know Von Helldorf?

MAX: The head of the storm troopers in Berlin.

GRETA: I don't believe it. You've actually *heard* of someone. Right. Second in command at the SA, immediately under Ernst Rohm.

RUDY: Oh. Ernst Rohm. I know him. [MAX *and* GRETA *stare at him.*] He's that fat queen, with those awful scars on his face, a real big shot, friend of Hitler's, runs around with a lot of beautiful boys. Goes to all the clubs; I sat at his table once. He's been *here* too, hasn't he?

MAX: Rudy, shut up.
RUDY: Why?
MAX: Just shut up, O.K.? [*To* GRETA] So?
GRETA: So Hitler had Rohm arrested last night.
MAX: You're kidding. He's Hitler's right-hand man.
GRETA: Was. He's dead. Just about anyone who's high up in the SA is dead. Your little scene on top of that table was *not* the big event of the evening. It was a bloody night. The city's in a panic. Didn't you see the soldiers on the streets? The SS. How'd you get here in your bathrobes? Boy, you have dumb luck, that's all. The talk is that Rohm and his storm troopers—Von Helldorf, Ernst, your blond friend, the lot— were planning a coup. I don't believe it. What the hell, let them kill each other, who cares? Except, it's the end of the club. As long as Rohm was around, a queer club was still O.K. Anyhow, that's who you had, baby—Wolfgang Granz. I hope he was a good fuck. What's the difference? You picked up the wrong guy, that's all.
RUDY: We can explain to somebody. It's not like we knew him.
GRETA: Sure. Explain it all to the SS. You don't explain. Not anymore. You know, you queers are not very popular anyhow. It was just Rohm keeping you all safe. Now you're like Jews. Unloved, baby, unloved.
RUDY: How about you?
GRETA: *Me?* Everyone knows I'm not queer. I got a wife and kids. Of course, that doesn't mean much these days, does it? But—I still ain't queer! As for this... [*Fingers his costume.*] I go where the money is. Was.
MAX: [*Gets up.*] Money.
GRETA: Right.
MAX: Money. Ah! Greta!
GRETA: What's with you?
MAX: How much?
GRETA: How much what?
MAX: How much did they give you?
GRETA: [*Laughs.*] Oh. [*Takes out a roll of money.*] This much.
MAX: And you told them where Granz was?
GRETA: Told them, hell—I showed them your building.
RUDY: Greta, you didn't.
GRETA: Why not? You don't play games with the SS. Anyhow, it's just what he would do, your big shot here. He's into money, too. He just isn't very good at it. Me, I'm dynamite. Here. I'll do you a favor. Take it. [*Holds out the money.*]

RUDY: No.
GRETA: It will help.
RUDY: We don't want it.
MAX: Shut up, Rudy.
RUDY: Stop telling me to —
MAX: Shut up! It's not enough.
MAX: We need more.
GRETA: So get more.
MAX: If they catch us, it won't help you.
GRETA: Oh? A threat? [*Pause.*] Tell you what. I'll do you a favor. Take some
    more. [*Holds out some more money.*] I've made a lot off your kind, so I'm
    giving a little back. Take it all.
RUDY: Don't take it.
MAX: O.K. [*Takes the money.*]
GRETA: Now get out.
MAX: [*To* RUDY] Come on . . .
RUDY: Where? I'm not leaving Berlin.
MAX: We have to.
RUDY: We don't have to.
MAX: They're looking for us.
RUDY: But I live here.
MAX: Come on . . .
RUDY: I've paid up for dance class for the next two weeks. I can't leave.
    And my plants . . .
MAX: Jesus! Come on!
RUDY: If you hadn't gotten so drunk . . .
MAX: Don't.
RUDY: Why'd you have to take him home?
MAX: How do I know? *I don't remember.*
RUDY: You've ruined everything.
MAX: Right. I always do. So you go off on your own, O.K.? Go back to
    dance class. They can shoot you in the middle of an arabesque. Take
    half. [*Holds out some money.*]
RUDY: I don't want it.
MAX: Then fuck it! [*Starts to leave.*]
RUDY: Max!
GRETA: Max. He can't handle it alone. Look at him. Stick together. [MAX
    turns back to RUDY.] Take his hand, schmuck. [RUDY *takes* MAX's *hand.*]
    That's right.

RUDY: Where are we going to go?

GRETA: *Don't.* Don't say anything in front of me. Get out.

[MAX *stares at* GRETA. *Then he tugs at* RUDY *and pulls him out of the room.* GRETA *removes his wig. He stares at his face in the mirror, as*

BLACKOUT]

Scene III

Lights up on a park in Cologne.

A middle-aged man, well dressed [FREDDIE] *sits on a bench. He is reading a newspaper.* MAX *enters. He sees the man and goes to the bench. The man looks up.*

FREDDIE: Sit down.

[MAX *sits.*]

FREDDIE: Pretend we're strangers. Having a little conversation in the park. Perfectly normal. [*Folds the newspaper.*] Do something innocent. Feed the pigeons.
MAX: There aren't any pigeons.
FREDDIE: Here. [*Hands* MAX *an envelope.*]
MAX: You look good.
FREDDIE: You look older.
MAX: What's in this?
FREDDIE: Your papers and a ticket to Amsterdam.
MAX: Just one?
FREDDIE: Yes.
MAX: Shit.
FREDDIE: Keep your voice down. Remember, we're strangers. Just a casual conversation. Perfectly normal.
MAX: One ticket. I told you on the phone . . .
FREDDIE: One ticket. That's all.
MAX: I can't take it. Damn it, I'd kill for this. Here. [*Gives the envelope back.*] Thanks anyway. [*Gets up.*]
FREDDIE: Sit down. It wasn't easy getting new papers for you. If the family finds out . . .

[MAX *sits.*]

FREDDIE: I have to be careful. They've passed a law, you know. We're not allowed to be fluffs anymore. We're not even allowed to kiss or embrace. Or fantasize. They can arrest you for having fluff thoughts.
MAX: [*Laughs.*] Oh, Uncle Freddie.
FREDDIE: It's not funny.
MAX: It is.
FREDDIE: The family takes care of me. But you. Throwing it in everyone's face. No wonder they don't want anything to do with you. Why

couldn't you have been quiet about it? Settled down, gotten married, paid for a few boys on the side. No one would have known. Ach! Take this ticket.

MAX: I can't. Stop giving it to me. [*Silence.*]

FREDDIE: Look over there.

MAX: Where?

FREDDIE: Over there. See him?

MAX: Who?

FREDDIE: With the mustache.

MAX: Yes.

FREDDIE: Cute.

MAX: I guess.

FREDDIE: Think he's a fluff?

MAX: I don't care.

FREDDIE: You've been running for two years now. Haven't you? With that dancer. The family knows all about it. You can't live like that. Take this ticket.

MAX: I need two.

FREDDIE: I can't get two.

MAX: Of course you can.

FREDDIE: Yes. I think he is a fluff. You have to be so careful now. What is it? Do you love him?

MAX: Who?

FREDDIE: The dancer.

MAX: Jesus!

FREDDIE: Do you?

MAX: Don't be stupid. What's love? Bullshit. I'm a grown-up now. I just feel responsible.

FREDDIE: Fluffs can't afford that kind of responsibility. Why are you laughing?

MAX: That word. Fluffs. Look, do you think it's been a holiday? We've tramped right across this country; we settle in somewhere and then suddenly they're checking papers and we have to leave rather quickly; now we're living outside Cologne, in the goddamn forest! In a colony of *tents* — are you ready for that? *Me* in a tent! With hundreds of very boring unemployed people. Except most of them are *just* unemployed; they're not running from the Gestapo. I'm not cut out for this, Uncle Freddie. I was brought up to be comfortable. Like you. O.K. I've been fooling around for too long. You're right. The family and I should make up. So. How about a deal? *Two* tickets to Amsterdam. And two new sets of identity papers. Once we get to Amsterdam, I ditch him. And they can have me back.

FREDDIE: Maybe they don't want you back. It's been ten years.

MAX: They want me. It's good business. I'm an only son. [*Pause.*] Remember that marriage Father wanted to arrange? Her father had button factories, too. I just read about her in the paper; she's an eligible widow, living in Brussels. Make the arrangements again. I'll marry her. Our button factories can sleep with her button factories. It's a good deal. You know it. And eventually, when all this blows over, you can get me back to Germany. If I want a boy, I'll rent him. Like you. I'll be a discreet, quiet…fluff. Fair enough? It's what Father always wanted. Just get us *both* out alive.

FREDDIE: I'll have to ask your father.

MAX: Do it. Then ask him.

FREDDIE: I can't do things on my own. Not now. [*Holds out envelope.*] Just this.

MAX: I can't take it.

FREDDIE: He's looking this way. He might be the police. No. He's a fluff. He has fluff eyes. Still. You can't tell. You better leave. Just be casual. Perfectly normal. I'll ask your father.

MAX: Soon?

FREDDIE: Yes. Can I phone you?

MAX: In the *forest?*

FREDDIE: Phone me. On Friday. [FREDDIE *puts the envelope away.* MAX *gets up.*]

MAX: You look good, Uncle Freddie. [MAX *leaves.* FREDDIE *picks up his newspaper, glances at it, puts it down, and turns to look again at the man with the mustache, as*

BLACKOUT

Scene VI
The forest.

In front of a tent.

RUDY *sits in front of a fire. He has some apples, cheese, and a knife. He calls back to the tent.*

RUDY: Cheese! Max! [MAX *comes out of the tent, sits down.*]
MAX: Where'd you get cheese. Steal it?
RUDY: I don't steal. I dug a ditch.
MAX: You *what?*
RUDY: Dug a ditch. Right outside of Cologne. They're building a road. You can sign on each morning if you get there in time. They don't check your papers. It's good exercise too, for your shoulders. I'm getting nice shoulders. But my feet...no more dancing feet. Oh, God. Here. Have some.
MAX: I don't want to eat. You shouldn't have to dig ditches. I want some real food, for Christ's sake. [*Takes the cheese.*] Look at this. It's lousy cheese. You don't know anything about cheese. Look at all these tents. There's no one to talk to in any of them. [*Eats a piece of cheese.*] It has no flavor.
RUDY: Then don't eat it. I'll eat it. I have apples, too.
MAX: I hate apples.
RUDY: Then starve. What did you do today, while I was ditch digging?
MAX: Nothing.
RUDY: You weren't here when I got back.
MAX: Went to town.
RUDY: Have fun?
MAX: I'm working on something.
RUDY: Really?
MAX: Yeah. A deal. [*Takes an apple.*]
RUDY: Oh. A deal. Wonderful.
MAX: I might get us new papers and tickets to Amsterdam.
RUDY: You said that in Hamburg.
MAX: It didn't work out in Hamburg.
RUDY: You said that in Stuttgart.
MAX: Are you going to recite the list?

Rudy: Why not? I'm tired of your deals. You're right. This cheese stinks. I
   don't want to eat it. [*Pushes the food aside.*]
Max: You have to eat.
Rudy: Throw it out.
Max: You get sick if you don't eat.
Rudy: So what?
Max: O.K. Get sick.
Rudy: No. I don't want to get sick. [*Eats a piece of cheese.*] If I get sick,
   you'll leave me behind. You're just waiting for me to get sick.
Max: Oh — here we go.
Rudy: You'd love it if I died.
Max: Rudy! I just want to get us out of here. These awful tents. There's no
   air. We're *in* the air, but there's still no air. I can't breathe. I've got to
   get us across the border.
Rudy: Why don't we just cross it?
Max: What do you mean?
Rudy: This guy on the job today was telling me it's easy to cross the
   border.
Max: Oh sure it's simple. You just walk across. Of course, they shoot you.
Rudy: He said he knew spots.
Max: Spots?
Rudy: Spots to get through. I told him to come talk to you.
Max: Here?
Rudy: Yes.
Max: I told you we don't want anyone to know we're here, or that we're
   trying to cross the border. Are you *that* dumb?
Rudy: I'm not dumb.
Max: He could tell the police.
Rudy: O.K. So I *am* dumb. Why don't we try it anyway?
Max: Because . . .
Rudy: Why?
Max: I'm working on a deal.
Rudy: Who with?
Max: I can't tell you. I can't talk about it before it happens. Then it won't
   happen. I'm superstitious.
Rudy: Then why'd you bring it up?
Max: So you'd know that . . .
Rudy: What?
Max: That I'm trying.

RUDY: This is crazy. We're in the middle of the jungle —
MAX: Forest.
RUDY: Jungle. I'm a dancer, not Robin Hood. I can't dance anymore. I've walked my feet away. But you don't mind. You're working on deals. You worked on deals in Berlin, you work on deals in the jungle.
MAX: Forest.
RUDY: Jungle. I want to get out of here. I could have. I met a man in Frankfurt. You were in town "working on a deal." He gave me a ride. He was an old man, rich too. I could have stayed with him. I could have got him to get me out of the country. He really wanted me, I could tell. But no, I had to think about you. It wasn't fair to *you*. I'm dumb, you're right. You would have grabbed the chance. You're just hanging around, waiting for me to die. I think you've poisoned the cheese.
MAX: It's *your* cheese. Choke on it. Please, choke on it. I can't tell you how much I want you to choke on it. Christ! [MAX *gets up.*]
RUDY: Where are you going?
MAX: I have to get out of here. I can't breathe. I'm going for a walk.
RUDY: You can't. There's no place to walk. Just tents and jungle.
MAX: I have a fever.
RUDY: What?
MAX: I have a fever! I'm burning up.
RUDY: It's a trick. [*Gets up, goes to him, tries to feel his forehead.*]
MAX: [*Pulls away.*] I know. I'm lying. Get away.
RUDY: Let me feel. [*Feels* MAX's *forehead.*] You have a fever.
MAX: It's the cheese. *You* poisoned *me*. What the hell. I'll die in the jungle. [*Sits down again.*]
RUDY: Forest. [*Sits.*]

[*Silence.*]

MAX: Remember cocaine?
RUDY: Yes.
MAX: I'd like cocaine.
RUDY: Yes.
MAX: What would you like?
RUDY: New glasses.
MAX: What?
RUDY: My eyes have changed. I need a new prescription. I'd like new glasses.
MAX: In Amsterdam.

RUDY: Sure.
MAX: In *Amsterdam*. Cocaine and new glasses. Trust me. Plants. You'll have plants. Wonderful Dutch plants. And Dutch dance classes. Your feet will come back. And you won't dig ditches. You'll have to give up your new shoulders, though. And you know what? We can buy a Dutch dog. Everyone should have a dog. I don't know why we didn't have a dog in Berlin. We'll have one in Amsterdam. [*Silence.*] Trust me.

[RUDY *looks at* MAX *and smiles.*

Silence.]

RUDY: How's your fever?
MAX: Burning.

[RUDY *touches* MAX*'s forehead; leaves his hand on the forehead.*]

MAX: Don't.
RUDY: I'm sorry, Max. [*Strokes his forehead.*]
MAX: Don't.
RUDY: I really love you.
MAX: DON'T. [*Pulls* RUDY*'s hand away.*] If they see us...from the other tents...they're always looking...they could throw us out...for touching...we have to be careful...we have to be very careful...
RUDY: O.K. [*Pause — starts to sing.*]
Streets of Berlin,
I must leave you soon,
Ah!

MAX: What are you doing?
RUDY: Singing. We're sitting around a campfire, that's when people sing. This must be the way the Hitler Youth does it. They sing old favorites, too. I'm sure they're not allowed to touch either.
MAX: Don't be so sure.
RUDY: Well, it's unfair if they can, and we can't. [*Sings.*]
Streets of Berlin,
I must leave you soon,
Ah!

[MAX *takes* RUDY*'s hand, holds it, on the ground, where it can't be seen, and smiles.*]

MAX: Shh!

[*They laugh. They both sing.*]

MAX and RUDY: Will you forget me?
Was I ever really here?
VOICE: [*From the darkness*] There! That's them! [*A bright light shines on* MAX
and RUDY.]
ANOTHER VOICE: [*From darkness*] Maximilian Berber. Rudolf Hennings.
Hands high in the air. You are under arrest.

BLACKOUT

Scene V

A train whistle is heard.

Sound of a train running through the night. A train whistle again.

A circle of light comes up.

It is a prisoner transport train. We see one small corner. Five prisoners are in the light — two men in civilian dress, then RUDY *and* MAX, *then a man, in his twenties, wearing a striped uniform, with a pink triangle sewn onto it.*

A GUARD *walks through the circle of light. He carries a rifle.*

Silence.

RUDY: Where do you think they're taking us?

[*Silence.*

The other prisoners look away.

The GUARD *walks through the circle of light.*

Silence.]

RUDY: [*To the* PRISONER *next to him*] Did you have a trial? [*The* PRISONER *doesn't answer.*]
MAX: Rudy!

[*Silence.*

RUDY *and* MAX *look at each other. They are both terrified.* RUDY *starts to extend his hand, then withdraws it.*

A scream is heard — off, beyond the circle. RUDY *and* MAX *look at each other, then turn away.*

Silence.

The GUARD *walks through the circle of light.*

Silence.

Another scream.

Silence.

The GUARD *walks through the circle of light. An SS* OFFICER *enters. The circle slightly expands. The* OFFICER *looks at the prisoners one by one. He stops at* RUDY.]

OFFICER: Glasses. [*Silence.*] Give me your glasses. [RUDY *hands the* OFFICER *his glasses. The* OFFICER *examines them.*] Horn-rimmed. Intelligensia.

RUDY: What?

OFFICER: [*Smiles.*] Stand up. [*Pulls* RUDY *up.*] Step on your glasses. [RUDY *stands—petrified.*] Step on them. [RUDY *steps on the glasses.*] Take him.

RUDY: Max! [RUDY *looks at* MAX. *The* GUARD *pulls* RUDY *off—out of the circle. The* OFFICER *smiles.*]

OFFICER: Glasses.

[*He kicks the glasses away.*

The OFFICER *leaves the circle of light.*

The light narrows.

MAX *stares ahead.*

The GUARD *walks through the circle of light.*

Silence.

A scream is heard—off, beyond the circle. RUDY'S *scream.* MAX *stiffens.*

Silence.

RUDY *screams again.*

MAX *moves, as if to get up.*

The man wearing the pink triangle [HORST] *moves toward* MAX. *He touches him.*]

HORST: Don't.

[*He removes his hand from* MAX *and looks straight ahead.*

The GUARD *walks through the circle of light.*]

HORST: Don't move. You can't help him.

[RUDY *screams.*

Silence.

The GUARD *walks through the circle of light.*]

MAX: This isn't happening.
HORST: It's happening.
MAX: Where are they taking us?
HORST: Dachau.
MAX: How do you know?
HORST: I've been through transport before. They took me to Cologne for a propaganda film. Pink triangle in good health. Now it's back to Dachau.
MAX: Pink triangle? What's that?
HORST: Queer. If you're queer, that's what you wear. If you're a Jew, a yellow star. Political—a red triangle. Criminal—green. Pink's the lowest.

[*He looks straight ahead.*

The GUARD *walks through the circle of light.*

RUDY *screams.*

MAX *starts.*]

MAX: This isn't happening. [*Silence.*] This can't be happening. [*Silence.*]
HORST: Listen to me. If you survive the train, you stand a chance. Here's where they break you. You can do nothing for your friend. Nothing. If you try to help him, they will kill you. If you try to care for his wounds, they will kill you. If you even *see*—see what they do to him, *hear*—hear what they do to him—they will kill you. If you want to stay alive, he cannot exist. [RUDY *screams.*]
MAX: It isn't happening. [RUDY *screams.*]
HORST: He hasn't a chance. He wore glasses.

[RUDY *screams.*]

HORST: If you want to stay alive, he cannot exist.

[RUDY *screams.*]

HORST: It *is* happening.

[HORST *moves away.*

The light focuses in on MAX's *face.* RUDY *screams.* MAX *stares ahead, mumbling to himself.*]

MAX: It isn't happening…it isn't happening…

[*The light expands.*

The GUARD *drags* RUDY *in.* RUDY *is semiconscious. His body is bloody and mutilated. The* GUARD *holds him up. The* OFFICER *enters the circle.* MAX *looks away. The* OFFICER *looks at* MAX. MAX *is still mumbling to himself.*]

OFFICER: [*To* MAX] Who is this man?
MAX: I don't know. [*Stops mumbling, looks straight ahead.*]
OFFICER: Your friend? [*Silence.*]
MAX: No. [RUDY *moans.*]
OFFICER: Look at him. [MAX *stares straight ahead.*] Look! [MAX *looks at* RUDY. *The* OFFICER *hits* RUDY *on the chest.* RUDY *screams.*] Your friend?
MAX: No. [*The* OFFICER *hits* RUDY *on the chest.* RUDY *screams.*]
OFFICER: Your friend?
MAX: No. [*Silence.*]
OFFICER: Hit him. [MAX *stares at the* OFFICER.] Like this. [*Hits* RUDY *on the chest.* RUDY *screams.*]
OFFICER: Hit him. [MAX *doesn't move.*] Your friend? [MAX *doesn't move.*] Your friend?
MAX: No. [*Closes his eyes. Hits* RUDY *on the chest.* RUDY *screams.*]
OFFICER: Open your eyes. [MAX *opens his eyes.*] Again. [MAX *hits* RUDY *on the chest.*] Again! [MAX *hits* RUDY *again and again and again . . .*] Enough. [*Pushes* RUDY *down to the ground, at* MAX'*s feet.*] Your friend?
MAX: No.
OFFICER: [*Smiles.*] No.

[*The* OFFICER *leaves the circle of light. The* GUARD *follows him.*

The light focuses in — on MAX'*s face.*

The train is heard running through the night.

The train whistles.

RUDY *is heard — meaning — and calling* MAX'*s name.*

MAX *stares ahead.*

RUDY *calls* MAX'*s name. The name merges with the whistle.*

MAX *takes a deep breath.*]

MAX: One. Two. Three. Four. Five. [*Takes another deep breath.*] Six. Seven. Eight. Nine. Ten.

[Rudy *calls* Max*'s name.*

Max *stares ahead.*

The lights dim on Max, *almost to* blackout —*then, suddenly, they expand and include the three other prisoners. A morning ray of sunlight.*

Rudy *lies at* Max*'s feet.*

The Guard *walks through the circle of light.*

Silence.

The Officer *comes into the circle. He looks at* Max.]

Officer: Stand up. [*Stares at* Max.] We'll see. [*To* Guard] Take him. [*Kicks* Rudy*'s body; it rolls over—looks down at it.*] Dead.

[*The* Officer *leaves.*

The Guard *pushes* Max *with his rifle. They walk out of the light.*

The lights dim on the prisoners.]

blackout

Scene VI

Lights up, on one side of the stage. A large barrel is on the ground. A prisoner-foreman [Kapo] *stands behind the barrel, with a huge ladle. He stirs it. The* Kapo *wears a green triangle on his prison uniform. Prisoners come up, one by one, with bowls in their hand, to be fed. They all wear prison uniforms.*

[*A* Prisoner *with a yellow star enters. The* Kapo *stirs the soup.*

He fills the Prisoner's *bowl. The* Prisoner *leaves. A* Prisoner *with a red triangle enters.*

The Kapo *stirs the soup.*

He fills the Prisoner's *bowl. The* Prisoner *leaves.* Horst *enters. The* Kapo *does not stir the soup.*]

Horst: Only soup. You skimmed it from the top. There's nothing in it but water. No meat, no vegetables... nothing.
Kapo: Take what you get.
Horst: [*Reaches for the ladle.*] Give me some meat.
Kapo: [*Pushes him back.*] Fucking queer! Take what you get!

[blackout.

Lights rise on other side of the stage.

A tight little corner at the end of the barracks. Horst *crawls in and sits huddled with his bowl. He drinks the soup.*

Max *enters, crawling in next to* Horst. *He carries a bowl. He wears the prison uniform. On it is a yellow star.*]

Max: Hi. [Horst *looks at him; says nothing;* Max *holds up his bowl.*] Here.
Horst: Leave me alone.
Max: I got extra. Some vegetables. Here. [*Drops some vegetables from his bowl into* Horst's *bowl.*]
Horst: Thanks. [*They eat in silence.* Horst *looks up. Stares at* Max's *uniform.*] Yellow star?
Max: What?
Horst: Jew?
Max: Oh. Yeah.
Horst: I wouldn't have figured it. [*Silence.*] I'm sorry about your friend.
Max: Who?
Horst: Your friend.

MAX: Oh. [*Silence.*]
HORST: It's not very sociable in these barracks. [*Laughs.*] Is it?
MAX: [*Points to* HORST'*s pink triangle.*] How'd you get that?
HORST: I signed a petition.
MAX: And?
HORST: That was it.
MAX: What kind of petition?
HORST: For Magnus Hirschfeld.
MAX: Oh yeah. I remember him. Berlin.
HORST: Berlin.
MAX: He wanted to . . .
HORST: Make queers legal.
MAX: Right. I remember.
HORST: Looked like he would, too, for a while. It was quite a movement.
Then the Nazis came in. Well. I was a nurse. They said a queer
couldn't be a nurse. Suppose I had to touch a patient's penis! God
forbid. They said rather than be a nurse, I should be a prisoner. A more
suitable occupation. So. So. That's how I got my pink triangle. How'd
you get the yellow star?
MAX: I'm Jewish.
HORST: You're not Jewish, you're a queer. [*Silence.*]
MAX: I didn't want one.
HORST: Didn't want what?
MAX: A pink triangle.
HORST: Didn't *want* one?
MAX: You told me it was the lowest. So I didn't want one.
HORST: So?
MAX: So I worked a deal.
HORST: A deal?
MAX: Sure. I'm good at that.
HORST: With the Gestapo?
MAX: Sure.
HORST: You're full of shit. [*Silence.*]
MAX: I'm going to work a lot of deals. They can't keep us here forever.
Sooner or later they'll release us. I'm only under protective custody,
that's what they told me. I'm going to stay alive.
HORST: I don't doubt it.
MAX: Sure. I'm good at that.
HORST: Thanks for the vegetables. [*Starts to crawl away.*]
MAX: Where are you going?

Horst: To sleep. We get up at four in the morning, I'm on stone detail. I chop stones up. It's fun. Excuse me...

Max: Don't go.

Horst: I'm tired.

Max: I don't have anyone to talk to.

Horst: Talk to your landsmen.

Max: I'm not Jewish.

Horst: Then why are you wearing that?

Max: You told me pink was the lowest.

Horst: It is, but only because the other prisoners hate us so much.

Max: I got meat in my soup. You didn't.

Horst: Good for you.

Max: Don't go.

Horst: Look, friendships last about twelve hours in this place. We had ours on the train. Why don't you go and bother someone else.

Max: You didn't think I'd make it, did you? Off the train?

Horst: I wasn't sure.

Max: I'm going to stay alive.

Horst: Yes.

Max: Because of you. You told me how.

Horst: Yes. [*Pause.*] I did. [*Pause.*] I'm sorry.

Max: About what?

Horst: I don't know. Your friend.

Max: Oh. [*Silence.*] He wasn't my friend. [*Silence.*]

Horst: You should be wearing a pink triangle.

Max: I made a deal.

Horst: You don't make deals here.

Max: I did. I made a deal.

Horst: Sure. [*Starts to leave again.*]

Max: They said if I... I could... they said...

Horst: What?

Max: Nothing. [Horst *crawls past* Max.] I could prove... I don't know how...

Horst: What? [*Stops, sits next to* Max.]

Max: Nothing. [*Silence.*]

Horst: Try. [*Silence.*] I think you better. [*Silence.*] Try to tell me.

Max: Nothing. [*Silence.*]

Horst: O.K. [*Moves away.*]

Max: I made... They took me... into that room...

Horst: [*Stops.*] Where?

MAX: Into that room.

HORST: On the train?

MAX: On the train. And they said... prove that you're... and I did...

HORST: Prove that you're what?

MAX: Not.

HORST: Not what?

MAX: Queer.

HORST: How?

MAX: Her.

HORST: Her?

MAX: They said, if you... and I did...

HORST: Did what?

MAX: Her. Made...

HORST: Made what?

MAX: Love.

HORST: Who to?

MAX: Her.

HORST: Who was she?

MAX: Only... maybe... maybe only thirteen... she was maybe... she was dead.

HORST: Oh.

MAX: Just. Just dead, minutes... bullet... in her... they said... prove that you're... and I did... prove that you're... lots of them, watching... laughing... drinking... he's a bit bent, they said, he can't... but I did...

HORST: How?

MAX: I don't... I don't... know. I wanted...

HORST: To stay alive.

MAX: And there was something...

HORST: Something...

MAX: Exciting...

HORST: Oh God.

MAX: I hit him, you know. I kissed her. Dead lips. I killed him. Sweet lips. Angel.

HORST: God.

MAX: She was... like an angel... to save my life... just beginning... her breasts... just beginning... they said he can't... he's a bit bent... but I did... and I proved... I proved that I wasn't... [*Silence.*] And they enjoyed it.

HORST: Yes.

MAX: And I said, I'm not queer. And they laughed. And I said, give me a yellow star. And they said, sure, make him a Jew. He's not bent. And they laughed. They were having fun. But...I...got...my...star...

HORST: [*Gently*] Oh yes.

MAX: I got my star.

HORST: Yes. [*Reaches out, touches* MAX's *face.*]

MAX: *Don't do that!* [*Pulls away.*] You mustn't do that. For your own sake. You mustn't touch me. I'm a rotten person.

HORST: No...[HORST *touches* MAX *again.* MAX *hits him.*]

MAX: Rotten.

HORST: [*Stares at* MAX.] No. [*Crawls away, and leaves.*]

MAX: [*Is alone. He takes a deep breath. He closes his eyes. He takes another deep breath. He opens his eyes.*] One. Two. Three. Four. Five. [*Takes another deep breath.*] Six. Seven. Eight. Nine. Ten.

BLACKOUT

End of Act One

Act Two

Scene I
One month later.

A large fence extends across the stage. In front of the fence, on one side, lies a pile of rocks. On the other side—far over—a deep pit.

MAX is moving rocks. He carries one rock from the pile to the other side and starts a new pile. He returns and takes another rock. The rocks are carried one by one. He wears a prison uniform and hat.

A GUARD enters with HORST. HORST also wears a prison uniform and hat. The GUARD is very officious.

GUARD: Here. You will work here.
HORST: Yes sir.
GUARD: He'll explain.
HORST: Yes sir.
GUARD: I'm up there. [*Points off, and up.*]
HORST: Yes sir.
GUARD: I see everything.
HORST: Yes sir.
GUARD: No laying about.
HORST: No sir.
GUARD: I see everything.
HORST: Yes sir.
GUARD: [*To* MAX] You.
MAX: [*Puts down his rock.*] Yes sir.
GUARD: Tell him what to do.
MAX: Yes sir.
GUARD: No laying about.

MAX: No sir.
GUARD: I see everything.
MAX: Yes sir.
GUARD: [*To* HORST] You.
HORST: Yes sir.
GUARD: Every two hours there is a rest period.
HORST: Yes sir.
GUARD: For three minutes.
HORST: Yes sir.
GUARD: Stand at attention.
HORST: Yes sir.
GUARD: Don't move.
HORST: No sir.
GUARD: Rest.
HORST: Yes sir.
GUARD: Three minutes.
HORST: Yes sir.
GUARD: A bell rings.
HORST: Yes sir.
GUARD: [*To* MAX] You.
MAX: Yes sir.
GUARD: Explain it to him.
MAX: Yes sir.
GUARD: No laying about.
MAX: No sir.
GUARD: [*To* HORST] You.
HORST: Yes sir.
GUARD: When the bell rings.
HORST: Yes sir.
GUARD: Don't move.
HORST: No sir.
GUARD: Three minutes.
HORST: Yes sir.
GUARD: He'll explain.
HORST: Yes sir.
GUARD: [*To* MAX] You.
MAX: Yes sir.
GUARD: You're responsible.
MAX: Yes sir.

GUARD: I'm up there.
MAX: Yes sir.
GUARD: [*To* HORST] You.
HORST: Yes sir.
GUARD: I see everything.
HORST: Yes sir.

[*The* GUARD *leaves.* HORST *watches carefully, until he is far gone.*]

HORST: We had a kid like that in school. Used to lead us in Simon Says.
MAX: O.K. I'll explain.
HORST: O.K.
MAX: Hey — we can't stand here. We have to move rocks.
HORST: Yes sir.
MAX: You see those . . .
HORST: Yes sir.
MAX: You take one rock at a time.
HORST: Yes sir.
MAX: And move it over there.
HORST: Yes sir.
MAX: And then when the entire pile is over there, you take one rock at a time, and move it back.
HORST: [*Looks at* MAX. *Silence.*] And move it back?
MAX: Yes.
HORST: We move the rocks from there to there, and then back from there to there?
MAX: Yes sir.
HORST: *Why?*
MAX: Start moving. He's watching. [MAX *continues to move rocks.* HORST *does the same. They do so in different rhythms, at times passing each other.*]
HORST: O.K.
MAX: It's supposed to drive us crazy.
HORST: These are heavy!
MAX: You get used to it.
HORST: What do you mean, drive us crazy?
MAX: Just that. It makes no sense. It serves no purpose. I figured it out. They do it to drive us crazy.
HORST: They probably know what they're doing.
MAX: But it doesn't work. I figured it out. It's the best job to have. That's why I got you here.

Horst: *What?* [*Puts down his rock.*]

Max: Don't stop. Keep moving. [Horst *picks up the rock and moves it.*] A couple more things. That fence.

Horst: Yes.

Max: It's electric. Don't touch it. You fry.

Horst: I won't touch it.

Max: And over there — that pit.

Horst: Where?

Max: There.

Horst: Oh yes. It smells awful.

Max: Bodies.

Horst: In the pit.

Max: Yes. Sometimes we have to throw them in.

Horst: Oh. Well, it will break the routine. What do you mean you got me here?

Max: Don't walk so fast.

Horst: Why?

Max: You'll tire yourself. Pace it. Nice and slow.

Horst: O.K. This better?

Max: Yeah.

Horst: What do you mean you got me here?

Max: I worked a deal.

Horst: I don't want to hear. [*Silence.*] Yes, I do. What the hell is this? You *got* me here? What right do you have —

Max: Careful.

Horst: What?

Max: You drop the rock.

Horst: No I'm not. I'm holding it, I'm holding it. What right do you have —

Max: You were at the stones?

Horst: Yes.

Max: Was it harder than this?

Horst: I guess.

Max: People get sick?

Horst: Yes.

Max: Die?

Horst: Yes.

Max: Guards beat you if you didn't work hard enough?

Horst: Yes.

Max: [*Proudly*] So?

Horst: So? So what?

Max: So it was dangerous.

Horst: This isn't?

Max: No. No one gets sick here. Look at all those guys moving rocks over there. [*Points off.*] They look healthier than most. No one dies. The guards don't beat you, because the work is totally non-essential. All it can do is drive you crazy.

Horst: That's all?

Max: Yes.

Horst: Then maybe the other was better.

Max: No, I figured it out! This is the best work in the camp, if you keep your head, if you have someone to talk to.

Horst: Ah! I see! Someone to talk to! Don't you think you should have asked me . . .

Max: Asked you what?

Horst: If I wanted to move rocks, if I wanted to talk to you . . .

Max: Didn't have a chance. They moved you.

Horst: Thank heaven.

Max: Your new barracks, is it all pink triangles?

Horst: Yes. They're arresting more queers each day; they keep pouring into the camp. Is yours all yellow stars now?

Max: Yes.

Horst: Good. You might go all religious. There was an old man at the stones. A rabbi. Really kind. It's not easy being kind here. He was. I thought of you.

Max: Why?

Horst: Maybe if you knew him you could be proud of your star. You should be proud of *something*. [*Silence.*]

Max: Don't keep looking at me. As long as they don't see us look at each other they can't tell we're talking. [*Silence.*]

Horst: Where do the bodies come from?

Max: What bodies?

Horst: The ones in the pit.

Max: The fence. The hat trick.

Horst: Oh. What's that?

Max: Sometimes a guard throws a prisoner's hat against the fence. He orders him to get the hat. If he doesn't get the hat, the guard will shoot him. If he does get the hat, he'll be electrocuted.

Horst: I'm really going to like it here. Thanks a lot.

Max: I'm really doing you a favor.

HORST: Some favor! You just want someone to talk to so you won't go crazy. And I'm the only one who knows your secret.

MAX: What secret?

HORST: That you're a pink triangle.

MAX: No. I'm a Jew now.

HORST: You are not.

MAX: They think I am.

HORST: But it's a lie.

MAX: It's a smart lie.

HORST: You're crazy.

MAX: I thought you'd be grateful.

HORST: That's why you like this job. It can't drive you crazy. You're already there.

MAX: I spent money getting you here.

HORST: Money?

MAX: Yes. I bribed the guard.

HORST: Where'd you get money?

MAX: My uncle sent me some. First letter I ever got from him. He didn't sign it, but it had money in it.

HORST: And you bribed the guard?

MAX: Yes.

HORST: For me?

MAX: Yes.

HORST: Used *your* money?

MAX: Yes.

HORST: You'll probably never get money again.

MAX: Probably not.

HORST: You are crazy.

MAX: I thought you'd be grateful.

HORST: You should have asked me first.

MAX: How could I ask you. We're in separate barracks. Do you think it's easy to bribe a guard? It's complicated. It's dangerous. He could have turned on me. I took a risk. Do you think I didn't? I took a risk. I thought you'd be grateful.

HORST: I'm *not* grateful. I liked cutting stones. I liked that old rabbi. This is insane. Twelve hours of this a day? I'll be nuts in a week. Like you. Jesus!

MAX: I'm sorry I did it.

HORST: *You're* sorry?

MAX: You haven't figured out this camp, that's all. You don't know what's good for you. This is the best job to have.

HORST: Moving rocks back and forth for no reason. Next to a pit with dead bodies and a fence that can burn you to dust. The best job to have?

MAX: Yes. You don't understand.

HORST: I don't want to understand. I don't want to talk to you.

MAX: You have to talk to me.

HORST: Why?

MAX: I got you here to talk.

HORST: Well, tough. I don't want to talk. Move your rocks, and I'll move mine. Just don't speak to me.

[*They both move their rocks.*

A long silence.]

MAX: I thought you'd be grateful.

BLACKOUT

Scene II

The same. Three days later.

MAX *and* HORST *are moving rocks. It is very hot. Their shirts lie on the ground.*

A long silence.

HORST: It's so hot.
MAX: Yes.
HORST: Burning hot.
MAX: Yes.

[*Silence.*]

MAX: You talked to me.
HORST: Weather talk, that's all.
MAX: After three days of silence.
HORST: *Weather* talk. Everyone talks about the weather. [*Silence.*] Anyhow. [*Silence.*]
MAX: Did you say something?
HORST: No.

[*Silence.*]

HORST: Anyhow.
MAX: Anyhow?
HORST: Anyhow. Anyhow, I'm sorry. [*Stands still.*] Sometimes in this place, I behave like everyone else—bloody awful. Cut off, mean, not human, I'm sorry. You were doing me a favor. This is a good place to be. And the favor won't work unless we talk, will it?
MAX: *Move!*
HORST: What?
MAX: Talk while you're moving. Don't stop. They can see us.
HORST: [*Starts to move the rock again.*] It's hard to talk when you're going one way and I'm going the other. God, it's hot.

[*Silence.*]

HORST: Somebody died last night.
MAX: Where?
HORST: In my barracks. A moslem.

MAX: An Arab?

HORST: No. A moslem. That's what they call a dead person who walks. You know, one of those guys who won't eat anymore, won't talk anymore, just wanders around waiting to really die.

MAX: I've seen them.

HORST: So one really died. In my barracks. [*Silence.*] God, it's hot. [*Silence.*]

MAX: We'll miss the Olympics.

HORST: The *what?*

MAX: Olympics. Next month in Berlin.

HORST: I knew there was a reason I didn't want to be here.

MAX: Maybe they'll release us.

HORST: For the Olympics?

MAX: As a goodwill gesture. It is possible, don't you think?

HORST: I think it's hot. [*Silence.*]

MAX: Heard a rumor.

HORST: What?

MAX: We get sardines tonight.

HORST: I don't like sardines.

MAX: It's only a rumor. [*Silence.*]

HORST: God, it's hot. [*Silence.*]

MAX: Sure is. [*Silence.*]

HORST: Sure is what? [*Silence.*]

MAX: Sure is hot. [*Silence.*]

HORST: Suppose... [*Silence.*]

MAX: What? [*Silence.*]

HORST: Suppose after all of this... [*Silence.*] We have nothing to talk about.

[*A loud bell rings.*

MAX *and* HORST *put down their rocks and stand at attention, staring straight ahead.*]

HORST: Shit! I'd rather be moving rocks than standing in the sun. Some rest period.

MAX: It's part of their plan.

HORST: What plan?

MAX: To drive us crazy. [*Silence.*] Was I awful to bring you here?

HORST: No.

MAX: I was, wasn't I?

HORST: No.

MAX: I had no right...

HORST: Stop it. Stop thinking how awful you are. Come on, don't get depressed. Smile. [*Silence.*] You're not smiling.

MAX: You can't see me.

HORST: I can feel you.

MAX: I wish we could look at each other.

HORST: I can feel you.

MAX: They hate it if anyone looks at each other.

HORST: I snuck a glance.

MAX: At what?

HORST: At you.

MAX: When?

HORST: Before.

MAX: Yeah?

HORST: A couple of glances. You look sexy.

MAX: Me?

HORST: Without your shirt.

MAX: No.

HORST: Come off it. You know you're sexy.

MAX: No.

HORST: Liar.

MAX: [*Smiles.*] Of course I'm a liar.

HORST: Sure.

MAX: I've always been sexy.

HORST: Uh-huh.

MAX: Since I was a kid.

HORST: Yes?

MAX: Twelve. I got into a lot of trouble when I was . . .

HORST: Twelve?

MAX: Twelve.

HORST: Your body's beautiful.

MAX: I take care of it. I exercise.

HORST: What?

MAX: At night I do push-ups and knee bends in the barracks.

HORST: After twelve hours of moving rocks?

MAX: Sure. I figured it out. You got to keep your entire body strong. By yourself. That's how you survive here. You should do it.

HORST: I don't like to exercise.

MAX: You're a nurse.

HORST: For other people, not myself.

Max: But you have to think of survival.
Horst: Sleep. I think of sleep. That's how I survive. Or I think of nothing. [*Silence.*] That scares me. When I think of nothing. [*Silence.*]
Max: Your body's nice, too.
Horst: It's O.K. Not great.
Max: No, it's nice.
Horst: Not as nice as yours.
Max: No. But it's O.K.
Horst: How do you know?
Max: I looked. I snuck a few glances, too.
Horst: When?
Max: All day.
Horst: Yes?
Max: Yes. [*Silence.*]
Horst: Listen, do you…
Max: What?
Horst: Miss…
Max: What?
Horst: You know.
Max: No, I don't.
Horst: Everyone misses it.
Max: No.
Horst: Everyone in the camp.
Max: No.
Horst: They go crazy missing it.
Max: No.
Horst: Come on. No one can hear us. You're not a yellow star with me, remember? Do you miss it?
Max: I don't want…
Horst: What?
Max: To miss it.
Horst: But do you? [*Silence.*]
Max: Yes.
Horst: Me too. [*Silence.*] We don't have to.
Max: What?
Horst: Miss it. [*Silence.*] We're here together. We don't have to miss it.
Max: We can't look at each other. We can't touch.
Horst: We can feel…
Max: Feel what?

HORST: Each other. Without looking. Without touching. I can feel you
  right now. Next to me. Can you feel me?
MAX: No.
HORST: Come on. Don't be afraid. No one can hear us. Can you feel me?
MAX: Maybe.
HORST: No one's going to know. It's all right. Feel me.
MAX: Maybe.
HORST: Feel me.
MAX: It's so hot.
HORST: I'm touching you.
MAX: No.
HORST: I'm touching you.
MAX: It's burning.
HORST: I'm kissing you.
MAX: Burning.
HORST: Kissing your eyes.
MAX: Hot.
HORST: Kissing your lips.
MAX: Yes.
HORST: Mouth.
MAX: Yes.
HORST: Inside your mouth.
MAX: Yes.
HORST: Neck.
MAX: Yes.
HORST: Down . . .
MAX: Yes.
HORST: Down . . .
MAX: Yes.
HORST: Chest. My tongue . . .
MAX: Burning.
HORST: Your chest.
MAX: Your mouth.
HORST: I'm kissing your chest.
MAX: Yes.
HORST: Hard.
MAX: Yes.
HORST: Down . . .
MAX: Yes.
HORST: Down . . .

MAX: Yes.
HORST: Your cock.
MAX: Yes.
HORST: Do you feel my mouth?
MAX: Yes. Do you feel my cock?
HORST: Yes. Do you feel...
MAX: Do you feel...
HORST: Mouth.
MAX: Cock.
HORST: Cock.
MAX: Mouth.
HORST: Do you feel my cock?
MAX: Do you feel my mouth?
HORST: Yes.
MAX: Do you know what I'm doing?
HORST: Yes. Can you taste what I'm doing?
MAX: Yes.
HORST: Taste.
MAX: Feel.
HORST: Together...
MAX: Together...
HORST: Do you feel me?
MAX: I feel you.
HORST: I see you.
MAX: I feel you.
HORST: I have you.
MAX: I want you.
HORST: Do you feel me inside you?
MAX: I want you inside me.
HORST: Feel...
MAX: I have you inside me.
HORST: Inside...
MAX: Strong.
HORST: Do you feel me thrust...
MAX: Hold.
HORST: Stroke...
MAX: Strong...
HORST: Oh...
MAX: Strong...
HORST: Oh...

MAX: Strong...
HORST: I'm going to...
MAX: Strong...
HORST: Do you feel...I'm going to...
MAX: I feel us both.
HORST: Do you...
MAX: Oh yes...
HORST: Do you...
MAX: Yes. Yes.
HORST: Feel...
MAX: Yes. Strong...
HORST: Feel...
MAX: More...
HORST: Ohh...
MAX: Now...
HORST: Yes...
MAX: Now! [*Gasps.*] Oh! Oh! My God! [*Has orgasm.*]
HORST: Ohh!...Now! Ohh!...[*Has orgasm.*]

[*Silence.*]

HORST: Oh.

[*Silence.*]

HORST: Did you?
MAX: Yes. *You?*
HORST: Yes. [*Silence.*]
MAX: You're a good lay.
HORST: So are you. [*Silence.*]
MAX: It's awfully sticky. [*Silence.*]
HORST: Max?
MAX: What?
HORST: We did it. How about that—fucking guards, fucking camp, we did it.
MAX: Don't shout.
HORST: O.K. But I'm shouting inside. We did it. They're not going to kill us. We made love. We were real. We were human. We made love. They're not going to kill us. [*Silence.*]
MAX: I never...
HORST: What?
MAX: Thought we'd...

Horst: What?
Max: Do it in three minutes.

[*They laugh.*

The bell rings.]

BLACKOUT

Scene III
The same. Two months later.

MAX *and* HORST *are at attention, wearing shirts.*

HORST: I'm going crazy. [*Silence.*] I'm going crazy. [*Silence.*] I'm going crazy. I dream about rocks. I close my eyes and I'm moving rocks. Rocks never end. Never end. [*Silence.*] I'm going crazy.

MAX: Think of something else.

HORST: I can't think. I've been up all night.

MAX: Up all night?

HORST: Come on, didn't you hear? Our barracks had to stand outside all night.

MAX: No.

HORST: Yes. We stood at attention all night long. Punishment.

MAX: What for?

HORST: Someone in our barracks killed himself.

MAX: A moslem?

HORST: Of course not. It doesn't mean anything if a moslem kills himself, but if a person who's still a person commits suicide, well…it's a kind of defiance, isn't it? They hate that—it's an act of free will.

MAX: I'm sorry.

HORST: Sure. Yellow star is sorry. [*Silence.*]

MAX: Heard a rumor.

HORST: What?

MAX: Sardines tonight.

HORST: I hate sardines! I hate all food. Scraps. Sardine scraps. That's all we get anyhow. Not worth eating. Didn't know you could have sardine scraps. [*Silence.*] I'm going crazy.

MAX: O.K. O.K. You're going crazy. I'm sorry. It's my fault.

HORST: What do you mean *your* fault?

MAX: For bringing you here. Because you make me feel so guilty. And you should. This job is the worst. I figured it wrong. I'm sorry.

HORST: I'm glad to be here.

MAX: Oh sure.

HORST: I am.

MAX: How can you be?

HORST: That's my secret. [*Pause.*]

[*Bell rings.* MAX *starts to move rocks.* HORST *remains still.*]

HORST: Maybe if I closed my eyes...
MAX: Heard a rumor.
HORST: What? [*Starts to move rocks.*]
MAX: We may get potatoes.
HORST: When?
MAX: Tomorrow.
HORST: I don't believe it.
MAX: They said so in my barracks.
HORST: Who's they?
MAX: Some guys.
HORST: Are they cute?
MAX: Cut it out.
HORST: You should be with us, where you belong.
MAX: No. But you shouldn't be *here.*
HORST: I want to be here.
MAX: Why would you want to be here — are you crazy?
HORST: Of course I'm crazy. I'm trying to tell you I'm crazy. And I want to be here.
MAX: Why?
HORST: Because. Because I love rocks. [*Pause.*] Because I love you. [*Silence.*] I do. I love you. When I'm not dreaming about rocks, I'm dreaming about you. For the past six weeks, I've dreamed about you. It helps me get up. It helps me make sure my bed is perfectly made so I'm not punished. It helps me eat the stinking food. It helps me put up with the constant fights in the barracks. Knowing I'll see you. At least out of the corner of my eyes. In passing. It's a reason to live. So I'm glad I'm here.

[MAX *is at one pile of rocks, moving them into symmetrical piles.*]

HORST: What are you doing?
MAX: Arranging these neatly. We've gotten sloppy. They can beat you for it. [*Silence.*] Don't love me.
HORST: It makes me happy. It doesn't harm anyone. It's my secret.
MAX: Don't love me.
HORST: It's my secret. And I have a signal. No one knows it. When I rub my left eyebrow at you, like this... [*Rubs his left eyebrow.*]... it means I

love you. Bet you didn't know that. I can even do it in front of the guards. No one knows. It's my secret. [*Starts to cough.*] It's cold. It was better hot. I don't like it cold.

MAX: Don't love me.

HORST: I can't help it.

MAX: I don't want anybody to love me.

HORST: That's tough.

MAX: I can't love anybody back.

HORST: Who's asking you to?

MAX: Queers aren't meant to love. I know. I thought I loved someone once. He worked in my father's factory. My father paid him to go away. He went. Queers aren't meant to love. They don't want us to. You know who loved me? That boy. That dancer. I don't remember his name. But I killed him. See—queers aren't meant to love. I'll kill you too. Hate me. That's better. Hate me. Don't love me.

[MAX *finishes arranging the rocks. He returns to moving the rocks.*

Silence.

HORST *starts to cough again.*]

MAX: Why are you coughing?

HORST: Because I like to.

MAX: Are you catching cold?

HORST: Probably. Up all night. In the wind.

MAX: Winter's coming.

HORST: I know. [*Silence.*] I just want to close my eyes…

MAX: Heard a rumor.

HORST: I don't care.

MAX: Don't you want to hear it?

HORST: Stuff your rumors. [*Coughs again. Slips. Drops the rock and falls to the ground.*]

MAX: Horst! [*Puts down his rock.*]

HORST: Shit. [MAX *starts toward him.*] Don't move! He's watching. The guard. Don't help me. If you help me, they'll kill you. Get back to your rock. Do you hear me, get back! [MAX *returns, picks up his rock, but stands looking at* HORST; HORST *is coughing—looks up at* MAX.] Move! [MAX *moves the rock.*] Right. I'm O.K. I'll get up. I'll get up. Don't ever help me. [*Pulls himself up.*] I'm up. It's O.K. [*Picks up his rock.*] These bloody things get heavier and heavier. [*Starts to move the rock.*] The guard was watching. He'd kill you if you helped me. Never notice. Never watch.

Remember? I love you. But I won't help you if *you* fall. Don't you dare help me. You don't even love me, so why are you going to help? We save *ourselves*. Do you understand? Do you?

MAX: Yes. I understand.

HORST: Promise me. Come on. Promise me. We save ourselves.

MAX: O.K.

HORST: Promise me!

MAX: YES!

HORST: You're a fool. I don't love you anymore. It was just a passing fancy. I love myself. Poor you, you don't love anybody. [*Silence.*] It's getting cold. Winter's coming. [*They walk, moving the rocks, in silence.*]

BLACKOUT

Scene IV

The same. Two months later.

MAX *and* HORST *are moving rocks. They wear jackets.* HORST *is slower than ever, as if dazed. He is holding the rocks with difficulty.*

HORST *has a coughing spell.*

MAX: You have a barracks leader. [HORST*'s coughing continues.*] He can get you medicine. [*Coughing continues.*] He can try to get you medicine. [*Coughing continues.*] You have to ask him. [*Coughing continues.*] You have to get help. [*Coughing continues.*] You have to stop coughing—damn it. [*The coughing spell slowly subsides.*]

HORST: It doesn't matter.

MAX: If you're nice to the kapo...

HORST: It doesn't matter.

MAX: Some sort of medicine.

HORST: What for? The cough? How about the hands?

MAX: I told you what to do. Exercise.

HORST: They're frostbitten.

MAX: So exercise.

HORST: It doesn't matter.

MAX: Every night, I move my fingers up and down, one at a time, for a half hour. I don't do push-ups anymore. Just fingers.

HORST: It doesn't matter.

MAX: You're losing weight.

HORST: I don't like sardines. [*Starts to cough again. It goes on for a minute, then subsides.*]

MAX: It's getting worse.

HORST: It's getting colder.

MAX: You need medicine.

HORST: Stop nagging me.

MAX: See your kapo.

HORST: He doesn't care.

MAX: Ask him.

HORST: He wants money.

MAX: Are you sure?

HORST: It doesn't matter.

MAX: I thought you cared about yourself.

HORST: You don't know anything.
MAX: I thought you loved yourself.
HORST: It's too cold.
MAX: You know what? [*Silence.*] You know what? You're turning into a moslem. I'm scared.
HORST: Who isn't.
MAX: For you.
HORST: Be scared for yourself.
MAX: Why don't you listen to me?
HORST: Moslems don't listen.
MAX: You're not a moslem.
HORST: You said I was.
MAX: I didn't mean it. You're not a moslem.
HORST: You're not a Jew.
MAX: Can't you ever forget that?
HORST: If I forget that...then...I am a moslem.

[*The bell rings.*

They both drop their rocks and stand at attention, side by side, looking straight ahead.]

HORST: Look, I'm just cold. My fingers are numb. I can't stop coughing. I hate food. That's all. Nothing special. Don't get upset.
MAX: I want you to care.
HORST: I would. If I was warm.
MAX: I'll warm you.
HORST: You can't.
MAX: I know how.
HORST: No. You don't.
MAX: I do. I'm terrific at it. You said so.
HORST: When?
MAX: I'm next to you.
HORST: Don't start.
MAX: I'll make love to you.
HORST: Not now.
MAX: Yes. Now.
HORST: I have a headache. I can't.
MAX: Don't joke. I'll make love to you.
HORST: No.
MAX: I'll make you warm. [*Pause.*]

HORST: You can't.
MAX: You'll feel the warm...
HORST: I can't.
MAX: You'll *feel* it. [*Pause.*]
HORST: In my fingers?
MAX: All over.
HORST: I can't.
MAX: I'm kissing your fingers.
HORST: They're numb.
MAX: My mouth is hot.
HORST: They're cold.
MAX: My mouth is on fire.
HORST: My fingers...
MAX: Are getting warm.
HORST: Are they?
MAX: They're getting warm.
HORST: I can't tell.
MAX: They're getting warm.
HORST: A little.
MAX: They're getting warm.
HORST: Yes.
MAX: My mouth is on fire. Your fingers are on fire. Your body's on fire.
HORST: Yes.
MAX: My mouth is all over you.
HORST: Yes.
MAX: My mouth is on your chest...
HORST: Yes.
MAX: Kissing your chest.
HORST: Yes.
MAX: Making it warm.
HORST: Yes.
MAX: Biting your nipple.
HORST: Yes.
MAX: Biting...into it...
HORST: Yes.
MAX: Harder...harder...harder...
HORST: Hold it! That hurts!
MAX: Harder...
HORST: No, hold it. I'm serious. You're hurting me. [*A pause.* MAX *catches his breath.*]

Max: You pulled away.

Horst: Damn right.

Max: It was exciting.

Horst: For *you* maybe. I don't try to hurt you.

Max: I like being hurt. It's exciting.

Horst: It's not. Not when you're rough.

Max: I'm not being rough.

Horst: Yes you are. Sometimes you are.

Max: O.K. So what? It's exciting.

Horst: Why'd you have to spoil it? You were making me warm. Why can't you be gentle?

Max: I am.

Horst: You're not. You try to hurt me. You make me warm, and then you hurt me. I hurt enough. I don't want to feel more pain. Why can't you be gentle?

Max: I am.

Horst: No you're not. You're like them. You're like the Gestapo. You're like the guards. We stopped being gentle. I watched it, when we were on the outside. People made pain and called it love. I don't want to be like that. You don't make love to hurt.

Max: I wanted to make you warm. That's all I wanted. I can't do anything right. I don't understand you. I used to do things right.

Horst: You still can.

Max: People liked it when I got rough. Most. Not everybody. He didn't.

Horst: Who?

Max: The dancer. But everyone else did. Just a little rough.

Horst: Did you like it?

Max: I don't remember. I could never remember. I was always drunk. There was always coke. Nothing seemed to matter that much.

Horst: Some things do matter.

Max: Not to you.

Horst: They do.

Max: I don't understand you. All day long you've been saying nothing matters...your cough, your fingers...

Horst: They matter.

Max: I don't understand anything anymore.

Horst: They matter. I'm not a moslem. You're not a Jew. My fingers are cold.

Max: I want you to be happy.

Horst: Is that true?

MAX: I think so. I don't know. [*Pause.*] Yes.
HORST: Then be gentle with me.
MAX: I don't know how.
HORST: Just hold me.
MAX: I'm afraid to hold you.
HORST: Don't be.
MAX: I'm afraid.
HORST: Don't be.
MAX: I'm going to drown.
HORST: Hold me. Please. Hold me.
MAX: O.K. I'm holding you.
HORST: Are you?
MAX: Yes. You're in my arms.
HORST: Am I?
MAX: You're here in my arms. I promise. I'm holding you. You're here...
HORST: Touch me.
MAX: No.
HORST: Gently...
MAX: Here.
HORST: Are you?
MAX: Yes. Touching. Softly... I'm touching you softly... gently... You're safe... I'll keep you safe... and warm... You're with me now... You'll never be cold again... I'm holding you now... safe... and warm... As long as you're here, as long as you're with me, as long as I'm holding you, you're safe...

BLACKOUT

Scene V

The same. Three days later.

MAX *is moving rocks.* HORST *is putting the rock pile into neat order.*

HORST: The air is fresh today. Clean.

> [MAX *hands* HORST *a needle and a thread as he passes the rock pile.*
>
> HORST *starts to cough — continues coughing — then stops.*]

MAX: It sounds better.
HORST: It does.
MAX: Loosening up.
HORST: It is.
MAX: The medicine is helping.
HORST: Yes. [*Silence.*] Thank you. [*Silence.*] Why don't you tell me.
MAX: Tell you what?
HORST: How you got it.
MAX: Told you. Spoke to my barracks leader. He took me to an officer.
HORST: Which one?
MAX: Some captain. The new one.
HORST: He's rotten.
MAX: You know him?
HORST: I've heard about him. You gave him money?
MAX: Yes.
HORST: I don't believe you.
MAX: Why?
HORST: You don't have any money.
MAX: Why don't you ever believe me?
HORST: Because I can tell when you're lying. You think you're so terrific at it. You're not. Your voice changes.
MAX: It *what?*
HORST: Changes. Sounds different.
MAX: Bullshit.

> [*Silence.*]

MAX: Hey . . . Guess who I saw?
HORST: Where?
MAX: In my barracks.

HORST: Marlene Dietrich.

MAX: No. My landlord. From Berlin. Rosen.

HORST: Oh.

MAX: Nice man.

HORST: I thought you hated him.

MAX: Sure, I used to think he was what I was supposed to think he was.

HORST: What was that?

MAX: A lousy Jew.

HORST: He probably thought you were a lousy queer.

MAX: Probably.

HORST: Now he thinks you're not a queer. He must be very confused. It's a shame.

MAX: It's not a shame. Don't start in. [HORST *has a coughing spell.*] You *are* taking the medicine?

HORST: [*The coughing subsides.*] Of course I am. [*Silence.*] Of course I am. Max. I'm glad you got it.

MAX: So am I. [*Silence.*]

HORST: Wish I knew how, though.

MAX: I told you.

HORST: You're a liar. [*Silence.*]

MAX: I never met anyone like you. Can't make you believe anything.

HORST: How'd you get it?

MAX: Won't just be grateful.

HORST: Am I ever?

MAX: Suppose you don't like the answer.

HORST: I'll chance it.

MAX: Then when I tell you, you'll nag me about *that.*

HORST: You chance it.

MAX: I went down on him.

HORST: What?

MAX: I told you you wouldn't like it.

HORST: That SS captain?

MAX: Uh-huh.

HORST: He's the worst bastard in the —

MAX: I know.

HORST: You went down on him?

MAX: I had to. I didn't have any money.

HORST: You touched him?

MAX: No. I just went down on him. That's what he wanted. And I needed the medicine.

HORST: I'd rather cough.

MAX: No you wouldn't.

HORST: Is he queer?

MAX: Who knows? Just horny maybe. Sure, he could be queer. You don't like to think about that, do you? You don't want *them* to be queer. [*Silence.*]

HORST: I guess not. Well... what the hell. There *are* queer Nazis. And queer saints. And queer mediocrities. Just people. I really believe that. That's why I signed Hirschfeld's petition. That's why I ended up here. That's why I'm wearing this triangle. That's why you should be wearing it.

MAX: Do you think that ss bastard would let a queer go down on him? Of course not. He'd kill me if he knew I was queer. My yellow star got your medicine.

HORST: Who needs it?

MAX: Then give it back. Throw it away. Throw it away, why don't you? And die. I'm tired of being told I should have a pink triangle.

HORST: He remember you?

MAX: Who?

HORST: Rosen?

MAX: Yes. He said I owed him rent.

HORST: What's Berlin like? Did he say?

MAX: Worse.

HORST: I miss it.

MAX: Yes. [*Pause.*]

MAX: Greta's Club?

HORST: No.

MAX: Good. You had taste. The White Mouse?

HORST: Sometimes.

MAX: Surprised you never saw me.

HORST: What were you wearing?

MAX: Things that came off. I was conspicuous.

HORST: Why?

MAX: Because I was always making a fool of myself. Did you sunbathe?

HORST: I loved to sunbathe.

MAX: By the river.

HORST: Sure.

MAX: And you *never* saw me?

HORST: Well, actually, I did. I saw you by the river. You were making a fool of yourself. And I said, someday I'll be at Dachau with that man, moving rocks.

MAX: I didn't like Berlin. Always scared. But I like it now. I miss it.

HORST: [*Finishes straightening the rocks and resumes moving the rocks.*] We'll go back someday.

MAX: When we get out of here?

HORST: Yes.

MAX: We will, won't we?

HORST: We have to. Don't we?

MAX: Yes. Horst?

HORST: What?

MAX: We can go back together.

[*An SS* CAPTAIN *enters. The* GUARD *is with him.* MAX *and* HORST *look up for a second, then continue with their task.*

The CAPTAIN *stares at* MAX *for a long time, then* HORST, *then* MAX *again.*]

CAPTAIN: [*To* MAX] You. Jew.

MAX: [*Stands still.*] Yes sir?

CAPTAIN: Feeling better?

MAX: Sir?

CAPTAIN: Your cold?

MAX: Yes sir.

CAPTAIN: Remarkable.

MAX: Yes sir.

CAPTAIN: You seem so strong.

MAX: Yes sir.

CAPTAIN: Not sick at all.

MAX: No sir.

CAPTAIN: No?

MAX: Not now, sir.

CAPTAIN: Carry on.

[MAX *resumes moving rocks. The* CAPTAIN *watches* MAX *and* HORST. *He paces up and down.* MAX *and* HORST *move the rocks. The* CAPTAIN *paces.* HORST *coughs. He catches himself and tries to stifle it.*]

CAPTAIN: Ah. [HORST *stops the cough.*] You. Pervert.

HORST: [*Stiffens, stands still.*] Yes sir?

CAPTAIN: Are you ill?

HORST: No sir.

CAPTAIN: You have a cough.

HORST: No sir.
CAPTAIN: I heard you cough.
HORST: Yes sir.
CAPTAIN: Some thing caught in your throat?
HORST: Yes sir.
CAPTAIN: From breakfast?
HORST: Yes sir.
CAPTAIN: Ah. Carry on.

[HORST *resumes his work.* MAX *and* HORST *move the rocks. The* CAPTAIN *stands watching them. He takes out a cigarette. The* GUARD *lights it. The* CAPTAIN *smokes the cigarette and watches* MAX *and* HORST.

MAX *and* HORST *continue moving rocks.* HORST *coughs again, attempting to strangle it, but the cough comes through.*]

CAPTAIN: You. Pervert.
HORST: [*Stands still.*] Yes sir.
CAPTAIN: You coughed.
HORST: Yes sir.
CAPTAIN: You're not well.
HORST: I am, sir.
CAPTAIN: I see. [*To* MAX] You. Jew.
MAX: [*Stands still.*] Yes sir.
CAPTAIN: Watch.
MAX: Watch, sir?
CAPTAIN: Yes. Watch. [*To* HORST] You.
HORST: Yes sir.
CAPTAIN: Put down that rock.
HORST: Yes sir. [*Puts down the rock.*]
CAPTAIN: Good. Now take off your hat. [*A long pause.*]
HORST: My hat, sir?
CAPTAIN: Yes. Your hat.
HORST: My hat, sir?
CAPTAIN: Your hat.
HORST: Yes sir. [HORST *removes his hat.* MAX's *hand moves.* HORST *shoots him a warning stare.*]
CAPTAIN: [*To* MAX] You.
MAX: Yes sir.
CAPTAIN: Relax.
MAX: Yes sir.

CAPTAIN: And watch.

MAX: Yes sir.

CAPTAIN: [*To* HORST] You.

HORST: Yes sir.

CAPTAIN: Throw your hat away. [HORST *flings his hat on the ground.*] Not there.

HORST: Not there, sir?

CAPTAIN: No. Pick it up.

HORST: Yes sir. [*Picks up his hat.*]

CAPTAIN: Throw it on the fence.

HORST: The fence, sir?

CAPTAIN: The fence. [HORST *starts to cough.*] That's all right. We'll wait. [*The cough subsides.*] Are you better?

HORST: Yes sir.

CAPTAIN: Nasty cough.

HORST: Yes sir.

CAPTAIN: On the fence. Now.

HORST: On the fence. Yes sir. [HORST *glances at* MAX, *another warning stare, then throws his hat on the fence. The fence sparks.*]

CAPTAIN: [*To* MAX] You.

MAX: Yes sir.

CAPTAIN: Are you watching?

MAX: Yes sir.

CAPTAIN: Good. [*To* HORST] You.

HORST: Yes sir.

CAPTAIN: Get your hat. [*The* CAPTAIN *motions to the* GUARD. *The* GUARD *points his rifle at* HORST.]

HORST: Now, sir?

CAPTAIN: Now.

HORST: Are you sure, sir?

CAPTAIN: Quite.

HORST: Could I do without my hat, sir?

CAPTAIN: No.

HORST: [*Is silent for a moment. Feels* MAX *watching and gives him another quick glance, his eyes saying, don't move. Turns to the* CAPTAIN.] Yes sir.

[HORST *looks at* MAX. *He takes his hand and rubs his left eyebrow.*

He turns and stares at the CAPTAIN. *The* CAPTAIN *waits. The* GUARD *is pointing his rifle.*

HORST *turns toward the fence. He starts to walk very slowly to his hat. He almost reaches the fence, when, suddenly—*

He turns and rushes at the CAPTAIN. *He screams in fury.*

The GUARD *shoots* HORST. HORST *continues to lunge at the* CAPTAIN. *His hand is out. He scratches the* CAPTAIN'*s face.*

The GUARD *shoots* HORST *in the back. He falls, dead.*

Silence.

The CAPTAIN *holds his face.*]

CAPTAIN: He scratched me. [*To* MAX] You. Jew. [MAX *is silent.*] You!
MAX: Yes sir.
CAPTAIN: I hope the medicine helped. [*Turns to leave, turns back.*] Get rid of the body. [*Silence.*]
MAX: Yes sir.

[*The* CAPTAIN *leaves. The* GUARD *points the rifle at* MAX, *lowers it, then walks off, after the* CAPTAIN.

MAX *stares at* HORST.

Silence.

MAX *opens his mouth to cry out. He can't.*

Silence.

MAX *walks to* HORST'*s body. He tries to lift it. It is heavy. He manages to pull the body partly up,* HORST'*s head resting against* MAX'*s chest. He looks away. He takes* HORST, *feet dragging on the ground, toward the pit.*

The bell rings.]

MAX: No! [*He looks up—off—at the* GUARD, *then back at* HORST. *He stands at attention.* HORST *starts to fall.* MAX *pulls him up. He stands still, staring in front of him, holding on to* HORST.] It's O.K. I won't drop you. I'll hold you. If I stand at attention, I can hold you. They'll let me hold you. I won't let you down. [*Silence.*] I never held you before. [*Silence.*] You don't have to worry about the rocks. I'll do yours, too. I'll move twice as many each day. I'll do yours, too. You don't have to worry about them. [*Silence.*] You know what? [*Silence.*] Horst? [*Silence.*] You know what? [*Silence.*] I think . . . [*Silence.*] I think I love you. [*Silence.*] Shh!

Don't tell anyone. I think I loved...I can't remember his name. A dancer. I think I loved him, too. Don't be jealous. I think I loved... some boy a long time ago. In my father's factory. Hans. That was his name. But the dancer. I don't remember. [*Silence.*] I love you. [*Silence.*] What's wrong with that? [*Silence.*] What's wrong with that?

[*He starts to cry.*

The bell rings.

He drags HORST*'s body to the pit. He throws it in the pit.*

He turns and looks at the rocks. He takes a deep breath.

He walks over the rocks and picks one up. He moves it across to the other side. He takes another deep breath. He stands still.]

MAX: One. Two. Three. Four. Five. [*Takes another deep breath.*] Six. Seven. Eight. Nine. Ten.

[*He picks up a rock. He moves it across to the other side.*

He moves another rock.

He moves another rock.

He moves another rock.

He pauses. He takes a deep breath.

He moves another rock.

He moves another rock.

He stops. He tries to take another deep breath. He can't. His hand is trembling. He steadies his hand. He picks up another rock and starts to move it.

He stops. He drops the rock. He moves toward the pit.

He jumps into the pit.

He disappears.

A long pause.

MAX *climbs out of the pit.* MAX *holds* HORST*'s jacket with the pink triangle on it. Puts the jacket on.*

MAX *turns and looks at the fence.*]

MAX *walks into the fence.*

The fence lights up. It grows brighter and brighter, until the light consumes the stage.

And blinds the audience.]

End of Act Two

Background Information
Events leading to the Nazi persecution of homosexuals and the atrocities of the concentration camps

1871   King Wilhelm established the Second Reich and adopted the Bavarian code. Paragraph 175 of this code outlawed "lewd and unnatural behaviour," prescribing prison sentences ranging from one day to five years.

1897   Adolf Brand, Magnus Hirschfeld and Max Spohr established the first Gay Rights organization—the Scientific Humanitarian Committee.

1898   A petition of 900 signatures was submitted to the Reichstag demanding the repeal of Paragraph 175. The petition failed. More petitions were submitted throughout the next ten years.

1910   The Government proposed outlawing Lesbian acts.

The bill failed to pass.

1919   Hirschfeld opened the Institute for Sexual Science in Berlin.

1920   Hirschfeld (Jewish as well as homosexual) was attacked by Anti-Semites in Munich. Later in the same year he was attacked by Nazis and left on the pavement with a fractured skull.

1921   Eros Theatre, the first homosexual theatre, was started by Bruno Mattusek in Berlin. The SA, Storm troopers, the original Nazi paramilitary organization was founded.

1923   Fascists shot and wounded several members of an audience for Hirschfeld's first pro-homosexual film *Different from the Others* in Vienna.

1925   Reconstruction of the National Socialist Workers Party (the official title of the Nazi party).

Summer: Formation of the first SS units.

Ernst Röhm, one of Adolf Hitler's chief advisers, and a homosexual, pressed charges against a 17 year old hustler who had robbed him the 'morning after.'

1928   The National Socialist Party issued their official view of homosexuals on May 14th: "It is not necessary that you and I live, but it is necessary that the German people live. And it can live if it can fight, for life means fighting. And it can only fight if it maintains its masculinity. It can only maintain its masculinity if it exercises discipline, especially in the matters of love. Free love and deviance are undisciplined. Therefore, we reject you, as we reject anything which hurts our people. Anyone who even thinks of homosexual love is our enemy."

Reichstag Committee, by a vote of 15 to 13, approved the Penal Reform Bill which abolished all homosexual crimes.

1929   The Stock Market crashed.

Penal Reform Bill set aside before taking effect.

The Nazis were swept to power.

1930   Ernst Röhm made head of Storm troopers.

1933   *January*: Hitler becomes Reich Chancellor.

March: Dachau concentration camp set up.

April: Formation of the Gestapo (secret state police), Berlin. Hirschfeld's Institute of Sexual Science ransacked by Nazis.

1934   *June*: *The Night of the Long Knives*: Röhm shot dead. Hitler issued an order to purge all homosexuals from the Army, 200 SA leaders were rounded up in Berlin and massacred. *July*: Gay Rights activist Kurt Hiller was arrested and sent to Oranienburg concentration camp.

A law was passed condoning, the sterilization of all homosexuals, schizophrenics, epileptics, drug addicts, hysterics and those born blind or malformed. By 1935, 56,000 people had been thus 'treated'.

In actual practice, the homosexuals were literally castrated rather than sterilized. All activities of Hirschfeld's League of Human Rights were banned, and the homosexual movement was crushed.

1935 On the first anniversary of the Röhm Putsch, Paragraph 175 was revised: ten possible homosexual 'acts' were punishable, including a kiss, an embrace and even homosexual fantasies.

1936 Excerpt from the speech by Heinrich Himmler: "In our judgment of homosexuality—a symptom of degeneracy which could destroy our race—we must return to the guiding Nordic principles 'extermination of degenerates'" "Protective custody"—internment in concentration camps—begins for civilian offenders, including homosexuals. The early concentration camps were detention centers: they were turned into extermination camps after 1940.

It is estimated that between a quarter and half a million homosexuals died in the concentration camps. The exact figure is not known because the Allies retained Paragraph 175A as a functioning law. A pink triangle surviving the war could not reveal why he had been incarcerated—it was still against the law and he could be returned to prison. The law was abolished in 1969, but the courts ruled that imprisoned homosexuals were still to be considered criminal and not political inmates, and thus were not entitled to restitution.

As Is

William Hoffman

In memory of

R.A.
S.A.
Fortunato Arico
M.B.
Michael Baseleon
Francis Brady
Stephen Buker
Phil Carey
Gregory Y. Connell
Daniel Corcoran
Wilfredo Davilla
Arthur Ellenbogen
Bill Elliot
Tom Ellis
Timothy Farrell
Christian Fincke
Neil Flanagan
George Harris
Mark Johnson
Charles Ludlam
Ed Lynch
André Mathis
J. J. Mitchell
John Murphy
Pierre Murue
Arthur Naftal
Stephen Pender
Glenn Person
Russell Redmond
L.S.
Tony Serchio
Giulio Sorrentino
Larry Stanton
David Summers
Rick Wadsworth
Larry Waurin
Stuart White

Special thanks

Jerry Vezzuso, Beth Allen, Nestor Almendros, John Bishop, George Boyd, Victor Bumbalo, John Corigliano, David Courier, Penny Dashinger, Barry Davidson, East End Gay Organization, Gay Men's Health Crisis, Barbara Grandé-LeVine, Jay Harris, Stephen Harvey, Joel Honig, Reed Jones, Daniel Irvine, David Kapihe, Robert Kubera, Rodger McFarlane, Terrence McNally, Barbara Myers, Claris Nelson, Constance Mary O'Toole, Kent Paul, Candida Scott Piel, David Richardson, Luis Sanjurjo, Mary Scarborough, June Stein, Paul Theobald, Dr. Kenneth Unger, Tobin Wheeler, Lanford Wilson, the New York Foundation for the Arts, Albert Poland, and Marshall W. Mason.

As It Was

"It must be the combination of quiche and leather," I think I joked to a friend over the phone the first time I heard about the mysterious new disease attacking gay men. It was 1980, '81, I'm not sure. I think it was early spring and I was sitting in my office, drinking my first decaffeinated espresso of the morning. I had just finished reading the previous days *New York Times*. I like to have my news a little stale so I don't get too alarmed at the state of the world. I told my friend the article was absurd: a disease capable of distinguishing between homo- and heterosexual men? Come on.

At the time, I was in the midst of writing Act One of the libretto to *A Figaro for Antonia*, which the Metropolitan Opera had commissioned, and when I wasn't writing I was jogging. So, for a period, I was totally immersed in work. When I came back up for air it registered that my roommate's best friend, Tim, was dying in a hospital in San Francisco. He had a pneumonia that antibiotics couldn't touch, and wild viral infections of the brain. He finally fell into a coma and succumbed.

But was it really surprising, I asked myself, that Tim would get ill? A terrific person, generous, funny, warm, but definitely in the fast lane. And when Freddy went into the hospital I told myself that he had been looking for trouble: I mean, he practically lived at the gay bathhouses. People like me were not going to come down with AIDS. I wasn't going to the baths. I didn't drink or take drugs. And I was running twenty to thirty miles a week. I felt invulnerable.

And then Larry took sick: mild ailments that wouldn't clear up, not bothersome enough to stop him from running the marathon faster than I could conceive of doing. Larry was younger than I, and he didn't drink or take drugs. A few months later he died.

And then Brian, who lived over in the East Village. And then George, the kid from the early Caffe Cino days of Off Off Broadway. And then Freddy the cellist. And then that guy who ran the flower shop on Sixth—what was his name?

I was busy writing a comic opera as daily the news got worse. My close friend, Stephen came down with a chronic case of swollen glands, which was labeled an "AIDS-related complex." It seemed as if the disease were closing in on me personally. I was reminded of the pre-Salk-vaccine polio epidemic of my childhood, when you avoided movie theaters and swimming pools. I remembered Wally, the boy upstairs who liked to bully me, until infantile paralysis made him weak and stupid, and I remembered classmates who suddenly stopped coming to school.

But during the polio epidemic, as during the Tylenol and Legionnaire's Disease scares, the media and the government committed themselves whole-heartedly to the side of the victims. In the early eighties, with few exceptions, the main concern of people outside the gay community was reassuring themselves that it was only happening to "them," and not to "us." I felt isolated from society in a way I never had before.

As the mortality figures mounted, and as I heard stories of people with AIDS being abandoned by friends and families, mistreated by health workers, and evicted from apartments (in one case being thrown from a window), stories of the Holocaust came to my mind. Most of my family in Europe had perished during the war. As far as I know they never made it to the concentration camps, but were murdered on the street by their Polish and Latvian neighbors. I knew intellectually that the epidemic was *not* the Holocaust, but I had no other experience of mass death and public indifference and brutality to compare it with.

I was writing about the rebellion of Figaro and the tragedy of Marie Antoinette when I learned that my favorite uncle, Wolf, had cancer. And my father was not recovering from his stroke as fully as I had hoped. All around me there was illness and death. I fell into a depression.

So, sometime in 1982, as a sort of a therapy, I started to express my feelings on paper. I decided to write a play about a man named Rich—a writer and runner—who comes down with AIDS; his former lover, Saul; and their friends and families.

I did my research. I visited friends who had the disease; I talked with a hospice worker; I went to support groups; I attended lectures; I made field trips to the Gay Men's Health Crisis (the most important organization dealing with the disease in New York City); I spent hours eavesdropping in gay bars, taking the public pulse.

I was willing to go to any lengths for my play, except to imagine myself having AIDS. I was not afraid of contracting the disease through casual physical contact with those who had it. I was well aware that AIDS is transmitted only by an exchange of body fluids. But on a deep irrational level, I was terrified of catching it by identifying with those who had it.

Consequently, for a long period, my central characters, Rich and Saul, were shadowy and undeveloped, compared with the background figures. But one day I realized the depth of my fear and asked God to protect me as I wrote the play. He did.

All along my characters cracked jokes, which I tried to suppress. People were in the process of expiring, and here I was laughing. I mean, this was supposed to be a *serious* play. Well, I had to do something to keep my spirits up, I rationalized.

Half hoping to depress myself, I'd call up my uncle, and to my chagrin he'd make me smile with some reminiscence of the Yiddish theater. (He was a playwright and poet, like me.) And my father was always eager for a joke, the dirtier the better—and he was in his eighties.

I was having dinner with my friend Constance Mary O'Toole, who was a hospice worker at St. Vincent's Hospital in Greenwich Village, in the heart of New York's gay community, when it finally dawned on me that maybe humor was a key to my play. She said, "We tell a lot of jokes in my line of work." I also began to realize that among the people with AIDS that I was meeting, those with a sense of humor were doing better than those without.

I permitted the play to be funny. I found that audiences at the Circle Repertory Company, where I was workshopping sections of the piece as I wrote them, responded to the humor. It enabled them to accept the pain of the sadder material.

Encouraged by my director Marshall W. Mason and producer John Glines, I also allowed the spirit of *A Figaro for Antonia* to infiltrate *As Is*. I asked myself, "Why should I write a totally realistic play, when I take extravagant liberties with time and space in musical theater? Why can't I allow my characters to speak eloquently, when I'm planning to let them do that at the Met?"

By the time we moved from our Off Broadway home at the Circle Rep to the Lyceum Theater on Broadway, the good humor and the good spirits of some of the people with AIDS that I had met, their lovers and families, people like Connie O'Toole, and my family (my father and uncle died in 1984) had completely subverted the depression that prompted the writing of the play.

Facing my own worst fears has made me feel...What do I feel now? Sad at the loss of friends. Frustrated by my powerlessness over a force of nature. Angry at those who have the power to help and won't. But I'm pretty comfortable with people who have AIDS. I'm sane on the subject of my own health. And when I'm frightened in this time of trouble, I'm loving to myself.

—William M. Hoffman

Lou Liberatore (Pat), Jonathan Hogan (Rich), Lily Knight (Lily), Ken Kliban (Brother), and Mark Myers (Clone) in *As Is*, at the Lyceum Theatre, 1985. (Photograph reprinted with permission from the John Willis Theatre World/ Screen World Archive.)

Jonathan Hogan (Rich), Jonathan Hadary (Saul), and Lily Knight (Lily) in *As Is*, at the Lyceum Theatre, 1985. (Photograph reprinted with permission from the John Willis Theatre World/Screen World Archive.)

As Is was developed in the Circle Repertory Company playwrighting and directing workshops under the leadership of Daniel Irvine. It was directed by George Boyd.

As Is was presented Off Broadway at The Circle Repertory Company on Wednesday, February 27, 1985. It was produced by The Circle Repertory Company and The Glines. The director was Marshall Mason, the set was by David Potts, and the lighting was by Dennis Parichy. The costumes were by Michael Warren Powell, the associate director was George Boyd, the sound was by Chuck London Media/Stuart Werner, and the stage manager was Fred Reinglas.

Cast

Hospice Worker, Business Partner, Nurse	Claris Erickson
Chet	Steven Gregan
Saul	Jonathan Hadary
Rich	Jonathan Hogan
Brother/Barney	Ken Kliban
Lily	Lily Knight
Clone/Pat/Orderly	Lou Liberatore
Clone	Mark Myers

As Is transferred to the Lyceum Theatre on Broadway on Friday, April 26, 1985 and opened on Wednesday, May 1, 1985. It was produced by The Circle Repertory Company, John Glines/Lawrence Lane, Lucille Lortel, and The Shubert Organization (Gerald Schoenfeld, Chairman; Bernard Jacobs, President). The set was by David Potts, the lighting was by Dennis Parichy, and the costumes were by Michael Warren Powell. The associate director was George Boyd, the sound was by Chuck London Media/Stuart Werner, the associate producer was Paul A. Kaplan, the general manager was Albert Poland, the company manager was Claire Abel, the wardrobe was by Joan E. Weiss, and the hairstylist was Patrik D. Moreton. Casting was by Eve Battaglia, the stage manager was Denise Yaney, and the press was by Betty Lee Hunt/Maria Cristina Pucci.

Cast

Hospice Worker . . . . Claris Erickson
Rich . . . . Jonathan Hogan
Saul . . . . Jonathan Hadary
Chet . ♠ . . . . Steven Gregan
Lily . . . . Lily Knight
Brother . . . . Ken Kliban
Business Partner . . . . Claris Erickson
Clones . . . . Mark Myers
                                                   Lou Liberatore
Pat . . . . Lou Liberatore
Barney . . . . Ken Kliban
Nurse . . . . Claris Erickson
Orderly . . . . Lou Liberatore

STANDBYS:

Hospice Worker, Lily, Nurse . . . . Patricia Fletcher
Saul, Chet . . . . Reed Jones
Rich, Brother, Barney, Pat, Orderly . . . . Bruce McCarty

ALSO: Doctors, TV Commentator (Prerecorded), Average People, Drug Dealers and Customers

A note on the text: The present script is from the June 1987 revival at the Circle Repertory Company, directed by Michael Warren Powell.

Production note

In approaching the original production of *As Is*, I felt it was important to find a visual stage life for the play that permitted the freedom of time and place that the text suggests. David Potts, the designer, and I came up with an open stage that suggested simultaneously the stature of the classical Greek theater and the frankness of Brecht and still allowed the audience, with a little imagination, to see the realistic studio apartment of a New York photographer. I feel it is important that the actors remain on stage as much as possible, to witness as a community the events of the play in which they do not participate as characters. The audience must be kept from feeling "safe" from this subject, so the actors of the "chorus" must act as a bridge between the fictional characters and the real theater event, and also as an unconventional kind of "threat"—keeping the audience aware that entertaining as the play may be, its subject is deadly. The desired effect is to assist the audience in a catharsis, as they are required to contemplate our common mortality.

—Marshall W. Mason

The "Red Death" had long devastated the country. No pestilence had ever been so fatal, or so hideous... The scarlet stains upon the body... were the pest ban which shut the victim out from the sympathy of his fellow-men... But the Prince Prospero was happy and dauntless and sagacious. When his dominions were half depopulated, he summoned to his presence a thousand hale and light-hearted friends... and with these retired to the deep seclusion of one of his castellated abbeys... A strong and lofty wall girdled it in. The wall had gates of iron. The courtiers brought furnaces and massy hammers and welded the bolts... With such precautions the courtiers might bid defiance to contagion. In the meantime it was folly to grieve, or to think. The Prince had provided all the appliances of pleasure. There were buffoons, there were improvisatori, there were ballet-dancers, there were musicians, there was Beauty, there was wine. All these and security were within. Without was the "Red Death."

—Edgar Allan Poe, *The Masque of the Red Death*

My tale was heard, and yet it was not told;
My fruit is fallen, and yet my leaves are green;
My youth is spent, and yet I am not old;
I saw the world, and yet I was not seen;
My thread is cut, and yet it is not spun;
And now I live, and now my life is done.

—Chidiock Tichborne, "Elegy"

Characters

SAUL

RICH

Depending on the budget and the skills and aptitudes of the performers, at least four other men and two women play the following:

HOSPICE WORKER

CHET

BROTHER

BUSINESS PARTNER

LILY

TV ANNOUNCER (Prerecorded)

DOCTORS (5)

BARTENDER

PICKUPS (2)

MARTY

VINNIE

CLONES (3)

PEOPLE WITH AIDS (4)

AVERAGE PEOPLE (6)

HOTLINE COUNSELORS (2)

NURSE

HOSPITAL WORKER

DRUG DEALERS and CUSTOMERS (5)

Except for short exits, the actors remain onstage for the whole play. There is no intermission.

Time: *The present.*
Setting: *New York City.*

Stage right is SAUL's *fashionable loft space, suggested by a sofa, Barcelona chair, bench, and area rug. Upstage center is a bar; stage left, a bench.*

The HOSPICE WORKER, *a dowdy middle-aged woman, walks downstage center and addresses the audience.*

HOSPICE WORKER: Mother Superior always used to say, "Watch out for the religious cranks, Sister Veronica." When I started working for the hospice I had a touch of the crank about me. I think maybe that's why they gave me the old heave-ho from the convent. But I've kept my vow of chastity and I've made a pilgrimage to Lourdes.

My job is to ease the way for those who are dying. I've done this for the last couple of years. I work mainly here at St. Vincent's. During the day I have a boring secretarial job, which is how I support my career as a saint.

I was much more idealistic when I started. I had just left the convent. I guess I thought working with the dying would give me spiritual gold stars. I thought I'd be able to impart my great wisdom to those in need of improvement. I wanted to bear witness to dramatic deathbed conversions, see shafts of light emanating from heaven, multicolored auras hovering above the heads of those in the process of expiring. I always imagined they would go out expressing their gratitude for all I had done.

A quick joke: Did you hear about the man who lost his left side? He's all *right* now. All right now. [*She laughs.*] We tell a lot of jokes in my line of work. [*She takes her seat. Lights come up on two casually dressed men in their thirties seated in the living area.*]

RICH: You take Henry.
SAUL: Cut him in half.
RICH: You can keep him.
SAUL: What are we going to do about him?
RICH: I said he's yours.
SAUL: You found him.
RICH: I don't want him.
SAUL: Chet doesn't like cats?
RICH: I knew this would happen. Don't start in.
SAUL: We gotta get things settled.

RICH: Then let's. How 'bout if we simplify things: sell everything and split the cash.

SAUL: Even the cobalt glass?

RICH: Yes.

SAUL: And Aunt Billie's hooked rug? Say, how's she doing?

RICH: She's on medication. Sell the rug.

SAUL: I will not sell the manikin heads. I don't care what you say.

RICH: Then take them.

SAUL: And the chromium lamp? I love that lamp.

RICH: Take it.

SAUL: And the Barcelona chair?

RICH: The Barcelona chair is *mine!* [*Beat.*] Fuck it. Take it. Take everything. I won't be Jewish about it. [*He rises to go.*]

SAUL: Why didn't you warn me we were going to play Christians and Jews today? I would have worn my yellow star.

RICH: I've gotta go. [RICH *is leaving.*]

SAUL: Where're you going?

RICH: I'm not feeling so hot. Let's make it another day.

SAUL: [*blocking his way*] Sit down.

RICH: [*pushing his hand away*] Don't push me.

SAUL: Sorry. I don't like this any more than you, but we gotta do it. It's been six months. [*Lightening things up.*] A divorce is not final until the property settlement.

RICH: Saul . . . ? [*He's about to say something important.*]

SAUL: What, Rich? [*He waits expectantly.*] What?

RICH: Never mind.

SAUL: What? . . . What? . . . You always do that!

RICH: I want the chair.

SAUL: You can have the fucking Barcelona chair if Chet wants it so bad! . . . What about the paintings? Do you want to sell the Paul Cadmus?

RICH: Yes.

SAUL: You love the Cadmus. [*Silence.*] And who's going to buy the Burgess drawings? Did you hear that Kenny had a heart attack?

RICH: We'll donate them to the Metropolitan.

SAUL: Just what they always wanted: the world's largest collection of Magic Marker hustler portraits. [RICH *nods.*]

RICH: They're yours.

SAUL: But you commissioned them. We'll split them up: I get the blonds and you get the blacks — or vice versa.

RICH: All yours.

SAUL: Then you get the Mickey Mouse collection.

RICH: Sell it.

SAUL: You don't sell collectibles. Not right now. What's with this money
    mania? Between the book and the catering, I thought you were
    doing well.

RICH: I want to build a swimming pool.

SAUL: You don't swim.

RICH: I want a Mercedes.

SAUL: You don't drive. Its Chet—he'll bankrupt you! [*Beat.*] I don't believe
    I said that... [*Sincerely.*] Your book is beautiful.

RICH: I never thanked you for the cover photograph.

SAUL: [*shrugging off the compliment*] How's it selling?

RICH: Not bad—for short stories. Everyone mentions your photo. Ed
    White said—

SAUL: Your book is terrific. Really.

RICH: I'm glad you like it.

SAUL: One minor thing.

RICH: What's that?

SAUL: I thought the dedication was a bit much.

RICH: Why are you doing this?

SAUL: Don't you think quoting Cavafy in Greek is a little coy?

RICH: Please!

SAUL: Why didn't you just say, "To Chet, whose beautiful buns inspired
    these tales"?

RICH: Jesus Christ!

SAUL: I'm sorry! [*Silence.*]

RICH: I sold the IBM stock. You were right about it. You have always been
    right about money. [*He hands* SAUL *a check.*] This includes the thousand
    I borrowed for the periodontist.

SAUL: You sure?

RICH: Take it.

SAUL: I'm not desperate for it.

RICH: It's yours.

SAUL: I don't want it.

RICH: Damn it!

SAUL: [*taking the check*] Okay.

RICH: That makes us even now.

SAUL: [*examining the check*] Clouds and trees.

RICH: Let's get on with this.

SAUL: Is he waiting for you downstairs? You could have told him to come up.

RICH: Shit. No! Can it. [*Beat.*] I won't be wanting the copper pots.

SAUL: Why not? When you and Chet move to your space you'll want to cook again.

RICH: I just don't want them! People change. [*Silence.*] I'm eating out a lot.

SAUL: Chet can't cook?

RICH: [*deciding not to respond with a bitchy comment*] You keep the rowing machine.

SAUL: Have you lost weight?

RICH: And the trampoline.

SAUL: There's some Black Forest cake in the fridge. [SAUL *goes toward the kitchen to get the cake.*]

RICH: Stop it.

SAUL: Stop what?

RICH: Just stop.

SAUL: I can't.

RICH: We're almost through.

SAUL: I have feelings.

RICH: You have only one feeling.

SAUL: He won't make you happy.

RICH: Here we go again. [RICH *gets up to go.*]

SAUL: Don't!

RICH: Keep everything.

SAUL: I'm not myself.

RICH: Nothing is worth this.

SAUL: I've been upset.

RICH: I mean it.

SAUL: Don't go. Please. [RICH *sits. Long pause.*] I visited Teddy today at St. Vincent's. It's very depressing…He's lying there in bed, out of it. He's been out of it since the time we saw him. He's not in any pain, snorting his imaginary cocaine, doing his poppers. Sometimes he's washing his mother's floor, and he's speaking to her in Spanish. Sometimes he's having sex. You can see him having sex right in front of you. He doesn't even know you're there. [*Pause. Both men look down at their feet.*] Jimmy died, as you must have heard. I went out to San Francisco to be with him the last few weeks. You must have heard that, too. He was in a coma for a month. Everybody wanted to pull the plug, but they were afraid of legal complications. I held his hand. He couldn't talk, but I could see his eyelids flutter. I swear he knew I was with him. [*Pause.*] Harry has K.S., and Matt has the swollen glands. He went for tests today…I haven't slept well for weeks. Every morning I examine my body for swellings, marks. I'm terrified of every pimple, every rash. If I cough I think of Teddy. I wish he would die. He *is* dead. He might as well be. Why can't he die? I feel the disease closing in on me. All my activities are life and death. Keep up my Blue Cross. Up my reps. Eat my vegetables.

Sometimes I'm so scared I go back on my resolutions: I drink too much, and I smoke a joint, and I find myself at the bars and clubs, where I stand around and watch. They remind me of accounts of Europe during the Black Plague: coupling in the dark, dancing till you drop. The New Wave is the corpse look. I'm very frightened and I miss you. Say something, damn it. [*Beat.*]

RICH: I have it. [*Immediately the lights come up on the left side of the stage.*]

CHET: [*a handsome, boyish man in his early twenties*] You what?

LILY: [*a beautiful woman, thirtyish*] You have what?

BROTHER: [*to his wife, whom we don't see*] He has AIDS.

SAUL: I don't think that's funny.

PARTNER: Don't be ridiculous.

RICH: That's the bad news.

PARTNER: You ran the goddamned marathon.

LILY: Darling!

RICH: The good news is that I have only the swollen glands. [*Two doctors appear in white gowns.*]

DOCTOR 1: We call it a "Pre-AIDS Condition."

DOCTOR 2: "AIDS-related Complex."

RICH: And I've lost some weight.

SAUL: I'm in a state of shock.

LILY: Move in with me. Chet doesn't know how to take care of you.

RICH: I tire easily. My temperature goes up and down.

DOCTOR 1: Your suppressor cells outnumber your helper cells.

BROTHER: I don't care what he has, Betty, he's my brother.

CHET: You're my lover.

LILY: You're my buddy.

PARTNER: Rich and I started the business about a year ago. But now word got out that Rich has this disease. I tried to explain: he doesn't touch the

BROTHER: I'm not in the habit of kissing my brother. I touched

food; I do all the cooking. But they won't listen.

him on the back when I arrived and when I left.

PARTNER: Why would they? I wonder if I'd use a caterer who had AIDS.

SAUL: Doctors make mistakes all the time.

DOCTOR 2: There are a number of highly experimental treatments.

DOCTOR 1: Of highly experimental treatments.

LILY: I got this job.

CHET: If you don't mind, I'll sleep on the couch tonight. You've been sweating a lot.

LILY: I can't turn it down. The work is pure dreck, and who wants to tour Canada in January, but they're paying a fortune. I'll be back in four weeks.

BROTHER: When he offered me a cup of coffee I told him I'd have a can of beer.

PARTNER: I can understand what he's going through. Myself, I've been wrestling with cancer for a while.

SAUL: Remember when they told my niece she had skin cancer?

It turned out to be dry skin.

PARTNER: I'm winning.

CHET: I hope you don't mind, but I'll use the red soap dish and you'll use the blue.

RICH: Christ! I've been putting the blocks to you nightly for months and now you're worried about sharing the fucking soap dish?

BROTHER: Christ, I didn't even use the bathroom, even though I had to take a leak so bad I could taste it. Now, that's paranoid.

PARTNER: I wonder if it's safe to use the same telephone, or whether I'm being paranoid.

CHET: I know I'm being paranoid.

LILY: They're flying me out to the Coast.

I hate that place.

RICH: Chet, you've been out every night this week. Do you have to go out again?

BROTHER: I know you're scared, Betty, but I will not tell my own brother he's not welcome in my house.

CHET: Need something from outside?

BROTHER: He's spent every Christmas with us since we got married, and this year will be no exception.

RICH: Forget I said anything: just don't wake me up when you get in.

BROTHER: You're forcing me to choose between you and my brother.

CHET: See you later.

LILY: I've been dating this guy
Mick — can you imagine *me*
dating? Well, he's very nice, and
he's got a lot of money, and he's
not impressed with my life in
the theater and he's straight —   CHET: You know I'd do anything for
and that's why I haven't been   you.
up to see you. Rich?   RICH: You're walking out on me.

BROTHER: We're going to Betty's mother's for Christmas.

CHET: I need more space to get my head together.

SAUL: What did you expect?

RICH: Chet, please, I need you! [RICH *tries to put his arms around* CHET. *Everyone except* SAUL *pulls back terrified.*]

CHET, BROTHER, LILY, PARTNER, DOCTORS: Don't touch me! [*Beat.*]

LILY: Please forgive me!

CHET: This thing has me blown away.

BROTHER: If it weren't for the kids.

PARTNER: I don't know what the hell we're going to do.

SAUL: Bastards! [CHET, BROTHER, PARTNER, *and* LILY *put on white gowns and become doctors.*]

RICH: [*to* DOCTOR 1] Doctor, tell me   TV COMMENTATOR: [*prerecorded*]
the truth. What are my chances?   Since 1981, nearly 32,000
DOCTOR 1: I don't know.   Americans have been diagnosed
RICH: [*to* DOCTOR 2] Doctor, tell me   with AIDS (use current fatality
the truth. What are my chances?   figures) and about sixty percent
DOCTOR 2: I don't know.   of them have died. Scientists
RICH: [*to* DOCTOR 3] What are my   project that by 1991, some
chances?   54,000 people will be dead. So
DOCTOR 3: I just don't know.   far, nine out of ten patients have
RICH: [*to* DOCTORS 4 *and* 5] Am I   been homosexual or bisexual
going to make it, doctors, yes   men or intravenous drug users.
or no?!   Experts estimate that from four

DOCTORS 4 and 5: I'm sorry, we just don't know.

SAUL: Rich?

DOCTORS: We don't know.

SAUL: And for three months you kept this from me. [*The doctors exit. We're back in* SAUL's *apartment.*]

to seven percent of all adult patients were infected through heterosexual intercourse. When will science conquer this dreaded plague? We don't know. We don't know. We simply don't know. Don't know. (Etc.)

RICH: I don't want your pity.

SAUL: You're my friend. You'll stay with me till you feel better.

RICH: Aren't you afraid I'll infect you?

SAUL: Maybe you already have.

RICH: And maybe I haven't.

SAUL: Maybe I gave it to you.

RICH: Maybe you did.

SAUL: We'll take precautions.

RICH: Paper plates, Lysol, face masks — no, I'd prefer to live alone, thank you.

SAUL: You need me.

RICH: Besides, if I live with you, where am I going to bring my tricks?

SAUL: You pick up people?

RICH: [*standing at the bar*] I go to bars . . . I pick up guys . . . but I give them a medical report before we leave . . . [*Without a pause, we're in a bar.* RICH *is talking to a stranger.*] I should tell you something.

PICKUP 1: You like something kinky. Whips? Golden showers? Fist?

RICH: It's not like that.

PICKUP 1: I once picked up a guy who liked to be yelled at in German. The only German I know is the "Ode to Joy" from Beethoven's Ninth. [*Yelling like an enraged Nazi.*] "*O Freude, schöner Götterfunken, Schweinehund, Tochter aus Elysium, Dummkopf!*"

RICH: I have a very mild case of lymphadenopathy.

PICKUP 1: What's that?

RICH: An AIDS-related condition.

PICKUP 1: Oh, shit.

RICH: Just the swollen glands —

PICKUP 1: No way. Uh-uh . . . Good luck . . . Oh, man . . . [PICKUP 1 *exits. We're back with* RICH *and* SAUL.]

RICH: So I stopped telling them.

SAUL: You mean you take them home and don't tell them?

RICH: We do it there in the bar.

SAUL: How can you?

RICH: I lurk in dark corners where they can't see my lumps. I'm like a
shark or a barracuda, and I snap them up and infect them.

SAUL: How can you joke about this?

RICH: I don't care. I'm going to die! I'll take as many as I can with me.
And I've pissed in the Croton Reservoir. I'm going to infect the
whole fucking city! Wheeeee!

SAUL: No fucking around, give me a straight answer. Do you still pick up
people?

RICH: Maybe I ought to wear a sign around my neck and ring a bell:
"AIDS, I've got AIDS, stand clear!" Would that make you happy?
Or maybe I should dig a hole in the ground, douse myself with
kerosene, and have a final cigarette. No muss, no fuss. Is that what
you want?

SAUL: Forgive me for not trusting you. It's just that I'm frightened of it.
Don't know what I'm saying half the time.

RICH: How the fuck do you think I feel? My lover leaves me; my family
won't let me near them; I lose my business; I can't pay my rent. How
the fuck do you think I feel?

SAUL: You'll stay here with me.

RICH: Till death do us part.

SAUL: I love you.

RICH: I don't want your love!

SAUL: Take what you can . . . (get)! I didn't mean that. I love you. I always
have. You have nowhere to go. You've got to stay with me.

RICH: Shit shit shit.

SAUL: You were kidding about picking up people.

RICH: What do you think? What would you do in my place?

SAUL: I wouldn't . . . I'd . . . Therapy! . . . I don't know what I'd do.

[*We're back in the bar.*]

PICKUP 2: Jesus, I've told you all about myself. I've really spilled my guts to
you. I *needed* to do that. Maybe I shouldn't say this, but Christ, you
know something? I like you very much. Even though you *are* a
writer . . . Would you like to come home with me?

RICH: I'd like to very much . . . [*he checks his watch*] but I have an
appointment.

PICKUP 2: Then tomorrow, how about tomorrow? I don't want to lose
track of you. I don't know when I've had such a good time. I can
talk to you.

RICH: I've enjoyed myself, too.

PICKUP 2: Then maybe we'll have dinner, maybe go to the movies. Do you like the movies? There's an Alfred Hitchcock festival at the Regency. Or maybe we could see the new Mark Morris —
RICH: Thanks, but I have to tell you something. I have —
PICKUP 2: You have a lover. I knew it. You're too nice to be unattached.
RICH: I have … I have … I have a lover.

[*We're back with* SAUL.]

SAUL: You have a lover.
RICH: I don't even know where he is.
SAUL: I don't mean Chet. I mean me. [RICH *turns away. He's back in the bar with another stranger,* CLONE 1, *who is wearing a leather jacket and reflecting aviator glasses.* SAUL *continues to plead to* RICH'S *back.*] What about me? [RICH *tries in vain to get* CLONE 1'*s attention.*]
RICH: Pardon me.
SAUL: What about me?
RICH: Yo. Yoo-hoo. Hello.
SAUL: What about *me*?!
RICH: [*to* CLONE 1] What about me?!
CLONE 1: What about you?
RICH: I'm a very interesting guy. You look like a very interesting guy. Let's talk. And if you don't want to talk, let's go back there and let's … [RICH *stares* CLONE 1 *straight in the face.*] I'll do anything you want. Anything.
CLONE 1: I want you to get the fuck out of my face. Can't you see I'm cruising that dude over there? [*We notice for the first time an identically dressed man standing across the room.*]
RICH: Well, fuck you.
CLONE 1: What's that, buddy? [RICH *turns his back on* CLONE 1 *and starts talking loudly to the bartender.*]
RICH: Gimme a Jack Daniels straight up — *no* ice — make it a double, and a Heineken chaser.
BARTENDER: Double Jack up, Heinie back. [CLONE 2 *has moseyed on over to* CLONE 1. *They stand side by side, facing the audience, feigning indifference to each other.*]
CLONE 2: Your name Chip?
RICH: No ice!
BARTENDER: No ice.
CLONE 1: Chuck.
RICH: Hate ice.

CLONE 2: [*extending his hand*] Chad. [*The clones shake hands.*]

RICH: [*to the bartender*] Put 'er there, Chet—I mean Chump. You come here often? [*He downs the shot and beer as quickly as he can.*]

CLONE 2: Thought you were this guy, Chip, I met here on Jockstrap Night.

CLONE 1: Haven't been here since the Slave Auction.

CLONE 2: Look familiar. [*With synchronized actions the clones turn to look at each other, then turn away.*]

CLONE 1: Go to the Spike?

CLONE 2: Been there.

RICH: [*to the bartender*] Quiet for a Friday...

CLONE 1: I know where.

RICH: Not much action.

CLONE 2: Palladium?

RICH: [*offering his glass*] Same...

CLONE 1: Nah.

RICH: Probably's this disease thing.

CLONE 1: Bookstore on Christopher. Ever go there?

CLONE 2: Stopped going since this disease thing.

CLONE 1: Gotta be real careful.

RICH: No use getting hysterical.

CLONE 2: Right. Me, I'm HIV negative.

CLONE 1: Can you prove it? [*He punches* CLONE 2 *on the arm.*] Kidding.

CLONE 2: Gotta be real careful. Run six miles a day.

RICH: My philosophy is: you've got it, you've got it. Nothing you can do about it. [*He offers his glass.*] Same.

CLONE 1: [*tweaking* CLONE 2's *nipple*] So what're you up for?

CLONE 2: Come right to the point, don't you? [*The clones perform a macho mating ritual of arm wrestling, punching, and ass grabbing to determine who is the "top man."*]

RICH: Poor bastards that got it: cancer, pneumonia, herpes all over. I mean, I'd kill myself if I had to go through all that shit. Get a gun and perform fellatio on it...

CLONE 2: What're you up for, Daddy?

RICH: Slash my wrists *with* the grain...

CLONE 1: Me top.

RICH: Subway tracks?

CLONE 1: Got some beautiful...[*He snorts deeply to indicate cocaine.*]

CLONE 2: Ever do opium?

CLONE 1: I have a water pipe. We'll smoke it through some Southern Comfort.

RICH: Or maybe I'd mix myself a Judy Garland: forty reds and a quart of vodka. [*He hands his glass to the bartender.*] Fuck the beer!

CLONE 1: We're roommates now. What about you?

RICH: [*the ecstatic drunken poet*] "Glory be to God for dappled things..."

CLONE 2: I'm free, white, and twenty-four.

RICH: "For skies of couple-colour as a brinded cow..."

SAUL: I know it sounds stupid, but take care of your health.

RICH: "For rose-moles all in stipple upon trout that swim..."

CLONE 2: In bed, I mean.

RICH: I don't care what anybody says, I believe that somewhere, you know, *deep* down. [*He holds out his glass.*]

CLONE 1: I'll do anything you want.

RICH: Beyond all this incredible pain and confusion, anxiety, fear, terror... [*He holds out his glass.*]

BARTENDER: No ice.

CLONE 2: Anything?

RICH: I believe that there might be... [*searching for words to describe the Supreme Being*] that there could be... that there is—

CLONE 1: Safe sex!

SAUL: You're drinking too much.

RICH: I believe in a perfect... [*He is having a booze-fueled vision of the Godhead.*]

CLONE 2: Mirrors...

RICH: Shining...

CLONE 1: Chains...

RICH: Powerful...

SAUL: Vitamins...

RICH: Pure... [*A third clone appears.*]

CLONE 3: Condom...

CLONE 1: Dildo...

SAUL: Diet...

RICH: Free...

CLONE 2: Dungeon...

SAUL: Acupuncture...

RICH: Truthful...

CLONE 3: Ten inches...

SAUL: AZT...

RICH: Beautiful...

CLONE 3: [*approaching the bar, to the* BARTENDER] Beer! [*He accidentally spills beer on* RICH.]

CLONE 2: Watersports.

RICH: [*raging drunkenly*] Asshole!

CLONE 1: Hey!

RICH: I'll kill ya, faggot!

SAUL: [*intervening*] Hey!... He's been drinking.

BARTENDER: Get that jerk outta here!

RICH: What's a matter, can't you fight like a man?

SAUL: [*gently but firmly*] Rich.

RICH: Fuck all that shit!

SAUL: Rich.

RICH: Let Him cure me!

SAUL: [*trying to distract him*] Did you hear the one about the faggot, the black, and the Jew?

RICH: [*to God in the sky, shaking his fist*] You hear me, motherfucker?

SAUL: How did that go?

RICH: Cure me! [*They are out on the street by now.*]

SAUL: C'mon, keep moving.

RICH: I'm a very bad person.

SAUL: You're an asshole.

RICH: I wanted to go to bed with that guy.

SAUL: I practically beg you to move in—

RICH: I wasn't going to tell him about me or anything.

SAUL: And what do you do?

RICH: But you want to know something?

SAUL: You disappear for two weeks.

RICH: I wouldn't do that. I would *never* do that.

SAUL: I almost called the cops.

RICH: You believe me?

SAUL: Believe what?

RICH: I never never never would ever do that.

SAUL: Do you remember the one about the Polish Lesbian?

RICH: Never.

SAUL: She liked men. [*The joke pretty much sobers* RICH *up.*]

RICH: You asshole.

SAUL: You schmuck.

RICH: You prick.

SAUL: God, I miss talking dirty.

RICH: Talking dirty makes it feel like spring. [*He is the superstud.*] Suck my dick, faggot.

SAUL: [*superstud*] Kiss my ass, cocksucker.

RICH: Sit on it, punk.

SAUL: Lick boot, fruit.

RICH: God, how I used to love sleaze: the whining self-pity of a rainy Monday night in a leather bar in early spring; five o'clock in the morning in the Mineshaft, with the bathtubs full of men dying to get pissed on and whipped; a subway john full of horny high school students; Morocco—getting raped on a tombstone in Marrakesh. God, how I miss it.

SAUL: I miss my filthy old ripped-up, patched button-fly jeans that I sun-bleached on myself our first weekend on the Island. Remember? It was Labor Day—

RICH: Memorial Day.

SAUL: And we did blotter acid. Remember acid before they put the speed in it? And we drank muscadet when we got thirsty.

RICH: Which we did a lot.

SAUL: Remember?

RICH: Remember Sunday afternoons blitzed on beer?

SAUL: And suddenly it's Sunday night and you're getting fucked in the second-floor window of the Hotel Christopher and you're being cheered on by a mob of hundreds of men.

RICH: And suddenly its Friday a week later, and he's moved in, sleeping next to you, and you want him to go because you've met his brother Rod or Lance—

SAUL: [*practically sighing*] Miles.

RICH: —late of the merchant marines, who's even humpier.

SAUL: Orgies at the baths—

RICH: Afternoons at the Columbus Avenue bookstore. [*They are in the back room of a gay porno shop, or "bookstore." They play their favorite bookstore habitués.*] More! *Give* it to me!

SAUL: Give it to *you*? Give it to *me*! Get out of my way, he's mine!

RICH: No, he's mine! Keep your hands off my wallet!

SAUL: [*a black queen*] Sistuhs, theyuh's plenty heah fo' ivrybody.

RICH: [*a tough New York queen*] Hey, Mary, the line forms at the rear.

SAUL: And whose rear might that be, sugar? [*Two other men appear in the bookstore.*]

MARTY: Hey, Vinnie?

VINNIE: Marty?

MARTY: What are you doing here? You said you were gonna buy the papers.

VINNIE: You said you were gonna walk the dogs.

MARTY: You trash! [*They exit, bickering.*]

SAUL: I always knew when you were fucking around.
RICH: You did your share.
SAUL: *Moi?*
RICH: I knew why Grand Union wouldn't deliver to our house. [*They have returned to the loft.*]
SAUL: God, I used to love promiscuous sex.
RICH: Not "promiscuous," Saul, nondirective, noncommitted, non-authoritarian—
SAUL: Free, wild, rampant—
RICH: Hot, sweaty, steamy, smelly—
SAUL: Juicy, funky, hunky—
RICH: Sex.
SAUL: Sex. God, I miss it. [RICH *lowers his eyes.* SAUL *nods and goes to* RICH. *He takes* RICH'S *face in both hands and tries to kiss him square on the mouth.* RICH *pulls away frantically.*]
RICH: No!
SAUL: Its safe!
RICH: You don't know what you're doing!
SAUL: It's my decision!
RICH: [*shaking his head*] No. Uh-uh. No! [SAUL *sits on the sofa.* RICH *tries to take* SAUL'S *hand, but* SAUL *pulls it away. Beat.*] The best times for me were going out with you on shoots.
SAUL: I thought you found them boring.
RICH: I enjoyed them.
SAUL: I was always afraid of boring you.
RICH: Remember staying up all night shooting the harvest moon at Jake's place?
SAUL: My fingers got so cold I could barely change film.
RICH: It was almost as bright as daylight. Remember the apple tree stuck out in the middle of the pasture, how the moonlight drained it of color?
SAUL: I remember the smell of the blanket we took from the barn.
RICH: Remember, I bet you I could find five constellations?
SAUL: You found six . . . I never wanted us to break up.
RICH: Passive aggression.
SAUL: I wanted things to always remain the same. I'm still like that. I even like eating the same things day after day.
RICH: Pork chops, French fries—
SAUL: No change. I used to love our routine together. I'd go to work and then you'd be there when I got home, writing—

RICH: Drinking.

SAUL: I'd do this and you'd do that, and then we'd... [*he makes a graceful gesture to indicate making love*] for a while—while *Mission Impossible*'d be on low in the background.

RICH: And then *Star Trek*.

SAUL: I never got tired of the same—

RICH: We were stagnating.

SAUL: —day after day the same, so we'd have a structure to fall back on when life dealt us its wild cards or curve balls. I want to be just half awake, like at the seashore, watching the waves roll in late in the afternoon, hypnotized by the glare of the sun, smelling the sea breeze and suntan lotion. [*Beat.*]

Mom is what? She's lying there next to Dad on the Navaho blanket, with white gunk on her nose, and my baby sister has finally stopped screaming and is sucking on the ear of her dollie. And Aunt Ellie—the one who said she thought I had good taste when she met you—is snoring next to husband number three. Her bazooms are going up and down, up and down, almost popping out of her bathing suit. It's so peaceful. [*Long pause.*]

I was at the St. Mark's baths soaking in the hot tub when I first heard about AIDS. It was how many years ago? My friend Brian—remember him?—was soaking, too, and he told me about a mutual friend who had died the week before. It was "bizarre," he said... [*A group enters, quietly talking.*]

1ST MAN: The first person I knew who had AIDS was George. I had just seen him at the movies—*Mommie Dearest*—and we had a big laugh together. I remember he had a little cough. I ran into his mother it couldn't have been a week later and she told me he had died. It was absurd. I had just seen George.

1ST WOMAN: The first time it really hit me was when my boss got ill. When Roger got out of the hospital I didn't know what to say. I said, "You look so much

It hit home after that.

2ND WOMAN: The first time I heard about it I was standing in my kitchen. I was about to go out shopping for my youngest's birthday party. The phone rang. It was this doctor calling me about my son Bernard. He used all these words I can't pronounce. And then he said, "Do you understand what I've told you?" I said yes. Right before he hung up he said, "So you know he has AIDS." That's the first time I heard that word.

I turned white.

3RD MAN: [*a cop*] The word never really registered in my mind until they transferred this guy with AIDS to our unit. Maybe I thought AIDS was like Legionnaires Disease

or Toxic Shock Syndrome — one of those rare diseases you

taller." He said, "Well, I've lost about forty-five pounds."

1ST MAN: Do you understand what I've told you?

1ST WOMAN: So you know he has AIDS.

JOHN: The first time I heard about AIDS was in 1980. I was on the seven A.M. shuttle to Boston, trying to make a nine o'clock appointment in Cambridge. I was looking over the shoulder of the man next to me, at his newspaper, and I caught the words "cancer," "promiscuous," "homosexual."

read about in the papers. Anyway, the guys on the job were up in arms that they were going to expose us to it. I didn't know what to think. I got used to Bobby though. He wanted to keep working very badly.

I think he had a lot of courage.

2ND WOMAN: He was in the theater.

3RD MAN: I couldn't figure it out.

1ST WOMAN: ... Fortunato ...

3RD MAN: ... Stephen ...

4TH MAN: ... Phil ...

1ST WOMAN: ... Arthur ...

2ND WOMAN: ... Neil ...

1ST WOMAN: ... John ...

2ND WOMAN: ... Julie ...

3RD MAN: ... Luis ... Larry and his lover Danny ... Stuart ... J.J. ... Maria ... Jamal ...

2ND WOMAN: ... David ... Stuart ... J.J. ... Maria ... Jamal ...

[_The group exits._]

1ST and 2ND MEN: I think he had a lot of courage.

4TH MAN: The first memorial service I went to was on the set of _Oh Calcutta!_ It was for Bill. He was in the theater. They filled the house. He had hidden the fact that he was ill for a year. A while before he asked me if I wanted his dog—a beautiful huskie. I couldn't figure it out. He loved that dog ... Since that time I've been to how many memorial services? Seth ... Robby ...

2ND WOMAN: ... Francis ...

2ND MAN: ... Greg ...

2ND WOMAN: ... Freddie ...

1ST MAN: ... Tom ...

2ND MAN: ... André ...

3RD MAN: ... Glen ...

1ST and 4TH MAN and 1ST WOMAN: ... Russell ... Luis ... Larry and his lover Danny ... David ... Stuart ... J.J. ... Maria ... Jamal ...

2ND MAN: ... Larry ... David ... Stuart ... J.J. ... Maria ... Jamal ... Charles ...

SAUL: ...and he told me about a mutual friend who had died the week before. It was "bizarre," he said. Brian died last week of the same thing. And he and I once soaked in the same hot tub, making a kind of human soup.... That's all I ever wanted to do was relax. [*Long pause.*] You'll stay with me. I won't bother you.

RICH: Just until I feel better.

SAUL: I understand: you're not coming back to be my lover.

RICH: Right. Is that okay?

SAUL: Schmuck. [*Mimicking him.*] Is that okay? Is that okay? It's *okay*! Asshole. Who the fuck wants you anyhow? And when I have guests stay the night, you disappear into your room. Right?

RICH: Right. Understood. [*Offhand.*] You seeing somebody?

SAUL: I said when I have guests.

RICH: You planning an orgy?

SAUL: Just so we understand each other.

RICH: I should mention one thing.

SAUL: No, you do not have to spend Passover with the tribe.

RICH: I miss your father.

SAUL: Then go live with him. He *likes* you. The two of you could be very happy together.

RICH: One thing.

SAUL: He's never really liked me.

RICH: Saul.

SAUL: He's always been polite but—

RICH: Are you finished?

SAUL: No, I will not bring you coffee in bed. I only do that for lovers. Besides, I broke your blue mug.

RICH: Saul, please.

SAUL: On purpose.

RICH: One thing. I'm embarrassed. I'm just about broke. The doctors. Tests.

SAUL: I thought you were insured.

RICH: They're pulling a fast one.

SAUL: We'll sue. I'll call Craig. He'll know what—

RICH: Craig told me not to have high hopes.

SAUL: We'll get by. You'll see.

RICH: I'll keep track of every cent you spend on me. You'll get it all back when I can work. I swear.

SAUL: Not to worry, I'll take it out in trade.

RICH: Saul, I'm frightened! [SAUL *takes him in his arms.*]

SAUL: We'll be okay, we'll be okay... [*They hold each other.* LILY *walks into the scene with* CHET. *She's dressed in evening wear and is carrying a number of accessories, including a mirror and a shawl.* CHET *is dressed in cutoffs and a sweatshirt. We are in a flashback.*]

LILY: Rich, congratulations! It's fantastic that they're going to publish your book. [SAUL *tries to break from the clinch, but* RICH *holds him back.*]

RICH: No autographs, please.

LILY: Its wonderful, it really is, but can you guys celebrate later?

SAUL: [*to* RICH] Let me go. [*To* CHET:] How do you do? I'm Saul.

LILY: Shit. Saul, Rich — my cousin Chet.

SAUL: [*trying to shake hands*] Hi, Chet. [*To* RICH:] You're strangling me.

CHET: Hi.

RICH: [*to* SAUL] It's your last chance to kiss the author before he becomes famous and goes straight.

SAUL: Straight to the bars. [*To* CHET:] So how do you like New York?

CHET: I only got here yesterday. Lily's taking me to a show tonight.

RICH: Do you think success will change me?

SAUL: God, I hope so.

LILY: I know I'm being a pig, but I need head shots by six o'clock. [*She lowers a roller of colored background paper.*] It's a dazzling role for me and [*to* SAUL] you're such an artist.

SAUL: Rich is the "artiste" in the family.

LILY: Chet, be an angel and bring Saul his camera. It's by the bar. [CHET *looks for the camera.*]

SAUL: [*to* CHET] Don't let your cousin push you around the way she does me.

LILY: Come on, Saul, make click-click.

SAUL: Unless you like that sort of thing.

RICH: That's all I get?

LILY: [*to* RICH, *about* SAUL] Leave the boy alone.

RICH: A hug and a bitchy remark?

SAUL: [*to* RICH] That and a subway token.

RICH: [*to* SAUL] No "Gee, Rich, I'm so proud of you"?

SAUL: [*smiling falsely*] Gee, Rich, I'm so proud of you.

RICH: I finally have some good news and he's annoyed.

CHET: [*to* LILY, *holding the camera*] What should I do with this?

SAUL: Well, your brother called, while you were out guzzling lunch with your agent, Dr. Mengele. Call him back.

RICH: What'd he have to say?

SAUL: Call him and ask him. I'm not your secretary.

RICH: [*imitating him*] I'm not your —

SAUL: He forgot my fucking name again. How long we been together?

RICH: Too long. Forget my brother. It's my first fucking book. Let's celebrate.
SAUL: You celebrate.
LILY: I'll throw a party.
RICH: What'll you serve, organic cabbage juice?
SAUL: [*to* LILY] His brother's a scumbag.
RICH: He likes you, too.
CHET: [*to* SAUL, *still holding the camera*] Do you want this?
SAUL: [*to* CHET] Thanks, Chuck.
CHET: Chet. [SAUL *accepts the camera from* CHET, *but ignores the correction.*]
LILY: [*fondly, to* RICH] You're such a lush.
RICH: Whatever happened to my old drinking buddy?
LILY: Did you know they have gay A.A. meetings? [RICH *makes a face.*]
SAUL: [*to* RICH, *trying to be nice*] It's great news, babes, really.
RICH: You really don't give a fuck.
SAUL: Just how many copies you think a book of "fairy tales" will sell?
LILY: I picked a fine day to have my picture taken.
SAUL: If you only knew how much I love doing head shots.
RICH: [*to* SAUL] Ah, fuck it, I guess I'm being childish.
SAUL: I shouldn't have said that. I'm thoughtless. [RICH *shrugs.*]
LILY: And I'm Sneezy. No, really, I'm selfish. But I want that role so bad. I play the ghost of Marie Antoinette. [*To* SAUL, *throwing the scarf around her neck and taking a tits-and-ass pose*:] How do you like this, hon? "Let them eat . . ." [*She drops the pose immediately as* SAUL *starts to photograph her.*]
SAUL: Move your head a little to the . . . [*She moves her head.*] Good. [SAUL *snaps her.*]
RICH: [*going to the living area, followed by* CHET] I'm going running. [RICH *changes into jogging clothes.*]
CHET: How far do you run?
RICH: Depends. I'm in training for the marathon.
CHET: The marathon! Hey, that's great. I run, too.
RICH: Oh, yeah? [LILY *and* SAUL *are busy taking pictures in the other side of the loft. They can see* RICH *and* CHET, *but they can't easily hear them.*]
LILY: How's this?
CHET: Congratulations on the book.
RICH: Thanks.
SAUL: That's right.
LILY: I forget the director's name. He's Lithuanian.
CHET: That poem of yours that Lily has hung up in her kitchen, I read it. I think its great.
SAUL: Great.

629

RICH: You don't much look like the poetry type.
LILY: Bulgarian.
CHET: I'm not. I just love your poem.
RICH: Are you a student?
CHET: Just graduated from San Francisco State.
LILY: Everybody in the play is dead.
SAUL: Your cousin's hot. Is he gay?
LILY: I don't know. I'll ask him. [*Yelling to* CHET.] Chet, are you gay?
SAUL: Christ.
RICH: That's what I call tact.
LILY: Well?
CHET: [*loud, to* LILY] Yes.
LILY: Thanks, hon.
SAUL: Give us a little more cheek...
CHET: There's a line of your poem I don't understand.
RICH: Only one? I have no idea what any of it means.
CHET: "The final waning moon..."
SAUL: Don't smile.
RICH: "And the coming of the light."
CHET: I love the way it sounds.
SAUL: Smile.
CHET: "The final waning moon/And the coming of the light."
SAUL: [*indicating to* LILY *that he wants a sexy pose*] He loves you.
CHET: Oh, I get it.
RICH: Lily tells me you're looking for a place to stay.
CHET: New York is so expensive.
SAUL: He lusts for you.
RICH: A friend of mine wants someone to take care of his loft while he's in L.A.
SAUL: He wants to ravage you.
CHET: I'll do it.
RICH: He has eight cats.
CHET: Eight tigers, I don't care.
LILY: I love that play.
RICH: It's in Tribeca.
SAUL: [*yelling to* RICH] I apologize about the book. [RICH *and* CHET *ignore* SAUL.]
CHET: Where's Tribeca?
SAUL: Did you hear me?

RICH: On the isle of Manhattan.
CHET: We're on the isle of Manhattan.
RICH: We are.
LILY: The main characters are all ghosts.
CHET: I know that.
SAUL: I'll throw him a party.
RICH: That's about all you have to know.
SAUL: A big bash.
CHET: Is it?
LILY: We'll do it together.
RICH: I'll tell you a few more things.
CHET: Will you?
SAUL: I'll even invite his brother.
RICH: You bet your ass I will.
SAUL: [*snapping up the roller of background paper*] Finished. [LILY, RICH, *and* CHET *leave.* SAUL *goes to the sofa. The* HOSPICE WORKER *comes forward.*]
HOSPICE WORKER: A woman is told by her doctor that she has cancer and has only a month to live. "Now wait just one minute," she tells the doctor. "I'll be wanting a second opinion." To which the doctor replies, "Okay, you're ugly, too."

David told me that one. He was an old Jewish man who had survived the Lodz ghetto in World War II. He'd seen everything in his life, and when the time came for him to go, he accepted it. The doctors wanted to go to obscene lengths to keep his body alive, but he refused. I loved him.

But most of my people are more like Margaret. She was in her nineties. She half accepted the fact that she was dying. One moment she'd be talking to you about which nephew she was definitely going to cross out of her will, and the next she'd be telling you about the summer vacation she was planning in Skibbereen. She had terminal cancer! But I always go along with what they have to say. My job is not to bring enlightenment, only comfort.

Which reminds me: Margaret's family saw her as some kind of prophet. The whole clan was in the room waiting to hear her last words. She had developed a distinct dislike for her family, so I was sitting closest to her when she went, and therefore I could hear what the poor soul was whispering. After it was all over, they asked me what prayer she had been uttering. I told them the Lord's Prayer. I didn't have the heart to tell them that what she was saying was "Oh, shit, oh, shit, oh, shit."

I've worked with thirty-five people altogether. About a third of them had AIDS. It *is* the Village. [*She exits. Lights come up on left area. An* AIDS *support group is in session.*]

PERSON WITH AIDS 1: Funny thing is, I wasn't at all promiscuous.
PWA 2: Oh, please.
PWA 1: I swear. And I never drank much—once in a while a beer with Mexican food—and I don't smoke, and drugs, forget… I met Jerry in my sophomore year—we shared the same dorm room at Hofstra—and we fell in love, and that was it for me. When the sex revolution thing happened, I remember I felt retarded. Everybody was doing all those wild things. Me, I was going to the opera a lot. As far as I know, Jerry didn't screw around. He swore he didn't. But then… he's not around for me to cross-examine. He left me.
RICH: Well, I…
PWA 3: What?
RICH: No.
PWA 4: [*a young housewife, eight months pregnant*] At least when I come here I don't have to lie. Like "Bernie's doing better. I'm fine." I can even crack up if I want to. Don't worry, I won't do it two weeks in a row. I mean, who's there to talk to in Brewster? These things don't happen in Brewster. Police officers don't shoot up heroin, cops don't come down with the "gay plague"—that's what they call it in Brewster. I can't talk to Bernie. I'll never forgive him. Have a chat with the minister? "Well, Reverend Miller, I have this little problem. My husband has AIDS, and I have AIDS, and I'm eight months pregnant, and I…" You guys know what I mean. You're the only people in this world who know what I mean.
PWA 5: I know what you guys are going to tell me: I'm suffering from the homophobia that an oppressive society blah blah blah. I never felt good about being gay.
PWA 2: Oh, Mary.
PWA 5: Gay was grim. It was something I did because I had to. Like a dope fiend needs his fix. It always left me feeling like shit afterward. And that's the truth. I felt guilty. I still feel that way. [PWA 4 *leans over to put a consoling hand on him. He pulls away.*]
PWA 2: I was part of a team trying to teach robots how to use language. [*He moves and talks like a robot.*] "I'm Harris, your android model

632

3135X. I can vacuum the floors, cook cheeseburgers, play the piano."
It's much harder to teach robots to understand. [*Instructing a backward
robot.*] "Joke." [*The robot responds dutifully.*] "Noun: a clash of values or
levels of reality, producing laughter. Example: Have you heard about
the disease attacking Jewish American princesses? It's called MAIDS. You
die if you *don't* get it. Ha. Ha." My co-workers asked me to leave. They
were afraid of contracting AIDS through the air, or by my looking at
them. You see, they are scientists. My last act before I left was program-
ming one final robot. [*He behaves like a robot again.*] "Good morning.
This is Jack — [*he suddenly becomes a flamboyantly gay robot*] but you can
call me Jackie — your *fabulous* new android model 1069. If you wish to
use me — and I *love* being used — press one of those cunning little
buttons on my pecs. Go on, press one — [*he switches from a campy tone to
an almost angry, accusatory one*] or are you afraid of me, too?" That was
my stab at immortality.

RICH: I'm not sure I have it anymore. I feel guilty saying this, like
somehow I'm being disloyal to the group. I'm getting better, I know
it. I just have these lumps, which for some reason won't go away, and a
loss of weight, which has made me lighter than I've been for years.

PWA 3: Lose weight the AYDS way!

RICH: But anyway, I feel great. I feel the disease disappearing in me. Only a
small percentage of those with the swollen glands come down with
the rest. I'm going to *not* come here next week. I'm sorry.

PWA 3: Rich?

SAUL: [*calling to* RICH *as if he were in the next room, while feeling the glands in
his neck and armpits*] Rich?

RICH: [*still to group*] Why do I keep on apologizing?

SAUL: Rich?

RICH: If I *really* thought that I was coming down with it . . . We all have
options.

PWA 2: Rich?

SAUL: Rich.

RICH: [*entering* SAUL'*s area*] What?

SAUL: Here, feel my glands.

RICH: You are such a hypochondriac.

SAUL: Do you think they're swollen?

RICH: [*placing his hands around* SAUL'*s neck*] They feel okay to me.
[*Transylvanian accent.*] But your neck — eet is grotesquely meesshapen.
[*Suddenly mock-strangling* SAUL.] Here, let me feex it. [*They start wrestling
on sofa.*]

SAUL: Not fair!
RICH: You're such a hypochondriac.
SAUL: Ow! *I'm* such a hypochondriac. You and your vitamins!
RICH: You and your yoga!
SAUL: You and your yoghurt!
RICH: Its working. My ratio's up.
SAUL: All right! [*To the tune of "New York, New York."*]
    T-cells up,
    The suppressors are down.
    New York, New York . . .
RICH: Hey, I love you! You know that?
SAUL: If you love me, get off my chest!
RICH: I don't dare. You'd try and get even. You're that way.
SAUL: We'll call a truce. One, two, three . . .
RICH and SAUL: Truce. [*As* RICH *climbs off* SAUL's *chest,* SAUL *pulls him down, lifting his shirt, and gets him in a hammerlock.*]
SAUL: You were right. You never should have trusted me.
RICH: Unfair . . . foul . . . most unfair!
SAUL: Fuck fair. The winner gets his way with the loser. [*They tussle until* RICH *gives up.*] Having vanquished the good ship *Socrates*, the savage pirate chief Bigmeat takes the first mate as his captive.
RICH: [*in falsetto*] No, Captain Bigmeat, no!
SAUL: I've had me eye on ye since that time we met in Bangalore. Ye can't escape me now, matey. I shall ravish ye fer sure. [SAUL *tickles* RICH.]
RICH: No! . . . I'm pure of blood and noble born! [*Gradually their play turns more and more sexual, which* RICH *resists at first.*] No! . . . No! . . . [*Relents.*] Perhaps . . . Please!
SAUL: Now I got ye, boy-o . . . boy-o . . . boy-o . . . Oh, boy! [*Finally* RICH *stops struggling.* RICH *and* SAUL *are close together, panting, exhausted.* SAUL *is about to make love to* RICH *when he notices a mark on his back.*]
RICH: What? [SAUL *ignores him and looks at the mark carefully.*] What? You seduce me, you finally succeed in getting me hot and bothered, and what do you do as I lie here panting? You look at my birthmark. [SAUL *looks at* RICH's *back. He touches some marks.*]
RICH: What is it?
SAUL: Nothing.
RICH: What is it? Tell me!
SAUL: I'm sure it's nothing!
RICH: What! WHAT! *What!* . . . [*Immediately, the* HOSPICE WORKER *draws a curtain that surrounds the entire living area of* SAUL's *loft, hiding it from view.*

Overlapping the closing of the curtain, we hear the ringing of two telephones. Lights up on two men sitting side by side, answering multiline telephones.]

PAT: Hotline, Pat speaking.

BARNEY: Hotline. This is Barney. [*To* PAT, *covering the phone:*] Oh, no, it's her again.

PAT: Are you a gay man?

BARNEY: Didn't we speak a few days ago? [*To* PAT, *covering the phone:*] She doesn't stop.

PAT: We're all worried.

BARNEY: Is he bisexual?

PAT: Calm down, first of all. [*The third line rings.*]

BARNEY: Is he an IV drug user?

PAT: It's not all that easy to get it — *if* you take a few precautions. [*To* BARNEY, *covering the phone:*] Okay, I'll get it. [*He speaks into the phone.*] Please hold on. [*He presses a button.*]

BARNEY: It wasn't my intention to insult you.

PAT: Hotline . . . Shit. [*To* BARNEY, *pressing a button:*] Lost him. Fucking phone.

BARNEY: So what makes you think he has AIDS?

PAT: [*to phone*] Hello.

BARNEY: He is what?

PAT: The disease is spread through the blood and the semen.

BARNEY: American Indians are *not* a risk group. [*To* PAT, *covering the phone:*] American Indians?

PAT: So wear a condom.

BARNEY: There's half a zillion diseases he has symptoms of.

PAT: Make *him* wear a condom. [*The phone rings.*]

BARNEY: Please hold. [*He presses a button.*]

PAT: Kissing is acceptable.

BARNEY: Hotline . . . [*In response to a hate call.*] And your mother eats turds in hell! . . . Thank you. [*He presses a button.*]

PAT: Myself, I don't do it on the first date.

BARNEY: I would definitely check it out with a physician.

BARNEY: Spots? I'm not a doctor . . .   PAT: Stroking, holding, rubbing, mir-
Go to a doctor.   rors, whips, chains, jacking off,
                                                             porno — use your imagination.
BARNEY: I'm sorry you're lonely.

PAT: Our motto is: "On me, not in me."

BARNEY: Madam, we're busy here. I can't stay on the line with you all day.

PAT: You have a nice voice, too, but I'm seeing someone.

BARNEY: Hello?

PAT: Thanks.

BARNEY: [*to* PAT] Thank God.

PAT: Good luck. [*They hang up at the same time.*]

BARNEY: Spots. I love it.

PAT: [*to himself*] I am not seeing anyone.

BARNEY: What are you talking about?

PAT: I was saying how much I love being celibate. [*He kisses his palm.*] So how the fuck are you?

BARNEY: Tired, broke, depressed, and Tim is moving out this afternoon. Well, you asked. I hear you have a new PWA.★

PAT: Sorry about Tim. Yes, I have a new baby, a writer. Why do I get all the tough customers?

BARNEY: Because you're so tough.

PAT: So butch.

BARNEY: So mean.

PAT: Weathered by life like the saddle under a cowboy's ass.

BARNEY: Ooooh. I could never be a CMP.★★ Where do you get your energy?

PAT: Drugs. I don't do that anymore either. What *do* I do? I wait tables, answer phones, and work with ingrates like Rich. Boy, is he pissed. He calls me Miss Nightingale or Florence and throws dishes and curses his roommate and won't cooperate with the doctor and won't see his shrink and isn't interested in support groups *and he shit in the fucking bathtub!* He shit —

BARNEY: Is he incontinent?

PAT: Fuck, no. He ain't that sick yet. He said it was "convenient." I don't know why he shit in the tub.

BARNEY: A real sweetheart.

PAT: I'm going out of my mind. Thank God they put him in the hospital.

BARNEY: First time?

PAT: Yep.

BARNEY: I'd probably be a real bastard.

PAT: I wouldn't take it lying down.

BARNEY: You'd take it any way you can get it.

PAT: Go on, girlfriend.

BARNEY: Me, if I learned I had it, I'd shove a time bomb up my tush and drop in on Timmy for tea and meet his new lover: Jimmy.

★ Person with AIDS.

★★ Crisis Management Partner.

PAT: Jimmy?

BARNEY: I swear: Jimmy. [*Visiting* TIMMY *and* JIMMY *for high tea.*] "Timmy has told me so much about you. I've been *dying* to meet you." And kaboom! There goes Timmy and Jimmy.

PAT: Timmy and Jimmy? [*The telephone rings.*]

BARNEY: Ain't it a gas?

PAT: Gag me, for sure.

BARNEY: For sure.

PAT: [*answering the phone*] Hotline. Pat speaking.

BARNEY: [*raging*] When are we going to get some more help around here??!! I'm going out of my mind! [*Suddenly, sweet and sultry as he answers the phone.*] Hotline, Barney speaking.

PAT: Are you a gay man?

BARNEY: Are you a gay man? [*The lights quickly fade on the two men. The curtain opens, revealing a hospital room, with bed, chair, and bed table. The loft space and bar have disappeared.* RICH *is in bed.* LILY, SAUL, *and a* NURSE *are standing nearby.*]

NURSE: Temperature and blood pressure, Mr. Farrell.

LILY: Can you come back later?

SAUL: He's had some bad news.

NURSE: He's last on my rounds.

RICH: [*to* SAUL] You lied to me.

SAUL: I didn't know.

LILY: He didn't know. I swear.

NURSE: It'll just take a minute.

RICH: What other little details are you keeping from me? They let him lie there like a dog. What else? [*A Hispanic hospital worker comes in to empty the waste basket.*] You! *Váyase!* Get the wetback out of here! *Váyase!*

HOSPITAL WORKER: I not do nothing! He crazy.

RICH: You, get out of here before I breathe on you! *Ahora! Ahora! Váyase!*

NURSE: Mr. Farrell, please.

SAUL: Come back later. *Más tarde, por favor.*

RICH: Go back to your picket line. [*To* SAUL:] They want a wage hike, no less. He tried to get me to bribe him to clean my room—

HOSPITAL WORKER: *Qué coño estás diciendo?* (What the fuck are you saying?)

NURSE: Please cooperate.

LILY: He didn't say anything.

RICH: He won't go near my bed, but he's not afraid to touch my money.

SAUL: You misunderstood him.

RICH: *El dinero está limpio, ah? Tu madre.* (Money is clean, huh, mother-fucker?)

HOSPITAL WORKER: *Maricón.* (Faggot.)

RICH: [*to* SAUL] They're unionizing primates now.

LILY: [*to* RICH] Sh!

HOSPITAL WORKER: *No entiendo.* (I don't understand.) I going. [*He exits.*]

LILY: [*aside to* SAUL] I shouldn't have told him about Chet.

SAUL: [*aside to* LILY] Better you than someone else.

RICH: [*imitating* LILY *and* SAUL] Bzzz bzzz bzzz.

NURSE: [*trying to put a blood pressure cuff on* RICH'*s arm*] Will you be still a moment so I can check your blood pressure?

RICH: Are you a union member, too?

NURSE: [*to* SAUL] What shall I do?

LILY: A good friend of his just passed away.

NURSE: AIDS? [*She resumes struggling with the cuff.*]

RICH: The undertakers' union. Go away, I'm on strike, too; I refuse to participate in the documentation of my own demise.

SAUL: She's only trying to help you.

RICH: [*to the nurse, ripping off the cuff*] Go find another statistic for the Center for Disease Control.

NURSE: [*to* SAUL] I'm a patient woman, but he wants me to lose it. I swear that's what he's after.

RICH: Lady, fuck off!

SAUL: [*to the nurse*] Please. Can't you see he's upset?

NURSE: [*to* RICH] Okay, you win. I'm losing it. Are you happy? I'm *angry*, angry, Mr. Farrell.

LILY: Will you please go!

NURSE: A person can take only so much. I give up. I don't have to put up with this shit. I'm gonna speak to my supervisor. [*The* NURSE *exits.*]

RICH: [*applauding*] Three gold stars for self-assertion!

LILY: [*to* SAUL] I should have kept my mouth shut.

RICH: Having brought Romeo the news that Juliet is dead, Balthasar makes a tearful exit.

LILY: I don't know what to say. [LILY *looks at* RICH, *then* SAUL.]

RICH: I said: Balthasar makes a tearful exit.

LILY: I know how you're feeling.

RICH: No matter. Get thee gone and hire those horses.

LILY: I loved Chet, too.

RICH: Tush, thou art deceived.

LILY: He told me he was sorry for the way he treated you.

RICH: Do the thing I bid thee.

LILY: He didn't belong in New York. He thought he was so sophisticated, but he was just a kid from Mendocino. I'm sorry I let him go home.

RICH: The messenger must go. The hero wishes to be alone with his confidant. [RICH *turns his back on* SAUL *and* LILY.]

LILY: I'll be back tomorrow. [*Aside to* SAUL:] I've got half a crown roast from Margo. She went vegetarian. I'll be up. I have to have a talk with Mick. He's irrational on the subject of AIDS. He can go to hell. If he's so afraid, let him move out. [*To* RICH:] I won't let him come between us. You're my buddy. [SAUL *indicates that* LILY *should leave. She gathers up her belongings, mimes dialing a telephone, and blows* SAUL *a kiss.*] Rich? [SAUL *shakes his head no. She leaves.* SAUL *tries to think of something to say to* RICH. *He abandons the effort and picks up the Sunday* New York Times *crossword puzzle.*]

SAUL: "African quadruped." [*Writing.*] G–n–u … "Hitler's father." [*Counting on his fingers.*] One, two … five letters. Let's see: Herman? Herman Hitler? [*Counting.*] That's six … Otto? … Werner? … Rudi? … Putzi? [*He shrugs.*] Fuck. [*He reads on.*] Thank God: "Jewish rolls." Starts with a *b*, six letters: bagels. [*He starts to write it in.*] Shit, that won't work. I need a *y*.

RICH: [*without turning*] Bialys.

SAUL: B-i-a-l-y-s.

RICH: Short for Bialystok, a large industrial city in eastern Poland … [*turning to* SAUL] hometown of Ludwig Zamenhof, inventor of Esperanto, an artificial international language. Alois Hitler! *A-l-o—*

SAUL: [*putting down the puzzle*] Outclassed again. Why do I bother? He knows everything.

RICH: When I was a kid I used to spend all my time in libraries. My childhood was—

SAUL: If I had a father like yours I would have done the same thing.

RICH: But thanks to that son of a bitch I could tell you how many metric tons of coal the Benelux countries produced per annum, and the capital city of the Grand Duchy of Liechtenstein.

SAUL: I give up.

RICH: Vaduz.

SAUL: Miss Trivial Pursuit.

RICH: I knew to which great linguistic family the Telegu language of South India belongs.

SAUL: Telegu? Isn't that the national dish of Botswana?

RICH: [*ignoring him*] The Dravidian. [SAUL *straightens up the bed table.*] I've

always loved words…I wrote poetry when I was a kid. My brother
used to make fun of me…
Winter, winter,
How you glinter,
With holidays' array.
And the snow
We all know
Is here all day.

[SAUL *smiles.*] I was eight, nine when I wrote that. I had just come in
from sledding down Indian Hill—a steep road that connects Jefferson
Heights to the valley.

SAUL: You showed it to me on our grand tour of West Jersey.

RICH: It was a late afternoon just before sundown and the sky was
intensely blue and intensely cold and you could see the stars already.
For some reason nobody was home when I came back, so I stood
there at the stamped enamel-top kitchen table dripping in my frozen
corduroys and wrote that poem.

SAUL: Are you comfortable? [RICH *shrugs.* SAUL *fixes his pillows.*]

RICH: I was a good kid, but I was lonely and scared all the time. I was so
desperate to find people like myself that I looked for them in the
indexes of books—under *H.* I eventually found them—

SAUL: But not in books.

RICH: The next thing you know I moved to the city and was your typical
office-worker-slash-writer. I hated my job, so I grew a beard and wore
sandals, hoping they would fire me and give me permanent unemployment. I wanted to stay at home in my rent-controlled apartment and
drink bourbon and write poems. I did that for a period. I loved it. The
apartment got filthy and I did, too, and I'd go out only at night—to
pick up guys. And then I found you—in a porno theater—[*he takes*
SAUL's *hand*] and we semi-settled down and you took my picture and I
started to jog. We bought a loft—

SAUL: And raised a cat—

RICH: —and loved each other. But that wasn't enough for me. I don't think
you ever understood this: you weren't my muse, you were…[*he
searches for the word*] Saul. [SAUL *rises and looks out the window.*] I loved
you but I wanted someone to write poems to. During our marriage I
had almost stopped writing and felt stifled even though our loft had
appeared in *New York* magazine. And then I met Chet and left you in

the lurch and lived with him at the Chelsea Hotel. He was shallow, callow, and selfish, and I loved him, too.

We did a lot of coke and I wrote a lot of poetry and the catering was booming and the *New Yorker* published a story of mine and I ran in the marathon. I was on a roll. [*With mounting excitement as he relives the experience.*] I remember training on the East River Drive for the first time. I didn't realize how narrow and dark the city streets were until I got to the river and all of a sudden there was the fucking river. The sky was the same color as that twilight when I was a kid. I came from the darkness into the light. I'm running downtown and I make this bend and out of nowhere straight up ahead is the Manhattan Bridge and then the Brooklyn Bridge, one after another, and my earphones are playing Handel's *Royal Fireworks Music.* It can't get better than this, I know it. I'm running and crying from gratitude. I came from the darkness into the light. I'm running and telling God I didn't know He was *that* good or *that* big, thank you, Jesus, thanks, thanks... [*He slumps back, exhausted from the effort.*]

The next morning I woke up with the flu and stayed in bed for a couple of days and felt much better. But my throat stayed a little sore and my glands were a little swollen... [*Long silence. Casually.*] Saul, I want you to do something for me. Will you do something for me, baby?

SAUL: Sure, babe.
RICH: Now listen. I want you to go out of here and go to the doctor and tell him you aren't sleeping so hot—
SAUL: I'm sleeping okay.
RICH: Sh! Now listen: you tell him you want something to make you sleep and Valium doesn't work on you, but a friend once gave you some Seconal—
SAUL: *No!* I won't do it!
RICH: [*pressuring* SAUL *relentlessly*] I tried hoarding the pills here, but every night the nurse stays to watch me swallow them down.
SAUL: I can't do that.
RICH: I don't want to end up like Chet.
SAUL: I won't listen.
RICH: If you love me, you'll help me. I have something that's eating me up. I don't want to go on. I'm scared to go on.

SAUL: Don't do this to me! I can't handle it. I'll go out the window, I swear, don't do this—

RICH: Don't you see, it's the only way. Just get the pills.

SAUL: No!

RICH: Just have them around. You'll get used to the idea. And when the lesions spread above my neck so that I don't look the same, you'll want me to have them.

SAUL: Help me, help me!

RICH: It's all right. Not now.

SAUL: No.

RICH: Tomorrow.

SAUL: No.

RICH: The day after.

SAUL: No.

RICH: We'll see. [RICH's brother, wearing a surgical mask, gown, and gloves and carrying a small shopping bag, tiptoes in, stopping when he notices RICH and SAUL.]

SAUL: Oh, my God. I think it's your brother.

BROTHER: I'll come back later.

SAUL: [pulling himself together] No, I was just going.

BROTHER: It's all right, really.

SAUL: I've been here for a while.

BROTHER: I'm interrupting.

SAUL: Really.

RICH: [to his BROTHER] Unless you're planning to come into intimate contact with me or my body fluids, none of that shit you have on is necessary.

BROTHER: The sign says—

RICH: But please restrain your brotherly affection for my sake; who knows what diseases you might have brought in with you? [The BROTHER removes the mask, gown, and gloves]

SAUL: You two haven't seen each other in a while, so why don't I just—

RICH: By all means. You need a break, kid. Think about what I said.

SAUL: It stopped raining. I'll take a walk.

RICH: Have a nice walk.

BROTHER: Good seeing ya…? [He has forgotten SAUL's name.]

SAUL: Saul. Yeah. [SAUL exits. Beat.]

BROTHER: I owe you an apology… [RICH won't help him.] I was very frightened…I'm afraid I panicked…Please forgive me.

RICH: Nothing to forgive.

BROTHER: [*brightly*] Betty sends her love. She sent along a tin of butter crunch. [*He offers* RICH *a tin, which* RICH *ignores.*] You're not on any special diet? I told Betty I thought maybe you'd be on one of those macrobiotic diets. I read in the papers that it's helped some people with...

RICH: AIDS.

BROTHER: Yes. I keep a file of clippings on all the latest medical developments. [*He takes a clipping out of his wallet.*] Looks like they're going to have a vaccine soon. The French—

RICH: That's to *prevent* AIDS. I already *have* AIDS.

BROTHER: They have this new drug, AZT.

RICH: That's for pneumonia. I don't have pneumonia.

BROTHER: Right...So how are you doing?

RICH: [*smiling cheerfully*] I have Kaposi's sarcoma, a hitherto rare form of skin cancer. It's spreading. I have just begun chemotherapy. It nauseates me. I expect my hair will fall out. I also have a fungal infection of the throat called candidiasis, or thrush. My life expectancy is...I have a greater chance of winning the lottery. Otherwise I'm fine. How are you?

BROTHER: I'm sorry...[*Brightly again, after a long pause.*] Mary Pat sends her love. She won a school swimming competition and I registered her for the South Jersey championship. Oh, I forgot, she made this for you... [*He takes a large handmade fold-out card from the shopping bag. It opens downward a full two feet.*]

RICH: Say, have you heard about the miracle of AIDS?

BROTHER: What?

RICH: It can turn a fruit into a vegetable. What's the worst thing about getting AIDS? [*The* BROTHER *lets the card fall to the floor.*]

BROTHER: Stop it!

RICH: Trying to convince your parents that you're Haitian. Get it?

BROTHER: I came here to see if I could help you.

RICH: Skip it. So what do you want?

BROTHER: I don't want anything.

RICH: Everything I own is going to Saul—

BROTHER: I don't want anything.

RICH: Except for the stuff Mom left us. I told Saul that it's to go to you. Except for the Barcelona chair—

BROTHER: I don't care about—

RICH: I'm leaving Saul the copyright to my book—

BROTHER: Why are you doing this to me?

RICH: So you don't want my worldly possessions, such as they are; you want me to relieve your guilt.

BROTHER: Stop it.

RICH: [*making the sign of the cross over his* BROTHER, *chanting*] I hereby exonerate you of the sin of being ashamed of your queer brother and being a coward in the face of—

BROTHER: Stop! Don't! [*The* BROTHER *grabs* RICH'S *hand.*]

RICH: No!

BROTHER: Richard, don't!... [*He attempts to hug* RICH, *who resists with all of his strength.*] I don't care...I don't care!...Rich!...Richie...Richie... [RICH *relents. They hug.*]

RICH: I'm so... (frightened)

BROTHER: Forgive me. Forgive me.

RICH: I don't want to... (die)

BROTHER: It's all right. I'm here...I'm here... [*They hold each other close for a beat. The* HOSPITAL WORKER *rushes into the room.*]

HOSPITAL WORKER: Psst. *Oye.* Psst. [RICH *and his* BROTHER *notice the* WORKER.]

RICH: What do you want now?

HOSPITAL WORKER: [*shakes his head no*] *Viene. Viene.* He come. He come. [*He pulls the* BROTHER *from* RICH.]

RICH: Who come?

HOSPITAL WORKER: *Su amigo.* Your freng. He no like.

BROTHER: What's he saying? [RICH *starts to laugh. Enter* SAUL. *The* WORKER *starts sweeping and whistling with an air of exuberant nonchalance. The following is overlapping.*]

RICH: [*laughing*] He...he...

SAUL: What's going on?

BROTHER: Richie, what's so damned funny?

RICH: He thought we... [*he breaks up*] that he and I were cheating on you.

BROTHER: He thought that you and I were... [*He laughs.*]

RICH: He came in to warn me that you were coming! [*He laughs. To the worker.*] *Gracias! Muchas gracias!*

SAUL: He thought you two were... [*He laughs.*]

HOSPITAL WORKER: [*to* RICH] *De nada.* (You're welcome.) Why you laugh? [*The* WORKER *laughs.*] *Como hay maricones.* (What a bunch of faggots.)

RICH: *Es mi hermano.* (He's my brother.)

HOSPITAL WORKER: *Coño.* (Fuck.)

RICH: *Perdona por lo que dije antes. Yo* [*pointing to himself*] *era mucho estupido.* (Forgive me for what I said to you before. I was being very stupid.)

HOSPITAL WORKER: *De nada. Somos todos estúpidos, chico.* (We're all stupid, my friend.) [*He exits. The giggles subside.*]

BROTHER: [*checking watch, stiffening his spine*] I've got to be going now.

RICH: I'm glad you came by.

BROTHER: I'll be back tomorrow with Mary Pat. She's been dying—wanting to come by. She's been writing poetry and—

RICH: I'd love to see her. And tell Betty thanks for the...?

BROTHER: Butter crunch. [*Exiting, shaking hands with* SAUL.] Good seeing ya...? [*He has forgotten* SAUL's *name again.*]

SAUL: Saul.

BROTHER: Sorry. Bye. [*He exits.*]

SAUL: I won't get upset. I won't get upset.

RICH: What's the matter?

SAUL: It's *my* problem.

RICH: What?

SAUL: Rich, I've thought about things.

RICH: What?

SAUL: [*suddenly exploding*] Goddamn it! That prick doesn't know my name after—how many years are we together?

RICH: *Were* together.

SAUL: Pardon me, I forgot we got an annulment from the pope. Fuck it, I won't get upset.

RICH: [*overlapping*] My brother finds it hard to deal with the fact that—

SAUL: I said fuck it.

RICH: Don't you see, it was a big step for him—

SAUL: Your brother hates my fucking guts. Haven't you ever told him I didn't turn you queer?

RICH: My brother—

SAUL: I didn't give you AIDS either.

RICH: My brother—

SAUL: Why're you always defending him? What about me?

RICH: My brother's got a few feelings, too, even if he isn't a card-carrying member of the lavender elite.

SAUL: Let's hear it for our working-class hero.

RICH: You've never tried talking to him. You're so self-centered that it never occurred to you—

SAUL: I'm self—Now wait one minute! I'm so self-centered that I was willing to buy the pills for you.

RICH:You have the pills? [*The other actors create the sleazy atmosphere of Christopher Street near the Hudson River.*]

DEALER 1:Yo, my man.

SAUL: I was willing to go down to Christopher Street, where all the drug dealers hang out.

DEALER 2:What's 'attenin', what's 'attenin'? [SAUL *turns his back to* RICH *and immediately he is on Christopher Street.*]

SAUL: [*to* Dealer 2] Nice night.

RICH: I told you to go to the doctor's.

DEALER 1: Smoke 'n' acid, MDA 'n' speed, Smoke 'n' acid, MDA 'n' speed...   DEALER 2: Smoke 'n' coke, smoke 'n' coke, smoke 'n' coke...

SAUL: [*to* Dealer 1] I said, "Nice night."

DEALER 1: Real nice. What's shakin', babe?

RICH: All you would've had to say to the doctor was "My roommate has AIDS and I'm not sleeping well."

SAUL: [*to* Dealer 1] I'm not sleeping well.

DEALER 1: I have just the thing. Step right into my office.

DEALER 3: Speed, acid, mesc, ups, downs, crack...

SAUL: I'll take one hundred.

DEALER 1:Two dollars a cap.

RICH: Forty's enough.

SAUL: I wanted enough for both of us.

DEALER 1:You got the cash, I got the stash.

RICH:Tristan and Isolde.

DEALER 1: Hey, man, you want them or not?

SAUL:You don't understand anything!

DEALER 1: Look, man, I can't handle all that emotiating.

SAUL: [*near the breaking point*] You've never understood anything!

DEALER 1: Gimme the greens, I'll give you the reds.

RICH:The widow throws herself on her husband's funeral pyre.

SAUL: [*hitting the bed with his fists. If* RICH *were the bed he'd be dead*] SHIT! SHIT! SHIT! You selfish bastard!

RICH:What stopped you?

SAUL: From hitting you?

RICH: From buying the pills.

SAUL:The pills? Nothing stopped me. I bought them.

RICH:Thank you. Where are they?

SAUL: I threw them away.

RICH:Why?

SAUL: Let me help you live!

RICH: What's so hot about living when you're covered with lesions and you're coming down with a new infection every day? . . . If it gets too bad, I want to be able to quietly disappear.

SAUL: I won't argue the logic of it. I can't do what you want me to do.

RICH: I just want them around. You keep them for me — just in case.

SAUL: I won't.

RICH: Then I'll get them myself. I'll go out of here and get them. [*He climbs out of bed. He's shaky.*]

SAUL: You're crazy.

RICH: I don't need you to do my dirty work. [*He takes a few steps.*] Where're my clothes? Where'd they put them?

SAUL: Get back in bed!

RICH: I want to get out of here! [*He puts on his robe.*] This place is a death machine! [*He starts to leave but collapses on the floor.*]

SAUL: [*rushing to his aid*] You idiot.

RICH: [*catching his breath*] Well, here we are again. [SAUL *tries to help him back to bed.*] No. Let me sit . . . Fuck . . . [*He sits in chair.*] "Dependent": from the Late Latin "to hang from."

SAUL: I tried to do what you asked me to do. Just like always.

RICH: You don't have to apologize.

SAUL: I want you to understand something.

RICH: I understand.

SAUL: It's important. Listen. I had made up my mind to give you half of the pills and keep the other half for myself. I was walking past Sheridan Square. It was starting to drizzle again. You've never seen Sheridan Square look grungier: a drunk was pissing on the pathetic little flowers. And that crazy lady — you know the one that sings off-key at the top of her lungs — she was there, too. And my favorite, the guy with his stomach out to here —

RICH: I get the picture.

SAUL: There I was walking with the pills in my pocket, contemplating our suicides. And I was getting wet and cold. As I passed the square, Seconal seemed too slow to me. You don't have a monopoly on pain.

RICH: I never thought —

SAUL: Shut up. Anyway, I had stopped in front of the Pleasure Chest. I looked up and there in the window were sex toys and multicolored jockstraps, lit by a red neon sign. I said, "Help me, God." Which is funny coming from an atheist, let me tell you . . . I said it out loud.

RICH: And you could walk again.

SAUL: Well, it wasn't exactly a miracle.

RICH: Thank God.

SAUL: Anyway, there I was in front of a sex shop, and I looked down and there was a puddle. Now this'll sound stupid.

RICH: Couldn't sound stupider than the rest.

SAUL: In this dirty little puddle was a reflection of the red neon sign. It was beautiful. And the whole street was shining with the incredible colors. They kept changing as the different signs blinked on and off...I don't know how long I stood there. A phrase came to my head: "The Lord taketh and the Lord giveth."

RICH: You blew your punch line.

SAUL: It's the other way around. Anyway, there went two hundred bucks down the sewer.

RICH: Take it off your taxes.

SAUL: Don't you see, I just don't have the right to take your life or mine.

RICH: The Miracle of the Pleasure Chest.

SAUL: Hang in there, Rich.

RICH: Our Lady of Christopher Street.

SAUL: Maybe I'm being selfish, but I want you here. I need you.

RICH: My future isn't exactly promising.

SAUL: I'll take you as is.

RICH: But what happens when it gets worse? Its gonna get worse.

SAUL: I'll be here for you no matter what happens.

RICH: Will you?

SAUL: I promise.

RICH: Shit.

SAUL: What do you want me to say?

RICH: You're so goddamned noble.

SAUL: How do you want me to be?

RICH: I can't afford to be noble. The only thing holding me together is rage. It's not fair! Why me?

SAUL: Why *not* you? Maybe I'm next. No one knows.

RICH: I reserve the right to put an end to all this shit.

SAUL: All right, but if you kill yourself they won't bury you in hallowed ground and you'll go to hell with all us Jews.

RICH: I bet they have a separate AIDS section in the cemetery so I don't infect the other corpses. [*Beat, then suddenly he speaks fiercely.*] Do you promise to stick with me no matter what happens?

SAUL: I do.

RICH: _Do you?_ [_He searches_ SAUL's _face for the answer._] I need you. [_Long silence. He releases_ SAUL.] Paradise in a puddle.

SAUL: You couldn't resist that, could you?

RICH: Prodigies and signs, why not? It's the end of an era.

SAUL: What do you think'll come next?

RICH: Next? After I'm gone?

SAUL: Don't be maudlin. You know I didn't mean that.

RICH: I know you didn't... I've been wondering what happens after I die... Do you think things go on and on? I don't know. Is this all the time I have? I hope not... Do you think anywhere out there is a place as sweet as this one? I like it here—even though right now I am going through a lot of... [_searching for the word_] difficulty. [_He goes back to bed._] And if we get to come back, where do we get to come back to? I don't feature leaving here and going to a goddamned naphtha swamp in the Z sector of some provincial galaxy to live as some kind of weird insect... But if life is a kind of educational process in which each piece of the universe eventually gets to discover its own true divine nature, if it is, then a methane bog on Jupiter might serve just as well as a meadow in the Berkshires... I want to be cremated and I want my ashes to fertilize the apple tree in the middle of Jake's pasture. When you take a bite of an apple from that tree, think of me.

SAUL: You'd be the worm in it.

RICH: Saul?

SAUL: What, Rich?

RICH: There's a café way over by Tompkins Square Park, off of B. It holds maybe ten tables and has the scuzziest art on the walls.

SAUL: What about it?

RICH: I want to read my work there.

SAUL: You turned down the Y.

RICH: People go there, gay, straight, with their weird hair and their ears pierced ninety-nine different ways, they go there late in the evening, and there's a guitarist, and they sit there politely and listen. They look newborn, but slightly depraved. I want to read there when I get out of here. And you'll take pictures. Okay?

SAUL: Sounds okay. Sounds good to me.

RICH: Forgive me for being such a fuck.

SAUL: You really are a fuck.

RICH: I'm a real prick.

SAUL: You're an asshole.

RICH: You're a faggot.

SAUL: You're a fruit.

RICH: You know, if we took precautions…

SAUL: If what? What? You always do that.

RICH: I don't know.

SAUL: Would you like to?

RICH: If we're careful. Do you want to?

SAUL: I'd love to. What do you think?

RICH: I think it'd be okay.

SAUL: What'll we do?

RICH: I don't know. Something safe.

SAUL: We'll think of something.

RICH: Close the curtain.

SAUL: Do you think we should?

RICH: Well, we can't do it like this.

SAUL: Right.

RICH: Right.

SAUL: What if someone comes in?

RICH: So what?

SAUL: Right. [SAUL *doesn't move.*]

RICH: So what are you waiting for?

SAUL: I'm scared.

RICH: So am I. Do you think we should?

SAUL: God, I want to.

RICH: Well, close the fucking curtain! [*The* HOSPICE WORKER *ends the impasse by closing the curtain.*] Thanks.

SAUL: Thanks. [*When the curtain is completely shut, the* HOSPICE WORKER *walks down center.*]

HOSPICE WORKER: I have a new AIDS patient. Richard. He still has a lot of denial about his condition. Which is normal. I think most of us would go crazy if we had to face our own deaths squarely. He's a wonderful man. He writes extraordinarily funny poems about the ward. His lover's there all the time, and he's got a lot of friends visiting, and both families. I only hope it keeps up. It's only his second time in the hospital. They get a lot of support at first, but as the illness goes on, the visitors stop coming—and they're left with only me.

But something tells me it's not going to happen in his case. You should see how his lover takes care of him. God forbid they treat Rich badly, Saul swoops down and lets them have it. He's making a real pain in the ass of himself, which is sometimes how you have to be in this situation.

Rich should be out of the hospital again in a week or so. For a while. He's a fighter... The angry phase is just about over and the bargaining phase is beginning. If he behaves like a good little boy, God will do what Rich tells Him to do... I certainly hope that God does.

I don't know anymore. Sometimes I think I'm an atheist. No. Not really. It's more that I'm angry at God: how can He do this? [*Pause.*] *I* have a lot of denial, *I* am angry, and *I* bargain with God. I have a long way to go towards acceptance. Maybe its time for me to resign. Maybe I'm suffering from burnout.

But what would I do if I didn't go to St. Vincent's? And it's a privilege to be with people when they are dying. Sometimes they tell you the most amazing things. The other night Jean-Jacques—he's this real queen, there's no other word for it—he told me what he misses most in the hospital is his corset and high heels. I mean he weighs all of ninety pounds and he's half-dead. But I admire his spirit. The way they treat him. Sometimes they won't even bring the food to his bed. And I'm afraid to complain for fear they take it out on him! Damn them!... I've lost some of my idealism, as I said. Last night I painted his nails for him. [*She shows the audience her vividly painted fingernails.*] Flaming red. He loved it.

Love! Valour! Compassion!

Terrence McNally

Love! Valour! Compassion! was originally produced by The Manhattan Theatre Club with funds provided by AT&T: On Stage on November 1, 1994.

For performance of songs, arrangements and recordings mentioned in this play that are protected by copyright, the permission of the copyright owners must be obtained.

Author's note

Plays are meant to be seen, not read, and yet we playwrights are always moaning how difficult it is to get our plays published. In fact, we moan about that almost as much as we moan how difficult it is to get our plays produced. Of course, the thing we moan about most is how difficult it is to write them.

That's a lot of moaning.

The truth is probably that none of it has ever been easy — writing, production or publication — but in these last fleeting moments of the twentieth century the voices of those who claim that the theater is not only dying but actually dead and just doesn't know it yet are particularly strident and, to some ears, persuasive, so that a single playwright's moans may seem just that more poignant and urgent than in Shakespeare's day or in Ibsen's.

Significantly, none of those voices belongs to a working playwright. Our moans are pretty small potatoes by comparison. They're saying the party's over; we're saying give us the opportunity and we'll show you it's just begun. A lot of very good plays are being written right now. They're being produced; they're even being published. The only thing they're not is easier to write.

Very few of them are being produced on Broadway, however, which has led to the false conclusion that they aren't being written at all. Not true. The American theater has never been healthier. It's Broadway that's sick. The American theater is no longer Broadway. It is Los Angeles, it is Seattle, it is Louisville, it is everywhere but the west side of midtown Manhattan.

Just look around. For the first time in our history, we have a *national* theater — regional theaters are in the vanguard of producing the world premieres of our best playwrights. Twenty-five years ago regional theaters produced New York's hits, period. Now New York is host to the best work of the not-for-profit regional theater.

I was recently asked to appear on a panel saluting "The Golden Age of Gay Theatre." Nonsense. This is a golden age for the American theater, gay *and* straight. The good new plays are being written and produced as I write this introduction. Take it from someone who toils in the trenches: The energy being generated by American playwrights, directors, actors and designers is seismic. With a little luck you'll be reading about them and seeing them and reading them by this time next year. With no luck at all you'll be aware of them in two or three or maybe five years, but I promise you, they're coming soon to a theater near you. The American theater is on a roll, and there is no stopping us.

I wouldn't be a playwright today if it weren't for the regional theater. My regional theater is the Manhattan Theatre Club. I'm a regional theater playwright who just happens to live in New York.

Without the unconditional love of MTC (*support* seems too meager a word), this play would never have been written. Knowing that they are committed to me as a writer and not as a playwright who is expected to provide them with "hits" has given me the confidence to write each play as I wanted, not what I think *they* wanted based on expectations from the last play. Thanks to MTC I don't have to compete with myself. There was never any danger that I would be tempted to write *Lips Together, Teeth Apart 2* or *Frankie and Johnny Go to Paris* or *Revenge of the Lisbon Traviata.*

And while I write and dream my next play, I know that I will have a production of it at MTC regardless of its likelihood to succeed with audiences and critics. I may be the only playwright in America who has such an arrangement with a producing theater. Because of it, I know I am the luckiest. I owe Lynne Meadow, Barry Grove and Michael Bush my artistic life. In a profession strewn with too many orphans, they have given me a home that in truth feels more like a fairy tale palace. I have a theater!

Good fortune has allowed me to work with the best actors, directors and designers of these times. The play in hand is no exception. *Love! Valour! Compassion!* had no specific moment of inspiration. The title comes from an entry in John Cheever's journals. I think I wanted to write about what it's like to be a gay man at this particular moment in our history. I think I wanted to tell my friends how much they've meant to me. I think I wanted to tell everyone else who we are when they aren't around. I think I wanted to reach out and let more people into those places in my heart where I don't ordinarily welcome strangers. I think a lot of things about this play, but mainly I think it's much too soon to know what they are. These things take time.

I know for certain, however, that the play was given a definitive production by Joe Mantello and seven remarkable actors: Nathan Lane, Stephen Spinella, John Glover, Stephen Bogardus, John Benjamin Hickey, Justin Kirk and Randy Becker. Loy Arcenas took an impossible design situation and made it seem as easy as it was inevitable.

Manhattan Theatre Club had done it again for me. No wonder I have never been tempted, not once, in all these years, to roam. I like to think I'm smart, too.

So once again I am wallowing in some kind of playwright's heaven. If I'm not careful, I'll forget to moan. This book should have come out months ago. The *Love! Valour! Compassion!* cast hasn't been signed to life-indenturing contracts. The theater was too cold last night. The night before, it was too hot. There, that feels much better. The truth is, I'm worrying about the next play. Will it be any good? What's really scary is that Manhattan Theatre Club will produce it all the same. I have no one to blame if it fails but me. That's terrifying.

Moaning is easier.

—Terrence McNally
New York City, 1995

Nathan Lane (Buzz) and Randy Becker (Ramon) in *Love! Valour! Compassion!* at the Walter Kerr Theatre, 1995. (Photo by Martha Swope. Reprinted with permission from the John Willis Theatre World/Screen World Archive.)

Love! Valour! Compassion! was first presented Off Broadway at Stage I at the Manhattan Theatre Club on November 1, 1994, with funds provided by AT&T. It was produced by the Manhattan Theatre Club (Lynne Meadow, Artistic Director; Barry Grove, Managing Director) and directed by Joe Mantello. The sets were by Loy Arcenas, the costumes by Jess Goldstein, the lighting was by Brian MacDevitt, and the sound was by John Kilgore. The choreography was by John Carrafa, the production stage manager was William Joseph Barnes, and the stage manager was Ira Mont.

Cast

Gregory Mitchell . . . . Stephen Bogardus
Arthur Pape . . . . John Benjamin Hickey
Perry Sellars . . . . Stephen Spinella
John Jeckyll/James Jeckyll . . . . John Glover
Buzz Hauser . . . . Nathan Lane
Bobby Brahms . . . . Justin Kirk
Ramon Fornos . . . . Randy Becker

Love! Valour! Compassion! transferred to the Walter Kerr Theatre on Broadway and opened on February 14, 1995. It was directed by Joe Mantello, the sets were by Loy Arcenas, the costumes were by Jess Goldstein, the lighting was by Brian MacDevitt, and sound was by John Kilgore. Choreography was by John Carrafa, the general manager was Victoria Bailey, the company manager was Denise Cooper, the stage managers were William Joseph Barnes and Ira Mont. The press agents were Kevin P. McAnarney/Helene Davis, and Amy Lefkowitz, and the photographer was Martha Swope.

Cast

Gregory Mitchell	Stephen Bogardus
Arthur Pape	John Benjamin Hickey
Perry Sellars	Anthony Heald
John Jeckyll/James Jeckyll	John Glover
Buzz Hauser	Nathan Lane
Bobby Brahms	Justin Kirk
Ramon Fornos	Randy Becker

UNDERSTUDIES:

Perry, Buzz, Arthur	Steven Skybell
John, James	Gregory Mitchell
Perry	Kirk Jackson
Bobby, Ramon	David Norona

For Nathan Lane
Great heart
Great soul
Great actor
Best friend

The Players

BOBBY BRAHMS: *early twenties*
RAMON FORNOS: *early twenties*
BUZZ HAUSER: *mid-thirties*
JOHN JECKYLL: *late forties*
JAMES JECKYLL: *his twin*
GREGORY MITCHELL: *early forties*
ARTHUR PAPE: *late thirties, early forties*
PERRY SELLARS: *late thirties, early forties*

The action takes place in a remote house and wooded grounds by a lake in Dutchess County, two hours north of New York City, on Memorial Day, Fourth of July, and Labor Day weekends, respectively.

Act One

Bare stage.

There are invisible doors and traps in the walk and floor.

Lights up.

The seven actors are singing "Beautiful Dreamer" by Stephen Foster to a piano accompaniment.

GREGORY *turns out and addresses us.*

GREGORY: Um. I love my. Um. House. Everybody does. I like to fill it with my friends. Um. And walk around the grounds at night and watch them. Um. Through the lighted windows. It makes me happy to see them inside. Um. Our home. Mine. Um. And Bobby's. Um. I'm sorry. Um. I don't do this. Um. On purpose. Um.

ARTHUR: It's okay, Gregory.

GREGORY: It was built in 1915 and still has most of the. Um. Original roof. The wallpaper in the dining room. Um. Is original, too. So is. Um. A lot of the cabinet work. You'd have to be a fool. Um. To change it. This sofa is my pride. Um. And joy. It came with the house. It's genuine. Um. Horsehair. It's itchy but I don't care. I love it.

PERRY: Tell them about the sled.

GREGORY: Jerome Robbins gave me this sled.

PERRY: Mutual admiration, he said. One master choreographer to another.

GREGORY: It's flat here, I said. No hills. Um. What am I going to do with a sled? It's not a sled, Gregory, he told me. It's an antique.

JOHN: It's not an antique, Gregory. It's a piece of junk.

GREGORY: I hope you. Um. Appreciate detail. That. Um. Wainscoting there.

This finial here. The main stairs. Um. Have a very gentle rise. Everyone comments how easy it is to. Um. Climb them.

BUZZ: I love your stairs, Gregory. They're so easy.

ARTHUR: Don't tease him like that.

BUZZ: Who's teasing? I wasn't teasing!

GREGORY: They don't build houses like this anymore. Um. The golden age. Um. Of American house building.

BUZZ: If this is going to be Pick On Buzz weekend . . . !

GREGORY: Not architecture, mind you, but house building. This house. Um. Was meant. Um. To stand. Welcome. Make yourself at home. [*As the men begin to break apart, and drift to their various bedrooms, we see that two of them are kissing furiously:* BOBBY *and* RAMON.]

BOBBY: No. No. No. [*They continue. Now it is* PERRY *who turns to us.*]

PERRY: Anyway. Bobby had gone downstairs for cookies, Pepperidge Farm Brussels, and a glass of milk. Whether Ramon had followed him or was waiting for him quiet like a cat, bare feet cold on the bare wood floors, I don't know. I was upstairs, asleep with my Arthur.

BUZZ: I was upstairs, asleep with myself. All this I heard later that summer—when everything changed, for good and bad but forever—but I wouldn't have been surprised.

BOBBY: Don't. Stop. Please. [*They continue.*]

PERRY: Anyway. I prefer the latter: the waiting. It implies certainty. That Bobby would wake up and steal from Gregory's bed and make his way down to their country kitchen—

BUZZ: Which actually was in the country. You're in Dutchess County, two hours north of the city.

PERRY: —and feel unfamiliar arms surround his bare chest from behind, raking his nipples, and in his surprise drop the milk bottle and break it—[*Sound of a bottle of milk breaking.*]

GREGORY: Bobby?

PERRY: —splattering milk and shards of glass everywhere—[*A pool of spilt milk is forming around them.*]

ARTHUR: What was that?

PERRY: —pinning them to that spot where they found themselves in the dull light of the still-open Frigidaire door. [JOHN *sits up in bed.*]

JOHN: Ramon?

BOBBY: Just tell me, who is this? [RAMON *whispers in his ear.*]

PERRY: What name did Ramon whisper in Bobby's ear that first night? His? One of the others'? Mine? [*One by one the other four men resume singing.*] Anyway. They stood like this for quite some time and achieved some sort of satisfaction. After he'd come, Ramon whispered more words of love and passion into Bobby's ear, and stole quietly back up the stairs and into the bed he was sharing with John.

JOHN: Where were you?

RAMON: I couldn't sleep.

PERRY: Bobby cleaned up the mess on the kitchen floor, the whole time wondering what an episode like this meant, if, indeed, it meant anything at all. [ARTHUR *has come into the kitchen area.*]

ARTHUR: What happened?

BOBBY: Perry?

PERRY: That's me.

ARTHUR: It's Arthur.

PERRY: Arthur's my lover. We're often —

ARTHUR: What happened?

PERRY: It's very annoying.

BOBBY: Be careful. There might be broken glass.

ARTHUR: I'm okay, I'm wearing slippers.

PERRY: Arthur is always wearing slippers.

BOBBY: I think I got it all. Did I?

ARTHUR: I can't tell.

PERRY: Bobby is blind.

ARTHUR: Do you mind if I turn the light on? I'm sorry.

BOBBY: It's all right.

PERRY: People are always saying things like that to him. Me, too, and I've known him since he and Gregory got together. Bobby doesn't seem to mind. He has a remarkably loving nature.

ARTHUR: You know the refrigerator door is open?

BOBBY: Thanks. I was just going up. That's all we needed: a refrigerator filled with spoiled food and a house full of guests.

PERRY: See what I mean? Never puts himself first. I don't understand people like that.

ARTHUR: You're not going anywhere. Sit.

BOBBY: What's the matter?

ARTHUR: You cut yourself. Hang on, I'll be right back.

BOBBY: I'm fine.

ARTHUR: Sit [ARTHUR *turns his back to* BOBBY. *We hear running water and the sound of a piece of cloth being torn to make a bandage.*] I read an article that said most blind people hated to be helped.

BOBBY: We love to be helped. We hate to be patronized. It's people assuming we want help that pisses us off. I'm standing at a corner

667

waiting for the light to change and some jerk grabs my elbow and says, "Don't worry, I've got you." It happens all the time. People think blindness is the most awful thing that can happen to a person. Hey, I've got news for everybody: it's not.

PERRY: I'm not in this conversation. I'm upstairs sleeping in the spoon position with my Arthur. Well, thinking I'm sleeping in the spoon position with my Arthur. Arthur's down in the kitchen expressing his remarkably loving nature to Bobby. [PERRY *goes to his and* ARTHUR'*s bed. He hugs a pillow and tries to sleep.*]

BOBBY: "Really, I'm fine," I said.

PERRY: I would have taken him at his word. When someone tells me he's fine, I believe him. But now we're getting Arthur's Mother Teresa.

GREGORY: Don't make yourself sound so cynical, Perry.

PERRY: That's Gregory expressing his remarkably loving nature. Shut up and go back to sleep. It was nothing. [GREGORY *rolls over.*]

JOHN: Americans confuse sentimentality with love.

PERRY: That's John, expressing his fundamentally hateful one. [JOHN *is standing with his back to us. We hear the sound of him relieving himself as he turns over his shoulder and addresses* PERRY, *who is trying to sleep.*]

JOHN: It's true, duck. [ARTHUR *turns around.*]

ARTHUR: I'll try not to hurt. [*He kneels and begins to dress* BOBBY'*s foot.* ARTHUR *is attracted to* BOBBY.]

BOBBY: Ow!

ARTHUR: Sorry.

PERRY: John is sour. He wrote a musical once. No one liked it. There or here. I don't know why they brought it over.

JOHN: Retaliation for losing the War of Independence. [*He follows* RAMON.]

PERRY: He's usually funnier than that.

JOHN: I missed you. I said I missed you.

RAMON: I heard you. Ssshh. Go back to sleep.

JOHN: *Te quiero, Ramon Fornos. Te quiero.*

PERRY: Does everyone know what that means? "I love you, Ramon Fornos. I love you." Anyway, the show closed, John stayed.

JOHN: Some people liked it. Some people rather liked it a lot, in fact. Not many, but some. The good people.

RAMON: Hey, c'mon, it's late!

PERRY: He's Gregory's rehearsal pianist now. When he's not pounding out *The Rite of Spring* for Gregory's dancers, he's working on a new musical-theater project for himself.

JOHN: The life of Houdini. It's got endless possibilities. I've written thirteen songs.

PERRY: John is always working on a new musical-theater project, I should hasten to add.

JOHN: What do you mean, you "should hasten to add"? Is that a crack?

RAMON: I'm going to find another bed if you keep this up.

PERRY: Anyway!

BUZZ: [*stirring*] Did somebody say something about musicals? I distinctly heard something about musicals. Somebody somewhere is talking about musicals! [*He sits up with a start. PERRY holds him.*] I was having a musical comedy nightmare. They were going to revive *The King and I* for Tommy Tune and Elaine Stritch. We've got to stop them!

PERRY: Buzz liked John's musical.

BUZZ: It had a lot of good things in it.

PERRY: Buzz likes musicals, period.

BUZZ: I'm just a Gershwin with a Romberg rising in the house of Kern.

PERRY: [*to us*] He's off.

BUZZ: I was conceived after a performance of *Wildcat* with Lucille Ball. I don't just love Lucy, I owe my very existence to her. For those of you who care but don't know, *Wildcat* was a musical by Cy Coleman and Carolyn Leigh with a book by N. Richard Nash. It opened December 16, 1960, at the Alvin Theatre and played for 172 performances. Two of its most-remembered songs are "Hey, Look Me Over!" and "Give a Little Whistle." For those of you who care but know all that, I'm sorry. For those of you who don't know and don't care, I'm really sorry. You're going to have a lot of trouble with me. So what's up, doc?

PERRY: Buzz, you weren't awake for this.

BUZZ: If I was, I don't remember it.

PERRY: You weren't.

BUZZ: Okay. [*He rolls over and goes back to sleep.*]

PERRY: If it isn't about musicals, Buzz has the attention span of a very small moth. That wasn't fair. Buzz isn't well. He makes costumes for Gregory's company and does volunteer work at an AIDS clinic in Chelsea. He says he's going to find the cure for this disease all by himself and save the world for love and laughter.

BUZZ: It sounds ridiculous when you say it like that.

PERRY: I know. I'm sorry. [*He kisses BUZZ on the head, goes back to his own bed, picks up a pillow, and hugs it close to him.*] None of us were awake for this. [*Gentle snoring begins—or humming, maybe. ARTHUR has stopped*

bandaging BOBBY*'s foot. He is just looking at him now. His hand goes out and would touch* BOBBY*'s bare chest or arms or legs, but doesn't.*]
BOBBY: What are you doing?
ARTHUR: I guess you should know: there's a rather obvious stain on your pajamas.
BOBBY: Thanks.
ARTHUR: I didn't know I could still blush at my age.
BOBBY: That's okay. Your secret is safe with me.
ARTHUR: So is yours.
BOBBY: I'm the one who should be blushing, only blind men don't blush.
ARTHUR: That sounds like the title of one of Perry's detective novels.
BOBBY: I had sort of an accident.
ARTHUR: What you had was a mortal sin. I hope you both did. You know what we used to call them back in Catholic boys' school? Nocturnal emissions. It's so much nicer than "wet dream." It always made me think of Chopin. Nocturnal Emission in C-sharp Minor.
BOBBY: I don't want Greg to know.
ARTHUR: I swear to God, I only came down here for a glass of milk.
BOBBY: I swear to God, I did, too.
ARTHUR: We don't have to have this conversation at three A.M. We don't have to have this conversation ever.
BOBBY: Okay.
ARTHUR: We can talk about you and Greg. We can talk about me and Perry. We can talk about John and his new friend. We could even go back to bed.
BOBBY: It was Ramon.
ARTHUR: I figured.
BOBBY: Why?
ARTHUR: Who else would it be?
BOBBY: I shouldn't have. I'm not very strong that way.
ARTHUR: Most people aren't. [*They start walking up the stairs to their bedrooms.*]
BOBBY: Is he attractive?
ARTHUR: I'm not supposed to notice things like that. I'm in a relationship.
BOBBY: So am I. Is he?
ARTHUR: I think the word is "hot," Bobby. Okay? I love these stairs. They're so easy.
BOBBY: Everyone says that. Have you ever…? On Perry…?
ARTHUR: Yes. I don't recommend it.

BOBBY: Did he find out?

ARTHUR: No, I told him and it's never been the same. It's terrific, but it's not the same. Here we are. End of the line. [*He looks at* BOBBY.] Don't fuck up. You are so… [*He hugs* BOBBY.] He's not that hot, Bobby. No one is.

BOBBY: I know. Thanks. Goodnight. [*He goes into* GREGORY'S *room.* GREGORY *is awake.* ARTHUR *joins* PERRY *in their room.* PERRY *is still clutching his pillow.*]

GREGORY: Are you all right?

BOBBY: Ssshh. Go to sleep.

ARTHUR: Sorry. [*He lies next to* PERRY.]

GREGORY: Where were you?

ARTHUR: Bobby cut himself.

BOBBY: Downstairs.

ARTHUR: He dropped a milk bottle.

BOBBY: I cut myself.

ARTHUR: Remember milk bottles?

BOBBY: I dropped a milk bottle. [*He lies next to* GREGORY.]

ARTHUR: Only Gregory would have milk bottles.

GREGORY: Are you—?

BOBBY: I'm fine. Arthur took care of me. Go to sleep.

ARTHUR: Are you awake?

GREGORY: I missed you. [BOBBY *snuggles against* GREGORY.]

BOBBY: Ssshh. [ARTHUR *rolls over, his back to* PERRY *now.* BUZZ *and* RAMON *are snoring.*]

ARTHUR: He is so young, Perry!

GREGORY: I had a dream. We were in Aspen. The company. We were doing *Wesendonck Lieder.*

ARTHUR: I wanted to hold him.

GREGORY: The record got stuck during "Der Engel." [*Music starts.*] I had to do it over and over and over.

ARTHUR: Desire is a terrible thing. I'm sorry we're not young anymore. [GREGORY *begins to sing: very softly, not well, and never fully awake.*]

GREGORY: In der Kindheit frühen Tagen

Hört'ich oft von Engeln sagen, [JOHN *sits up, while* RAMON *sleeps beside him, and listens.* GREGORY *is beginning to drift off. At the same time we will hear a soprano singing the same words, her voice gently accompanying his.*]

die des Himmels hehre Wonne,

tauschen mit der Erdensonne... [GREGORY *sleeps. He and* BOBBY *roll over in each other's arms.* JOHN *has left* RAMON *and come out of their room. The soprano continues. All the men are snoring now.*]

JOHN: I am that merry wanderer of the night. Curiosity, a strange house, an unfaithful bedfellow drive me. Oh, there are other distractions, too, of course. A dog barking in the distance. Bed springs creaking; perhaps love is being made on the premises. The drip of the toilet on the third floor. Can they not hear it? But it's mainly the curiosity. I am obsessed with who people really are. They don't tell us, so I must know their secrets. [BUZZ *moans in his sleep.*] I see things I shouldn't: Buzz is sleeping in a pool of sweat. They've increased his medication again. And for what? He's dead. [*He puts his hand on* BUZZ'S *shoulder, then moves to where* PERRY *and* ARTHUR *are sleeping.*] Arthur has begun to sleep with his back to Perry, who clutches a pillow instead. I overhear what was better left unsaid: Arthur's sad confession of inappropriate desire. I read words I often wish were never written. Words that other eyes were never meant to see. [*He moves to where* GREGORY *and* BOBBY *are sleeping, takes up a journal, and reads.*] "Memorial Day Weekend. Manderley. Out here alone to work on the new piece. We've invited a full house and they're predicting rain. We'll see if Fred Avens has fixed that leak on the north side porch this time. Thought he would never get around to taking down the storm windows and putting up the screens. The garden is late. Only the cukes will be ready. Everything else will have to come from the A&P." This isn't quite what I had in mind. [BUZZ *appears. He is carrying a knapsack.*]

BUZZ: Where is everybody?

JOHN: Did you know Gregory has only three places he feels safe? His work, in Bobby's arms, and in his journal.

BUZZ: That's disgusting.

JOHN: What is? The weather? Or the startling unoriginality of naming your house Manderley, after a kitsch-classic movie?

BUZZ: Reading someone's journal.

JOHN: Did you just get here?

BUZZ: Yes. Where's Gregory?

JOHN: Down by the lake. Are you alone?

BUZZ: No, I have Michael J. Fox in here. Are you?

JOHN: No. "I've rounded up. Um. The usual suspects. Um."

BUZZ: That's not funny. You're a guest in his home.

JOHN: "I think I'll make my special ginger soy vegetable loaf Sunday night." You see why I do this? Gregory's cooking. There's still time to buy steaks.

BUZZ: If I thought you'd ever read anything I wrote when we were together, I'd kill you. I mean it.

JOHN: "I'm stuck on the new piece. Maybe the Webern was a bad choice of music."

BUZZ: I hate what you're doing. [*He grabs the journal from* JOHN.]

JOHN: I'm puzzled. What kind of statement about his work do you think a choreographer is making by living with a blind person?

BUZZ: I don't know and I don't care. It's not a statement. It's a relationship. Remember them?

JOHN: Nevertheless, the one can't see what the other does. Gregory's work is the deepest expression of who he is—or so one would hope—and Bobby's never seen it.

BUZZ: That's their business. At least they've got someone.

JOHN: Speak for yourself.

BUZZ: So you got lucky this weekend. Don't rub it in. Who is he? Anyone I know?

JOHN: I doubt it.

BUZZ: Is he cute?

JOHN: Yes.

BUZZ: I hate you. I really hate you. What does he do?

JOHN: He's a dancer.

BUZZ: How long have you been seeing him?

JOHN: Three weeks.

BUZZ: Is it serious?

JOHN: In three weeks?

BUZZ: I get serious in about three seconds. People say "What's your rush?" I say, "What's your delay?"

JOHN: What happened to you and—?

BUZZ: I got too intense for him. That's my problem with people. I'm too intense for them. I need someone like Dennis Hopper. A cute, young, gay Dennis Hopper. In the meantime, I'm through with love and all it meant to me.

JOHN: Are you going to be holding that when they come back? [BUZZ *hasn't resisted stealing a glance at* GREGORY's *journal.*]

BUZZ: Perry's work for Greg is *pro bono?*

JOHN: Arts advocacy is very in.

BUZZ: He does the clinic, too.

JOHN: So is AIDS. I'm sorry.

BUZZ: That's five dollars. Anyone who mentions AIDS this summer, it'll cost them.

JOHN: Who made this rule up?

BUZZ: I did. It's for the kitty. Cough it up. [JOHN *holds his hand out for the journal.*]

BUZZ: Did you?

JOHN: Did I what?

BUZZ: Ever read anything I wrote?

JOHN: I don't know. Probably. I don't remember. If you left it out, yes.

BUZZ: I would hardly call a journal left on someone's desk in their own room in their own home while they took the other guests swimming "out." [*He returns the journal.*]

JOHN: People who keep journals—thank you—expect them to be read by people like me. They just pretend they don't. Freud was on to them like that! [*He snaps his fingers while continuing to skim the pages of the journal. We hear thunder. It will increase.*]

BUZZ: Shit, it's going to rain.

JOHN: Here's something about you.

BUZZ: I don't want to hear it.

JOHN: "It's Buzz's birthday. We got him an out-of-print recording of an obscure musical called *Seventeen*."

BUZZ: I have *Seventeen*.

JOHN: "They assured us he wouldn't have it."

BUZZ: Don't worry, I'll act surprised.

JOHN: "It cost seventy-five dollars." You better act more than surprised.

BUZZ: I just paid a hundred and a quarter for it. They said it was the last copy.

JOHN: Calm down. You can exchange it.

BUZZ: For what? *Call Me Madam?* I mean, how many copies of a forgotten musical that opened in 1951 and ran 182 performances at the Broadhurst Theatre are they going to sell in one week? Do you know what the odds are against this sort of thing? This is like the time Tim Sheahan and Claude Meade both got me *Whoop-Up!* [JOHN *has resumed reading in the journal, but* BUZZ *continues, speaking to us.*]

You may wonder why I fill my head with such trivial-seeming information. First of all, it isn't trivial to me, and second, I can contain the world of the Broadway musical. Get my hands around it, so to speak. Be the master of one little universe. Besides, when I'm alone, it gives me great pleasure to sing and dance around the apartment. I especially like "Big Spender" from *Sweet Charity* and "I'm Going Back Where I Can Be Me" from *Bells Are Ringing*. I could never do this with anyone watching, of course. Even a boyfriend, if I had one, which I don't. I'd be too inhibited.

So, when I'm not at the clinic thinking I am single-handedly going to find the cure for this fucking scourge (it doesn't sound ridiculous when I say it, not to me!), I am to be found at my place in Chelsea doing "Rose's Turn" from *Gypsy*. I can't think of the last time I didn't cry myself to sleep. Hey, it's no skin off your nose. I think that is so loathsome of you, John. [GREGORY *and* RAMON *return from swimming.*]

GREGORY: Hello! We're back! Where is. Um. Everybody?

JOHN: I'd better return this.

BUZZ: We're up here.

GREGORY: John?

JOHN: Coming.

GREGORY: You don't know. Um. What you're missing. The lake is. Um. Wonderful.

RAMON: Don't believe him. It's freezing! [He drops his towel.] *¡Ay! ¡Coño! ¡Madre de Dios!*

GREGORY: Did. Um. The others get here?

JOHN: Just Buzz!

BUZZ: Hello.

GREGORY: Buzz!

RAMON: My nuts. Where are they? I have no nuts. They're gone.

GREGORY: They're not gone. Um. They're just. Um. Hiding. [JOHN *and* BUZZ *have returned.*]

RAMON: I had enormous nuts. I was famous for my nuts. Where are my fabulous nuts?

JOHN: I warned you, sweetheart. They got so cold in Gregory's lake they fell off and one of those goddamn snapping turtles is eating them as we speak.

GREGORY: My turtles don't. Um. Snap, Ramon. This is Buzz.

RAMON: Hi, Buzz. I had balls. He doesn't believe me. Tell him about my balls, John.

JOHN: Ramon had legendary balls up until twenty minutes ago.

BUZZ: I know. I've been following them for the last two seasons. From a tiny performance space in the East Village all the way to the Opera House at BAM. The three of you have come a long way, baby.

JOHN: Do you believe this man and I were an item?

BUZZ: A wee item, Ramon.

JOHN: You don't want to go there, Buzz.

BUZZ: But seriously (and don't you hate people who begin sentences "But seriously"?), are you guys going to be back at the Joyce? That last piece was sensational.

GREGORY: You mean *Verklärte Nacht?*

BUZZ: Speak English! The man can barely get a whole sentence out and then he hits us with *Verklärte Nacht!* [*Then to* RAMON] I don't suppose you want to get married?

RAMON: No, but thank you.

BUZZ: Just thought I'd get it out there. Anyway, *Verklärte Schmatta*, whatever it is, was a thrilling piece. It blew me away. And you were fantastic.

RAMON: Thank you.

BUZZ: Your balls weren't bad, either. I stood.

GREGORY: It was wonderful work. Wonderful. Um. Energy.

RAMON: You saw us, Mr. Mitchell?

GREGORY: I wanted to know. Um. What all the. Um. Shouting was about.

RAMON: I would have freaked if I'd known you were out there, Mr. Mitchell.

GREGORY: It's Gregory, please. You're making me feel. Um. Like. Um. An old man with "Mr. Mitchell." It was great. You reminded me. Um. Of me. Um. At your age.

BUZZ: "So what's next for you guys?" he asked in a casual, bantering voice, though his heart was beating so hard he was sure everyone could hear it.

RAMON: Right now we're all just hoping there will be a next season. We're broke.

GREGORY: Every company is, Ramon.

RAMON: Not yours, surely.

BUZZ: It's "Gregory." He doesn't like "Shirley." I'm sorry. Ignore me.

JOHN: He is.

BUZZ: What you people need is a Diaghilev.

RAMON: What's a Diaghilev?

BUZZ: A rich older man who in return for certain favors funds an entire ballet company.

RAMON: Where is this rich older dude? I'm all his.

JOHN: Don't you want to know what these favors are first?

RAMON: I'm a big boy. I have a pretty good idea.

GREGORY: I'm in line first for him, Ramon.

BUZZ: Gregory, your dancers love you. We all do. We'd work for you for free.

GREGORY: I won't let you. Artists should be paid.

RAMON: Right on. The only thing an artist should do for free is make love.

JOHN: Now you tell me. Now he tells me! This is getting entirely too artsy-fartsy/idealistic/intellectual for me. Can we go upstairs and fuck?

GREGORY: I'm going to start. Um. Dinner. They should be here soon. I thought. Um. I'd make my special. Um. *Penne Primavera.* [*He goes.*]

BUZZ: I brought those sketches you wanted. I've got. everyone in Lycra. Lots and lots of Lycra. I'm entering my Lycra period. You still know how to clear a room, John. [*He goes.*]

RAMON: I didn't appreciate that fucking remark in front of your friends.

JOHN: I don't appreciate you flapping your dick in everybody's face, okay? Are you coming upstairs?

RAMON: Maybe. [JOHN *heads upstairs.* GREGORY *looks at his watch and begins to chop onions.* BUZZ *covers his eyes with some computer printouts and rests.* JOHN *waits upstairs while* RAMON *sits downstairs.* ARTHUR, PERRY, *and* BOBBY *come into view. They are driving in heavy traffic.*]

PERRY: Cunt! Goddamn cunt. Fuck you and your ultimate driving machine!

ARTHUR: Perry!

PERRY: Well, they *are* when they drive like that.

ARTHUR: Don't use that word.

PERRY: Men are cunts when they drive like that. Did you see how she just cut right in front of me?

BOBBY: Are you talking to me? Sorry, I was reading the life of Ray Charles. What happened?

PERRY: Some asshole-whore-cunt-bitch-dyke with New Jersey license plates and Republican candidates on her bumper practically took my fender off at seventy miles an hour.

BOBBY: It sounds like an extremely cunt-like maneuver, Batman.

PERRY: You see? Boy Wonder agrees with Bruce.

ARTHUR: I think you're both disgusting. If I had any convictions I'd ask you to let me out right here.

PERRY: You have too many convictions. That's your trouble.

ARTHUR: Maybe you have too few and that's yours.

PERRY: They're just words. They don't mean anything.

ARTHUR: Can I quote him, Batboy?

PERRY: I was mad. Words only mean something if you say them when

677

you're not mad and mean them. I agree: "Nancy Reagan is a cunt" is an offensive remark.

BOBBY: I wouldn't go that far, Bruce.

PERRY: But "Cunt!" when she grabs a cab in front of you after you've been waiting twenty minutes on a rainy night and she just pops out from Lutèce is a justifiable emotional response to an enormous social injustice.

BOBBY: You're right. He's right. Let's all kill ourselves.

ARTHUR: All I'm saying is, it's never right to use words to hurt another person.

PERRY: How did I hurt her? She didn't hear me. She's halfway to Poughkeepsie by now, the bitch. Don't get me started again. I was just calming down.

ARTHUR: We hurt ourselves when we use them. We're all diminished.

PERRY: You're right. I don't agree with you, but you're right.

ARTHUR: Of course I'm right, you big fairy. And what are you laughing at back there, you visual gimp? There's no really good insulting word for a blind person, is there?

BOBBY: I think you people decided nature had done enough to us and declared a moratorium.

PERRY: Do you ever wonder what Gregory looks like?

ARTHUR: Perry!

BOBBY: It's all right. I don't mind. I know what he looks like.

PERRY: No, I mean, what he really looks like.

BOBBY: I know what he really looks like. He's handsome. His eyes shine. He has wonderful blond hair.

PERRY: But you've never seen blond hair. You have no concept of it.

BOBBY: In my mind's eye, I do, Horatio.

ARTHUR: That shut you up.

BOBBY: That wasn't my intention. In my mind's eye, I see very clearly the same things you and Perry take for granted. Gregory's heart is beautiful.

PERRY: What do we look like?

ARTHUR: Perry!

BOBBY: Like bookends.

PERRY: Is that a compliment?

BOBBY: I think you've come to look more and more like each other over the years.

PERRY: You haven't known us that long.

ARTHUR: That's not what he's saying.

Bobby: I think you love each other very much. I think you'll stick it out, whatever. I think right now you're holding hands—that when Perry has to take his hand from yours, Arthur, to steer in traffic, he puts it back in yours as soon as he can. I think this is how you always drive. I think this is how you go through life.

Arthur: Don't stop.

Bobby: I think you're both wearing light blue Calvin Klein shirts and chinos.

Perry: Wrong!

Arthur: Look out for that car—!

Perry: I see it, I see it! What color is my hair?

Bobby: What hair? You're totally bald.

Perry: Wrong again. What color?

Bobby: I wanted to be wrong. I don't like this game. It's making me afraid.

Ramon: Okay. [*He stands up.*]

John: He's coming. [Ramon *starts up to* John's *room.*]

Perry: I'm sorry. I didn't . . . [*They drive in silence.* Ramon *comes into the bedroom.* John *is sitting on the bed.*]

John: Hello.

Ramon: Hi.

John: I'm sorry.

Ramon: Look, I'm sort of out of my element this weekend. He's Gregory Mitchell, for Christ's sake. Do you know what that means? You're all old friends. You work together. You have a company. I'm just somebody you brought with you. I'd appreciate a little more respect, okay? I'm being honest.

John: Okay.

Ramon: Thank you. What's wrong with your neck?

John: Would you be an angel and massage my shoulders?

Ramon: Sure. Just show me where. [Ramon *works on* John.]

Bobby: Now it's my turn. I want you to tell me what someone looks like.

Perry: Don't tell me, let me guess: Tom Cruise, Willard Scott. I give up, who?

Bobby: John.

Arthur: John Jeckyll?

Bobby: What does he look like? Describe him. After all this time, I still can't get a picture.

Perry: Can you visualize Satan, Bobby?

Arthur: Don't start.

Perry: Do you have a concept of evil?

Bobby: A very good one, actually.

ARTHUR: Not everyone shares your opinion, Perry. Perry has a problem with John, Bobby.

PERRY: I don't have a problem with him. I can't stand him and I wish he were dead.

JOHN: Don't stop.

PERRY: Beware him, Bobby. People like you are too good for this world, so people like John Jeckyll have to destroy them.

ARTHUR: You can't say these things, Perry.

PERRY: Yes, I can. He doesn't have to believe them.

BOBBY: I'm not so good. If anything, this world is too good for us.

PERRY: What do you care what John Jeckyll looks like anyway?

BOBBY: I just wondered. People like that intrigue me.

PERRY: What? Shits?

ARTHUR: It's going to be a wonderful weekend.

PERRY: What does that mean?

ARTHUR: John had nowhere to go, so Gregory invited him.

BOBBY: Didn't Gregory tell you?

PERRY: No, he did not. Probably because he knew I wouldn't come if he did. Shit! Why would Greg do this to me?

ARTHUR: He didn't. He told me. I elected not to tell you.

PERRY: Why?

ARTHUR: "Why?"!

PERRY: I assume he's coming alone.

ARTHUR: Why would you assume that?

PERRY: Who would willingly spend Memorial Day weekend at a wonderful big house in the country on a gorgeous lake with John Jeckyll when they could be suffocating in the city all by themselves?

BOBBY: He's bringing someone.

ARTHUR: A new boyfriend?

PERRY: One of the Menendez brothers.

BOBBY: A dancer.

ARTHUR: Someone from the company?

BOBBY: No. I think Greg said his name was Ramon. Ramon Something.

ARTHUR: Sounds Latino.

PERRY: "Something" sounds Latino? Since when?

BOBBY: He's Puerto Rican.

PERRY: A Third World boyfriend. So John Jeckyll has gone PC.

ARTHUR: I don't think Puerto Rico qualifies as Third World.

PERRY: This is like Adolf Hitler shtupping Anne Frank.

ARTHUR: You are really over the top this afternoon!

PERRY: Wait till the weekend's over! Here's the driveway.

You're home, Bobby. [*Sounds of the car approaching. Everyone in the house reacts to the sound of it.*]

GREGORY: They're here! Buzz, John! They're here! I hear the car!

PERRY: Any other surprises for us, Bobby?

JOHN: I guess they're here. Perry and Arthur are lovers. Bobby is Greg's.

RAMON: I'm terrible with names.

GREGORY: Buzz, wake up, they're here!

BUZZ: I was dreaming about a vacuum cleaner. I need to get laid. [GREGORY, BUZZ, JOHN *and* RAMON *go to greet the others, who are carrying bags.*]

GREGORY: I was beginning to. Um. Worry. How was the. Um. Traffic?

PERRY: Terrible. Especially before Hawthorne Circle.

ARTHUR: I told him to take the Thruway, but no!

BUZZ: The train was horrendous. I should have waited for you. But guess who I saw? Tony Leigh and Kyle. Together again. A handshake? What is this shit? I want a hug, Martha.

GREGORY: Where's my. Um. Angel?

BOBBY: Hi. Have you been working?

GREGORY: I didn't leave. Um. The studio. Um. All week.

BOBBY: How did it go?

GREGORY: Great. Don't ask. Terrible. [*They embrace and withdraw a little.*]

JOHN: Hello, Perry. Arthur. You both look terrific. Don't you two put on weight? Ever? Anywhere?

ARTHUR: Look who's talking! I'd love to see the portrait in his closet.

JOHN: No, you wouldn't. Ramon, Arthur and Perry.

PERRY: He's Arthur, I'm Perry. He's nice, I'm not. Hi.

ARTHUR: We're both nice. Don't listen to him.

BUZZ: So what are you driving now, boys? A Ford Taurus?

PERRY: What do you care, you big fruit? I don't know. I just get in, turn the key, and go. When they stop, I get a new one.

JOHN: You should see the wreck we rented.

ARTHUR: It's a Mazda 626, Buzz.

PERRY: He's so butch.

ARTHUR: Someone had to do it. That's why he married me. Can you change a tire?

PERRY: No.

ARTHUR: Neither can I.

BUZZ: That's from *Annie Get Your Gun.* "Can you bake a pie?" "No."
"Neither can I." Ethel Merman was gay, you know. So was Irving
Berlin. I don't think English is Ramon's first language.

GREGORY: I missed you.

BOBBY: It's so good to be here. The city is awful. You can't breathe. They
still haven't fixed the dryer. Flor was in hysterics. Here. I've got your
mail in my backpack.

GREGORY: What's this?

BOBBY: The CDs you wanted. And I got your sheet music from Patelson's.

GREGORY: You didn't have to.

BOBBY: I wanted to.

GREGORY: John, look, the Elliott Carter!

RAMON: [*to* BOBBY.] Hi, I'm Ramon.

GREGORY: I'm sorry! [RAMON *puts his hand out to* BOBBY.] Bobby doesn't.
Um. See, Ramon.

RAMON: I'm sorry. I didn't—

BOBBY: Don't be sorry. Just come here! [*He hugs* RAMON.] Welcome.
Ramon, is it?

RAMON: Right.

BOBBY: Latino?

RAMON: Yes.

BOBBY: *Mi casa es su casa.* I bet you were wishing I wasn't going to say that.

BUZZ: We all were, Bobby.

PERRY, ARTHUR and **BUZZ:** We all were!

RAMON: Listen, that's about as much Spanish as I speak.

BOBBY: You're kidding.

RAMON: Sorry to disappoint you. The Commonwealth of Puerto Rico is a
territory of U.S. imperialism.

JOHN: No speeches, please, Ramon. No one's interested.

RAMON: We speak American. We think American. We dress American. The
only thing we don't do is move or make love American.

BOBBY: I've been like this since birth, Ramon. Gregory and I have been
together four years. I get around fine. It'll surprise you. Any more
questions?

RAMON: [*Off guard.*] No. [*They separate.*]

GREGORY: Let me. Um. Show you. Um. To your room.

ARTHUR: After all these years, I think we know, Gregory. If those walls
could talk!

BUZZ: They don't have to. We've all heard you.

ARTHUR: What room are you in?

Buzz: That little horror under the eaves. I call it the Patty Hearst Memorial Closet.

Arthur: Give me a hand with these, will you, Perry?

Perry: I told you not to take so much.

Arthur: It's my hair dryer.

Perry: You don't have enough hair to justify an appliance that size.

Arthur: Has it ever occurred to you that I stopped listening to you at least ten years ago?

Ramon: Here, let me.

Arthur: Thank you. [*They will start moving to the house.*]

Gregory: We're having. Um. *Salade Nicoise.* Um. For lunch.

Buzz: You know I'm allergic to anchovies.

Gregory: We just. Um. Swam the float out. Me. Um. And Ramon.

Buzz: He knows I'm allergic to anchovies.

Perry: I'm not going in that lake until you get it heated.

Gregory: I hope you brought. Um. Your swimsuits.

Arthur: No one is wearing swimsuits. We're all going skinny-dipping after lunch. What are we? Men or wimps?

Buzz: You just want to see everyone's dick.

Arthur: I've seen everyone's dick. Answer the question.

Buzz: Sometimes we're men and sometimes we're wimps. You haven't seen Ramon's dick.

Arthur: You're a troublemaker.

Buzz: I'm not a troublemaker. I'm an imp. A gay imp. [*He goes. The new arrivals are beginning to settle in.* **Perry** *and* **John** *remain for the following until indicated.*]

Perry: Anyway. Gregory knew he'd left Bobby downstairs and outside the house.

Gregory: Does everyone. Um. Have towels?

Perry: It was their ritual. Whenever they arrived at the house from the city, Bobby liked to be alone outside for a while, even in winter. Gregory never asked what he did.

Bobby: Hello, house.

Arthur: Greg! We need some towels.

Perry: No, we don't. We brought our own. Remember?

Bobby: Hello, trees.

Arthur: Never mind! That's right, we hate his towels.

Bobby: Hello, lake.

Gregory: Who said they needed towels?

Perry: Greg's house is very large.

ARTHUR: Too large. I get sick of shouting. We're fine! Forget the towels!

BOBBY: I bless you all.

PERRY: None of us saw Ramon when he returned to the driveway, the parked cars, and Bobby. Arthur and I were settling in. [RAMON *has returned to where* BOBBY *is standing. He watches him.*]

JOHN: I was on the phone to London with my brother, James.

PERRY: I didn't know you had a brother.

JOHN: A twin brother. We're like *that*. [*He opens his arms wide.*] He's not well.

PERRY: I'm sorry.

JOHN: This is about them. [*He nods toward* BOBBY *and* RAMON.]

PERRY: Minutes passed. Gregory fussed. Buzz washed salad greens in his hosts' pricey balsamic vinegar. He's very diligent about germs. He has to be. Ramon looked at Bobby.

BOBBY: Thank you. God.

RAMON: Excuse me?

BOBBY: Who's that?

RAMON: I'm sorry.

BOBBY: You startled me.

RAMON: It's Ramon. I'm sorry. I thought you said something.

BOBBY: I was thanking God for all this. The trees, the lake, the sweet, sweet air. For being here. For all of us together in Gregory's house.

RAMON: I didn't mean to interrupt or anything.

BOBBY: I'm not crazy. I'm happy.

RAMON: I understand.

GREGORY: Here are the towels you asked for.

ARTHUR: Thank you.

GREGORY: Anything else?

ARTHUR: We're fine.

GREGORY: Perry?

PERRY: We're fine.

GREGORY: Um. I'm glad. Um. You're both here.

RAMON: Do you need a hand with anything?

BOBBY: No, thanks.

BUZZ: Pssst! Gregory!

GREGORY: What?

BUZZ: John is on the phone to his brother in London. I didn't hear him use a credit card or reverse the charges.

GREGORY: Um. I'm sure he'll. Um. Tell me.

BUZZ: Don't you ever believe the worst about anyone?

GREGORY: No. [RAMON *hasn't moved. He scarcely breathes. He has not taken his eyes off* BOBBY.]

BOBBY: You're still there, aren't you? What are you doing? What do you want? Don't be afraid. Tell me. All right. Don't. Stay there. I'll come to you. Just tell me, should I fall (which I don't plan to), what color are my trousers? I think I put on white. I hope so. It's Memorial Day.

PERRY: I don't know why, but I'm finding this very painful.

BOBBY: Children play at this and call it Blindman's Bluff. Imagine your whole life being a children's birthday-party game!

JOHN: Painful, erotic, and absurd.

BOBBY: I can feel you. I can hear you. I'm getting warm. I'm getting close. I like this game. I'm very good at it. I'm going to win. You haven't got a chance.

PERRY: Bobby didn't see the rake. [BOBBY *trips and falls. He hurts himself. There will be a gash on his forehead.*]

RAMON: Oh!

BOBBY: He speaks! The cat has let go his tongue. I wouldn't say no to a hand. [RAMON *goes.* BOBBY *calls after him.*] At least tell me, what color are my trousers?

PERRY: [*moved.*] White. White.

BOBBY: Sometimes I get tired of behaving like a grown-up. Ow! Gregory! [*At once, everyone converges on the scene and surrounds him.*]

GREGORY: What happened?

BOBBY: I'm okay. Just—

GREGORY: The rake! You tripped. It's my fault. Um.

PERRY: Take his other arm.

BOBBY: I'm fine. I want Gregory to do it.

BUZZ: Who would leave a rake out like that?

ARTHUR: Shut up, will you?

JOHN: He's cut.

BOBBY: I'm not cut.

JOHN: His forehead.

BOBBY: What color are my trousers?

GREGORY: White.

BOBBY: Are there grass stains on them?

BUZZ: Bobby, you are the only fairy in America who still wears white pants on the first holiday of summer.

BOBBY: I was hoping I was the only person in America who still wears white pants on the first holiday of summer.

PERRY: White pants were before my time even, and I'm pushing forty.

BUZZ: Not. You pushed forty when *Chorus Line* was still running.

PERRY: That's not true. I was born in 19 —

ARTHUR: We have an injured person here. [RAMON *returns*.]

BOBBY: I'm not injured.

JOHN: Where have you been?

RAMON: Down by the lake. What happened?

BOBBY: Nothing happened. Who's that?

BUZZ: The new kid on the block.

RAMON: Is he all right?

BOBBY: I fell. Big deal. I do it all the time.

GREGORY: No, you don't. No, he doesn't.

BOBBY: Now everyone back off. Everyone but Gregory. I can feel you all crowding around me.

GREGORY: One!

BOBBY: What are you doing?

BUZZ: Rhett picks up Scarlett and carries her up the stairs.

GREGORY: Two!

BOBBY: No, I don't want you to.

GREGORY: Three! [*He tries to pick* BOBBY *up but can't. He staggers with the weight, then sets him down. The others look away in embarrassment.*] I couldn't get a good. Um. Grip.

BOBBY: It's not you. It's all that ice cream I've been eating.

GREGORY: That's never happened. Usually I — I feel so —

BOBBY: It's okay, it's okay. [BOBBY *and* GREGORY *go into the house. The others hang behind somewhat sheepishly.*]

BUZZ: [*singing*] "Just a weekend in the country."

RAMON: Is that a joke?

BUZZ: Come on, I need you in the kitchen. I'll explain the entire Sondheim oeuvre to you while we peel potatoes. I'm borrowing your humpy boyfriend, John. I love the way I said that. Oeuvre. I'm quite impressed. Oeuvre. Say it with me. Oeuvre. [BUZZ *and* RAMON *go.*]

ARTHUR: Don't ever try to pick me up.

PERRY: It's lucky for you I did.

JOHN: I'd rung off from my brother feeling a rage and a desolation I didn't know how to cope with. "Didn't"? I never have.

ARTHUR: What's the matter?

JOHN: My twin brother. The National Theatre seamstress. He wants to come over. He's not well. He needs me and I don't like him.

ARTHUR: That's a tough order. I don't envy you. Perry, I'm going to take a canoe out. You want to come?

PERRY: I promised Greg I'd go over some company business with him.

ARTHUR: It's your last chance to get rid of me.

PERRY: No, it's not. [ARTHUR *goes. Only* PERRY *and* JOHN *remain.*] I work with quite a few AIDS organizations.

JOHN: Thank you.

PERRY: They can help him find a doctor.

JOHN: Thank you.

PERRY: It never ends.

JOHN: No.

PERRY: How does Buzz look to you?

JOHN: I don't know. How does he look to you?

PERRY: I can't tell anymore.

JOHN: He wouldn't tell me if things were worse.

PERRY: I can't look at him sometimes.

JOHN: Anyway.

PERRY: [*pleasantly*] You got that from me, you know.

JOHN: Got what?

PERRY: The "anyway."

JOHN: It's a word in the dictionary. Page 249. You can't copyright the English language, duck.

PERRY: Hey, I'm trying! Fuck you. [*He goes.*]

JOHN: Anyway. *En tout cas!* The weekend had begun. Everyone was in place. Old wounds reopened. New alliances forged. For fifteen minutes, while I helped Arthur wash their car, he was my best friend in the entire world. Later that afternoon, after too much picnic, when I came upon him and Perry all cozy in a hammock on the porch, he barely gave me the time of day. The hours until dinner seemed endless. [*The other men are reassembling for after-dinner after a very big meal.*]

PERRY: No, Gregory. It's out of the question. Jesus, I hope this isn't why you invited us out here for the weekend.

GREGORY: I've. Um. Committed us.

PERRY: Well *un*commit us!

GREGORY: It's too late.

PERRY: Leave it to me. I'll get you out of it.

GREGORY: No, I want to. Um. Do it. It's for a good cause.

PERRY: I don't care if it's the greatest cause in the history of Western civilization, which it's not, you are not going to find six men, nondancers

all, to put on tutus and do *Swan Lake* for another AIDS benefit at
Carnegie Hall. You're not going to find one man!

BUZZ: Speak for yourself. Perry.

PERRY: Well, *you!* The love child of Judy Garland and Liberace.

ARTHUR: When is it, Greg?

GREGORY: Um. It's. Um. Early September, right after Labor Day.

PERRY: Bobby, tell your lover he is not going to find six men to make fools
of themselves like that.

BOBBY: How would they be making fools of themselves?

PERRY: By dressing like women. Men in drag turn my stomach.

RAMON: Why?

ARTHUR: Don't start. Perry.

BUZZ: You wouldn't be in drag. I'd have you in tulle, lots and lots of tulle. A
vision of hairy legs in a tutu and toe shoes.

PERRY: This will go over big at the NEA, Gregory. That's all we need. A
picture of you looking like some flaming fairy in the Arts and Leisure
section.

GREGORY: I. Um. I am a flaming fairy. I thought we all were.

PERRY: You know what. I'm talking about.

BOBBY: Don't yell at him. It was my idea I thought it would be funny.

PERRY: What do you know about funny? I'm sorry, Bobby, but sometimes
boyfriends should stay boyfriends.

GREGORY: Sometimes. Um. Lawyers should stay. Um. Lawyers.

PERRY: You've done enough for AIDS. We all have.

GREGORY: Nobody's done enough. Um. For AIDS.

BOBBY: It's okay, Gregory.

GREGORY: Never mind, Perry. I'll ask someone else. Now who wants what?

ARTHUR: We're all fine.

PERRY: No, we're not.

JOHN: People are bloody sick of benefits, Gregory.

PERRY: That's the truth.

BUZZ: Not the people they're being given for.

GREGORY: *Basta*, Buzz. The subject is closed.

ARTHUR: Dinner was delicious. The mashed potatoes were fabulous, Gregory.

BUZZ: The mashed potatoes were mine. [*He sings from* The King and I★.] I
don't know why I've bothered to perfect a flawless imitation of
Gertrude Lawrence when none of you cretins has even heard of her!

JOHN: We've heard, luv. We don't care.

★See note on songs and recordings on page 654.

BOBBY: Who's Gertrude Lawrence?

PERRY: A British actress.

GREGORY: She was. Um. Gay, you know.

BUZZ: That's not funny. Julie Andrews made a rotten film about her.

ARTHUR: Isn't Julie Andrews gay?

BUZZ: I don't know. She never fucked me. Don't interrupt. Gertrude Lawrence wasn't an actress. She was a star. Hence, the rotten film, *Star!*, but don't get me started on movies. Movies are for people who have to eat popcorn while they're being entertained. Next question? Yes, you, at the end of the table with the lindenberry sorbét all over his face.

RAMON: Who's Julie Andrews?

BUZZ: I should have seen that one coming. I was born in the wrong decade, that's my problem.

RAMON: I was kidding. I saw *Mary Poppins*. But who's Liberace?

BOBBY: Who's Judy Garland? Who are any of those people? [BOBBY *and* RAMON *laugh together.*]

ARTHUR: You want me to clear up, Gregory?

BUZZ: Who's Ethel Merman? Who's Mary Martin? Who's Beatrice Lillie? Who's anybody? We're all going to be dead and forgotten anyway.

BOBBY: Gregory's not.

BUZZ: I'm talking about mattering!

PERRY: I just don't want to be dead and forgotten in my own lifetime.

ARTHUR: Nattering?

BUZZ: Mattering! Really mattering.

ARTHUR: Oh, I thought you said "nattering"!

JOHN: You admit people like Gertrude Lawrence don't really matter?

ARTHUR: I thought he said "nattering."

BUZZ: I cannot believe a subject of the U.K. could make a remark like that. Gertrude Lawrence brought pleasure to hundreds of thousands of people. You wrote a musical that ran for eleven performances.

JOHN: I have United States citizenship.

RAMON: I know who Barbra Streisand is.

BUZZ: She'll be very pleased to hear that.

BOBBY: I don't know who most of those people are, either.

PERRY: When did you take out U.S. citizenship?

JOHN: Nine years ago. October 25.

BUZZ: Barbara Cook's birthday. "Who's Barbara Cook?" No one. Nobody. Forget it. Die listening to your Madonna albums. I long for the day when people ask "Who's Madonna?" I apologize to the teenagers at the table, but the state of the American musical has me very upset.

Perry: The state of America is what should get you upset.

Buzz: It does. It's a metaphor, you asshole!

Perry: Now just a minute!

Buzz: I have a picture of a starving child in Somalia over my desk at the clinic. He's covered in dust.

John: We all know the picture.

Perry: It doesn't justify you calling me an asshole.

Buzz: The child has fallen forward on his haunches, he's so weak from hunger, he can barely lift his head.

Perry: Buzz, we know the picture. It was in every magazine and paper.

Buzz: Clearly, the kid is dying. He's got what? Five minutes? Ten? Five feet away a vulture sits. Sits and waits. He's not even looking at the kid. He's that confident where his next meal is coming from. There's no way this kid is going to jump up and launch into a number from *Oliver!* or *Porgy and Bess*.

Perry: We've all seen the picture!

Bobby: [*quietly*] I haven't. [Gregory *takes his hand.*]

Perry: What is your point?

Buzz: Point? I don't have a point. Why does everything have to have a point? To make it comfortable? I look at that picture every day and I get sick to my stomach and some days I even cry a little. The newspaper has already yellowed, but the nausea and the occasional tears keep coming. But so what? So fucking what? That kid is dead meat by now.

John: That's disgusting.

Buzz: You bet it is.

John: Your language.

Buzz: So sue me. That's from *Guys and Dolls*, for you kiddies.

Ramon: Happy Memorial Day.

Perry: I think the point is, we're all skiing around here talking about something, pretending to care.

Arthur: No one's pretending.

Perry: Pretending to care, when the truth is there's nothing we can do about it. It would hurt too much to really care. You wouldn't have a stomach ache, you'd be dead from the dry heaves from throwing your guts up for the rest of your life. That kid is a picture in a newspaper who makes us feel bad for having it so good. But feed him, brush him off, and in ten years he's just another nigger to scare the shit out of us. Apologies tendered, but that's how I see it.

Arthur: Apologies not accepted.

GREGORY: Don't, you two.

ARTHUR: I hate it when he talks like that.

PERRY: You'd rather I dissembled, sirrah? (I wasn't an English major at Williams for nothing!)

ARTHUR: Yes. I'd rather you would. Rather the man I shared my life with and loved with all my heart, rather he dissembled than let me see the hate and bile there.

PERRY: The hate and bile aren't for you, love.

ARTHUR: That's not good enough, Perry. After a while, the hate and bile are for everyone. It all comes around. [*He starts clearing the table.*]

PERRY: Anyway.

ARTHUR: I hate that word. You use it to get yourself out of every tight corner you've ever found yourself in. Shall I load the washer?

GREGORY: Just rinse and stack. Thank you, Arthur.

RAMON: Do you need a hand?

ARTHUR: No, thank you. [*He goes.*]

PERRY: The younger generation hasn't put in their two cents, I notice.

RAMON: As a person of color, I think you're full of shit. As a gay man, I think—

JOHN: No one cares what you think as a gay man, duck. That wasn't the question. What do you think as a member of the human race?

RAMON: As a gay man, I think you're full of shit. [*We hear a door slam. ARTHUR isn't back. Everyone reacts.*] I think the problem begins right here, the way we relate to one another as gay men.

JOHN: This is tired, Ramon. Very, very tired.

RAMON: I don't think it is. We don't love one another because we don't love ourselves.

JOHN: Clichés! Clichés!

RAMON: Where is the love at this table? I want to see the love at this table.

BOBBY: I love Gregory.

GREGORY: I love Bobby.

PERRY: I love Arthur. I love Gregory. I love Bobby. I love Buzz. Right now I love you, your righteous anger.

BUZZ: I sure as hell don't love anyone at this table right now. All right. Bobby and Greg. A little bit, but only because they're our hosts.

JOHN: I love the Queen; she's been through hell lately. My Aunt Olivia in Brighton in a pensioners' villa—old-age home, you call them? My Welsh Corgi, Dylan, even though he's been dead lo these eleven years (I'm surprised his name came up!). And my job.

GREGORY: Thank you.

RAMON: Everything you love is dead or old or inanimal. Don't you love anything that's alive and new?

JOHN: Of course I do, but I choose not to share them around a dinner table. And you mean "inanimate."

PERRY: That's honest.

JOHN: I thought that's what we were all being. Otherwise, what's the point? Are you satisfied, Ramon?

RAMON: None of you said yourself.

PERRY: Maybe it goes without saying.

JOHN: We were waiting for you, Ramon. How do you love yourself? Let us count the ways.

RAMON: I love myself. I love myself when I dance.

JOHN: That's one.

RAMON: I love myself when I'm dancing. When I feel the music right here. When I'm moving in time and space. Gregory knows what I'm talking about.

GREGORY: Yes, yes, I do.

RAMON: When I dance I become all the best things I can be.

JOHN: Ramon loves himself when he dances. That's still only one, Chiquita. One and counting.

RAMON: I love myself when I'm making love with a really hot man. I love myself when I'm eating really good food. I love myself when I'm swimming naked.

JOHN: That's four.

RAMON: The rest of the time I just feel okay.

PERRY: I'm jealous. We don't reach such an apotheosis at the law firm of Cohen, Mendelssohn and Leibowitz.

RAMON: But most of all I love myself when I'm dancing well and no one can touch me.

JOHN: Is this as a gay dancer, luv?

RAMON: Fuck you, John.

BUZZ: You tell him, sweetheart. That's right: Fuck you, John.

JOHN: Americans use that expression entirely too often.

BUZZ: Everybody!

ALL BUT JOHN: Fuck you, John!

JOHN: In England we think it nearly as often as you do, but we don't actually say it to someone's face. It would be too rude. Half the people who are being knighted at the Palace every year are thinking "Fuck you" as they're being tapped with that little sword, but they don't come right out and say it, the way an American would, which is why we don't knight Americans, the only reason—you're too uncouth.

ALL BUT JOHN: Fuck you.

JOHN: What do you mean when you tell another person "Fuck you"?

RAMON: Fuck you, John. And don't you ever call me Chiquita again.

BUZZ: This is good.

JOHN: I think you mean several things. Mixed signals, I believe they're called in therapeutic circles. "I hate you. Get out of my life." At least. "I hate you, get out of my life for the moment."

RAMON: Fuck you.

JOHN: "I love you, but you don't love me. I want to kill you, but I can't so I will hurt you instead. I want to make you feel small and insignificant, the way you've made me feel. I want to make you feel every terrible thing my entire life right up until this moment has made me feel." Ah, there's the link! I knew we'd find it. The common bond uniting this limey and the Yanks. The resolution of our fraternal theme.

RAMON: I said "Fuck you."

JOHN: But until we recognize and accept this mutual "Fuck you" in each of us, with every last fiber of my fading British being, every last ounce of my tobaccoed English breath, I say "Fuck you" right back. Fuck you, Ramon. Fuck you, Buzz. Fuck you, Perry. Fuck you, Gregory. Fuck you, Bobby. Fuck all of you. Well, I think I've said my piece. [*He moves away from the others, who remain at the table.*] I feel like playing, Gregory. Did you have your mighty Bechstein tuned in honor of our royal visit?

GREGORY: The man. Um. Was just here.

JOHN: What would you like to hear?

PERRY: I don't think anyone much cares.

JOHN: I'll play very softly.

BUZZ: I don't suppose you know *Subways Are for Seeping*?

JOHN: Would anyone say no to a little Chopin?

RAMON: I would.

JOHN: One of the nocturnes. [*He goes into the next room.*]

RAMON: I'm still saying "Fuck you," John!

BUZZ: What brought that on?

PERRY: His brother?

BUZZ: That's no excuse. Play something gay. We want gay music written by a gay composer.

PERRY: There's no such thing as gay music, Buzz.

Buzz: Well, maybe there should be. I'm sick of straight people. Tell the truth, aren't you? There's too goddamn many of them. I was in the bank yesterday. They were everywhere. Writing checks, making deposits. Two of them were applying for a mortgage. It was disgusting. They're taking over. No one wants to talk about it, but it's true. [John *starts playing the piano, off.*]

John: [*off*] This is for you, Buzz. It's by Tchaikovsky. Peter Ilitch. One of us. Can't you tell? All these dominant triads are so, so gay! Who did he think he was fooling, writing music like this? [*Melancholy music fills the room. They listen.*]

Buzz: I like this. It's not Jerry Herman, but it's got a beat. [Perry *gets up.*]

Gregory: Where. Um...?

Perry: I'd better find Arthur. [*He goes.*]

John: [*off*] This is depressing. How's this, Gregory? [*He starts playing the* Dance of the Little Swans *from* Swan Lake.]

Buzz: That's more like it.

Gregory: That's the. Um. Music. *Swan Lake.* The benefit. The *Pas des Cygnes.* Thank you, John. [Gregory *stands up from the table. He begins to dance the* Pas des Cygnes *from* Swan Lake. *He is an entirely different person when he moves: free, spontaneous, as physically fluent as he is verbally inhibited.*]

Buzz: What are you doing?

Gregory: The *Pas de Cygnes.*

Buzz: I don't do *Pas de Cygnes.* What is it?

Gregory: The *Dance of the Swans.* Come on. I can't do it alone. Ramon!

Ramon: No, thanks.

Gregory: Come on, Buzz!

Buzz: Why are you holding your arms like that? [*Indeed, as* Gregory *dances he holds his arms crossed in front of him, each hand on its opposite side, ready to link hands with another person and form a chain.*]

Gregory: I'm waiting for you to take my hand.

John: [*off*] What are you doing in there?

Gregory: We're dancing! Don't stop! Take my hand, Buzz. [Buzz *tentatively takes his hand and will try to follow* Gregory's *steps.*]

Bobby: What are they doing?

Ramon: Now they're both dancing.

Bobby: How do they look?

Buzz: Ridiculous. What do you think?

Bobby: You see? I knew it would be funny. [Ramon *and* Bobby *begin to laugh.* Gregory *and* Buzz *continue to dance while* John *plays the piano from another room.*]

GREGORY: That's it, Buzz, that's it.

BUZZ: My admiration for Chita Rivera has just become boundless!

RAMON: You should see this.

BOBBY: I can imagine.

JOHN: Can I stop?

THE OTHERS: No!!

GREGORY: Now you've got it!

BUZZ: Eat your heart out. Donna McKechnie! [*Their arms linked,* GREGORY *and* BUZZ *dance themselves out of the house and out onto the grounds.*]

BOBBY: What happened?

RAMON: They're gone. They danced themselves right out onto the lawn. [PERRY *has joined* ARTHUR *down by the lake.*]

PERRY: Listen to them up there. We're missing all the fun.

ARTHUR: We better talk.

PERRY: Okay. I brought you a sweater.

ARTHUR: Thank you.

PERRY: And one of their blankets. I thought we could spread it and look at the sky. The stars are incredible. Thick as . . . whatever stars are thick as. "Molasses" doesn't sound right.

ARTHUR: Thieves? No. Diamonds! Thick as diamonds on a jeweler's black felt!

PERRY: I love you.

ARTHUR: I know. Me, too.

PERRY: I'm sorry we don't always understand each other. I hate it when we're not in sync. I hate what I said at the table.

ARTHUR: I hated it, too.

PERRY: I just get so frightened sometimes, so angry.

ARTHUR: It's all right, Perry, we all do.

PERRY: Don't give up on me.

ARTHUR: No. I thought you were coming down here with me. It's spectacular. I can see Orion's Belt and both Dippers.

PERRY: That's not the Dipper. That's the Dipper. [*The piano music stops.* JOHN *comes back into the room where* BOBBY *and* RAMON *are.*]

JOHN: Where is everyone?

BOBBY: They were last sighted heading for the boathouse. Gregory was very pleased with himself.

JOHN: You see, I'm good for something. I'm not entirely bad!

BOBBY: No one is, John.

JOHN: Thank you. I can't tell you how good that makes me feel. I was a shit tonight and I'm not even drunk. I'm sorry, Ramon. Am I forgiven?

BOBBY: Ramon?

JOHN: "Am I forgiven?" I said.

RAMON: Yes.

JOHN: Thank you. Forgiveness is good. We all need it from time to time. It's this business with my brother. [*He goes back into the adjoining room and begins to play a Beethoven sonata.*]

BOBBY: Are you still there?

RAMON: Yes.

BOBBY: What are you doing?

RAMON: Nothing.

JOHN: [*off*] This one is for me.

ARTHUR: He plays beautifully, the son of a bitch. The devil's fingers.

PERRY: So many stars, so many stars! Say a prayer for Buzz.

BUZZ: Arthur and Perry lay on blankets and looked at the heavens and talked things out. Gregory danced on by a couple of times. John played a melancholy piano until the wee small hours of the morning. Bobby and Ramon sat quietly talking across the deserted dining table — empty glasses, soiled napkins between them. All in all, there was a lot of love in Gregory and Bobby's house that first night of the first holiday weekend of the summer. It didn't start raining till the next morning. It didn't stop until the drive back home on Monday night. It rained all weekend.

BOBBY: It was raining when Buzz started crying in the middle of a movie on AMC and couldn't stop.

RAMON: It was raining when Gregory sat alone in his studio for six hours listening to a piece of music and didn't move from his chair.

BUZZ: It was raining when Ramon waited for Bobby by the refrigerator and he dropped the bottle.

ARTHUR: It was raining when John wanted Ramon to fuck him the next afternoon anyway.

PERRY: Anyway! There's that word again. And he's wrong, this one. I don't say "anyway" when I'm cornered. I say it when I'm overcome. I love you, Arthur Pape. [*He kisses* ARTHUR *on the lips.* GREGORY *and* BUZZ *will dance by again. They are having a wonderful time.* BOBBY *and* RAMON *remain at the dining table.* JOHN *is playing a Chopin nocturne. The lights fade. The music swells.*]

Act Two

Lakeside. Blaze of noon.

The **MEN** *are singing "In the Good Old Summertime."*

As they move apart, they reveal RAMON *sprawled naked on an old-fashioned wooden float at a distance offshore.*

One by one, they stop singing, turn around, and take a long look back at RAMON *splayed on the raft.*

Even BOBBY.

Finally, only JOHN *and* RAMON *remain.*

JOHN: Anyway. [*He turns away from* RAMON *and takes out* GREGORY's *journal and begins to read.*] "Fourth of July weekend. Manderley. Promise of good weather. After Memorial Day we deserve it. John Jeckyll is arriving with his twin brother, James. Perry has already dubbed them James the Fair and John the Foul. John will also have Ramon Fornos, a superb young dancer, in tow. I thought they were over. Chances of finishing the first section of the new piece before they all descend on us looking slim. Bobby says he will stand sentry outside the studio while I work. I tried to tell him our guests aren't the reason I — Too late. They're here." [*Lights up on* PERRY, ARTHUR, GREGORY, *and* BUZZ *making ready to play tennis doubles.* ARTHUR *and* GREGORY *are partners. So are* BUZZ *and* PERRY. JOHN *is free to walk among them as he reads.*]
BUZZ: Which end of the racquet do I hold?
PERRY: That's it! Change partners. You show him, Gregory! [*He crosses to* ARTHUR.]
BUZZ: Good teachers are patient. [ARTHUR *is looking off to* RAMON.]

PERRY: What are you looking at out there?

ARTHUR: Nothing. [GREGORY *has his arms around* BUZZ *in the classic "teacher's" position.*]

GREGORY: Here, Buzz. Make a. Um. V with your thumb. Um. And forefinger.

BUZZ: Thank you. See how I respond to human kindness?

GREGORY: You bring your arm back like this, step into the ball, and pow! [*They continue.*]

JOHN: "Buzz arrived alone again. We were hoping he'd bring someone. He looks thinner."

PERRY: Try to keep your eye on this ball, not those.

JOHN: "Perry and Arthur asked if the could celebrate their anniversary with us. I warned them John would be here."

ARTHUR: That wasn't called for.

JOHN: "Poor John. People don't like him." [*He closes the journal and becomes "visible" to the others.*]

PERRY: I don't want to fight. I want to beat them in tennis.

JOHN: Who's winning?

BUZZ: We are. We're killing them.

JOHN: I can't believe it.

PERRY: You can't believe it?

BUZZ: Look who I have for a coach and partner. Why can't you have a twin brother?

ARTHUR: Don't make Gregory blush!

JOHN: What's wrong with mine?

BUZZ: He looks too much like you and acts too much like me. Where are all the men? There are no eligible men!

PERRY: Will you keep your voice down?

BUZZ: For what? We're in the middle of nowhere! Will I keep my voice down! You're a martyr, Arthur, a genuine martyr. I would have pushed him off your tasteful lower Fifth Avenue balcony ten years ago.

JOHN: Ramon is eligible, gentlemen.

BUZZ: I don't date dancers. I've made it a rule. It's very simple. Dancers don't want to date me. So fuck 'em.

JOHN: In Ramon's case, you don't know what you're missing. Does anyone want anything from the house?

GREGORY: There's tea in the. Um. Fridge.

JOHN: I'll send James down with it. [*He goes.*]

PERRY: I've got another one: the Princes of Light and Darkness.

ARTHUR: Could we concentrate on winning this set?

Buzz: So what's the score? A thousand to one? I'm really getting into this.

Perry: [*annoyed*] Love-forty! [*He cranks up for a serve.*]

Buzz: Getting ready to serve now, the ever-lovely Dr. Renee Richards. [**Perry** *flubs.*]

Gregory: Double fault. Game! Change sides.

Perry: Fuck you, Buzz.

Buzz: What did I do? Who won?

Gregory: We did.

Buzz: We did? We didn't do anything. I love tennis. [*They change sides.*]

Perry: You heard John: he's eligible!

Arthur: Perry.

Perry: Lighten up. Your serve, Martina. [*The game. continues.* **John** *is heard playing the piano, off.* **Ramon** *raises up and looks around. He shields his eyes with his hand, scans the horizon, and lies back down.* **Bobby** *appears. He is wearing a robe. He will advance to the stage apron.*]

Bobby: When Gregory told me he thought John and Ramon were over and was surprised that John would be bringing him again, I didn't tell him that they were and that Ramon was coming with him because of me. I didn't tell him that when the phone rang Monday night, and then again Thursday, and there was no one there, and he kept saying "Hello? Hello? Who is this?" I didn't tell him it was Ramon on the other end. [*He falls off the stage.*] Don't anyone touch me. I don't want help. [*He climbs back onto the stage.*] And I didn't tell him what Ramon's mouth felt like against my own. I didn't tell him the last time we made love I thought of it. I didn't tell him Ramon whispered to me this morning. He would be waiting for me on the raft when I swam out there. [*He drops his robe and goes out into the lake.* **James** *appears, wheeling a serving cart with iced tea and potato chips.*]

James: It's not who you think. I'm the other one. When John stops playing the piano, you can start getting nervous again.

Perry: Ball!

James: My brother gave me the most, extraordinary book. *Outing America: From A to Z.* I'm absolutely riveted.

Perry: Ball, please!

James: It gives the names of all the gay men and lesbians in this country in alphabetical order, from the pre-Revolutionary period (Pocahontas, I think her name was) right up to now, someone called Dan Rather.

Perry: Bail, please!

Arthur: Which one of them is it?

Buzz: It must be James. The grass isn't turning brown.

ARTHUR: I think he's attractive, Buzz.

BUZZ: Yeah?

PERRY: Goddamnit! [PERRY *retrieves the tennis ball.*] Thanks for nothing.

JAMES: I'm sorry?

PERRY: Just wait till you say, "Ball, please!"

JAMES: I haven't the vaguest notion what you're talking about, luv.

PERRY: Skip it. [*He goes.*]

JAMES: I must say, and I hope you take this in the best possible way, for a young country, you've turned out an awful lot of poufters. In two and a half centuries you've done almost as well as we have in twenty. John Foster Dulles. Who is that? Is it a juicy one? Benjamin Franklin. Him we've heard of. Very into kites. Knute Rockne. Lady Bird Johnson. Americans have the most extraordinary names! Booker T. Washington. Babe Ruth. Buzz Hauser. [*He settles himself to read as* PERRY *rejoins the others.*]

BUZZ: Whose serve is it?

PERRY: Still yours. Don't patronize us.

ARTHUR: We can always stop.

PERRY: No!

BUZZ: [*to* GREGORY] What's the matter? Are you okay?

GREGORY: I'm fine. [*He's not. He's tired.*]

BUZZ: Are you sure?

GREGORY: I'm fine!

BUZZ: What's wrong?

GREGORY: I don't. Um. See Bobby.

PERRY: Are we playing or what?

BUZZ: Time. Is that legal? Can I call time?

GREGORY: I saw him go into the lake. Um. He doesn't like me to. Um. Watch him swim. It's an honor. Um. System. And I'm not. Um. Very honorable.

BUZZ: Ramon's out there. He'll be fine.

PERRY: What is the problem, people?

GREGORY: There he is! [BOBBY *appears at the side of the raft. He is winded from the swim and just hangs there.*]

BOBBY: Hello? Anyone aboard? [RAMON *doesn't move.*] Ramon? [RAMON *still doesn't move.*]

RAMON: This time I would let him find me. I waited, not daring to breathe, while his hands searched for me on the raft. I prayed to our Holy Blessed Mother I wouldn't get a hard-on.

BOBBY: Ramon?

RAMON: My prayers weren't being answered. I thought I would explode.

BOBBY: Ow! [*He's gotten a splinter from the raft.*]

GREGORY: Ow! [*He's twisted something running for a ball and falls heavily to the ground.*]

BUZZ: Are you hurt?

GREGORY: No. Yes. Ow! [BUZZ, PERRY, *and* ARTHUR *help him to his feet.*] Get some ice.

BUZZ: What is it? Your ankle?

GREGORY: My ankle, my knee, everything.

BUZZ: Careful with him.

PERRY: Take his other arm.

ARTHUR: I've got you. Get him to the house. [*They are helping him off.*]

GREGORY: No, the studio. I've got ice packs there. [*They help him off in another direction.* BUZZ *looks out across the lake to the raft.*]

BUZZ: Bobby! [BOBBY *is still hanging on to the raft with one arm. He works on the splinter with his teeth.* RAMON *sits up and gently takes hold of* BOBBY'S *wrist.*]

BOBBY: Oh! Who's that? [RAMON *takes* BOBBY'S *finger, puts it in his mouth, sucks out the splinter, and spits it out.*]

BUZZ: Bobby! Come in! It's Gregory! He's hurt!

BOBBY: They're calling me.

RAMON: I waited for you last night. I thought you'd come down. Meet me somewhere tonight.

BOBBY: I can't.

RAMON: I'll be in the garden after supper.

BOBBY: Not the garden. The boathouse. [BOBBY *kisses* RAMON *this time, passionately, and then disappears back into the lake.* RAMON *watches him disappear. After a while, he will lie back down and sleep.* BUZZ *joins* JAMES *in the shaded area.*]

JAMES: No! I won't even say it. It's not possible. Do you think? Dare we dream?

BUZZ: What?

JAMES: This book says John F. Kennedy, Jr., is gay.

BUZZ: That explains it. [*He has seen the rolling tray of refreshments.*] Is that for us? [*He goes to it.*]

JAMES: That explains what?

BUZZ: I've seen him in the Spike. It's a leather bar in Chelsea. He comes in with friends. Daryl Hannah, the Schlossbergs, Willy Smith.

JAMES: I don't believe it.

BUZZ: I'm the wrong person to ask. I think everyone is gay, and if they're

not, they should be. [*He calls off to the raft:*] Ramon! Noon! Teatime!
[RAMON *doesn't react.*] He doesn't hear me. He's going to burn to a
crisp. Ramon! If that was my boyfriend, I would swim out there and
drag him in by the hair.

JAMES: If he were my boyfriend, he could do anything he wanted.

BUZZ: I know what you mean. Maybe that's why I don't have a boyfriend.
I'm too caring. [*They are both looking out across the lake to* RAMON.]

JAMES: My brother has always had a good-looking man in his life.

BUZZ: Thank you.

JAMES: I beg your pardon?

BUZZ: He didn't tell you? It was when he First came to this country. Short
and sweet. Six months, tops.

JAMES: I'm sorry. What happened?

BUZZ: We were both very young. I was too needy. He wasn't needy enough.

JAMES: I don't think John can love anyone.

BUZZ: Now you tell me!

JAMES: Perhaps one of us had better go out there and tell Ramon.

BUZZ: I'll let you break it to him. I don't think I'm his type.

JAMES: I don't think either of us is. [*They are both still staring out across the lake
to* RAMON *on the raft.*] I enjoy looking, though. [BUZZ *and* JAMES *sigh.*]

BUZZ: Is there a British equivalent for "machismo?"

JAMES: No. None at all. Maybe Glenda Jackson.

BUZZ: Do you have a boyfriend over there?

JAMES: Not anymore. What about you?

BUZZ: [*shaking his head*] When the going gets tough, weak boyfriends get
going. Or something like that.

JAMES: I can't honestly say I'm minding. Last acts are depressing and
generally one long solo.

BUZZ: They don't have to be. [BUZZ *finally looks at* JAMES.] How sick are you?

JAMES: I think I'm in pretty good nick, but my reports read like something
out of Nostradamus. [*He looks at* BUZZ.] I should have died six months
ago.

BUZZ: Try eighteen. Do you have any lesions?

JAMES: Only one, and I've had it for nearly a year.

BUZZ: Where is it?

JAMES: In a very inconvenient spot.

BUZZ: They're all inconvenient. May I see it?

JAMES: It's—All right. [*He pulls up his shirt and lets* BUZZ *see the lesion.*] I
have a lesbian friend in London who's the only other person who's
ever asked to see it. I was quite astonished when she did. Touched,

actually. Mortified, too, of course. But mainly touched. Somebody loves me, even if it's not the someone I've dreamed of. A little love from a woman who works in the box office at the Lyric Hammersmith is better than none. Are you through? [BUZZ *kisses the lesion.*] Gwyneth didn't go that far. It doesn't disgust you?

BUZZ: It's going to be me.

JAMES: You don't know that.

BUZZ: Yes, I do.

JAMES: You learn to make friends with them. Hello, little lesion. Not people you like especially, but people you've made your peace with.

BUZZ: You're very nice, you know.

JAMES: Frankly, I don't see how I can afford not to be.

BUZZ: No, I mean it.

JAMES: So are you.

BUZZ: I didn't mean to interrupt your reading.

JAMES: It was getting too intense. They just outed George and Ira Gershwin.

BUZZ: Wait till they get to Comden and Green. Would you like me to bring you a real drink down? I know where they hide the good liquor.

JAMES: An ice-cold martini. Very dry. With a twist.

BUZZ: Is that going to be good for you?

JAMES: Of course not.

BUZZ: Does this make me an enabler?

JAMES: No, but it makes me your slave for life. I'll snitch a frock out of National Theatre storage for you. Something of Dame Edith Evans'.

BUZZ: What's the matter?

JAMES: I'm waiting for you to tell me she was gay.

BUZZ: She wasn't, actually. One of the two British actresses who isn't. I think Deborah Kerr is the other one. But all the rest—galloping lezzies! [*He goes.* JAMES *looks after him and does not resume reading for quite some time.* GREGORY's *leg is being tended to by* ARTHUR. PERRY *watches squeamishly.* BOBBY *is with them.*]

ARTHUR: How's that?

GREGORY: Ow.

PERRY: Jesus, Gregory! I never really looked at your body before. I mean, except when you're on stage in a costume and lights and I'm in the fifth row.

GREGORY: Well, don't start now.

PERRY: It's amazing.

GREGORY: It's just old. Um. And very used.

PERRY: Your legs are like knots. And your feet. I can't even look at them. Doesn't everything hurt?

GREGORY: Yes. They have for years.

PERRY: Why do you to it?

GREGORY: I don't know– I just know I don't know what I'd do if I didn't.

ARTHUR: Why do you practice law?

PERRY: Law doesn't do that to me.

BOBBY: Gregory says a dancer's body is the scars of his dancing.

GREGORY: Bobby.

BOBBY: Isn't that what you say?

GREGORY: To you. Now it sounds pretentious.

ARTHUR: It's not pretentious, Greg.

BOBBY: The dances are gone, but his body's effort to do them isn't. Show them, Gregory.

GREGORY: Here's the Philip Glass.

ARTHUR: Look, Perry.

PERRY: I can't.

GREGORY: Here's the Bach-Schoenberg. Here's the Ravel. The Sam Barber. Here's the best one of all: the David Diamond. [BUZZ *enters.*]

BUZZ: I can't leave you kids alone for a second! Bobby bwana, you be having a phone call in the Big House.

BOBBY: Thanks, Buzz. Show them *Webern Pieces.*

GREGORY: There are no. Um. *Webern Pieces* yet.

BOBBY: There will be.

PERRY: There better be. We've signed the contracts.

BUZZ: I can understand not having a phone down here, but what has he got against an intercom? [BUZZ *and* BOBBY *go.*]

PERRY: While Arthur tended Gregory and I gaped at his life's wounds (his body didn't look old; it looked exhausted, spent—like that barren soil of Africa that can't produce anymore), and while James waited with more anticipation than he realized for Buzz to return, and while Ramon bronzed his already bronzen body even bronzer, Bobby was learning via a very iffy connection with a not very forthcoming sub-attaché at the American consulate in Jaipur that his sister, two years his senior, was dead. Valerie, I think her name was. Just like that.

BOBBY: What? I can't hear you. You'll have to speak up.

PERRY: It was a freak accident.

BOBBY: What?

PERRY: Something to do with a faultily installed ride at a fun fair at a religious festival celebrating the god Shiva.

BOBBY: How? [GREGORY *will join* BOBBY *and put his arms around him from behind while he talks on the phone.*]

PERRY: A sort of swing you sat in that spun around a sort of maypole. [ARTHUR *joins him.*]

ARTHUR: We never got the full story. [*He rests his head on* PERRY's *shoulder.* JAMES *stops reading.* BUZZ *comes out of the kitchen, mixing bowl in hand.* RAMON *sits up on the raft.*]

BOBBY: Thank you for calling. [*He lets the phone drop.*]

GREGORY: Oh, honey, I'm so sorry.

PERRY: No one knew whether to stay or go. There is nothing quite like the vulnerability of weekend guests.

BOBBY: It's all so fucking fragile. So fucking arbitrary.

GREGORY: I know, I know.

ARTHUR: It's not what we want. It's what Bobby wants.

BOBBY: I want you to stay.

RAMON: We stayed.

BOBBY: Let's go upstairs. [BOBBY *and* GREGORY *leave. There is a silence. From the house* BOBBY *is heard howling his grief: a wild, uncontainable animal sound.*]

JAMES: Poor lamb. I'm afraid those martinis have made me quite, quite maudlin. I'm all teary. [JOHN *is heard playing the piano, off: the* Pas des Cygnes *from* Swan Lake.]

PERRY: *Swan Lake.* My blood just ran cold. Gregory is serious about that goddamn benefit.

JAMES: So many costumes, so little time.

PERRY: [*calling off*] Give it a rest, will you, John? [*He gives up.*]

JAMES: Gregory says you're a good sport and you'll do it in the end.

PERRY: Gregory is wrong.

ARTHUR: I'm working on him, James.

PERRY: And you're not getting up in any goddamn tutu and toe shoes either.

ARTHUR: My lord and master here. Do you want to go for a swim?

PERRY: I want to get some sun.

ARTHUR: We can swim and sun.

PERRY: You just want to visit your boyfriend on the raft.

ARTHUR: You want to talk about giving something a rest? [JAMES *buries himself in his book and begins to read aloud.*]

JAMES: "No one who had ever seen Catherine Morland in her infancy would have supposed her born to be a heroine." [BUZZ *has entered with more refreshments. He is wearing an apron, heels, and little else.*]

Buzz: They said the same thing about me.

Perry: Jesus Christ, Buzz.

Buzz: What?

Perry: You know goddamn well what.

Buzz: No. What? This? [*He flashes* **Perry**.]

Perry: Put some clothes on. Nobody wants to look at that.

Buzz: That? You are calling my body "that"?

Perry: You're not at a nudist colony. There are other people present.

Buzz: I thought I was among friends.

Perry: I'm sure James here is just as uncomfortable as we are, only he's just too polite to say so.

James: James here is still reeling from the news about the Kennedy boy. You could all be starkers and I wouldn't bat an eyebrow.

Perry: Tell him, Arthur.

Arthur: It's not bothering me.

Buzz: Thank you, Arthur. I'm glad Isadora Duncan and Sally Kirkland did not live entirely in vain.

Perry: Please, Buzz.

Buzz: No. Close your eyes. Take a walk. Drop dead.

Perry: What brought this on?

Buzz: Nothing brought it on. Some people do things spontaneously. It's a beautiful day. The sun feels good. I may not be around next summer. Okay? This is what I look like, Perry. Sorry it's not better. It's the best I can do. Love me, love my love handles.

Arthur: That's what I keep telling him!

Perry: None of us may be around next summer. [**Arthur** *starts undressing.*] What do you think you're doing?

Arthur: Come on, I'll race you out to the raft.

Perry: Go to hell.

Arthur: I can't believe you actually lived through the sixties, Perry. We only read about them in Kansas, and I'm less uptight than you.

Perry: You know, I could walk around like that, too, if I wanted to.

Buzz: Who's stopping you?

Perry: I just don't want to.

Buzz: I think she's got it. By George, she's got it! [**Buzz** *and* **Arthur** *do a little celebratory twirl before he braves the lake waters.*]

Perry: I give up. I hope your dick gets a sunburn.

Arthur: Yadda, yadda, yadda.

Buzz: That's the spirit. The world loves a good sport. [**Arthur** *goes into the lake and starts to swim out to the float.*]

PERRY: Both your dicks!

BUZZ: I forgot my sunblock!

PERRY: Would you bring mine? It's on our dresser. The lip balm should be right with it.

BUZZ: I thought you were mad at me. I see! Get me waiting on you hand and foot and all is forgiven.

PERRY: Oh, and the Walkman. There's a Bob Dylan tape with it.

BUZZ: Bob Dylan? You sure you don't want Rosa Ponselle? Get a life, Perry. They've invented penicillin. You can actually pick up a phone and talk to someone in New Jersey now.

PERRY: I still like Bob Dylan — and don't tell me he's gay.

BUZZ: For his sake, I hope he's not. Would you date him?

PERRY: That's cruel.

BUZZ: I know. So's dating. [*He goes.* ARTHUR *has reached the raft. He is winded from the swim.*]

RAMON: I'll race you back in!

ARTHUR: What? No. I just got here.

RAMON: Aw, c'mon.

ARTHUR: No, I said. Give me a hand. [RAMON *helps* ARTHUR *onto the raft.*]

RAMON: I'll let you catch your breath. Then we'll race.

ARTHUR: My breath is fine. We're not racing. [*He flops on the raft.* RAMON *stays in a sitting up position.*]

RAMON: I hate the country. I fucking hate it. There's no cabs to get you fucking out of it. I like mass transportation. I like the fucking pavement under my feet. I like places that sell food that stay open all night. I fucking hate it.

PERRY: Should I be trusting my lover skinny-dipping with a horny Puerto Rican modern dancer?

JAMES: It depends on what makes you suspicious. Horny, Puerto Rican, modern, or dancer?

PERRY: All of them.

JAMES: How long have you two been together?

PERRY: Fourteen years. We're role models. It's very stressful.

JAMES: Two or three years was the most I ever managed. Mutual lack of attention span. [BUZZ *returns.*]

BUZZ: Here's your desperate attempt to stay young, Mr. Sellars. *Blood on the Tracks.* Wasn't this originally released on 78s?

PERRY: Bob Dylan will go down in history as one of the great American songwriters. [*He puts on the headset and lies back.*]

BUZZ: He's no Lerner and Loewe! [*He is getting ready to settle down, too.*]

Wake me if I doze off. I have a VCR alert for AMC. *Damn Yankees* at one-thirty. Gwen Verdon is hosting. Poor James, you don't have a clue what I'm talking about.

JAMES: I seldom know what any American is talking about. [*Reading:*] "No one who had ever seen Catherine Morland in her infancy would have supposed her born to be a heroine."

BUZZ: I love being read to. I feel five years old. [PERRY *sings along with his Dylan tape.* JAMES *reads to* BUZZ. JOHN *is playing the piano.* RAMON *smacks* ARTHUR *on his bare ass.*]

ARTHUR: Ow!

RAMON: You had a fly on you. You know, you got a nice ass for someone your age.

ARTHUR: Thank you.

RAMON: You both do.

ARTHUR: Thank you.

RAMON: I really hate it. [GREGORY *and* BOBBY *are in their room.*]

GREGORY: When is the body—?

BOBBY: Not until Tuesday.

GREGORY: So long?

BOBBY: Red tape. She always said there was nothing worse than Indian red tape. We're meeting it in Dallas. I'll fly down Monday.

GREGORY: I think we should both fly down tonight.

BOBBY: No. You stay here and work. I want you to finish the piece. It's more important.

GREGORY: It's all important. Why don't you want to go down there tonight?

BOBBY: We've got a houseful.

GREGORY: I'll manage.

BOBBY: We'll see. Do you know what this music is?

GREGORY: No. But it's Russian. It's definitely Russian. There are times I wish you could see me.

BOBBY: I see you, Gregory.

GREGORY: See me looking at you. The love there. I'm not—

BOBBY: I know.

GREGORY: It only happens when I'm alone with you. It s like a little present. I know this is a terrible thing to say right now, but I am so happy, Bobby. Thank you, God, for him.

BOBBY: You know how we tell each other everything, even when it's hard?

GREGORY: Yes.

BOBBY: I'd like to make this one of those times.

GREGORY: All right.

BOBBY: Memorial Day weekend.

GREGORY: Yes.

BOBBY: Something happened.

GREGORY: Why do I have a feeling I don't want to hear this?

BOBBY: Ramon and I.

GREGORY: Don't, Bobby. Don't.

BOBBY: We made love. I didn't want it to happen, but it did.

GREGORY: Is there more?

BOBBY: No. I'm sorry.

GREGORY: So am I.

BOBBY: This was better than not telling you, Gregory. [*GREGORY is starting to have difficulty speaking again.*]

GREGORY: It's Scriabin. Um. The music, it's. Um. It's definitely Scriabin.

BOBBY: Talk to me, Gregory.

GREGORY: Have you. Did you. Do you. Want to. Again?

BOBBY: No, I'm with you.

GREGORY: You're. Um. Very lucky you. Um. Can't. Um. See right now, Robert. Go to Texas tonight. I don't want you in our house.

BOBBY: Where are you going?

GREGORY: Down to the lake. Don't. Um. Come. Um. With me. Um. It's back. That was brief. [*He goes.* BOBBY *comes forward to us.*]

BOBBY: Do you believe in God? Don't worry, I'm not going to fall off this time! Do you? I think we all believe in God in our way. Or want to. Or need to. Only so many of us are afraid to. Unconditional love is pretty terrifying. We don't think we deserve it. It's human nature to run. But He always finds us. He never gives up. I used to think that's what other people were for. Lovers, friends, family. I had it all wrong. Other people are as imperfect and as frightened as we are. We love, but not unconditionally. Only God is unconditional love, and we don't even have to love Him back. He's very big about it. I have a lot of reservations about God. What intelligent, caring person doesn't lately? But the way I see it, He doesn't have any reservations about me. It's very one-sided. It's unconditional. Besides, He's God. I'm not. [*He goes.* ARTHUR *stirs on the raft.*]

ARTHUR: Sun like this makes you want to never move again. I feel nailed to this raft. Crucified on it.

RAMON: Sun like this makes me horny.

ARTHUR: Well . . .

RAMON: I bet I can hold my breath underwater longer than you.

ARTHUR: I bet you can, too.

RAMON: Come on, you want to see?

ARTHUR: No! If you're so bored...

RAMON: Come on!

ARTHUR: I don't want to. Play with someone else.

RAMON: Come on! *Venga*, baby, *venga!*

ARTHUR: I'm resting. It's a national holiday.

RAMON: Come on! You know you want to! Don't be an old fart! Who knows? We get down there together, who knows what might happen? Yeah? [*He jumps off the raft and goes under the water.*]

ARTHUR: Damn it. You got me all—Shit. I was nice and dry. I'm not going in there. I don't care how long you stay under. You can drown, Ramon. I hope you can hear me down there. You're not getting me in. All right, Ramon. That's enough. Come on. Stop. [GREGORY *appears at the side of the raft. He hangs there.*]

PERRY: I remember when Gregory bought this place. I was dead against it. "It's in the middle of nowhere. What are you going to do for fun?" Now it seems like bliss. No one for miles and miles. We could be the last eight people on earth.

BUZZ: That's a frightening thought.

JAMES: Not if you're with the right eight people. Who's that out there on the raft?

BUZZ: It looks like Gregory.

PERRY: Where's Arthur? He was out there.

BUZZ: You're looking good, Gregory!

PERRY: Arthur? Arthur? He was with Ramon.

BUZZ: We'd better put a stop to that. Arthur! Your mother wants you. Arthur! The *MacNeil/Lehrer Report* is on. Arthur! [*To* PERRY *and* JAMES:] Help me. One, two, three.

BUZZ, PERRY, JAMES: Arthur!! [BUZZ *starts coughing. He can't stop.*]

JAMES: Are you all right?

BUZZ: Ooooo!

JAMES: Here.

BUZZ: Thank you.

JAMES: Just get your breath. Lean on me. There you go.

BUZZ: Look at Gregory out there. He's lucky. He is so lucky.

JAMES: So are we.

BUZZ: Not like that. Not like that. [*In the silence, we will begin to notice the throbbing, humming sounds of summer's high noon. The figure of* GREGORY *on the raft glows, shimmers, irradiates in the bright light. Nothing moves.*]

JAMES: Listen. What's that sound?

PERRY: Nature.

JAMES: It's fearful.

PERRY: It's life.

BUZZ: It's so loud.

PERRY: Because we're listening to it. Ssshh.

BUZZ: I never —

JAMES: Ssshh.

PERRY: Arthur and I were in Alaska once. We flew out to a glacier. When the pilot cut the engine, it was so quiet you could hear the universe throbbing. I didn't know it did that. It was thrilling. [*Tableau. The three men do not move.* JAMES *has his arm around* BUZZ. GREGORY *is sitting on the raft with his knees pulled up to his chin. He is crying. There is a distant but ominous roll of thunder.*] Five minutes later, it was raining buckets. Thunder, lightning, wind. Everybody scattered. James, take the hammock in. Gregory! Come in! Lightning!

BUZZ: Auntie Em! Auntie Em!

PERRY: Buzz, run the flag down. Where is my Arthur? Arthur!! [ARTHUR *appears, fully dressed and dry. He will join* PERRY.]

ARTHUR: Your Arthur was gasping for breath on the other side of the lake. [RAMON *appears; he is not dressed and he is still wet. He is laughing and playful.*]

RAMON: I knew I'd get you in!

ARTHUR: You scared me. I thought something had happened to you.

RAMON: I wanted to stay down there forever. I wished I was a fish.

ARTHUR: He was sitting on the bottom of the lake. When I swam up to him he pulled me towards him and kissed me on the mouth.

RAMON: I was goofing.

ARTHUR: Then he swam away.

PERRY: In all the excitement, the tragedy of Bobby's sister was quite forgotten. Where were you?

ARTHUR: Nowhere. I was swimming. Their door is still closed. You were right, Perry, we should have left.

PERRY: Don't do that.

ARTHUR: Do what?

PERRY: Disappear.

RAMON: [*holding a magazine*] Okay, here he is, I found him. Gather round, gentlemen.

BUZZ: It was after lunch and Ramon was having a hard time convincing us of an adventure he claimed to have had on the island of Mykonos.

RAMON: That's him. I swear on my mother's life.

BUZZ: And I had sex with the ghost of Troy Donahue.

PERRY: First you said he was the model for Calvin Klein's Obsession. Now he's the model for—

RAMON: I can't keep all those names straight, but I don't forget a face and body like that.

BUZZ: You all know the picture.

ARTHUR: And you found this person in the same position sleeping adrift in a fishing boat?

RAMON: Yes. You ever been to Greece? There are a lot of fishing boats. Why won't you believe he was in one of them?

PERRY: And you made love to him?

RAMON: Not in the fishing boat. It started raining. We went ashore. We found sort of a cave.

JAMES: This is very Dido and Aeneas. I'm calling Barbara Cartland. [*He goes.*]

RAMON: Why would I make up a story like that? It's too incredible.

PERRY: You're right, it is.

RAMON: Fuck you, all of you. I don't care. But the next time you see his picture or you're tossing in your beds thinking about him, just remember: somebody had him and it wasn't you. I know how that must burn your asses.

BUZZ: Go to your room! [*He goes. The others stay with the magazine.*]

ARTHUR: Do you think he's telling the truth?

BUZZ: No, do you?

PERRY: The thought of Ramon and his possible encounter with the Obsession Man hung over the house like a shroud. We all wanted him and never would—

BUZZ: I bet he's got a rotten personality.

PERRY: Anyway. There is nothing like the steady drumming of a summer rain on wooden shingles to turn even this pedantic mind into a devil's workshop. I've' got an idea. [*He whispers to* ARTHUR *and* BUZZ, *who surround him.* RAMON *and* JOHN *are seen in their room.*]

RAMON: I don't know people like you and your friends. I don't know what you're talking about half the time. Who the fuck are Dido and Aeneas? We used to beat up people like you where I grew up.

JOHN: Come here.

RAMON: Do you believe me?

JOHN: Do you want me to believe you?

RAMON: Maybe.

JOHN: So come here. [RAMON *will take his time coming over to where* JOHN *is.*]

PERRY: Unfortunately, John and Ramon were not alone. Buzz and I had hidden in their closet. Our plan was to leap out at the moment of maximum inopportunity and embarrassment and then regale the rest of the household with what we'd seen and heard.

BUZZ: It'll serve John right.

PERRY: What does that mean?

BUZZ: Never mind. Squeeze!

RAMON: What? [JOHN *kisses* RAMON.]

PERRY: It was a terrible idea. Arthur would have no part of it.

ARTHUR: Happy anniversary to you, too, Perry! [*He goes.*]

PERRY: Is today the — I'm sorry, Arthur. Oh, shit.

JOHN: What's the matter?

RAMON: I thought I heard something.

PERRY: That was our last chance. We should have taken it.

JOHN: Sit down.

RAMON: You want to? Now?

JOHN: Sit.

RAMON: I'm a little sunburned.

JOHN: Sit.

RAMON: Aren't you going to lock the door?

JOHN: It's locked. Sit. [RAMON *sits in a straight-back chair.*] Put your hands behind your back. Feet apart. Head down. Ready for interrogation. My beautiful bound prisoner. Look at me. You look so beautiful like that. I think I could come without even touching you.

BUZZ: Oh!

RAMON: I think I could, too. Let me go.

JOHN: No.

RAMON: Please. The rope. It's too tight. My wrists, the circulation.

JOHN: Go on, struggle.

RAMON: I can't get loose.

JOHN: Look at me. Don't take your eyes from mine. Who do you see?

RAMON: No one. You! Let me touch you.

JOHN: Not yet. Who do you see? Who do you wish I were?

RAMON: No, I won't tell you.

JOHN: Yes, you will. Who? Look at me. Look at me! Who? Who do you wish I were?

RAMON: Kiss me. Gag me with your mouth. [JOHN *kisses him.*]

PERRY: We knew what they were doing. We didn't have to see.

BUZZ: I was singing "99 Bottles of Beer on the Wall" silently to myself. It's a very hard song to sing silently to yourself.

RAMON: Who do you see? Who do you want in this chair?

JOHN: I don't know.

RAMON: Yes, you do. Everybody does. Who do you see? Who do you want here like this? Tell me, it's okay, John.

JOHN: I can't.

RAMON: Who? Come on, baby, who?

JOHN: Don't make me.

RAMON: I can't make you do anything. I'm your fucking prisoner, man. You got me tied up here. Gagged. Mmmm. Mmmm.

JOHN: His name was Padraic. The Irish spelling.

RAMON: Fuck the spelling!

JOHN: Padraic Boyle. He was seventeen years old. I was nineteen.

RAMON: I hear you. Seventeen and nineteen!

JOHN: He will always be seventeen years old and I will always be nineteen. Neither of us grows old in this story.

RAMON: What did he look like, this hot fucking stud Irishman?

JOHN: He was a fierce-looking ginger Irishman with big powerful shoulders and arms with muscles with big veins in them. You could see them blue through the white skin of his biceps. Always in hip boots and a vest.

RAMON: A vest? He was wearing a fucking vest?

JOHN: I'm sorry—undershirts, you call them.

RAMON: That's more like it. Fucking Fruit of the Looms, fucking BVDs, fucking Calvins.

JOHN: He worked for us. So did his father. We owned a fleet of coaches. Padraic and his father washed them. But that didn't matter. We were friends. He liked me. I know he liked me.

RAMON: Cut to the chase.

JOHN: Cut to what chase? There wasn't any chase.

RAMON: It's a movie expression. Get to the good part.

JOHN: It's all good part.

RAMON: Get to the sex. One night...!

JOHN: One day we started wrestling. It was summer. He was washing a coach (that's a bus), and—

RAMON: I know what a coach is. I've been to London.

JOHN: And Padraic squirted me with a hose and I got him with a bucket of water and then we started fooling around, and one thing led to another and we started wrestling, we were in the garage now, and suddenly Padraic put his hand down there and he could feel I was hard and he said, "What is this? What the bloody hell is this, mate?"

RAMON: What did you do?

JOHN: I put my hand on him down there and he was hard and I said, "And what the bloody hell is that, mate?" and we both laughed, but we didn't move.

PERRY: Even from the closet, we were beginning to share Ramon's impatience.

PERRY and **BUZZ:** Cut to the fucking chase!

JOHN: He stopped laughing. "Do you know what we're doing?" I had no idea, so I nodded yes. He took off my belt and wrapped it around my wrists. He raised my arms over my head and hung them to a hook along the wall. I probably could have freed myself. I didn't try. He took out a handkerchief and gagged me with it. Then, and this frightened me, he ripped open my shirt. Then he unfastened my trousers and let them drop to my ankles. Then he undressed himself and took a chair, very like this one, and sat in it, maybe five feet away from me. He had some rope. He wrapped it around his wrists like he was tied to the chair. He'd gagged himself, too, with his own knickers. He looked right at me. He didn't move. Not even the slightest undulation of his hips, and then he came and all he'd let out was this one, soft "oh" After a while, he opened his eyes, asked me how I was doing and cleaned himself up. Then he stood up and kissed me lightly on the lips. No man had ever kissed me on the lips before. I wanted to kiss him back, but I didn't dare. He moved to whisper something in my ear. My heart stopped beating. He was going to tell me he loved me! Instead, he said, "I've doused this place with petrol. I'm lighting a match. You have three minutes to get out alive. Good luck, 007." And then he laughed and walked out whistling. He never wanted to play again. The last time I saw him he was overweight, the father of four and still washing our coaches. But that's who I still see there. Every time. And that's why we hate the bloody Irish!

PERRY: Clearly the mood was broken. I felt a certain relief. [GREGORY *appears outside their door.*]

GREGORY: Knock, knock!

JOHN: Yes?

GREGORY: Can I. Um. Get in there a sec?

JOHN: Sure.

RAMON: [*playfully*] Maybe Greg can rescue me. [*He puts his arms behind him, struggles again.*] Mmmmm. Mmmmm, Help.

JOHN: Stop that. [GREGORY *comes into the room.*]

GREGORY: Sorry. I need to. Um. Get a suitcase. Um. For Bobby.

RAMON: [*playfully*] Mmmmmm! Mmmmmm!

JOHN: Ignore him. [GREGORY *opens the closet and sees* PERRY *and* BUZZ.]

PERRY: [*to* GREGORY] Ssshh. please. I'll explain.

JOHN: Was it in there?

GREGORY: No. Wrong closet.

RAMON: Help! Mmmmm. [GREGORY *goes.* BUZZ *manages to exit with him without being seen by* JOHN *or* RAMON.] It sounds like Bobby's leaving. I want to say goodbye. Do you mind if we don't—

JOHN: Suit yourself.

RAMON: I'm not Padraic.

JOHN: And I'm not Bobby. *C'est la vie.*

RAMON: I don't know what you're talking about. [*He goes.*]

JOHN: Wait up. I'll go with you.

PERRY: I suppose the next few moments could be called out of the closet and into the fire. John had forgotten his wallet. People like John don't feel fully dressed unless they're carrying their wallets, even on Fourth of July weekends on forty-plus acres.

JOHN: You son of a bitch.

PERRY: I'm sorry.

JOHN: You miserable son of a bitch.

PERRY: It was a joke. It was supposed to be funny.

JOHN: You scum. You lump. You piece of shit. How dare you?

PERRY: I wasn't thinking. I'm sorry, John. I have never been sorrier about anything in my entire life.

JOHN: How fucking dare you?

PERRY: I will get down on my knees to you to ask your forgiveness.

JOHN: What did you hear?

PERRY: Nothing.

JOHN: What did you hear?

PERRY: I won't tell anyone. Not even Arthur. I swear on my mother's life, I won't. [JOHN *spits in* PERRY*'s face.*]

JOHN: I hope you get what my brother has. I hope you die from it. When I read or hear that you have, then, then, Perry, will I forgive you. [*He goes.*]

PERRY: I don't know which was worse. His words or his saliva. Right now I can't think of anything more annihilating than being spat upon. I could feel his hate running down my face. So much for the unsafe exchange of body fluids. [ARTHUR *is trimming the hair in* PERRY*'s ears.*]

ARTHUR: I'm glad you're getting your sense of humor back. I'd like to flatten that limey motherfucker. I'm tired of "limey." Aren't there any other hateful words for those cocksucking, ass-licking, motherfucking, shit-eating descendants of Shakespeare, Shelley, and Keats?

PERRY: Come on, honey. Let's drop it.

ARTHUR: I don't go around hitting people or using words like "mother-fucker," but that's how mad I am.

PERRY: Let it go. I love my bracelet. Thank you.

ARTHUR: Happy anniversary.

PERRY: I'm sorry I forgot. What do you want?

ARTHUR: Towels.

PERRY: Towels? That's not very romantic.

ARTHUR: The last time your mother stayed with us I could see she thought the towels were my responsibility. It's one thing for her son to be gay just so long as he's not the one who's doing the cooking. Towels and a Mixmaster!

PERRY: Who wound you up?

ARTHUR: That asshole did. Don't get me started again. He's just lucky I'm a big queen.

PERRY: Don't forget the left ear.

ARTHUR: And you're really lucky I'm a big queen.

PERRY: One thing you're not, Arthur, and never will be is a big queen.

ARTHUR: I know. I'm butch. One of the lucky ones. I can catch a ball. I genuinely like both my parents. I hate opera. I don't know why I bother being gay.

PERRY: I was so sure you weren't that first time I saw you. I came this close to not saying hello. [PERRY *suddenly kisses one of* ARTHUR'S *hands.*]

ARTHUR: Where did that come from?

PERRY: Are we okay?

ARTHUR: We're fine. Don't rock de boat. It don't need no rocking. Fourteen years! Make you feel old?

PERRY: No, lucky.

ARTHUR: My first time m New York. You had your own apartment in "Green-wich Village." Exposed brick. I was so impressed.

PERRY: It's pronounced Greenwich. You're lucky you were so cute.

ARTHUR: The Mark Spitz poster right out where anyone could see it. [BUZZ *crosses the room.*]

BUZZ: He's gay, you know.

ARTHUR: He is?

BUZZ: They're all gay. The entire Olympics.

PERRY: This is my roommate, Buzz. Buzz, this is—I'm sorry—

ARTHUR: Arthur.

PERRY: Oh come on, I didn't—

ARTHUR: You did.

PERRY: Why are we whispering?

BUZZ: I've got someone in my room. He's a Brit. I'm getting him tea. [*Now* JOHN *crosses the room.*]

JOHN: Don't mind me, ducks. Just nipping through. Is that the loo? [*He goes.*]

BUZZ: Don't say anything. Perry. I think he's cute. He's written a musical. I think I'm in love.

PERRY: Take it easy this time, will you?

BUZZ: Perry likes it rough, Arthur—really, really rough. [*He goes.*]

ARTHUR: He was right—you did.

PERRY: Look who's talking! Do you want me to do your ears now?

ARTHUR: That was John? I'd completely forgotten. He and Buzz met the same night we did. We lasted, they didn't.

PERRY: I thought you were the most wonderful looking man I'd ever seen.

ARTHUR: Did you? Did you really think that?

PERRY: Unh-hunh.

ARTHUR: Ow!

PERRY: Sorry. When was the last time I did this?

ARTHUR: Don't make a face.

PERRY: I'm not making a face.

ARTHUR: I can hear it in your voice.

PERRY: I wouldn't do this for anyone but you.

ARTHUR: You know, if you really think about it, this is what it all comes down to.

PERRY: What? Trimming the hair in your boyfriend's ears? Oh God, I hope not. [BUZZ *and* JAMES *appear. They are ready for a tutu fitting.* JAMES *motions* ARTHUR *and* PERRY *to come close.*]

ARTHUR: That and helping your best friends out by putting on a tutu for five minutes in front of three thousand people in Carnegie Hall. [BUZZ *and* JAMES *have put a tape measure around* PERRY'S *waist.* BUZZ *drapes him in tulle.*]

PERRY: You're wasting your time, Buzz, I'm not going to do it. [BUZZ *writes down the measurements.*]

BUZZ: She's a classic *Giselle* size, I should have guessed. Thirty-six! Whose measurements are these?

JAMES: Yours, luv.

ARTHUR: Is that good or bad?

JAMES: For a tutu it's a little big. For a gay man it's a disaster.

BUZZ: I'm not thirty-six! What metric system are you on? Let me see that.

What are you laughing at? You're next. [BUZZ *and* JAMES *pursue* ARTHUR *off.*]

PERRY: Anyway. The heavens cleared. The sunset was spectacular. The next day would be glorious. We would have a fabulous Fifth of July, sodden fireworks and strained relationships notwithstanding. Only the evening lay ahead. [*The sound of crickets.* BOBBY *is waiting in the yard with his suitcase. It is night.* RAMON *appears.*]

RAMON: Hi.

BOBBY: Hi. Betty's Taxi is living up to their reputation. "We're on our way, Mr. Brahms." Five minutes, she promised, and that was twenty minutes ago.

RAMON: I have a sister, too. I love her very much. I'm sorry.

BOBBY: Thank you, Ramon.

RAMON: Where's your cowboy boots? They told me home for you was Texas. I thought you'd be in boots and a Stetson.

BOBBY: Home for me is right here. My folks are in Texas. Paris, Texas.

RAMON: Aw, c'mon. There's no such place.

BOBBY: French is my second language.

RAMON: You're kidding.

BOBBY: I'm kidding. The settlers had delusions of grandeur. [RAMON *takes his hand.*] Don't.

RAMON: I'm sorry. [*He lets go of* BOBBY'S *hand.*]

BOBBY: A part of me is, too. I can't.

RAMON: Does Gregory—?

BOBBY: No.

RAMON: That night by the refrigerator . . . ?

BOBBY: Any of it. [GREGORY *appears outside the house.*]

GREGORY: You're still here?

BOBBY: They're on their way.

RAMON: Safe trip, amigo. I'm really sorry. [*He goes back into the house.*]

GREGORY: I would have driven you. Um. In. Um.

BOBBY: We've got guests.

GREGORY: We both need time to think.

BOBBY: I don't. I'm sorry. I love you.

GREGORY: [*he is angry*] Are any of you. Um. Gardeners? I'm especially. Um. Proud of what I've done here. Um. It's a. Um. Seasonal garden. Always something blooming. Um. Just as another dies. That's a. Um. Bobby knows the names of everything. *Dianthus barbatus.* That's the Latin name. Um. I can't think of the. Um. Common one.

BOBBY: Sweet William. It's Sweet William. And this one is rue. Bitter. Very bitter. Buzz says I would make a great Ophelia if I wouldn't fall off the stage.

GREGORY: He shouldn't. Um. Say things like that. Um. To you. [*He is crying.*]

BOBBY: And this is. Wait. Don't tell me.

GREGORY: It's a rose.

BOBBY: I know it's a rose. Connecticut Pride Morning Rose.

GREGORY: I'll never understand it. The will to know the names of things you'll never see.

BOBBY: It's one way of feeling closer to you. [GREGORY *embraces* BOBBY, *but they don't kiss.*]

GREGORY: Hurry back to me. [*He goes back into the house.* BOBBY *will stay in the yard until his cab comes. The other men have gathered in the living room. The* TV *is on.*]

BUZZ: It's not my turn to clear up. I'm waiting for the musical remake of *Lost Horizon.* I never miss a chance to watch Liv Ullmann sing and dance.

JAMES: May I join you? [*He sits next to* BUZZ.]

ARTHUR: What's this?

PERRY: Open it.

ARTHUR: You didn't forget. You had me fooled.

JAMES: What are we watching?

BUZZ: The *Dinah Shore Classic.* Dykes playing golf in the desert.

PERRY: Do you like it?

ARTHUR: I love it. Look, guys. A solar-power calculator.

PERRY: For your work. Arthur's an accountant.

RAMON: Very nice.

BUZZ: Switching channels! [*We hear* BOBBY'*s cab tooting off.* BOBBY *takes up his suitcase and goes to it.* GREGORY *watches him through the window.*] Oh, look, the President's on MTV! He's made a video.

PERRY: Only in America!

BUZZ: He's gay, you know.

PERRY: Dream on, Buzz.

BUZZ: Why not? We could have a gay president.

PERRY: It'll never happen.

BUZZ: We're going to have a gay president in this country, you'll see.

PERRY: It's the Fourth of July, Buzz, no gay rights stuff, please. [RAMON *gives the appointed "signal."*]

RAMON: Are we having dessert or what?

BUZZ: No dessert. You're too fat. We're all too fat.

RAMON: My friend in the fishing boat didn't think I was too fat.

BUZZ: Stay out of that kitchen. We're all on diets. [BUZZ, JAMES, *and* RAMON *go into the kitchen.*]

ARTHUR: Go to CNN.

PERRY: Not a moment too soon. I'd like to know what's going on in the world. [GREGORY *is apart from the others.*]

ARTHUR: Cheer up, Gregory. He's coming back.

GREGORY: Thanks, Arthur.

ARTHUR: That looks like Gore.

PERRY: It's a gay demonstration in Seattle. The Vice-President is out there speaking up for endangered species. I don't think we were included. Jesus! Did you see that? He whacked that guy with his nightstick right against his head. Motherfucker!

GREGORY: What's happening? [*He joins them in front of the TV set.*]

PERRY: Why do they have to hit them like that? Jesus! [*They watch in silence. Appalling sounds of violence are coming from the television.*]

ARTHUR: I can't watch this.

GREGORY: Um. Um. Um.

ARTHUR: It's okay, Greg, it's okay. Turn that off. will you?

PERRY: What is wrong with this country? They hate us. They fucking hate us. They've always hated us. It never ends, the fucking hatred. [*The lights in the room go off.* BUZZ, JAMES, *and* RAMON *bring in a cake with blazing candles.*]

BUZZ, JAMES, RAMON, GREGORY: [*singing*]
Happy anniversary to you,
Happy anniversary to you,
Happy anniversary, Arthur and Perry,
Happy anniversary to you.
Make a wish. Speech, speech.

PERRY: I'm married to the best man in the world, even if he doesn't put the toothpaste cap back on and squeezes the tube in the middle. I wish him long life, much love, and as much happiness as he's brought me.

ARTHUR: Ditto.

PERRY: Ditto? That's it? Ditto? [*They begin a slow dance together.*]

JAMES: That's nice.

BUZZ: You don't have to go all Goody Two Shoes on us.

ARTHUR: Everybody dance. All lovers dance.

BUZZ: What about us single girls? [*To* JAMES:] You know you're dying to ask me. [*He starts dancing with* JAMES. *There are two couples dancing now.*]

PERRY: So what was your wish? [ARTHUR *whispers something in his ear.*] No fucking way, José. He still thinks you're going to get me into one of

those fucking tutus. [PERRY *now leads* ARTHUR. *They dance very well together.* BUZZ *and* JAMES *are dancing closer and closer in a smaller and smaller space. Pretty soon they're just standing, holding on to each other, their arms around each other.* GREGORY *sits apart.* RAMON *watches them all.*]
Arthur, look.

ARTHUR: What?

PERRY: Answered prayers. [*The two couples dance.* RAMON *and* GREGORY *sit staring at each other. The lights fade swiftly. The music continues until the house lights are up.*]

Act Three

Dawn. GREGORY *is alone in his studio.* PERRY *is sleeping with* ARTHUR. JAMES *and* BUZZ *are walking by the lake.* RAMON *and* BOBBY *are both awake.*

PERRY: Gregory was stuck. He had been since the beginning of summer. And here it was Labor Day weekend. You'd think he'd move on, but Gregory is stubborn. I don't know if I admire that. [RAMON *steals from his bed.*]

RAMON: Bobby?

PERRY: So was Ramon.

RAMON: Bobby?

PERRY: I don't know if I admire that, either.

ARTHUR: You're taking all the covers.

RAMON: Bobby, it's me.

PERRY: You hear that? They are up to something.

ARTHUR: Mind your own business.

RAMON: He's out in the studio. I can see the lights. I won't do anything. I just want to.... Fuck it. I'll be downstairs making coffee. [*He goes.*]

PERRY: I wonder if Gregory had counted on Ramon showing up with John. I remembered the time Arthur had been unfaithful and how badly I'd handled it. I don't know what to say anymore and I certainly don't know what to do. "Don't ask, don't tell." No, that's something else. I prayed for good weather, took a Unisom, and wrapped myself around my Arthur. [*He rolls over and sleeps with* ARTHUR.]

ARTHUR: No funny stuff. Go back to sleep. [GREGORY *puts on the* Webern Opus 27 *and plays the same passage over and over.*]

BOBBY: Gregory's not stubborn. He's scared. He's started telling people the new piece is nearly done when the truth is there's nothing there. I want to tell him to just stay in the moment, not to think in finished dances. That it doesn't have to be about everything. Just to let it come from here. But when I do he says, "What do you know about it?

You're blind. You betrayed me." It hasn't been easy since I got back from Texas.

GREGORY: Shit.

BOBBY: I wish it were just the two of us this weekend. [JOHN *appears with* GREGORY'*s journal.*]

JOHN: The lawns were brown now, the gardens wilted. The autumnal chill in the air was telling us this would be our last weekend. Soon it would be "back to school." Manderley had changed once again, but I hadn't. Still hung up on Ramon and our rituals. Still reading what other eyes were never meant to see. [*Reading from the journal.*] "James Jeckyll has decided to stay in this country. Buzz says he will get much better care here. He will also get Buzz. They are in love. I'm glad it happened here. Who could not love James? We have all taken him to our hearts. It will be a sad day when the light goes out."

GREGORY: Shit, shit, shit, shit, shit!!! [*He stops dancing in a rage of utter frustration. He picks up a chair and smashes it again and again until it is in pieces. He falls to his knees and begins to cry.*]

PERRY: I can't sleep. You didn't hear that?

ARTHUR: Will you leave them alone?

PERRY: Who?

ARTHUR: Other people. All of them. You're as bad as John. And stop taking all the covers.

PERRY: I'm not as bad as John. No one is as bad as John. I smell coffee. Do you smell coffee?

ARTHUR: That's it! I want a divorce.

PERRY: Are you awake now?

ARTHUR: Thanks to you.

PERRY: I'll bring you up some. How do you want it?

ARTHUR: Black with eleven sugars. How do I want it?

PERRY: You take it with milk, with Equal.

ARTHUR: Why is he torturing me? [PERRY *rolls out of bed.*]

PERRY: It looks like rain. [*He goes.*]

JAMES: I'm so cold, I'm so cold.

BUZZ: I'm right here.

JAMES: Two hours ago I was drenched in sweat.

BUZZ: Tonight'll be my turn.

JAMES: We're a fine pair.

BUZZ: We're loverly. I wouldn't have it any other way.

JAMES: I left England for this?

BUZZ: How are you feeling?

JAMES: Not sexy.

BUZZ: How are you feeling, really?

JAMES: "We defy augury."

BUZZ: What does that mean?

JAMES: I don't know. It's from a Shakespearean play we did at the National. The actor who played it always tossed his head and put his hand on his hip when he said it. I think he was being brave in the face of adversity.

BUZZ: Would this have been Lady Derek Jacobi or Dame Ian McKellen?

JAMES: I believe I have the floor! So, whenever I don't like what's coming down, I toss my head, put my hand on my hip, and say "We defy augury."

BUZZ: Shakespeare was gay, you know.

JAMES: You're going too far now.

BUZZ: Do you think a straight man would write a line like "We defy augury"? Get real, James. My three-year-old gay niece knows Shakespeare was gay. So was Anne Hathaway. So was her cottage. So was Julius Caesar. So was Romeo and Juliet. So was Hamlet. So was King Lear. Every character Shakespeare wrote was gay. Except for Titus Andronicus. Titus was straight. Go figure.

JAMES: People are awake.

BUZZ: I'll get us some coffee. [*He goes to the upstairs bathroom, where* PERRY *is standing with his back to us.* RAMON *is making coffee and singing a Diana Ross song.* GREGORY *comes into the kitchen.*]

RAMON: Good morning, Gregory. The coffee's brewing. I woke up in my diva mode and there is no greater diva than Diana Ross. [*Sings a Diana Ross song.*] I figured you were working out there. I saw the lights. I didn't want to disturb you. How's it going. Don't ask, hunh? [*He sings a Diana Ross song and undulates. He's terrific.*] These are the exact movements that won me my high school talent contest. My big competition was a girl in glasses — Julia Cordoba — who played "Carnival in Venice" on the trumpet. Next to "You Can't Hurry Love" she didn't have a chance. But just in case anybody thought I was too good at Diana, I went into my tribute to Elvis, the title song from *Jailhouse Rock*★. [*He sings from the title song from* Jailhouse Rock *and dances. He's electric. He remembers the choreography from the movie perfectly.*] I was turning the whole school on. Girls, boys, faculty. I loved it. If I ever get famous like you, Greg, and they ask me when I decided I wanted to be a dancer — no, a great dancer, like you were — I am going to answer, "I remember

---

★ See note on songs and recordings on page 654.

the exact moment when. It was on the stage of the Immaculate
Conception Catholic High School in Ponce in the Commonwealth of
Puerto Rico when—" [*He slows down but keeps dancing.*] What's the
matter? What are you looking at? You're making me feel weird. Come
on, don't. You know me, I'm goofing. "Great dancer you *are*." I didn't
mean it, okay? [*He dances slower and slower, but he has too much machismo
to completely stop.*] Fuck you then. I'm sorry your work isn't going well.
Bobby told me. But don't take it out on me. I'm just having fun.
Sometimes I wonder why we bother, you know? Great art! I mean,
who needs it? Who fucking needs it? We got Diana. We got Elvis. [*He
has practically danced himself into* GREGORY *and is about to dance away from
him at his original full, exuberant tempo when* GREGORY *grabs his wrist.*]
Hey! [GREGORY *leads him to the sink.*] What are you doing? Let go.
[GREGORY *throws a switch. We hear the low rumble of the disposal.*] What
are you doing? I said. I don't like this. [GREGORY *turns off the disposal.
He grabs* RAMON*'s other arm and twists it behind his back. At the same time
he lets go of his wrist.*] Ow!
GREGORY: Put your. Um. Hand down the drain.
RAMON: Fuck you, no!
GREGORY: Do it.
RAMON: No, I said. Ow! Ow!
GREGORY: I said, do it!
RAMON: What for?
GREGORY: You know what for.
RAMON: I don't.
GREGORY: You know.
RAMON: Because of Bobby.
GREGORY: Because of Bobby? Did you say "Because of Bobby"? What,
   because of Bobby?
RAMON: Nothing. Nothing because of Bobby.
GREGORY: [*slowly and deliberately*] Put your hand down the drain.
RAMON: No. Ow!
GREGORY: Do it or I'll break it fucking off.
RAMON: You're crazy. You're fucking crazy. [PERRY *enters the kitchen area.*
   BUZZ *is right behind him.*]
PERRY: Jesus, Gregory. What are you—?
RAMON: He wants me to put my fucking hand down the drain.
GREGORY: Tell them why.
RAMON: I don't know.
GREGORY: Tell them why.

RAMON: He thinks me and Bobby . . .
GREGORY: That's why.
PERRY: Somebody's gonna get hurt fooling around like this.
BUZZ: Let him go, Greg.
RAMON: Ow!
GREGORY: I'll break it.
RAMON: All right, all right. I'll do it, I'll do it. [RAMON *puts his hand down the drain.*] Go ahead, turn it on, cut my fucking fingers off. [GREGORY *lets go of* RAMON's *arm.*]
GREGORY: Is that coffee. Um. Ready yet?
BUZZ: That wasn't funny, Greg.
PERRY: Are you all right?
RAMON: That wasn't about me and Bobby. That was about me and you.
GREGORY: Coffee, Perry?
PERRY: Thank you.
RAMON: You're old and you're scared and you don't know what to do about it.
GREGORY: Buzz?
BUZZ: Sure.
RAMON: I'm young and I'm not scared and I'm coming after you.
GREGORY: Ramon?
RAMON: That's what it was about. Yes, please, with milk.
GREGORY: One *café con leche* for Ramon.
RAMON: Thank you.
PERRY: Anyway. My stomach is up in my throat.
RAMON: I knew he wouldn't do it. I knew you wouldn't do it.
BUZZ: Macho man herself here.
RAMON: He's just lucky I didn't pop him one. [GREGORY *turns on the disposal. Everyone jumps a little.*]
GREGORY: Sorry. Coffee grounds.
BUZZ: You're not supposed to put them down there.
GREGORY: Live dangerously. That's my. Um. Motto.
PERRY: Anyway. The incident was never mentioned again. Funny, the things we sit on, stuff down. The simplest exchanges take on an entirely different meaning.
GREGORY: Ramon. Would you. Um. Take this up to. Um. Bobby. Thank you.
PERRY: No, not funny. Amazing. [GREGORY *returns to the studio, puts the music on, and goes back to work*]. Anyway. We spent all day in bed. We napped, we cuddled. Arthur read the life of Donald Trump. Don't ask. We listened to the rain.

ARTHUR: It's stopped.

PERRY: Of course it's stopped. The day is shot. We'll all go out and get a good moonburn tonight.

ARTHUR: It's not shot. Come on, we're going canoeing.

PERRY: It's dusk. It's practically dark, Artie. No. Absolutely not. We went canoeing. [*They begin to paddle.*]

ARTHUR: I don't believe the rain this summer. First Memorial Day, then the Fourth.

PERRY: It's simple. God doesn't want you to beat me in tennis anymore.

ARTHUR: That's not what it means. It means He doesn't want us to develop skin cancer from overzealous exposure to His sun in our overzealous pursuit of looking drop-dead good to one another. Look out for that log.

PERRY: That's big of Him. I see it.

ARTHUR: After AIDS, he figures we deserve a break.

PERRY: That's five dollars!

ARTHUR: I think we've stopped playing that game.

PERRY: Who won?

ARTHUR: Not Buzz and James.

PERRY: How did we manage?

ARTHUR: Depends on who you slept with.

PERRY: Fourteen years. I haven't been perfect. Just lucky.

ARTHUR: I've been perfect.

PERRY: Sure you have!

ARTHUR: Do you ever feel guilty?

PERRY: No, grateful. Why, do you?

ARTHUR: It used to be nearly all the time. No, first I was just scared. Then the guilt. Massive at first. Why not me? That lingers, more than the fear. We've never really talked about this. Paddle.

PERRY: I'm paddling.

ARTHUR: Every time I look at Buzz, even when he's driving me crazy, or now James, I have to think, I have to say to myself. "Sooner or later, that man, that human being, is not going to be standing there washing the dishes or tying his shoelace."

PERRY: None of us is. Are. Is. Are?

ARTHUR: I don't know. Are. You're right. It's no comfort, but you're right.

PERRY: Will be. None of us will be.

ARTHUR: Paddle, I said.

PERRY: Why not, not you?

ARTHUR: That's a good question. I wish I could answer it. [JAMES *and* BUZZ *come into view in a canoe.* BUZZ *is doing the paddling.* JAMES *is up front.*]

PERRY: Can we drift a while? Look, there's Buzz and James. Hello!

ARTHUR: Can we finish something for a change?

JAMES: I feel guilty. You're doing all the paddling.

BUZZ: Good, I want you to. Look at the turtle!

JAMES: I'm going to miss all this.

BUZZ: Sshh. Don't say that. Sshh. Don't even think it.

JAMES: There's Perry and Arthur.

BUZZ: I don't want to talk to anyone. Just us.

ARTHUR: I think we're back to zero with this thing, but I'm willing to bend my shoulder and start all over again. What I else am I going to do with my time? But the fellow next to me with his shoulder to the same wheel isn't so lucky. He gets sick, I don't. Why is that? I think we should both go together. Is that gay solidarity or a death wish?

PERRY: Don't talk like that.

ARTHUR: I will always feel guilty in some private part of me that I don't let anyone see but you, and not even you all of it; I will always feel like a bystander at the genocide of who we are.

PERRY: You're not a bystander.

ARTHUR: If you didn't save the human race you're a bystander.

PERRY: That's crazy. You sound like Buzz.

ARTHUR: That's how I feel.

PERRY: You're not a bystander.

JAMES: Buzz, could we go back now?

BUZZ: Sure, honey.

JAMES: Right away. I'm not feeling terribly well.

BUZZ: You're there.

ARTHUR: Hello! They see us.

BUZZ: We'll see you at dinner!

PERRY: [*to* BUZZ *and* JAMES] You want to race?

ARTHUR: Perry!

BUZZ: What?

ARTHUR: Jesus.

PERRY: I'm sorry. I wasn't thinking.

BUZZ: [*to* PERRY] What did you say?

PERRY: Nothing! It's all right!

ARTHUR: Let's go in. [*They paddle.*]

PERRY: You're not a bystander.

BUZZ: Grace. I thought he said something about grace.

JAMES: I think I soiled myself.

BUZZ: We're almost there. [*He paddles.*]

PERRY: Anyway. Anyway. That evening. I'm sorry. [*He can't continue.*]

JAMES: That evening it rained harder than ever. I'll do it. (I hate making someone cry.) There was talk of tar-and-feathering the weatherman.

PERRY: I'm sorry.

JAMES: A slight case of the runs, Perry. I'm fine now. My bum is as clean as a baby's. The best is yet to come. The real horror.

BUZZ: We don't know that.

JAMES: Yes, we do.

PERRY: I don't know what came over me.

ARTHUR: It's all right, come on, Perry. [*They go.*]

JAMES: I thought I put it very politely. I mean, I could have said, "I shit myself."

BUZZ: We're all walking on eggshells. I'll draw your bath, luv.

JAMES: Was that "luv" or "love," luv?

BUZZ: For people who insist on spelling "valor" with a *u* and using words like "lorry" and "lift," you're lucky we have a lenient immigration. [*He goes.*]

JAMES: Anyway. (If I'm going to fill in for Perry here, I might as well try to sound like him. Bloody unlikely!) After my bath, Buzz (and I never remotely thought in my wildest imaginings that I would be making love to someone called Buzz and saying things like "I love you, Buzz," or "How do you take your tea. Buzz?"), this same, wonderful Buzz wrapped me in the biggest, toastiest bath sheet imaginable and tucked me safely into that lovely big chair by the window in the corner of our room. I fell asleep listening to my brother play Rachmaninoff downstairs. I would wake up to one of the most unsettling, yet strangely satisfying, conversations of my long/short life. And I will scarcely say a word. [*He closes his eyes. The piano music stops. He stands up and looks down at the chair. He is* JOHN.]

JOHN: There's no point in pretending this isn't happening. You're dying, aren't you? There are so many things I've never said to you, things we've never spoken about. I don't want to wait until it's too late to say them. I've spent my life waiting for the appropriate moment to tell you the truth. I resent you. I resent everything about you. You had Mum and Dad's unconditional love and now you have the world's. How can I not envy that? I wish I could say it was because you're so much better looking than me. No, the real pain is that it's something so much harder to bear. You got the good soul. I got the bad one. Think about leaving me yours.

They have names for us, behind our back. I bet you didn't know that, did you? James the Good and John the Bad, the Princes of Charm and Ugly. Gregory keeps a journal. We're all in it. I don't come off very well in there, either. So what's your secret? The secret of unconditional love? I'm not going to let you die with it.

My brother smiled wanly and shook his head, suggesting he didn't know, dear spectators. And just then a tear started to fall from the corner of one eye. This tear told me my brother knew something of the pain I felt of never, ever, not once, being loved. Another tear. The other eye this time. And then I felt his hand on mine. Not only did I feel as if I were looking at myself, eyes half-open, deep in a winged-back chair, a blanket almost to my chin, in the twilight of a summer that had never come, and talking to myself, who else could this mirror image be but me?, both cheeks wet with tears now, but now I was touching myself. That hand taking mine was my own. I could trace the same sinews, follow the same veins. But no! It brought it to other lips and began to kiss it, his kisses mingling with his tears. He was forgiving me. My brother was forgiving me. But wait!—and I tried to pull my hand away. I hated you. He holds tighter. I. More kisses. I. New tears. I wished you were dead. He presses his head against my hand now and cries and cries and cries as I try to tell him every wrong I have done him, but he just shakes his head and bathes my hand with his tears and lips. There have never been so many kisses, not in all the world, as when I told my brother all the wrongs I had done him and he forgave me. Nor so many tears. Finally we stopped. We looked at each other in the silence. We could look at each other at last. We weren't the same person. I just wanted to be the one they loved, I told him. [JOHN *sits in the chair.*]

JAMES: And now you will be. [*Lights up on* GREGORY *dancing in the studio.* PERRY *returns to the stage.*]

PERRY: Gregory was working! The lights in his studio had been burning all that night and now well into the next day. Bobby shuttled food and refreshment from the main house while keeping the rest of us at bay. None of us had ever seen Gregory at work. He'd always kept the studio curtains closed. But this time it was as if he wanted us to watch.

ARTHUR: We shouldn't be doing this.

RAMON: Hey, c'mon, quit crowding me.

ARTHUR: I'm sorry.

RAMON: Watch Gregory. He is so good. He is so fucking good. I'd give my left nut to work with him.

PERRY: Ouch.

ARTHUR: Did you ever tell him that?

RAMON: I'm in a company.

ARTHUR: Not his. And I think the expression is "right arm," Ramon. He told Perry he thinks you're a magnificent dancer.

RAMON: He never told me.

ARTHUR: What are you two having? A withholding contest? Duck! He'll see us.

RAMON: I think he knows we're out here.

BOBBY: Someone's out there, Gregory.

ARTHUR: He's going to kill you. [*He goes.* GREGORY *finishes the dance. He is exhausted.*]

PERRY: When Gregory finished, he knew he had made something good, something he was proud of.

GREGORY: It's done, Bobby. It's finished.

BOBBY: The whole thing? Beginning, middle, and end?

GREGORY: Yes! It's even got an epilogue. Give me a hug, for Christ's sake! No, give me a chair. You got an old boyfriend, honey.

PERRY: He also knew he would never be able to dance it. Not the way he wanted it to be danced.

BOBBY: What's the matter?

GREGORY: I can't do this anymore.

BOBBY: Your legs just cramped. Here, let me. [*He massages* GREGORY's *legs.*]

PERRY: It wasn't just his legs. It was everything. Gregory had begun to hurt too much nearly all the time now. He knew he'd never make it through a whole performance.

GREGORY: Ramon!

BOBBY: You let him watch?

GREGORY: I wanted him to watch. Ramon! [RAMON *comes into the studio.*]

RAMON: I'm sorry, Gregory, I couldn't help myself. But Jesus, where does stuff like that come from? I would give my life to dance something like that solo one day.

PERRY: Ramon had obviously reconsidered his priorities.

BOBBY: What are you doing, Gregory?

PERRY: Gregory was suddenly a forty-three-year-old man whose body had begun to quit in places he'd never dreamed of, looking at a twenty-two-year-old dancer who had his whole career ahead of him.

GREGORY: You're good, Ramon. You're very good. You're better than I was at your age, but that's not good enough, you should be better.

RAMON: Don't you think I know that?

PERRY: What Gregory next said surprised everyone, but no one more than himself.

RAMON: You mean your solo? In rehearsal? So you can see how it looks?

GREGORY: It would be your solo at the premiere. New York. Early December.

RAMON: I don't know what to say.

PERRY: I can't believe people really say things like that. I mean, all your life you wait for the Great Opportunity and you suddenly don't know what to say. It reminds me of the time I —

RAMON: Where are you going to be?

GREGORY: Out front. Watching you.

RAMON: What about . . . ? [*He motions toward* BOBBY.]

PERRY: Someone had to bring it up. It wasn't going to be any of us.

BOBBY: What about what?

GREGORY: Ask him.

BOBBY: What's happening? Don't do this to me.

RAMON: I'm asking you.

GREGORY: I'm fine, Ramon. Are you?

BOBBY: What's happening?

RAMON: When do we start?

GREGORY: The fifteenth. Ten A.M.

RAMON: I'll be there on the first.

GREGORY: You won't be paid.

RAMON: Is this a secret? I mean, can I tell people? I want to call my mother. Is that okay? She'll shit. She won't know what I'm talking about, but she'll shit. [*His enthusiasm is spontaneous and infectious. He runs off yelling.*] Eeeeeowww! ¡Dios mio!

GREGORY: We always said I would stop when it's time.

BOBBY: Time. I hate that word, "time."

GREGORY: It's time, Bobby.

PERRY: You should have seen this man ten years ago, even five. No one could touch him. He's always been some sort of a god to me.

GREGORY: I just want to stay like this, my eyes closed, and feel you next to me, our hands touching. Two blind mice now. I didn't know I was going to do this, honey.

PERRY: Ever since I'd known Gregory, he'd been a dancer. I didn't think I would mind this moment so much.

BOBBY: You did the right thing. [*They stay as* GREGORY *has described them.* JOHN *appears and stands very close to them.*]

JOHN: This is what Gregory wrote in his journal that day. "Bobby and I made love. We kissed so hard we each had hickeys afterwards. I don't think I'll tell him. When I feel his young body against my own, I feel lucky and happy and safe. I am loved."

GREGORY: Okay.

BOBBY: You ready? [BOBBY *and* GREGORY *get up and slowly leave the stage.* JOHN *stops reading, closes the book, and looks in the direction* BOBBY *and* GREGORY *have gone.*]

JOHN: "And I am all alone." That's from a song. What song? Anyway. [*He sits and stares straight ahead.*]

PERRY: Anyway. [BUZZ *has returned.*] How's James?

BUZZ: Don't ask. Like ice. I'm running his tub.

PERRY: Poor guy. How are you?

BUZZ: Weary and wonderful. [GREGORY *appears.*]

GREGORY: Who's using all the hot water?

BUZZ: We are, Gregory, I'm sorry.

GREGORY: That's all right, that's all right. I'll shower later. Really, Buzz, it's fine. [*He goes.*]

BUZZ: If this were a musical, that would be a great cue for "Steam Heat." "Really, Buzz, it's fine." "I've got ding! ding! steam heat!" Of course, if this were a musical, there would be plenty of hot water, and it would have a happy ending. Life and Gregory's plumbing should be more like a musical: Today's Deep Thought from Buzz Hauser.

PERRY: Musicals don't always have happy endings, either.

BUZZ: Yes, they do. That's why I like them, even the sad ones. The orchestra plays, the characters die, the audience cries, the curtain falls, the actors get up off the floor, the audience puts on their coats, and everybody goes home feeling better. That's a happy ending, Perry. Once, just once, I want to see a *West Side Story* where Tony really gets it, where they all die, the Sharks and the Jets, and Maria while we're at it, and Officer Krupke, what's he doing sneaking out of the theater? — get back here and die with everybody else, you son of a bitch! Or a *King and I* where Yul Brynner doesn't get up from that little Siamese bed for a curtain call. I want to see a *Sound of Music* where the entire von Trapp family dies in an authentic Alpine avalanche. A *Kiss Me Kate* where's she got a big cold sore on her mouth. A *Funny Thing Happened on the*

Way to the Forum where the only thing that happens is nothing and it's not funny and they all go down waiting—waiting for what? Waiting for nothing, waiting for death, like everyone I know and care about is, including me. That's the musical I want to see, Perry, but they don't write musicals like that anymore. In the meantime, gangway, world, get off my runway!

PERRY: You're my oldest friend in the world and next to Arthur, my best.

BUZZ: It's not enough sometimes, Perry. You're not sick. You two are going to end up on Golden Pond in matching white wicker rockers. "The loons are coming, Arthur. They're shitting on our annuities."

PERRY: That's not fair. We can't help that.

BUZZ: I can't afford to be fair. Fair's a luxury. Fair is for healthy people with healthy lovers in nice apartments with lots of health insurance, which, of course, they don't need, but God forbid someone like me or James should have it.

PERRY: Are you through?

BUZZ: I'm scared I won't be there for James when he needs me and angry he won't be there for me when I need him.

PERRY: [*comforting him*] I know, I know.

BUZZ: I said I wasn't going to do this again. I wasn't going to lose anyone else. I was going to stay healthy, work hard for the clinic, and finish cataloging my original cast albums. They're worth something to someone, some nut like me somewhere. That was all I thought I could handle. And now this.

PERRY: I know, I know. But it's wonderful what's happened. You know it's wonderful.

BUZZ: Who's gonna be there for me when it's my turn?

PERRY: We all will. Every one of us.

BUZZ: I wish I could believe that.

JAMES: [*off*] Buzz, the tub!

BUZZ: Can you promise me you'll be holding my hand when I let go? That the last face I see will be yours?

PERRY: Yes.

BUZZ: I believe you.

PERRY: Mine and Arthur's.

BUZZ: Arthur's is negotiable. I can't tell you how this matters to me. I'm a very petty person.

PERRY: No, you're not.

BUZZ: I've always had better luck with roommates than lovers.

PERRY: I think this time you got lucky with both.

735

JAMES: [*off*] Buzz, it's running over.

BUZZ: I adore him. What am I going to do? [*The other men are assembling in the living room.*]

GREGORY: All right, everyone. This is your five-minute call. This is a dress. [BUZZ, BOBBY, ARTHUR, RAMON, *and* GREGORY *will get ready to rehearse the* Swan Lake Pas des Cygnes. *This time they will put on tutus and toe shoes. They will, help each other dress. Think of a happy, giggly group of coeds.* PERRY *watches from the side.*]

GREGORY: John? Are you ready in there?

JOHN: [*off*] All set. [*He starts playing.*]

GREGORY: Not yet! Not yet!

RAMON: Okay, let's do it!

GREGORY: Lord, but you. Um. Have big feet, Bobby.

BUZZ: You're heartless. Picking on the handicapped.

BOBBY: I'm not handicapped. Not anymore. I'm visually challenged.

BUZZ: I'm sorry, doll.

BOBBY: That's all right, doll. It took me forever.

GREGORY: John, are you still ready?

JOHN: [*off*] Yes, Gregory.

GREGORY: Tuck it in, Arthur.

ARTHUR: I beg your pardon.

PERRY: You see? That's what I keep telling him.

ARTHUR: If you're just going to sit on the sidelines and be a kibitz.

RAMON: Kibitz? What's a kibitz?

BUZZ: It's a place where very old gay Jewish couples go. [GREGORY *claps his hands with a choreographer's authority.*]

GREGORY: All right, gentlemen. Line up. From the top.

BUZZ: We're in big trouble.

GREGORY: John? Are you ready?

JOHN: [*off*] Yes, for the eighty-fifth time! [GREGORY *claps his hands again.*]

GREGORY: Okay, everybody. This is a take. All set, John. [JOHN *begins to play off-stage and they begin to dance. They have improved considerably since they started rehearsing.*] Very good. Very good.

RAMON: Ow! Buzz kicked me.

BUZZ: Tattletale. Shut up and dance.

ARTHUR: That's from *Gypsy*.

BUZZ: That's amazing from an accountant.

BOBBY: How are we looking?

PERRY: Actually, you look like you're having fun.

BOBBY: Well, come on then! [JAMES *enters. He has put on his tutu.*]

JAMES: You started without me.

BUZZ: We thought you were resting.

JAMES: Don't stop. Let me in. [*He links arms with* BOBBY *and joins in the dance. The others are apprehensive about his participation but try not to show it.*] Left! I always want to go right on that step.

BUZZ: If you do and I hear about it…! That was the punchline to a politically incorrect joke nobody dares tell anymore.

ARTHUR: But you will.

BUZZ: Absolutely. Hervé Villechaize, the deceased midget, was talking to Faye Dunaway.

ALL: She's gay, you know.

BUZZ: Keep trying, guys. One of these days you'll get it. Anyway. Hervé and Faye.

PERRY: Anyway. While my friends rehearsed and laughed and I watched and felt envious of their freedom (I couldn't believe that was my Arthur with them! My button-down, plodding Arthur!), something else was happening, too. Something awful. James collapsed. [*Everyone stops as* JAMES *falters.* JOHN *keeps playing the piano, off.*]

JAMES: I'm fine. I said, I'm fine! Everybody, please. Back off. I just want to lie down a little.

BUZZ: I'll—

JAMES: No. I'm fine. Don't stop. Go on. You need all the rehearsal you can get. [*He goes.*]

GREGORY: John, will you stop. John, goddamnit! [*The music continues.*]

RAMON: I'll tell him. [*He goes.*]

ARTHUR: Buzz, maybe you should go with him.

BUZZ: Maybe you should mind your own business.

ARTHUR: I'm sorry. [RAMON *returns.*]

RAMON: John's gone up to him.

BUZZ: Put on the record. That's how we're going to perform it anyway. The piano is for stop-and-start. We're beyond stop-and-start.

ARTHUR: We're one short again.

BUZZ: We'll live. [*He starts taking charge, his way of being in denial about* JAMES*'s condition.*] Let's go. Places, ladies. From the top.

RAMON: You're being replaced, Gregory.

BUZZ: Did anyone object to me calling them ladies? Speak now or forever hold your peace.

PERRY: I object.

BUZZ: You're not in this piece. [*He claps his hands. This time we hear the Tchaikovsky in the full orchestral arrangement. They being the dance again. The dance continues.*]

PERRY: I wanted to join them. I couldn't. I just couldn't. I was a dancer once. I was a good dancer. What happened?

GREGORY: Come on. Um. Perry. We need. Um. You. It's a. Um. *Pas de six.*

BUZZ: That sounds dirty. I wish it were. [*As the dance proceeds, one by one the men will stop dancing, step forward, and speak to us.*]

PERRY: I have twenty-seven years, eight months, six days, three hours, thirty-one minutes, and eleven seconds left. I will be watching *Gone With the Wind* of all things again on television. Arthur will be in the other room fixing me hot cocoa and arguing with his brother on the phone. He won't even hear me go.

ARTHUR: You insisted on keeping the TV on so loud. Wouldn't buy a hearing supplement.

PERRY: I hate that word, "supplement." They're aids. Hearing aids. They're for old men.

ARTHUR: Three years later, it's my turn. On the bus. The M-9. Quietly. Very quietly. Just like my life. Without him, I won't much mind.

GREGORY: You're getting behind, Arthur, catch up!

BUZZ: I don't want to think about it. Soon. Sooner than I thought, even. Let's just say I died happy. They'd reissued *Happy Hunting* on CD and I'd met Gwen Verdon at a benefit. She was very nice and I don't think it was because she knew I was sick. Perry and Arthur said, "You know what Ethel Merman is going to do to you, telling everyone she was a big dyke?"

GREGORY: On the beat, Buzz, on the beat. [JAMES *appears.*]

JAMES: I wasn't brave. I took pills. I went back home to Battersea and took pills. I'm sorry, Buzz. [*He goes.*]

RAMON: I don't die. I'm fucking immortal. I live forever. Until I take a small plane to Pittsfield, Massachusetts. I was late for a concert. Nobody else from my company was on it. Just me and a pilot I didn't bother to look at twice.

BOBBY: I don't know.

GREGORY: You—

BOBBY: I don't want to—

GREGORY: You won't be with me.

BOBBY: I'm sorry.

GREGORY: What was his name?

BOBBY: Luke.

GREGORY: That's right, Luke.

BOBBY: You knew that. He knew that. He does that just to. . . . What about you?

GREGORY: There was no one else. Not even close. You were the last.

BOBBY: I'm sorry, Gregory.

GREGORY: It was my age.

BOBBY: No.

GREGORY: It was my age.

BOBBY: Yes.

GREGORY: You —

BOBBY: I said I don't want to know.

GREGORY: Don't be afraid.

BOBBY: I'm not.

GREGORY: It will seem like forever.

BOBBY: I'm sorry I couldn't stay with you.

GREGORY: I. Um. Bury every one of you. Um. It got. Um. Awfully lonely out here. [*JOHN appears.*]

JOHN: I didn't change. And I tried. At least I think I tried. I couldn't. I just couldn't. No one mourned me. Not one tear was shed. [*Long pause. No one moves. Finally:*]

PERRY: Anyway. [*The dance resumes and the Tchaikovsky is heard again. By this final reprise of the dance their precision and coordination is as good as it's going to get.*] It was just about now when the lights went out. [*The music stops and the lights go off abruptly.*] Violent thunderstorms are taken for granted in this neck of the woods. So are power failures when you live as remotely as Gregory. [*Already matches are being struck and candles lit.*] The benefit rehearsal would have to wait.

BUZZ: There will be no performance of *Ze Red Shoes* tonight. [*More and more candles are being lit.*] When do you expect the power back?

BOBBY: Are the lights still out? Aaaww! It could be forever.

BUZZ: You don't have to sound so cheerful. [*The stage is ablaze with lit candles by now.*]

ARTHUR: You know what's going to happen, don't you? We'll all be sound asleep and the lights will come back on and the music will start playing and we'll all be scared to death. Why is it that when the lights go off the telephones usually still work? Hunh?

BUZZ: Gay people aren't expected to answer questions like that.

PERRY: Speak for yourself.

BUZZ: I was. I usually do. Whose turn is it to do the dishes?

BOBBY: I'll start.

PERRY: You cooked.

ARTHUR: Hey, no fair.

BOBBY: Who said life was fair? It certainly wasn't a blind person. [JOHN *enters.*]

BUZZ: How is he?

JOHN: He's sleeping but he's better. He's a little better. You've all been so.... There aren't words enough. Can I give anyone a hand? I want you to like me. [JOHN *exits.*]

ARTHUR: Look out there. It's clearing up. There's a full moon.

PERRY: This is why people have places in the country.

BUZZ: Even gay people, Perry.

ARTHUR: Drop it, you two.

RAMON: You could practically read by that moonlight. The dishes can wait. Come on, Bobby.

BOBBY: It's wasted on me. Go on down to the lake. All of you. Make them, Greg. I'll join you.

BUZZ: He's a saint. He's gorgeous and he's a saint.

GREGORY: John? We're all going down to the lake.

PERRY: What's the weather supposed to be tomorrow?

ARTHUR: More rain. [PERRY, RAMON, ARTHUR, BUZZ, *and* GREGORY *move to the rear of the stage, where they sit with their backs to us looking at the moonlight on the lake.* ARTHUR *begins to sing "Shine On, Harvest Moon." The others will join in.* BOBBY *is clearing up.* JAMES *enters. He is wearing a robe. He watches* BOBBY.]

BOBBY: Who's there? Somebody's there.

JAMES: It's me. Forgive me for staring. You looked very handsome in the moonlight. Very handsome and very graceful. You took my breath away. I'm going to remember you like that. It's James.

BOBBY: I know. Are you supposed to be down here?

JAMES: No. And neither are you. There's a full moon and everyone's down by the lake. I saw them from my window. Come on. I'll go with you. [*He takes* BOBBY *by the arm.*] I have a confession to make. I've never been skinny-dipping in the moonlight with a blind American. You only live once.

BOBBY: If you're lucky. Some people don't live at all. I thought you were scared of that snapping turtle.

JAMES: I'm terrified of him. I'm counting on you.

BOBBY: Let's go then.

JAMES: I have another confession to make. I'm English. I've never been skinny-dipping in the moonlight with anyone.

BOBBY: I knew that. [*They leave. The front of the stage and main playing area are bare. Everyone is taking off his clothes to go swimming now. One by one we see the men at the rear of the stage undress and go into the lake. As they go into the water and swim out, the sound of their voices will fade away. Silence. Empty stage.* JOHN *enters. He looks back to the lake. He looks up at the sound of a plane overhead. He looks out to us.*]

JOHN: Anyway. [*He looks straight ahead. He doesn't move. The lights fade.* BLACKOUT.]

BEN HODGES is associate editor to John Willis on *Theatre World*, the definitive pictorial and statistical record of the American theatre, and serves as executive producer of the Theatre World Awards, the oldest awards given for Broadway and Off-Broadway debuts. He is an actor, director, and producer, and has worked as a casting director for the theatre, television, and film. He currently serves as executive director for Fat Chance Productions and the Ground Floor Theatre in New York City and is vice president of Fat Chance Films. Ben received his B.F.A. in Acting/Directing from Otterbein College. He lives in New York City.